C0-GHL-182

Native Tongues

Portrayals of National Identity in Five Classic Novels

Francis Goskowski

Strategic Book Publishing and Rights Co.

Copyright © 2023 Francis Goskowski. All rights reserved.

No part of this book may be reproduced or transmitted in any form or by any means, graphic, electronic, or mechanical, including photocopying, recording, taping, or by any information storage retrieval system, without the permission, in writing, of the publisher. For more information, send an email to support@sbpra.net, Attention Subsidiary Rights Department.

Strategic Book Publishing and Rights Co., LLC
USA
www.sbpra.net

For information about special discounts for bulk purchases, please contact Strategic Book Publishing and Rights Co. Special Sales, at bookorder@sbpra.net.

ISBN: 978-1-68235-754-5

Book Design: Suzanne Kelly

DEDICATION

To Kathy and Ron
With Love and Gratitude

TABLE OF CONTENTS

PREFACE

What is now known as Western civilization evolved during the Middle Ages within territories formerly organized and governed as provinces of the Roman Empire in the west. Portions of France, Great Britain, Germany, Austria, Spain, and Italy coalesced as independent nation-states in the centuries following the end of the reign of the last Roman Emperor in 476 CE. In varying degrees, these nations have reflected ever since the lasting influence of Roman colonization in language, law, art, governance, and religion. In the regions of Eastern and Southeastern Europe that constituted the Eastern Roman or Byzantine Empire until its collapse in 1453, a similar diffusion of Greek-inspired political, linguistic, legal, artistic, and religious paradigms and conventions can be traced. In Russia, under the leadership of Czar Peter I (1672–1725), later to be designated "the Great," European science, technology, and performing arts were introduced and blended with native traditions to give this nation some recognizably Western features. In the North American colonies first settled by English-speaking explorers and migrants, a more thorough Westernization occurred, with the culture of the indigenous peoples largely suppressed by the colonists and their successors.

Western civilization is not, however, revealed and embodied everywhere in the same forms and with the same standards in values and belief systems, lifestyles, preferences, aspirations, and ideals. The nations whose peoples have adopted over time distinctively Western perspectives have embraced aspects of this inheritance idiosyncratically. Their contributions to the culture of the West as a whole are like the individual patterns, color schemes, emblems, and signs that harmonize in a tapestry. The essays that follow explore in detail how the characters and their interactions with the worlds portrayed in five great works of the Western canon of literature, one each from the United States, France, Great Britain, Russia, and Germany, illustrate differences in the ways the foundational principles of the West are understood and brought into relief through emphases, nuances, concepts, and points of departure peculiar to each national tradition.

Mark Twain's *The Adventures of Huckleberry Finn* recounts an adolescent boy's growth in awareness and character over several months' experience in frontier America before the Civil War. Huck has had little formal education, but he manages to escape danger and overcome all manner of challenges a world populated by fallen humanity presents, through native common sense, cleverness, quick thinking, and imagination. These virtues and skills enable young Huck to leave settled life and his father's abuse, striking out on his own no matter how difficult this will be. While on the run, he meets Nigger Jim, a slave in his aunt's household, who is also on the run. The two bond, something not countenanced in slave-holding societies. Huck, nevertheless, lets conscience and natural empathy guide his actions, bringing into sharp focus American culture's preference for individual choice rather than strict adherence to social conventions in how one person relates to another. The two will become involved with murderous feuding families, con artists, vigilantes, and even with book-smart but manipulative Tom Sawyer, Huck's erstwhile companion and friend. They overcome all the obstacles these encounters bring. Jim is freed finally, and Huck moves on, chastened by all that has happened. He is wounded, with his innocence tarnished and his spirit weakened. He will flee to the territories in the West, where he can start over again alone, relying on self-reliance and conscience to carry him through.

The French novelist Stendhal illustrates in *The Red and the Black* how rationality comes into conflict with anarchic sexual urges to derail the clerical career a precocious student, Julien Sorel, is planning to pursue mainly to rise in the world. Unlike Huck, who has little interest in society or money, the boy who has memorized the New Testament in Latin is intent on "conquering" through force of intellect all that stands in the way of his ambitions. But passion dictates otherwise, making the young man obsess over sexual conquests. He seduces first a married woman whose children he is hired to tutor and then a young woman of noble descent, with whom he fathers a child. The tensions between the two aspirations cannot be reconciled. Julien enjoys a measure of success in Paris, interacting with wealthy and privileged benefactors, but ultimately all he has striven for disappears when he loses self-control and commits a crime of passion that leads to the guillotine.

The English writer Charles Dickens lowers the temperature in *David Copperfield.* David overcomes childhood abuse and neglect to mature into a man of solid British character. He controls the emotions that tear Sorel apart and never looks to conquer. He stays firmly within the boundaries of moderation, the *via media* so valued by his people, and grows steadily in moral awareness. David is loyal and generous, grateful to all who help him on his way and wary of any who threaten to throw him off balance. Throughout the novel, Dickens's brilliant characterizations bring colorful personalities to life with quirks, habits, speech, and style uniquely their own, aligning himself with predecessors like Chaucer and Shakespeare in recognizing diversity and respecting human nature in all its variety.

An altogether different dynamic animates Russian culture. Leo Tolstoy's *War and Peace* is a long account of discovering and coming to terms with one's identity. The Russian tradition stresses the need for acceptance of and resignation to one's fate. This posture, however, is not synonymous with weakness or apathy. Whatever one's fate may be, he or she should embrace it joyfully and grow to love it (*amor fati*), trusting in God's will. The novel's main character, Pierre Bezukhov, does just that, ultimately rejecting the lure of foreign influences like Freemasonry and liberalism in favor of the native autocracy and the Orthodox faith. In this regard, he becomes one with his people, particularly the mostly peasant soldiers, who rise up in opposition to Napoleon's invading armies in 1812 to preserve the motherland, the monarchy, and the church. Their steadfastness prevails, forcing the invaders to go back the way they came, a terrible journey in a harsh and hostile land that destroys the no longer *Grande Armee.*

German culture emphasizes the need to strive, to go beyond, to reach realms of the Spirit (*Geist*) and the Absolute. Goethe's Faust exemplifies this drive to break the bonds keeping humanity dependent, signing in blood a pact with Satan to gain superhuman power and experience transcendence at the expense of eternal damnation. In the years immediately after World War II, Thomas Mann used the Faust tale as the framework for *Doctor Faustus*, the story of Adrian Leverkuhn, a fictional composer so intent on achieving a "breakthrough" in his art, he agrees to a similar pact. In addition to eternal torment, Leverkuhn also renounces all forms of love in this life, confirming his commitment to Satan alone. This is German striving in the service of personal distinction and glory, not moral betterment or understanding. Such corruption infects not just Leverkuhn, but his nation as well. The novel links Adrian's life story with repeated commentary on the German people's experience from the later nineteenth century through World War I, the rise of Nazism, and the catastrophe of World War II. As the novel proceeds, it becomes clear that both Adrian and his nation have succumbed to the same dark forces, leading to moral degeneration and tragedy on a grand scale.

These expressions of national ideals and ways of living and dealing with the world and others are not mutually exclusive. Though they may be more prominent and pronounced among certain nationalities, they are not tribal perspectives foreign to other peoples. In *Doctor Faustus*, for example, the narrator of Adrian Leverkuhn's life story is his friend from youth, Dr. Serenus Zeitblom. Serenus is a man formed by middle-class values, such as moderation in political and religious commitment, self-discipline, charity, and respect for law and civic order. He is deaf to the siren song of Aryan superiority and uncomfortable with his friend's attempts to make music that soars into the realm of *Geist*. He is, in other words, a German adhering to the *via media* so identified with British culture and exemplified by David Copperfield. Huckleberry Finn and Nigger Jim are two innocents, who, trusting in their good sense and decency, become as one, making their way through thick and thin and surviving all kinds of challenges and threats. In the same way, the unschooled peasant soldiers who bond with each other to resist the French army's relentless attacks at Borodino are sustained throughout by native courage and a willingness to sacrifice that ultimately saves their nation. An older man of the people, Platon Karateyev, relies, like Huck, Jim, and the soldiers, on folk wisdom and simple skills to get him through a harsh imprisonment, all the while impressing to no end his cell mate, the cosmopolitan aristocrat Pierre Bezukhov.

In other words, the five voices speaking to us in the great national contributions to Western literature discussed in the pages that follow are distinctive but also harmonious. They blend like the members of a quintet who sing the parts that in vocal range and style best reflect their national identity, creating the effect of a unity built upon diverse elements. Western civilization is such a unity.

THE UNITED STATES

Mark Twain
The Adventures of Huckleberry Finn

INTRODUCTION

Americans are portrayed in myth and in literature as "new" people. Unlike the national cultures of Western Europe and Russia, whose identities and value systems evolved over many centuries and in response to powerful influences like the Roman and Byzantine Empires, the territories that first recognized themselves as distinctively "American" took shape along the Atlantic coast between the early seventeenth and the mid-eighteenth centuries, far later than their continental predecessors. Even though Western Europeans and their descendants made up the majority of America's original settlers, these immigrants were largely detached from and, in many cases, hostile to the established political and ecclesiastical structures of the nations they had left. Among the country's most prominent early colonists, for instance, were English religious dissenters determined to create in Massachusetts a godly "New Kingdom" that would nurture and guide authentic believers newly freed from the tyranny and corruption of the old ecclesiastical establishment. They would be joined in coming years by English Catholic settlers in Maryland and Quakers in Pennsylvania, both groups likewise eager to profess their beliefs without interference. This diversity in religious commitment and practice led inevitably to widespread tolerance, introduced first within colonies that would later coalesce as states. With this principle established, religious identity ceased to be something that a state could somehow mandate and became instead solely a matter of individual choice.

The nation itself was created "new" in the eighteenth century when revolutionaries threw off British colonial rule and formed a republic; in the process, the Founding Fathers made every effort to stamp out all traces of traditional European governing systems and perquisites, including state churches, titled families, and special powers and privileges for an elite upper class. The evolution of American society after the 1789 Constitution reveals ever-broadening opportunity, as more and more "new" groups and individuals, such as workingmen and women, slaves, and "huddled masses" of poor migrants, who, over time and not without struggle, would steadily earn the means to realize life's possibilities in ways hitherto unimagined. The American people, as a result, became defined not by their countries of origin, not by their religion, race, or gender, not by their social class or family, not by their degree of professional success or level of education, not by anything extraneous to their identity as American citizens. The American is, in reality, what Rousseau sketched in theory: a new being arising in a New World and free as no one before him or her ever could be. The American is born free, not only in the political sense but also as a thinker and agent. The American is indeed childlike even into adulthood, because most of that which matures a person in stratified societies is absent in his or her experience. Unlike Latin America, where Spanish colonists recreated a mostly Old-World religious, political, and social system characterized by centralized authority, orthodox faith, privileged land-owning families, and strong military presences, America north of the Rio Grande gave an individual ample room to develop outside such influences and to be open to new ways of thinking. In the one region where large estates were built, slaves toiled in the fields, and rich families became for a while almost a separate caste, the Civil War of 1861–65 made illegal or illegitimate all forms of bondage and inherited privilege, giving to the American South in later years a character very much like the rest of the country.

Americans had to be new and innovative in their thinking. The vast territory predominantly white Anglo-Saxon Protestants explored initially, and Irish, German, Polish, Italian, and related groupings entered afterwards, dwarfed anything these people had ever known before and called into question the verities of their ancestral cultures. In Europe, after all, most men and women became what their families either desired them to become or what their circumstances compelled them to become. For the upper classes and the ambitious bourgeois, to be sure, development led to acceptable results. An elaborate system of training and education took boys and girls through prescribed lessons in language, history, science, and theology, supplemented by music and dancing for the girls and horseback riding and hunting for the boys. The drawing room and the theater provided carefully orchestrated occasions for the sexes to meet and mingle. For budding craftsmen, the guilds offered a stage-by-stage training program in various skills and processes that produced highly competent workers in wood and metals. The military services followed similar patterns to transform raw recruits into disciplined professional soldiers and sailors, while in the seminaries of the different religious bodies, several years of prayer and study led men to ordination as licensed clerics and women to profession as vowed members of religious orders. The rural and urban poor had to settle for rudimentary education and tutelage in agricultural labor or basic trades from parents and older relatives. No matter the profession or the class, training and education adhered to rigid patterns and time-honored principles. Many, it is true, rebelled against or disdained such a regimented and rule-driven upbringing, but these were never regarded as anything other than miscreants or mavericks.

In America, by contrast, these straitjacketed systems did not take hold or become normative. Throughout most of its history, this nation's economy and society have been too dynamic, too fluid, too prone to upheaval and "creative destruction" for any of these slow-moving and inadaptable programs to flourish. Colleges and academies were built, and mostly affluent families, at first, sent their sons and daughters to them, but nothing like an educated elite emerged from them to dominate American culture. Today, a much larger student body fills the seats in institutions ranging from community colleges and trade schools to Ivy League universities; across this broad landscape, however, the curricula are so diffuse, the standards so varied, and the outcomes so unpredictable, that for the typical student formal education has taken on the character of a rite of passage rather than a serious preparation for a lifelong vocation. The same holds true for the guilds. Except for a brief period toward the end of the nineteenth century, when the American Federation of Labor gave craft union workers a status comparable to guild members in Europe, American workers have preferred to "freelance" in the labor market, trusting to experience as a guide rather than training mechanisms. The poor and the unconnected, in particular, have utilized freedom of movement to pursue economic opportunity in a country that places few barriers to mobility. In short, rather than allowing impersonal systems, where all is prescribed, to mold their characters and determine their careers, Americans from Franklin to Lincoln to Edison to Bill Gates have made their mark through exploitation of situations and possibilities and application of native ingenuity, making the innovator and pioneer more common than the academician in American cultural history.

The American tradition has set great value on practical wisdom. For this reason, "classical" studies emphasizing acquisition of knowledge, per se, or the adoption of models of behavior and social intercourse derived from approved works of the past, have not established themselves in America as standard academic pursuits. They have not been able to guide or inspire Americans as they could Europeans, whose languages and lived experience are so much closer to ancient models. Shakespeare and Milton do not have the same resonance in multi-ethnic Chicago, for instance, as they do in Cambridge. Alexander the Great and Julius Caesar were undeniably masters of the art of war, but could their tactics have been of much help to an American cavalry officer in a remote western territory facing rugged tribesmen unmatched in their knowledge of the land, their horsemanship, their skill in surprising and sudden attack, and their fearsome weaponry? Beethoven and the great masters of European instrumental music require well-trained musicians to give their compositions proper performances, but until the twentieth century, instrumental ensembles were not to be found outside the largest American cities. As for opera, which demands superbly trained singing actors and stage technicians for full realization, foreign-born artists have been preferred for many of the leading roles on American stages.

Emerson recognized early that the American scholar could not adopt forms and styles not native to him or her and that offered irrelevant or inappropriate sustenance to intellects hungering for guidance in a human and natural environment unparalleled in its challenges. The American scholar would do better to study nature in all its thunderous glory and read with a creative spirit rather than as a disciple if he or she wished to influence significantly his country's intellectual development. The philosopher Charles Peirce later codified such thinking within his concept of "pragmatism." This way of approaching the world and making choices and decisions differs markedly from the teachings advanced by traditional European philosophical schools of thought, which give to abstraction and to a quasi-mathematical quest for certainty priority in reasoning. The pragmatic emphasis makes what is effective and what is useful more important than what is rationally provable as a guideline for life choices. Medieval philosophers, for instance, made great efforts to demonstrate how theological teachings derived mainly from biblical authority were compatible with conclusions drawn by pagan philosophers such as Aristotle, who based their theories on rigorous observation of the natural world and its regularities expressible in mathematical formulae. To a pragmatist, such exertions are beside the point, since in everyday living scientific principles and religious formulations are embodied in concrete experiences and become important when they have an impact on how such experiences make living better or worse. Prior to Mephistopheles's visit, for instance, Faust labors alone in his study trying to grasp and formulate eternal truths; he suffers because on his own he cannot scale the philosophical heights such an ambition requires. For the pragmatist, a better approach would be to find significance in applying principles to practice, as, for instance, seeing if, in real life, evidence of God's existence and presence is apparent rather than struggling to prove such through abstract reasoning.

The mind alone is not the supreme arbiter of truth. Body, heart, and soul must also play their roles in influencing an individual to reach judgments on existential issues. What works for one person in this realm may not do much for another, so a degree of modesty should govern one's thinking on all matters of vital significance.

All of this leads the American to be perpetually young and innocent. He (and in American literature this iconic character is almost always male) cannot grow wise or rich with experience when the wisdom he is presented and the experience he is supposed to find instructive are foreign to him. The American is thrown back on his own resources, his native good sense and trustworthy instinct to guide him through a world that previous generations in far different environments could not have known. The novel that brings all these matters into high relief and that gives us a character whom Americans of every age, sex, race, and way of thinking instantly recognize as one of us is *The Adventures of Huckleberry Finn* (New York: New American Library, 1959).

PART ONE

Huckleberry Finn is Rousseau's "noble savage" in American frontier dress, complete with authentic accent and dialect, devoted companions, fondness for and skill in dealing with nature's perils and traps, and instincts that lead invariably to good decisions and sympathetic understanding. Huck is innocent of all that in Rousseau's conceptions corrupts the innate goodness of "natural" man. He has little formal education to twist his thinking into socially conforming patterns; his religious upbringing has been much abbreviated, so he still has an uncomplicated conscience, knowing right from wrong instinctively, and he cares little for such proprieties as proper dress, proper table manners, proper speech, and so on, allowing him to express and present himself without artificiality or pretense.

The novel is a memoir told in the first person and placing its subject, Huck, in a series of situations and interactions that threaten his innocence. It is not a *Bildungsroman* like *David Copperfield*, charting a character's growth and development from childhood to adulthood. The "adventures" Huck narrates take place over just a few months as the boy enters adolescence. They lead, nevertheless, to important conclusions and judgments and to a growth in awareness that will set Huck apart in a distinctively American way. The novel has three distinct sections. The first of these introduces us to the two strong family influences vying for control of Huck's future: the proper elderly women who try to raise the wild child to be respectable, and the primitive and avaricious father, for whom Huck counts for nothing except as a source of unearned income for a destitute ne'er-do-well. In coping with these competing influences, Huck remains a work in progress who manages to resist the pressures of both forces.

The opening chapters highlight Huck's discomfort in the home he shares with the Widow Douglas, who strives to "sivilize" the "poor lost lamb" (11) in her care. Thus, when Huck hears "a bell for supper," he has "to come to time" (12) and refrain from eating until grace is said. The widow's sister, Miss Watson, "a tolerable slim old maid" (12), assists with spelling lessons and moral instruction, focusing on the virtues that will keep Huck on the right path toward "the good place," where he will be privileged "to go around all day long with a harp and sing, forever and ever" (13). The moral compass for these small-town church ladies is the Bible. Its teachings, embedded in exemplary tales and stories and made explicit in commandments and laws governing behavior, should guide a youngster firmly, so no hazards, temptations, or challenges in life can ever deflect him or her from the straight and narrow. For women like these, the Bible's teachings are divinely ordained, as relevant in nineteenth century rural America as they were in ancient Israel.

To Huck, however, "Moses and the Bullrushers" (12) mean little. He is a resourceful, independent young boy who sets "no stock on dead people" (12). He is doubtful, too, about the desirability of eternal happiness in heaven. When, for instance, Miss Watson tells him his friend Tom Sawyer could "not by a considerable sight" be joining Huck in the good place, her charge decides the other eternal destiny will be better because "I wanted him and me to be together" (13). His teacher reacts to Huck's indifference with exhortations to prayer, assuring him that God will grant "whatever [he] asks for" (20). Huck wonders how this could be, since others of his acquaintance clearly have not gotten what they most obviously have needed. Miss Watson has to modify her assurance. Huck will gain "spiritual gifts" through his prayers that will encourage him to become more charitable and "never think about [himself]" (20). To Huck's way of thinking, though, such a practice can bring no personal advantage, benefiting only those like Miss Watson, who would gain from his solicitude and selflessness. So much for prayer. The young pragmatist will dispense with heavenly aid and deal with whatever comes his way by choosing the most practical and most useful course of action.

Here in a nutshell are cherished beliefs and expectations of nineteenth century American fundamentalist churches "reduced to the absurd." The ladies' struggle to convince Huck that whatever the Bible says must be so for no other reason than the Bible says it, anticipates the grueling experience of William Jennings Bryan as he tried to respond to Clarence Darrow's harshly rationalistic questioning of biblical "facts" during the Scopes trial in 1925. The values espoused so sincerely in the widow's household appear even more grotesque when they are followed by a disquisition on ghosts "Miss Watson's nigger, Jim" (26) presents in chapter 3. It is as if one superstition leads to another. Near the end of the novel, Huck reflects on all that has transpired and realizes that if he had followed the church's guidance, he would not have violated the law by helping Jim elude capture after he had run away. Mark Twain's savage irony makes such established teachings positively evil:

> *There was the Sunday School, you could 'a' gone to it; and if you'd 'a' done it they'd 'a' learnt you there that people that acts as I'd been acting about that nigger goes to everlasting fire.* (208)

No book, not even the "Good Book," and no school will form Huck's conscience. He will never grow into a solid citizen of Main Street precisely because he will trust himself and the instincts that form the bedrock of his innocence.

Huck is also indifferent to money, the great corrupting agent of burgeoning American capitalism. He entrusts the treasure trove he had acquired in his earlier adventures with Tom Sawyer to Judge Thatcher, not only to keep his greedy father from pilfering the lode but also because money is, in general, burdensome to him. He and Tom earn "a dollar a day apiece all the year round" (11) in interest, but Huck has no desire for the things money can buy; he travels light, caring only for the trinkets and tools that will assist him in his various locales or in his interactions with friends.

His friends are boys like himself, most notably Tom Sawyer. Tom is different, however. He has been "schooled" more thoroughly. His life experience has included the confusion and awkwardness of awakening love, the limitations of conventional family life, the need to strive and excel to impress the powerful, and the allure of utilizing craft and guile to exploit others for adventure's sake. Tom is much more familiar than Huck with the literature of romance and daring. When, for instance, he gathers a group of boys around him in the dark woods to form a band of robbers, he makes each swear "a real beautiful oath" and sign "his name in blood" as the "pirate books and robber books" (17) prescribe. Indeed, in Huck's eyes, Tom is all-knowing as he explains how his gang will not be "burglars" but rather "highwaymen," who will "stop stages and carriages on the road with masks on and kill the people and take their watches and money" (18) like a "high-toned" (17) enterprise should. In indulging such fantasies, Tom is still clearly a boy, but he is one who is preparing to go places as a man. On the one hand, we can see him as a George Bailey type successful businessman or politician, a worldly-wise up and coming leader who will use his wits to get ahead. On the other hand, if life throws Tom a curve or two, we can picture him plausibly as a con artist. While it is hard to imagine Tom Sawyer sinking to the level of the king and the duke, the two flim-flam artists who attach themselves to Huck as he travels down the Mississippi, his gifts are compatible with theirs.

Tom's innocence is real but already compromised; he will, for better or for worse, gradually lose it as life goes on. Huck's is a permanent possession. Huck resists Tom's ways just as he does those of his guardians. He shows intermittent desire to learn to read, largely to separate himself from his father's brutishness, but not to the extent of Tom, who has immersed himself in boys' tales of derring-do. Huck also has little interest in being a leader or in impressing the girls. Only one young lady stirs his emotions in the novel, Mary Jane Wilks, whom he meets during his river journey. To Huck, her beauty and simplicity are beyond telling. She is the virtuous child, the Cordelia of her household. When she is about to leave for good, he muses:

> *And when it comes to beauty—and goodness, too—she lays over them all. I hain't ever seen her since that time that I see her go out that door; no, I hain't ever seen her since, but I reckon I've thought of her a many and a many a million times, and of her saying she would pray for me: and if I'd 'a' thought it would do any good for me to pray for her, blamed if I wouldn't 'a' done it or bust.* (189)

This is the idealizing love of the young and the innocent.

If Huck resists Tom's family's attempts to civilize him and Tom's example of leadership through bookish style, he is equally opposed to his father's cruel and exploitative way of life. Huck's "Pap" is not a Hollywood dad come upon hard times and gone bad. He is bad to the bone, an outlier whose parasitic relationship to society is like that of the ancient nomads to agricultural settlements and commercial towns: whatever is fixed and established is fair game for expropriation. Huck's strongest memory of his father reinforces this identity: "He used to always whale me when he was sober and could get his hands on me" (21). Pap is also aloof, socially inept, and indifferent. He too knows the forests and rivers and can survive quite well without domestic comforts, provided alcohol is available. He is rough, plain-spoken, and harsh in his judgments but clever enough to understand how law and convention function, especially where parents' and children's rights and duties are concerned.

As chapter 3 begins, Huck has not seen his father "for more than a year" (21), and indeed there is a possibility he has died in a drowning accident. But Huck, the child of nature who has learned the realities of life through rich experience, knows that that possibility cannot be considered because of one detail in the report of the drowning: "a drownded man don't float on his back" (21). This conclusion is proven correct when Huck walks into his room one night and sees his father in the candlelight. Pap looks weathered and beaten, as a lifelong alcoholic would, but there is something else in his gaze, something so sinister in its bloodless pallor it would "make a baby sick . . . make a baby's flesh crawl—a tree-toad white, a fish-belly white" (27). This is the stare of an ice-cold sociopath, whom a baby, pure innocence, recognizes immediately as its polar opposite and recoils from instinctively. Pap could have appeared as one of the dark antagonists in a Hawthorne morality tale or as a character like Melville's Claggart, another pale monster whose burning hostility dooms Billy Budd, so like Huck in his guilelessness.

With his overriding self-absorption, his father does not have Huck's instinctive respect for other people's feelings and points of view. When he first bursts on the scene, Pap becomes immediately jealous of Huck, threatening to take him "down a peg" for thinking he is "better'n your father" and "putting on frills" (28) by going to school and learning to read. He sees his son as an object, not a fellow human being. He is incapable of paternal love; his concept of father/son relations emphasizes the parent's authority to rule his child. In Pap's case, the rule is despotic. He calls himself "boss of his son" (30), but he is more like a slave-owner of his son. Just as the master is free to exploit his human "property" as he sees fit, so Pap sees himself as entitled to every liberty in his relentless pursuit of the one object that makes his son important to him: the fortune Huck gained in the earlier novel and in this one entrusts to Judge Thatcher to keep from Pap. In his exertions to claim the money for himself, Pap subjects Huck to abuse that would earn him a jail sentence today: "He said he'd cowhide me till I was black and blue if I didn't raise some money for him" (30). As if his threats and maneuverings to force the transfer of Huck's fortune to himself were not enough, Pap goes so far as to make his son a captive by imprisoning him in a deserted shed deep in the woods for days on end as he conducts his legal challenge to Judge Thatcher and binges away idle hours.

Today, this monstrous behavior would be held up as exceptionally vicious. In the nineteenth-century frontier world Twain evokes, however, it is understood as part of the primitivism that always threatens to overwhelm the civilized stability embodied in a stable community's churches, schools, and law enforcement. The great Hollywood director John Ford shows a similar contrast in *The Man Who Shot Liberty Valance*, where James Stewart's character, so decent, wholesome, and comfortable with the domestic values that have tamed the once Wild West, is made to confront Lee Marvin's Liberty Valance, a sadistic and dangerous throwback to the lawless past. Pap's hostility to civilized society and its institutions is profound, expressing itself in drunken monologues that punctuate the hours he and his captive son are together in the woods, an environment as cruel as Hobbes's state of nature. In one rambling harangue, the perpetually resentful Pap rants about the evils of the "wonderful govment" (35) that will not allow him to collect the money that really should be his and not Huck's. Pap underlines his point by remembering once seeing and hearing about "a free nigger there from Ohio—a mulatter, most as white as a white man" (35). He was told this well-dressed and articulate gentleman was "a p'fessor in a college and could talk all kinds of languages, and knowed everything" (35). This man, furthermore, "could *vote* when he was at home" (35), a fact Pap considers proof positive of the civil law's deviation from nature's law. He asks in amazement, "why ain't this nigger put up at auction and sold?" (35) Pap then learns the astonishing fact that "he couldn't be sold till he'd been in the state six months, and he hadn't been there that long yet" (35). The man who is already apoplectic over the injustice being perpetrated against him can barely contain his rage over what he has just heard:

> *They call that a govment that can't sell a free nigger till he's been in the state six months. Here's a govment that calls itself a govment, and lets on to be a govment, and thinks it is a govment, and yet's got to set stock-still for six whole months before it can take a-hold of a prowling, thieving, infernal, white-shirted free nigger . . .* (35–36)

Huck will later come to very different conclusions on the subject of race, reflecting the innate sense of justice and tolerance guiding his untutored conscience. For the moment, though, he needs to escape the situation he is in, but not by trying to return to the widow and Miss Watson, where all he can think of is being forced "to wash, and eat on a plate, and comb up, and get up regular" (32). One morning as Pap sleeps off another bender that includes a frightening attack of delirium tremens, during which he tries to assault his son "with a clasp knife" (37), Huck has the good fortune afterwards of seizing an empty canoe as it rolls down the river near his camp. He decides quickly to hide the canoe and, when an opportunity presents itself, use it to "get so far away that the old man nor the widow couldn't ever find me any more" (34). In other words, Huck will separate himself completely from both the junglelike environment he is stuck in with his father and the oppressive feminine regimentation of the widow's home back in town. He has his chance when Pap leaves him abruptly one afternoon with a load of loose timbers he expects to sell for a nice profit. Left alone, Huck piles into his canoe supplies his father has left behind and then uses Pap's rifle to kill a hog he chances upon shortly after. It occurs to Huck that the best way to keep from being followed is to fake his death at the hands of robbers, for which blood from the slaughtered animal will provide evidence. He calculates how his disappearance will be dealt with in a passage revealing the native intelligence of this child of nature, concluding with confidence: "They won't ever hunt the river for anything but my dead carcass. They'll soon get tired of that, and won't bother no more about me" (42). Under cover of darkness, Huck makes his way down the Mississippi to Jackson's Island, a perfect hideaway because "nobody ever comes there" (42).

As Huck awakens the next morning, however, he discovers that a number of people are indeed coming near the island. He hears the sound of cannon fire "away up the river" (44) and realizes that what he anticipated is coming to pass: "You see, they was firing cannon over the water, trying to make my carcass come to the top" (44). As the noise gets louder, Huck sees a "ferryboat full of people floating down" (44), and everyone staring at the river expecting a body to rise to the surface through the power of the blasts. When the boat comes near the shore, Huck recognizes many on board, including "Pap, and Judge Thatcher, and Joe Harper, and Tom Sawyer, and his old Aunt Polly, and Sid and Mary, and plenty more" (45–46). If it takes a village to raise a child, Huck's village in cameo is passing by, all convinced that their child has been taken from them long before their work has been completed. As the boat leaves the vicinity, Huck is, for that community, only a memory, but for himself, now liberated to make his way in the world as his conscience and instincts dictate, a boy born again free. He will begin an odyssey down the Mississippi that will expose him to people, situations, difficulties, and challenges that will all together be decisive in forming the character and world view he will acquire through these experiences.

At the very start, he will be faced with a choice that literally involves life and death. On the island that no one ever visits, Huck meets none other than "Miss Watson's Jim" (49), who confesses, with some trepidation, that he has "run off" (50). He had to do so because around the time of Huck's disappearance, Jim overheard "old missus," that stern teacher of Christian morality and virtue, "tell de widder she gwyne to sell me down to Orleans, but she didn't want to, but she could git eight hundred dollars for me, en it 'uz sich a big stack o' money she couldn' resis" (50). Before Jim gives this explanation, he makes Huck promise not to reveal the truth to anyone: "But you wouldn't tell on me ef I 'uz to tell you, would you, Huck?" (50). When Jim asks him to reaffirm his vow of silence, Huck does so with firm resolve:

> *Well, I did. I said I wouldn't, and I'll stick to it. Honest injun, I will. People would call me a low-down Abolitionist and despise me for keeping mum—but that don't make no difference. I ain't a-going to tell, and I ain't a-going back there, anyways."* (50)

Huck's words mark a critical turning point in his tale and in his life. By assisting a fugitive slave escape capture, he is breaking the law. But in Huck's innocence, the natural impulse to help someone in desperate need trumps conventional strictures and must be honored. Here is Rousseau's child asserting, in essence, that "all men are created equal" and as such are entitled to "life, liberty, and the pursuit of happiness" no matter their color, sex, or life circumstances. Huck is making a leap forward and applying in his day standards of value typical of the post-civil rights era, even if, as he is well aware, the dogs and the horsemen scouring the region for Jim will, if they find the two, arrest both as criminals. None of these concerns matter now, however, because in this situation, Huck and Jim must bond as brothers, two survivalists who are equals in tracking, hunting, fishing, and, above all, evading capture. Their travels together will turn out to be life-transforming, not only through their encounters with other people and their adaptations to nature's challenges, but also in the simple fact that they have to become partners to maximize their chances for survival. Huck is unwavering in his care and concern for the man he considers a friend and soul mate. He anticipates and lives up to the resolution writer E. M. Forster called upon when, in the politically charged England of the 1930s, he stated that if given the choice between betraying his country or betraying his friend, he hoped he would have "the courage to betray his country." Huck's "country" is the Mississippi Valley of the early nineteenth century; by refusing to "betray his friend," Huck is certainly defying that country's law and turning upside down all that custom and convention have taught concerning relations between the races.

In their long ride up and down the Mississippi, which comprises the novel's long middle section, Huck and Jim meet characters and face situations that force both to use their wits and native good sense to the utmost to escape harm. Over the course of their journey, the adventures they are thrust into are of a character similar to those Tom Sawyer reads about in boys' tales, where intrepid youths face and overcome obstacles and antagonists almost magically. Thus, while the dialogue and settings in the novel are those of real people and places, Huck and Jim's numerous escapes from danger through means of rescue appearing out of nowhere are characteristic of the self-inflating heroism of boyish imagination, where fantasy overcomes reality regularly. For instance, while the two are still on Jackson's Island, they see "a frame house" (56) floating down the river, apparently swept away by storms and flooding. As if this were nothing out of the ordinary, Huck and Jim row out to the structure, make their way inside, discover a body on the floor "shot in the back" (56), and an enormous quantity of useful items like furnishings, clothing, tools, bedding, candles, and "a bran-new Barlow knife worth two bits in any store" (57). They manage to load all of this into their canoe, which does not capsize, and return to their island "home all safe" (58). Even though this kind of providential discovery and appropriation of essentials has all the elements of myth, it and similar manna-from-heaven instances abound to keep Huck and Jim whole. Then, as if finding this cache just when most needed were not coincidence enough, Huck will learn at novel's end that the dead man is Pap, whom Jim recognizes and tells Huck not to "look at his face—it's too gashly" (57).

As the two hunker down on the island, Huck realizes that they are vulnerable to a surprise capture if slave hunters on the prowl for Jim stumble upon their camp. He decides to take a chance and "slip over the river" (60) to try to pick up any information he can about search parties in the area. Jim suggests Huck "dress up like a girl" (61) for this exploration to keep from being recognized. This vaudevillian turn is easily exposed by the first and only person he encounters, a woman new to the region who detects decidedly non-girlish traits in her guest as they talk. Among other peculiarities is the way Huck flings "a bar of lead twisted up into a knot" (65) at a stray rat roaming the premises. He throws "from the wrist and elbow, with . . . arm out to one side, like a boy" (68). Nonetheless, the lady is kind to Huck and sympathetic as he spins out a melancholy tale about being forced to escape from "a mean old farmer in the country thirty mile back from the river" (66), who cruelly abused him. As their conversation proceeds, the woman unwittingly reveals exactly the news Huck is seeking. She knows Jim ran away the day after Huck disappeared, and now, like everyone else in town, is sure "the runaway nigger" (63) had to have killed the poor boy. Furthermore, she had seen what appeared to be smoke rising above Jackson's Island several days earlier. In consequence, her husband and another man this very night are planning to "slip around through the woods and hunt up his [Jim's] campfire" (65) and grab him before he can get away. They will immediately surrender him to the authorities and collect "three hundred dollars" (64) in reward money.

Huck exits instantly, making his way back to the camp in a panic. When he arrives, he sees with relief that his companion is alone and unharmed. Taking no chances, the two pile whatever they will need into their raft and leave in a hurry, hoping to put distance between themselves and any pursuers. Under cover of darkness, they manage to avoid detection and then begin a pattern of traveling and hiding that persists for the rest of their journey. Because they cannot risk being spotted in the daylight, they cruise by night, "drifting down the big, still river . . . looking up at the stars" (70). As the sun begins to rise, Huck and Jim will head for the shore, where they can conceal their raft and lie low until dark.

Together and alone in nature, they flourish. Except for a snake bite Jim suffers in a cave on Jackson's Island, they face few threats from animals or sea creatures. The worst challenges arise from weather changes, particularly when storms stir up the river, reducing visibility and making navigation difficult. Most of these incidents are temporary and controllable. Huck and Jim also feel no need for clothing in the summer heat: "we was always naked, day and night, whenever the mosquitoes would let us" (121). This detail highlights the innocence of these two youths, who are free to think and act like individuals living in a state of nature and shunning all the restraints and complications of settled society. They are a masculine duo living like Adam and Eve before the Fall. As such, they can look upon their majestic surroundings with naïve awe:

> *Sometimes we'd have that whole river to ourselves for the longest time. Yonder was the banks and the islands, across the water; and maybe a spark—which was a candle in a cabin window; and sometimes on the water you could see a spark or two—on a raft or a scow, you know; and maybe you could hear a fiddle or a song coming over from one of them crafts. It's lovely to live on a raft. We had the sky up there, all speckled with stars, and we used to lay on our backs and look up at them, and discuss about whether they was made or only just happened.* (121)

Metaphysical speculations aside, these boys are living life to the fullest in a virgin world. They can breathe free only on the great river, the one steady and constant resource and refuge in the novel. They resemble the Native Americans, who settled the continent first and established the most sensitive and symbiotic relationships with nature North America has ever supported. For Huck and Jim, even when "civilization" intrudes, the effect is fleeting and evanescent, as nature easily absorbs even a dramatic intervention:

> *Once or twice of a night we would see a steamboat slipping along in the dark, and now and then she would belch a whole world of sparks up out of her chimbleys, and they would rain down in the river and look awful pretty; then she would turn a corner and her lights would wink out and her powwow shut off and leave the river still again; and by and by her waves would get to us, a long time after she was gone, and joggle the raft a bit and after that you wouldn't hear nothing for you couldn't tell how long, except maybe frogs or something.* (121–22)

The two fugitives bond naturally and care for each other like brothers, confirming Rousseau's contention that primitive simplicity promotes equality. As far as moral character is concerned, though Huck's conscience is a reliable guide, he can sometimes fail to be as sensitive to Jim's feelings as a friend should be. On one occasion, as they are floating down the river in the night fog, Huck falls overboard. Jim fears the worst and drifts to sleep despairing that he will ever see Huck again. Huck, though, survives and suddenly reappears before the groggy-eyed Jim, apparently no worse for the experience. Not content to reassure his mate that all is well, Huck lets his penchant for storytelling get the best of him as he tries to convince Jim that he must have been dreaming that Huck had been in the water. When the truth is finally revealed, Jim shows how deeply Huck's deception has hurt him:

> *When I got all wore out with work, en wid de callin' for you, en went to sleep, my heart waz mos' broke bekase you wuz los', en I didn' k'yer no'mo' what become er me en de raf'. En when I wake up en find you back ag'in all safe en soun', de tears come, en I could 'a' got down on my knees en kiss yo' foot, I's so thankful. En all you wuz thinkin' 'bout wuz how you could make fool uv ole Jim wid a lie'. Dat truck dah is trash; en trash is what people is dat puts dirt on de head er dey frien's en makes 'em ashamed."* (90)

This rebuke stings, like a reprimand from a respected teacher or clergyman. Huck is chastened, apologetic, and determined to do "no more mean tricks" (90).

Jim possesses other virtues that set him apart. He cares about his family, for instance, who are separated from him by the cruelty of a system that has no concern about keeping black families intact and together. As a child of his time, albeit an exceptional one, even Huck finds Jim's solicitude hard to credit, but living so closely with him, he knows it is genuine: "I do believe he cared just as much for his people as white folks does for there'n. It don't seem natural, but I reckon it's so" (155). The irony of "natural" in Huck's musing is noteworthy. If natural is equated with "conventional," as it was in the thinking of the great majority of Huck's white compatriots, Jim's tender feelings are remarkable. But if natural is understood in the sense of Rousseau, it is to be expected that Jim should suffer so when he thinks about his absent loved ones. As a "child of nature" uncontaminated by a degraded society, Jim responds instinctively and therefore authentically to the need to care for those closest to him.

In the same scene, Jim explains more fully why he is particularly morose while thinking of family members. He tells Huck about an episode with his little daughter in which he behaved badly. He remembers telling her repeatedly to shut the door behind her. Each time he asked, she made no effort to comply. Becoming exasperated by what seemed like flagrant disregard for paternal authority, Jim began shouting his commands. Still his daughter stayed put, seemingly oblivious to him. Finally, thoroughly enraged, Jim slapped her hard on the side of the head and stormed away. He returned shortly after to find his daughter in tears. Just then the wind blew the door shut with a loud crash. The girl, however, with her back to the door remained perfectly still despite the noise. Jim then realized to his horror that, far from being defiant, his little girl had not closed the door because she had never heard his words: "Oh, she was plumb deef en dumb, Huck, plumb deef en dumb—en I'd been a-treat'n her so" (156). While he recounts this tale, Jim too is in tears as he begs God's forgiveness for his rash tantrum. Jim's guilt can be compared to Huck's in the previous excerpt, but its emotional weight is much heavier. Jim's conscience is acutely sensitive: "he never gwyne to fogive hisself as long's he live" (156). He is torn apart by this memory, and his sorrow and contrition are profound.

Jim is loyal to a fault as well. His bond with Huck is unbreakable, of course, but he is just as firmly attached to "Mars Tom Sawyer," whose passion for literature, as we shall see, will lead to so many delays in "freeing" Jim later in the novel.

At one point in this last section, Tom is actually wounded as a posse of slave hunters open fire on the trio. While Tom is lying in pain, Jim forcefully reminds Huck of their need for a doctor and adamantly refuses to leave Tom's side until one arrives, despite the danger he faces from his pursuers. He is eloquent in his brave stand: "I doan' budge a step out'n dis place 'dout a *doctor*; not if it's forty year" (267). Huck draws the absolutely incorrect conclusion that this extraordinary courage proves that Jim is really "white inside" (267), an ironic commentary that Huck's whole experience with Jim cannot completely dispel.

If the days and nights Huck and Jim spend by themselves floating on the river and camping near the shore are akin to a sojourn in Eden, the times when circumstances force them to separate, with Jim having to hide and Huck having to interact with various people in the villages and towns bordering the Mississippi, their experiences are more like sojourns in the netherworld. Humanity on dry land is decidedly "fallen," with lying, cheating, stealing, hating, bullying, and even killing common and acceptable. This is the environment that has shaped the life of Huck's pap, leaving him permanently scarred, friendless, suspicious, and hostile. The society Huck has to navigate, however reluctantly, is a playground for Satan, a community the Father of Lies regards as his to infect and corrupt freely.

What Huck witnesses and has to endure is similar to what Young Goodman Brown undergoes in Nathaniel Hawthorne's short story of that title. Brown tries to live as a "good man" among the godly in his hometown of Salem, originally settled by religious dissidents eager to create a New Jerusalem in a New World. Over time, however, Satan has so thoroughly distorted the belief systems of so many of Brown's neighbors that their godliness is for the sake of appearance only. Deep down they are Satan's minions. During one terrible night, as the young man looks on in horror, townspeople he respects as pious and respectable men and women take part in a ceremony that features prayers and hymns grossly twisted out of their Christian context and redirected toward devil worship. The young man's innocent acceptance of the religious values he has been taught to uphold is shattered that night by the very people who supposedly profess and model them. The experience culminates with Brown's young wife, aptly named Faith, appearing as a candidate for "baptism" into this company's terrifying cult. Brown's life from this point on will be tinged with bitterness, sorrow, and gloom.

Huck does not witness a nocturnal spectacle like this, nor does he betray any of the principles his conscience has instilled in him as he tries to cope with what fallen humanity throws at him. Throughout his time away from the river and in whatever situation, Huck remains the moral center of the novel, always acting "with malice toward none and charity toward all" no matter the circumstances he is in or the people he encounters. In three distinct adventures on shore, he prevails in the face of staggering challenges. These encounters resemble in their numerous fantastic details and scarcely credible interventions and rescues, the adventures of Huck and Jim as they travel on the river, escaping capture or disaster through quick wit and resourcefulness.

The first begins when a steamboat rams the raft one dark night, and the boys are thrown overboard into the river. Huck manages to make it to the shore, but without Jim, who he is sure must have swum to the opposite side. After making his way through the undergrowth, Huck arrives at a stately looking home and decides to approach the door. As he proceeds, a number of dogs converge on him, barking and yelping furiously. The home's inhabitants shoo them away and invite Huck inside. They do so, however, without warmth or friendliness; in fact, three of the men point guns at the boy. They hold a candle in front of Huck's face and carefully "take a good look at" (101) their visitor, declaring finally in unison, "Why *he* ain't a Shepherdson—no, they ain't any Shepherdson about him" (101). This conclusion melts the ice, and the family members become hospitable. They are the Grangerfords, consisting of the patriarch, Colonel Grangerford, "a gentleman all over" (108), his wife, three sons, and two daughters. "This was all there was of the family now, but there used to be more—three sons; they got killed; and Emmeline that died" (109). The sons perished because of the Grangerfords' obsessive and irrational hostility to all the members of a neighboring clan, the Shepherdsons, with whom they and their forbears have been feuding for generations for reasons never made clear. Here, in essence, is an American version of a Shakespearean noble family poisoned in its potential for gracious living and normal relationships by a tradition that defies all logic and distorts everyday experience lethally. Mark Twain once observed that Sir Walter Scott bore a great deal of responsibility for the American Civil War since Scott's chivalrous heroes and noble ladies served as role models for Southern gentry intent on keeping their culture and "peculiar institution" undefiled by modernity. These grandees went to war enthusiastically, blind to the realities ignored in romances and seeing only the compelling need to defend aristocratic values against vulgar commerce. The Grangerfords could fit this model; in their failure to dispense with out-of-date thinking and their propagating to death the purity of their cruel inheritance, they reveal the cold emptiness of gentrified "family values." Such values ensure the extinction of a family, not its preservation.

Death, indeed, broods over the family. Daughter Emmeline, for instance, "kinder pined away and did not live long" (107). Throughout her short life, she became known far and wide for her poetry, almost all of which was elegiac: "Every time a man died, or a woman died, or a child died, she would be on hand for her 'tribute' before he was cold" (107). Col. Grangerford and his sons radiate an aristocratic fearlessness that can lead to suicidal confrontations if Shepherdsons are in the vicinity. The youngest son, Buck, who befriends Huck, complains at one point that he "don't get no show" (101), that is, no opportunity to shoot it out with the Shepherdsons. These characters are "grotesques," extreme types compelled by blood, status, mental or physical deformity, eccentric gifts, poverty, or superstition to live in one-dimensional service to the peculiarity shaping their lives. Emmeline's morbidity, the colonel's hauteur, the sons' reckless courting of danger are all characteristic of the Southern Gothic literary tradition, exemplified by writers like Poe, Faulkner, Flannery O'Connor, and Carson McCullers. We shall meet other examples as Huck's peregrinations continue.

Huck's time with the Grangerfords ends in a hail of gunfire. The tensions and suspicions keeping the feuding families constantly on alert build to a climax when Sophia Grangerford elopes with Harney Shepherdson, igniting rage and bloodlust within both households. Unlike Romeo and Juliet, Sophia and Harney escape unharmed to begin a new life far away. Others are not so fortunate. The men of the families go to war with each other. The colonel and two of his sons are killed, along with "two or three of the enemy" (117). Huck climbs a tree and hides while Buck and "his cousin Joe" (117) are wounded and then chased by a crowd of Shepherdsons "singing out, 'Kill them, kill them!'" (117). This savagery is too much for Huck. His last thoughts on the spectacle and the feud are like Goodman Brown's on his neighbors:

> *It made me so sick I most fell out of the tree. I ain't a-going to tell all that happened—it would make me sick again if I was to do that. I wished I hadn't ever come ashore that night to see such things. I ain't ever going to get shut of them—lots of times I dream about them.* (117)

Prior to this deadly affair, Huck has been reunited with Jim, who implausibly swam behind him after the accident but stayed quiet in the water and has kept out of sight on land "because he didn't want nobody to pick him up and take him into slavery again" (114). In another bit of heaven-sent relief, Jim was able to rescue the boys' raft and make it seaworthy again since "dey warn't no great harm done" (115) by the steamboat. Thus, the two are able to leave the bloody scene and take up with relief their happy life on the river once more:

> *We said there warn't no home like a raft, after all. Other places do seem so cramped up and smothery,*

> *but a raft don't. You feel mighty free and easy and comfortable on a raft.* (119)

One morning, however, things change when Huck paddles his canoe "over a chute to the main shore" (122) to pick berries. As he does so, two men clearly in a panic approach and ask him to help "save their lives" (122). Though "they hadn't been doing nothing . . . there was men and dogs a'coming" (122). These two turn out to be con artists, who are being chased by outraged victims of one of their schemes. These include phony temperance meetings "for ten cents a head, children, and niggers free," as well as quasi-religious miracle cures "for cancer and paralysis and sich things" (123). They boast about how they can "do lots of things—most anything comes handy, so it ain't work" (123). Their pretensions are breathtaking. One claims to be "the rightful Duke of Bridgewater" (125), while the other asserts a royal lineage by identifying himself as "the pore disappeared Dauphin, Looy the Seventeen, son of Looy the Sixteen and Marry Antoinette" (126). Intrigue and revolution at home have forced these exalted personages into exile in frontier America, where they scrape by any way they can. Jim is impressed and defers to the king, in particular. Thanks to his native good sense, though, Huck sees through both: "It didn't take me long to make up my mind that these liars warn't no kings nor dukes at all, but just low-down humbugs and frauds" (127). Nevertheless, like an indulgent parent of spoiled children, Huck lets "them have their own way" (127) to avoid conflict.

Huck sees the king in action when he and his companions discover that just about everyone in "a one-horse town about three mile down the bend" (131) from their raft is at a huge camp meeting in a nearby grove. For the king, such an event does not induce religious feeling, only the prospect of quick profit. The meeting's atmosphere is highly charged as a preacher whips up his audience with "his arms and his body going all the time, and shouting his words out with all his might" (132), while his listeners react by "groaning and crying and saying amen." (132). This is just the setting the king relishes. He goes "a-charging up onto the platform" (133) and receives permission to speak. He offers personal testimony to God's saving grace, telling everyone he had been robbed the night before and had to come "ashore off of a steamboat without a cent" (133). This was actually providential, though, because it has reinforced the king's determination as "a changed man" (133) and reformed pirate to return to the Indian Ocean without money or possessions and spend "the rest of his life trying to turn the pirates into the true path" (133). Granted, even if "it would take him a long time to get there without money, he would get there anyway" (133) and fulfill God's plan.

The people are so moved they demand that the king walk among them with hat in hand to gather the necessary funds for an immediate voyage. He leaves the crowd with "eighty-seven dollars and seventy-five cents" (134). On the way back to the raft, as a bonus, he grabs "a three-gallon jug of whiskey" (134) lying under someone's wagon. To the glib imposter, this haul "laid over any day he'd ever put in in the missionarying line" (134). For someone claiming to have given up piratical ways, the king's trickery has all the hallmarks of a heist on the high seas. Even Jim has seen and heard enough. That evening, he asks Huck if "we gwyne to run acrost any mo' kings on dis trip," and is greatly relieved to hear Huck reply, "I reckon not" (135).

The duke is not to be outdone. The next caper will be a performance of excerpts from Shakespeare's plays. Since the king has had little experience in theatrics, let alone Shakespeare, his partner has "to learn him over and over again how to say every speech" (136), a tutorial he enjoys. The duke also shows the king how to be expressive:

> *So he went to marching up and down, thinking, and frowning horrible every now and then; then he would hoist up his eyebrows; next he would squeeze his hand on his forehead and stagger back and kind of moan; next he would sigh, and next he'd let on to drop a tear. It was beautiful to see.* (137)

The duke is eager to have his student recite Hamlet's soliloquy "To be or not to be," punctuating the words with histrionic sounds and gestures inspired by the duke's example. Since he has no published text of the soliloquy, the duke has to "piece it out from memory" (137). He pulls back "from recollection's vaults" (137) these opening lines:

To be or not to be; that is the bare bodkin
That makes calamity of so long life;
For who would fardels bear, till Birnam Wood do come to Dunsinane,
But that the fear of something after death
Murders the innocent sleep . . . (137)

Two dozen more chaotic lines follow, making the king's star turn a hilarious mishmash the two frauds have no shame or hesitation presenting.

Continuing to sail "pretty well down the state of Arkansaw" (138), the thespians and the boys come to another "one horse town in a big bend" (138) that may offer good possibilities for the Shakespeare farce. They are encouraged when they hear that a circus is in town as well, because such a show will draw people from far and wide. What they observe as they walk through the muddy streets past dilapidated buildings behind fences that "had been whitewashed some time or another, but the duke said it was in Columbus's time like enough" (140), is a venue ripe for exploitation. The locals seem like just the kind of good ol' boys the frauds are used to fleecing:

There was empty dry-goods boxes under the awnings, and loafers roosting on them all day long, whittling them with their Barlow knives; and chawing tobacco, and gaping and yawning and stretching—a mighty ornery lot. They generly had on yellow straw hats most as wide as an umbrella, but didn't wear no coats nor waistcoats; they called one another Bill, and Buck, and Hank, and

> *Joe, and Andy, and talked lazy and used considerable many cusswords.* (140)

With supreme confidence and cynicism, the king and the duke make their extravaganza work. Posing as London stage professionals, they perform to packed houses for two nights. The audiences, however, leave the shows angry and perplexed, complaining that the brief and disjointed excerpts are not what they expected such artists to offer. On the third and last night of "The Royal Nonesuch," as patrons are filing in, Huck can smell "sickly eggs by the barrel, and rotten cabbages and such things" (152) that the rubes undoubtedly intend to use on "them tragedians" (152). The duke, however, has anticipated this outcome, so right before the program is to begin, he and Huck slip away to the safety of the raft, apparently deserting the poor king by so doing. But the king greets them on the raft, not having "been uptown at all" (153). Huck can hardly believe what has occurred: "Them rapscallions took in four hundred and sixty-five dollars in that three nights. I never see money hauled in like that before" (153). "Greenhorns, flatheads" (153) and the like are clearly no match for bandits like these "and the king and the duke fairly laughed their bones loose over the way they'd served them people" (153).

The king and the duke obviously live by lying. They have no clear identities, no professions, no purpose other than to create schemes that in their outrageousness will attract the interest and the funds of the ignorant herd among whom these men of superior breeding always find themselves. None of their deceptions bring anything of real value, and whatever money the frauds weasel out of their victims is quickly squandered, mostly on alcohol. Notwithstanding, their misadventures highlight an important aspect of the "civilization" Huck resists. When Huck first meets them, the two are carrying "big, fat, ratty-looking carpetbags" (123), very appropriate luggage. The king and the duke indeed bear a resemblance to those northern sales and businesspeople who swept into Southern towns and villages after the Civil War with all sorts of mostly bogus commercial propositions and deals. Today they would be promoting Ponzi schemes and other too good to be true investment prospects, as well as fraudulent insurance and retirement plans and the like. Herman Melville imagined a similar type, giving him multiple incarnations and endlessly plausible proposals in *The Confidence Man*, where true to American innocence, the victims all react with dumb amazement and pitiful credulity to every approach. The king and the duke play on this gullibility, particularly when they caricature European cultural ideals and types.

Nineteenth century America was still very much in thrall to Europe, England especially, when it came to the essentials of fine living. Despite the fact that the American revolutionaries had cut all political ties to Britain and had opened up the American heartland to exploration and settlement that should have distanced most citizens from Continental cultural influences, Americans still believed European standards were essential in molding character and promoting a sophisticated appreciation of literature and the arts and that European institutions, such as the theater and the opera, should be brought to major cities and, through touring companies, to the hinterland as well. The king and the duke are aware of this instinctive American veneration of all things European. Therefore, when they present themselves as actors and offer to perform excerpts from Shakespeare, they naturally spark interest within the coastal towns. The Marx Brothers-like caricatures they offer are hilarious in their error-prone grandiosity, but in mocking their audiences, they call into question the relevance of classical English theater to the American experience. The audience can be bamboozled because of the difficulty any plain-spoken rustic would have had in interpreting poetic drama in a setting thousands of miles away from and four centuries past this literature's place and time. Even had the townspeople perfect command of the language and the plays, the fraudsters likely would have been received with the same incomprehension. Just as Tom Sawyer's "by the book" applications of the romance novelists' "rules" make the models ridiculously inappropriate to his world, and just as

Miss Watson's instruction in Bible stories renders them equally questionable as guides to current living, so the assault on Shakespeare by the two con men disconnects even the greatest of playwrights from the life experience of the men and women of the Mississippi Delta.

What about these rustic citizens? Are they more authentic in their simplicity and naturalness, and do they therefore present attractive contrasts to the feuding grandees and the pretentious duo? Not really. They may be exploited by cynical con artists, and they may be pitied in their poverty, but the glimpses we have of the bumpkins' lifestyle and values are not inspiring. Huck observes another sickening spectacle that arouses these people just as he is leaving town. It involves Colonel Sherburn, the "heap best dressed man," (142) he has seen so far. For some time, the colonel has been regularly and publicly abused by a loud-mouthed but harmless local alcoholic named Boggs, who claims he has been swindled by Sherburn. Boggs is especially vocal this day, perhaps because, with the circus, more people than normal are present. Sherburn appears and, in deference to the man who clearly lords it over everyone, "the crowd drops back on each side to let him come" (142–43). Speaking "mighty ca'm and slow" (143), the colonel threatens Boggs with instant death if he says anything derogatory about him after a certain time. Everyone feels intimidated except Boggs. As the zero hour draws near, no one can get the drunken loudmouth to cease. In fact, he gets worse: "He cussed away with all his might, and throwed his hat down in the mud and rode over it, and pretty soon away he went a-raging down the street again, with his gray hair a-flying" (143). In desperation, onlookers send someone to bring Boggs's daughter to the scene because "sometimes he'll listen to her. If anybody can persuade him, she can" (143). While Huck watches "a young girl coming on the run" (143), he sees simultaneously Sherburn "standing perfectly still in the street" with "a pistol raised in his right hand" (143), looking for all the world like a duelist. Huck now stares in disbelief as Sherburn brings his arm level, fires, and murders Boggs with two well-aimed shots as his daughter looks on helplessly.

A mob forms to bring the killer to justice. This is a rare occurrence because, as a rule, only cruel sport can rouse these people from torpor:

> *There couldn't anything wake them up all over and make them happy all over like a dogfight—unless it might be putting turpentine on a stray dog and setting fire to him or tying a tin pan to his tail and see him run himself to death.* (141)

But when the townspeople arrive at the colonel's home, all hot for quick action, they are stopped in their tracks by the shotgun the old man points at them and by the icy contempt his withering glance radiates:

> *Sherburn run his eyes slow along the crowd; and wherever it struck the people tried a little to outgaze him, but they couldn't; they dropped their eyes and looked sneaky. Then pretty soon Sherburn sort of laughed; not the pleasant kind, but the kind that makes you feel like when you are eating bread that's got sand in it.* (146)

After listening to the colonel deride their courage ("the average man's a coward" (146)), their manhood ("But a mob without any *man* at the head of it is *beneath* pitifulness" (147)), and their humanity ("Now the thing for *you* to do is to droop your tails and go home and crawl in a hole" (147)), they quickly disperse. Huck's reaction, "I could a stayed if I wanted to, but I didn't want to" (147) sums up the revulsion he feels both for these "average" men and women who tolerate abuse sheepishly and the fearsome tyrant who despises them. He has had a vision of hell on earth.

The success the king and the duke have enjoyed in the "one horse town" goes to their heads. A short while after this escapade, the king learns from a stranger that one Peter Wilks, whom he has never known nor met, has died and will be buried the following day. The stranger reveals numerous details about the deceased and his family, especially regarding Peter's inheritance, that the king eagerly absorbs. A key point is the fact that two of Wilks's brothers, one a clergyman and the other a deaf mute, and both living in England, are traveling to the Wilks's funeral. They are expected to arrive by steamboat in time for the service, although this is not a certainty.

The king can hardly believe his luck. He rushes back to the raft and shares this information with the duke. They decide immediately to impersonate the brothers and persuade Wilks's daughters to let them dispose of their father's money and property on their behalf, all the while hoping the real brothers will be delayed. The scheme is daring and outlandish, but they very nearly succeed, largely because they play their parts so convincingly. Huck watches with mounting disgust as they weep uncontrollably over Peter's casket: "Well, if ever I struck anything like it, I'm a nigger. It was enough to make a body ashamed of the human race" (162). The first time they meet the Wilks daughters the two carry on in the same way, leading Huck to conclude, "I never see anything so disgusting" (163). The daughters, though, are totally trusting, allowing the king, in true Tartuffe style, to do as he pleases with their inheritance. They also let him secure title to the Wilks's three slaves. The day after the funeral, the king brazenly sells them, breaking up a family in the process. Huck cannot bear the spectacle unfolding in front of him:

> *I thought them poor girls and them niggers would break their hearts for grief; they cried around each other, and took on so it most made me down sick to see it . . . I can't ever get it out of my memory, the sight of them poor miserable girls and niggers hanging around each other's necks and crying . . .* (181)

Huck knows that the king's sale of the slaves will not be deemed legitimate and they will be returned soon enough, but the expropriation of the daughters' assets could be carried through if he does not intervene. One of the daughters, Mary

Jane, is too kind and too attractive to Huck to be led down a road to impoverishment: "I says to myself, *this* is a girl that I'm letting that old reptile rob her of her money" (173). He resolves to foil the frauds' plans: "I felt so ornery and low down and mean that I says to myself, my mind's made up; I'll hive that money for them or bust" (173). With wit and resourcefulness and through a byzantine series of breathtaking maneuvers and complications, Huck manages to keep the daughters' money and property out of the imposters' hands and back within the family's control.

But Huck is not yet finished with the king and the duke. Returning to the raft alone after he has saved the daughters' inheritance, he opens the wigwam where Jim has been hiding by day and is shocked to find it empty. Behind his back, he later discovers, the king has sold ever loyal and faithful Jim, like he did the Wilks's slaves, for a pittance:

> *. . . here it was all come to nothing, everything all busted up and ruined, because they could have the heart to serve Jim such a trick as that, and make him a slave again all his life, and amongst strangers, too, for forty dirty dollars.* (207–08)

This devil's deed will be the two thieves' undoing. Jim's new owner is Tom Sawyer's uncle, a kind and decent gentleman. Jim tells him all about the king and the duke and their propensity to swindle cash out of unsuspecting victims, like the audience members for the Shakespeare performances. The owner spreads the word about the two, and soon everyone is on the lookout for them. The king and the duke are now to be served frontier justice. They post their bills for "The Royal Nonesuch" in the nearby town shortly after Huck and Tom Sawyer have been reunited. On the night of the performance, Tom and Huck hurry to the site, with Huck hoping he can warn the two to get away before they are exposed and manhandled. They are too late. On their way, the boys run into "a raging rush of people with torches" leading "the king and the duke astraddle of a rail;" and "they was all over tar and feathers, and didn't look like anything in the world that was human—just looked like a couple of monstrous big soldier-plumes" (225). Despite all the two fraudsters have done, Huck remains true to character, feeling only shame and compassion as he beholds this painful and humiliating sight:

> *Well, it made me sick to see it; and I was sorry for them poor pitiful rascals, it seemed like I couldn't feel any hardness against them any more in the world. It was a dreadful thing to see. Human beings can be awful cruel to one another.* (225)

This scene culminates Huck's experience in the fallen world of humankind. He even blames himself for somehow letting the awful thing occur. Even though he could not get to the two in time, his conscience still disturbs him; "But that's always the way; it don't make no difference whether you do right or wrong, a person's conscience ain't got no sense, and just goes for him *anyway*" (226). This sensitive and demanding conscience nevertheless keeps Huck whole and true to his best self. In Nathaniel Hawthorne's short story, *"My Kinsman, Major Molineaux,"* young Robin watches as his uncle, an official in the hated British governor's service, is paraded past him in "tar and feathery dignity" with a frenzied mob howling. When the uncle and the boy look at each other, the boy, who has always respected him, laughs like the others. Robin loses at that instant the innocence Huck still retains.

This innocence, however, is now more strained and more fragile as a result of all Huck has seen and experienced in his days in the Delta towns. His pent-up disenchantment will lead Huck to a momentous decision after one final episode, where he joins with Tom Sawyer in an elaborate scheme to free Nigger Jim, whom Tom's Uncle Silas has shackled in a shed as a runaway slave. The story of the boys' exertions to "steal that nigger out of slavery" (228) takes up the entire third and final section of the novel. It need not have done so, because

Jim's bonds are easily loosened, a concession to their captive Uncle Silas and Aunt Sally, who are "kind as they could be" (241), make readily. Huck is eager to liberate Jim for all the right reasons. He and Jim have become like brothers, have worked together as equals, and have evaded dangers and trials through mutual support, quick thinking, and spirited action. Allowing Jim to return to servitude would undo all the two have worked so hard to achieve. Therefore, when Tom asks Huck how they should proceed, his partner is supremely practical and straightforward, proposing that "the first dark night that comes [they] steal the key out of the old man's britches after he goes to bed, and shove off down the river on the raft with Jim, hiding daytime and running nights" (227) like before. But this simple and quick expedient is too prosaic for Tom. The maestro of calculated adventurism rejects it out of hand and offers instead a highly complex and exhausting scheme modeled on the old boys' tales of derring-do and intrigue he has spent his youth absorbing. The setting is the rural South in the early nineteenth century, but for Tom the parties might as well be in Paris in the Middle Ages, another instance of European models having no connection to the New World. Nevertheless, Huck cannot help admiring Tom's artistry, admitting that his friend's genius has produced a masterful plan of escape for Jim "worth fifteen of" (227) Huck's. He defers to Tom from this point on, as the two embark on one last escapade that will be an "over the top" tour de force in conception and realization.

What Huck does not know, however, as the two begin their "by the book" labors, is that there is no need to worry at all about Jim's returning to slavery. Not until the end of a long and incredibly detailed series of inventive and picturesque processes derived from accounts of prisoners enchained or wearing iron masks in fortress-like dungeons, does Huck learn that Jim's owner, Miss Watson, has died and has freed Jim in her will. Tom has known this all along but will still compel Huck and Jim to go through all the hoops his imagination has conjured up just because of the "*adventure* of it" (280). Tom's adventure includes back-breaking digging, the introduction of rats and snakes into Jim's cell, inscriptions signed in Jim's blood, and a final race for the raft under gunfire. As was noted earlier, Tom himself is wounded while being chased, but his vainglory turns the injury into a badge of honor. Tom's craving for attention and his egocentric character actually victimize Jim; instead of being an equal as with Huck, he becomes a creature under Tom's control and direction at all times. He tells his Aunt Sally later that she "can't think *half* the fun it was" (278) to subject Jim to extraordinary rigors and pressures simply for Tom's amusement. This is slavery of a different sort but slavery, nonetheless. Jim remonstrates, but to no avail, concluding at one point that he has to endure what Tom and a compliant Huck require, because, as Huck records, "we was white folks and knowed better than him" (242). Such self-abasement was not apparent when he and Huck sailed down the Mississippi River in happier days. Tom has been fatally compromised by a "civilized" upbringing that countenances using another human being to satisfy selfish needs or whims. Tom enjoys his ring master's role so much that he tells Huck he wishes "we could keep it up all the rest of our lives" (242).

Something else is apparent in Tom's style, something Huck and Jim have seen before. Keeping Jim bound and confined as he does, Tom acts like the king and the duke, who kept Jim hidden and bound in a wigwam on the raft for days on end, ostensibly to convince any curious slave hunters Jim was a captured runaway, but really to secure him for use at a propitious time in a later sale. Tom's motives are not at all mercenary, but the fact is he is forcing Jim to adhere to a regimen wholly inappropriate to the circumstances mainly to satisfy his fantasies and his wish to be entertained. In addition, just like the two frauds, Tom is in over his head and verging on the grotesque as he tries to employ specific aspects and features of his escape literature to Jim's altogether different world. The following extract is Tom's attempt to create for Jim a knightly "inscription and coat of arms":

> *On the scutcheon we'll have a bend or in the dexter base, a saltire murrey in the fess, with a dog, couchant, for common charge, and under his foot a chain embattled, for slavery, with a chevron vert in a*

> *chief engrailed, and three invected lines on a field azure, with the nombril points rampant on a dancette indented; crest, a runaway nigger, sable, with his bundle over his shoulder on a bar sinister; and a couple of gules for supporters, which is you and me; motto, Maggiore fretta, minore atto. Got it out of a book—means the more haste the less speed.* (251)

The sheer audacity of Tom's attempt to assemble all the necessary elements of what must be the one and only coat of arms of "a runaway nigger," whose current master certainly eschews haste," is as bold and imaginative as it is ludicrous. Huck is awed, but when he asks Tom to explain what terms like "fess" and "bar sinister" mean, his imperious friend is not forthcoming. Huck charitably ascribes this refusal not to Tom's lack of knowledge but to his mercurial character: "If it didn't suit him to explain a thing to you, he wouldn't do it" (252). The king and the duke in their heyday behaved likewise whenever they mounted the "The Royal Nonesuch" in the small towns they visited with Huck.

Tom's back-and- forth with Huck is typical of their interactions throughout this last joint adventure. Tom Sawyer rules and Huck follows. This dynamic marginalizes Huck, making the whole faux rescue of Jim Tom's production and showpiece. The boy whom civilization has made a leader will eventually make the boy who has resisted civilization's lure a loner. Once all the strands of the boys' last hurrah are tied up and everything is resolved happily, one might expect things to return to normal, i.e., as portrayed in the novel's opening chapters. After all, Jim is at last free, Tom is back in the good graces of his aunts, Tom's and Huck's money is intact, and Pap is dead. But for Huckleberry Finn, these facts lead in an altogether new direction. His transformative journey down the big river and through the shore towns has forced this archetype of American innocence to move on, chastened and scarred by all that has happened to him. Huck cannot go back to the order and security of domestic life with the likes of Aunt Sally, who wants to adopt and "sivilize" (283) him so that he can become like Tom and company. Instead, he will "take to the open road" like Walt Whitman and "light out for the territory ahead of the rest" (283), hoping by this bold assertion of independence to nurture whatever remnants of fairness, decency, kindness, and care remain in heart and conscience while he is still young and still alone.

PART TWO

The bedrock conviction that unites Americans is Rousseau's assertion that man was created pure, wholesome, and innocent and that only as a result of misguided social processes and developments has he become corrupted. With proper redirection and education, these processes could be reversed and the innocence of primitive humankind restored in the New World. As we shall see, this faith animates Americans' approach to politics, education, and social life; it does not, however, resonate with the country's writers, Mark Twain especially. The world Huck Finn has to navigate is dark, depraved, and violent. He retains his innocence by following his conscience and his instincts, not by conforming to the values and practices he encounters in his travels. By starting again in the sparsely populated and still rugged territories, he can reproduce the American experience in microcosm. He will do so, however, as a boy-man wounded in spirit. Huck has gone through a fiery furnace that other emblematic characters in American literature know well. Stephen Crane's Henry Fleming, J. D. Salinger's Holden Caulfield, Ernest Hemingway's Frederick Henry, and Upton Sinclair's Jurgis Rudkus, to name a few, are burned by the world's ugly realities and purged of self-deception and illusion in similar ways. Though they survive their trials, like Huck, they do so at the expense of their former selves' innocence. Henry Fleming goes from untested recruit, who cannot perform as required in his baptism of fire, to hard-charging veteran free of all fears and restraints, a transformation we are all too familiar with after Vietnam, Iraq, and Afghanistan. We can imagine Fleming as one of the "hard cases" these conflicts have produced and continue to produce; we can envision him with beard and bandana, ostentatiously throwing away his decorations and cruising the country on a motorcycle preaching an end to war. After a near seduction by a male teacher, Holden Caulfield retreats to pastoral fantasy, and after his lover dies prematurely, Frederick Henry walks away in the rain to live with the "wound" that can never heal. In a kind of melting pot reversal, the son of recent immigrants, Jurgis Rudkus, leaves Chicago and all its miseries and heads for the hills to resume the agrarian existence his forbears strove so hard to transcend.

Nathaniel Hawthorne's Reverend Arthur Dimmesdale survives also, but his purgatorial cleansing is exceptionally painful. He labors among his people as a spiritual leader. When he follows his natural instincts and allows himself to fall in love with an unhappy married woman, the result is catastrophe. The dark forces of the world, where "fallen" man reigns and where a bitter husband plots his vengeance, overpower these two who have fallen from grace. Their sin must be exposed, their patina of romantic innocence erased, their shame made visible to all in the stocks and through a public branding. Unlike the great lovers of French literature, who are energized by sexual desire, these two are led haltingly and guiltily to their union, which takes on the character of a ruinous moral lapse bringing lifelong consequences.

Herman Melville's Billy Budd faces deadly consequences when he tries to cope with dark forces emerging in the closed world of a crew at sea. There is no escape to the raft for Billy. The irrational jealousy and provocations of Master-at-Arms Claggart doom the "handsome" young sailor; lashing out in righteous anger over this mistreatment, he kills Claggart with one blow. Though everyone knows he has been victimized, Billy must die to preserve law and order. He forgives the ship's captain just before he is executed, confirming the goodness and purity of heart that cannot cope with the assaults of fallen humanity.

F. Scott Fitzgerald's Jay Gatsby is Horatio Alger gone awry. He is self-made through steady application and disciplined habits; however, instead of virtuous fulfillment, these exertions lead to exploitation by and association with a corrupt gambler.

Gatsby retains his faith in himself and his naivete, enjoying riches and possessions the way a child would toys. Like Dimmesdale, he becomes involved with a married woman and suffers not just humiliation but death at the hands of the wronged husband. He dies unaware and uncomprehending, encased in a protective idealism that proves blinding. This tale is set in the Roaring Twenties, the time when mid-American virtue and small-town values of the type Jay Gatsby grew up with were overcome by the larger society's flirtation with Hollywood glamor, urban sophistication, and motorized affluence; it is nevertheless timelessly American in its portrayal of innocence corrupted and destroyed.

Huck has been affected by the forces that caused these characters' tribulations, but by remaining firmly boyish, he can at least attempt to navigate through "the world." Like Natty Bumpo, he will try to remain a creature of the earth, sky, and woods, and let native virtue and simplicity guide him in the jungle that a corrupt civilization has substituted for Eden. Such resolve resonates throughout his nation's history.

The Adventures of Huckleberry Finn mirrors American thought and activity so well it is almost a textbook for national self-understanding. Its cartoonish exaggerations and contrived plot elements notwithstanding, a reader can sense under its surface almost exactly what he or she has thought about various subjects or how he or she has acted with respect to certain causes. Let us explore some of these.

Huckleberry Finn is a boy who comes of age by coping with experience; in essence, he has raised himself. He has not been conditioned by formal education, family values, or social conventions. As a result, he can view people and consider ideas with fresh eyes and points of view, precisely as his forbears had to do once they began life in the New World. Almost as soon as the Pilgrims on the Mayflower disembarked with their famous Compact in hand, European immigrants have had to come to terms with their environment guided not by throne, altar, or custom, but by their own thinking. Traditional European society relied on established institutions for the maintenance of law, order, and morality. They also valued the patronage state and church could extend to artists, scientists, explorers, and entrepreneurs, who had no other means to support their activities. A superstructure of well-established authorities gave order and meaning to all those born under the particular flag and particular ecclesiastical emblem controlling their corner of Europe. Even as late as Mark Twain's time, with the exception of France, where Republicans, Royalists, and Bonapartists still fought over the legacy of the 1789 Revolution, Europe from London to Moscow was ruled by dynastic houses and catechized by state-sanctioned churches.

For Huck Finn, all of this is foreign with a capital F. His experience with the king and the duke, to an exaggerated degree, is the American experience with inherited privilege, real or imagined. As we have seen, Huck has no illusions about them and defers to their pretensions as one does to those of madmen, hoping that by humoring them, they will cause no harm. Huck has no fear of these puffed-up phonies; since they need him more than he needs them, he is the decision-maker on the boat. Only his innate kindness allows the two frauds to enjoy succor and protection for most of the trip, and his ingenuity and resourcefulness save them again and again. Huck's tolerance has limits, however. As the two perpetrate crime after crime, Huck moves from bemused observer to sickened antagonist, going out of his way to foil their schemes as best he can. Americans fear the exercise of royal or, in our day, dictatorial power because over the centuries too much innocent blood has been shed through fiat or whim. When George Washington refused to become King George I of the United States and settled for serving a fixed term as an elected and constitutionally restricted federal executive, he set the tone for all subsequent American responses to untrammeled power. Huck, therefore, knows that in America one's stature rests on achievement, not on accident of birth, and that the king and the duke are setting themselves firmly against the American grain in highlighting the advantages birth should have conferred on them. He tries to explain to Jim what real kings do, and despite errors that make for hilarious reading (comparable to the phonies' Shakespearean mess), manages to convince Jim that the "rapscallions" on their boat are not very different from the real dynasts: "All I say is kings is kings and you got to make allowances. Take them all around, they're a mighty ornery lot. It's the way they're raised" (154).

America is the great leveler. While the French Revolution raged, *émigré* nobles tried to set up a retreat for Queen Marie Antoinette in rural Pennsylvania, presuming that the revolutionary government would be happy to see her in exile rather than as a perpetual prisoner. Nothing of the sort took place, of course, and the noble builders soon abandoned this establishment, known as the French Azylum, because they could not bring themselves to perform the manual labor needed to maintain the outpost. As the king and the duke persist in their follies, they continually resist the conclusion that this exemplary tale reinforces: the titles and honors that confer so much abroad have no cachet here.

American political history shows the same tendency to bring down the mighty from their thrones. The War Between the States, for instance, was won by the anti-slavery, free soil, free labor, and free enterprise North, which also sponsored the Homestead Act, encouraging small farmers to move west, and the construction of the Union Pacific Railroad, providing connections to mass markets for livestock, grain, fruit, and vegetable producers all over the West. America fought against the Spanish in 1898 and the Germans and Austrians in 1917, not to defend the homeland but to liberate foreign peoples oppressed by imperial rule. In 1941, the United States was provoked into similar action against two states, Japan and Germany, ruled by militarists and tyrannical political extremists. After 1945, America intervened in Korea, South Vietnam, Iraq, and Afghanistan out of genuine fear that political or religious fanaticism, fueled by despotic regimes, would create far-reaching global discord. If ever an anti-authoritarian personality could be said to be reflected in a nation, the United States would be that nation.

Americans have viewed and continue to view military action as a last-resort option undertaken with only limited means and strict rules of engagement. Because the foe either has deliberately provoked a bellicose response to outright attack or invasion (the firing on Fort Sumter, the bombing of Pearl Harbor, the incursion into South Korea) or has generated resistance to its loudly threatened disturbance of the peace and stability of an entire region through military and political aggrandizement (Iraq's attempted conquest of Kuwait, Serbia's ethnic cleansing in Bosnia, the Austro-German threat in 1917, and the Nazi menace in 1941), American military interventions have taken on the character of crusades. An overarching moral purpose in each instance has given meaning and direction to the fighting. Julia Ward Howe saw the Civil War in just such a context:

> *Mine eyes have seen the glory of the coming of the Lord,*
> *He is trampling out the vintage where the grapes of wrath are stored.*
> *He hath loosed the fateful lightning of his terrible swift sword,*
> *His truth is marching on.*

Whereas Lincoln and his northern political and military associates entered the conflict in 1861 with only one goal, to preserve the federal union and system, as time went on, the overriding moral imperative to abolish slaveholding and assimilate its displaced victims within a reconstituted and cleansed nation became the paramount objective of the Union Army and its civilian leadership. Therefore, though the former Confederate states were integrated back into the federal republic shortly after armed conflict ceased, they were readmitted under the condition that they accept the thirteenth, fourteenth, and fifteenth amendments to the Constitution, acknowledging the freedom, citizenship, and voting rights of former slaves. While it took almost an additional century for these Reconstruction measures to be implemented uniformly nationwide, their binding force was affirmed again and again in the postwar period, with no serious attempt to repeal the three amendments ever undertaken.

The crusading spirit Americans bring to war making is *sui generis*. As we shall see in the later chapters of this book, European monarchs and chancellors have looked upon war as an accepted instrument of state policy. They have declared and waged war for reasons of state that, with the exception of the campaigns of forces like Cromwell's New Model Army, rarely have included anything like moral earnestness as an influencing factor. French statecraft is illustrative in this regard. In the midst of the conflicts spawned by the Reformation, Francis I, styled the Most Christian King, actually allied with the Ottoman sultan just to weaken the power of Catholicism's leading warrior and Francis' rival, the Holy Roman Emperor Charles V. In the seventeenth century, Louis XIV declared war on the Netherlands to avenge a slight on his honor the Dutch had somehow inflicted. Louis XVI sent ships, troops, and money to the American colonists in 1782 to help defeat Britain, which had expelled France from all of North America in 1763. Napoleon I engaged in constant conflict with most of the European great powers in the years following the French Revolution. At first, these hostilities were motivated by the need to defend France and preserve the reforms of the revolutionaries. Later, however, as victories multiplied and new territories were conquered, despite a pretext of republican principle, imperial ambition became all-consuming. Crowned emperor in 1804, Napoleon waged war to assert power and secure submission, leading inevitably to overreach, such as the 1812 invasion of Russia, an act of pointless machismo so reminiscent of earlier royal excesses. Later in the century, Napoleon III declared war on Germany, largely to erase a diplomatic humiliation that was later exposed as a deliberate deception orchestrated by the German Chancellor, who wanted to go to war but not as an aggressor. These and other examples that could have been cited highlight the selfish, petty, calculating, treacherous, and opportunistic governing style one European nation's leaders brought to inter-state politics over the span of four centuries. Without even a hint of moral sensitivity or conscience in any of the thinking surrounding these acts, they clearly emanate from a radically different mental universe than that inhabited by Americans.

The crusades America's military forces have engaged in are paralleled by the political or moral initiatives its many special interest groups have pursued doggedly since the foundation of the republic. Apart from the numerous revivals religious congregations have sponsored since the Great Awakening of the eighteenth century, Americans have promoted throughout their history a host of causes affecting a wide range of personal behaviors and ethical imperatives. These have attracted enormous interest and popular support. Abolitionism comes immediately to mind. Without the intense pressure this mostly New England-led movement brought to bear in favor of immediate and unconditional emancipation, the Civil War may not have taken on its anti-slavery crusading character at all. A Northern victory might have resulted in a negotiated settlement restoring the status quo ante: allowing the Southern states to return without prejudice to the federal union, banning slavery in the territories but not where it was already established, and agreeing on some form of indemnification to cover the unprecedented expense in lives and property brought by the war. Abolitionists, however, citing the moral necessity to treat all as equals and inspired by the Old Testament's chronicle of the divinely led liberation of the Jewish people from Egyptian bondage, would not let the Civil War become a struggle over states' rights alone. The epochal conflict had to be purgative; its outcome had to lead to moral regeneration and irreversible social change.

The same had to be the case after World War II. American idealism required prosecution of those responsible for the greatest injustices and crimes its defeated enemies had perpetrated. Consequently, trials of Nazi and Japanese officers and officials who had enabled atrocities to occur had to take place, and the people who had suffered the most and had been singled out for special condemnation, the European Jews, had to be accorded a nation-state of their own, Israel, to make any future Holocaust impossible. That this state would return the Jews to the Promised Land for the first time since the Roman expulsions of the first century made this particular moral duty emotionally compelling for millions of Americans, schooled as they were in biblical thought patterns. In addition to making provision for the Jews, postwar American policy promoted the creation of a new supranational body, the United Nations, that would, in theory, safeguard the rights of peoples threatened by powerful neighbors or by oppressive forces within their borders. This body would rise above ethnic, ideological, religious, or tribal interests to serve as a nonpartisan referee, or, if necessary, as a police power guaranteeing the maintenance of law and order and the functioning of peaceful processes for political, social, or economic change in all member states. Within the UN's halls, arguments would be heard and disputes between or among various parties would be adjudicated objectively; if problems persisted, the whole weight of international opinion and power would be brought to bear in the form of sanctions to enforce the body's mandate. Should even these prove ineffective, a multinational peacekeeping force would be assembled and placed in an embattled zone to resist aggressors' encroachments and ensure the restoration of order. The United Nations thus would have powers and enforcement mechanisms that the League of Nations, President Woodrow Wilson's answer to the strident nationalism that had caused such misery in the 1914–18 war, fatally lacked.

On a much less lofty scale, after the Civil War, Americans lent themselves to idealistic causes affecting the most private and intimate aspects of a person's life experience. The temperance movement, for instance, took a page from the abolitionists' playbook to advocate for the ultimate in universal moral transformation, abstention from all alcoholic beverages, not just by certain exceptional persons but by the entire citizenry. Allying, in many cases, with women's groups striving for civil rights and an end to alcohol-fueled abuse and with the conservative Evangelical churches of the Bible Belt, the movement grew steadily and enjoyed broad-based appeal. The passage of the Volstead Act in 1917, though prompted by the need to divert resources to the war effort rather than to civilian consumption, brought national endorsement to what had seemed heretofore a local, rural, and mostly feminine movement. From 1917 to 1933, despite furious opposition and widespread evasion of the law, the manufacture and distribution of alcoholic beverages was illegal in the United States, making America, almost overnight, into something like a radical Islamic state.

In our time, the anti-abortion movement has a similar character. Pro-life advocates regard abortion, in almost all instances, as tantamount to murder, so no compromise position on the issue is possible. Should its zealous proponents ever prevail, it is conceivable that abortion will be outlawed, its medical providers sanctioned, and its supporters stigmatized as baby killers. Here again, the state is being asked to preempt personal decision-making on the most intimately personal of matters.

What distinguishes America's crusading spirit from the popular movements of past times and other places is its combination of idealism (or innocence) and absolute conviction. In contrast, for instance, to the militant street fighters of the European revolutionary parties, such as the Nazis, Fascists, and Communists of the post-Versailles era, who joined hatred of the old order to a ruthless determination to overcome all opposition by any means, American reform movements have been and continue to be largely nonviolent, avoiding hate-mongering and choosing to achieve desired goals through legitimate processes. The American crusader is usually young, unsophisticated, drawn to a cause by a generous aspiration to bring about something good for the benefit of all, and unaware of or indifferent to considerations that might complicate the public's reception of the proposed benefit. He or she is, like Huck Finn, guided by an innate perception of what is good, trusting to instincts that trump any cautions education or worldly experience might offer, and true to the simple code of mutual good will and aid that he, she, and their peers follow without question or doubt. European reformers knew that they could not bring about fundamental change in religious understanding and practice, political structure, or economic life without overcoming entrenched authorities. Simply going out and spreading the good word was not enough; an organized movement had to coalesce, win important popular support and some influential allies from the opposing sides, and prevail through struggle. Once in control of governments, such revolutionaries had to maintain their regimes through the empowerment of police or spy agencies and the recruitment of newly radicalized armed forces.

Apart from the Civil War, which as noted earlier began as a political dispute and only took on its crusading character later, America's reform groups have achieved their aims by legitimate means, through persuasion and appeal to conscience. A classic example is the civil rights movement of the 1950s and 1960s, which disavowed violence from the start, using Gandhi's success in India as a model, and moved the American people to its support and the American Congress to legislative redress by actions such as sit-ins at segregated restaurants, peaceful demonstration parades through segregated towns or neighborhoods, powerful televised sermons and speeches, and constant exhortations to conscience. These were acts of civil disobedience that Huck Finn would have understood well. Their powerful impact 2succeeded in emancipating a whole race (this time in reality and not just in theory), just as Huck's acts of conscience ultimately give one slave freedom.

Such successes notwithstanding, however, American history is littered with the consequences of failed idealism or innocence betrayed. In political and foreign affairs, some of America's greatest statesmen experienced rejection and defeat when their high-minded principles came up against the "dark" forces its greatest writers recognized as inherent in the nature of society. In his first inaugural address, Abraham Lincoln asked Southern secessionists to heed the admonitions of "the better angels of our nature" and refrain from any rash and lawless actions; by the time of his second inaugural, after three years of hard fighting, Lincoln asked why the "better angels" had been ignored and could only conclude that the "judgments of the Lord" required that the sins of slavery be expiated in blood.

Shortly thereafter, the blood of this great and greatly chastened man of iron principle would be shed too. In 1919, Woodrow Wilson arrived in Paris in triumph, convinced that a League of Nations could be created that would make armed conflicts between nations impossible in future years. But the narrow and selfish interests of his hardened European allies and the ambitious leaders of newly formed nation states stripped his League of real-world power or even legitimacy, while Wilson's political opponents in the United States humiliated him by denouncing the whole concept of a supra-national authority as an infringement on American sovereignty. Wilson's presidency and his idealistic proposals went up in smoke as a result. This stubborn and strong-willed statesman who had worked so hard to make the Great War the last of its kind, spent his final days in office crippled by a stroke and embittered by the way his generous efforts on behalf of international amity had been stymied. Franklin Roosevelt suffered likewise when Josef Stalin continually and brutally blocked implementation of Roosevelt's equally visionary proposals for national reconstruction and reconciliation along democratic lines in Central and Eastern Europe. The new supra-national United Nations, created through mostly American pressure to prevent such oppression, failed like the League of Nations to prohibit member states' misuse of power or influence. Lyndon Johnson could not extricate himself from the morass of Vietnam, as obdurate anti-colonial and nationalist forces resisted this most socially fair-minded President's repeated attempts to end a conflict that was bleeding his country dry. He left office in 1968 just as hollowed out as Wilson and Roosevelt had been. George W. Bush underestimated the power of ethnic and sectarian militancy when he mistook military victories in Iraq and Afghanistan for successful nation-building. Nothing like representative democracy or free market capitalism has been made to operate smoothly in either place, and violent internal conflict seems persistent.

Americans have reacted and continue to react to such disappointments and setbacks by maintaining their principles and, if anything, proclaiming them even more fervently. They do so, however, from an increasingly detached posture. The retreat to isolation (Huck's final choice) is a constant temptation. Americans see themselves as special, a people created pure and innocent in a New World, so it is natural that they would resist involvement in the affairs of much older, tradition-bound, poorly educated, and xenophobic territories and peoples. Washington, after all, famously warned against foreign entanglements; Lincoln resisted aggressive action against Europeans meddling in Civil War politics; and General Douglas MacArthur, on his deathbed, warned President Lyndon Johnson not to engage in a land war in Asia. After the fiasco of Versailles, isolationism became a valid foreign policy position for over twenty years, complicating America's response to the European dictators and the Japanese imperialists. Some of the same sentiment inspired the anti-immigrant agitation that led to nativism in the mid-nineteenth century and later to severe restrictions on Chinese and Central and Southern European immigration. Today, the same exclusionary rhetoric is aimed at desperate Hispanic migrants who cross the southern border illegally.

America is isolated (or unique) in at least two other important endeavors. Inspired by post-Reformation religious dissenters whose faith commitments were unequivocal and welcoming all varieties of religious enthusiasts whose public meetings have usually exceeded in passionate affirmation anything in the European heartland, America since its founding has been and still is by far the most openly religious and biblically literate society in the Western world. Americans, however, particularly in rural and small-town communities, profess their Christianity in ways that mainline European denominations do not recognize. The most popular exegetical approach in the United States, for instance, is literalism, a position not endorsed by the Greek or Latin church fathers, the medieval scholastics, the original reformers, the nineteenth-century liberal scholars, or Catholic, Orthodox, or non-Evangelical Protestant interpreters today. This insistence on treating all of the Old and New Testament chronicles and prophecies as historically accurate and factual separates most Americans from the European Christian mainstream. Literalism has also led to embarrassments, such as the Scopes trial, and to contemporary controversies over the contents of school textbooks, wherein outraged parents take on the weight of scientific scholarship in increasingly strident attempts to give creationism the same status as natural selection in the story of human development over time. Long after the rest of the Christian world made its peace with science and formally rehabilitated Galileo, American fundamentalists continue to wage a rear-guard assault on Darwin and his successors (as well as on the scientists who assert that global warming is a clear and present danger) that seems more appropriate to the seventeenth than to the twenty-first century.

Likewise, apart from arguments about content, Americans' approach to education in general is idiosyncratic. Ever since the end of World War II, when the GI Bill made college education an option for many who were formerly excluded, Americans have worked tirelessly to realize in practice the egalitarian concept of universal access to and universal success in attaining the standards of primary, secondary, and post-secondary academic education. In contrast again to European models, which evaluate young people at various ages and assign them to curricula best suited to their abilities and promise, Americans insist that no child should be "left behind," that is, all should be taught to master the same knowledge and skills, all should earn the same diploma, and all should be able to take advantage of the same post-secondary opportunities. As a result, faculty at every level have had to adjust course requirements and adopt pedagogies that best enable all students in a class to make at least the minimum progress mandated by state or federal agencies. These adaptations have caused a general lowering of expectations, to the extent that students in other nations, who have been selected out already, are routinely assimilating in middle school what the average American is learning in high school.

College and university professors must deal with the knowledge and skill deficiencies such a system generates. Since approximately 80 percent of a typical American high school's graduating seniors choose to attend some type of post-secondary institution, dealing with widely divergent achievement levels is urgent. Remedial coursework is the most common institutional response to this diversity. "Higher learning" is, as a result, deferred for these underachievers until they can, at least in theory, demonstrate mastery of fundamental language and mathematical skill sets. For the vast majority of so-called developmental students, however, demonstrating this mastery is next to impossible, since poor preparation, a native language other than English, and too many competing pressures and responsibilities work against whatever their best classroom efforts can produce. While America, therefore, boasts the highest rate of college attendance in the developed world, its college retention and completion rates, particularly for "at risk" students, are among the lowest. If he were alive today, Huck Finn would be one such casualty. He would be a good candidate for a GED certificate and for admission to his local community college, where he probably would be placed in a developmental track initially. Given his contempt for the formalities of spoken and written English, as well as for the intricacies of algebra, however, it is hard to envision his staying in college for very long. Try as they might, American educators cannot generate positive outcomes when so many of the students in their classrooms are, like Huck, outliers. They do not conform to the model and so make the egalitarian dream one more quixotic American pursuit.

The innocence and idealism that distinguish Huck Finn are therefore baked into the entire nation's DNA. For better or for worse, and, as we have noted, American history offers numerous instances of both outcomes, its people continue to affirm the exceptional character of the Puritan founders' "city on the hill" that inspires everyone looking for guidance and assurance that aspiration and striving can bring about an enhanced personal and community life. At the same time, however, the godliness such endeavors aim to reenforce is repeatedly challenged by the dark forces infecting fallen humanity, making the struggle to embody the grand principles of truth, justice, equality, and charity in the life experience of both the individual and the larger society a process fraught with pain, disillusionment, and sorrow.

FRANCE

Stendhal
The Red and the Black

INTRODUCTION

The nation we know as France emerged from the Gallic provinces of northwestern Europe conquered by Julius Caesar and settled by successive generations of Roman colonists. This blending of native and colonizing peoples produced a national culture showing two distinctive tendencies: a centralizing focus characteristic of the Roman political occupation and a strongly assertive counterforce emphasizing local independence more characteristic of the native Frankish populace. The first tendency manifests itself again and again in French history, beginning in the Middle Ages with Clovis, the Frankish leader who brought neighboring tribesmen into the Franks' kingdom and into the Catholic Church. Charlemagne continued this pattern, creating a centralized empire that included parts of what is now Belgium, Luxembourg, and Germany that all jurisdictions from the pope on down recognized as the successor of the Roman Empire in the west. The Valois and Bourbon monarchs who followed brought the governing classes together within a hierarchical structure centered around Paris and Versailles. After the 1789 Revolution, successive republics refined and streamlined these federating processes, so that today France is, for all intents and purposes, governed by civil servants who take their marching orders from Paris.

Not only is French political history highlighted by the progressive amalgamation of diverse peoples and traditions within a strict legal and administrative framework emphasizing order and uniformity, so also in intellectual and artistic life, the French display a preference for clarity, rationality, and logic. Descartes is the French thinker par excellence, so closely identified with his nation's way of thinking that the adjective "Cartesian" is used frequently to describe a typically French theoretical or artistic creation. Descartes' groundbreaking work in mathematics and philosophy highlighted rationality: his world is one whose constituent elements move in a clockwork order best expressed and understood through mathematical formulae. Therefore, a student who wants to explore the workings of natural systems should eschew emotion, passion, and personality and embrace reason, logic, and impersonal science as his/her instruments. The philosophers of the eighteenth century Enlightenment reinforced such thinking, stressing that "enlightenment" could come only when reason and science displaced prejudice and superstition as guiding principles in the formation of young people. Humanity could become "perfected" over time, and law, order, and peace within and among nations could then prevail. In literature, the tragedian Racine strove for formal perfection in the construction of drama, making sure that the "unities" are observed and that every word spoken is right for its context, not just in meaning but in sound or rhyme as well. In modern times, Cartesian emphases are apparent in French structuralism, the theory that requires one to probe beneath spoken or written words or beneath transient political or social events to discover the permanent realities that determine meaning in literature and development in history.

The French carry this insistence on rationalizing experience into most areas of human endeavor. One must never let spontaneity or impulse govern his/her approach to social life; there is an art to conversation, to dining, to friendship, and to relations between the sexes. To be successful in a world where time-tested rules and precepts guide conduct, a man or woman must model "best practices." Likewise, in relations between organized groups, an art of diplomacy, greatly influenced by French statecraft, requires that communication between and among parties is civil, and in cases where this art is unavailing and groups engage in conflict, an art of war similarly governs activity. When any of these arts is exercised well, the result is admirable, a thing of beauty no less. The French, consequently, respond to beauty, refinement, elegant manners, and well-chosen phrases or flashes of wit or insight (*apercus*) as do few other nationalities.

There is more to the French identity, however, than *l'esprit geometrique*. Along with their rationalism and aestheticism, the French are fiercely proud of their independence and passionately committed to its preservation. Thus, while rulers since Charlemagne have made great strides in centralizing authority and administration along the lines of the Roman model, Gallic *élan* has never allowed this centrifugal pressure to suppress completely the rich traditions of provincial life or the native spirit of resistance sometimes aroused by overreach from Paris. In religion, for instance, France has fondly assumed the title "Eldest Daughter of the Church," bestowed by the Vatican in gratitude for this nation's many contributions to and support of Catholicism since the time of Clovis. French Catholicism, nevertheless, has not held sway over the centuries without major challenges from both within and outside its ranks. In the thirteenth century, the Cathars and Albigensians stubbornly maintained heretical beliefs and unorthodox practices in the southern region of Languedoc. These movements were politically threatening as well as religiously divisive, so their suppression by the French king's forces and the pope's missionaries was regarded as altogether justified. In the sixteenth century, however, a far more challenging crisis almost led to the disintegration of France as a centralized politico-religious state. Reformers inspired mainly by Jean Calvin, a priest from Picardy much influenced by Martin Luther and his fellow protesters, formed breakaway sects in various parts of France that attracted significant support from local notables.

With the Valois monarchs after Francis I unable to stamp out these Huguenot cells, and with powerful elements of the nobility taking up their cause, it appeared for a time as if France would soon go the way of its neighbor, Germany, where Calvinist, Lutheran, and Catholic churches had to coexist under the protection of sympathetic princes. Civil war raged from 1562 to 1598 as Catholic forces led by nobles loyal to the established church and monarchy fought against Huguenot separatists. The conflicts ended finally with the accession of the Bourbon King Henry IV, who, though Protestant by conviction, accepted Catholicism, was crowned in

Paris, and issued the Edict of Nantes, granting non-Catholics a degree of religious freedom. His Bourbon successors, most notably Louis XIII (and his chief minister, Cardinal Richelieu) and Louis XIV, resumed the centralizing policies of their predecessors, gradually weakening the edict until it was set aside altogether in 1685. But though on the surface it appeared as if Catholicism had triumphed once and for all, dissenters had gained breathing space and legitimacy as a result of all this upheaval. In 1789, discontent with the established order would flare up once again, and this would lead to far-reaching change.

Before this cataclysmic series of events, however, the French monarchy reached the zenith of its power and influence, both within and outside France. King Louis XIV brought the restless French nobility under tighter control by forcing all those interested in favors or in state service to dance attendance around him in Paris or in his palace at Versailles, where he and his court gave grand entertainments that attracted all who wanted to be seen in the best company, as well as playwrights, actors, singers, and musicians who wished to be noticed. Smaller fetes took place in Paris, where influential aristocratic women presided over *salons*. These were social clubs that also gave writers, artists, and ambitious bourgeois a chance to make a good impression on the men and women of the only class that could promote their interests or careers. The "society" that all such patrons belonged to and jealously kept exclusive would become over time the essential training and proving ground for all those provincials whose manners were crude, whose conversation was dull, whose worldly experience was limited, and whose talents were still dormant. Versailles would succor the likes of Rameau, Couperin, and Racine, while Paris would support Moliere and the philosophers of the Enlightenment. Between 1685 and 1789, therefore, names like these made monarchical France the cultural capital of Europe.

The political upheaval that began with the calling of the Estates General in 1789, at least initially, moved in the opposite direction. By giving priority to French national needs and feelings, and by bringing together in one place and time men and women from all over the nation, the revolution that followed changed France decisively. Whereas members of the nobility and high-ranking church prelates had held sway in political, ecclesiastical, economic, military, and cultural affairs for most of the previous two centuries, after the revolutionaries created the French Republic, they endowed the Third Estate and its dependencies—that is, most of the rest of the population—with unprecedented power and influence. The result was a change in perspective and emphasis from the Roman-inspired feudal rule of the monarch and the state-supported church to a more inclusive and popular conception of France as a community of "citizens," bound to each other by fraternal ties and governed by representatives obligated to promote and defend the sovereign people's interests at all times. France became more nativist; it cut its ties to the rest of the continent and with the Roman Church, replacing the monarch with a National Assembly and reinventing France's religious identity by introducing in place of Catholicism a cult of reason modeled on contemporary philosophy. France became, in consequence, unique in a Europe where all other nations still adhered to hereditary rule and upheld only established Christian churches.

Such extreme departures from tradition could be maintained and defended only through fervent commitment and zeal. The "*furia Francese*" associated with French war-making never was more evident than in the revolutionary decade of 1789–99. The Jacobins of Paris, who proudly embraced radicalism, attacked and persecuted any who professed contrary views as enemies of the new order, worthy of extermination. They rallied the common people, forming them into a National Guard, which eventually kept the professional troops of the Hapsburg emperor from invading French territory and crushing the revolutionaries. When refractory elements of the rural population, centered in the Vendee, organized a counter-revolutionary force, the authorities in Paris suppressed it violently, even though its adherents were common people like themselves.

Conflict and terror, however, could not persist. With the rise of Napoleon Bonaparte, whose military talents rivaled those of Julius Caesar, order and stability were finally restored. Napoleon reasserted Roman principles. He made peace with the pope and restored Catholicism as the "religion of France" through the Concordat of 1802. He invited the nobility and high clergy, who had fled the country in droves in the previous decade, to return to France without penalty and to reestablish themselves as legitimate citizens. Through aggressive military operations, Napoleon defeated Austrian, Prussian, and Russian armies that threatened to roll back the French Revolution and resurrect the monarchy; in the process, he and his troops spread republican concepts in all the territories they marched through, guaranteeing that the Revolution's driving principles would take root among progressives outside France. But while no monarchy would be reimposed in France at this time, something very much like the old regime would come into being in 1804 in Notre Dame Cathedral, when Napoleon, in the presence of Pope Pius VII and wearing regalia going back to Charlemagne, crowned himself emperor of the French. This deliberate return to the Roman paradigm kept the fierce nationalism that had endangered French survival under tight control so long as the empire held firm.

Of course, it did not. Napoleon's revival of Charlemagne's Christian imperium lasted barely ten years. Military overreach, culminating in the disastrous invasion of Russia in 1812, a strong allied coalition of nations and empires focused unwaveringly on Napoleon's defeat, and France's inability to control the Atlantic and Mediterranean shipping lanes, doomed the regime and forced Napoleon into exile permanently after the Battle of Waterloo in 1814. At the Congress of Vienna, the victors dictated peace terms that restored the Bourbon monarchy in France and the various royal and princely houses that Napoleon's armies had displaced in conquered European states. For all intents and purposes, the clock had swung back to the days preceding the calling of the Estates General. Time, however, moves only one way. Even though the post-Napoleonic world was, on the surface, a familiar patchwork of hereditary rulers and docile subjects, as we will see when discussing *The Red and the*

Black, forms and protocols associated with feudalism were being superimposed upon societies that had been fundamentally changed. In France at least, it would be only a matter of time before the monarchy, the church, the military, high society, and all the other restored establishments of old France would be either marginalized or swept away entirely.

The world that "hero" Julien Sorel, strives so hard to master is one where the traditional structures still exist but are open to new blood and new ways of thinking. High society and the church hierarchy, for instance, remain deeply attached to Roman ideals but lack the power they once had to enforce their values on a people newly liberated and aspiring to a respectability they see as linked inextricably with money. The common people figure in *The Red and the Black* mostly as cartoonish vulgarians, incapable of appreciating life's finer things and crippled by acquisitiveness and an obsession with status. In later French works, such as *Madame Bovary* and in parts of *Remembrance of Things Past*, the bourgeois are a leveling force of sinister intent. Nevertheless, their rise to political dominance after the failure of the restored monarchy to take new root is the most important fact of post-Napoleonic French history. These often despised but dedicated and talented sons and daughters of the *lycées*, the technical colleges, and the convent schools brought the amenities of civilization to the masses, even if this progress did not occur universally until after the Second World War. The Revolution's progeny also transformed the church and the military, the two avenues to power and fame the aristocracy once utilized exclusively.

As Julien enters the seminary in Besancon to begin studies for the priesthood, he is not impressed by his fellow students. As we shall see, Julien's character is quintessentially French: he is intellectually superior, proud, touchy, and egocentric. For him, the priesthood will be a means to move up the social ladder by mastering all obstacles or persons standing in the way, nothing else. The young men he meets in the seminary are different: born into poverty, most are striving to pass their courses and be ordained in order to gain a measure of security and respectability in the towns and villages they will eventually serve. Their ambitions are modest; Julien's are titanic. When he is diverted from his studies by a prominent nobleman in need of his services, Julien does not look back. He will use other means to advance his interests. The rough-edged characters he leaves behind, however, included in real life men of talent. One such was Jean Baptiste Lamy, archbishop of Santa Fe, New Mexico, from 1853 to 1885. Born in the hard-scrabble countryside, he left his parents and home once and for all as a teenager to enter a seminary not much different from Julien's. After volunteering to serve as a missionary in the American West, by dint of hard work, pastoral zeal, exemplary piety, and force of intellect, he eventually won appointment as the Catholic metropolitan of the American Southwest. Archbishop Lamy became over time well-known and respected by all, from the initially hostile Protestant political and commercial establishment to the mostly poor Spanish-speaking minority that made up a great part of his flock, to the indigenous peoples, who came increasingly to rely on him as a spokesperson and advocate. The church hierarchy that before the Revolution was dominated by noblemen who held almost every influential position, was, after its restoration by Napoleon, much more diverse and much more influential in the Catholic world. The liturgical revival associated with the humble monks of the Abbey of Solesmes and the revival of scholastic philosophy and theology begun by Cardinal Mercier in Belgium but promoted vigorously by French clergy in university circles and in Rome, are just two of the important nineteenth-century initiatives priests of the type known to Julien bequeathed the universal church. On the other hand, in some of Julien's classmates, the prototypes of less enlightened and less scrupulous provocateurs may be seen, such as the many clerical journalists and pseudo-historians who fanned the flames of French anti-Semitism, leading to the shameful persecution of Captain Alfred Dreyfus in the 1890s. The record is mixed, but there is no denying the fact that the church of Julien's day offered to the poor the possibilities of advancements never even dreamed of by earlier generations.

The military likewise underwent a great transformation in the nineteenth century. Ever since the Paris revolutionaries rallied the peasantry and the urban poor throughout France for the defense of the fatherland in 1791–92, and ever since the citizen army thus created withstood the pressure of well-trained foreign troops and held the frontiers, the French army from the officer corps to the lowest ranks was the people's force. Widespread hostility to the aristocracy, as well as their members' virtual absence from national life after 1792, made it possible for sons of the lower classes to rise in the ranks strictly on merit; this process led to the emergence afterwards not only of Napoleon Bonaparte but also of the majority of his officers, including those of outstanding ability, such as Murat and Ney. When the *émigrés* were repatriated, aristocratic influence increased, as illustrated by the ease with which the Marquis de la Mole secures a commission for a wholly untrained Julien late in the novel, but, as with the church, the landscape had changed permanently as a result of the Grande Armee's extraordinary accomplishments. Napoleon's breathtaking conquests left a rich legacy. For young Frenchmen like Julien, without influence or connection to power, Napoleon's meteoric ascent proved that anything was possible, that obscure peasants' sons could win glory and that a type of all-conquering heroism once associated strictly with ancient exemplars, like Alexander the Great or Julius Caesar, could be achieved today.

In contrast to Julien's seminarians, the summit of whose ambitions is "to dine well and to have good clothing in winter" (*The Red and the Black*, trans., Lloyd C. Parks, New York: The New American Library, 1970, p. 188), after Napoleon, soldiers of France, imbued with an *elan* that would surmount any challenge, could imagine themselves once again occupying Europe's capitals and imposing their will on the populace. Their hero had, after all, captured the Emperor Francis and abolished his creaky Holy Roman Empire; he had humiliated the pope, the patriarch of the West, and disregarded his paternal sovereignty; he had triumphed over the tsar's forces and set himself up in Moscow as the nation's de facto ruler, betrayed only by weather and the fanaticism of an enemy incapable of understanding or appreciating the reforms Napoleon was prepared to introduce. In the imaginations of ardent romantics like Julien, this history could be repeated, and ambitious men like himself could come out of nowhere and win glory.

All of the forces outlined above have a marked bearing on Julien Sorel's thoughts, aspirations, decisions, and actions. In him, Stendhal has created the archetypal Frenchman because all the prominent qualities the French have manifested over the centuries are seen in him in some form. He mirrors the dualities of France. He is, on the one hand, fiercely proud, like the Gauls whom Caesar and his legions had to work so hard to conquer. The Abbé Pirard, rector of the seminary in Besancon where Julien has studied, knows this well. When the Marquis de La Mole asks the rector about Julien, whom he would like to employ as a secretary, the priest warns him that "this young man is high-spirited; he will be of no use in your affairs if you try to curb his pride; you will make him stupid" (218).

With this pride, though, comes a calculating shrewdness that Julien relies on to govern his words and actions in every situation that may impact his perpetual quest for advancement. This is characteristic of the Roman careerist, so sensitive to opportunity, to favor, to subtle shifts in political and social affairs. Julien is sexually aggressive, too, despite his seminary stint, just as were most of the leaders of the Revolution, who gloried in their liberation from the restraints of conventional morality, but he is careful to conduct his seductions according to plan, succeeding, he believes, like a Cartesian thinker, in disciplining and channeling his passions through artful dialogue, surprise, and maneuver. Julien is Napoleonic in conquering through strategy and imperious assertion. He displays the most refined sensibility in the midst of his relentless quest for self-advancement, but he is not an artist. He responds to beauty in whatever form it appears, but beauty is part of the background for Julien, a necessary accompaniment to the hard business of coping successfully in a world that values power and privilege above all else. Julien knows to get on, he must master the challenges of the drawing room and the company of the privileged, and he does so eventually, becoming a "dandy" after his tutelage in the aristocratic de la Mole household, but this achievement leaves him cold. He takes little pleasure in exchanges of wit or insight; his focus is always on overcoming the next hurdle and on playing the part that circumstances require. Over the course of the novel, Julien displays all the skills and subtlety of a great French classical actor, knowing what to say and how to say it to produce the greatest impact. Uniting all these conflicting tendencies and drives is the dominant French quality: the will to conquer. Julien strives above all for mastery. He feels he has been born to lead, born to triumph, born to rule. There is no one better, and the world must ultimately recognize this fact.

PART ONE

The Red and the Black is divided into two sections. Book I introduces us to Julien Sorel, an immensely talented, proud, and ambitious young man, whose birth and upbringing in a harsh family environment have excited in him a fierce determination to pursue every avenue to self-advancement. Julien's father is a logger in Verrieres, a small town in northeastern France. Of peasant extraction, he is not poor, but his avarice and selfishness create household conditions not much different from those of his poverty-stricken rural neighbors. Unlike his brothers, Julien has little interest in or aptitude for his father's vocation; indeed, when we first meet him at the workplace, he is perched on a platform above the saws reading Napoleon's *Memoires* and paying no attention to the processes going on below. His father, exasperated, strikes him roughly, nearly knocking him into the cutting apparatus underneath. He responds to his son's distress with characteristic scorn:

> *So, good-for-nothing! You will keep on reading your damned books when you're supposed to be watching the saw? Read in the evening when you go and waste your time at the curé's house . . . a fine thing!* (27)

Julien's father is the classic small-town entrepreneur, impatient with dreamy types like his son, focused almost entirely on the here and now, mercenary, shrewd in commercial dealings, and unsentimental. Julien is the boy born for higher things. Like James Joyce's Stephen Daedalus, he is the antithesis of father and family, a prodigy who has memorized the New Testament in the Vulgate Latin; a student so gifted his pastor and tutor, Abbé Chélan, can only marvel; and a military romantic whose conversations with a veteran of Napoleon's army inspire the most alluring visions. Unlike Huck Finn, who prefers to live on the edge of civilized communities, Julien is eager to make his mark and be recognized in society, whether through military advancement or, more realistically, through the priesthood, an honored calling everywhere in the Catholic world and one where Julien can apply his intellectual gifts fully to rise in status. Throughout the novel, he will strive to master every situation and take advantage of every opportunity to advance his interests, being careful always to take on the character his surroundings require, speak the language his peers are used to hearing, wear the garments and make the gestures expected of him, all the while masking his true motives and true feelings.

In this respect, he is truly French. A Frenchman who looks to move ahead in life does not generally expect to do so as an independent individual, such as the American self-made man or the English merchant or the German small farmer. The French prefer to make their way through the organizational ranks of large institutions like the army, the church, the civil service, or the diplomatic corps. This is the Roman model, imposed at first by conquerors but then assimilated by the French over so many centuries and so many generations, it became their own. This model demands that the individual submerge his idiosyncrasies, his peculiarities, his personal likes or dislikes within a pre-ordained pattern of thought and behavior. He (and it is always "he" in the nineteenth century) must mold himself to correspond as closely as possible to the paradigm already established. The French, as a rule, have mastered this art more successfully than most. Their military leaders over the centuries have projected the most confident, fastidious, and authoritative *hauteur* (De Gaulle); their diplomats have always been masters of style, knowledge, and smooth calculation (Talleyrand); their prominent clergy have been urbane and scholarly gentlemen who, when called upon, have executed political or religious responsibilities with *panache* (Richelieu). Julien knows all of this instinctively and so strives always to play the role he has been assigned.

In Book I, he is given two opportunities to learn the ropes, so to speak. The first comes when M. de Renal, the mayor of Verrieres and a local notable, offers the precocious Julien the chance to become part of his household. He has three young sons who would derive great benefit from Julien's guidance and instruction. In return, Julien will receive a generous stipend and enjoy rare privileges as the family's live-in guest. Julien is not aware of the mixed motives M. de Renal has in securing his services; the fierce social competition between de Renal and Monsieur Valenod, another local worthy with aspirations to high living, has made Julien a prize catch. M. de Renal, however, is not prepared for the proud young man's demands. Far from jumping at the prospect of becoming associated with one of his region's richest families, Julien hesitates at first, worried, for instance, that he might have to dine with the servants, as no less a luminary than Mozart had to do in the archbishop of Salzburg's palace.

Old Sorel is astonished by such assertiveness and horrified that his son's "airs" will upset the arrangement he has negotiated with M. de Renal. True to form, however, he recovers and, skillfully playing on the mayor's eagerness to bring Julien in, Sorel hastily brokers a new agreement explicitly confirming that "his son was to eat with the master and the mistress of the house, and on days when there was company, in a room apart with the children" (31). Sorel also wins for Julien a much higher stipend than M. de Renal had proposed originally (pocketing the first month's installment as a kind of "finder's fee") and has the pleasure of seeing a boy he considers useless taken out of his home and off his books, probably for good. The two will have no meaningful contact afterwards, until Julien is in prison awaiting execution. Their last conversation will concern money and will be without affection or strong emotion.

Stendhal dwells on these all too human weaknesses, jealousies, fears, and sensitivities because they govern the inner lives of the people of Verrieres. What matters in the provinces of post-revolutionary France is money and all that it may bring.

The anonymous narrator of *The Red and the Black* knows this well, as early on he advises a traveler in the vicinity of Verrieres to contemplate the scenic "hills of Burgundy" if one wishes to take his or her mind off "the town's foul atmosphere of petty concern about money" (14). Mme. de Renal, educated in a convent and secure in her family's status, senses this in the men she must interact with all the time:

> *Coarseness and the most brutal indifference about any question that did not involve money, precedence or a cross, and a blind hatred for every argument that opposed their interests, these things seemed to her as natural in the male sex as wearing boots and a felt hat.* (46)

While cupidity motivates his father, jealousy of Julien's preferment and his healthy stipend so inflames his brothers that one day "they beat him and left him unconscious and all bloody" (44). Fear of somehow losing face, losing a position, or being outmaneuvered by rivals makes everyone from bourgeois social climbers to the saintly parish priest constantly walk on eggshells.

Proud, aloof, and unworldly, Julien scorns the mercenary intrigues that are part of the fabric of provincial life. He is repelled by M. de Renal's tendency to boast about his position or possessions, and though he has been granted the privilege of joining de Renal and his bourgeois guests at table, he is not comfortable in their presence or attuned to their concerns. For them he is a *rara avis*, a phenomenon they just marvel over. One evening, notables rush to M. de Renal's house just "to see the wonder" (42) and listen to his Latin recitations. For "the wonder" such guests are tiresome: "Julien answered them all with a gloomy look that kept them at a distance" (42). He soon senses they can do nothing for him since their preoccupation with social standing and influence is as alien to him as his family's similar passion for money. This realization leads Julien to a depressing conclusion:

> *The position in which he had found himself all of his life was duplicated at the mayor of Verrieres' fine house. There, as at his father's sawmill, he utterly despised the people with whom he lived, and was hated by them . . . His comment to himself was always, What monsters, or What fools!* (50)

Julien takes refuge in his pride, recognized and admired by Mme. de Renal: "In the drawing room, however humble his bearing might be, she read in his eyes an attitude of intellectual superiority toward all who came to her house" (51). To compensate for his diminished condition, he continues to fantasize about power, glory, and acclaim. The example of Napoleon inspires him: "For many years now, scarcely an hour of Julien's life had gone by without his telling himself that Bonaparte, an unknown and penniless lieutenant, had made himself master of the world by his sword" (33-34). The de Renal household is agreeable when he is with the children and their beautiful mother is nearby, but it is a dead end otherwise.

For relief, Julien looks toward a change of scene. He asks for and receives permission to visit his friend Fouqué, a woodcutter and merchant who lives in the mountains alone. Fouqué lives in a way Julien's other role model, the Jean-Jacques Rousseau of *The Confessions*, would recognize and extol. He is honest, hard-working, kind, and loyal. He resembles Tiberge in *Manon Lescaut*, one totally devoted to his friend's welfare. Fouqué knows how business works, how certain influential individuals have to be placated, how dealing should proceed, and he navigates accordingly, but he is personally detached. He maintains a degree of independence that enables him literally and imaginatively to transcend the mundane and not become "lost in the weeds" of his business affairs, like de Renal and his associates. He sees in Julien a kindred spirit, so, to the latter's complete surprise, he proposes that Julien partner with him, creating a joint venture with the potential to make them both wealthy. Julien is taken aback by all of this; as Stendhal notes wryly, "This offer put Julien in a bad mood; it interfered with his mania" (82). Nevertheless, Julien considers his prospects with Fouqué carefully, reveling in the beauty of his mountain surroundings, the charm of his friend's rustic cottage, the sincerity of his feelings, and the total absence of the disagreeable concerns that repel him in the town below. He finds himself reacting to Fouqué's generous spirit not with his usual suspicion and disinclination, but as an *honnete homme*: "This individual, for whom hypocrisy and a total lack of human sympathy were the usual means of self-preservation, could not, in this instance, bear the thought of the slightest dishonesty with regard to a man who loved him" (83).

Julien realizes, however, that the hard labor a life with Fouqué would demand and the solitary virtue his friend models and would expect his partner to embrace cannot be fulfilling. He reflects ruefully on how such a life would extinguish the love of glory that drives his ambitions:

> *And after I had humbly earned a bit of money by running to all these timber sales and by currying favor with a few crooked subalterns, who can say whether I would have the sacred fire by which one makes a name?* (83)

Julien longs to master his fate, to be the leading player on whatever stage life presents.

A stage demands an audience. Fouqué is content to live as if no one else in the world matters. Julien must live as if everyone in the world matters and is watching with keen interest the drama of his life. He believes in his destiny: "But this young peasant saw nothing standing between him and the most heroic deeds but a want of opportunity" (81).

Fouqué provides opportunity, but not the sort that will lead to glory. Julien returns to Verrieres, therefore, still unsatisfied.

Julien resumes the life of a poor scholar and tutor. He continues to teach the children and participate in the de Renal household's social life. The proud young man, however, cannot succumb to the dull life of a provincial nobody. He has urges that compel him to acts of daring that highlight his superior character. Though he is supposed to be preparing for an ecclesiastical career, Julien lacks an essential element for such a profession: he cannot submit to the rigors of celibacy. In this respect, Julien is the French protagonist par excellence; he responds to the sexual attractions and desires other cultures downplay or ignore. In contrast to Huck Finn, whose boyish innocence has not yet been tested by sexual awakenings and David Copperfield, whose relationship with Dora is proper and undisturbed by passion, the twenty-year-old Julien is drawn to the beautiful Mme. de Renal almost from the beginning of his time with the family. The moment he first lays eyes on her, he is nonplussed: "Amazed at her beauty, he soon forgot everything, even what he had come for" (36).

Like his countrymen, Julien sees women as essential to a full life. They exist to be not so much loved as desired and won. Desire must be satisfied, so a woman who attracts a man must be conquered. Ever since Abelard and Eloise, the drama of seduction has been portrayed over and over in French literature as a balletic exercise demanding extraordinary sensitivity to nuance and subtlety. A look, a soft touch, a certain gait, a tone of voice all convey essential knowledge. A lover's quest can be as daunting as climbing Mount Everest (Proust's Marcel and Albertine) or as coldly calculated as a military siege and attack (Rodolphe's seduction of Madame Bovary). Marital bonds do not bring any special immunity from a lover's interest; indeed, the fact that a beautiful woman is engaged or married usually makes her more desirable. Julien's experience in the de Renal household recalls that of Adolphe and Ellenore, the lovers in Benjamin Constant's 1816 novel, *Adolphe*. Like Julien, Adolphe, a young man of parts, falls in love with an older married woman whose husband has been generous to him. Adolphe's youthful passions override conventional morality and the laws of hospitality. He and Ellenore embark on a life together that takes them ultimately to Poland, where Ellenore dies and Adolphe, whose life lacks purpose and whose only achievement has been winning his lover's lifelong devotion, bitterly mourns her passing and his failures. This is a cautionary tale, showing passion as an all-consuming force leaving only ruin in its wake.

Julien is too young and too far removed from the circles that indulge in dalliances as a matter of course to understand what is happening to him or to take any precautions; he behaves like headstrong men consumed by passion do. The boy who treasures just two books, Napoleon's *Memoires* and Rousseau's *Confessions*, acts as a disciple of both guides. From Napoleon he draws the conclusion that life is a perpetual war where one must conquer or be overwhelmed by all the conventional forces lined up to crush an ambitious upstart. From Rousseau he learns that quasi-maternal care, as Madame de Warens provided, can inspire deep devotion. Julien decides that a Napoleonic "conquest" of his employer's beautiful wife is not only desirable but *de rigeur* for a young man in his position. He will go Rousseau one step further and seduce his patroness, fancying this action as akin to unsentimental military duty: "The idea of a duty to be performed, and the ridicule, or rather, the feeling of inferiority to be incurred if he should fail, suddenly drove every pleasurable sensation out of his heart" (60).

Mme. de Renal at first treats the poor and nervous young man who has come into her home with maternal solicitude: "Julien had never known anyone so well dressed, especially a woman with such a dazzling complexion, to speak to him gently" (36–37). Soon, however, she is noticing his striking features and admiring his naturalness: "Mme. De Renal was struck by Julien's extraordinary good looks. The almost feminine cast of his features and his embarrassment did not seem ridiculous to a woman who was extremely shy herself" (38). She is innocence incarnate. Like Madame Bovary, "Mme. De Renal, wealthy heiress of a pious aunt and married at sixteen to a fine gentleman, had never experienced or seen anything that bore the least resemblance to love" (51). In her "angelical sweetness" (53), she is "perfectly happy, incessantly concerned about Julien, and far from blaming herself the least bit" (52) as matters develop.

They develop steadily. One evening, Mme. de Renal is relaxing with Julien and her friend Madame Derville. With a boldness he has forced himself to assume, Julien takes Mme. de Renal's hand in his and squeezes it "convulsively" (63). Mme. de Renal makes a weak effort to wrest it away, but then allows herself to relax, basking in the glow of a new emotion:

> *As for Mme. de Renal, her hand in Julien's, she hadn't a thought in the world; she was letting herself live. For her the hours they spent beneath the great lime tree, which as local tradition would have it, had been planted by Charles the Bold, were a time of bliss.* (63)

These moments become more frequent as both she and Julien grow less and less cautious. They culminate in a scene right out of grand opera, when after midnight one night, Julien climbs a ladder to Mme. de Renal's bedroom window, jumps inside, and, against all odds and all restraints, makes love to his patron's wife. More secret assignations will follow. For the first time in her life, Mme. de Renal experiences the bliss and turbulence of passionate love. Her adultery brings severe stress, as she torments herself with guilt, going so far as to believe that a serious illness her young son contracts during the affair is a special punishment from God. Mme. de Renal is a female type extolled in the French provinces: submissive to her husband; devout and deferential to the clergy; focused on child-rearing and all the details of comfortable domestic living; secure in her social status; and indifferent to any idea or point of view that defies accepted thinking. Stendhal exposes the emotional power that passion and desire can unleash in the most respectable of women, something Racine had done previously in *Phedre*, where an older woman also falls hopelessly in love with a younger man, and which Flaubert and Proust would explore with great subtlety later. This is one of the signal contributions the French have made to Western self-understanding. In other cultures, sexual desire and passion are acknowledged but are never probed with the frankness the French have brought to this theme. The great critic, Erich Auerbach, argued in *Mimesis* that love between men and women was never portrayed realistically before Stendhal did so in this novel.

Julien's feelings toward Mme. de Renal are strong and genuine, but because the brilliant young man has had more experience with books than with women, he proceeds in fits and starts, not sure how to act or think because the "art" of love the French adhere to is still a foreign language and territory for him. Clearly, he should return the love Mme. de Renal extends to him. Julien, however, despite moments of supreme happiness, cannot let love into his heart; he lacks the "courage to be sincere" (103), so he steels himself against emotional commitment and forces himself to act in the only way he believes a seducer can: he must conquer his prized lady as Napoleon did an enemy army. He ties himself up in doubt, insecurity, resentment, and self-contradictory justification throughout the relationship, telling himself at one point, for instance, that Mme. de Renal is "kind and gentle, her feeling for me is very strong," but due to her social position, she "has been raised in the enemy camp" (103), and must therefore be subdued rather than loved. In this regard, Julien is firmly in the French tradition, as exemplified, for instance, by Choderlos de Laclos's Vicomte de Valmont, who describes his "conquest" of Mme. de Tourvel, a pious and faithful wife who has resisted his advances for months but, finally, has succumbed:

> *Judge me then as you would Frederic or Turenne. I forced the enemy to fight when she wished only to refuse battle; by clever manoeuvres I obtained the choice of battlefield and of dispositions; I inspired the enemy with confidence, to overtake her more easily in retreat; I was able to make terror succeed confidence before joining battle; I left nothing to chance except from consideration of a great advantage in case of success and from the certainty of other resources in case of defeat; finally, I only joined action when I had an assured retreat by which I could cover and retain all I had conquered*

before. (*Dangerous Acquaintances.* Trans., Richard Aldington, New York: A New Directions Paperback, 1957, p. 279)

Julien's fumblings match Mme. de Renal's innocence. Both move blindly and battle inner demons: Julien's pride and egotism and Mme. de Renal's moral guilt. They navigate the way people engulfed by passion try their best to do, relying on no other guidance than everyday experience and books of doubtful relevance may offer. As their affair continues, they become like a true couple, compensating for each partner's weaknesses and building up each one's strengths. Stendhal captures this complementarity frequently, as in this passage:

> *At those times when the presence of too-intelligent children confined them to speak the language of cold reason, Julien would sit perfectly docile and look at her, his eyes aglow with love, and listen to her explain the ways of the world . . . Didn't she have constantly to answer his questions about a thousand simple things that any wellborn child knows by the time he's fifteen? An instant later she would look up to him as her master. Sometimes she was even frightened at his genius; she thought she could see the future great man every day in this young priest.* (105–06)

In the midst of the lovers' idyll, the people of Verrieres learn that a foreign monarch will soon be passing through their town on his way to pray at the shrine of St. Clement, only a short distance away. This news has the impact of a boulder hurled into a still pond. Everyone scrambles to find a way to observe or, better, take part in the spectacle about to unfold. No one is above politicking to enhance his or her candidacy for a favored position or to keep someone else out. The town's worthies consider it essential that they participate noticeably in this heaven-sent visitation, preferably as members of the guard of honor that will escort the king and his entourage through the town. Mme. de Renal finds "her drawing room filled with the wives of Liberals"; one of these supposed anti-monarchists begs that her husband be chosen lest he "go bankrupt out of grief" (108). Clergy in the vicinity also welcome the chance to accompany and, perhaps, be noticed by the newly appointed Bishop of Agde, who will conduct the religious ceremony that will culminate in his showing the king the precious relic of St. Clement. The Abbé Maslon, the curate who has replaced Abbé Chélan, Julien's patron, tries furiously to keep his predecessor away: "I will be dishonored here and in Besancon [the episcopal see] . . . if he shows up among my priests. A Jansenist, good God!" (109)

Even though Julien has given political or religious affairs little thought while enjoying the affections of Mme. de Renal, he too becomes caught up in the excitement. His influential patroness would very much "like to see him put off, if only for a day, his dreary black outfit" (108). She pulls some strings and has Julien appointed to the honor guard, entitling him to wear "one of those beautiful sky-blue uniforms, with a pair of colonel's epaulettes in silver" (109) that she will have specially made for her lover. Julien is delighted by this stroke of good fortune and makes the most of it. Though he has no social pedigree and no experience riding, he carries himself magnificently on the great day, inspiring in some of the observers extreme resentment toward the wrong person: "There was an outcry against the mayor, especially from the Liberals. What, just because that little workman dressed up as a priest was his brats' tutor, he had the nerve to make him a guard of honor" (110).

Julien's good fortune leads to a special privilege. Despite the Abbé Maslon's opposition, the well-connected Abbé Chélan has received an invitation to join the clergy assisting at the ceremony in the chapel. The priest has asked that Julien be invited as well, so he could serve as his chaplain. The request has been granted. Thus, the moment the king's party reaches the chapel, Julien dismounts, changes from riding dress to cassock and surplice, and quickly joins the Abbé Chélan and the rest of the clergy preparing to lead the bishop into the church. This coup makes the logger's son the only resident of Verrieres to have a prominent role in both the civic and the religious segments of the royal visit.

Abbé Chélan is the senior cleric of the local chapter. As such, he has the responsibility of informing the bishop that the procession into the chapel is about to begin. When all are in line and ready, he sends Julien to the area where the bishop is waiting to alert him that the clergy are preparing to process. This is obviously another honor, particularly since Julien has never met the Bishop of Agde. After they have been convinced Julien is really Abbé Chélan's delegate, the bishop's aides allow him to enter the prelate's private quarters to deliver the message. As he prepares to do so, Julien is surprised by what he sees:

> *A young man wearing a violet robe and a lace surplice, but bareheaded, had stopped three feet from the mirror. This piece of furniture seemed strangely out of place and had, no doubt, been brought there from town. Julien thought the young man looked irritated; with his right hand he was solemnly making the sign of benediction at the mirror.* (113)

It is a while before Julien realizes this is indeed the Bishop of Agde and, clearly, he is very young ("six or eight years older than I at the most" (113)) and inexperienced. Far from being repelled, however, by what appears to be excessive vanity, Julien is impressed by the young man's determination to perform this gesture as perfectly as possible. The concern for proper form that the bishop's refined upbringing (he is the nephew of a marquis) has instilled makes the man sensitive to what may be called one's presentation of self. The bishop fusses over his miter in the same way, placing it on his head carefully so it is neither too far back ("would look a bit foolish") nor too far forward ("[not] an officer's shako" (114)). Julien is dazzled by this man's presence, by the charming style of his conversation and by the gracious tone he assumes toward one whom he could have dismissed after just a few seconds. For the first time, Julien has a glimpse of a way of acting and living far more elegant than anything the provincial society he has grown tired of can produce.

As the procession makes its way into the church, Julien manages to stay close to the bishop and note with admiration his exquisite deportment:

> *Julien was stupefied with admiration at such a beautiful ceremony. His ambition roused again by the example of the bishop's youth, Julien couldn't tell which pleased him more, this prelate's sensitivity or his exquisite manners. This politeness was a very different thing from M. de Renal's, even on his good days.* (115)

The Bishop of Agde goes on to conduct the service splendidly, delivering an inspiring sermon directed mainly to a group of admiring young girls brought close to the relic's repository. Julien is swept away, not only by the young bishop's star-quality performance but also by the incense and chant that create such an exalted atmosphere. An ecclesiastical career that can lead to a bishop's appointment and can include radiant moments like this suddenly takes on more allure than ever before.

These festive days are a turning point. Life in the de Renal household afterwards is not the same. Mme. de Renal's youngest son, a favorite of Julien's, remains seriously ill, and her mother is convinced only a rupture with Julien can restore Stanislas's health. She gives vent to her grief-stricken self-reproach: "My crime is hideous, and I went on living with no sense of guilt. That was the first sign I had forsaken God; I ought to be punished twice as much" (121).

Julien's reaction is perceptive but coldly egocentric: "She believes she is killing her son by loving me, and yet this unhappy woman loves me more than her son. That, I am certain, is the regret that is killing her" (121). This disconnect is symptomatic. Stanislas eventually recovers, but the lovers' relationship does not. Its springtime quality has vanished, as Julien and Mme. de Renal quickly realize:

> *Their happiness might have seemed greater than ever in the eyes of the world. But they could never again find the delightful serenity, the unclouded felicity, the easy contentment, of the first stages of their love, when Mme. de Renal's only fear was that Julien might not love her enough. Sometimes their happiness wore the face of crime.* (125)

Stanislas's sickness is one of several complications occurring in quick succession. The love that seems criminal to Mme. de Renal soon looks potentially lethal when her husband receives an anonymous letter detailing all that has been going on under his nose. This bombshell upends all the arrangements the lovers once enjoyed. Mme. de Renal uses tact and diplomacy to maintain her position. She persuades her husband that his hated rival, Valenod, is behind the slander. However, rather than challenging him publicly and therefore allowing the story to spread, M. de Renal should send Julien away to Verrieres for a time and let matters cool. Her performance in dialogues with her husband is worthy of the stage. It includes comments such as this:

> *That little peasant, whom we've showered with favors and even presents, may be innocent, but he is nonetheless the cause of the first insult I have received . . . Sir! when I read that filthy note, I promised myself that either he or I would leave your house.* (138)

Julien resolves to make the most of his exile by reconnecting with Abbé Chélan and accepting invitations from society families, including M. and Mme. Valenod, who are eager to meet the boy who was a Guard of Honor. With his patented New Testament recitations and intellectually stimulating conversation, Julien shines:

> *Before leaving, Julien received four or five invitations to dine. "That young man is an honor to our department,"*

> *cried all the guests at once in very high spirits. They even went so far as to talk about a pension to be voted against the public funds, which would allow him to carry on his studies in Paris.* (149)

This interlude ends abruptly. The Abbé Chélan learns of Julien's affair when he hears the confession of Elsa, Mme. de Renal's former chambermaid, who in fact instigated the anonymous letter. The abbé responds decisively, ordering Julien to pack his bags immediately and leave for the seminary in Besancon, where he has made all the arrangements for his admission. The conscientious pastor's motives are pure: he wants to keep his prized pupil away from Mme. de Renal's caresses and M. de Renal's vengeful clutches through a radical change of scenery and lifestyle. For their own reasons, M. and Mme.de Renal endorse this initiative. Though Julien may seem an improbable candidate for holy orders, Abbé Chélan knows that with God all things are possible, so Julien's vocation may be rescued. Hardly in a position to resist such an intervention, Julien bids farewell to Mme. de Renal, who by now is barely sentient: "Far from responding to her lover's eagerness, she was like a cadaver" (166).

Julien is anything but eager to embrace the new life that has been offered to him. Upon catching sight of the seminary's walls, he reacts with despairing resentment: "So there it is, that hell on earth I won't be able to leave" (174). For one as brilliant, proud, aesthetically sensitive, sexually active, and skeptical as Julien, walking through the gate and climbing the steps of the grim seminary compound is like entering prison. He is so repelled by the cold ambience and by the harsh manner of the rector, Abbé Pirard, he actually passes out briefly and falls out of his chair as he is being interviewed. Notwithstanding, his obvious talents, revealed in a long theological dialogue with the rector conducted almost entirely in Latin, as well as the effusive recommendation of Abbé Chélan, an old friend Abbé Pirard greatly respects, are enough to win him admission as a scholarship recipient. Julien's seminary days and his "on again/

off again" attraction to religious life are reminiscent of Des Grieux's in *Manon Lescaut*. Des Grieux excels at Saint-Sulpice, one of France's premier theological colleges for potential priest scholars, but never completes his program because his love for the mercurial Manon is unquenchable.

Julien likewise stands out. Because his preparation in Latin, Scripture study, church history, and dogma is so extensive, he is far ahead of his classmates in almost every course. This achievement, however, is not as noteworthy as it might seem, given the quality of his fellow students: "Most were peasants' sons; they preferred earning their bread by reciting a few words in Latin to digging up the ground" (182). Julien quickly concludes that in such company he will so stand out as to become "a vicar-general" (182). Before such ambitions can be entertained, though, Julien needs to master the seminary's unwritten code, which is as strict and detailed as that of households like the de Renal establishment. He stumbles at first: "Though he thought himself cautious, all of our hero's first steps . . . were blunders" (182). Being first in every class, for instance, excites more envy than admiration in the "types in whose midst he would have to distinguish himself" because intellectual distinction is "in their eyes nothing but a 'resplendent' sin" (183). Julien is in a closed world; he might as well be on a ship in the ocean for all the contact he has with society outside his walls. As he interacts with students and staff, he barely avoids fatal errors. With his impetuosity and pride, he could well have become another Billy Budd. His worst fault is his self-confidence and indifference to authority: "In their eyes, he stood convicted of an egregious vice: *he thought, he judged for himself*, instead of blindly following *authority* and example" (185). His peers deride his achievements, mock his superior airs, and label him "Martin Luther" in their furious resentment.

Julien tries to save himself by assuming a much lower profile. Just as his dissembling and cunning ruses allowed him to flourish in the de Renal household despite his misconduct, so here too he will use his actor's ability to modify tone, style, and gesture to dispel the others' hostility. Julien studies his fellow students' habitual behaviors, carefully noting how they walk, speak, kneel, recite, and dine, the last being especially important because with the majority of seminarians coming from poor families, "happiness . . . consisted above all in dining well" (188). He makes heroic efforts to simulate a serenity only the blessed can assume:

> *What trouble he gave himself to achieve that beatific and sanctimonious expression, that countenance of a blind and fervent faith, which is ready to believe everything and to undergo anything, that one finds so frequently in Italian monasteries, and of which, for us laymen, Guercino has left such perfect models in his religious paintings.* (187)

Such exertions have only a limited impact, however, because Julien cannot recast himself entirely. He is who he is:

> *Several young seminarists had rosier complexions and might be considered better looking than Julien; but he had white hands and could not hide certain habits of fastidious cleanliness. This virtue was really not one in the dreary house into which fate had cast him.* (194)

From this nadir of hope and expectation, a quick succession of events and experiences lifts Julien's spirits and elevates his stature. One of Julien's professors is Abbé Chas Bernard, who doubles as master of ceremonies at the cathedral in Besancon. He invites Julien, whose talents he recognizes, to assist him in decorating the huge church for the upcoming Corpus Christi celebrations. This is the first mark of favor Julien has received since entering the seminary. The opportunity to excel without fear of giving offense energizes him. His urge to master every situation takes hold, and soon he is "directing the local upholsterers" and showing up the conceited Parisian decorators, specially brought in for the occasion, by climbing up a steep ladder himself to place a bouquet perfectly "on the crown-shaped ornament at the center of the baldequin" (197). The master of ceremonies is delighted: "Never had the Abbé Chas seen his church so beautiful" (199). He then entrusts Julien with the duty of patrolling the north aisle of the cathedral's nave during and after the ceremonies to be sure none of the valuable decorations can be pilfered. As he takes up position, Julien's aesthetic sensitivity responds to the splendor of the service being enacted before him. Just as at St. Clement's with the Bishop of Agde, Julien is swept away by all he sees and hears:

> *As he [Abbé Chas] finished speaking the clock struck eleven forty-five; at the same time the great bell began to toll. It was ringing at full peal. These sounds, so full and so solemn, thrilled Julien. His imagination had left earth. The fragrance of incense and of rose leaves, scattered before the Blessed Sacrament by little children dressed up as St John, brought his exaltation to a pitch.* (198)

While all this is proceeding, Julien happens to look back at the confessionals in the rear of the church, because, as the abbé had warned: 'That's where thieves have their women spies watch out for the moments our backs are turned" (198). Julien, however, sees no spy lurking behind the curtain. Instead, he is thunderstruck by the sight of Mme. de Renal, beautiful as ever, kneeling devoutly and awaiting absolution. Her companion, Madame Derville, intervenes and shoos Julien away. But the moment is electric, arousing in Julien long-suppressed tender emotions that carry him away from the present just as powerfully as the service had. The Abbé Chas drops plans to present his protégé to the bishop because Julien looks "half dead" and is "shaking so" (200–01).

Nevertheless, despite this shock at the end, the cathedral interlude has done Julien a great deal of good: it has offered an opportunity for him to excel and be noticed, to experience religious exaltation once more, and to renew contact, if only for an instant, with the source of his most intensely passionate feelings. His purgatorial trials behind the seminary walls are coming to an end at long last.

Their end is hastened by what occurs next. Shortly after returning to the seminary, Julien is unexpectedly summoned to the rector's office. The Abbé Pirard is about to resign his post, and aware of all that Julien has had to endure and bothered in conscience over his failure to address the seminarians' spiteful conduct, the rector resolves before he leaves to "do something" for Julien, in whom he sees "a spark that must not be neglected" (202). Abbé Pirard then informs an astonished Julien that he is making him "assistant master of the New and the Old Testament" (202). This is the second special favor accorded Julien in just a matter of days. The rector's parting counsel is characteristically biblical: "Let your conduct be flawless; that is the only resource I see for you. If you hold to the truth with an invincible grasp, sooner or later your enemies will be confounded" (203).

But his enemies are confounded almost immediately, and for reasons that have nothing to do with flawless conduct. Julien's promotion has changed the landscape permanently. As a master, he is a superior being who has privileges and power, whose teachings must be accepted as authorized truths, and whose commands must be obeyed. With regard to obedience, the seminarians are like the recruits who swelled the ranks of the great European national and imperial militaries of the era. They obeyed their officers without question or cavil, lest they suffer the most severe punishments. Julien has become the equivalent of an officer, someone to look up to, an authority figure and a role model:

> *To his great amazement, Julien observed that he was less hated; he had anticipated, on the contrary, an increase of hatred. His secret desire that no one should speak to him, which was all too obvious and had won him so many enemies, was no longer taken as a sign of absurd arrogance. In the eyes of the coarse creatures who surrounded him, it sprang from a just sense of his own worth. Hatred waned appreciably, especially among*

> *the youngest of his companions, now his students, whom he treated with a great deal of courtesy. In due time he even began to have a following; it came to be in bad taste to call him Martin Luther.* (203)

Julien's stature is further enhanced when Abbé Pirard entrusts to him the special and delicate task of hand-delivering to the Bishop of Besancon himself the rector's carefully composed letter of resignation. Julien carries out this task with aplomb. Though the abbé describes the bishopric and its tenants as "a den of wolves" (209), Julien is not repelled. While awaiting the bishop, he admires "the pious magnificence" (210) of the drawing room, so different in style from the austere seminary furnishings. The Bishop of Besancon is old and indifferent about the future, but he is of aristocratic background, so he takes special care to put his young guest at ease. Julien senses that he is in the company of a *grand seigneur*, whose questions and conversation are supported by broad familiarity with the classics. Julien quickly concludes that he will "try to shine" (211) in the bishop's eyes. He does so by displaying, as is his wont, immense learning, both in dogma and in literature. Julien even gently corrects His Grace when he falters with Horace: "The prelate quoted several odes, but his memory was sometimes lazy, and with a modest air Julien would recite the ode in its entirety on the spot" (211). The prelate can only conclude, "It is not possible to be better educated" (211). He presents Julien with an eight-volume collection of Tacitus's writings and insists "on writing in his own hand, on the title page of the first, a Latin inscription to Julien Sorel" (212).

The bishop clearly inhabits a different world than Julien and his rough peers. This is a world dominated by Roman models, classical in structure and style, authoritarian but careful and restrained in the exercise of power, open to young men like Julien whose intellects set them apart, and refined in lifestyle so that the art of living is modeled daily. Julien responds to the aesthetics of this existence: "Julien was astonished at the bishop's extreme politeness above all else. He had no conception of such urbane manners combined with so natural an air of dignity" (213). The bishop is an ambassador from the highest echelons, a man whom Julien could one day succeed, a man who lives as a great lord should, and who makes devotion to ecclesiastical duty positively joyful. Julien is beginning to see light at the end of the tunnel as his star continues to rise.

The seminarians' reaction to all of this is predictable: "They knew everything down to the smallest details. From that moment there was no more jealousy. Julien's favor was basely courted" (214). Once again, through sheer assertion of will and intellect, Julien has overcome challenges that would have overwhelmed most young men of his type. He has not just survived; he has flourished. From his new eminence, he can view his now sycophantic associates with all the *hauteur* of a Roman official in ancient Gaul, commenting sourly about how "their fawning merely disgusted him and gave him not the least pleasure" (214).

Julien in the seminary is clearly a French type, of whom Charles Talleyrand is perhaps the supreme embodiment. Talleyrand was born to wealth and privilege, so from the start he could dispense with any need to ingratiate himself with seminarians, professors, or rectors. His path was laid out the moment he chose to become a priest: he would use connections and influence wherever necessary to rise in the ecclesiastical ranks of Bourbon France. Income, honor, and prestige would follow. In 1789, he was made Bishop of Autun, a post that could serve as a steppingstone to further advancement. For Talleyrand, as for many of his aristocratic episcopal peers, high church office did not require a prelate to forsake mistresses, dinner parties, hunting expeditions, and other pursuits deemed "worldly" then and now. Like a Roman governor, a bishop enjoyed virtually unlimited authority in his diocese, regardless of how he ruled or lived.

In 1789, though, something else occurred that would make ecclesiastical advancement quickly fade as a realistic goal. The calling of the Estates-General changed everything for ambitious men like the Bishop of Autun. Talleyrand realized early that he had no future in a church fighting for its institutional life in a country trying to reinvent itself as a republic. He, therefore, coolly and shamelessly abandoned his diocese and his vocation to join forces with the revolutionaries and their successors, the Bonapartists. Though Napoleon himself famously referred to him as "*merde* in a silk stocking," Talleyrand proved not only useful but indispensable as the emperor's foreign minister. When Napoleon went into exile and the Bourbon monarchy was restored, Talleyrand might reasonably have expected to face a firing squad, like Marshall Ney. Instead, he managed to land on his feet, becoming foreign minister once again and ably representing France at the Congress of Vienna. Talleyrand worked through what seems like a bewildering series of role and wardrobe changes in an ongoing epic drama by mastering the diplomatic art, whose intricacies Julien has been forced by circumstances to learn through trial and error. The bishop turned state servant knew how to charm, how to flatter, how to be witty at one moment and coldly silent the next, how to gain advantage or concession through subtle hint rather than harsh assertion, and, above all, how to exploit opportunity. If, as is said of doctrinaires, "they never let reality interfere with their ideas," Talleyrand never let principle impede his multiple career trajectories. Julien may not realize it at the time, but in the seminary at Besancon, he is well on his way to accelerating exactly this type of ascendancy.

Suddenly, however, fate intervenes to take Julien, now at the height of prestige and influence, in an entirely different direction. Just as his seminary studies began abruptly when his dalliance with Mme. de Renal was exposed, so now they will end abruptly when the Abbé Pirard departs as rector. Once the abbé does so, he quickly secures appointment as pastor of a fashionable parish in Paris. This comes about not through normal church channels, but because the Marquis de la Mole, a powerful landowner with connections to ecclesiastical decision-makers, has pulled the right strings behind the scenes. The marquis and the abbé have had a long association; somewhat improbably, the austere priest with Jansenist leanings has acted for years as the Marquis de la Mole's spokesman and legal advisor in protracted litigation with another priest over properties in eastern France. The other priest is none other than the Abbé Frilair, the all-powerful vicar-general of the diocese of Besancon. Julien had met him at the bishop's palace the night he delivered Abbé Pirard's letter of resignation and had been struck by Abbé Frilair's good looks and elegant dress. Only "the great cunning apparent in certain features" (210) tempered Julien's admiration.

From today's perspective, two priests at loggerheads over property rights is off-putting, but as the example of Talleyrand has shown, French clergy, particularly those not sequestered in monasteries, have involved themselves over the centuries in all sorts of business, legal, and political affairs. The Bourbon monarchs, for instance, regularly nominated cardinals as ministers of state. In the towns and villages of pre-industrial France, it was only natural for priests, who were among the best-educated and most influential local dignitaries, to assist parishioners and friends in need of services that only accomplished writers, scholars, or speakers could provide. The fact that most priests could be compensated for such work with what today would be called an honorarium rather than a salary or fee, made them even more valuable to the laity. Some priests, like the Abbé Frilair, took such advantage of their connections as to accumulate money and power far beyond what their vocations alone could have generated. Their families would reap unheard of benefits upon their deaths.

In any case, the marquis becomes acquainted with Julien through Abbé Pirard. The marquis is in need of a competent copyist cum secretary and asks the abbé, whose talents he knows and appreciates to take on this additional work, assuring him he will make it his business to hold his "fine parish" for him until the day they "no longer suit one another" (217). A priest first, the abbé declines the offer but suggests an alternative. "In the depths" (217) of his seminary in Besancon is Julien Sorel, whose prospects are unclear:

> *As of now, the young man knows nothing but Latin and Holy Scriptures; but it is not impossible that he will one day display great talents, be it for preaching, be it for the guidance of souls. I don't know what he'll do; but he has the sacred fire, he may go far.* (217)

It so happens that the marquis knows of Julien; though they have never met, the marquis once secretly accorded him a large cash gift after hearing the abbé praise him highly. The job will be his. As noted earlier, Abbé Pirard cautions the marquis about taking offense if Julien's prickly pride and sensitivity strain their working relationship, but the marquis assures the priest he will have no issue with high spirits and pride. Julien will take an extended leave from the seminary and join the household at the Hotel de la Mole, in the Faubourg Saint Germain, Paris. "At last, he [Julien] was going to make his appearance on a scene where great events took place" (219).

Before he makes his Parisian debut, Julien cannot resist a daring parting appearance in Mme. de Renal's Verrieres bedroom. With melodramatic zeal and enterprise, he procures a ladder and, for the last time, silently enters the chamber where he once enjoyed the greatest happiness and the most memorable conquests. He and his former lover reunite after "fourteen months of cruel separation" (221). Both experience a welter of passionate and conflicting emotions. For Julien, the first moments with his former mistress bring back the tenderness that he has been forced to suppress in the seminary, where "all feeling had vanished from his heart save love" (223). Mme. de Renal, however, has spent a long time with Abbé Chélan, to whom she has revealed the details of her affair. She is, consequently, cold and distant, dwelling on repentance rather than renewed love. True to his character, Julien cannot bear to leave without overcoming this resistance: "What a shame for me if I am sent packing! The regret would poison my whole life" (224). He must triumph; he must show mastery: "In that moment, all that was heavenly about Julien's situation quickly lost its influence over his heart" (225). He becomes "calculating and cold", focused only on breaking down Mme. de Renal's scruples. Julien plays "his last card" when he tells her he will soon be leaving for Paris, "never to return" (225). As Julien then moves toward the window as if to go quickly, Mme. de Renal rushes to stop him. They embrace passionately, but, having required so much craft and artifice, the outcome is equivocal, "nothing more than a triumph" (226). The masterful young man, nonetheless, revels in "all the pleasures of pride" as he caresses his "lovely woman," while she rejoices that he is "showing proof of so much love" (227). This disconnect, unfortunately, is emblematic of their entire relationship.

Their time together extends over several days, with Mme. de Renal becoming more and more reluctant to be away from Julien even briefly and he marveling at her courage and *élan* in deceiving the whole household: "she was recklessness itself" (230). This interlude ends dramatically. M. de Renal's servant has found Julien's ladder, and all are in an uproar as its owner is sought. Julien escapes like one of Dumas' heroes, jumping out the window at the last possible moment and dodging rifle shots as he scurries away. Book I ends with Julien's walking toward Geneva to throw his pursuers off. From there, he can reenact Jean-Jacques Rousseau's progress to Paris and fame.

PART TWO

Book II of the novel chronicles Julien's life with the de la Mole family and its aftermath. This family's colorful history has been punctuated over the centuries by scandal, illicit love, political intrigue, and religious zealotry. The son of the carpenter of Verrieres, like Rousseau, will now enter the *haute monde*. Though this environment is clearly outside his comfort zone, Julien will continually strive to meet its challenges, just as he has done with the provincial bigwigs and the seminarians. In the process, he will indeed master its code and rise to a scarcely to be believed status as a Parisian dandy. At the height of his success, this determined Gallic provincial will have used his native intelligence, connections, and guile in Paris to earn a military commission, property, and funds for himself, his wife, and his soon to be born son. All such honors, recognitions, and triumphs will, however, vanish in an instant as a crime of passion leads to a tragic end for one who had dared greatly and always prevailed.

Julien's service with the Marquis de la Mole begins well. He is clearly the kind of bright young man older men and women, even against their better judgment, like to guide and mentor. Abbé Pirard is one of these, though he is careful to be stern and commanding in tone to assuage his "pangs of conscience about liking Julien" (241). He has known the marquis and his family for some time and can speak with some authority on how Julien should comport himself in this aristocratic household:

> *You will live in the marquis' house; he's one of the greatest lords of France. You will wear black, but like a man in mourning, not as a clergyman . . . Every day at noon you will install yourself in the marquis's library; he means to have you write letters about his lawsuits and*

> *other business. In the margin of each letter he receives, the marquis jots down a summary of the answer to be made. I claimed that at the end of three months you would know how to write out these replies, so that out of every twelve letters you presented for the marquis' signature, he might be able to sign eight or nine. At eight o'clock in the evening you will put his desk in order, and at ten you will be free.* (240)

Julien should also be discreet and careful in conversation: "You must be useful. If I were in your place, I would speak little and, above all, never talk about anything of which I was ignorant" (240). Abbé Pirard also reminds Julien that he is "the son of a carpenter from Verrieres" and likely to be looked down upon by some in the family, particularly "young Count de la Mole" (241). If that is the case, though, Julien may never realize how the man really feels because he and his friends will veil their contempt "in exaggerated compliments" (241). Mme. la Marquise de la Mole deserves special attention:

> *That great lady is a kind of scale model, in high relief, of what is most basic to the character of women of her rank. She lets it be known, she does, that to have had ancestors who went on the Crusades is the only distinction she respects. Money comes a long way after; that surprises you? We are no longer in the country, my friend.* (242)

When Julien expresses doubt that he will be able to navigate in Paris for any length of time, the abbé reminds him of a basic truth: "There is no way to fortune for a man of our cloth save through the great lords" (242). In gratitude for the almost paternal concern the abbé has shown, Julien for once lowers his guard and allows real feeling to influence his words: "I have been hated by my father since birth; that is one of my great sorrows; but I will never again complain about my luck. I have found a second father in you, sir" (243).

Abbé Pirard is touched by Julien's words but too embarrassed by his pupil's emotional tone to respond in kind. As he escorts Julien into the Hotel de la Mole, he resumes his admonitory warnings, alerting him first to the nature of the company he will have to deal with:

> *Remember that this crowd of lackeys, seeing you installed here, will try to make a fool of you; they will look upon you as an equal set above them unfairly. Behind a show of good-naturedness, of good advice, of a desire to be helpful, they will try to lead you into committing some gross blunder.* (245)

A "gross blunder" is easy to commit in this environment. Just as with the seminarians and their teachers, unspoken rules and protocols govern relations among not only the lackeys but also the privileged. The abbé counsels Julien to be prudent and careful, particularly if lured into conversation by the marquis's family and guests: "Another thing, don't let these Parisians hear the sound of your voice. If you say a word, they will find a way to make fun of you. They have a talent for that" (247). The abbé's words have an impact. Julien approaches the de la Mole household as he had the de Renal household and the seminary—that is, with resentment and mistrust.

He is pleasantly surprised, however, when he is introduced to the Marquis de la Mole. The master of the house is not at all overbearing. Indeed, he is reminded of the one man whose style until now has had no parallel in Julien's experience: "But Julien soon noted that the marquis' manners were even more agreeable to the interlocutor than those of the Bishop of Besancon himself" (246). The marquis talks with him for only a few minutes, but in this span, he arranges for Julien to acquire two new suits, to begin dancing lessons, and to order twenty-two shirts. Though he has reservations about "this little abbé from Franche-Comte" and is distressed by a spelling error Julien makes in one of his first documents, the marquis reveals no sign of displeasure with his newest employee as he graciously squires Julien through his first day at the residence. Julien is appreciative and impressed: "He was touched by the marquis' kindness, which reminded him, by contrast, of M. de Renal's offensive manner" (248).

Julien meets other members of the marquis's family and retinue when they gather in the evening "in a drawing room resplendent with gilding" (249). He is struck by Mlle. de la Mole, the marquis's daughter, whose expressive eyes he struggles to describe, settling finally on "scintillating" (250). The marquis, by contrast, "scarcely bothered to look at him" (249). Count de la Mole, the marquis's son, whom Abbé Pirard had cautioned him about, appears at first sight "charming" (249) and "admirable in every way" (250).

Others behave more like the "lackeys" Abbé Pirard alluded to earlier. The young Bishop of Agde is present but "not at all eager to recognize this provincial" (249). Several academics, regular guests of the marquis, engage Julien in discussions about classical literature, language, history, and politics, always with the intention of exposing what they hope is his essential boorishness. But Julien performs expertly, using his experience with the Bishop of Besancon and his knowledge of Horace et al. to parry anyone's attempt to trip him up. Though Julien knows little about current writers or political situations, when the conversation concerns the ancients, he is in his element:

> *But it escaped no one's attention that whenever a question came up about an event that had occurred in Rome, and knowledge about it could be inferred from the works of Horace, or Martial, or Tacitus, etc., he had an undeniable superiority. Julien lay hands boldly on several ideas he learned from the Bishop of Besancon, in the famous discussion he had had with that prelate; they were by no means the least relished.* (251)

Julien emerges triumphant from this intellectual trial by fire: "He had handsome eyes, which a trembling shyness, or happiness when he answered well, made twice as bright. The company thought him agreeable" (250-251). Julien offers "fresh insights" even if, like Rousseau, he "does not know the language they speak in Paris" (251) and cannot therefore display wit, which is prized so highly in these circles, especially by Mlle. de la Mole. These deficiencies will be addressed over time. For now, Julien has earned the household's approval. Even the marquis, "who made it a law unto herself to admire anything that entertained her husband, deigned to look at Julien" (252).

This opening scene at the Hotel de la Mole will typify Julien's entire experience in Parisian society. Though he will never become completely comfortable in the de la Mole household ("All of their ways seemed strange to him and he was always doing the wrong thing" (256)), Julien emerges quickly as a young man with talent and prospects; he earns the Marquis de la Mole's favor; he impresses the marquis's son and daughter, who show special interest in him for different reasons; and he takes the measure of the aristocratic network and its dependents that the de la Mole clan is tied to and helps sustain. Over the course of Book II, variations on these themes will be acted out in a multitude of contexts and settings, all of them highlighting Julien's steady progress toward mastering this world.

The day after this successful "opening night," Count Norbert invites Julien to accompany him on a horseback ride. Julien is at first apprehensive, having, he says, been on a horse "no more than six times" (254) in his entire life. Norbert, who is "courtesy itself" (253), insists he take the challenge. Julien does and, despite one mishap, manages not only to stay erect in the saddle through to the end but also to look good doing so, since "he had style without knowing it" (254). The marquis is delighted: "I augur well of this little priest" (254). Julien rises in his estimation because he surmounts an obstacle and then talks about it charmingly, as if to the Parisian manner born. This is no easy task in the presence of titled notables, old and young, and their entourages. In their midst, Julien stands out: "If everything about the Hotel de la Mole's noble drawing room seemed strange to Julien, the pale young man in black likewise struck everyone who bothered to notice him as very odd" (257). The contrasts are in more than wardrobe or physiognomy.

The young aristocrats who frequent the de la Mole drawing room have resonant names: "the Marquis de Croisenois, the Count de Caylus, the Viscount de Luz" (260), and so on. Despite their social eminence, however, they are, in important ways, very much like the seminarians Julien could barely endure. They are not crude, backward, or boorish, of course. They have been raised by parents who have seen to it that they possess all the social graces and skills. But their surface charms mask characters that are basically timid, passive, and unimaginative. Just as the seminarians have been so schooled in obedience, they cannot entertain an unscripted thought; the aristocrats stay always within a circumscribed social and intellectual milieu that permits only conventional concepts, words, and sentiments to be expressed in drawing room conversation:

> *Any idea with the least bit of life in it seemed an indecency. Despite the good tone, perfect politeness, a desire to please, boredom was stamped on every forehead. The young people who came out of a sense of duty, fearful lest they say something that might cause them to be suspected of an idea, or betray their knowledge of some prohibited book, kept silence after a few elegant remarks about Rossini or the weather.* (258)

Julien finds them lacking in the will to give life to their etiolated convictions. In contrast to the Spanish Liberal, Count Altamira, who lives with a death sentence over his head for having acted on his convictions and who will so impress Julien later, de Croisenois and his friends can only mumble platitudes and maneuver for political favor.

While the young men who gather in the Hotel de la Mole make little impression on Julien, the marquis's daughter, Mathilde, overawes him. At first entranced by her beauty and her stylish manner, Julien soon begins to appreciate her piercing wit (which scares most of the young men who vie for her attention lest it be directed at one of them), her romantic fixation on heroic ancestors, her refined tolerance (she attends

Mass daily but reads Voltaire secretly), and her self-confidence. She is a kindred spirit and an equal. They take pleasure in each other's company and conversation. Julien respects and admires Mathilde's commanding manner, so Parisian and so different from Madame Renal's modest charm, while Mathilde sees in Julien a potential hero, a throwback to the French nobles of the Wars of Religion, so passionately engaged and so courageous in combat. The young man who reproaches himself for not having yet achieved any triumphs comparable to Napoleon's at the same age, is about to become the intimate companion of a young woman who is like a free-thinking Joan of Arc in her dismissal of all the weak young aristocrats who fawn on her.

As alluded to earlier, in *Mimesis,* the great twentieth-century critic Erich Auerbach deconstructs a dialogue between Julien and Mathilde, concluding that it is the first realistic depiction of love between the sexes in European literature. He could have expanded his scope and reiterated his thesis a hundred times over by considering the entirety of their time together. What Stendhal does throughout Book II is portray as none before him ever did, the swirling waves and eddies of passionate attachment. Julien and Mathilde experience desire and shame, pride and humility, the urge to dominate and to be enslaved, the ecstasy of passion fulfilled and the *ennui* of passion spent, the need to love and the need to be free of all entanglements—in other words, the whole range of powerful and conflicting realities in the ballet two young lovers perform over the course of their time together. Julien's affair with Mme. de Renal includes these emotional swings, but that relationship is between an older woman in a settled life and a young man eager to assert himself sexually but still fundamentally innocent. It does not have the intensity, volatility, romance, and potential for triumph or tragedy that the affair between two equally brilliant and strong-willed young people has. Many years later, Marcel Proust would probe even more deeply the agonies of unfulfilled relationships, laying bare the subtlest gradations of emotion a passing thought, a glance, an unexpected word or gesture, could provoke in one who loves but cannot possess another. This sensitivity is uniquely French.

No other European literary tradition even comes close to French artistry in the depiction of love between the sexes, and, as in so many other aspects, Stendhal's portrayal of Julien and Mathilde's affair of the heart highlights the French character.

The French strive always for mastery, but love between equals makes mastery impossible; the more one partner strives to gain control of the other's emotional life, the more that partner resists. The relationship becomes a roller-coaster ride of alternating elation and depression, with the level of feeling growing more and more intense as the couple engage each other. Neither can win this contest, but neither can walk away. The sexual excitement each inspires in the other and the allure each discovers in the other's every word, deed, and feature, create endless fascination and provoke the most intimate fantasies. Julien and Mathilde embody all these complexities. They are, on the surface, an unexpected pairing. Mathilde is the daughter of a marquis and the descendant of a long line of proud and brave nobles. Julien is a carpenter's son on leave from a seminary and totally dependent on Mathilde's father for daily sustenance. Yet he is as proud as she. In her case, pride is natural given her pedigree, her beauty, her intellect, and her glittering prospects. Julien has no pedigree, but he is strikingly handsome, brilliant, and capable of great accomplishment. Mathilde is drawn to him almost against her will. At a grand ball at the Hotel de Retz, she gives most of her attention to Julien. He attends at the invitation of her brother and is not quite prepared for what awaits the hotel's guests. The setting is reminiscent of the richly decorated churches he has been in on festive occasions; only this time the celebration is non-religious:

> *That night, when he arrived for the ball, he was impressed by the magnificence of the Hotel de Retz. The front courtyard was covered by a huge awning made of crimson twill spangled with gold stars: nothing could be more elegant. Beneath this awning, the courtyard had been transformed into a grove of orange trees and oleander in flower. Since care had been taken to bury the*

> *tubs sufficiently, the oleanders and orange trees looked as if they were growing in the ground. The drive over which the carriages rolled had been graveled.* (287)

Julien is once again in "enemy territory" and behaves accordingly. He assumes a wary and detached pose, limiting contact and conversation with the mostly titled company, who are, in any case, focused only on Mathilde. The comments of these gentlemen are admiring, as in this speculation: "And who could be worthy of the sublime Mathilde? . . . Some ruling prince, handsome, witty, well built, a war hero, and twenty years old at the most" (288). To the astonishment of the "young men with mustaches" (289), Mathilde at first engages only one, twenty-year-old Julien, in conversation. She speaks directly to him about the opinions and character of Jean-Jacques Rousseau, from whose *Confessions* she has learned obscure biographical details. Julien, too, knows this philosopher's memoir very well, so he is not fazed. He responds to her probing observations with equally knowledgeable citations. Mathilde, who has been and will continue to be bored at the ball by the young men Julien dismisses as "stuffed dolls" (288), is delighted by Julien's command of the facts but is annoyed by his "coldness." She notes ruefully that it is "she who was used to producing this effect in others" (289).

What should diminish any attraction between this apparently ill-matched pair actually increases interest. Far from being repelled by Julien, Mathilde becomes more and more fascinated. They have another conversation about a historical figure, this time, Danton. Mathilde is struck by Julien's decisive and independent manner: "He's not always thinking of what he is going to say! He is not like Caylus or Croisenois. Sorel has something of that air my father imitates so well when he goes to a ball dressed as Napoleon" (295). For his part, Julien is certainly flattered by the "Queen of the Ball's" special favor, but his pride bristles at the thought that she is making him perform for her by taking advantage of her position: "He seemed to be saying: 'I am paid to answer you and I live on my pay'"

(295). He then does what no other young man ever does in Mathilde's presence: he walks away to be with another guest. Instead of leaving him in a fury, Mathilde follows, determined to listen in on Julien's conversation with none other than Count Altamira, a legendary figure. The count is a Spanish noble who has been condemned to death in his own country and faces extradition from France for plotting against the Spanish regime. For Mathilde, Altamira is the embodiment of reckless daring and death-defying resolution. This kind of courage is not to be found in post-revolutionary France. As Mathilde gazes at the young suitors who accompany her every move but are too timid to meet her gaze ("they dreaded the explosion of some sharp remark that would be hard to answer." (292)), she concludes that high birth "atrophies those qualities of the heart which cause a man to be condemned to death" (292). This is all the more reason to hover over the lowborn young man who "has the look of a prince in disguise" (295) and the heroic revolutionary. She finds their conversation riveting as both denounce the period they live in for diminishing valor and ambition and allowing mercenary mediocrity to rule, to the detriment of honor and integrity. As the dialogue reaches emotional heights and Julien proclaims his willingness to "have three men hanged to save the lives of four" (298), Mathilde meets his gaze and is astounded that "his contempt, far from changing into a gracious and civil look, seemed to increase" (298). But she is under his spell; she has now met a man who can give as well as he gets and whose character is as fully developed along heroic lines as is hers. It is "no longer in her power to forget Julien" (298).

The next day, Mlle. de la Mole, almost under compulsion, visits Julien in her father's library. Julien, however, is still preoccupied with Count Altamira and the other men of decisive action their conversation has called to mind. When he notices Mathilde, who has not been in his thoughts at all, he reacts with indifference:

> *He was so stirred by his admiration for the great virtues of Danton, Mirabeau, Carnot, men who knew*

> *how to avoid defeat, that he stared at Mlle. de la Mole without reacting to her, without greeting her, almost without seeing her. When his big eyes opened so wide finally registered her presence, his look grew dull. Mlle. de la Mole noted this bitterly.* (300)

Mathilde is, of course, furious not only with Julien but also with herself. She laughs in "an attempt to hide her embarrassment" (301), but then, to her astonishment, she asks Julien to tell her what he has been thinking about, promising like a schoolgirl not to tattle: "I'm dying to know. I won't repeat it; I swear" (301). She is actually "pleading with an inferior" (301) and is horrified. Julien responds with a Nietzschean rant about the need for a genuine leader to "move like the whirlwind and do evil as if by chance" (301) to further the emancipation of the masses. Mathilde is "frightened" and cannot "bear his gaze," but she leaves the library "with a light step" (301), having provoked in Julien a reaction that confirms her fascination with and attraction to the only young man she knows who has the capacity for true heroism.

Julien, for a time afterwards, continues to be repelled by Mathilde, despite her beauty and regal bearing, because, unlike Madame de Renal, she is not "natural" (303). Like Rousseau in Paris, he has encountered "cold and arrogant vanity, every shade of conceit, and nothing more" (303). But Mathilde is so charismatic Julien cannot remain coldly aloof. His attitude changes:

> *He was beginning not to take that kind of beauty which is accompanied by a noble bearing for coldness of heart. He had long conversations with Mlle. de la Mole, who, during the fine days of spring, would sometimes stroll with him after dinner in the garden, alongside the open windows of the drawing room.* (305)

Julien is flattered by her attention and by the fact that she "was condescending to speak to him in a manner that might almost be taken as friendly" (305). He soon abandons "his dreary role of plebeian in revolt" (306) and entertains the amazing thought that "she has taken a fancy" (307) to him. Still determined not "to be offended once by this haughty girl" (307), he nevertheless relishes his ability to attract the one female every gentleman in the vicinity of the Hotel de la Mole is hoping to marry. Julien fears Mathilde may be toying with his feelings, but he refuses to deny what is taking place before his eyes:

> *No! Either I am crazy, or she is making up to me; the more I treat her coldly and respectfully, the more she seeks me out. This could be deliberate on her part, an affectation; but I see her eyes light up whenever I appear unexpectedly. Do Parisian women know how to sham to that extent? What do I care? Appearances are for me; let's enjoy the appearances. My God, she's beautiful! How I love those big blue eyes from close up, and looking at me as they often do!* (308)

Julien ends this reverie with a sudden resolution: "I will have her; I'll run away afterwards, and woe to him who tries to stop me!" (309). He then begins to obsess over her just as she has been obsessing over him. This very French conclusion comes like a rifle shot at the end of chapter X, in Book II. It will determine Julien's conduct for the rest of the novel.

Both, however, still have to get over lingering doubts and fears. Each is clearly enthralled by the other, but each remains wary and on guard lest his or her feelings be betrayed. Mathilde is infatuated by French and family history. For her, the man she loves must somehow approach the stature of her ancestor, Boniface de la Mole, "adored lover of Queen Marguerite de Navarre" (304) and heroic martyr for the Bourbon party in sixteenth-century France. She wears black every year on the anniversary of his execution. For her, Julien is star-crossed, someone who, alone of her male acquaintance, is capable of great deeds. Yet a bonding between the two, by its very nature, brings the possibility of shame, humiliation, and personal and family disgrace, since Julien is a carpenter's son, a seminary student, and a dependent of her father. The social distance between them is unbridgeable, but the intellectual excitement they share, their compulsion to stand out from the crowd, their fierce pride, and their powerful emotions make mutual attraction natural. Mathilde characteristically places her passion for Julien within the historical context she reveres:

> *With Julien and me there's no question of signing a contract, no lawyer at a bourgeois ceremony; with us, everything is heroic; everything will be the offspring of chance. Noble birth apart, which he lacks, it is the love of Marguerite of Valois for the young La Mole, the most distinguished man of his day.* (314)

This romanticism must constantly compete with Mathilde's sense of herself and her station. Even if "her greatest pleasure was to gamble with her fate" (311), she will not do so for a man who may not be as great as she imagines:

> *There is already something great and venturesome about daring to love a man so far removed from me by his social position. Will he continue to deserve me? We shall see. At the first sign of weakness, I will drop him. A girl of my birth, with the chivalrous character people so readily ascribe to me . . . ought not to behave like a simpleton.* (313)

Julien is likewise conflicted. He cannot deny his feelings for Mathilde, based though they are mostly on appearances:

> *It was only after losing himself in reveries over the elegance of Mlle. de la Mole's figure, her excellent taste in dress, the whiteness of her hand, the beauty of her arm, the disinvoltura of her movements, that he found himself in love.* (321)

He admits he knows "nothing about her character" and that her interest in him "might be nothing more than a show" (321). Even when he receives a letter from Mathilde that is nothing less than "a declaration of love from a great lady" (324), and he is at first overjoyed, Julien cannot allay his suspicion that this is all part of an elaborate aristocratic plot to bring a "poor peasant" (324) to his knees. He gets himself so tied up in these suspicions that his joy turns to hostility. He ends by exploding in Iago-like fury: "One must admit that Julien's gaze was atrocious, his face hideous: it was instinct with unalloyed crime. He was the unhappy man at war with all society" (327).

Before this outburst, Julien has made one telling observation. Just after reading Mathilde's letter, he says to himself with pride that he has kept his "dignity" by never having said he "was in love" (324). For this typically French young man, to admit one's love prematurely is to risk everything. It is best to elicit such an admission from the other; one can then relish his/her conquest and let tender feeling express itself freely later. Until such a conquest can be achieved through a sexual union, a relationship must be carried on as if it were a military operation, complete with strategies specially designed to win victory. For young men, typically, this operation's objective is to persuade a girl to give up her virginity, so important a possession in Catholic France. Julien gives voice to such thinking when he muses, "In the battle that is preparing" . . . "pride of birth will be like a high hill, forming a tactical position between her and me. It's up there that I'll have to maneuver" (331).

Mathilde's perspective is affected by her aristocratic lineage, but given her consuming passion for Julien, the restraints instilled by her convent school upbringing are soon overcome. In writing and sending the letter, she has lowered herself to being "the *first*" (330) to declare her love. If this is revealed, she will incur "everlasting dishonor" (330) because the men and women of her class should not stoop to conquer. Notwithstanding, the "pride which, as long as she had known herself, had reigned absolute in her heart" has been overwhelmed by "her passionate feeling" (328) for the carpenter's son. Once over the edge, as it were, Mathilde casts all hesitations aside by following up her original letter with a second one that implores Julien to climb up a ladder at one in the morning to enter her bedroom through an open window so that she may speak to him on matters of great urgency.

This recreation of his seduction in Verrieres throws Julien into a panic, as suspicion, speculation, fear, self-satisfaction, and triumph alternately color his reactions. He still worries that "someone is out to ruin him" (334) but quickly realizes that if "Mathilde were acting in good faith" and he failed to appear, he "would be playing the part of a perfect coward" (335). Better to be "shot full of holes by a servant" than to be "dishonored" (336). He decides finally "it would be cowardly not to go" (336), particularly when his doing so will humiliate de Croisnois and his friends, but he packs two pistols just in case he is walking into a trap. Julien compares his personal drama to a "duel" (336) with swords, and he is exactly right. Mathilde has made a daring move, one that exposes her vulnerability; it is up to him to know how to "parry every thrust" (336) effectively. Since his dueling partner is formidable, and since the consequences of failure could be fatal, all Julien's resources of intellect, skill, and experience must be summoned to win.

Julien arrives as scheduled and climbs to Mathilde's bedroom without obstruction. What happens inside, however, does not correspond to either's expectations, revealing the impossibility of orchestrating the powerful emotions passion brings into play. As Julien enters the room, he draws a blank, "embarrassed, he didn't know how to act; he felt no love at all" (340). Mathilde is likewise confused, moving between "feelings of reserve and shyness so natural in a well-bred girl" (340) to admiration for Julien's courageous act: "Ah! How worthy is this man of all my love!" (341). Her approbation inspires in Julien "the keenest happiness of crowned ambition" (342), but he forces himself to acknowledge this since he can feel nothing else. They make love for the first time, yet rather than crowning the night's adventures, these embraces are more like a play's denouement, the main action having already taken place. Mathilde has yielded in recognition of Julien's extraordinary exertions on her behalf. She has done so, however, as if in a coma, unable "to redeem the harsh constraint under which she found herself" (344). Mathilde suffers so since "her reason was horrified at the piece of sheer madness she had just committed" and her resurgent pride had been "offended by [Julien's] air of triumph" (343). She ends the night questioning the depth and sincerity of the love that has compelled all these actions. Julien senses these complications. He feels he has been "lifted to an immense height" but is not emotionally moved because "Mathilde, in her behavior with him, however strange it may sound, had been fulfilling a duty" (344). Such are the complexities, contradictions, and surprises these two young lovers experience.

Stendhal reveals the unexpected reality that underlies what should be the summit of emotional fulfillment in conventional thinking. The groping, uncertain, and mutually guarded moves and countermoves that characterize this scene and, for the rest of the novel, this relationship, include as much high-strung competition as they do romantic attraction. But relationships in real life have the same chess-like character. Stendhal, like the great French writers, is attuned to emotional give and take. Nothing is simple when passion brings two strong people together, and no rules can govern how they will think, feel, or act. The French like to believe that an "art of love" will guide them through passion's treacherous swirls, but their writers mock this notion. At one point later in Book II, Julien receives a series of graded letters that a Russian associate has prepared for men who wish to conduct a well-managed and artful seduction of a woman. Julien uses them to carry on a mock affair with an influential lady just to excite jealousy in Mathilde, who, characteristically, has turned cold toward him. The exchange of letters offers comic relief. Julien is so careless that he uses the wrong name in one. They produce only confusion and have no impact on his real love affair. Julien is on his own. Like Madame Bovary, led to her doom by romantic fantasy; like Racine's Phedre, led to her doom by illicit passion; like Proust's Swann, led to endless misery by a doomed love for a courtesan;

Julien defies logic, morality, hospitality, and common sense by engaging in a passionate romance with a brilliant and seductive beauty whom he openly suspects incapable of loving him more than a week.

The French know that one does not choose to fall in love; the rationality they prize plays little role in the mysterious alchemy that brings lovers together. Nor does morality or religious conviction bring any serious resistance to passion's imperial sway. As noted earlier, Madame de Renal discovers this when Julien visits her for the last time. She is overcome by grateful desire when, as is his wont, he bravely climbs to her bedroom at a time when the house is filled with family members and servants who would like nothing better than to hurl him out the window to his death. Despite her repentance and her confessor's counsel and constant spiritual care, "resolutions fortified by a year's constancy had not been able to withstand his courage" (226). Likewise, Mathilde, though emotionally torn and unexpectedly burdened by scruple, yields to the intrepid lover who has performed the same feats of derring-do in her home. Passion can be channeled or tamed, as in bourgeois marriage, but it cannot be extinguished. It can be aroused at any time, at any age, by any person, and it can leave wreckage in its wake. Law and order mean nothing to one in its power. Julien and Mathilde are inseparably linked, even if they are so mismatched no objective observer could ever consider them a suitable couple.

Julien and Mathilde continue to deal with their inner demons as they move through the next days. Following their night together, Mathilde turns cold, yielding again to her pride and trying to repair the damage to her self-image an affair with an inferior has created. Julien reacts to her aloofness with despair as his fears about her sincerity once more take hold. When, after three days of silence, he tries to speak with her, Mathilde puts on airs:

> *"Very well, sir, so you think you have acquired some great authority over me," she said to him with*

> *barely restrained anger, "since in opposition to my clearly expressed will, you claim the right to speak with me? . . . Do you realize no one has ever presumed so far . . . ?"* (346)

Resigned now to "eternal estrangement" (347), Julien prepares to take a long-delayed trip to Languedoc to assess the condition of some of the Marquis de la Mole's properties. The day before his scheduled departure, Julien goes to the library where he customarily works undisturbed. This time, however, Mathilde is present. His rage boils over when Mathilde reproaches herself for losing her virginity "to the first man who came along" (347–48). Julien pulls down from the wall a medieval sword and scabbard, feeling he would be "the happiest of men if he could have killed her" (348). He draws out the sword but quickly comes to his senses. Far from being terrified, though, Mathilde is "delighted at so new a sensation" (348) and happy that Julien has shown himself capable of murder: "The idea carried her back to the finest years in the reign of Charles IX and Henry III" (348). Long before Sigmund Freud, Stendhal portrays the turmoil of passion by crafting a scene highly charged with phallic symbolism as Julien unsheathes the sword and Mathilde experiences sexual arousal. He also foreshadows the novel's climactic end, when Julien, in a furious rage, will actually commit a crime that nearly results in the murder of his former mistress.

Julien's travel plans change abruptly when the marquis denies him permission to leave. Caught up in political intrigues, he needs to have Julien, who has become indispensable, on the premises and available for stenographic services whenever he and his confederates decide to confer. Hoping to inspire another outburst, Mathilde plays with Julien's tenderest emotions. On the one hand, she makes a great show of confiding in him, while on the other hand she talks mostly "about the passing fits of enthusiasm she had once felt for M. de Croisenois, and then for M. de Caylus" (351). Julien is sure he has loved and lost and will be talked about in the same way when Mathilde embraces someone new. Mathilde is "beginning to wonder, after what had happened, why he did not take offense at her revelations" (353). Julien, instead, blurts out in anguish, "So you don't love me anymore, and I adore you!" (353). This is entirely the opposite reaction, and Mathilde is scornful: "His remark, so frank but so foolish, changed everything in an instant; now sure of his love, Mathilde despised him thoroughly" (353). In the eyes of sentimentalists, Julien's declaration should have ended his torture; it prolongs it because a passionate and egocentric Parisienne is looking for an angry and even threatening response from an equally passionate and egocentric lover. Nevertheless, despite her repulsion, Mathilde cannot abandon Julien. She ends this episode by looking forward to their life together and to how she can make him rich and herself famous: "In her thoughts, she was treating Julien somewhat as an inferior whose fortune one intends to make when and how one wishes, and about whose love one does not permit oneself to have the slightest doubt" (355). Such are the twists and contortions passionate feeling can produce.

Julien's declaration of love may have diminished him in Mathilde's eyes, but he is still head and shoulders above the titled suitors she sees around her. Though she may have tormented Julien by recounting largely imaginary "passing fancies" (357) for one or the other of these, Mathilde is definite in measuring their prospects against his: "Ah! if he but knew how little danger there is from that quarter! How sickly they seem to me, all pale copies of one another compared with him" (357). Julien confirms this high opinion when, in a last-ditch effort to regain his mistress's favor, he once again climbs the ladder to her bedroom window at one in the morning and presents himself to an astonished Mathilde "more dead than alive" (361). Mathilde is thrilled by his extraordinary exertions, which elicit, as with the sword, an intense sexual response. The two enjoy an ecstatic night together, with Mathilde unable to restrain her rhapsodies: "Yes, you are my master. Rule over me forever, punish your slave harshly if she tries to rebel" (361). She almost goes so far as to cut off "a whole side of her hair" (361) and offer it to Julien as a token of her submission. These seemingly irrational outbursts and acts are induced by the delirium her sexual awakening has produced. The woman whose intellect and beauty have made her a superior being is acting foolishly, as if possessed.

In the cold light of day, Mathilde is nonplussed by what went on the night before. At lunch, she is coldly unapproachable, evoking in Julien, as after their first night together, "terrible doubts, astonishment, despair" (364). Mathilde struggles with conscience and pride:

> *That morning, the remorse of virtue and that of pride made her equally miserable. She was, as it were, dumbfounded by the thought of having given certain rights over herself to a little abbé, a peasant's son.* (368)

Unable to resolve these inner conflicts, she directs her sharpest barbs at Julien, whom she now detests as the author of her misery: "For the first time in his life, Julien found himself subjected to the onslaught of a superior mind, set against him by the most violent hatred" (368). He begins to think he is as despicable as she insinuates. But he and she are bound to each other by the most passionate ties. Even when he is sure his love for Mathilde is hopeless, Julien cannot put her out of his mind or his heart:

> *"She's mad, it's true," he told himself; "is she less adorable for that? Can a girl be prettier? Haven't all the keen pleasures that the most elegant civilization has to offer been united, as if in a competition with one another, in the person of Mlle. de La Mole?"* (370)

In the midst of all this, as it were, bipolar turmoil, Julien receives a summons from the Marquis de La Mole. Coming almost as a relief after Mathilde's withering verbal assaults, this discussion with the marquis reaffirms his importance to the household and the confidence in which he is held. The marquis orders Julien to work with him on preparing a concise memorandum summarizing the conclusions the marquis and a group of associates will reach in an upcoming conference. As soon as the document is finished, Julien will commit its contents to memory and then travel out of the country to meet with an eminent *émigré* dignitary. Julien will recite every word of the memo to this man and return immediately. The journey will not be an easy one, since spies and agents will be looking to thwart him; there may, in fact, be some "who would like nothing better than to take a potshot at the Abbé Sorel" or slip some opium into his drink "one night in some good inn" (372) while they search his belongings.

Julien is not deterred; on the contrary, he welcomes this opportunity to do his patron a service that can perhaps "make up for all the sorrow" he "may one day cause him" (377). Secrecy shrouds all aspects of this conference and its aftermath. Julien is not told where he will be going or to whom he will be revealing the memo's statements; in like manner, on the night of the conference, the marquis does not tell the cabman the street where they will disembark, and as they and others enter the drawing room where the meeting will take place, no one is announced by name. Julien recognizes only one participant, none other than the Bishop of Agde, who, just as he did at the Hotel de la Mole, does not acknowledge him. Julien fears that he is being drawn into "what is a conspiracy at the very least" (377), but this company is not sending out assassins or plotting against the current regime. What Stendhal presents in the earnest dialogue that ensues is French intrigue par excellence. The twelve luminaries are engaged in what the gathering's chairman calls a "holy cause" (377). Though it is 1830 and a king reigns in France once more, all in this conference, which includes monarchists and a few Bonapartist sympathizers, live still in the shadow of 1789, as, in their anxiety and insecurity, they consider the likelihood of another revolutionary outburst. They call to mind the numerous aristocratic exile groups that devised schemes to free Louis XVI and Marie Antoinette from their confinement in Paris but lacked the means and mettle to move beyond talk. The small team that actually succeeded in whisking the royal family away used staples of French intrigue, bribery, and dashing deception to bring this off, only to be foiled on the way to Varennes by the kind of missteps and mishaps that doom complicated missions.

The men Julien meets are decidedly like the exiles; he finds them "mediocre-looking" and out of touch with contemporary France. They devote most of their discussion to ways to combat and contain another popular uprising. One option, calling for foreign assistance, is problematical: "England hasn't a sou to spare for the good cause" (379), and though Austria, Prussia, and Russia "have courage," without money they cannot sustain "more than one or two campaigns against France" (380). They will, however, be more inclined to assist if they know "twenty thousand gentlemen are ready to take up arms and open the gates of France to them" (382). France, therefore, must be saved from a resurgent Jacobinism by Frenchmen. Most agree that a kind of royalist national guard, made up of "five hundred devoted men in each department," must be organized to save "the Throne, the Altar, [and] the aristocracy" (381).

As the conference winds down, clerics dominate the discussion. A cardinal insists "that in 1830 only the clergy led by Rome, can reach the masses" (384); therefore, if an armed contingent must be raised in each province, the clergy nationwide have to serve as recruiters. The cardinal is sure that, for this purpose, concerted preaching is the best strategy: "Fifty thousand priests will repeat the same words on a day designated by their leaders, and the people, who, after all, supply the soldiers, will be more deeply touched by the voice of its priests than by all the light verse in the world" (384) The Bishop of Agde, hitherto portrayed as the embodiment of courtesy and grace, concludes the conference by summarizing the major points. He does so, however, "with the concentrated and restrained zeal of the most exalted fanaticism" (386). He ends by sounding like Cato denouncing Carthage: "Paris alone, with its newspapers and drawing rooms, has done the harm. May the new Babylon perish" (386). Paris needs to be "sacrificed"

(386) so the French nation can live again in godliness. Only if the Paris that nurtured the revolutionaries and continues to spew anti-clerical and anti-monarchical propaganda is somehow swept away, can, as a previous speaker proclaimed, "noble France . . . reappear almost as our ancestors made her and as our eyes still saw her before the death of Louis XVI" (380). Paris stands for modernity, specifically for rationalism, secularism, and democratic liberalism. This is precisely the point of view Julien and, to the extent she can, Mathilde embrace, in sharp opposition to the straightjacketed seminarians and the timid "boobies" who crowd the Hotel de La Mole like Penelope's ancient suitors.

These men are well-educated and well-connected, but they rely too much on intellectual insight to achieve their ends. Their intrigue is typically French in that its participants expect to control and eventually master public affairs through force of intellect alone. They are armchair doctrinaires, too confident in their ability to motivate and manipulate a French people notably more diverse in thought and experience than those of any previous generation. The people the cardinal expects to follow the clergy's lead have been permanently changed by the revolution and their service across Europe with Napoleon. There are more young men like Julien in the provinces than the speakers realize. Even among the seminarians in Besancon, by Julien's estimate, close to a third are studying to be priests only because they are drawn to the clergy's comparatively affluent lifestyle, not because they are true believers. Men like these certainly cannot be counted on to serve Throne and Altar without question or hesitation. The conference's atmosphere is secretive, fearful, and fanatical because the prominent men involved, despite high-sounding declarations, sweeping geopolitical projections, and impassioned evocations of the world before 1789, are not strong enough, brave enough, or influential enough to have any real impact on the world of 1830.

That world, ostensibly, is akin to the vanished kingdom the intriguers love. A king has recently been crowned at Rheims, and he reigns over a nation finally at peace. Yet none of the speakers Julien records has any sense of security. They are, to a man, expecting more civil unrest and conflict. Their enemies are not vanquished, only awaiting opportunity for renewed revolutionary agitation. Far from being like the old France these reactionaries dream of restoring, this is a France filled with tensions, resentments, and lingering hostilities. Charles X's court is artificial, more like something created by stagecraft rather than an organic and popular arm of government. It cannot command the nation's loyalty or love. In fact, ever since the revolutionaries forcibly transferred Louis XVI and Marie Antoinette from Versailles to Paris, where, except for their brief escape to near the border, they would remain until their executions, royalty in France has been eclipsed by other forces and other actors. The likes of Danton, Marat, and Robespierre asserted power and commanded followers far beyond anything Louis XVI could summon as he lost control of events, while Napoleon roamed over Europe like another Charlemagne, subjugating rival empires and nations that had never been ruled by France. Only when a war-weary, bankrupt, and occupied France succumbed after Waterloo to a peace imposed by to its leagued enemies, all monarchies, did the Bourbon heir return from exile. In comparison to the men who moved heaven and earth in the preceding years, he is decidedly ordinary. As a boy, Julien dreams of glory and makes the young Napoleon his role model; he never mentions or pays the slightest attention to the king. The men who talk so earnestly about restoring the old regime are thinking of Louis XIV and Richelieu, who did not just go through the motions of governing but ruled authoritatively.

Nothing would come of these men's self-important exertions, just as nothing would come of their successors' machinations. In France, up until 1945, groups like these would continue to meet furtively and create castles in the air, while France would become more like the Paris the Bishop of Agde execrates. Aristocratic notables would go into a kind of internal exile, like successive generations of pretenders waiting for a call to return to their rightful places at the head of civil and political society, or they would turn their backs on intrigues and power plays and take interest only in the pleasures and privileges afforded by fashionable society, as the blue bloods in Proust's novels so obviously do. Such marginalization, becoming clearly apparent in Julien's day, was more or less the fate of the pre-revolutionary ruling class. At times, though, such as at the height of the Dreyfus Affair and during the Vichy regime, reactionary elements actually would achieve a measure of power and influence. What resulted, however, during such periods was political action so chauvinist, racist, regressive, and repressive that no self-respecting Frenchman could look back on these episodes without shame.

Julien does his duty. His mission is to end not in Rome, as he had initially presumed, but at Strasbourg, in Alsace, near the German border. On his journey there, Julien faces counter-intrigue. The Abbé Castanede, leader of the congregation, one of the most powerful politico-religious organizations in France, very nearly exposes him as a courier for a rival grouping when he rifles through a drugged Julien's belongings during a stopover outside of Metz. The clerical "chief of police for the whole northern frontier" (390), however, finds nothing incriminating, and Julien goes on to deliver his memo word for word to a German duke. A few days later, by prearrangement, he meets the duke again and receives his response, one that will later deflate the Marquis de La Mole, who is "most disconcerted" (397) when Julien relays it. The machinations of the little cabal have obviously led nowhere.

While waiting to see the duke again, Julien has some idle time in Strasbourg. He, of course, dwells on Mathilde, "mistress absolute of his happiness as of his imagination" (391). By this point, "Mathilde had absorbed his whole life; he found her everywhere in his future" (391). In her absence, Julien becomes gloomy and self-doubting, fearful once more that Mathilde may have forgotten about him. While thus preoccupied, Julien runs into a man whose demeanor radiates *joie de vivre*. Prince Korasoff is a Russian dandy Julien first met when he transacted some business for the marquis in London. He is a master of the "fundamentals of high-class foppery" (392). Shallow and carefree though he surely is, Julien is drawn to the fop:

> *"A happy nature!" he said to himself. "How well his pants fit; how elegantly his hair is cut. Alas! If I had looked like that, perhaps after having loved me for three days she wouldn't have taken a dislike to me."* (392)

Julien still has not gotten over his admiration for high-class grace and style, even if these are exhibited in a person of little consequence. He also takes note of "the graceful way he rode his horse" (392), remembering perhaps his own misadventures on horseback with Mathilde's brother. Julien confesses his despair to Prince Korasoff, albeit without naming Mathilde or revealing anything of their relationship. The prince is eager to help, and because he finds Julien stimulating company, impulsively offers him "the hand of one of his cousins, a rich heiress in Moscow," who, with the prince's help, can secure Julien an officer's commission "in two years" (396). Though it is tempting, Julien realizes upon reflection that he cannot accept the offer, since "the thought of leaving France and Mathilde seemed to him a punishment worse than death" (396). He does, however, agree to a plan B. The prince allows Julien to make copies of "fifty-three carefully numbered love letters," a series guaranteed to win the heart of "the most sublimely and most cruelly virtuous" (395) woman, provided she receives them in their properly graded order. Julien decides to send them to the "Field Marshall de Fervaques' widow" (395), in order to inspire in Mathilde, first, jealousy and then renewed affection for him.

We are now in the world of *Les Liaisons Dangereuses*, where the art of love plays out in endless correspondence. As with Julien's interlude among the political plotters, we see him succumbing to the same French obsession, the need to reduce human experience to rational principles and to control such inherently turbulent and unpredictable excitements as war or love through the application of such principles. In this case, the effect is clumsy and comic. Julien's heart is not really in the game. At one point, he thoughtlessly copies Korasoff's name as the person of interest rather than the widow's and delivers the letter without ever catching the slip. This is understandably confusing to the recipient, who nevertheless suspects nothing. But Julien persists in this farcical proceeding because the real subject of his act, Mathilde, cannot help noticing that something is amiss, and that is to Julien's advantage. It does not hurt, either, that Mme. de Fervaques' uncle, a bishop with immense influence on church appointments throughout France, could be of great service to Julien if, improbable as it may seem, he were forced back into an ecclesiastical career.

Julien is, therefore, "faithful to the letter about observing the line of conduct laid down by Prince Korasoff" (402). Such conduct includes lingering in the garden outside the Hotel de La Mole and engaging Mme. de Fervaques in animated conversation directly in front of the French windows, so that should Mathilde walk by, she will see them together. Julien also stations himself close to Mme. de Fervaques' armchair every evening, even though once he does so, he cannot "find a word to say" (403). The letters themselves are prolix and dull, but Julien copies them precisely and delivers each like an actor in a comic opera, following these instructions exactly:

> *These letters are to be delivered personally: on horseback, black ruff, blue frock coat. One should hand the letter to the porter with a contrite air, deep melancholy in one's gaze. If one happens to see a chambermaid, one wipes one's eyes furtively. Say a few words to the chambermaid.* (406)

Far from being annoyed by these artificial creations, Mme. de Fervaques is enchanted. After reading through the first letter, for instance, "a mystical and religious philosophical dissertation" (406), she concludes that "there is unction, deep seriousness, and a great deal of conviction in this young Levite's prose" (407). She quickly decides Julien should be a candidate for a diocese no less. Julien plays his part to perfection, calling on his accomplished hypocrisy once again: "What astonished her most was his perfect falseness; he never said a word to the widow, but it was a lie, or at least an abominable disguise for his true opinion, which Mathilde knew perfectly well on every subject" (414). When the widow begins to reply to Julien, she has no idea that her letters are never opened and is blind to the fact "that there was so little connection between his replies and her letters" (417).

Mme. de Fervaques is merely a pawn in an elaborate charade, the whole purpose of which is to win by art the elusive "guarantee" of Mathilde's love Julien cannot secure through sincere devotion. The letters and staged conversations finally do provoke a response from Mathilde, but true to her character and true to life, the response creates further emotional turmoil rather than a change of heart. Mathilde enters the library one morning, only to discover Julien preoccupied with his copying. As she turns away from him, she happens to see on his table, just delivered, a letter to Julien from Mme. de Fervaques. Mathilde finds more of these in the drawers, all of them unopened. This leads to a fiery outburst: "So," she shouted, beside herself, "Not only are you on good terms with her, you despise her as well. You, a nobody, to scorn the Field Marshall de Fervaques' widow!" (419). Immediately thereafter, however, perhaps relieved that Julien really has no interest in the widow, Mathilde implores Julien: "Ah! Forgive me, my dear . . . Scorn me if you wish, but love me; I cannot live any longer without your love" (419). She thereupon falls "to the floor in a dead faint," and Julien, like a victorious gladiator, stands over "that haughty woman" (419) in triumph.

A little later, in the privacy of his room, Julien will, uncharacteristically, cover "the love letters Prince Korasoff had given him with kisses" (426) in gratitude for the magic he thinks they have produced. A proud, passionate, and, above all, mercurial nature like Mathilde's, though, is not to be mastered by artifice. The French faith in reason may sometimes create the illusion that the mind can rule the heart and guide the passions into approved channels, but the great French writers know better. Like Proust's Marcel, who strives mightily to possess Albertine but never can, Julien contemplates the love of his life without joy or gratitude, despite her declaration. After all, Mathilde is still Mathilde, so her constancy is still in doubt. Her dramatic protestations Julien has heard before; he also has had to endure their after-effects, such as disdain, aloofness, and cruel witticisms that have always plunged him into despair. Therefore, shortly after reviving Mathilde, the apparently triumphant Julien acts as if nothing has really happened. He vows to remain unmoved and impassive: "In a little while those eyes will show nothing but the coldest disdain . . . if I let myself be swept away by the happiness of loving her" (421). In other words, despite feeling "pierced with love to the heart's core" (421), he will keep Mathilde at bay and even toy with her emotions by insinuating he may still be attracted to Mme. de Fervaques, to whom he will continue to send letters. As has been evident throughout their affair, Julien's touchy pride and hypersensitivity about his status in the Hotel de La Mole make him just as reluctant as Mathilde to risk emotional ruin and ridicule by declaring love too openly or too thoughtlessly. "Love," in fact, is radioactive; it can burn one up if mishandled. Julien and Mathilde are back in the chess match. If Mathilde "was almost happy that day, for she was all love" (423), Julien is walking on eggshells, worried that "a careless word" may cause "despair" to "begin all over again" (422).

Julien remains aloof and inscrutable. What he needs above all is a "guarantee" that Mathilde's renewed affections for him "will hold for more than two days" (422). He seems to be seeking, in essence, a promise of commitment that engaged couples make, even though this romantic pair both scorn such formalities. Julien is burning with love but fears to express his feelings; Mathilde is showing her love, finally, but has to suffer the kind of doubts about her lover she used to inspire. These intense emotions are taking their toll. For Julien, particularly, some kind of climactic resolution must occur since he is "nearly as much out of his head as Mathilde" (421–22). He decides to attend the *opera buffa* and accept Mme.de Fervaques' invitation to sit in her loge. Julien is sure his being there with the widow will be reported to Mathilde. It turns out that Mathilde and her mother are also in attendance, even though it is "not their day for the opera" (424). When Julien leans out to acknowledge them, he sees Mathilde's eyes "glittering with tears" (423). Julien moves immediately to her side:

> *The first thing that crossed his sight was Mathilde's tear-filled eyes; she was weeping without stint... Mathilde put her hand on Julien's; she seemed to have lost all fear of her mother. Almost choked with weeping, she said but one word to him: "Guarantees!"* (425)

This is Julien's moment of victory. He has compelled Mathilde to confirm with tears her love for him exclusively. The girl whom all the young aristocratic men of his acquaintance adore, pine for, and fear is his. The carpenter's son has wrung from a marquis's daughter "guarantees" that no lawyer could ever have secured. When he returns home, however, he is still ill at ease. He calms his restlessness by reading in Napoleon's *Memoires* and concluding that he must behave harshly toward his conquered "enemy" to insure her obedience. Though Julien feels an "immense happiness" (427), he masks it and lets his guard down only gradually. In later meetings with Mathilde, he is cursed by memories of her "fickleness" and the grief it always has caused him. His "present happiness" may have "put an end to his atrocious suffering" (428), but he still copies Korasoff's letters and sends them to the widow, which disgusts Mathilde. Julien's triumph is proving hollow and fleeting. He cannot savor the possession, and certainty he appears to have won nor can he rid himself of nagging doubt and bad memories. Julien has conquered but is still as wary and nervous as a combatant.

But then, with a suddenness that astounds, the landscape changes. In the most matter-of- fact way, without any preparation or warning, Stendhal states flatly, "She discovered that she was pregnant and informed Julien delightedly" (431). Now the chess game is rendered irrelevant as the unmarried couple face the complications their situation has created. Julien's coldness melts, at least initially, as he approaches the mother of his child with kindness and concern. He is relieved to end the charade of cruelty: "It was with happiness that the tender side of his nature seized upon the pretext of Mathilde's state to excuse himself from making cruel remarks to her" (432).

The pace of the narrative accelerates from this point on. Mathilde sends a moving letter to her father detailing her condition and its causes. She nobly accepts responsibility for all that has occurred, absolving Julien ("for it is I who loved first, it is I who seduced him") and reminding the marquis that he himself had recognized Julien's gifts ("That young Sorel is the only person who knows how to amuse me." (433)). She assures her father that she and Julien will live modestly at first as he begins "teaching Latin and literature" in Besancon, but she has no doubt "he will rise" and "if there is a revolution . . . he will play an important part" (434). Of course, six thousand francs from the marquis would make things easier.

The Marquis de La Mole reacts to this earthquake announcement with predictable fury. He is so abusive when he meets Julien shortly after receiving Mathilde's letter that the new father offers him his life: "Kill me," said Julien, "or have me killed by your valet" (436). Nothing so drastic occurs, however. Instead, as the dust settles and as cooler heads, like that of Abbé Pirard, prevail, what began as a calamity turns into nothing short of a blessing. Obsessed with his daughter's future and still dreaming of a "stool" (439) for her at the foot of the queen of France, the marquis is soon "dreaming of building a brilliant fortune" (443) for Julien. In short order, he deeds the couple his estates in Languedoc, which Julien has been managing so well they will "bring in 20,600 francs yearly" (441). With the connivance of the Abbé Pirard, the marquis also creates a title for Julien, who will be known henceforth as "the Chevalier de la Vernaye" (448). The carpenter's son will reach the summit of glory a short time later when he receives a lieutenant's commission in the "Fifteenth Regiment of Hussars, one of the most splendid in the army" (448). Finally, he has been "acknowledged" (448), and Julien exults in his new role like an eagle finally allowed to soar:

> *His impassive air, his severe and almost wicked look, his pallor, his unalterable coldness, made a reputation for him at the outset. A while later, his impeccable courtesy and reserve, his skill with pistol and sword, which he demonstrated without too much affectation, discouraged any idea of joking aloud at his expense. After wavering for five or six days, public opinion in the regiment declared itself in his favor.* (448)

Such military distinction is, in Julien's mind, only the beginning of a spectacular trajectory that will end in a quasi-Napoleonic triumph. His imagination goes into overdrive as he speculates on his prospects:

> *His horses, his uniforms, his servants' livery, were all kept up with a correctness that would have done credit to the punctiliousness of a great English lord. Lieutenant for barely two days, and through a favor, he had already calculated that in order to be commander-in-chief of an army by thirty, at the latest, like all the great generals, he would have to be more than lieutenant at twenty-three. He had thoughts for nothing but glory and his son.* (449)

At this very moment, however, the young conqueror is brought back to earth. What seems like the starting point for a grand career is, in reality, its termination. Julien's commission is the apogee of his worldly success and the only instance of his reaching even the first rung in a Roman-style progress up the ladder. He will go no further because his whole world is about to come crashing down. The Marquis de La Mole had been advised by Julien himself to contact Madame de Renal should he require additional information on Julien's past and/or a character reference. The marquis has done so. Julien, though, is unaware that his former lover has undergone yet another religious awakening under the tutelage of "a virtuous and fervent young clergyman newly arrived from Dijon" (453). This priest has guided Mme. de Renal's response to the marquis. The resulting letter is the opposite of Mathilde's. Mme. de Renal reveals all that took place between them, lays the blame squarely on Julien, and cites unscrupulous motives as the originating cause: "Poor and covetous, it was by means of the most consummate hypocrisy and through the seduction of a weak, unhappy woman that that man sought to further himself and become somebody" (450).

Julien is indignant. The woman he remembers with affection as kind and loving has turned on him with vengeful fury, threatening all that so recently has come to him. She has also shown that she is anything but submissive and discreet, as he had once imagined her to be, in contrast to his *élan*. His honor traduced and his love apparently betrayed, the Chevalier de Vernaye rushes back to Verrieres. Compelled to take action even as "the sight of that woman who had loved him so made Julien's arm tremble" (451), he loses all self-control as he fires shots at Mme. de Renal while she kneels in prayer in the parish church. This significant action takes barely one page to record.

Julien is apprehended immediately and imprisoned. Mme. de Renal is wounded, but her life is not in danger, a fact she does not find reassuring: "For a long time she had sincerely wished to die" (453), as she suffered through Julien's absence and her confessor's strictures. Julien is also prepared to die: "Yes, in two weeks the guillotine . . . or else, kill myself between now and then" (452). The two are tasting the bitter dregs passion leaves in its wake. Passionate attraction culminating in sexual union is, to the French, the most intense and life-enhancing experience a man or woman can have, but it is ultimately fatal unless domesticated. Julien has acted quickly and impulsively, just as he did when he challenged a stranger to a duel and when he waved the old sword in Mathilde's face. Mme. de Renal's words demanded "satisfaction" for the offense they caused to his pride and honor. This is all typically French, but the passion that animates Julien is not a momentary loss of control. Passion has been the driving force of his entire emotional life; even in the depths of the seminary, he had striven passionately for honors and preferment. But the sexual passion that led him to seduce Mme. de Renal and the passion that led her to love him in return, has brought ruin. The French crave conquest and have great faith in their intellect, sure that they can artfully gain their objective through clever application; desire, however, cannot be controlled, mastered, or reasoned away. It feeds on itself, growing more imperious the more it is denied.

In Julien, we see the duality of French culture brought to life vividly. The French intellect is one of Europe's treasures. It has elevated art and the experience of beauty to the level of a national resource and has made French citizens more respectful of intellectual or artistic distinction than most of their neighboring peoples. But the confidence that comes with superior intellect and culture declines appreciably when love is aroused. Julien displays sureness and finesse once he masters the environment at the de Renal estate, in the seminary, and at the Hotel de La Mole. He moves swiftly and rises in the estimation of important people through judicious application of natural talents and liberal education. Despite his skepticism, he could have completed his seminary studies and been ordained; we can envision him, like a shrewd Roman official, using talents, contacts, and opportunity to move up the hierarchical ladder and becoming an influential cleric in a church badly in need of gifts like his. Likewise, we can accept any of the possibilities his marriage to Mathilde could bring, such as an estate in a rich province, a military command, even a political career, again with real convictions masked. Julien has been nothing short of masterful in assimilating the qualities, sensitivities, and associations a successful priest, diplomat, business manager, or officer must possess to be effective.

Yet he fails. He has been brought down by what his superior intellect cannot control or channel. In his short life, he has loved two women foolishly, intensely, uncomprehendingly. Normally sure-footed and careful to exploit opportunity only when the moment is right, he has plunged into sexual affairs without moderation or restraint. Blinded by the need to master beautiful women as he has mastered men who could further his ambitions, Julien stumbles. Only a seminary scholarship saves him from the wrath of M. de Renal; indeed, he is nearly shot dead when he recklessly pays a last visit to Mme. de Renal. In a tragic reversal, Julien dooms himself and shatters all hope of a prosperous marriage and career the moment he fires at his former lover. The passions excited by love are stronger, more contradictory, and more lethal than any level of reasoning can deal with.

Ought we to conclude then that Julien should have avoided temptation and steered prudently clear of Mme. de Renal and Mathilde de La Mole? Would it have been better for him to have stayed with Fouqué in his mountain cabin and become a partner in his logging business? Questions like these, however, presuppose that Julien actually could have made such choices freely. Stendhal's brilliant portrayal denies such possibilities. For him, as for French writers in general, love is not a choice. It is an overpowering reality that men and women can neither reject nor deny. All who wish to live fully must take the plunge, no matter the hazards, and the more capable and confident one is, the more challenging will love prove, because it tests a person to the core. Nothing, for instance, is as intimidating to Julien as climbing the ladders, first to Mme. de Renal's bed chamber, and then to Mathilde's. He is less afraid of being shot in a duel than he is of appearing cowardly in the eyes of these women. These are not moments when a genius for the right word or the elegant gesture carries weight. These are tests of Julien's manliness that provoke the most emotional reactions. Only by overcoming his fears can he compare himself to Napoleon.

As Julien's trial approaches, the men and women who have played important roles in his young life appear again. All behave in character, as if they were stage actors taking one last turn as Julien's dramatic tale rushes to its end. Fouqué, whose genuine and disinterested friendship has never wavered, visits Julien in his cell and immediately pledges to "sell everything he owned, bribe the jailer, and rescue Julien" (461). Aged and infirm, barely able to walk and overcome with grief, Abbé Chélan, who has treated Julien as a son, pours out his tears as the man he tutored kisses his hands. Mathilde arrives in disguise and is swept away by the boldness of his deed: "She was studying her lover, whom she found very superior to anything she had imagined. Boniface de La Mole seemed to have returned from the dead, only more heroic" (465). In her ardor, she resolves to use her money and her connections to the utmost to save the man who will have fathered her child. She approaches Abbé Frilair, the all-powerful vicar general. This worldly cleric coldly calculates the benefit to himself of pulling strings on Julien's behalf. He concludes that the advantages of working with the de La Mole clan could include a possible episcopal appointment, so he agrees to bribe enough jurors to keep Julien from the guillotine. Mme. de Renal sends to "each of the thirty-six jurors in her own hand" (477) an eloquent appeal for mercy. She praises Julien's virtues in terms exactly opposite to those dictated by her confessor in the letter to the marquis:

> *The whole town of Verrieres, all our neighbors at Vergy, where we spend the summer months, my whole family, the subprefect himself, will do justice to his exemplary piety; he knows all of the Holy Bible by heart. Would an ungodly man have applied himself for years to learn the Holy Book?* (478)

Mme. de Renal also wonders how Julien merits a death sentence while she "is still alive" (478), a subject never fully clarified in the indictment. She attributes Julien's crime to "one of those moments of derangement that even my children used to notice in their tutor" (478), in other words, what we today would call "temporary insanity" and what French justice, typically, designates as a "crime of passion." She then comforts her former lover maternally in his cell each day before the trial, in spite of her husband's order to stay away. By contrast, Julien's father visits him only once and offers reproaches instead of comfort. The only way Julien can mollify him is to assure old Sorel he will leave him, as well as the brothers who beat him, a share of his estate upon his death. The carpenter shows no gratitude. Instead, he reminds his son that he is owed more than the brothers: "There's still the cost of your food and your education, which I advanced, and to which you haven't given a thought" (498).

Julien also stays in character as his life ebbs away. Since his character, however, is complex, including, as it does, the leading elements of the national identity, Julien reveals sometimes contradictory aspects at different times. His initial reaction after his imprisonment is regret for all that has caused his life to take such a fatal turn:

> *His ambition was gone. He rarely thought about Mlle. de La Mole. Remorse preoccupied him a great deal and often showed him a vision of Mme. de Renal, especially during the silence of the night.* (457)

He looks back on his days with Mme. de Renal, especially the summers at Vergy, with nostalgia, not realizing at the time how happy he then was and might still have been had his fierce determination to advance himself not inclined him elsewhere.

This mood does not persist. Upon learning that Mme. de Renal will survive, Julien recovers his spirit. Now he preoccupies himself with summoning up the courage to meet his judgment not with apathetic resignation but with the pride and self-possession that will enable him to conquer his fate. He will triumph, even over death, just as he has triumphed over the life circumstances that conspired against him. His very French response to this ultimate adversity invigorates Julien as he strives to prepare himself, like an athlete, for the moments when the public, whom he despises, will see him face the court, the jury, and, if he must, the guillotine, without fear. This pride, however, is not the romantic heroism Mathilde imagines he possesses. That ascription is largely her invention, prompted by his wife's egotism and "haughty spirit":

> *Amidst all her anguish, all her fears for the life of this lover, whom she did not wish to survive, she had, so Julien felt, a secret need to astonish the public by the immoderateness of her love and the sublimity of her undertakings.* (471)

His once great passion for Mathilde is fading as well: "In fact, I am happier alone than when that beautiful girl is sharing my solitude" (475). He dwells more on his serene vacations with Mme. de Renal than on his tempestuous days with Mathilde.

When he finally appears in court, Julien is himself again. He knows all eyes are on him, and he welcomes this interest. As the lawyers drone on, Julien studies the galleries, filled by "women, most of them were young and seemed to him very pretty" (481). He even notices the "elegance of the architecture" (481) in the courtroom. Clearly, his aesthetic sensitivity stays with him despite the stressful environment. Julien's dress and coiffure are appropriate too: "That day you would have said that he wasn't twenty years old; he was dressed simply but with perfect grace; his hair and forehead were charming; Mathilde had insisted on presiding over his toilet herself" (481).

The proceeding is brief, and sentiments in the courtroom clearly favor Julien. When at the end the judge asks the defendant if he has anything to say, Julien, "ablaze with the idea of duty," (483), launches into a long statement combining defiance and acceptance of responsibility but concluding without an appeal for mercy. His tone is superior but aggrieved. Julien describes himself as "a peasant in revolt against the baseness of his lot" (483). He admits his guilt:

> *I had the heart to make an attempt on the life of a woman who is worthy of every kind of respect and homage. Mme. de Renal had been like a mother to me. My crime is abominable and it was premeditated.* (483)

The word "premeditated" undermines the basis for a crime-of-passion defense. Julien is unfazed. He knows the jury is made up of those who, welcoming a chance to take their revenge on one whom they have always despised as thoroughly as he has despised them, will not be moved by anything he says:

> *Yet even if I were less guilty, I see men here who, not to be stopped by any consideration of mercy that my youth might deserve, would like to punish through me and discourage forever a whole class of young men who, born to an inferior position in society and, so to speak, oppressed by poverty, have had the luck to acquire a good education and the audacity to mingle with what the rich in their pride call society.* (483)

Julien concludes that he is being judged by "outraged burghers" (483), who want to make an example of him because his gifts allowed him to rise above the strict limits class has imposed on men like him.

Julien's is not a noble or inspiring appeal, although it brings many of the women to tears. Its quasi-revolutionary allegations do not ring true, since Julien has been largely favored by those of the upper-middle and aristocratic classes he has encountered. The speech is more like a *cri de coeur* of a young man sure of his talents, spurred by ambition, and brought down by his own excesses, rather than by the weight of the society he has striven so hard (and so successfully) to join. Julien seals his fate by speaking thus. Because his words are provocative, indeed, almost incendiary in the conservative French countryside, Julien understands they will offend the jurors, who will have no choice except to convict the young firebrand, notwithstanding the Abbé Frilair's maneuvering and Mme. de Renal's pleas. Nevertheless, despite its consequences, Julien's speech achieves a measure of the glory he has always sought since it highlights his disdain for death. Julien has triumphed over fear and cowardice one final time; he has not disgraced himself by begging for mercy. Instead, he has preserved his honor and asserted once more his superiority over those who would judge him by refusing to abase himself before them.

He has only days to live. Julien alternates between remorse over his conduct toward Mme. de Renal and regret over the possibilities his impetuosity has caused him to squander. Thus he can, at one point, proclaim his undying love for Mme. de Renal in spite of his shots and admit he has blundered badly in choosing "all that glitters" over "simple and modest worth" (487) and, a moment later, lament the loss of a "glittering" future: "And yet, what prospects I had! . . . Colonel in the Hussars, had we gone to war; secretary of a legation in peacetime; after that, ambassador" (487).

He sees Mathilde shortly after the verdict. She is enraged that her intrigues have produced no positive results. Julien by now is beyond caring, emphasizing instead his courageous statement to the court. In so doing, he plays on Mathilde's "character with the coolness of a skilled pianist," asking her, "Do you think Boniface de la Mole handled himself any better in front of his judges?" and vows that "no human eye shall see Julien weak" (488). In this exalted mood, Julien declines to appeal his conviction, thereby depriving Mathilde of a last opportunity to save him through her influence. She abuses him for such obstinacy, even though his refusal is in accord with her romantic conceptions of how men under duress should behave:

> *She adored him, and for a full quarter of an hour he recognized in her imprecations against his character, in her misgiving about having loved him, all of that haughty spirit which had once heaped him with such cutting abuse in the library at the Hotel de La Mole.* (489)

Her tirade makes Julien feel even more longing for Mme. de Renal. He is sure she will mourn him in spite of everything: "And the person whose life I tried to take will be the only one who will weep sincerely over my death" (490).

Mme. de Renal comes to see him the next day. She too begs him to appeal the verdict. In the course of their conversation, he discovers that her confessor had actually written the letter that led to Julien's crime; Mme. de Renal had merely copied his draft in her own hand. This leads the two to a rapturous reconciliation. Julien worries that his former lover's passionate attachment may lead her to attempt suicide after his execution. She agrees to forego any such desperate act provided he sign his appeal then and there, so she can deliver it personally to the attorney-general. Her devotion opens Julien's eyes to her truly selfless character: "He had just become aware, for the first time, of the full extent of the sacrifice she had made for him" (493).

Julien's life, as well as the long novel built around it, moves quickly now to its end. The condemned man endures a disagreeable session with a persistent priest, whom his jailer describes as a "holy man" (494), intent on hearing Julien's last confession and giving him his last communion. He is, in reality, a clone of the seminarians Julien had found unendurable: "That holy priest turned out to be horribly ugly; he was even dirtier" (495). Always suspicious of the clergy and sure the priest has some ulterior motive in wanting to counsel him, Julien sends him away to "offer a forty franc mass" (495) for his soul and declines the sacraments. Julien's greatest fear at the end is not death or the afterlife but cowardice. Confession and a last communion he sees as concessions to fear, and he is determined not to make any concessions. He continually reflects on the need to be resolute and to conquer death by staring it down:

> *I am isolated here in this dungeon; but I didn't live in isolation on the earth. I held to the powerful idea of duty. The duty I prescribed for myself, whether wrongly or rightly, has been like the trunk of a stout tree, which I could cling to during the storm. I wavered, I was shaken—after all, I am only a man—but I was not swept away.* (501)

He sees another priest, who argues that he must do all he can to win his appeal lest he be damned as suicidal. The priest advises him to undergo a "spectacular conversion" (505), which will win him support among the legal authorities and give religion in France a great boost: "The tears your conversion will cause to flow will wipe out the corrosive effects of ten editions of Voltaire's godless works" (506). Julien is unmoved: "But, generally speaking, I know I'd be thoroughly miserable if I lent myself to some piece of cowardice" (506). In spite of the fact that he does at least go through the motions of receiving the last rites as his end approaches, he remains steadfastly resolute. Julien is determined to die like the bravest of Napoleon's veterans, exclaiming in his last outburst before the sentence is carried out, "but as for fear, no; they won't see me turn pale" (507).

How he comports himself on the scaffold and how light or dark his complexion looks at the end, we do not know. Stendhal concludes with Julien's burial rites. Julien had asked Fouqué to take charge of his body and inter it in "a small cave in the tall mountain that looks down on Verrieres" (507). This is a place where Julien had been able to rest and refresh himself in the midst of nature's beauty. Fouqué, however, does not count on Mathilde's interference. Julien's imperious wife decides all the details of her husband's funeral. The descendant of Boniface de la Mole makes sure Julian is laid to rest in a style befitting lords of legend. Twenty priests offer a requiem mass illuminated by "countless tapers" and observed by "all the inhabitants of the small mountain villages" (508) the cortege had passed through. Mathilde stays behind afterwards to render a last ghoulish service: she buries "her lover's head with her own hands" (508) and, in so doing, reenacts the tale of Marguerite de Navarre and Boniface de La Mole.

Mme. de Renal is absent. She does not commit suicide but dies of grief "three days after Julien" (508).

PART THREE

The key to Julien's tragic end is his very French need to master his situation and dictate his fate. He must conquer. But because its power partakes of the irrational, one does not master passion as he or she does the drawing room. French history testifies to this truth. Clovis began the process of imposing Frankish rule and the Catholic faith on all of what is now France. He succeeded, although much blood was spilled as he proceeded. Charlemagne followed, going so far as to unite briefly the French and German peoples in an empire centered near the Rhine River and grounded in state Catholicism. This is imperial France as a well-organized, centralized, Romanized, bureaucratic, politico-religious entity. All the constituent parts come together to create a harmonious whole, with everyone from powerful nobles to unlettered peasants at least outwardly in accord on all essential issues. Julien mirrors this tradition as he strives to master the inner code and carve out a place for himself in the seminary and in the Faubourg Saint Germain. As we have seen, he largely succeeds, earning the respect and patronage of the Bishop of Besancon and the Marquis de La Mole, no less. Just before his fall, he has earned a reputation as a Parisian dandy, has married his aristocratic patron's daughter and fathered his grandson, and has received a commission in the Hussars. His cup runneth over. Once Mme. de Renal's letter arrives, however, Julien's triumphs evaporate. He has to endure the past resurrecting itself, the irrational overcoming logic and religious guilt obscuring cool reason. Julien reacts with equally irrational fury and begins his descent into the pit.

Charlemagne split his patrimony like King Lear, thinking that smaller portions would be easier to govern. The Franco-German union shattered as a result, leaving endless conflict in its wake. The Catholicism that the Franks upheld and propagated throughout the kingdom suffered attack after attack, first from heretical sects like the Albigensians of the Loire Valley, inheritors of the superstitions Gregory of Tours describes in his *History of the Franks*, and then from Huguenot Protestants inspired by the reformer Jean Calvin, of Picardy. In response to these outbreaks, as well as to the threats to legitimate power posed by elite secret societies such as the Knights Templar, French authorities outdid Julien in violently suppressing dissenters. They won only temporary victories. The forces of dissent, like the urges of the passions, could not be fully suppressed or controlled. They would ultimately rear up in a conflagration beginning in 1789 that would bring down the monarchy altogether, repudiating Charlemagne's legacy by ending royal rule and promoting a new faith based on reason and rooted in nature. All the efforts to restore the old regime, portrayed so vividly in *The Red and the Black*, would result in only equivocal successes, as the boorish seminarians took the place of the refined and influential courtly clergy and the Marquis de la Mole and his associates tried to substitute intrigue with foreign confederates for decisive action in defending the restored monarchy.

French intellectual life shows dichotomies similar to those affecting political life. In the seventeenth century, Descartes elevated reason above feeling, instinct, and blind faith in ascertaining truth. The man who famously said, "I think; therefore, I am" looked for an order and regularity in nature comparable to that of mathematics in science. The philosopher Pascal disagreed. His famous dictum, "The heart has its reasons, which the reason cannot know" gave importance to emotion and other nonrational realities in navigating life's multifaceted challenges. The great seventeenth-century playwrights, particularly Racine, brought the two tendencies together in solemn tragedies that overflowed with powerful emotion while proceeding in accord with strict aesthetic rules akin to mathematical formulae. In the eighteenth century, the *philosophes* attacked irrational beliefs, superstitions, and thoughtlessly accepted traditions, such as the use of torture against suspected criminals. Voltaire, in particular, condemned religious bigotry and intolerance as contrary to reason, which recognizes that human beings differ in the ways they understand religious teachings and in how they pray and worship. Suppressing those who see and do things differently, therefore, cannot be justified. Rousseau, however, French by adoption, questioned the efficacy of reason, arguing that inequality and injustice are as much a byproduct of advances in civilization led by reason and science as of primitive ignorance. He advocated a return to simple living and fellowship as exemplified by mankind in its infancy. Voltaire looked to monarchs liked Frederick the Great to bring enlightenment to the masses from above; Rousseau was happy with the commoners, who were closer to the ideals of the noble savage, the *avatar* of man in harmony with his surroundings and his fellows. After the Revolution, Chateaubriand extolled the medieval tradition of devout faith wedded to patriarchal social customs, while a few decades later, Emile Zola championed the emancipation brought by the overthrow of monarchy. These two forces clashed directly in 1894, when the French army unjustly condemned and exiled Jewish Captain Alfred Dreyfus on a trumped-up charge of treason. Most of Chateaubriand's medievalist clergy and royalist aristocracy sided with the military authorities in persecuting the "Jewish traitor"; Zola and his free-thinking associates worked diligently to expose the injustice Captain Dreyfus suffered and the Anti-Semitism that inspired it, ultimately securing the officer's release. Also, in the nineteenth century, the philosopher Auguste Comte advanced quasi-Cartesian logical positivism, and Henri Bergson countered with vitalism. In the twentieth century, Jean-Paul Sartre advocated existentialism, which gave priority to personal commitments like faith and moral choice, even if such were opposed to reasoned analysis, while Michele Foucault proposed structuralism, which emphasized the underlying and unchanging "structures" or patterns that determine the organization of knowledge and the development of history.

The Red and the Black paints with bright colors as it overflows with characteristic French themes, portraits, and types, all of them not just part of the landscape in 1830 but permanent components of the French sensibility and culture. Over and above all else, the French approach to life, love, and society demands assertion of will, leading to triumphant conquest. Julien needs to transcend his poverty and weakness by taking advantage of any opportunity to rise in the world and experience what Talleyrand called the "sweetness of life." He uses force of intellect and character to achieve his worldly successes and overcome obstacles. He comes to grief because his compelling need to master two beautiful women is unequal to the challenges such passionate attraction brings. His tragic end comes not from an excess of feeling but from fundamental misconceptions he shares with many of his countrymen. Julien's seductions arise from what he considers a "duty"; he must "have" Mme. de Renal and Mlle. de La Mole or lose all sense of self-worth. Only at the end of his life does he pause to reflect on his motivations, and only then does he wonder why he could not have been content with simple and unaffected love. But given his presuppositions, this is romantic fiction. It is inevitable that the complications of real-life relationships like theirs will entangle Julien, Mme. de Renal, and Mathilde hopelessly. Young tutors cannot expect to live happily ever after with their students' mother; ambitious young men from the provinces cannot abuse a titled patron's generous hospitality and live in harmony with a mercurial heiress who is going to bear his child. Passion, and the desire for conquest it incites, blinds one to all this. It is the enemy of rational thought and common sense, leading its victim to take reckless chances while he or she is bent on pleasure and triumph. Passion's consequences do not always entail death, as with Julien and Madame Bovary, but profound sorrow accompanies passion's course far more frequently than does ecstasy, as Proust's gentlemen know so well.

Around this central principle, Stendhal weaves in subsidiary themes that resonate as typically French. One is the overpowering effect of beauty. Julien is irresistibly attracted to aristocratic life and individuals because beauty pervades their world. The opposite is true in the provinces, even in sacred space. Julien nearly falls into a faint in Abbé Pirard's seminary office when its harsh décor and ambience repel him: "This is the violent effect of ugliness on a soul born to love the beautiful" (175). No European national culture has been as preoccupied as the French with capturing in art and literature the subtlest effects of beauty in form and feature, dress and speech, coiffure and ornamentation. The sexual electricity and the irresistible appeal of beautiful women, in particular, are constantly evoked in French art. In the nineteenth century, Delacroix's *Marianne*, leading the people to triumph, symbolized French *puissance*. In our time, the actress Catherine Deneuve, in her flawless and statuesque presence, has radiated a comparable mystique and become a national icon. In the novel, Julien is attracted to Mme. de Renal immediately, sensing in her features, dress, and manner perfect harmony. Mathilde is similar, with intellectual sophistication added in, making her interesting, challenging, and erotic. Julien clearly is responsive to feminine beauty and grace but is impressed also by the elegant manners and charm men of the higher classes habitually manifest. The Bishop of Agde, the Bishop of Besancon, and the Marquis de La Mole comport themselves with taste and polish. Men like these are almost from another planet than the one the crude seminarians, for instance, inhabit. Though he lacks faith, Julien is deeply moved by the beauty of the church's ceremonies, especially when they are conducted graciously by prelates like the Bishop of Agde or when special decoration and festivity enhance them, as in the Corpus Christi celebrations.

Julien is, of course, closest to the national ideal in his pride. As noted in this chapter's introduction, Louis XIV decided in 1666 that the Dutch had to be punished because they had somehow collectively injured his honor. In the war that followed, he fought the equivalent of a duel with an entire nation, just as Julien almost did with the employer of a coach driver who dared to violate the young man's *amour propre*. In 1870, Bismarck tricked Napoleon III into entering an ill-advised war with Prussia, knowing that the emperor had to respond aggressively to what seemed like a calculated diplomatic rebuff. French pride compels an aspiring gentleman like Julien to command his environment. In consequence, he approaches the world before him in terms of military assault; his father and brothers, M. de Renal and his flunkies, the seminarians, the titled suitors who dance attendance on Mathilde, the provincial jurors who will decide his fate, even Mme. de Renal and Mathilde, at first and periodically throughout their affairs, all are "enemies," and enemies must be conquered. He cannot overpower them by force, so he devotes endless energy and effort to learning and "mastering" the unwritten codes that govern life in closed worlds like the provincial and fashionable drawing rooms, the seminary, the military (briefly), and the bedrooms of beautiful women. He memorizes the New Testament in Latin, studies the odes of Horace, reads and meditates on Napoleon's *Memoires* and Rousseau's *Confessions*, learns to dance and dress stylishly, mounts horses for a parade and for recreation, and conducts a sham correspondence with a woman other than his mistress to gain every possible advantage in his campaign to rule by means of exceptional attainment. Julien does what he has to do; his pride gives him no options except to leave in the dust any who stand in his way. He is, in effect, Napoleon's heir.

Like his countrymen, Stendhal is preoccupied with intellectual analysis. The society he portrays is divided among parties and factions. Almost every major character except Julien is tied to one subgroup or coterie. Everyone with ambition seems to believe that advancement comes through clever manipulation. The Abbé Frilair, for instance, is constantly looking for opportunity to secure promotion to a bishopric through the interventions of influential people and their connections to decision-makers. The first thing that crosses his mind when Mathilde pleads for him to save Julien is how helping a wealthy heiress will serve such an end. He is moved by calculation, not Christian charity. The seminarians are no different. Julien hears many tales of how this cleric or that one amassed a fortune or won an appointment by exploiting his contacts. The students regard such activity as normal and even admirable. The thought of selflessly serving people in need of their ministrations is not uppermost in these men's code of conduct. The church in France in 1830 is like the civil service and the military; it is one of the approved means of upward mobility, which most often occurs through the right moves and the right connections. Priests like Abbé Chélan, who put conscience above calculation, are doomed to stagnate in poor parishes and suffer humiliating dismissal in old age. The aristocratic conspirators whom Julien assists are likewise convinced that with the right plans and the right timing, they can prevent a second revolution and preserve the old regime in perpetuity. What unites these characters from different backgrounds and professions is the very French conviction that worldly intelligence and its careful application in critical situations will bring results. The art of "getting on" depends not on good fortune or fate or God's will but on how well one has orchestrated men and events. The prizes go not to the fairest or the luckiest but to the smartest.

The Red and the Black, to sum up, delineates the French character. It does so in a style that is also characteristically French in its classical influences, worldly-wise tone, intellectual sophistication, and aristocratic disdain for the crass and the mercenary. Stendhal's narration brims over with witty asides, epigrammatic insights on a host of subjects, and, in almost throwaway fashion, bits of wisdom distilled into brief observations, the famous *apercus* that French writers are so fond of creating and that drawing room wits are always hoping to devise at just the right moments to enliven conversation. Stendhal uses all of this literary "artillery" to command whatever he surveys or considers, from brass tacks realities of ecclesiastical life to the protocols of high society as well as those of the provinces, to the intricacies, complications, ecstasies, and disappointments of passionate love. He is, in a word, masterful. What follows is a small assortment of the verbal felicities that abound in the novel.

Before she becomes deeply involved with Julien, Mme. de Renal reflects thus on romantic love: "Mme. de Renal had the same opinion of the passions that we have of the lottery: a cheat certainly and a happiness pursued only by fools" (56). Stendhal muses on the contrasts between a betrayed husband's options in the nineteenth century and the practices of simpler times in these words:

> *In spite of everything, an odalisk in a harem may love the sultan; he is omnipotent; she can have no hope of escaping his authority by a series of little ruses. The master's vengeance is terrible, bloody, yet military, generous. A blow of the dagger ends all. In the nineteenth century, a husband kills his wife with blows of public scorn; by closing every door to her.* (142)

On an entirely different note, when he rings the bell of the gate to the seminary in Besancon, Julien is greeted by an aged porter whose facial expression is striking: "The only sentiment that Julien's swift glance could discern on that long, pious face was a profound contempt for everything one might wish to speak with him about that was not concerned with heaven" (174). Later, as he looks out at the three hundred plus seminarians dining happily, Julien concludes that for the majority of them, the place he abhors is an oasis: "In their thatched cottages, they didn't eat meat more than five or six times a year. Like the Roman soldiers who thought of war as a time of rest, these coarse peasants are enchanted with the delights of the seminary" (183).

In his cell awaiting execution, Julian imagines how popular and how respected he will be if, as he marches to the gallows, he tosses out gold pieces to the good citizens of Verrieres lining the route: "My memory, associated in their minds with gold, will glitter" (455). The Marquis de La Mole is a prosperous landowner, but he needs Julien to manage his affairs: "Rich men who are high-spirited look for amusement in business affairs, not results" (270). Likewise, the Marquise de La Mole observes all the unwritten rules of fashionable Paris drawing rooms, being careful not to say anything original nor to tolerate anyone, like Julien, who is idiosyncratic: "The unexpected, arising from sensibility, is the aversion of great ladies; it is the antipode of good breeding" (270). Mathilde, though, is different. Her free-spirited style and sharp wit terrorize any who cross her in public:

> *When anyone offended Mlle. de La Mole, she knew how to punish him with a witticism so calculated, so well chosen, so proper in appearance, so timely launched, that the wound kept growing by the minute, the more one thought about it.* (310)

As Mathilde and Julien jockey for power and position throughout their affair, she contemplates him at one point in visible distress and pounces: "His pain was a keen delight for her. In it she saw her tyrant's weakness; she might thus permit herself to love him" (352). But Mathilde knows as well the *ennui* that privilege can bring: "She had been persuaded that with all her advantages of birth, fortune, etc., she ought to be happier than anyone else. This notion is the source of the boredom of princes, and of all their follies" (318).

Stendhal is hardly swept away by the delights of passion. Julien makes dashing and dangerous moves in his first sexual encounter with Mme. de Renal, an encounter he had long desired and had considered it his duty to pursue. Immediately afterwards, however, he feels numb: "He was in that state of astonishment and uneasiness into which a man who has just obtained what he has long desired may lapse. He is used to desiring, has nothing more to desire, and hasn't, as yet, any memories" (96). Mathilde is driven to her first sexual encounter in much the same way, and she reacts afterwards in similar terms:

> *If there was no tenderness in his heart, it was because Mathilde, in all her behavior with him, however strange it may sound, had been fulfilling a duty. There had been nothing unexpected for her in all the events of that night, except the wretchedness and shame she experienced, instead of that heavenly bliss of which the novels speak.* (344)

The novel is filled with melodrama and comic misadventure on the order of *opera buffa*. The following exchange could have come out of *The Marriage of Figaro*. Julien is with the Italian tenor Geronimo as he travels to Germany on behalf of the Marquis de La Mole and his partners in intrigue. The tenor is scheduled to perform before titled guests but is too sleepy to move: "They could give me the whole kingdom of Naples . . . and I wouldn't give up the voluptuous pleasure of sleep. But the seven sovereign princes! They can wait" (389).

GREAT BRITAIN

Charles Dickens
David Copperfield

INTRODUCTION

The British Isles are an integral part of Western Europe, but because England, Scotland, Wales, Ireland, and Northern Ireland are separated from the European mainland by miles of water, the British people over many centuries have developed philosophical, moral, religious, and literary concepts and values independently. Continental influences have been very strong, and unquestionably the British have been and are fundamentally European in how they live, think, and act, but they have given priority to certain values and have interpreted others in distinctive ways, so that the cultural, political, and religious patrimony they share with the rest of Europe has a distinctively British character.

The history of England and its sister commonwealths explains a great deal about the evolution of the British identity. The Romans under Julius Caesar invaded what is now southern England in 55 BCE, and, just as in the other territories they conquered, established towns, military camps, and fortresses and introduced political and legal systems that added a decidedly Mediterranean overlay to native Celtic customs and structures. Over time, intermarriage produced Romano-British citizens with ties to both the empire and the local tribes. The Romans also deliberately confined their colony to England and the Cornish Isles. Most significantly for the future, Hadrian's Wall effectively separated England and Scotland. The Scots and Picts were formidable warrior tribes, so a defensive line at the edge of their lands made strategic sense, particularly when in later years the Roman Empire came under increased pressure from barbarian peoples all along its frontiers and could not spare troops and resources to augment territory in a remote colony like Britannia. Scotland, therefore, was less affected by the

Roman model and ultimately became a kind of counterweight to what its leaders regarded as the imperializing tendencies of its southern neighbor.

As the military and administrative contingent declined in the latter days of the empire and dependents of the soldiers and civil servants departed with their household heads, representatives of a new force made their presence felt. Despite initial hostility and suspicion, Christianity had been making inroads throughout the Roman Empire ever since the Apostle Paul began his missionary outreach to the Gentiles a few decades after the death of Jesus of Nazareth. After the Emperor Constantine halted persecution of Christians and restored the beleaguered faith's churches and property in the fourth century, the leaders of an energized Catholic Church worked vigorously to spread the Christian faith near and far. Pope Gregory I dispatched Bishop Augustine to England in 597 ACE with a retinue of priests expressly to bring the island's population into full communion with Rome. Augustine established his headquarters at Canterbury, only a short distance from Lundinum, where he and his missionaries had disembarked. They made great headway, building churches, performing baptisms and other sacramental rites, and teaching and preaching throughout the land. Individual dioceses were sanctioned, usually in and around the largest cities and towns, with Canterbury serving as the hub of this ecclesiastical axis. With its ceremonies conducted in Latin and its Bible the Latin Vulgate, its archbishop answerable to the pope, and its clergy maintaining monasteries and schools where biblical commentary and classical texts held pride of place, the church reestablished among its clergy and people a close connection to Rome.

Nevertheless, despite centuries of political, legal, military, and ecclesiastical influence, the Roman imprint in Britain was not as profound as it was in Italy, France, Spain, and the German provinces along the Rhine and Danube rivers. Northern European peoples left their mark as well; Germanic tribesmen had been migrating to Britain in large numbers throughout the centuries following the collapse of the Western Empire. By the seventh century, they had melded so well with the Celtic Angles that today "Anglo-Saxon" is synonymous with "British" as an identifier for natives of the islands. The Saxons proved to be strong, industrious, and organized, reinvigorating civil society and the economy. They also overcame the challenges of the fearsome Norsemen, whose raids and plundering were very disruptive. Eventually, however, Danish warriors laid roots in Britain by integrating with the locals, accepting Christianity and carving out settlements mostly in the north of England. The Angles, the Saxons, and the Danes enriched the English language as well, competing strongly with Latin as an etymological source and guaranteeing that English would not become a Romance language.

In 1066, descendants of the Norsemen living in the French province of Normandy sailed to England in force, not to settle but to conquer. Led by the warrior king who would later become known as William the Conqueror, the Normans defeated a Saxon army in a decisive battle at Hastings. William then proclaimed himself King of England and by so doing created a dual monarchy; for the first time in history, England and major parts of France would be ruled by the same person. The affairs of England and France would be intertwined from this time until the sixteenth century. For the French, eager to see the entire French-speaking nation unified around the Paris-based monarchy, English claims to French territory were endlessly provocative. "Endless" is not an exaggeration. For over one hundred years, 1337 to 1453, England and France waged intermittent war, the longest sustained conflict in European history and the backdrop for one of Shakespeare's great plays, *Henry V*. England's political ties to France ended finally in 1558 with the loss of the port of Calais, the last French outpost of English rule, but the overall effect of centuries of contact between the two kingdoms was permanent. For England, the connection to one of Europe's great powers conferred privilege and status. The little island kingdom henceforth could show the much larger European dynastic states that it was a player in politics, commerce, religion, and military might, all hitherto dominated by the post-Roman continental states. The Normans also opened up to the English a rich cultural tapestry, as illustrated by such treasures as the illuminated manuscripts of this era and the French-inspired cathedrals, churches, and castles that began to dot the British landscape in subsequent centuries.

The period between the Norman Conquest and the English Reformation spans just over four and one-half centuries. We know it as the High Middle Ages, a time that contributed a great deal to the development of a characteristically British perspective and understanding. Late medieval literature is particularly revealing, with two themes standing out sharply: the irreducible significance of individual personality and the overriding importance of moral virtue, or the lack of such, in determining how personality forms character. The *Prologue* to Chaucer's *Canterbury Tales*, for instance, sketches personalities that, to this day, are recognizably British: the various church dignitaries, including friars, monks, and ecclesiastical agents, such as the pardon peddler, the bawdy wife of Bath, the knight, the cook, the miller, the man of law, and so on. Each personality produces a narrative that reflects his or her station in life, class, education, and values, yielding a portrait of character. The knight, for instance, calls upon Greek myth to chronicle the rivalry of two brothers of noble birth. Imprisoned after being captured in a battle with a powerful rival city-state, they both fall passionately in love with the same woman as they spy on her from the windows of their cells. After they manage their release, they meet in single combat to see who can win the maiden as his prize. The tale is long, replete with allusions to Homeric epic and inspired by the ideals of chivalry, which the knight has upheld in his life as a Christian warrior.

A longer knight's tale from roughly the same period, *Sir Gawain and the Green Knight*, focuses even more sharply on these themes, masterfully drawing out the consequences the famous Arthurian knight, Sir Gawain, suffers as a result of his failure, at a critical moment, to adhere to the chivalric code. When he faces a terrifying opponent, Gawain places his hopes and his fate not in the hands of God but in a piece of cloth that purportedly insures against injury. Though he survives his ordeal, his guilt and shame are profound. In contrast to these high-minded men of honor is the miller, whose crudity shines through his tale of vulgar prankstering. The pardon peddler, whose "entire purpose is geared to nothing but profit" *("The Pardon Peddler's Prologue,"* line 76, in *The Canterbury Tales*, trans. Burton Raffel. New York: The Modern Library, 2008) and who anticipates the actual pardoner, Tetzel, whose peddling of indulgences for hard cash so offended Martin Luther, tells a "moral" tale that shows expertly what can occur when men band together for criminal purposes but then yield to greed and something like paranoia when it comes time to divide their spoils. This moral wake-up call is presented by one whose cynicism about humanity makes the worst behavior seem normal.

The final tale is not a tale at all but a deeply felt meditation on sin, repentance, and true contrition. It is the pious parson's response to the pilgrims' wish to end their travels with an inspiring religious theme. True to his humble character, the parson warns his listeners at the start that with his "little knowledge of texts," his exhortation may not appeal to all since he can only "work with basic meanings" ("The Parson's Prologue," lines 57–58, *The Canterbury Tales*. Trans., Burton Raffel. New York: The Modern Library, 2008).

What follows, however, is anything but simplistic or commonplace. The rustic parson references the Bible with fluency and care and cites material from the Church fathers and later theologians with scholarly ease. Here is the model of Christian devotion and learning, living out his ministry in service to a congregation predominantly poor and uneducated but receptive to the best their pastor can offer. The parson treats the pilgrims the same way, offering a meditation the most erudite would commend. Though he speaks over a century before the Reformation, like the reformers, he stresses the need for Christians to repent sincerely for sin and to perform acts of contrition that fit the magnitude of their offenses and that are embraced freely and wholeheartedly. Contrition must be "universal and total" because "neither confession nor penance is worth anything whatever without contrition" (pp. 544–45). The parson ends his meditation and *The Canterbury Tales* with a penetrating analysis of the nature and power of each of the Seven Deadly Sins, going to great lengths to make the discourse relevant by illustrating in concrete terms recognizable to all the pilgrims (and all readers) how each of these sins can corrupt any person, no matter his or her status, and infect whole families, neighborhoods, and communities with its venom. "*The Parson's Tale*" is a guidebook and resource for living in conformity with principle and duty presented by one who models such living.

Chaucer's work contains all the themes that will later characterize English culture and literature. He reveals character through a multitude of detail, building a full portrait of each pilgrim by describing his or her dress, speech, style, interests, likes and dislikes. The pilgrims are not allegorical types; they are recognizably individual, with quirks and preoccupations all their own. The whole range of society is represented, with a knight and a parson intent on propagating cherished values, a merchant and a landowner eager to capitalize on business opportunities, a miller unashamed to advertise his vulgarity, an Oxford clerk ready to give up everything in his pursuit of knowledge, a nun fastidious in deportment, and a friar and a pardon peddler maximizing the social advantages and personal gain their positions afford. Chaucer's tolerance for human frailty and imperfection is very English; an acceptance and tolerance of diversity pervades *The Canterbury Tales*. "Tolerance" and "acceptance" do not, however, confer approval. The pilgrims' characterizations invite moral judgment. The nun, for instance, is too delicate and too concerned about her dress, speech, and authority to qualify as a bride of Christ. The Oxford clerk is a dedicated student, but his studies are so absorbing they detach him from everyday living. The knight, on the other hand, though more of a vagabond Christian soldier than a protector of home and hearth, is faithful to chivalric and crusading ideals, and the parson, though poor and marginalized in his remote parish, is supremely loyal to Gospel teachings, always putting the welfare of his humble flock ahead of his own comforts.

Indeed, the virtue the parson espouses in his preaching and embodies in his life is what the English most admire since lives lived according to conscience figure so prominently in the nation's history (Thomas More, John Milton, John Henry Newman). In literature, William Langland elaborated on this theme in *Piers Ploughman*, the story of a man of virtue, whose poverty, lack of education, and dim prospects cannot obscure or diminish his need to live out genuinely Christian values each day. Centuries later, the dissenting pastor John Bunyan crafted an allegorical variation on this same theme in *The Pilgrim's Progress*, which became, after the *King James Bible*, the most popular and influential literary work in the English-speaking world. Nevertheless, though virtuous living underlies English ideals, Chaucer's human comedy, in one incarnation or another, also reappears in British literature through the centuries. The Wife of Bath, for instance, is recreated as Molly Bloom in James Joyce's *Ulysses*; the Oxford clerk is recognizable in Matthew Arnold's Gypsy Scholar; and the friar is heard again in Dickens's Reverend Chadband, who never passes up an opportunity to indulge in food, drink, and sententious oratory in company with generous benefactors.

Chaucer's greatest successor, William Shakespeare, would create a whole gallery of such striking personalities, including Falstaff, Hotspur, Iago, and Mercutio, to name just a few in the great supporting roles, and Lear, Hamlet, Macbeth, and Richard II and III among the principals. The major characters prosper or fail according to whether or how they respond to moral challenges. Shakespeare's tragedies end in misery but not, as with the Greeks, because the gods have so decreed or the power of destiny has so determined. Hamlet suffers because he is not firm or forceful like his foreign counterpart Fortinbras. Instead of taking up his murdered father's cause immediately and confronting his dastardly uncle directly, he devises complicated schemes to expose Claudius's villainy, as if craft alone will avenge a father's assassination. The fault is in himself, not in the stars; Hamlet should be acting like a knight. Likewise, King Lear, against all precedence or prudence, cedes parts of his kingdom while still living and then is forced to endure humiliation at the hands of those he has foolishly endowed. He becomes petty and pitiful trying to navigate as one no longer regal. Macbeth lets his wife's overwhelming desire for power dominate his actions, and the result is bloodshed and political disorder on a grand scale. These are all downfalls due to failure to be what one ought to be. The failures are failures of character, nothing less.

The English literary emphasis on individual character as grounded in a person's perceptible characteristics is paralleled in philosophy. In contrast to their continental peers' abstract rationalism, English philosophers of the Middle Ages elevated "common sense" over theorizing. William of Occam taught that disputations would best be resolved through application of the simplest or most straightforward approach. His ruthless paring down of Scholasticism's metaphysical constructs by use of "Occam's razor" made questions that had seemed to require intense and complicated analysis yield conclusions breathtaking in their simplicity. William is the first to espouse empiricism, the philosophical perspective associated with English thinkers ever since. Like the Scottish philosopher John Duns Scotus, who criticized Thomas Aquinas for his uncritical acceptance of Aristotle's logic as granting access to truth by reasoning alone, William insisted that what the senses tell us of the world must be accepted as "given" and that any subsequent reasoning based upon sense experience must remain firmly grounded in and true to that experience. When, therefore, medieval thinkers speculated famously on how many angels could fit upon the head of a pin, Occam's razor would abort the inquiry immediately since by definition angels are incorporeal beings and therefore inaccessible to human senses.

In political matters, the Norman model, very much like the Roman, held sway for only a time. By 1215, local gentry had had enough of monarchical presumption and authoritarian rule. On the field at Runnymede, they formally compelled King John, successor to the legendary Richard the Lionhearted, to agree to a number of reforms and restrictions of royal prerogative specified in a document called *Magna Carta*. This is the first indication of the prudence and moderation in political matters that would characterize this nation's history going forward. The establishment of Parliament would eventually follow, giving first the gentry and then the people as a whole, a voice in determining how state policy in political, religious, and financial affairs would be formulated and executed. Just as in religion and culture, the English are distinctive in favoring a form of government that is consensual; popular opinion should be welcomed and honored, not disdained or feared. The individual is a person of sense and sensibility who can be trusted to understand serious issues and act upon them responsibly. The monarch must be respected and obeyed, but he or she is not all knowing and all powerful. A king or queen must reign in union with the nation's people, not isolated from them.

The Middle Ages ended violently in England. During the Wars of the Roses, powerful families, with their own quasi-militias, tore the social fabric apart in incessant conflict that did not cease until Henry Tudor defeated Richard III at Bosworth Field in 1485, ending the Plantagenet dynasty. The victor assumed the throne as Henry VII, beginning a new, immensely creative, and enduringly influential period in British history. The Tudor era accentuated all the tendencies in English history and culture noted previously and made them the dominant features of British identity. By the beginning of the sixteenth century, the Hundred Years War and the internal discord among factions within England had badly weakened the English hold on territory of the French mainland. The loss of Calais in 1558 ratified what had long been apparent: England would become once again an island kingdom only. The post-Norman concept of England as an appendage of France and parts of France as English fiefs could no longer be sustained. Tudor England capitalized on this separation, reasserting English exceptionalism and developing institutions and supporting a culture enriched by centuries of continental influence but freed now to grow independently.

The first manifestation of this independence occurred in religion. The Reformation began in 1516, when Martin Luther nailed his *95 Theses* to the door of the castle church in Wittenberg, Germany. Although English reformers and critics, such as John Wycliffe, in earlier years had raised objections to Catholic practices similar to Luther's, officially at least, England remained loyally Catholic in the opening years of the controversy. King Henry VIII even published a pamphlet denouncing the Reformers, earning from a grateful pope the title "Defender of the Faith." Everything changed, however, when for political reasons primarily, Henry petitioned Rome in 1527 for an annulment of his marriage to Queen Catherine of Aragon. Pope Clement VII, however, was in no position to grant the petition largely because in that same year, forces nominally loyal to Emperor Charles V had invaded Rome, sacked the city, ransacked the papal precincts, committed untold barbarities, and nearly captured Clement himself. Since Catherine was the emperor's aunt, insulting her nephew by annulling her marriage could well provoke a second sack of Rome.

The headstrong and impatient monarch would not wait for matters to settle or for clerical diplomats to work out a compromise. He did, instead, the boldest thing any European ruler had done since Charlemagne became emperor of the West. Henry VIII and a compliant Parliament forced the English bishops not only to annul his marriage but to sever all juridical and administrative ties to the Holy See; henceforth the English Church would be an independent and self-governing entity.

The new communion became known as the Anglican Church, and despite attempts by successors like Queen Mary Tudor to restore Catholicism as the state religion, the national church endured. Over the next century, Anglican leaders oversaw the translation of all liturgical prayers and rites from Latin to English, culminating in the *Book of Common Prayer* and the *King James Bible*, both of which would become immensely important cultural treasures and formative influences for generations to come. In typically English fashion, the church also took a moderate position on the most divisive theological controversies. Anglicans, therefore, would retain the priesthood but would abolish clerical celibacy; they would continue to celebrate the Eucharist but would substitute consubstantiation for transubstantiation in explaining how bread and wine are transformed into Christ's body and blood; and they would keep mitred bishops, boy choirs, and grand cathedrals but not object when King Henry's agents dissolved monasteries, sold off their properties, and emptied their treasuries.

But while the English Church followed a *via media* in theology and religious practice, the effect of its opening up of the Bible to all who were literate in English gave the greatest impetus to piety and to every variety of godly living. Rites and ceremonies were important and were conducted in the Anglican Church with care and sensitivity, but more important than churchgoing was virtuous living. Churchmen were not exempt; their leadership was effective only so long as they modeled the principles they preached. As we have seen, Chaucer portrays many varieties of hypocrisy in *The Canterbury Tales*, singling out ecclesiastics who are gluttonous, venal, vain, and conniving, and sparing from ridicule only the humble parson who lives the values of the gospel. This type of figure became in post-Reformation England an ideal for clergy and laity alike. Over time, emphasis shifted from what one professes to how one lives out his beliefs. There can be many "persuasions," since the richness of faith offers numerous approaches and expressions, but daily living according to a conscience formed by Scripture and pious guides compels one to stay on a straight and narrow path that is the same always and for all. Anthony Trollope's nineteenth-century novel, *The Warden,* focuses on a cleric who is clearly the spiritual brother of Bunyan's pilgrim couple, though they are at opposite poles theologically.

This emphasis differs from the major concerns among adherents of the various continental confessions. In Spain, mystical experience, coupled with a militant missionary Catholicism, dominated, as exemplified by St. John of the Cross, St. Theresa of Avila, and St. Ignatius Loyola, and their followers. The French highlighted intellectualism, subjecting all religious affirmation to the litmus test of reason, as Pascal did with his famous "wager." The Italians produced many great ecclesiastics during the Counter-Reformation, tying sanctity firmly to clerical orders and labors on behalf of the institutional church, as with St. Charles Borromeo, the reforming archbishop who made the education of his clergy a priority, and St. Philip Neri, who founded a new religious congregation. In Germany, among the Lutheran and Calvinist reformers, the focus was firmly on faith, which is fundamentally a gift to those possessing it and which should be cultivated and confirmed in clergy and laity alike over a lifetime of careful nurturing, involving prayer, study, Scripture reading, and instruction by preachers. While good works were certainly expected from those so gifted, in line with Luther's insistence on the priority of faith over works, they were not really essential for salvation. Faith in Christ's salvific sacrifice must be sincerely held to merit "justification"; without this, liturgical rites, acts of charity, and the like are not efficacious. As late as the nineteenth century, Kierkegaard, in *Fear and Trembling*, would portray the man of faith as happy, confident, cheerful, energetic, and in tune with all of life's possibilities, certainly not someone obsessing about moral lapses.

In England, a godly life radiated faith and conviction. Such a life is characterized by magnanimity and charity, not by extremism. Dr. Samuel Johnson once described Sir Thomas More, the Lord Chancellor who accepted death rather than endorse Henry VIII's break with Rome, as "the greatest man of virtue these islands ever produced." But martyrs like More are more admired than emulated in English history. The English upheaval included victims of conscience at both ends of the religious spectrum, from Calvinist-inspired Puritans on the extreme left to Jesuits on the extreme right, to borrow the dichotomy of the Estates-General. In relative terms, though, these extremists were not numerous or popular; the great majority followed the middle way of the established church. Indeed, whenever Catholics or Calvinists gained a political foothold, as they did under Queen Mary Tudor, on the one hand,

and Oliver Cromwell, on the other, popular sentiment quickly turned against each group.

Over time, the English Reformation's emphasis on authentic Christian faith manifested through good works, and avoidance of sin became less and less urgent and more and more something to be accepted but not acted upon with conscientious concern. As early as the eighteenth century, observers began to lament the decline in religious practice in England and the growing indifference of the public to traditional piety and ceremony. From the great churches of the cities to the small chapels in the countryside, services on Sundays and holidays attracted fewer and fewer congregants. Jonathan Swift, an Anglican clergyman as well as a brilliant satirist, tried to shock the populace into awareness of this reality by proposing that the "abolition of Christianity in England" be vigorously opposed and ultimately reversed. The French philosopher Montesquieu echoed Swift when, after a visit to England in the 1720's, he exclaimed, "There is no religion in England. If anyone mentions religion people begin to laugh" (As quoted in Kenneth Clark, *Civilisation.* New York: Harper & Row, 1969. 269). In the nineteenth century, clergy and laity associated with John Henry Newman, at one end of the religious spectrum, and John Wesley, at the other end, were united in advocating a return to Christian roots in response to society's drift toward a purely secular way of thinking and living. However, despite some early progress, neither the Methodist discipline promoted by Wesley nor the Anglo-Catholic Oxford movement inspired by Newman could make serious headway in restoring classic Anglican beliefs and values. Members of both groups soon went their separate ways, with Wesley and his followers forming an independent body, the Methodist Church, and Newman and many of his associates joining the Catholic Church, regarded then as a last bastion of tradition.

Those who remained in the Anglican Church, the great majority of the population, kept the two extremes in check. They wanted the church to reflect moderation and compromise in the same way society as whole did when it promoted the middle way as the preferred approach to balanced living for British citizens regardless of social class, birth, level of education, or economic status. This lifestyle emphasizes sober and steady effort, avoidance of ideological or emotional extremes, selfless adherence to duty, and a willingness to compromise whenever such will lead to harmonious interaction with others. This determination to reject extremes arises from the profound British conviction that no one possesses the whole truth, that modesty is more appropriate than self-display or self-aggrandizement, and that virtuous conduct is more to be valued than money, power, pleasure, or any worldly good. How this studied moderation plays out in the church is illustrated well by a novelist like the aforementioned Anthony Trollope, who produced a long series of novels, set in and around the cathedral city of Barchester, describing clerical life and society in the second half of the nineteenth century. In *Barchester Towers*, for instance, shortly after a new bishop is installed, his chaplain, Mr. Slope, delivers a sermon in the cathedral, with the bishop himself present, as well as the dean and clergy of the chapter, who organize and perform the services in this church. All listen in rapt attention as Mr. Slope boldly advances a decidedly evangelical, or Low Church, program for the cathedral going forward, one that deemphasizes ceremony and chant in worship in favor of plain statement:

> *The words of our morning service, how beautiful, how apposite, how intelligible they were, when read with simple and distinct decorum. But how much of the meaning of the words was lost when they were produced with the meretricious claims of melody.* (*Barchester Towers.* New York, New American Library, 1963, 58)

The Anglo-Catholic, or High Church, clergy, who have led the services for many years and love the "charms of melody," react with shock to such a proposal. They spend the rest of the novel looking for ways to thwart this point man of the opposite order, succeeding finally in having their nominee made Dean of the Cathedral and forcing the bishop to dispense with Mr. Slope altogether.

What is illustrated here is the yin and yang dialectic that kept the late-nineteenth-century church from moving too far away from its center of gravity. Mr. Slope's emphasis on inner conviction and comprehension is in accord with evangelical teaching dating back to Martin Luther, while the High Church party's insistence on preserving traditional chant and retaining dignified liturgical ceremony is in line with Catholic practice. Since neither group can silence the other, Anglican leaders opted to incorporate elements from both parties, continuing to pray with music and decorative embellishment in cathedrals but at the same time permitting simpler, less formal, more Scripture-centered rites in other venues. The British genius for compromise allowed each movement half a loaf.

This moderation is in marked contrast to the French Catholic world of Julien Sorel, where splendor is normal and expected. As was noted in the previous chapter, for the feast of Corpus Christi, for instance, Abbé Sorel helps arrange in the cathedral at Besancon floral bouquets, hangings, candelabra, and so on that are so ornate and elaborate that decorators from Paris have to be summoned to assist the locals. On another occasion, when a royal visitor arrives to pray at a nearby shrine, the event is celebrated with extraordinary ecclesiastical and civic pomp, as the entire town of Verrieres is bedecked with finery and dignitaries walk or ride to the shrine in a grand procession. Julien's funeral rites, which conclude *The Red and the Black*, are more than splendid; his aristocratic lover, Mathilde de la Mole, spares no expense and ignores canons of taste in memorializing the man she has loved, the man who has fathered her child, and the man whose severed head rests "on her lap" (508) throughout the obsequies. Julien is led to his grave "near the peak of one of the tall mountains in the Jura range in the middle of the night" (508). There, twenty priests perform a candlelit requiem identical to that offered in the sixteenth century for one of Mathilde's dashing ancestors, also guillotined like Julien. Later,

Julien's "rough cave was ornamented at great expense with marbles carved in Italy" (508). Nothing of such over-the-top grandeur, it is safe to say, could be accommodated within the Anglican *via media*.

The High Church/Low Church balance was sustained into the twentieth century, but as the years wore on, an accumulation of forces began to chip away at the church and called faith itself into question. Samuel Butler's *The Way of All Flesh*, published in 1903, highlights the change in thinking members of a rural clerical family experience over three generations. Theobald Pontifex, the son of a sturdy self-made entrepreneur, becomes an Anglican priest after completing his Oxford studies and becomes rector of a parish shortly thereafter. He has Low Church sympathies, including an attraction to grim Old Testament readings that encourage harsh parenting. In consequence, if his young son, Ernest, cannot recite his prayers or his lessons properly, he suffers beatings regularly. Ernest grows skeptical of a religion that permits these cruelties. He does not follow in his father's footsteps and become a priest; instead, he renounces religion completely, opting not to wrestle with theological difficulties at all but, rather, live happily and wholesomely in indifference. Butler's book was very influential, inspiring numerous defections of the same sort. In 1955, after the cataclysms of economic depression and global war, the poet Philip Larkin gave culminating voice to the prevailing pessimism about Christianity in "Church Going," a meditation on what churches once were and what they probably would become. As he walks through an empty church building, Larkin ponders its future in lines 21–27:

Wondering what to look for; wondering, too,
When churches fall completely out of use
What we shall turn them into, if we shall keep
A few cathedrals chronically on show,
Their parchment, plate, and pyx in locked cases,
And let the rest rain-free to rain and sheep,
Shall we avoid them as unlucky places?

This despairing concern is sincere and reflects the unmistakable decline all the English denominations have had to endure since the high point of commitment and devotion in the sixteenth and seventeenth centuries. But while customary practices faded, the fundamental English conviction that if one adheres to a religious persuasion his or her conscience must guide conduct and that everyday living must reflect whatever affirmations one professes, has remained embedded in English thinking to the present day. This conviction has animated reform movements, for instance, throughout English history. In the 1830s, when Newman and Wesley were so convinced of Christianity's lack of relevance in England, a politician could still be inspired by Christian principles to rally his countrymen in support of the abolition of slavery within the British Empire. In 1834, the efforts of William Wilberforce and his like-minded colleagues bore lasting fruit when Parliament confirmed emancipation. This occurred almost thirty years before Abraham Lincoln issued his own Emancipation Proclamation in a country considered far more serious about religion than England. Wilberforce also became connected to another reform movement, the Society for the Prevention of Cruelty to Animals, established in 1824 to advocate against the abuse of carriage horses. Just as the enslavement of fellow human beings could not in conscience be permitted, so the arbitrary and cruel abuse of innocent animals could not be tolerated in a society still animated by humane values. Similar zeal inspired the anti-colonial movements in the twentieth century, particularly in South Africa, where a native-born Anglican archbishop, Desmond Tutu, achieved international renown for his leadership in the effort to end apartheid. What these and other examples illustrate is how individual principle and conviction can inspire social changes leading to lasting advances in behavior and thinking. It does not take a multitude of believers to bring about victories for justice and decency, only a dedicated few. The majority of English citizens may have stopped going to church on Sundays and may have dispensed with prayer, psalm-singing, and Bible reading at home, but when leaders animated by moral zeal bring abuses to their attention, their consciences are awakened, and the people respond.

In domestic life, even where religious practice has become a matter of routine rather than fervent conviction, the power of everyday service and outreach can be overwhelming. Two examples from the nineteenth century illustrate the lingering impact of moral purpose in English culture. In *Bleak House*, Charles Dickens portrays Dr. Richard Woodcourt, who works selflessly among the poor, in terms that Chaucer's Parson would find commendable. At the end of the novel, the doctor's wife, Esther, another exemplar of quiet courage and dedication to principle, reflects on her life with Woodcourt as follows:

> *We are not rich in the bank, but we have always prospered and we have quite enough. I never walk out with my husband but I hear the people bless him. I never go into a house of any but I hear his praises or see them in grateful eyes. I never lie down at night but know that in the course of that day he has alleviated pain and soothed some fellow-creature in the time of need. I know that from the beds of those who were past recovery, thanks have often, often gone up in the last hour for his patient ministrations. Is not this to be rich?* (*Bleak House*. New York: New American Library, 1964, 880)

Dickens's contemporary, George Eliot, the unsurpassed chronicler of English provincial life, presents another perspective on this theme. We recall that in Catholic Europe a life of austerity and self-sacrifice was the preferred path to sanctity. One declared a "saint" was, in consequence, almost always a priest or a nun. Ever since Henry VIII shut down monasteries and convents, however, the English have had to strive for godliness not by detaching themselves from others but by immersing themselves fully in society and maintaining virtue in the midst of challenging people and situations. In Eliot's *The Mill on the Floss*, Maggie Tulliver discovers that this reality promotes personal growth. At one point, Maggie comes under the influence of Thomas à Kempis's *The Imitation of Christ*, a medieval devotional guide extolling the monastic virtues. At first, she embraces the teachings of the "small old-fashioned book":

> *With all the hurry of an imagination that can never rest in the present, she sat in the deepening twilight forming plans of self-humiliation and entire devotedness; and in the ardour of first discovery renunciation seemed to her the entrance into that satisfaction which she had so long been craving in vain.* (*The Mill on the Floss.* New York: New American Library, 1965, 306)

She realizes after a time, though, that "renunciation," taken to an extreme, leads not to a flowering of the spirit but to a quenching of individual hopes, desires, ambitions, and joys. It can make one retreat into a shell, obsessing only about the state of his or her soul. Maggie's mother finds her daughter transformed for the worse: "It was amazing that this once 'contrairy' child was become so submissive, so backward to assert her own will" (309). Submission and backwardness do not deepen one's experience or strengthen a person's capability of interacting successfully with a world that presents a multitude of challenges. Maggie's brother Tom is one such challenge. He is a trial whom renunciation can blot out but only at the cost of something like self-annihilation:

> *That is the path we all like when we set out on our abandonment of egoism—the path of martyrdom and endurance (where the palm branches grow) rather than the steep highway of tolerance, just allowance, and self-blame (where there are no leafy honours to be gathered and won.* (308–309)

Maggie returns to society, walking firmly up that "steep highway of tolerance, just allowance, and self-blame" where, in her very English way, she will let conscience be her guide as she navigates among personalities and trials that can daunt even the strongest.

English philosophy reenforces this insistence on engagement with the world. We have seen that William of Occam opposed medieval scholasticism's tendency toward abstraction by highlighting the primacy of what is simple and concrete. Since then, English thinkers have never wavered in their insistence that theory be grounded in the experience of the senses. The evidence of the senses is decisive, said John Locke, George Barkley, and David Hume, the three giants of English empiricism in the Age of the Enlightenment. They make a process akin to scientific method the only valid means of accessing truth in nature. Hume, in particular, questions the possibility that the laws governing nature and observable by all can ever be overcome, thereby placing all the miraculous elements in religious teaching under suspicion. In contrast to a German philosopher like Hegel, who, true to his pedigree, makes Spirit or *Geis*t the transcendent reality that creates and maintains all that is, English philosophers steer clear of metaphysics, remaining firmly grounded in the universe experience presents, whether to the ordinary man's five senses or to the professional enquirer's subtle instruments. English hard-headedness is illustrated well in the famous scene in Shakespeare's *Henry IV*, *Part 1*, when Owen Glendower, who reports "the earth did shake" when he was born, tells his cousin he can "call spirits from the vasty deep." With English good sense, Hotspur replies, "Why, so can I, or so can any man; But will they come when you do call for them?" (Act 3, Scene 1, 19, 51-53).

Common sense and aversion to ideology characterize English political history as well. Since the Middle Ages, English politics has been distinguished by its reliance on parliamentary rule—that is, rule by the majority party of the House of Commons as determined by popular vote. Over the centuries, the franchise has been steadily extended, so that today no one is excluded from voting because of his or her religion, race, class, ethnic origin, level of education, or any other factor extraneous to citizenship. A monarch reigns but does not rule, since constitutional restrictions make the king or queen head of state but not government. Ever since the great religious upheaval of the sixteenth century and the disorder and civil conflict it engendered, ending finally with the settlement of the Glorious Revolution of 1688, the English governing classes have been wary of monarchical overreach. The power of an aggressive king or queen to assert executive authority in defiance of parliamentary sentiment has been steadily curbed, particularly through Parliament's exclusive control of government finance. Consequently, political violence has not marred English history as it has that of France, with its St. Bartholomew's Massacre, bloody revolution of 1789, and military cabals and coups in the nineteenth century. Likewise, in contrast to Germany, where deep religious divisions worked against national unity for centuries, the British Isles have accepted English sovereignty without major crises since the eighteenth century, when Scotland was brought under English dominion. Catholics in Ireland have resented the English ever since King William's forces defeated the Catholic-leaning Stuart pretender in the Battle of the Boyne in 1690, but apart from open rebellion in 1916, the Irish remained loyal subjects until the island achieved independence in the twentieth century. The influence of England in continental Europe has been, on the whole, limited but positive. English restraint and insistence on a balance-of-power equilibrium among rival states kept aggrandizing powers like Spain and France at bay from the sixteenth through most of the eighteenth century. Only when diplomacy or financial intervention failed to prevent a continent-wide disturbance did Parliament authorize military intervention. In doing so against the Bourbon dynasty, Napoleon's Imperium, Kaiser Wilhelm's German coalition, and Hitler's Nazis, the British and their allies succeeded in keeping Europe empire free.

This is somewhat ironic because while Europeans were preoccupied by internal threats and tensions, almost by accident, the British acquired vast influence in the rest of the world, creating an empire of their own. In North America, Africa, Australia, and Asia, British traders, explorers, military and naval forces, and emigrants combined to establish colonies or, as in India, worked to unite small tribal or ethnic principalities into a nation-state transcending such divisions. In all regions under their rule, the British strove to create representative institutions; maintain the rule of law; support schools, hospitals, orphanages, and charities; reduce tensions and eliminate violent practices associated with ethnic or tribal traditions; and cultivate native talent. They did so, for the most part, by relying on reasonable persuasion, compromise, and negotiation rather than repression. As a result, though the empire no longer exists, today the English language is understood and spoken in most of the world, and governing bodies like Parliament and the judiciary conduct their affairs in ways that a British citizen would find familiar. With all respect to the Romans and the Spanish, the only empire-builders rivaling the British, the contributions to world civilization of the British Empire are unsurpassed.

PART ONE

The values, influences, and history sketched above are given expression through characters and incidents in *David Copperfield*. This novel, which Dickens called his "favorite child" and which purports to be his autobiography, is a *Bildungsroman*, a novel of education. The "education" David undergoes, however, does not so much involve intellectual growth or career training as it does development of character. David's progress from childhood to mature adulthood is a variant on the model laid out in Bunyan's *Pilgrim's Progress*, without, however, explicitly religious content or context. In the mid-nineteenth century world of this novel, as we have already noted, denominational Christianity has either been marginalized or become so distorted as to be a barrier to humane and magnanimous living rather than a stimulant to such. In *David Copperfield*, this toxic effect is associated mainly with the evangelical influence; it affects him profoundly when, after his young mother's death, David falls into the hands of the Murdstones, a brother/sister duo whose child-rearing is centered on "firmness," a euphemism for abuse. Likewise, in the school operated by Mr. Creakle, another rigid sectarian, boys are routinely beaten for the slightest infractions. David's life experience leads the other way, to the teachings of Chaucer's parson, that is, to growing tolerance, patience, decency, selflessness, and an adherence to principle without bigotry; by the end of the novel, he is a man who models the British people's ideals in ways that transcend particular faith traditions or socio-political categories. David's life choices move steadily toward the *via media*, the middle way between conservative traditionalism and evangelical righteousness.

David builds his character not through solitary study or meditation and not through random chance; he learns from the people he encounters in all the different families, schools, professions, and communities with which he comes into contact. Just as in Chaucer and Shakespeare, who create characters that stand out vividly as individuals and as embodiments of ruling virtues or vices, Dickens gives us characters notable for their peculiarities or eccentricities but always engaged with other personalities or in situations that compel moral judgment. For David, these men and women are touchstones; they show him what or how he should be or not be.

Even minor characters are brought vividly to full-bodied life through careful delineation of idiosyncratic detail, as in the following paragraph describing David's and his first wife's house page:

> *He appears to me to have lived in a hail of saucepan lids. His whole existence was a scuffle. He would shriek for help on the most improper occasions—as when we had a little dinner-party, or a few friends in the evening—and would come tumbling out of the kitchen, with iron missiles flying after him. We wanted to get rid of him, but he was very much attached to us, and wouldn't go. He was a tearful boy and broke into such deplorable lamentations, when a cessation of our connexion was hinted at, that we were obliged to keep him. He had no mother—no anything in the way of a relative that I could discover, except a sister, who fled to America the moment we had taken him off her hands—and he became quartered on us like a horrible young changeling. He had a lively perception of his own unfortunate state, and was always rubbing his eyes with the sleeve of his jacket, or stooping to blow his nose on the extreme corner of a little pocket-handerchief, which he never would take completely out of his pocket, but always economized and secreted.* (*David Copperfield.* New York: New American Library, 1962, 687).

This paragraph is followed by three more, detailing the page's salary; the difficulty of dismissing him despite a theft; his comprehensive knowledge of household irregularities perpetrated by the cook and the pot boy; his eventual trial and sentence; his final meeting with David's wife, Dora, who faints when the iron bars of the page's cell close behind her; and his new life as a "shepherd of 'up the country' somewhere" (689). Dickens's penchant for detailed characterization and the delight he takes in recording eccentricities are exceptional, even by nineteenth-century English standards, but they are typical of his culture's celebration of diversity. Great Britain, after all, in addition to England, includes Scotland, Wales, Cornwall, and Northern Ireland, with a close connection to the Irish Republic as well; each of these distinct communities has contributed its people, idioms, customs, faiths, and traditions to the patchwork we recognize as a peculiarly British style of thinking and acting. Given this diversity within the nation itself and the additional fact that because of its tolerance of minorities, Great Britain has been a magnet for immigrants from other parts of Europe, as well as from throughout its vast empire, it is hardly surprising that from Chaucer on, its writers have responded so sensitively to individual difference.

David's life, then, is formed by his experience as a social being. This may not seem unusual or notable, but in comparison with the other protagonists of this study, it is. Huckleberry Finn, for instance, has many young friends, notably Tom Sawyer and Nigger Jim, but the adult world he moves in is uniformly cold, hostile, or repellent. He learns nothing good and derives no comfort or encouragement from the grown-ups he meets or observes on his river journey, most of them manifesting the viciousness and vice of a fallen world. They are primarily why he has "to light out for the territory ahead of the rest" at the book's end. The same with Julien Sorel. With the exception of the two women he spends his young life pursuing, the numerous characters he interacts with are of negligible interest unless they can somehow be of use to him. Julien does not let moral scruple get in the way of his ambitions; he strives to master and to rule. Thomas Mann's Adrian Leverkuhn also seeks mastery, but not in a social context. He longs to surpass worldly limitations through intellectual and artistic achievement. His is a solitary pursuit for the most part; he responds to and communes with impulses and obstacles within himself. Tolstoy's Pierre Bezukhov, at first sight, appears more like David. He lives in a rich context of families, friends, and great events. But Pierre's life centers around his search for identity. He needs to come to terms with his Russian nationality while living in a world where, and in a time when, revolutionary concepts are calling all conventional wisdom into question and threatening the social and institutional fabric he was born into. Pierre is drawn to or repelled by others largely in terms of how they impact his self-exploration. They matter in his life only in this context. David's growth and development are different. He is repelled by some of those he sees, but he is inspired by so many others; with his anti-authoritarian personality, he yearns not for mastery or rule but for mutual respect and fellowship. He is clearly a talented writer, but his focus is on the here and now and the mundane, and he has no identity crisis to resolve since he is, in the best sense, British through and through.

David Copperfield is divided roughly into three parts: David's childhood (Chapters I—XIV); David's studies, apprenticeship, the beginning of his literary career, and his marriage (XV—XLIII); and David's mature years, involving the death of his wife, his second marriage, and the resolution of all the emotional, financial, and familial issues and conflicts raised earlier (Chapters XLIV—LXIV). One character dominates the entire book, provoking key events in each section. David meets James Steerforth when both are enrolled as young students in the Salem House boys' school presided over by the tyrannical Mr. Creakle. James is older than "Davy," but from the moment the youngster arrives, Steerforth, inspired by something like *noblesse oblige*, treats him kindly and protects David, not so much from the other boys' hazing as from Creakle and company. Since the headmaster and his staff try never to upset the imperious Steerforth, David is grateful he has been taken under his wing, but more than this, he is awed by his new friend. Steerforth is handsome, charming, witty, and confident; he is an only child who has been coddled and deferred to by a proud mother acutely conscious of her and her son's privileged status. He is all David aspires to be. In this respect, he is reminiscent of the promising young men memorialized in English elegies, notably Milton's *Lycidas*, Shelley's *Adonais*, Matthew Arnold's *Thyrsis*, and Tennyson's *In Memoriam*. Intense male friendship is characteristic of English culture, stimulated in part by schools like Creakle's, which are segregated by sex. This pattern often persists into adulthood, where men congregate in pubs and clubs, join each other in sports like hunting or riding, and work with mostly other men in the professions, in the trades, or, until recently, in agriculture, mining, or manufacturing.

While Steerforth's many gifts may seem to rank him among the "Golden Boys" the poets celebrate, he has profound moral weaknesses that disqualify him for accolades. The circumstances of his upbringing have corrupted his values and spoiled him almost beyond redemption. He has a conscience that reminds him of the rules in good British fashion, but he frankly will admit to David later in life that he cannot discipline his impulses, no matter how wayward. He laments the absence of a father in his upbringing; a male authority figure would have been better able than his doting mother to stiffen his resolve when ethically challenged. As it stands, though intelligent and perceptive, Steerforth resents having to do anything he regards as tedious. Thus, when one of the masters at Creakle's school, Mr. Mell, antagonizes Steerforth by insisting he remain silent during study time, the young man David idolizes shows his dark side. Not only does Steerforth take offense at being singled out, he defies Mr. Mell openly and deliberately humiliates him in front of everyone by highlighting the fact that the master's mother lives in the equivalent of public housing. Steerforth had learned of this in early conversations with David, who was met by Mr. Mell when he arrived in London and was introduced to his mother in her little apartment. Later on, as David and the kind-hearted Mell work together and the new boy begins making progress in his lessons, he grows to like this master, who is "never harsh" (87) to him. Now, to David's horror, Steerforth's outburst makes it appear as if David has betrayed the "master of Salem House," giving Creakle cause to dismiss David's mentor simply because Mr. Mell's "mother lives on charity in an alms-house" (108). This dramatic scene is an important moment in David's moral development. He is remorseful:

> *For myself, I felt so much self-reproach and contrition for my part in what had happened, that nothing would have enabled me to keep back my tears but the fear that Steerforth, who often looked at me, I saw, might think it unfriendly—. . . if I showed the emotion which distressed me.* (109)

Not bothered like David by "self-reproach and contrition," Steerforth tries to defuse the tensions he has created by offering to send Mr. Mell "some money" (109), a typical spoiled rich boy's answer to everything. This mollifies the other boys, who soon get over the regrets they had expressed when Mr. Mell was dismissed. But David is different. His guilt is not easily relieved:

> *But I must say that when I was going on with a story in the dark that night, Mr. Mell's old flute seemed more than once to sound mournfully in my ears and that when at last Steerforth was tired, and I lay down in my bed, I fancied it playing so sorrowfully somewhere, that I was quite wretched.* (110)

This guilt springs from conscience, whose imperatives leave painful after-effects when they are violated. This is like a "jump start" to moral sensitivity, which David will continue to cultivate throughout the years.

Steerforth's conduct leads to the most consequential event in the novel's long middle section. David's relationship with the extended family of his childhood nurse, Peggotty, is the most harmonious and comforting of his youth. After reuniting with Steerforth years after their time together at school, David thinks it only natural that his old friend, now at Oxford, should meet the members of this kind-hearted Yarmouth fishing clan as well. Steerforth and the sailoring men hit it off immediately, and soon the Oxford scholar and the "old" (Daniel Peggotty) and the "young" (Ham Peggotty) salts are enjoying each other's company on the water. Steerforth invests in his own boat, which he lodges with the family. He also makes the acquaintance of little Em'ly, David's childhood playmate and companion. Em'ly appears to be just the sweet and innocent young girl Steerforth once conjured up as "Davy's" most likely love interest. Like almost everyone else, Em'ly is charmed and fascinated by Steerforth, whose confidence and ease make him seem like a visitor from another planet. Even though she is engaged to Ham, Steerforth arouses in Em'ly ambitions that have long been suppressed. Though resigned to being a dutiful Yarmouth wife, Em'ly nurses an apparently hopeless longing to be a "lady," which would entail education in social graces, housekeeping, and the proper rearing of children, as well as an elevation in status and class. This is by no means a totally selfish aspiration; Em'ly envisions everyone in the Peggotty household deriving benefit from any improvement in her situation.

Generous though her motives may be, however, Em'ly is flirting with danger when she imagines herself among the privileged elite. Jane Austen gives us some fine examples of what can result when a fairly ordinary girl becomes, for instance, a parson's wife, such as Mrs. Elton in *Emma*. The change in status creates a change in style and manner that would be comical were it not so unpleasant. George Eliot's Maggie Tulliver also has ambitions to rise above her narrow family-centered world, albeit more in terms of intellectual distinction than anything else. She arouses the suspicions of female friends and neighbors as she appears to be "putting on airs" at a country fair; shortly thereafter, she finds herself universally condemned for having quite accidentally been alone with a young gentleman on a passenger boat that could not dock as planned. Neither she nor her family can shake off the shame such conduct elicits in the English countryside in the nineteenth century.

A young woman's ambitions can also lead to a tragic outcome. In Thomas Hardy's *The Return of the Native*, set in the heath country of southwest England the novelist called Wessex, Eustacia Vye reacts against the confinement and loneliness her rural surroundings impose. Beautiful and romantic, she is "a rare plant in such a wild place" (*The Return of the Native*, New American Library, 1959, 341). Instead of looking for ways to improve her lot and that of her neighbors and thereby make her straitened life morally admirable, Eustacia fantasizes about somehow escaping to a metropolis, where the style, wit, culture, and sophistication of fashionable acquaintances can transform her everyday existence. Like Em'ly, she lets imagination overpower good sense. When she meets Clym Yeobright, who has recently returned to his home on the heath after working in the jewel trade in Paris, Eustacia is swept away. The combination of "Paris" and "jewels" is irresistible. She resolves to marry him and begin an enchanting life with Clym in Paris. But Clym has had his fill of Paris and business; he is determined, instead, to begin a new career among the rough-hewn citizens of Wessex as a teacher and guide. He embraces the sturdy simplicity and virtue of his neighbors as happily as Eustacia does the *glitterati* of the *beau monde*. Nevertheless, Eustacia's charms and ardor are so alluring that, despite his mother's objections, Clym marries her, believing that his love and dedication will reconcile his wife to settling on the heath with him forever. Love, dedication, and ideals of service so consistent with the parson's words do not, however, resonate in the heart and soul of a passionate and willful young beauty bent on reinventing herself somewhere far away from the world Clym loves. After a former love interest, now married to Clym's cousin, inherits a considerable sum and offers to accompany her to and support her in Paris, Eustacia struggles with her conscience but ultimately consents to join him. The two do not go far. On a dark night, Eustacia loses herself on the heath, falls into a marsh, and drowns. Her partner suffers the same fate while trying to rescue her, thereby confirming that the "wages of sin are death." Clym spends the rest of his days alone, blaming himself for his wife's distress, and, as a kind of reparation, going out of his way, like Ham Peggotty will, to serve the people of the heath as an "itinerant open-air preacher and lecturer on morally unimpeachable subjects" (405).

The female ideal prevailing in this era and even into the early modern age is Christiana, the faithful wife and helpmeet of Christian who makes her own pilgrimage in the second half of *Pilgrim's Progress*. Christiana cultivates virtue, keeping herself pure and untainted by worldly attractions, such as power, wealth, or pleasure-seeking. She sees firsthand the horrors inflicted by the depraved inhabitants of Vanity Fair, who would rather execute the virtuous than have them in their midst, passing judgment on their corruptions by their charity and grace-filled lives. Em'ly has been raised to be one like Christiana, and she certainly displays charity toward the less fortunate in her circle. When her friend Martha chooses to live in the midst of "toils and snares" among the poor in London's dark byways, she does not join the rest of Yarmouth in condemning such a choice. Nevertheless, in her innocence, Em'ly is playing with fire by yearning to move up in the world.

Steerforth senses this, and, with his manservant's aid, executes a carefully laid-out scheme to whisk Em'ly away from family and friends, shattering the harmony and peace of Yarmouth and betraying David, as well as all those who have befriended him and succumbed to his charm. Steerforth is not amoral, like Rodolphe, for instance, who coldly appraises Madame Bovary's attractions as if she were a piece of livestock before seducing her. Steerforth needs stimulation and excitement; sweeping a modest but beautiful girl off her feet and beginning an adventure that will take the couple throughout Europe is irresistible to one who always has gotten what he has desired, regardless of consequences.

The consequences are severe. They occupy most of the rest of the novel. Daniel Peggotty, who has raised Em'ly almost since birth, embarks on his own pilgrimage dedicated to finding and rescuing his beloved girl; on the other side, Mrs. Steerforth disowns her wayward son and vows never to accept Em'ly as a legitimate daughter-in-law, thereby negating any possibility of Em'ly's becoming a "lady." Ham remains at home, never to marry or show any interest in someone other than Em'ly. He will stay firm in his determination to live out his tragedy with dignity and in service to others, but he will not move on or forgive the man who has wrecked lives because he could not help it.

But Ham's grim resolve leads to an unexpected ending in an event that climaxes David's tale and dominates the last third of the novel. By this time, Steerforth and Em'ly have grown apart, so much so that, almost in desperation, the man who was to make his paramour a "lady" tries to shift that responsibility to that paragon of respectability and gentlemanly deference, his manservant Littimer. At Steerforth's insistence, Littimer offers to marry Em'ly to "make things right"; in so doing, he will clean up the mess his master has created and free Steerforth from what has become burdensome. This tidy solution, however, proves unworkable, as Em'ly scornfully rejects any possibility of being treated as disposable property. Once she realizes her position, she escapes what now seems like bondage by walking away one night, never to be seen by either man again. Littimer also parts ways with his overbearing master, leaving Steerforth to navigate his future alone.

Steerforth's future is foreshortened considerably as he tries to return to England. He finds himself caught at sea near Yarmouth in the midst of a storm whose "wind was the greatest ever known to blow upon that coast" (784). This tempest is both a tremendous weather event and a symbol of the chaos, torment, and despair Steerforth has left in his wake. It is as if the Furies of Greek mythology have been let loose to do their apocalyptic worst. Steerforth faces his fate in character, wearing a bright red hat and waving bravely, a dashing style that David, observing from the shore, recognizes. He is clearly doomed as his vessel begins to break apart. At this point, none other than Ham Peggotty, the man he has so grievously wronged, begins to walk in the sea toward the ship in a last-ditch effort at rescue.

These two characters, so different in education, upbringing, and prospects, are brought together in mutual need despite the social chasm separating them. Steerforth needs help, and Ham needs to help; this is the stark reality compelling the one to reach out toward the other. Just as Ham is about to embrace Steerforth and rescue him, the powerful waves engulf the ship and pull both men to their deaths.

That near embrace is close to a reconciliation of opposites. For most of his life, Steerforth has had the world at his feet. His bravado and confidence, however, while attracting many, have led to his undoing; like a young Prince Henry Tudor, later to become King Henry VIII, Steerforth has relied on his good looks, self-assurance, and disdain for any obstacles standing in the way of his plans or pleasures to carry him through life. Had he lived at the time of the Great War's opening days, he would have joined thousands of his privileged peers in volunteering for service and heedlessly marching to early deaths in the face of an enemy whose firepower could no more be overcome by raw courage than the Yarmouth tempest could be. David is well aware of his friend's deficiencies of character and is shamed by his dalliance with Em'ly and his callousness toward the close-knit Peggottys. Still, with a detached judgment matured by experience and animated by charity, David writes, long before Steerforth's death, a valedictory that balances the sins of the past and the possibilities that might have been realized:

> *I am not afraid to write that I never had loved Steerforth better than when the ties that bound me to him were broken. In the keen distress of the discovery of his unworthiness, I thought more of all that was brilliant in him, I softened more toward all that was good in him, I did more justice to the qualities that might have made him a man of a noble nature and a great name, than ever I had done in the height of my devotion to him.* (457)

And then there is Ham, a man of simple habits, rough speech, devotion to duty and craft, and unshakeable resolve. He sees a man in distress and, ignoring everyone's advice, heads into the raging water to try to save him. More than stoic determination is at play here. By this time, Ham knows Em'ly has been found and is safe; there is no possibility of their marrying now and no need for Ham to remain stubbornly purposeful. He can be at peace and face danger with selfless bravery. His is not an act of reckless daring, such as that performed by the Light Brigade at Balaclava; Steerforth might be capable of charging into cannon fire, but Ham is not an adventurer. This is a man of the people doing what he considers his duty toward another in distress. The essential brotherhood and sisterhood of all in distress make the social distinctions separating people utterly meaningless. Ham has made his own pilgrim's progress, facing profound adversity with courage. David does not have to imagine how Ham might have achieved distinction; before David's eyes, Ham goes to a heroic death with his arms outstretched for a saving embrace of his worst enemy.

In contrast to Steerforth, who is born with every advantage but then allows caprice, indiscipline, and moral weakness to make his life trajectory show nothing but steady decline, David Copperfield overcomes whatever challenges life throws in his path and, like Bunyan's pilgrim, grows in moral stature and personal character through steady application and effort, becoming by the novel's end an English gentleman of distinction in the best sense. The road he travels is filled with character-building traps, deceptions, deviations, and temptations, and as David proceeds, he is forced to deal with a multitude of personalities and eccentrics representing the broadest section of the human comedy. David copes with each situation and each person as capably as he can, never making the same mistake twice, learning from his varied experiences, and becoming ever stronger in virtue and resolve. His trajectory steadily rises.

PART TWO

The first part of *David Copperfield* covers the subject's childhood. This childhood is, in a word, harsh. His father dies six months before David is born, and though the child he fathered is the light of his young mother's life, she is by no means totally absorbed in David. David's mother has some of the qualities Chaucer's parson warns against; she is susceptible to flattery, and she is conscious of the good impression her looks and charm make on men. Soon, she is keeping company with Mr. Murdstone, a suitor David instinctively dislikes right from the start:

> *He patted me on the head but somehow I didn't like him or his deep voice, and I was jealous that his hand should touch my mother's in touching me—which it did. I put it away as well as I could.* (29)

While some of this sentiment could be attributed to the natural suspicion and unease a child feels for one who will divert a good deal of his mother's attention away from himself, Mr. Murdstone soon bears out David's apprehensions. He is cold and hard-hearted. His constant concern is that he and everyone close to him should display "firmness" at all times. This is, in reality, another word for "inhumanity." Once he becomes David's stepfather, the effects of Mr. Murdstone's preoccupation become clear. He shows no affection, no empathy for a young boy's disorientation upon his entering the household permanently, no patience, and no flexibility. The impressionable young David is compelled to endure the following dialogue almost as soon as he learns Murdstone and his beloved mother have been married:

> *"David," he said, making his lips thin by pressing them together, "if I have an obstinate horse or dog to deal with, what do you think I do?"*
> *"I don't know."*
> *"I beat him."*
> *I had answered in a kind of breathless whisper, but I felt, in my silence that my breath was shorter now.*
> *"I make him wince and smart. I say to myself, 'I'll conquer that fellow,' and if it were to cost him all the blood he had, I should do it."* (56)

Mr. Murdstone and his spinster sister, Jane, who moves in with the family, exemplify a side of the British character that is more Scottish or Scotch-Irish than English. Its inspiration is John Knox and his grim Calvinism. This strain has influenced the evangelical wing of the Anglican Church, as Samuel Butler shows in *The Way of All Flesh*, but not the broad majority of believers. The English put up with Oliver Cromwell and his "firmness" for a time after the Civil War, but once he passed on, the people could not wait to restore the Stuart monarch, Charles II, dissipations and all. The Murdstones are like holdovers from a rigid and exclusive sect. They take perverse pleasure in condemning those who cannot or will not meet their demanding standards. David notes how Miss Murdstone radiates malice as she prays in church:

> *Again, I listen to Miss Murdstone mumbling the responses and emphasizing all the dread words with a cruel relish. Again, I see her dark eyes roll round the church when she says "miserable sinners," as if she were calling all the congregation names.* (62)

Alfred Hitchcock might have recalled this passage when he directed a scene in *The Thirty-Nine Steps*. The main character, Richard Hannay, is on the run in Scotland. He is handsome and charming, so it is not surprising that a pretty young farmer's wife offers him shelter for a night in her isolated cottage on the heath.

When he dines with her and her craggy husband, Hannay listens uncomfortably as the gentleman dwells on the words "miserable sinners" in his grace before the meal. Early the next morning, Hannay departs quickly, but not before exchanging a parting kiss with the wife, who has recognized but not betrayed him. Her mate later rewards her discretion by beating her severely. The Murdstones would undoubtedly endorse such "firmness."

David is repelled by the Murdstones but not crushed, as his mother is. Clara is soon sinking into self-abasement as she tries to appease her husband's need to dominate: "I have a great many defects, I know, and it's very good of you, Edward, with your strength of mind, to endeavor to correct them for me" (61). David sees her visibly weakening under the pressure of the Murdstones; his mother's step is "really not so light" anymore and "the gaiety of her beauty" is being "almost worried away" (62). In his despair, David finds some comfort in books, particularly romances and fantastic tales that let his imagination run wild and bring at least a temporary escape from his misery. A constant trial is the Murdstones's relentless tutoring. Though he is clearly intelligent and perceptive, David usually wilts when "the sight of these two" (63) causes all he has studied to vanish from memory. Mr. Murdstone is sure David's disabilities can be overcome through the application of firmness—that is, by a good beating. As he attempts to administer such punishment for the first time, however, David's stepfather discovers that his boy does not accept his blows with resignation, like a submissive animal, but with fury; David bites the hand that is abusing him, causing blood to flow. This extraordinary act of defiance, so characteristic of the English people's long-standing aversion to tyrannical political or religious authority, leads first to something like house arrest for David and then to the momentous decision to send David Copperfield away to boarding school. The establishment the Murdstones choose is a ramshackle operation run by one Mr. Creakle, another advocate of firmness, who considers himself a member of the "elect," that exclusive company of the saved in Calvinist Christianity. Notwithstanding such divine favor, Creakle regularly beats his charges without any twinge of conscience and takes pride in calling himself a "Tartar" (91).

Throughout his ordeal with the Murdstones, David has relied on the kindness of his mother's servant, Peggotty, when in distress. Peggotty's family is from Yarmouth, a small port city on the east coast of England. Here, her brother Daniel presides over an extended family like a *paterfamilias* of exceptional generosity and magnanimity. He has adopted "Ham and Emily . . . an orphan nephew and niece" and is sharing his home with Mrs. Gummidge, "the widow of his partner in a boat, who had died very poor" (44). The family are close-knit, instinctively kind, and respectful. Indeed, when David visits the clan in company with his nurse for a brief holiday, Mr. Peggotty treats him with the utmost deference, as a poor, unlettered working man would a young gentleman.

This episode is critically important in David's development. David is certainly anything but spoiled, yet he does have a sense of his own worth that will not allow him to accept any lowly station in life and that drives his ambitions. Like the millions of English-speaking migrants who peopled the New World and other parts of the British Empire, David is determined at a very young age to make something of himself and to become, in reality, the gentleman Mr. Peggotty instinctively recognizes. When, shortly after, David is forced to work at *Murdstone and Grinby's* "blacking factory" tearing labels off used wine bottles, he finds his fellow employees are mostly street urchins. David is not comfortable in their company and stays deliberately aloof. This is not the case with the Peggottys. In their kindness and charity, they break through David's defenses. He recognizes in them fellow human beings of remarkable decency; David appreciates their consideration, welcomes their attentions, and strives to reciprocate in kind. This is family life as it is supposed to be, with several generations under one roof performing individual duties and subordinating personal desires and needs to the common good. Chaucer's parson would recognize and commend this family; their virtues are those he would have asked his congregation of simple rustics to assimilate. The

Peggottys are without pride, class consciousness, or pretension. They do not speak or write the King's English, do not dress fashionably, and have little in the way of valuable possessions. They work and then relax in each other's company; this day-to-day routine is similar to how the poor live or have lived in any nation or era. What is distinctive about the Peggottys, though, is their virtue. In their simplicity, it shines through, and David is irresistibly attracted.

His sojourn with the Peggotty family prepares David not only to endure but, in many ways, enjoy his time at Mr. Creakle's school. Because he has been in close contact with kind and decent people, and because he has experienced the pleasure of companionship with Emily and Ham, the only young people he has been allowed to mingle with, David is open to all the possibilities of friendship the school's students can afford. Unlike Julien Sorel, who decides instantly that his fellow students in the seminary at Besancon are all enemies, David accepts eagerly the good will extended by his new acquaintances. He needs their good will because Murdstone and Creakle have done their best to make his first days in school miserable. Upon arrival at Salem House, David is forced to wear a placard with a sign on the back stating, "Take care of him. He bites" (88). However, instead of receiving no end of teasing and becoming the victim of rough horseplay, David is pleasantly surprised to find most of the boys "not so boisterous at my expense as I had expected" (93). He is also deeply relieved when the school's brightest star, the aforementioned J. Steerforth, declines to exploit his vulnerability:

> *Before this boy, who was reputed to be a great scholar, and was very good-looking, and at least half-a-dozen years my senior, I was carried as before a magistrate. He inquired, under a shed in the playground, into the particulars of my punishment, and was pleased to express his opinion that it was a "jolly shame," for which I became bound to him ever afterwards.* (93)

"Ever afterwards" is exactly right. The older boy's kindness at this critical juncture makes so powerful an impression on David that no matter what happens between them later, he will always regard Steerforth with respect and will cherish his memory. The possibility that justice, fairness, and empathy between peers can exist strongly reinforces David's experience with the Peggottys, as does the conduct of another Salem House pupil, Tommy Traddles. Traddles is a good-natured boy who also helps David get through his opening days unscathed, but unlike Steerforth, who is granted every liberty, Traddles is constantly being punished for little infractions: "He was always being caned—I think he was caned every day that half-year, except one holiday Monday when he was only ruler'd on both hands" (100)

Traddles puts up with this without complaint or anger; he is also "honorable" (100)—that is, he does not implicate others even if he is abused for their offenses. Traddles, too, will play a major role in David's development, behaving as a modest, steady, generous, and forgiving friend and colleague. He shows strength of character as well, even if by so doing, he provokes the wrath of the powerful.

Only Tommy Traddles, good-hearted, sensible, and sensitive to others' feelings, joins David in decrying Steerforth's attack on Mr. Mell. In contrast to David, he does so openly by shedding tears over the master's expulsion. For his sensitivity, he is caned once more by Creakle and called "Miss Traddles" by Steerforth when he reproaches the boy who has "hurt [Mr. Mell's] feelings and lost him his situation" (109). Traddles is not a natural leader or someone who can readily influence others; he is just an honest and honorable young man who speaks truth to power despite the consequences. This example of brave assertion of principle is not lost on David; he will turn to Traddles again and again in later life whenever in need of moral support or assistance. Just as with generations of young Englishmen, the bonds made by these boys in school will help carry them through the innumerable crises and challenges they will face as adults. One does not adroitly avoid the traps and temptations that can lure a pilgrim from his prescribed path without the aid and counsel only kindred spirits may offer.

David goes home for the holidays and rejoices to see his mother and nurse once more after their long separation. He and they, however, enjoy only a few uninterrupted hours in each other's company, since the Murdstones are constantly and oppressively at hand. For one evening, though, David, his mother, and his nurse are alone for several hours. Those precious hours will constitute for him ever afterwards a quiet valedictory: "We were very happy, and that evening, as the last of its race, and destined evermore to close that volume of my life, will never pass out of my memory" (123).

This reunion brings the only happiness David will feel in his old home. In his absence, Clara has given birth to a son, whom the Murdstones possessively coddle. In contrast to the Peggottys, who welcome all and share willingly, the Murdstones put up impenetrable walls around themselves, as if David and his mother carry a contagious illness. David soon finds that he is not on equal terms with the new addition to the family. Shortly after he arrives home for his month-long visit, he innocently takes the newborn from his mother's lap and holds him tenderly. Miss Murdstone is appalled: "The boy has got the baby!" (125), she screams, almost implying that David's mere touch will infect the Murdstone child. Later on, when his mother indiscreetly compares the two boys' appearances and declares "that the baby's eyes and David's are exactly alike" (125), Miss Murdstone erupts:

> *They are not at all alike. They are exactly unlike. They are utterly dissimilar in all respects. I hope they will remain ever so. I will not sit here, and hear such comparisons made.* (123)

David realizes his status in the Murdstone household is that of an intruder. He is forced to remain apart and to adopt a defensive wariness; so long as he stays out of their sight, he cannot irritate the Murdstones, or so he thinks. Even this posture, however, creates tensions. In spite of the fact that he and his sister's egotism has provoked David's detachment, Mr. Murdstone professes himself outraged by it: "You have kept your own room when you ought to have been here. You know now, once for all, that I require you to be here and not there" (127).

The holiday, mercifully, at last ends. As David leaves for London, he looks back from his carriage at his mother, who has just kissed him goodbye: "So I lost her. So I saw her afterwards, in my sleep at school—a silent presence near my bed—looking at me with the same intent face—holding up her baby in her arms" (129).

This is the last time he will see either mother or child alive.

The news of his mother's death comes just as David is settling in for the new school term. Mrs. Creakle tries to comfort David by stressing the melancholy fact that those we love must "pass away" and we must learn to accept and bear this harsh reality. David copes by sleepwalking his way through his mother's final rites, which end with her burial and that of her baby, who has died with her, to the total consternation of the Murdstones. As the days pass, David becomes listless and even more cut off as the Murdstones, closed off in their own grieving, give him little attention. Only Peggotty offers solace as she walks David through his mother's last hours and repeats her final request: "Let my dearest boy go with us to our resting-place,' she said, "and tell him that his mother, when she lay here, blessed him not once, but a thousand times" (141).

David's misery intensifies as he learns that Peggotty has been given her notice and that he will not be going back to Salem House. If there is an alternate plan for his education, it is not revealed since David "is never sought out or enquired for" (142). Peggotty thereupon intervenes to rescue him, at least temporarily, by inviting David back to Yarmouth for rest and renewal. On their way, she lightens the mood considerably by informing David she will be getting married soon to the coachman, Barkis. David is delighted because he had served the two as a message bearer when Barkis first showed interest in Peggotty. Barkis acknowledges this assistance laconically: "I'm a friend of your'n. You made it all right, first. It's all right" (146). Here is yet another illustration of the readiness of common people to express gratitude and to place a well-spoken young "gentleman" on a pedestal. In the company of Barkis, Peggotty, and the rest of the clan, David's spirits are lifted and his self-esteem restored. He can hope seriously to make a fresh start.

In Yarmouth, little Em'ly is a welcome presence, but the two are not as close as they were before. Em'ly is now "more of a woman" (151), with a job and friends and aspirations. She listens with special interest to David's description of Steerforth, whom Daniel Peggotty and Ham had met when they visited David at Salem House. David's words are colored by admiration and gratitude, but no insight; Steerforth's conduct toward Mr. Mell, for instance, is never mentioned:

> *"Then, he's such a generous, fine, noble fellow," said I, quite carried away by my favorite theme, "that it's hardly possible to give him as much praise as he deserves. I am sure I can never feel thankful enough for the generosity with which he has protected me, so much younger and lower in the school than himself."* (151)

Em'ly is clearly fascinated. David cannot help noticing "little Em'ly's face, which was bent forward over the table, listening with the deepest attention, her breath held, her blue eyes sparkling like jewels, and the color mounting in her cheeks" (151). In light of what will occur later, Em'ly's intense response reveals more than ordinary curiosity. A writer like Stendhal would have played up the sexual excitement Em'ly is experiencing as David speaks. Dickens, however, like almost all English authors before D. H. Lawrence, develops nothing in connection with this theme. English morality frowns on sexual experience outside of marriage and, even among the married, the less said about it the better.

This happy interlude ends with the wedding of Peggotty and Barkis and a renewed commitment by his old nurse to David's welfare: "Young or old, Davy dear, as long as I am alive and have this house over my head," said Peggotty, "you shall find it as if I expected you here directly minute" (156).

The Murdstone home is not like Peggotty's. David is about as welcome there as a long forgotten and despised relative. He immediately falls back into a depressing isolation. Only his books break the mood, allowing David, like young Tom Sawyer, to enter into fantasies of a more purposeful life. Mr. Murdstone, of course, cares nothing for fantasies and decides David should cease daydreaming and start working, because "to the young this is a world for action and not for moping and droning in" (159). He will become an employee of Murdstone and Grinby's, a large concern with a warehouse in London supplying "wines and spirits to certain pocket ships" (162). According to his stepfather, employment there will make David "conform to the ways of the working world, and to bend it and break it" (160). This daily combat will have the added effect of breaking something else, David's stubborn spirit, which Miss Murdstone knows must be "crushed" (160). For his own good, therefore, David will be sent away to "fight with the world" (160), and, not incidentally, walk completely out of the lives of the Murdstones.

David's time at *Murdstone and Grinby's* is the nadir of a young life already marked by abuse, neglect, sorrow, and loss. Stung by the failure to see nothing of the promise he knows he has and hurt so deeply by being "thrown away" (161), David approaches his new workplace with the same resignation Julien Sorel shows outside the seminary. The old warehouse is "literally overrun with rats" (162), and David's dreary work routine consists of nothing more than cleaning used wine bottles and pasting labels on new ones for hours on end day after day. His coworkers are about as compatible as Sorel's fellow seminarians. David gives anguished expression to his despair in one of the novel's most poignant sentences:

> *No words can express the secret agony of my soul as I sunk into this companionship, compared these henceforth everyday associates with those of my happier*

> *childhood, not to say with Steerforth, Traddles, and the rest of those boys, and felt my hopes of growing up to be a learned and distinguished man crushed in my bosom.* (163)

The boys sense that their new associate is different, referring to him as "the little gent" or "the young Suffolker" (170). To establish some kind of connection, David resorts to storytelling, something his friends at Salem House liked. This is, however, the extent of his interaction with them. He knows he is an outlier in this rough environment and must cope with his lot alone: "I led the same secretly unhappy life, but I led it in the same lonely, self-reliant manner" (174).

Though he is not close to his coworkers, David does develop a good relationship with the family with whom he boards while working at *Murdstone and Grimby's*. This is the Micawber family, headed by Wilkins, a man who, upon their first meeting, impresses David by displaying "a certain condescending roll in his voice, and a certain indescribable air of doing something genteel" (163). Wilkins Micawber is one of Dickens's great creations, a character who, in his excessive self-regard, magniloquent speech, and conviction of superiority despite the obviously strained circumstances of his and his family's daily existence, resembles the *miles gloriosus* of classical literature, the soldier whose actual achievements pale in comparison to his sense of himself as an unparalleled leader of men. Micawber projects no military airs, but his theatricality is just as riveting. David reacts to this, sensing he is in the presence of someone like an *émigré grand seigneur* reduced by the times to a needy state totally foreign to his birthright. In preparing to visit what will be his new home, David takes care to wash his "hands and face, to do the greater honor to his [Micawber's] gentility" (165).

The great man and his family are living hand to mouth in shabby, cramped surroundings they are forced to share with David to secure rental income, which is just about the only income the household can count on while its head perpetually waits for "something to turn up." Over the course of his time with them, David will assist the family in pawning dishes and other disposable items, and will move willingly to "a quiet back garret with a sloping roof" (174) in the neighborhood of King's Bench Prison when the Micawbers are sentenced there for debt.

His relationship with the Micawbers is trying, but it is important to David. In contrast to the Murdstones, who ignore his existence, the Micawbers treat David as a "young gentleman" and take him into their confidence. Their eagerness to assist him soon evolves into a need to be assisted by him. They become mutually dependent. David wants very much to help a genteel family improve its fortunes, and the Micawbers want very much to utilize his services. David recognizes this bond: "A curious equality of friendship, originating, I suppose, in our respective circumstances, sprang up between me and these people, notwithstanding the ludicrous disparity in our years" (171). The Micawbers make David feel needed and wanted. They induce him to share his time, talent, and meager resources with them, since they are the only people he cares about or who care about him in his current situation. He becomes for them what Peggotty always is for him, "an ever-present help in time of trouble." His dutiful concern and service allow him to feel empathy for others while enduring his own disappointments:

> *In my forlorn state I became quite attached to the family, and used to walk about, busy with Mrs. Micawber's calculations of ways and means, and heavy with the weight of Mr. Micawber's debts.* (170)

All of this manifests charity, the greatest of the theological virtues and the keystone of Christian living.

With the Micawbers in prison, David's decision-making must be a solitary exercise. There is value in this, however, since it contributes to the development of the self-reliance he has been nurturing ever since he left the Murdstones. This does not come without costs, as David realizes:

> *From Monday morning until Saturday night, I had no advice, no counsel, no encouragement, no consolation, no assistance, no support, of any kind, from anyone, that I can call to mind, as I hope to go to Heaven.* (167)

Painful as it is, this isolation compels David to determine what he will eat, what he will save, what he will do in the hours he is not at the warehouse, how he will assist the Micawbers, and so forth. The result is a steady acceptance of responsibility and an increased confidence in his own judgment. David may feel as if his "rescue from this kind of existence" (170) as a "common drudge" (180) is impossible, but the seeds of his emancipation are being planted. David has learned self-reliance as a survival mechanism, but it can also be a liberator.

While in prison, Mr. Micawber, who is subject to bipolar episodes, has not fallen into the kind of suicidal despair his mood swings frequently produce. Instead, he has spent considerable time preparing a petition "to the House of Commons, praying for an alteration in the law of imprisonment for debt" (175). The prisoners' "club" endorses this initiative, whereupon at an appointed day and time, all the club members, as well as the rest of the population, arrive to hear the petition read and to sign the appeal. Though this proceeding is more comical than practical, especially when a prison official insists on reading the entire document to anyone who wishes to hear it prior to signing, the petition is effective. The Micawbers are released just as the appeal is "ripe for hearing" (177), confirming, to some degree, Mrs. Micawber's unshakeable conviction that her husband "is a man of great talent" (178). This talent, she assures David, has a better chance of being recognized outside London, specifically at the Custom House in Plymouth, where her family has influence.

The departure of the Micawbers is pivotal. David, says Mr. Micawber, has "never been a lodger" but, rather, "a friend" (181), "who has the heart to feel for the distresses of his fellow creatures" (181). On the day the Micawbers leave, Mrs. Micawber does something only his late mother and his nurse Peggotty have:

> *. . . she beckoned to me to climb up, with quite a new and motherly expression in her face, and put her arm round my neck, and gave me just such a kiss as she might have given to her own boy.* (182–183)

David's kind, generous, and selfless nature has emerged through his acquaintance with the Micawbers, and what he calls their "commendation" (181) is the most heartfelt encouragement he has so far received.

Once they separate, David realizes he cannot return to a life without prospects or purpose in the wretched warehouse. He resolves to make a dramatic break with what has gone before. He rests his hope for regeneration on his imperious aunt, Betsey Trotwood, the story of whose kindness to his mother during his birth he has always treasured. David will walk to her cottage in Dover, introduce and identify himself to his aunt, and ask her for assistance in beginning a new life. Before this, however, he will go out of his way to make his employer whole and keep his conscience clear:

> *Being a very honest little creature, and unwilling to disgrace the memory I was going to leave behind me at Murdstone and Grinby's, I considered myself bound to remain until Saturday night, and, as I had been paid a week's wages in advance when I first came there, not to present myself in the counting house at the usual hour, to receive my stipend.* (184)

David does just as he promises, and then, with all his worldly goods packed into a box to be sent ahead, he begins his walk to freedom.

The journey will be long and difficult, not least because he is not sure exactly where his aunt lives or if she will even receive him. The long peregrination will also be important as a learning experience and a test of character. David will do in a few days what Bunyan's Faithful does over an adult lifetime, overcoming all kinds of obstacles and roadblocks and persevering in spite of the hostility of so many of those he meets on his way. He will have to cope with a segment of the "human comedy" harder and meaner than any of the boys in the warehouse, but in the midst of whom his native intelligence and newfound self-reliance will enable him to navigate successfully.

David starts out inauspiciously. Because his box is too heavy to carry to "the booking office" for transport to Dover, David asks a "long-legged young man with a very little empty donkey cart" (184) to help him. This is a classic encounter between a polite young "gentleman," who quickly apologizes for giving the impression he is staring at the other boy ("I stopped to assure him I had not done so in bad manners." (184-85)) and a street tough, who could easily have fit into a gang. The street-smart stranger agrees to transport the box in his cart. David is grateful and unsuspecting. As he pauses to tie the address card to the box, David places a half-guinea in his mouth to free his hands. His helper promptly strikes David under his chin, forcing the coin out and catching it in his hand. David is astounded and responds as a polite young man who believes in law, order, and good manners would: "You give me my money back, if you please," said I, very much frightened, "and leave me alone" (185). Having paid no attention, the young man quickly exits the scene, leaving David in tears and telling him to "come to the pollis" (186) if he is so upset. After a fruitless chase, he gives up. Nevertheless, despite losing his possessions and money, David remains firm in his determination to complete his journey, even if it means "taking very little more out of the world, towards the retreat of my aunt, Miss Betsey, than I had brought into it" (186).

This experience is one of several that will present David with a slice of life that thinks and acts differently and challenges all he upholds. David believes in honest dealing, so when he decides to sell his waistcoat at a little shop where "ladies' and gentlemen's wardrobes" are bought, he enters and offers to sell the item for "a fair price" (187). The proprietor asks David to name this price. Not used to this kind of bargaining, David replies, "Oh, you know best, sir" (187), respecting the shopkeeper's expertise and experience. But Mr. Dolloby knows he has a naïve youngster in his control and refuses. Once David is goaded into naming a price, the proprietor ostentatiously gives him the garment back and laments that he would be robbing his family if he were to give just half of what David proposes. Since he is desperate for cash, David offers to take the half, even if it pains him to be the cause of the family's suffering. "Not without some grumbling" (188), Mr. Dolloby pays him ninepence. David has stumbled into a world where values are fluid, prices are arbitrary, and craft, guile, and bluff prevail. The boy who could not shortchange his hated employer has to learn to maneuver in these unfamiliar surroundings without violating principle.

Soon he is tested again. David needs more money if he is to continue his journey without hunger or thirst. Since the clothes on his back are the only valuables he has, he decides to sell his jacket next. David stumbles into a shop "at the corner of a dirty lane" and is horrified when "an ugly old man" (190) "smelling terribly of rum" (191) grabs him by the hair and asks him "in a fierce, monotonous whine" (191) what he wants. "Trembling" (191), David offers to sell him his jacket. The wild-eyed proprietor proposes an exchange. David holds out for cash and resolves to wait for payment no matter how long it takes. It takes very long: "And I sat there so many hours, that the shade became sunlight, and the sunlight became shade again, and still I sat there waiting for the money" (192).

The proprietor haggles fiercely, even going so far as to threaten "to tear me in pieces" (192) if David will not take less and leave. Finally, he cuts his losses, accepts "fourpence" (193), and moves on. In the environment he is now in, valuations are what the stronger party says they are, not what a fair market exchange calculates.

David's final brush with the denizens of society's margins is brief but unnerving. Over the course of his odyssey, he has encountered "trampers," but has always been able to steer clear of them. The day after he sells his jacket, however, David is accosted by a young tinker and a woman with "a black eye" (193). The tinker demands that David stop in his tracks or face an assault ("I'll rip your young body open" (193)). After asking David if he is a "prig" and promising to do him bodily harm if he brags of his "honesty" (194), the tinker tears David's silk handkerchief from off his neck, claiming that it is really the property of the tinker's brother. As the tinker does so, his woman friend makes the mistake of laughing and then throwing the cloth back to David. She mouths the word "Go!" (194) to him while she is being manhandled by the tinker, who retrieves the handkerchief. David runs away immediately, but the sight of this kind woman "sitting on the pathway . . . wiping the blood from her face with a corner of her shawl," will be something he "never shall forget" (194).

He arrives at Dover at last. Here David experiences one more instance of gratuitous cruelty. As he asks "boatmen," fly-drivers," and shopkeepers" (195), the way to his aunt's home, they all react intemperately, allowing sarcasm, crude humor, or cold indifference to frustrate the boy's efforts to find the right route. David is very near the end of his rope by this time and wonders how he can ever reach his destination:

> *I felt more miserable and destitute than I had done at any period of my running away. My money was all gone; I had nothing left to dispose of; I was hungry, thirsty, and worn out, and seemed as distant from the end as if I had remained in London.* (195)

Luckily, a fly driver redeems the human race when he answers David's query honestly and gives the boy a penny as he resumes his travels. David reaches his destination forthwith, and after some initial surprise and suspicion, Miss Betsey welcomes him cordially. She is strong-willed and commanding, taking particular umbrage at young boys playing on her property or, worse, allowing horses to tear up her lawn. She also has borne a peculiar prejudice against David ever since his birth. Aunt Betsey had anticipated a girl's coming into the world on the evening his mother gave birth to David, taking great care to comfort and encourage her niece as she began her labor. When she learned "she" was really a "he" and obviously could not be named after her, Aunt Betsey left the scene abruptly, not to be seen again until now. Underneath her crusty exterior, however, Betsey is loving and affectionate. She is a *grande dame*, like Micawber is a *grand seigneur*, and though neither is living as such, they both respond to the imperatives of *noblesse oblige*. Aunt Betsey relies for advice on her live-in companion, Mr. Dick, a kind of *idiot savant* who plays the "fool" to his regal mistress, and like King Lear's witty retainer, in critical situations, gives common sense counsel that strikes his lady as heaven-sent wisdom. Thus, when Betsey asks Dick what should be done with David and Dick answers that he should be "put to bed" (205), David's future with his aunt is assured. Aunt Betsey knows one does not put a guest "to bed" if he or she is not welcome in the home, so, by her doing as Dick recommends, Betsey accepts David as her charge, insisting only that he call himself "Trotwood Copperfield" henceforth.

Throughout this first meeting, Aunt Betsey displays a confidence and sureness that will be her characteristic style throughout David's life with her. Her eccentricity, while as theatrical as Micawber's, can yield brilliantly perceptive insight, as when she deplores how David's mother had foolishly married "a Murderer—or a man with a name like it" (204). Aunt Betsey's motivations, however, are not marred by egotism or conceit. Her need is not to control but to expedite. Before David knows quite what has happened, therefore, he has bathed, been given new clothes, and offered a comfortable bed for some necessary rest. He expresses his gratitude in terms that highlight the selflessness his harrowing journey has reinforced:

> *I remember how I thought of all the solitary places under the night sky where I had slept, and how I prayed that I might never be houseless any more, and never might forget the houseless.* (206)

This concluding sentiment sums up David's young character. He has grown in empathy and magnanimity, while resisting resentment and bitterness. He has seen cold cruelty in the Murdstones and casual cruelty in Creakle and rejected these completely as contrary to nature. Though they have both alternately mistreated or neglected him, as later encounters will reveal, David bears no grudges. He will be civil, as a gentleman should be. By contrast, David has seen in the Peggotty family and in his schoolmate Traddles an openness to strangers, a willingness to share, a concern for others' feelings and comfort, and an indifference to self, all of which he embraces as right and good. Steerforth has entered his life like a bright comet trailing glory in its wake. The spectacle is so arresting it dazzles the beholder. This superstar has condescended to befriend "Davy" at a time when friendship was as essential to David as oxygen. For this, David was and will always remain deeply grateful. But Steerforth is a person of undisciplined habits and unpredictable mood and temper, the spoiled and touchy son of an adoring mother. When his vanity is aroused, as it is once Mr. Mell calls him out, Steerforth changes instantly. The charm and *bonhomie* vanish, to be replaced by arrogant self-assertion. David reacts against this behavior, particularly since he realizes he has been very much to blame for the terrible consequences befalling Mr. Mell. He is shamed and contrite, knowing a young gentleman should never be the cause of so much pain. And a young gentleman he will continue to be. David does not associate with his fellow workers at *Murdstone and Grinby's,* and he is repelled by the "low life" characters he meets on the way to Dover. Never is he tempted to descend into the depths of wretchedness they inhabit. He responds to those who are "to the manner born," like Micawber and Aunt Betsey, but show none of the vices of privilege. David inclines toward the Anglican "middle way," steering clear of lower-class lawlessness as well as upper class self-indulgence. In this approach to life, David will set himself apart from Julien Sorel, whose compulsion to master his world he can never share, and from Huck Finn, who follows conscience but cannot bear the wounds to innocence immersion in a harsh world inevitably causes. Young David learns to cope without surrendering basic decency, and in making the momentous decision to walk to Dover, he shows the gumption and self-reliance so admired in the English-speaking world. David has picked himself up by his bootstraps and moved forward. By the time he has arrived at his aunt's cottage, he is ready to take positive steps to improve his lot in life while being guided always by the virtues he has made his own.

PART THREE

The middle section of David *Copperfield* details David's steady progress toward becoming a person of note and his likewise steady advance in moral understanding and discrimination. Three strands make up this section: 1) The resumption of David's education and his slow realization of his vocation; 2) David's emotional experience, culminating in his marriage; and 3) David's renewed association with Steerforth, ending in Steerforth's betrayal of all David has invested in their friendship. In this long segment, new characters will appear, new locales will be explored, and new professional and romantic encounters will be highlighted. Nevertheless, the people and places that have played so important a role in David's youth will remain equally important to him as a maturing adult, giving continuity to the tale and keeping David firmly grounded in a familiar environment.

Once settled in, David is relieved to be with his aunt and wisely notes after observing her closely for several days: "There was something about my aunt, notwithstanding her many eccentricities and odd humours, to be honored and trusted in" (212). His faith is not misplaced. After a disagreeable meeting with the Murdstones, who still see David as incorrigible, Aunt Betsey takes responsibility for the boy's upbringing, welcoming the consequence Mr. Murdstone threatens: "If you step in between him and me, now, you must step in Miss Trotwood, forever" (217). Heeding Mr. Dick's suggestion, she arranges that David should be outfitted in a new suit, but she inscribes "Trotwood Copperfield" as its owner (221). This will be the name by which David will be known for some time, symbolizing a new beginning. David senses this and knows his life has taken an abrupt turn, but so much has happened so quickly, he is dazed:

> *The two things clearest in my mind were that a remoteness had come upon the old Blunderstone life—which seemed to lie in the haze of an immeasurable distance, and that a curtain had forever fallen on my life at Murdstone and Grinby's.* (221)

David now begins a life course fundamentally different from the treadmill repetitiveness of child labor. His aunt decides that he must be placed in a school focused on the full development of a child's potential. Returning to school is, in itself, remarkable, since only a tiny percentage of non-privileged children in mid-nineteenth century England completed an elementary education, but to be sent to something like a Victorian equivalent of a Montessori establishment makes David's experience practically unique. After hearing that Aunt Betsey wants David to attend the "best school," Mr. Wickfield, a lawyer friend who manages her financial affairs, recommends the one run by his friend, Dr. Strong, in Canterbury. Since no living quarters are currently available at this school, Mr. Wickfield offers to board David in his own home while he is enrolled there. Aunt Betsey concurs but insists upon paying for such. Knowing his client's pride, Mr. Wickfield assents, but, true to his own generous and open character, does not dwell on costs: "You shall not be oppressed by the receipt of favors, Miss Trotwood. You may pay for him, if you like. We won't be hard about terms, but you shall pay if you will" (228). Clearly, David is going to be in "a great, good place."

Both Aunt Betsey and Mr. Dick, whom David has grown fond of, are sad to see their ward leave them, even if his departure is in the boy's best interests. Mr. Dick gives him money for his personal use, just as Peggotty had, and Aunt Betsey admonishes him to be "a credit to yourself, to me, and Mr. Dick" (229). She also offers this sage addendum: "Never," said my aunt, "be mean in anything, never be false; never be cruel. Avoid these three vices, Trot, and I can always be hopeful of you" (229). What counts for Aunt Betsey is not money, power, pleasure, popularity, influence, or any other false ideal; in good English fashion, her parting words emphasize David's development of character.

David, or "Trot" as he will be known in his new circle, is receptive and takes his aunt's maxims to heart. His conduct since the disgrace of Mr. Mell has been a "credit" to everyone who cherishes him. David has also become much more "worldly wise" since his experiences in Creakle's school, in the blacking factory, and on the road. As he becomes acquainted with Mr. Wickfield and the members of his household and legal office, Trot responds perceptively to each, instinctively sensing upon first meeting, whether a person is someone to be cultivated as a mentor or friend or one to be watched closely as a potential Iago. Mr. Wickfield is clearly one of the former, extending aid and hospitality to Trot without hesitation or condition and making all the arrangements necessary to his studies. But Mr. Wickfield is at the service of all equally. He is not innocent or naïve, but he is guileless, not capable of seeing through complicated schemes until forced to acknowledge and deal with them too late. He is a man of steadfast virtue, like Chaucer's knight, honorable in all dealings and loyal to antique codes of conduct. Trot's first impression of him hints at the purity of his character:

> *He was very cleanly dressed, in a blue coat, striped waistcoat, and nankeen trousers, and his fine frilled shirt and cambric neckcloth looked unusually soft and white, reminding my strolling fancy (I call to mind) of the plumage on the breast of a swan.* (226)

His home/office complex is similar:

> *It was quite spotless in its cleanliness. The old-fashioned brass knocker on the low arched door, ornamented with carved garlands of fruit and flowers, twinkled like a star; the two stone steps descending to*

> *the door were as white as if they had been covered with fair linen, and all the angles and corners, and carvings and mouldings, and quaint little panes of glass, and quainter little windows, though as old as the hills, were as pure as any snow that ever fell upon the hills.* (224)

"Purity" is the most applicable term in any consideration of Mr. Wickfield's young daughter, Agnes. Trot sees something in her that suggests holiness:

> *I cannot call to mind where or when, in my childhood, I had seen a stained-glass window in a church. Nor do I recollect its subject. But I know that when I saw her turn round, in the grave light of the old staircase, and wait for us, above, I thought of that window, and I associated something of its tranquil brightness with Agnes Wickfield ever afterwards.* (229)

Agnes's ministrations to her father are gentle and sensitive, and his devotion to her is just as kind, so Trot, on his first evening with the Wickfields, sees the two at their most characteristic. Agnes's character reflects all the emphasis on feminine virtue so many contemporary English writers and commentators upheld. This has been attributed by many to the influence of Queen Victoria, whose relationship with her husband, Prince Albert, modeled for the entire nation proper wedded harmony. The royal example was certainly influential, but the English stress on modesty, virtue, and plain living among young women, especially, is integral to the culture. The poor, like Little Em'ly, the middle class, like Agnes, and the privileged, like Steerforth's mother, embrace the same ideal. The women in Jane Austen's and George Eliot's works adhere to this code without question, and, especially in Eliot's rural world, suffer terribly when even the most minor lapses occur. Sexuality does not come into play except as a demonic temptation. In contrast to Julien Sorel, who is typically French in responding strongly to the sexual attractiveness of the women he meets, Trot will not see Agnes as a possible sexual partner, and therefore mate, until nearly the end of the novel. For most of their time together, she dispenses advice, offers support and consolation, and guides Trot along paths of righteousness, all the while keeping under stern control any romantic attraction he exerts on her. This is a "chaste goddess" in the flesh.

Trot meets one more person in the Wickfield establishment who, on the surface, seems like a devoted son. Uriah Heep is Mr. Wickfield's clerk, a young man who lives with his mother in a little apartment and is aspiring by grit and application to rise in the legal profession. Uriah's situation, at first sight, reminds one of Mr. Mell's, albeit with an entirely different master. To Trot, however, there is really no such resemblance; he recoils from Uriah Heep as soon as the two are introduced, just as he did with Mr. Murdstone. Uriah twists himself like an eel upon making a new acquaintance, and Trot dislikes this ostentatious display of deference immediately. His experience with all sorts of odd behaviors in the menacing characters he had to deal with on the way to Dover, undoubtedly makes Trot wary of Uriah's motivations in abasing himself before him. Heep's features are also disturbing, particularly his eyes. Whereas purity radiates from Agnes and her father, only fire glows in Uriah's persistent gaze:

> *. . . it made me uncomfortable to observe that, every now and then, his sleepless eyes would come below the writing, like two red suns, and stealthily stare at me for I daresay a whole minute at a time . . . and whenever I looked towards those two red suns, I was sure to find them, either just rising or just setting.* (227)

As Trot will discover, Uriah operates like Chaucer's pardoner, a man forcing himself on the gullible and fearful, shaking them down shamelessly, and treacherously betraying associates if doing so will advance his ends. All of this will emerge over time; for now, Trot is only put off by this character's serpent-like presence:

> *As I came back, I saw Uriah Heep shutting up the office, and feeling friendly towards everybody, went in and spoke to him, and at parting, gave him my hand. But oh, what a clammy hand his was! As ghostly to the touch as to the sight! I rubbed mine afterwards, to warm it, and to rub his off.* (230)

Trot's new school is led by Dr. Strong, who might have been Mr. Wickfield's identical twin, given all the resemblance between them. He, too, is open and kind, making the same impression with his smile as Mr. Wickfield does at his ease, "for it was full of amiability and sweetness, and there was a simplicity in it, and indeed in his whole manner, when the studious, pondering frost upon it was got through" (233). Like Mr. Wickfield, who has "articled" Uriah at his own expense and senses nothing of his real nature, Dr. Strong is "good will to all" personified. Calling again upon his experience on the fringes of society, Trot can see quickly that "outside his own domain, and unprotected, he [Dr. Strong] was a very sheep for the shearers" (243), who include his grasping mother-in-law and her "world of poor relations" (242). Dr. Strong is also deeply attached to his young wife, Annie, who fusses over him as Agnes does Mr. Wickfield and whom the doctor likewise adores: "He had a fatherly, benignant way of showing his fondness for her, which seemed in itself to express a good man" (244).

Trot, at first, feels ill at ease at school. He realizes it has been some time since he has had to study, so he has to accept being "put into the lowest form of the school" (234); his classmates, too, are different from the youths he has been dealing with since he began work at the blacking factory. They are altogether removed from such settings, and are therefore more naïve about common humanity: "How would it affect them, who were so innocent of London life and London streets, to discover how knowing I was (and was ashamed to be) in some of the meanest phases of both?" (234) Although Trot may regard his immersion in the less attractive side of life as something like a disability that should be kept hidden, it is, as the reader realizes, an important advantage. His firsthand knowledge and experience are far better guides to evaluating people, places, and possibilities than any accumulation of textbook learning can provide.

Nevertheless, under the tutelage of Dr. Strong, "who was one of the gentlest of men" (235), Trot's uneasiness vanishes, and he begins to thrive. He is aided in his academic endeavors by the way Dr. Strong manages his enterprise. His style is, in a word, "enlightened":

> *Dr. Strong's was an excellent school, as different from Mr. Creakle's as good is from evil. It was very gravely and decorously ordered, and on a sound system, with an appeal, in everything, to the honour and good faith of the boys, and an avowed intention to rely on their possession of those qualities unless they proved themselves unworthy of it, which worked wonders.* (242)

Here is another example of the best qualities of the English character coming to the fore. At a time when corporal punishment in schools was common and severe, and when schoolmasters assumed all the power of petty tyrants and exercised it in ways that reduced students to dependency, Dr. Strong goes against the grain by empowering his charges. He trusts them to be the best they can be, and they reward his trust by living and working to the highest standards. The whole concept of self-government in political affairs is exemplified in microcosm in the operation of this school, as is the notion that virtue will govern conduct, not because of compulsion but because the path of virtue is the better choice for those schooled in responsibility.

Mr. Dick, Aunt Betsey's faithful companion, begins making regular visits to Trot at Dr. Strong's school. He soon develops the habit of accompanying the doctor on his daily walks. Dr. Strong is in the midst of a project that consumes his free hours. He is trying to compile a new dictionary, and is "always engaged in looking out for Greek roots" (243) to clarify etymologies. The work is slow, tedious, and seemingly endless. One of Trot's fellow students, "who had a turn for mathematics," has determined that it will take Dr. Strong "one thousand six hundred and forty-nine years" (243) to complete his task. Mr. Dick, too, is involved in a challenging project, "a memorial of his own history" that will be "submitted to the Lord Chancellor or the Lord Somebody or other" (211) when finished. This effort has been continuing for upwards of ten years, but King Charles I, the seventeenth-century "martyred king," keeps intruding in Mr. Dick's thoughts as he writes, forcing him to lose concentration and focus. These two from opposite ends of the human spectrum—one, a scholar and master, the other, one whom most would consider mentally challenged—form a bond as the doctor reads out portions of his tome to Mr. Dick, and Mr. Dick flies his kite with pages of the memorial pasted to it for broad dissemination as they detach. Though the dreams of each will never be fulfilled, they are as one in their passionate desire to leave some mark upon the world and to affirm their value. Differences in class, background, education, and the rest vanish as the master and the simpleton embrace their common purpose and share their common humanity. David loves them both, since in their kindness and simplicity they have restored his spirits and given him hope.

For very different reasons, Uriah would like to bond with David (as he will be known again). He begins by inviting "Master Copperfield" to meet his mother. David's instinctive distrust of Uriah and his "umbleness" makes this invitation unwelcome, but he accepts anyway. The scene portraying the three sharing tea and conversation in the Heeps' cramped lodging is reminiscent of David's meeting with Mr. Mell and his mother prior to his arrival at Creakle's school. This *tete-a-tete*, though, is very different. In contrast to Mr. Mell and his mother, who are open and frank with David, the Heeps do not confide in their guest anything of significance; instead, they draw David out at length about his life experience and his relations with Mr. Wickfield and Agnes. They do so by working as a team:

> *Uriah threw the ball to Mrs. Heep, Mrs. Heep caught it and threw it back to Uriah, Uriah kept it up a*

> *little while, then sent it back to Mrs. Heep, and so they went on tossing it about until I had no idea who had got it, and was quite bewildered.* (262)

The purpose is to suck David dry and file away whatever he has divulged that might be of use against him later. Uriah's great aim is one day to be Mr. Wickfield's son-in-law and successor. Given his favored situation as a boarder of the family and a student in Dr. Strong's school, David is a potential rival who has to be foiled lest he upset these best-laid plans. Any time, therefore, he reveals something that matters, David sees its impact in "the twinkling of Uriah's dented nostrils" (262). For mother and son, knowledge is power. The "umbleness" Uriah tries to radiate and his mother reinforces masks a vengeful resentment. Instead of accepting his past as a workhouse boy and striving to make the most of his current opportunity, as David is doing, Uriah is bent on raising his station at the expense of everyone else. Julien Sorel uses hypocrisy to advance his ambitions, but in circumstances where his gifts can shine, he demonstrates his talents with forthright candor. Uriah Heep never does, not only because his is a dull and plodding intellect but also because self-abasement makes him less threatening, the kind of person who ingratiates himself with others by appearing always ready to perform some service. With the exception of street-smart David, his victims let their guard down, never suspecting the intrigues this person is capable of spinning.

David sees Heep in action one more time as, later that evening, he watches Uriah walk by with none other than Mr. Micawber, who is in Canterbury looking for employment and has stumbled upon David and the Heeps quite by accident:

> . . . *it surprised me, and made me rather uneasy, to see Mr. Micawber and Uriah Heep walk past, arm in arm, Uriah humbly sensible of the honour that was done him, and Mr. Micawber taking a bland delight in extending his patronage to Uriah.* (267)

Micawber afterwards tells David that "your friend Heep is a young fellow who might be attorney-general" (268), indicating that he too has been gulled.

David learns that Mr. Micawber has made little progress in his search for suitable employment. As Mrs. Micawber remarks ruefully in connection with the Plymouth Custom House, "They would rather *not* have a man of Mr. Micawber's abilities. He would only show the deficiency of the others" (265). She is also upset by her family's failure to welcome her husband to Plymouth with enthusiasm: "They did not receive him with that ardour which he might have expected, being so newly released from captivity" (265). The contrast between what seems like the absurd pretensions of Mrs. Micawber and the reality of Mr. Micawber's situation is highlighted again and again in comical passages like the preceding, and even David has to confess to being "relieved" (270) when they leave him. Micawber, however, will have occasion later to display exceptional talent in exposing and unraveling the complicated financial manipulations Heep has been engaging in at the expense of Mr. Wickfield and David's aunt, among others. Just as Aunt Betsey's faith in Mr. Dick is amply justified by his sensible interventions, so too Mrs. Micawber's high estimation of her husband's gifts will be vindicated by events. Dick, Micawber, Mr. Wickfield, Dr. Strong, Mr. Mell, and the like are only temporarily ground down by circumstances or rogues; eventually they will "inherit the earth" because they live for others. This very English preference for common decency and respect for all, eccentric or weak notwithstanding, shines through Dickens's pages.

David, meanwhile, makes steady progress at Dr. Strong's school, earning plaudits from those he loves:

> *I am growing great in Latin verses, and neglect the laces of my boots. Doctor Strong refers to me in public as a promising young scholar. Mr. Dick is wild with joy, and my aunt remits me a guinea by the next post.* (272)

Soon he will become "the head boy" (273), a triumph for one who entered the school so disadvantaged. David is also becoming a young gentleman: "I wear a gold watch and chain, a ring upon my little finger, and a long-tailed coat, and I use a great deal of bear's grease" (273). He is also feeling the first stirrings of romantic attraction. Though he fantasizes about a girl at a neighboring school, David still keeps Agnes uppermost in his thoughts, submerging sexual desire in his admiration of her character: ". . . Agnes, my sweet sister, as I call her in my thoughts, my counsellor and friend, the better angel of the lives of all who come within her calm, good, self-denying influence, is quite a woman" (273).

How shocking it will be to David to learn that this pure soul will be Uriah Heep's love interest and that her father, to whom she is devoted, will become the target of his clerk's blackmail.

David leaves Dr. Strong's establishment ready and eager to make his way in the world, stressing that "my desire was to apply myself to some pursuit that would not lie too heavily upon her [Aunt Betsey's] purse and to do my duty in it whatever it might be" (279). His aunt is more than willing to subsidize his professional studies but insists that he must pursue his chosen career "with strength of character that is not to be influenced, except on good reason, by anybody, or by anything" (280). She need not worry. David's character is just what she hopes for, having been tried by the most challenging circumstances and made even more firm by the gentleman's code he has assimilated at Dr. Strong's school. As he begins a sabbatical to reflect on his future, David finds himself seated atop a stage to London that is taking him through places that stimulate strong memories. Like Bunyan's pilgrim, he realizes he has come through perilous situations unscathed:

> *It was curious and interesting, nevertheless, to be sitting up there behind four horses, well-educated, well-dressed, and with plenty of money in my pocket, and to look out for the places where I had slept on my weary journey. I had abundant occupation for my thoughts, in*

> *every conspicuous landmark on the road. When I looked down at the tramps whom we passed, and saw that well-remembered style of face turned up, I felt as if the tinker's blackened hand were in the bosom of my shirt again. When we clattered through the narrow street of Chatham, and I caught a glimpse, in passing, of the lane where the old monster lived who had bought my jacket, I stretched my neck eagerly to look for the place where I had sat, in the sun and in the shade, waiting for my money.*
>
> *When we came, at last, within a stage of London, and passed the veritable Salem House where Mr. Creakle had laid about him with a heavy hand, I would have given all I had for lawful permission to get down and thrash him, and let all the boys out like so many caged sparrows. (290)*

In London, David attends a stirring performance of *Julius Caesar* and then relaxes with some "porter and oysters" (292) afterwards. While he sits in his hotel's lobby, half-asleep and still dazzled by the play, he notices "the figure of a handsome, well-formed young man, dressed with a tasteful easy negligence" (292) entering the room. He realizes instantly that this is James Steerforth, who does not recognize David. When David introduces himself, Steerforth greets him cordially, calling him "little Copperfield" and "a very Daisy" (292-93). David loses his composure in his joy at seeing again this idol of his youth: "I grasped him by both hands, and could not let them go. But for very shame, and the fear that it might displease him, I could have held him round the neck and cried" (292). All the pride genuine accomplishment has brought him quickly deserts David as he falls over himself in greeting the ruler of Salem House, "so self-possessed, and elegant, and superior to me in all respects" (295). This superiority comes to David's aid once more in a way reminiscent of Steerforth's services in Salem House. The son of privilege, very much in character, berates a waiter for assigning his friend "a little lot over a stable" (294), an offense that is rectified immediately.

Steerforth and David enjoy their reunion at the hotel, although the class and status differences linger. As if they were still at Salem House, Steerforth addresses David as "Daisy" again and tells him he is his "property" (295), so he must fill the master in on what has transpired since they parted. As their conversation ends, Steerforth invites David to visit his home, where he can meet his mother. This will be the third time David will be meeting a young man's mother, and though style, décor, and deportment at Highgate are very different from the other two domiciles, Mrs. Steerforth will prove as doting a mother as Mrs. Mell and Mrs. Heep. Indeed, her devotion to her son is absolute and unwavering; David will conclude afterwards that "she seemed to be able to speak or think about nothing else" (300). Steerforth knows this and so places her in the same category of adults in his power as Mr. Creakle and the masters of Salem House.

Upon being introduced to Mrs. Steerforth, David notes immediately "her proud carriage and a handsome face" (296), reminding him of her son's bearing and features. She then explains an incongruity that strikes most readers of the novel early on, namely, how can a boy like Steerforth languish in a school as inferior as Creakle's. The answer sheds light on the kind of thinking prevailing in the Steerforth household: "My son's high spirit made it desirable that he should be placed with some man who felt its superiority, and would be content to bow himself before it, and we found such a man there" (301). Mrs. Steerforth associates David with the same deference, commenting that at the school he was "quite devoted" to her son and that upon meeting him the night before, David had shed "tears of joy" (301). She emphasizes to David that his sentiments are perfectly understandable and that she "cannot be indifferent to anyone who is so sensible of his [Steerforth's] merit," ending by assuring David that he can always "rely on [her son's] protection" (301), as he did at Salem House.

David meets a second member of the Steerforth household on this occasion. Rosa Dartle is Mrs. Steerforth's companion and aide. She is, David guesses, about thirty, has "an appearance of good looks," and would like to be married (297). These conclusions all prove correct, confirming once again the soundness of David's judgments about all types of people. Rosa is "all edge" (299), looking about with sharp eyes and interjecting skeptical commentary when someone offers an opinion, as if she needs special convincing. A notable exchange follows David's suggestion that Steerforth join him for a visit to the Peggotty clan in Yarmouth. Steerforth has been there once before during a school holiday and welcomes the chance "to see that sort of people together and to make one of 'em" (299) again. Rosa inquires about "that sort of people," wondering if they are "really animals and clods, and beings of another order" (299). Steerforth responds "with indifference":

> *They are not to be expected to be as sensitive as we are. Their delicacy is not to be shocked, or hurt very easily. They are wonderfully virtuous, I dare say. Some people contend for that, at least, and I am sure I don't want to contradict them. But they have not very fine natures, and they may be thankful that, like their coarse rough skins, they are not easily wounded.* (299)

David thinks, at first, "Steerforth had said what he had, in jest, or to draw Miss Dartle out" (299), but this is not the case. In fact, the reference to people like the Peggottys being "wonderfully virtuous" and to those "who contend for that" seems clearly an allusion to David's profound respect for Mr. Peggotty's "generosity and kindness" (298).

This exchange reveals prejudices similar to those that came to the surface during Steerforth's public denunciation of Mr. Mell. Their brutal insensitivity makes it possible for Steerforth to perpetrate an outrageous offense a short time later, causing Mr. Peggotty and company, supposedly "not easily wounded," to suffer beyond description. David enters a different world when he crosses the threshold of Mrs. Steerforth's "genteel old-fashioned home" (297). The distortions of character, thought, and judgment produced by the Steerforths' egotism and class consciousness are similar to those exhibited by contemporary racists in the antebellum American South. Steerforth is fixated on his superiority, just as Heep is on his inferiority. Both will be brought to ruin by their failure to move beyond the limitations of their respective upbringings. David has done this and is the better for it. He has learned to embrace those who extend themselves to others and to steer clear of those who do not. Only the magnetic appeal of Steerforth's charisma and the gratitude David feels for his old friend, who "protected" him when he most needed to be shielded, keep David from recoiling in horror from someone professing such views.

All this notwithstanding, David enjoys a pleasant week with the Steerforths. He meets and marvels over Littimer, Steerforth's manservant: "I believe there never existed in his station a more respectable-looking man" (303). Littimer's services are rendered with such perfection of form that David feels like "a boy again" (305) as this gentleman and the others work to gratify his every wish. With "the dashing way he had of treating me like a plaything" (306), Steerforth highlights even more this impression of childlike dependence. David does not mind, however; he believes his friend adopts this quasi-paternal style because David is "nearer to his heart than any other friend" (306). He cannot imagine at this stage that he may be being fussed over so that he can the more readily be used.

As the week comes to an end, Steerforth agrees to join David on his visit to Yarmouth, which he describes as "a good, queer, out-of-the-way kind of hole" (306). He looks forward to surprising everyone so David and he can observe "the natives in their aboriginal condition" (307). On the way to see Peggotty, now Mrs. Barkis, David stops at the shop of Mr. Omer, who had presided at the burial of his mother and her baby. David learns that one of Mr. Omer's employees is Little Em'ly, who is still little but with "such a face of her own that half the women in this town are mad against her" (309). These women also resent Em'ly's perceived desire "to be a lady" (310). David dismisses these criticisms, believing that Em'ly's aspirations are not selfish but meant to uplift her family as well. As he watches her at her work, David recognizes only the spirited girl with whom he used to play, sensing "nothing in her pretty looks . . . but what was meant for goodness and for happiness, and what was on a good and happy course" (311).

The stage is now being set for what will amount to high drama. David has a loving reunion with Peggotty, whom Steerforth charms so thoroughly "she had a kind of adoration for him before he left the house that night" (314). Steerforth has a similar effect on Mr. Peggotty and his family after David and he arrive at their boat home later. Even the dour Mrs. Gummidge spends the evening "continually laughing" and confessing to being "bewitched" (322) by the young gentleman. Steerforth meets Em'ly and her betrothed, the young fisherman Ham, whom Daniel Peggotty admires: "There's a man ashore there, iron-true to my little Em'ly, God bless her, and no wrong can touch my Em'ly while so be as that man lives" (318). But Em'ly's attention is not on Ham; she is dazzled by Steerforth, at whom exclusively "she looked, and listened, and her face got animated and she was charming" (321). In this regard, she is like David, another born with ambition to rise above circumstances who sees in Steerforth what he might yet become. Em'ly's urge to be a lady and bring the benefits of such a station to her poor relatives is likewise aroused by Steerforth's superior manner. David watches his friend perform and allows his usual perceptiveness to relax. Writing much later with the clarity of hindsight, he muses on Steerforth's "brilliant game, played for the excitement of the moment, for the employment of high spirits, in the thoughtless love of superiority," but admits that on that night, he would have rejected with "indignation" (315) the expression of any such reservations. Instead, as they leave the boat house and David hears Steerforth refer to Ham as "rather a chuckle-headed fellow for the girl," David convinces himself that the "laugh in his eyes" (323) betrays Steerforth's facetiousness. He then loses himself in a delusion bred by his blind devotion to his friend:

> *Ah, Steerforth! It's well for you to joke about the poor! You may skirmish with Miss Dartle, or try to hide*

> *your sympathies in jest from me, but I know better. When I see how perfectly you understand them, how exquisitely you can enter into happiness like this plain fisherman's, or humour a love like my old nurse's, I know that there is not a joy or sorrow, not an emotion, of such people, that can be indifferent to you. And I admire and love you for it, Steerforth, twenty times the more!"* (323)

Steerforth's response to this encomium is ominous: "Daisy, I believe you are in earnest, and are good. I wish we all were!" (323). The "we" of the last sentence refers to only one man, as with royalty. A plan is being hatched which will resist "Daisy's" earnestness and forever alter David's relationship with Steerforth. Before any of this comes to pass, though, David meets Steerforth late one evening "alone in Mr. Peggotty's home, sitting thoughtfully by the fire" (326). He is serious and sad, almost like Hamlet brooding upon fate: "There was a passionate dejection in his manner that quite amazed me. He was more unlike himself than I could have supposed possible," (326) says David. Unlike Prince Hamlet, however, whose late father was an overwhelming presence, Steerforth laments the absence in his life of "a steadfast and judicious father!" (327). Had such an authority figure been on the scene throughout his youth, Steerforth is sure he "would have been better guided!" (326). A more mature young man would then be disciplined enough to resist wayward impulses. Instead, with his mother, Rosa Dartle, and Littimer always at his beck and call, his every whim has been indulged. True, he has become a young gentleman whose gifts and station inspire so many others' admiration and envy, but on this night his discontent inspires only self-loathing. He sounds again like Hamlet as the prince compares himself to Fortinbras:

> *"It would be better to be this poor Peggotty, or his lout of a nephew," he said, getting up and leaning moodily against the chimney-piece, with his face to the fire, "than to be myself, twenty times richer and twenty*

> *times wiser, and be the torment to myself that I have been, in this Devil's bark of a boat, within the last half-hour."* (326–27)

Steerforth knows what will soon occur, that he and Littmer will whisk little Em'ly away on the pretense that "she was born to be a lady" (338), and that this seduction will bring untold shame and misery to her uncle and his household, not to mention Rosa and his mother. He is suffering pangs of conscience as he contemplates the ravages his selfish conduct will produce, confirming that for him, too, the stern British moral code still governs. Steerforth is too weak to stop himself, so nothing can assuage his guilt. He is responsible for his actions and their consequences because he knowingly and willfully has violated the code. A strong father may have done much to stiffen his spine in earlier years, but this son of privilege is now too far gone in egotism to remedy his conduct. In *Ulysses*, James Joyce's Stephen Daedalus, also brilliant and proud, contends with what he calls the "agenbite of inwit," or conscience, as he wanders in search of paternal guidance and succor. He eventually meets the very ordinary but very kind-hearted and decent Leopold Bloom, with whom he makes a connection. Steerforth is not so fortunate. He is too superior to embrace Daniel Peggotty, who has been surrogate father to so many in need and who has taught Steerforth so well he has become "a wonder" as a sailor. Instead, he will betray this good man's care and concern by robbing him of his most precious loved one, the young woman whose daily presence makes Daniel Peggotty's hard life happy and purposeful. Steerforth will offer compensation, just as he did after ruining Mr. Mell. He shows David a fishing boat he has bought and tells him "Mr. Peggotty will be master of her in my absence" (329). Since Steerforth expects to be permanently absent from Yarmouth, this boat is really a gift. He christens her "The Little Em'ly," (329) as if somehow a boat could reconcile Mr. Peggotty to his loss. Steerforth's gesture hardly justifies the action he has taken; it is, however, confirmation that he has a conscience, tender or not, and that like the rich and spoiled everywhere, he will try to use his wealth to make things right. Somehow, foul deeds can be redeemed through a judicious distribution of worldly goods. Chaucer's parson would have noted in Steerforth's beneficence the lack of repentance required for the forgiveness of sinful deeds, but self-reproach and appeals for mercy are not normally part of the inner makeup of the privileged. The best a man like Steerforth can do is to try to make amends with something tangible, not with prayers but with things.

David cannot see the forest for the trees. Steerforth's words he takes at face value, confirming his friend's description of him as "an amiable piece of innocence" (328): "I could not help showing in my face how much it [the boat's name] pleased me, but I said little, and he resumed his usual smile, and seemed relieved" (329). David then has a last encounter with little Em'ly and Ham. It is so unsettling it ought to have aroused the suspicions of a young man as perceptive as he. But when Em'ly bursts out saying "I am not as good a girl as I ought to be. Not near! Not near!" (344), and asks David for help, he is uncomprehending, ascribing Em'ly's emotion to the departure for London (and vice) of Martha, her workmate at Omer's. To David, Em'ly's pleas are not signs of guilt over what is about to happen but sympathetic tears for a friend who, against all her town's values, is preparing to plunge into the abyss of a great city's street life. As such, her distress enhances Em'ly's humanity, giving "her image a new grace" (345) in David's eyes.

Although there is little mystery about what is to happen, events move slowly. Steerforth and David leave Yarmouth together as if all is in order, and they can now consider other matters, mainly, David's choice of a career. David asks Steerforth's opinion of the profession of proctor, which David's aunt has suggested as a good avenue for his abilities and for advancement up the legal ladder. His dilettante's contempt for anything like steady employment in one field and one place leads Steerforth to joke that David "may as well do that as anything else" (347). He does, however, make the point that the proctors of Doctors' Commons in London "plume themselves on their gentility there" (348), an appealing feature for an aspiring gentleman like David. David's aunt is willing to finance his training and cover his living expenses, showing once again the magnanimity and generosity that characterize the English character at its best; Aunt Betsey, however, is also investing in David's future, always keeping in mind the main goal of helping David become "a good, a sensible, and a happy man" (351). When David questions the wisdom of her divesting herself of a thousand pounds for his "articles" alone, his aunt insists that the money could not be better spent because ever since his arrival at her cottage door "all dusty and way-worn," David has been "a credit" to her and "a pride and a pleasure" (352). She has every reason to believe he will continue to be near her as a proctor and will care for her in her "age" and "bear with" her "whims and fancies" (352). Like Daniel Peggotty, Aunt Betsey is finding fulfillment in surrogate parenting, and David is rewarding her maternal care by living up to the moral and character standards British society holds dear. Nothing could be more admirable than a young man embracing these standards and being ruled by them.

David and his aunt proceed to Doctors' Commons and the office of Francis Spenlow, the proctor who has prepared her will and who will mentor David. A dialogue between Spenlow and David ensues, which stands out as a first-rate example of Dickens's comic genius. David wants Mr. Spenlow to agree that the "premium" for his studies will be "a thousand pounds." (355). Spenlow is willing to accept such a fee, but, unfortunately, he has a partner, Mr. Jorkins, who is "implacable" and considers "a thousand pounds too little" (355). David asks if something like a rebate could be given later to one like himself, who, he is sure, will excel. Spenlow replies that while he might be open to something of the sort, Jorkins is "immoveable" (356). David can only conclude ruefully: "The heart and hand of the good angel Spenlow would have been always open but for the restraining demon Jorkins (356). Later on, after he has settled in with the partners, David meets the elusive Jorkins and finds him anything but demonic. He is, indeed, the meekest of men, not at all intimidating. Spenlow is another representative of the human comedy; his timidly grasping character is portrayed vividly through a simple conversation that reveals everything about him. What Chaucer's pilgrims illustrate through long tales is here shown in two pages of dialogue. Later on, Spenlow will confound David even more, when, after the proctor's sudden death, David discovers that he, the official who never has tired of preaching the necessity of everyone's having a will, has died intestate and in considerable debt. David's "education" is ongoing as he copes with and learns more about the complications and contradictions inherent in individuals and in the human condition in general.

David also navigates a male rite of passage when he hosts a gathering of friends in his new London lodgings. Steerforth is present, and David is once again awed, as if he is still the new boy at school who "bites": "I said I was delighted to propose his health. I said I owed him more obligations than I could ever repay, and held him in a higher admiration than I could ever express" (365).

David and his friends go on proposing toasts, since wine is their only relief from a decidedly unappetizing repast. When all decide to end their evening by going to the theater, David is so inebriated he falls down the steps leading out of his apartment. He then suffers the ultimate embarrassment: as he stumbles to his theater seat, he sees none other than Agnes Wickfield, the soul of purity, in the same box "shrink into her corner, and put her gloved hand to her forehead" (367). David thus experiences the double-edged sword of carefree dissipation. He loves the wonderful sense of belonging and the lack of restraint and inhibition that inclusion in a group of carousing friends brings, but then must endure "the agony of mind, the remorse, and shame" (368) that accompany one's recovery the morning after, as the clear daylight exposes all that was said and done in the night's darkness. Like Prince Hal, who faces serious responsibilities as heir to the throne and who must finally separate himself from Falstaff and his merry revelers if he is to prove a worthy monarch, David has to meet Aunt Betsey's high standards not just occasionally but regularly if he is to prove worthy of her favor. This episode is, consequently, a "one time only" deviation from moderate and virtuous living; it is for David one more learning experience and test of character on his pilgrim's way.

Agnes afterwards asks to see "Trotwood." As they converse, Agnes gives voice to conscience and, in her benevolence, speaks to him frankly. Her concern is not so much with the poor impression David made under the influence as with the effect his "bad Angel" (370) is having on his conduct and thinking. This is the first warning about Steerforth David has received, and he defends him as "a guide, a support, and a friend" (371). To Agnes, however, David's trust is naïve and dangerous, "not wise, and not hopeful" (371). Agnes has the instincts of the blessed, the moral insight that senses immediately how someone weighs in on the scale of virtue. Her razor-sharp evaluation of Steerforth is disturbing:

> *I am certain that what I say is right. I am quite sure it is. I feel as if it were someone else speaking to you, and not I, when I caution you that you have made a dangerous friend.* (372)

Agnes has anxieties about someone else as well, anxieties rooted in the same moral calculus. She confides to David her fear that Uriah Heep "is going to enter into partnership with Papa" (373). David is appalled; his estimate of Heep's character is as accurate as Agnes's of Steerforth. Both are of the devil's party, but Heep is far more obviously so in David's eyes, because Uriah lacks the charm and insouciance so natural to the privileged and so attractive to an aspiring gentleman like David. Agnes describes Heep's devious ways in terms David grasps readily:

> *He is subtle and watchful. He has mastered Papa's weaknesses, fostered them, and taken advantage of,*

> *until—to say all that I mean in a word, Trotwood—until Papa is afraid of him.* (373)

She tells David Uriah "professes humility and gratitude," but his sole aim is to acquire "a position . . . of power" over her father, of which he will make "a hard use" (374). Agnes is resigned to her father's "sacrifice" (374) and blames herself for Mr. Whitfield's troubles, since, in their time together, he has obsessed over her welfare to the detriment and neglect of all else. She ends, illogically, by begging David to "be friendly to Uriah" because "we know no certain ill of him" (375), thereby allowing charity to cloud moral judgment. Both David and Agnes have blind spots, David's arising from excessive admiration of Steerforth and Agnes's from fear that she has caused her father to be excessive in his care and solicitude. The *via media* of balanced living and impartial judgment has been transgressed, at least temporarily, by each in his/her own way.

Agnes's confidences have aroused in David emotional responses he is neither accustomed to nor comfortable with. Soon, he encounters Uriah at a small party, attended by David's school friend Thomas Traddles also, and, much against his will, but "in remembrance of the entreaty Agnes had made" (381) to him earlier, David invites Uriah Heep to his lodgings for late-night coffee. There the two engage in a dialogue that leaves David alternately furious and/or horrified as revelations of Heep's incredible personal and professional ambitions come pouring out. Like Steerforth, Uriah insists on addressing David as "Master" rather than "Mister," as if he is still the schoolboy whom Mr. Wickfield has taken to heart. This bit of malice gives the lie to Heep's constant flattery and expressions of humility; he is ever the combatant maneuvering for position through self-deprecation. David senses all of this but resists the temptation to send away this apparently harmless but supremely dangerous conniver with "his shadowless red eyes, which looked as if they had scorched their lashes off" (382). As Uriah speaks, two facts become clear: 1) Heep really is now a partner with Mr.

Wickfield, and 2) Heep is laying the groundwork for marriage to Agnes. Uriah justifies the partnership arrangement as a blessing in disguise for Wickfield, since the latter has been "imprudent" (382) and Heep will be at hand to save him from himself. With an air of revealing some super-secret indiscretions of Mr. Wickfield, Heep betrays his true posture toward his patron with a chilling gesture:

> *"It's a topic that I wouldn't touch upon to any soul but you. Even to you I can only touch upon it, and no more. If anyone else had been in my place during the last few years, by this time he would have had Mr. Wickfield (oh, what a worthy man he is, Master Copperfield too!) under his thumb. Un-der-his thumb," said Uriah, very slowly, as he stretched out his cruel-looking hand above my table, pressed his own thumb down upon it, until it shook, and shook the room.* (384)

What Heep is describing as a possibility his presence has prevented from occurring is, in reality, the current state of affairs between the partners. Knowing Mr. Wickfield is as far above venal "indiscretions" as any man can be, David reacts fiercely to Heep's calumny: "If I had been obliged to look at him with his splay foot on Mr. Wickfield's head, I think I could scarcely have hated him more" (384). But there is more, and hate will turn into murderous fury. Asking David not to "think the worse" of his "umbleness" as he continues, Heep begs to share with him a second confidence: "Oh, Master Copperfield, with what a pure affection do I love the ground my Agnes [Wickfield] walks on!" (385). Infuriated, David has the "delirious idea of seizing the red-hot poker out of the fire, and running him through with it" (385). The vision of Agnes and Uriah together is worse than Beauty and the Beast. Agnes's beauty lies in her virtue, far superior to anyone else's in David's eyes. With his flashing red gaze, splay foot, and viperish writhing, Heep is more satanic than human. Bringing the two together would be like mating good and evil, an impossible prospect.

Heep ends the conversation by pouring salt into David's emotional wounds. He makes clear why he has taken "Master Copperfield" into his confidence: "Oh, it's such a relief, you can't think, to know that you understand our situation, and are certain (as you wouldn't wish to make unpleasantness in the family) not to go against me" (387).

In other words, David is checkmated: he has to acquiesce in the "situation" Agnes, her father, and Heep are in, or Uriah will expose his partner's improprieties. These improprieties may be purely fictional, but neither Mr. Wickfield nor Agnes can bear any injury to the family's honor or reputation Heep's accusations would inevitably bring. Heep has tied David in knots, just as he has the Wickfields. He spends the night tossing and turning in an agony of dread and remorse, horrified that Heep's machinations could actually succeed, given Agnes's willingness to do anything to shield her father from disgrace.

On top of all this, David has invited his guest to spend the night at his lodgings, so as he awakens the next morning, he has to suffer the indignity of beholding "this creature" from the perspective of the previous night's revelations:

> *When I awoke, the recollection that Uriah was lying in the next room sat heavy on me like a waking nightmare, and oppressed me with a leaden dread, as if I had had some meaner quality of devil for a lodger.* (388)

"Meaner quality," notwithstanding, a devil is a devil, and, like Bunyan's pilgrim, who encounters and combats every variety of hell's denizens, David should not shrink from the challenges Heep presents. Rather than just watching impassively the next morning as Agnes's coach takes away the spidery Heep, who is "writhing on the roof, as if he had her [Agnes] in his clutches and triumphed" (390), David might have begun moving aggressively now to win Agnes's love for himself and convince Mr. Wickfield to let him work to extricate the lawyer from his difficulties by unraveling Heep's webs of deceit. Nothing of this sort occurs, however, because at this critical juncture, David is pulled in an entirely different direction. On the pretext of marking formally David's becoming "articled," Mr. Spenlow, who has taken a liking to this promising student, invites David to his "house at Norwood" (391) for a festive weekend. It so happens that Mr. Spenlow's daughter, Dora, is returning at the same time from studies in Paris, so she will join the celebration too.

This invitation is as noteworthy as Julien Sorel's to the Bishop of Besancon's residence. Mr. Spenlow, a widower, has been living apart from his Doctors' Commons clerks and associates for some time. Rumors about the elegance of his domicile and the lavish spread of his table have circulated, so when David is preparing to leave for Norwood in Spenlow's phaeton, "his very carpetbag was an object of veneration to the stipendiary clerks, to whom the house at Norwood was a sacred mystery" (391).

David has never met Dora, and no one has described her to him, but he is, nonetheless, filled with romantic expectations as he reaches the Spenlow property. He notices a well-kept garden and conjures up an image of "Miss Spenlow" walking there by herself (394). His excitement then knows no bounds as Mr. Spenlow introduces his daughter to him:

> *She was more than human to me. She was a Fairy, a Sylph, I don't know what she was—anything that no one ever saw, and everything that everybody ever wanted. I was swallowed up in an abyss of love in an instant. There was no pausing on the brink, no looking down, or looking back; I was gone, headlong, before I had sense to say a word to her.* (394)

Not even the presence of, of all people, Jane Murdstone, whom Mr. Spenlow has engaged as Dora's "companion and protector," (395) can chill David's ardor. The weekend flies by in a blur. David pays almost no attention to the surroundings, the food, the guests, or, after they agree basically to ignore each other, Miss Murdstone. He thinks only of Dora, finding her delightful as she sings gay French ballads, plays with her little dog, Jip, and strolls with David in the garden. David's feelings are intense, his longing deep and sincere, but his "intentions" are thoroughly respectable. He does not immediately begin plotting sexual conquest, *a la* Julien Sorel; rather, in good English fashion, he wonders what happiness can follow his becoming "engaged to this dear wonder" (397). From the mature perspective of later years, David judges his conduct in those bygone days extreme but acceptable:

> *There is no doubt whatever that I was a lackadaisical young spooney, but there was a purity of heart in all this still, that prevents my having a contemptuous recollection of it, let me laugh as I may.* (398)

This attraction is, nevertheless, an instance of passion getting the best of reason. Although David can say truthfully that lust did not disturb his thoughts or influence his actions on meeting Dora, the fact is, only sexual urging, however controlled or disciplined, can explain the instant and powerful response Dora provokes all that weekend. David is eager for connection, for love, for the ecstasy of intimacy. This is normal, given his age and Dora's coquettish style, but romantic infatuation is a stage in the process by which lust entangles a person. Little Em'ly can and soon will attest to that. For David, it is a challenge that the Christian pilgrim must surmount lest he fall by the wayside. David has been swept off his feet and fallen "madly" in love. The madness generated by eros is distorting and cruel. It makes its victim throw caution to the wind and become oblivious to all considerations but those promoting union with his or her loved one. The good sense, balance, careful weighing of cost, professional obligations, mutual needs, and necessary sacrifices, these and other mundane factors that go into the forging of lasting and fulfilling relationships are downplayed once the power of passion takes hold. Could he have been present to counsel David, Chaucer's parson would have warned him he has fallen into the grip of something British culture, in particular, has long kept severely domesticated, and his imprisonment will cost David dearly.

David's swooning over Dora is in sharp contrast to the experience of Tommy Traddles, the decent and much put-upon friend David made at Creakle's school and whom he visits shortly afterwards. Tommy is delighted to see David again, and they reminisce a bit as they renew acquaintances. David observes that their days at Salem House might have been "happier" (407) had Mr. Creakle spared the rod more often, a particularly pertinent reference for Traddles, who was always being caned. Tommy, however, is past all bitterness and resentment; with his good sense and good will and his refusal to bear any grudge against the cruel master, Traddles exemplifies the magnanimity of the true gentleman. When David reminds him how brutal Creakle was to him, Traddles responds with serene detachment, as if from a transcendent height: "Perhaps he was, rather. But it's all over, a long while" (407). Unlike Uriah Heep, for whom the past is ever-present, Traddles will not let himself be "bent out of shape" as an adult by something that happened long ago. He is similarly charitable when David asks about Traddles' uncle, who, for no good reason, disinherited his nephew shortly after Traddles left school: "It was an unfortunate thing, but he didn't like me at all" (407). Far from being defeated by such harsh circumstances, like David, Traddles is making his way steadily in the world, as he lays out with "an air of cheerful confidence" (408) the many side jobs he has taken to finance his legal studies. At the end of this recital, he informs David of one more interesting fact about himself: "Therefore, you must know that I am engaged" (409). His betrothed is a clergyman's daughter, "one of ten down in Devonshire . . . a little older than me, but the dearest girl!" (409). Traddles makes this announcement almost triumphantly, despite knowing that his "will be a long engagement" (409) and many practical difficulties still have to be overcome. Among these are the necessities of "housekeeping," such as "the table-cloths, and pillow cases, and articles of that kind" (409). Traddles and his partner, however, have "made a beginning" in acquiring what they lack, and have adopted a philosophy of patient resolve ("wait and hope") regarding the rest (409).

This is not romantic enthusiasm but down-to-earth simplicity, sound judgment, and modest expectation, the very model of Anglo-Saxon probity and good judgment. Jane Austen herself could not have offered a more compelling sketch of "sense and sensibility." Traddles is and will forever be David's trusted friend, whose virtues and talents he will rely on more and more as events unfold. Traddles' path to matrimony is characterized by kind affection rather than passionate desire and prosaic realities rather than fantasies; this path, though, leads to domestic contentment and virtuous living, marked by openness and welcoming, generous sharing and mutual sacrifice, and steady amelioration in living conditions and standards. This is the preferred British way of living.

Another example of conjugal love and devotion is presented when Mr. Micawber and his wife appear again; they have been living in a different apartment in Traddles' building but have been hiding from bill collectors throughout David's visit. This meeting with old friends leads David to invite the Micawbers and Traddles to a party at his rooms. As they all gather, David learns that while much time has passed since he and the Micawbers were together, the family's circumstances have not changed for the better. Mrs. Micawber has become pregnant again, prompting her family "to express their dissatisfaction at this state of things" (413). Mrs. Micawber does not allude to her "condition" in her conversations with David. She spends most of her time fretting over her husband's inability to secure suitable employment, blaming "society" for Micawber's plight and insisting that their best option now is to "advertise in all the papers" Mr. Micawber's immediate availability for hire. Included in the ad will be a listing of his qualifications, amounting to "genius," and a curt concluding note: "*Now* employ me on remunerative terms" (422). David and Traddles admire Mrs. Micawber's fortitude, David being reminded of "a Roman matron" who would do "all manner of heroic things, in times of public trouble" (424).

As with every encounter David has with the Micawbers, the contrast between the reality of their condition and the seemingly delusional fantasy through which they address the situation is matter for endless comic relief. In this instance, the comedy is darkened as David learns that Traddles has co-signed a note for Micawber on the latter's assurance that the obligation is "provided for" (426). This assurance proves false, and, as a result, the Micawbers are being evicted, and Traddles' personal property is being removed from the premises. Micawber is threatening suicide, and David is upset that his trusting friend has been pulled into Micawber's endlessly revolving debt schemes. But though the Micawbers test the patience and generosity of everyone, they are redeemed from farce and parasitism precisely by their exaggerated sense of worth. Theirs is a very British family pride that enables them to endure humiliation without loss of confidence or self-respect, rise above circumstances, have many children, and ultimately enjoy an improbable restoration as emigrants.

When David first meets Micawber, he is struck by his "gentlemanly' ways. He is florid, grandiloquent, courteous, and kind. He does not look down upon or exploit David; instead, Micawber defers to him almost as a peer, a young gentleman in the making. Micawber is a Falstaff who does much more than mix punch and offer toasts; over time, he will perform services of such value for David, Aunt Betsey, and Mr. Wickfield that when the time comes for the Micawbers to leave England, they will do so with the support and good wishes of all whom they have helped. Falstaff is sent away in sorrow and in shame as Prince Hal ascends the throne; Wilkins Micawber goes with head held high and *amour propre* intact.

Toward the end of David's party, Steerforth appears. He informs "Daisy" he has just returned from Yarmouth and brings sad tidings: Mr. Barkis is dying. Steerforth is not terribly upset over this, observing with his usual insensitivity that "the sun sets every day, and people die every minute, and we musn't be scared by the common lot" (429). What matters is renewed perseverance: "Ride on! Rough-shod if need be, smooth-shod if that will do, but ride on! Ride on over all obstacles and win the race!" (429). Coming from someone else, such advice might seem bracing, a very English exhortation to maintain a stiff upper lip. But Steerforth is planning a seduction and has been in Yarmouth with Littimer to iron out last details. His words and tone are cold and cruel, meaning something like "Do what you must do, right or wrong, and if others are hurt in the process, so be it. The important thing is to prevail." If this was spoken by Julien Sorel, we might be indulgent, since the French are so moved by *elan* and the potential for conquest, but English culture frames all behavior within the bounds set by virtue and morality. With his egotism and disrespect for Em'ly's family and friends, Steerforth is out of bounds. He is the epitome of spoiled privilege, a dangerous dilettante who has a "desperate way of pursuing any fancy" (430) and then moving on regardless of the turmoil and pain he leaves in his wake.

After hearing of Barkis's illness, David resolves to go to Yarmouth but yields to Steerforth's plea that he go with him and visit with his family at Highgate first. "Say the next day," he tells David, "and pass as much of tomorrow as you can with us. Who knows when we may meet again, else?" (431). In fact, they will not meet again in the land of the living.

The visit starts uneasily. Mrs. Steerforth, as a rule, is "particularly happy in her son's society," and this day he shows himself "particularly attentive and respectful" (435) to his mother. Rosa Dartle, though, is suspicious of Steerforth's intentions, especially as they imply an unknown romantic interest; she focuses attention at first on David, as if he is somehow complicit in Steerforth's waywardness: "Blameless as I was, and knew that I was, in reference to any wrong she could possibly suspect me of, I shrunk before her strange eyes, quite unable to endure their hungry lustre" (433). Rosa is onto something, since Steerforth and Em'ly probably never would have met had David not brought his friend to the Peggotty home. She has an obscure sense that David somehow is separating Steerforth from her. Rosa's is a love that needs to rule; she has the spinster's way of always appearing to oblige and serve, with the intent, however, of guiding her charge only to thoughts, feelings, and behaviors flattering to her. In this regard, she resembles Heep, that other master of someone else's home. Nevertheless, nothing emerges from her probing, as Steerforth turns on his well-known charm: "I saw her sharp glance soften, and her smile become quite gentle . . . and we all sat about the fire, talking and laughing together, with as little reserve as if we had been children" (437). Rosa ends the evening by playing "a most unearthly" (438) Irish tune on the harp, entertainment she has not provided in Steerforth's presence in a long time. The rendition suggests "something fearful" that "has sprung out of the passion" (438) Rosa feels for this dashing young man. In reality, with eerie clairvoyance, she has offered a dirge, one reminiscent of the heart-rending laments Mr. Peggotty and his Yarmouth fishermen are used to hearing when one of their own is lost at sea. Though neither Rosa nor Mrs. Steerforth can ever suspect such a thing, they too, sometime soon, will be joining the widows and orphans of the poor in mourning an identical loss.

Before David retires for the night, he engages in a poignant last conversation with Steerforth. His friend admits he likes to call David "Daisy," though it is hardly appropriate for an adult male, but he says with feeling, "I wish, I wish, I wish, you could give it to me!" (439). The name connotes freshness and purity, the bedrock virtue and decency of Bunyan's pilgrim which David manifests through thick and thin and Steerforth so conspicuously lacks. David cannot offer "it" as a gift; virtue must be chosen and cultivated within and lived out over an individual lifetime if it is to be genuine. Knowing this, the man David has looked up to for most of his life can only make a final plea:

> *Daisy, if anything should ever separate us, you must think of me at my best, old boy. Come! Let us make that bargain. Think of me at my best, if circumstances should ever part us.* (439)

Since David's feelings for Steerforth have never, up to this point, been anything but admiring, he assures him he will keep "that bargain" without question. Though he can hardly guess the nature of the "circumstances" that will part them forever, true to his character, when the time comes, David will think of Steerforth at his "best" and arrange last rites and obsequies with a friend's tender care.

David arrives in Yarmouth to see Barkis on his deathbed. They have a parting meeting, at the end of which Barkis regains consciousness briefly and then "distinctly, with a pleasant smile," utters his last words: "Barkis is willin" (447). He dies as the tide is going out, the appointed time for a coastal citizen. All of the Peggotty clan are affected by Barkis's passing, but none as much as Em'ly. They believe she and Ham would have been married by this time had not Barkis's death been imminent. Her employer, Mr. Omer, is sure that her listlessness at work is due to anxiety about Barkis, and her emotional embracing of her uncle over and over is simply Em'ly's way of comforting him:

> *"To see the clinging of that pretty little thing to her uncle," said Mr. Omer, "to see the way she holds onto him, tighter and tighter, and closer and closer, every day, is to see a sight."* (442)

As David arrives at the Peggotty home, Em'ly is leaning mournfully "upon his [Mr. Peggotty's] breast" (445) and hardly responding to David's extended hand. Her uncle appreciates her concern and devotion, saying that if ever he were "forced to lay down in a dyke," Em'ly would "go along with him" (446). Mr. Peggotty is not too worried about what seems like excessive grief, however, because he knows "there'll be someone else, soon," (446) for her to cling to, even if she appears to be avoiding Ham. The agony of guilt and fear Em'ly is suffering as she faces the prospect of separating herself from the only world she has ever known and violating the trust and faith every family member and friend has placed in her, is something no one in Yarmouth could credit. Her purity of character is so well known and respected it is inconceivable Em'ly, of all people, would participate willingly in an immoral action.

The stage is now set for the novel's most dramatic event. Since his is a retrospective account, author David has to recall his actions, reactions, thoughts, and feelings over the next days as accurately as he can. This is challenging; he admits that "a dread falls on me here" (449) as David reconstructs the swirling drama of emotion and incident following upon Em'ly's disappearance and how the steady professional progress and romantic joy life up to this point has brought him will be radically affected.

On the night after Barkis has been laid to rest, Em'ly has not returned to the Peggotty boathouse by the usual time. Instead, a letter has been left with Ham, with whose contents he is already familiar, and which David is asked to read aloud to Mr. Peggotty and the assembled family members. As David reads, his listeners are overcome by grief and shock. The letter is emotional, heart-breaking, and shattering. Em'ly informs everyone she will be far away by the time they read her letter and that she will "never" be back to her Yarmouth home and family unless "he brings me back a lady" (454). They soon determine who "he" is since Littimer "was seen along with our poor girl" (455) the previous night. The Peggotty family's reaction to this trauma is notably charitable and purposeful. Ham's life, for instance, has suddenly been turned upside down, but he nobly exempts "Davy" from any blame: "it ain't no fault of your'n—and I am far from laying of it to you" (455). This brotherly restraint and respect for a friend who could never have suspected such a result could occur after he brought Steerforth to Yarmouth is Christian virtue at its purest. Ham directs indignation solely toward Steerforth, "a damned villain" (455), whose perfidy deserves denunciation. Daniel Peggotty announces that henceforth he will make it his duty to "find my poor niece in her shame and bring her back" (456), thus beginning a lonely knight's quest to redress injustice. Though there is no doubt about Em'ly's "shame," her uncle's love is unconditional. Mrs. Gummidge hears this pledge and asks for Dan's forgiveness; she knows she has been a burden in her perpetual sadness and lassitude and vows to change her ways. This tragedy, in other words, brings out the best in all the members of the clan, uniting them in common resolve and willing cooperation. David feels a measure of relief. Their continuing good will allows him to assess what has happened objectively and to decide on a response unburdened by the family's condemnation.

The reaction of the townspeople to the news of Em'ly's flight is significant: "Many were hard upon her, some few were hard upon him" (457). Em'ly receives more criticism because her participation in Steerforth's scheme is an admission of co-responsibility. Even if she had not been aware of what could happen and had gone with the footman on what she thought would be a simple errand, she would be guilty of gross indiscretion at best and a flirting with temptation at the worst. As noted earlier, in George Eliot's *The Mill on the Floss*, Maggie Tulliver takes a boat trip with a male acquaintance that is supposed to end with a docking a few miles downriver; adverse weather conditions, however, force the ride to continue far beyond its original destination. Maggie could not have known something like this would occur, but in the eyes of rural England in 1850, she is still guilty of tempting fate by agreeing to accompany a gentleman on a journey unchaperoned. The moral code the British follow is strict and severe, particularly for women, whose chastity must be protected. Chaucer's pastor would have expatiated upon the mortal danger one faces simply by a coquettish glance or smile in male company. Em'ly's offense is compounded by her professed desire to become a "lady." Not only is this aspiration highly questionable in the context of Yarmouth society; it can become the motivating factor for the most compromising behavior, blinding its victim to the moral peril such conduct as Em'ly's brings. Better to strive sensibly and modestly to be the best one can be in the cultural, social, and economic environment he or she is born into than to lose one's head in fantasies about worldly advancement.

Steerforth's situation differs from Em'ly's in that he has been born to privilege, is receiving an Oxford education, and enjoys the best prospects for a successful career. Instead of sweeping off her feet an impressionable girl from the lower classes who would dearly love to rise in society, a man like Steerforth should be interested only in finding a suitable partner from among the eligible women of his social circle. But Steerforth is too spoiled and too willful to follow the well-worn path of gentlemanly discipline and decency. He is frivolous and fickle, a person of no firm grounding and no commitment to anyone or anything beyond himself, including his mother and Rosa. Em'ly is his current preoccupation, but he will move on to others. The man who has told "Daisy" it really does not matter what profession he enters because every calling offers basically the same tiresome duties and obligations, is not the man to swear eternal fealty and raise up in social standing a poor girl he barely knows. When he finally decides to move on, he gifts Em'ly to Littimer, his footman, as a prospective bride. The high-spirited girl is incensed that she could be thrown away like a no longer useful instrument and quickly runs away from both of the men. This heavy-handedness is characteristic of the person who has striven since he was a school boy "to make everything right" through bribes and gifts to those he has wronged. Em'ly, therefore, should have gratefully accepted Littimer, the man of impeccable manners, who could have taught her how to act like a lady. Steerforth's muddled manipulation and control are attributable to a pride that compels one to think he is above ordinary constraints and that whatever he desires he should have for no other reason than that he wants it.

PART FOUR

This episode ends the middle portion of *David Copperfield.* It affects David as nothing hitherto has. The contrasts with his own experience are marked. Em'ly turns her back, however tearfully and with whatever justification, on those who have raised her and love her. David never has done anything like this. He fled from the Murdstones and the blacking factory because he had to; all he encountered in both environments was contempt and hostility. Steerforth has violated his friend's confidence and shamelessly taken advantage of people he loves. David, however, does not turn against Steerforth in fury and outrage. He knows that their relationship is irretrievably broken, but he does justice to Steerforth's plea that, no matter what may transpire, David should always remember him at his best. The strength of David's character is nowhere more evident than in how he does, indeed, years later still cling to all that was best in Steerforth, as in this tribute cited before:

> *In the keen distress of the discovery of his unworthiness, I thought more of all that was brilliant in him, I softened more to all that was good in him, I did more justice to the qualities that might have made him a man of a noble nature and a great name . . .* (457)

David's consideration and good will, augmented by the Peggotty clan's refusal to condemn him for first bringing Steerforth to their household as an honored guest, are not accorded a similar respect by Steerforth's family. The fine distinctions, careful apportioning of responsibility, and unconditional love the Peggottys display are foreign to the thinking of Mrs. Steerforth and Rosa Dartle, whom David and

Daniel Peggotty call upon after the abduction. Mr. Peggotty has requested this meeting to try to determine how seriously Steerforth will work to fulfill Em'ly's ambition to return to Yarmouth "a lady"; in other words, he needs to be assured Steerforth can and will marry his niece. With her iron pride and cold contempt for Em'ly's "humble connexions" (470), Mrs. Steerforth abruptly and harshly sets the fisherman straight: "Such a marriage would irretrievably blight my son's career and ruin his prospects. Nothing is more certain than that it never can take place, and never will" (471). Then, just like her son would do in such a situation, she raises the subject of "compensation" (471), which Mr. Peggotty refuses with scorn. Mrs. Steerforth thereupon launches into a long lament, reviewing all she has done for her only child, all the hopes she has entertained for him, and all the emotional investment she has made in his life, sacrificing independence, identity, and authority in the process. His recent behavior has made all her efforts look futile, and she cannot bear this humiliation. Steerforth henceforth will be banned from his own home "unless, being rid of her [Em'ly] forever, he comes humbly to me and begs for my forgiveness" (471). To David, this uncompromising rigor has a familiar tone and style:

> *While I heard and saw the mother as she said these words, I seemed to see and hear the son, defying them. All that I had ever seen in him of an unyielding, willful spirit, I saw in her.* (472)

An event that has united David and the Peggottys in a common effort to rescue their loved one has divided the Steerforths, perhaps fatally. Rosa Dartle must be heard from as well. To her, the whole issue stems from one source, David. He should never have brought Mr. Peggotty to the Steerforth home and, by implication, should never have brought James Steerforth to the Peggotty houseboat. David is incredulous: "Miss Dartle," I returned, "you are surely not so unjust as to condemn me" (472). Since Miss Dartle's world is collapsing around her, with

Mrs. Steerforth banishing James and James not likely to beg forgiveness, David and his friend are convenient targets. Rosa's passionate attachment to James Steerforth provokes an outburst of passionate rage against Em'ly and the Peggottys: "They are a depraved worthless set. I would have her whipped" (473). She goes on in a similar vein, all the while seeming to project a demonic hatred. David reflects on this scene later: "I have seen passion in many forms, but I have never seen it in such a form as that" (473). Daniel Peggotty's virtue shines throughout this encounter, as he bears with dignity the insults, reproaches, and accusations hurled by both mother and companion. As David and he exit the Steerforth home, Mr. Peggotty has the last word:

> *I'm a-going to seek her [Em'ly] far and wide. If any hurt should come to me, remember that the last words I left for her was "My unchanged love is with my darling child, and I forgive her!"* (475)

This declaration comes from a moral height too lofty for his interlocutors to scale.

Mr. Peggotty will be as good as his pledge. He will spend the last third of the novel wandering through Europe, picking up intelligence about the couple, tracking down rumors, arriving at sites Steerforth and Emily have just departed, and everywhere impressing common people with his love and dedication, earning their praise and aid throughout. His long quest will end in London, where Em'ly has found help and lodging after escaping from Steerforth, who, in character, eventually tired of her companionship. This will be one of the three plot strands playing out in this part of the novel. A second involves Mr. Wickfield, Uriah Heep, Agnes, and Micawber, whose perpetual search for employment worthy of his talent leads him to Wickfield and Heep, thereby tying his and his family's destiny to those of the Wickfields and the Heeps. The third strand is David's continuing growth as a man of solid values and virtue and as a greatly influential professional writer. As such, this strand intersects with the others, as David, in company with his aunt, Mr. Dick, and Traddles, learns through continual observation of and interaction with all those whose life experiences in Yarmouth, Canterbury, Highgate, and London, form his character as a persevering pilgrim and test his fortitude and faith in a world filled with challenges to both.

After the ordeal at Highgate, David needs some relief from the stress Steerforth and Em'ly have caused him. He finds such only in thinking about and being with Dora. She becomes the equivalent in romantic attraction to Agnes in purity of character. His ardor knows no limit or restraint:

> *If I may so express it, I was steeped in Dora. I was not merely over head and ears in love with her, but I was saturated through and through. Enough love might have been wrung out of me, metaphorically speaking, to drown anybody in, and yet there would have remained enough within me, and all over me, to pervade my entire existence.* (475)

David's love for Dora is doubly important at this juncture. Not only does it provide emotional sustenance, it also makes his working life at Doctors' Commons more bearable. David has English good sense and strives toward balanced judgment in evaluating people and situations. He has little tolerance for hypocrisy or blind adherence to what is merely customary. Mr. Spenlow and his fellow proctors, along with the other legal professionals who fill the numerous offices attached to various courts, think differently, however. They go on day after day filing wills, issuing marriage licenses, and providing every other type of official certificate a petitioner asks for, so long as the required fees are paid in full. It matters little that the fees are excessive and that much of the documentation is redundant or irrelevant; this system generates income to support without undue strain a small army of officials, and that is the bottom-line reality that cannot be ignored. David sees that "justice" is of little importance in the Commons, as illustrated by the adjudication of a "divorce-suit" filed by one Thomas Benjamin.

With the connivance of a proctor, this gentleman had signed his marriage license "Thomas" only, hedging his bet on the durability of his marriage. The marriage did not turn out to be suitable, so the court issued a decree of divorce because the name on the license was incorrect (480). Spenlow and company are not disturbed by such chicanery, but David is. He is likewise baffled by the "Prerogative Office," where innumerable wills dating back three centuries are stored so haphazardly that no one could locate one without interminable searching. Moreover, the proctors who preside over this chaotic scene have no incentive to clean up and organize the collection, because they hold their offices as sinecures for life regardless of what they do or do not do. They are reminiscent of the politicians who, before the Reform Act of 1832, represented "rotten boroughs," whose tiny electorates returned them to office again and again, where they wielded disproportionate influence.

When David questions the propriety of these and other practices, Mr. Spenlow dismisses his concerns as arising from innocence and inexperience (echoing in his own way Steerforth's condescension toward "Daisy") and invokes national security in defending the system: "Under the Prerogative Office, the country had been glorious. Insert the wedge into the Prerogative Office, and the country would cease to be glorious" (482). From this world of mindless custom and endless busy work, David's moments with Dora become life-restoring interludes of unalloyed joy. He goes so far as to purchase an engagement ring for Dora and is nearly suicidal when she returns it. The intervention of Dora's lovelorn friend, Miss Mills, repairs the momentary breach, and the couple stay in close contact, awaiting only the right time and occasion to inform Mr. Spenlow of their intentions.

This happy time is all too brief. David cannot wait to tell his friends and family members the good news, and he is delighted when Agnes, by letter and Traddles and Peggotty in person, welcome his announcement. David is, however, disconcerted by Aunt Betsey, from whom he receives a surprise visit at his London lodgings. Betsey informs him first that she is "ruined"

(499), her investments with Mr. Wickfield having lost so much value that she is left virtually destitute. She assesses her changed circumstances, nevertheless, with sturdy English fortitude, blaming no one but herself and vowing to press on, another instance of positive response to adversity *a la* the Peggottys: "We must meet reverses boldly and not suffer them to frighten us, my dear. We must learn to act the play out. We must live misfortune down, Trot" (500).

As his conversation with his aunt continues, David hears unexpected reactions when he comments upon recent events. He expresses regret over "poor Em'ly," for instance, only to be told sharply, "Oh, don't talk to me about poor," returned my aunt, "She should have thought of that before she caused so much misery!" (503). This is the unsentimental judgment of those who uphold English moral standards, which is to say, of the great majority of Betsey's countrymen and women. David's charity toward Steerforth and his affection for Em'ly have not prepared him for such a clear and direct summing up of Em'ly's situation and her degree of responsibility for what has occurred. As if this astringency were not enough, his aunt also throws cold water on David's romantic fantasies. She asks if Dora is "silly" or "light-hearted," and then mutters "blind, blind, blind" after David insists he and Dora "love one another truly" (504). Betsey then compares David in his rapture to "poor Baby," his mother, ending with this characteristically English advice: "Earnestness is what that Somebody [David] must look for, to sustain him and improve him, Trot. Deep, downright, faithful earnestness" (505). Aunt Betsey has learned this lesson at great cost, having years ago married a man who later deserted her and who still reappears every so often as a creepy extortionist. The "earnestness" Betsey invokes is the opposite of what David loves in Dora. It connotes stability, good sense, modest devotion, reliability, and practical wisdom, all the qualities of a Christian helpmeet. Beauty, fashion, childlike dependence, and frivolity masking as charm are not the stuff of strong unions. David senses for perhaps the first time but certainly not the last, that Dora may lack elements essential for conjugal happiness and that in the fog generated by his ardor, he has, indeed, been blind to this possibility.

David is obviously shaken by what he has heard from his aunt, but he shudders at the thought of confiding these concerns to Spenlow and perhaps losing Dora. A better recourse is eminently practical and characteristically selfless. He decides to cancel his articles with Spenlow and Jorkins and try to recover some of the premium to help his aunt get through her current difficulties. David's alienation from the blood-sucking routines of Doctors' Commons has been growing, so this course of action is understandable. As he proceeds, however, he is forced to participate in another duet with Spenlow, who throws up his hands at any suggestion of a reimbursement, given Mr. Jorkins' immoveable opposition to any such adjustment. David then asks to appeal to Jorkins in person. The elusive partner is hard to pin down, but finally David manages to find him in his office. Jorkins is "a large, mild, smooth-faced man of sixty" (509,) addicted to snuff and ill at ease in conversation. Rather than come down heavily on David for daring to ask for a partial refund, Jorkins implies, through indirection and suggestion, that Spenlow is probably opposed to granting the request. David tries to dispute this, but Jorkins ends the interview quickly because of an "appointment at the Bank" (509). The partner is, in reality, weaker than Spenlow and even less willing to speak directly and assume responsibility. Both proctors are shackled to a way of thinking and to a system built upon deception, subterfuge, and connivance. Dickens milks fully the comic tergiversations these two proctors fall into as they, like Uriah and his mother, work in tandem to gain selfish ends, while the essential falsity and avarice of the system they serve is laid bare underneath the humor.

David's revulsion in the face of such conduct mirrors that of his nation. In contrast to the French, who, in good Roman fashion, view institutions such as the civil service, the church, and the military as preferred venues for personal achievement, advancement, and distinction, the English, as an island nation dependent on overseas commerce and trade for sustenance, are more inclined to look toward personal enterprise as the means to success. Napoleon derided this tendency in his great enemy's culture, labeling England "a nation of shopkeepers." David confirms this characterization throughout his London experience, particularly on the road to his aunt's cottage in Dover; his encounters with so many small merchants and vendors show how extensive business enterprise is in the capital and surrounding countryside. His career as a writer, which will begin with the publication of a few stories picked up by periodicals interested in original "wares," is a perfect example of how rewarding something prompted and sustained by nothing other than personal initiative can be. Likewise, at novel's end, the Peggottys and the Micawbers set sail for Australia with high hopes and determination, eager to begin anew in an environment that can repay handsomely investments in business enterprise, civic involvement, labor, or service. The two families flourish in their respective ways as they never could have had they stayed put.

In like fashion, generations earlier, poor families had left the British Isles to put down roots in the New World of North America; they became independent farmers, tradesmen, fishermen, merchants, artisans, and stock breeders, among many other callings. They populated their seaboard colonies with men and women used to making their own decisions, earning and spending their own money, marrying whom they pleased, worshiping as their consciences dictated, and cooperating closely with their fellow citizens in all matters requiring united effort. When the growth and expansion of their communities threatened the interests of the French settlements in the north and west, armed conflict broke out, ending in 1763 with French capitulation. One of the main reasons for the English-speaking colonists' success was superiority in numbers. The French territories in North America were populated by civil servants, military personnel, and priests, who were concentrated in the cities, and a small number of traders and trappers, who sailed the rivers and explored the vast countryside in search of fish, timber, fur-bearing animals, and anything else suitable for exchange. The French people did not migrate in significant numbers as potential colonists; the majority were content to work within the accepted national channels and remain at home. Thus, Napoleon, in 1803, finding himself in need of money, could agree to the sale of most French territory in the area between the Appalachians and the Spanish southwest, because outside of a few river ports, the lands were virtually empty of French-speaking settlers. The buyer was the United States of America, most of whose citizens at the time were descendants of the English "shopkeepers" he had once scorned.

David's trials continue after, first, Agnes, and then her father and Uriah Heep call on him and David's Aunt Betsey. Agnes informs the pair that things have changed radically since David was a tenant in the Wickfield home. His old rooms have been appropriated by none other than Uriah, now a partner in the firm, and his mother. Agnes is clearly uncomfortable with this situation and concerned about Heep's influence over her father, but the purity of her character exhibits the kind of charity and faith David has always known her to rely on in any difficulty: "But, if any fraud or treachery is practising against him [Mr. Wickfield], I hope that simple love and truth will be stronger, in the end . . . than any evil or misfortune in the world" (512). David's Aunt Betsey shows a similar restraint and forbearance when, to Agnes's great relief, she places the blame for her financial woes upon herself rather than upon Mr. Wickfield, "her man of business, who was not such a good man of business by this time, as he used to be" (513). Mr. Wickfield now appears with Uriah at his side, and David notices immediately that indeed he is not at all "the man he used to be" and not just in regard to business acumen. He has become more like a deferential junior partner to the all-powerful Heep:

> *. . . the thing that struck me most was that, with the evidence of his native superiority still upon him, he should submit himself to that crawling impersonation of meanness, Uriah Heep. The reversal of the two natures, in their relative positions, Uriah's of power and Mr.*

> *Wickfield's of dependence, was a sight more painful to me than I can express.* (516)

With smug self-satisfaction, Uriah underlines this new relationship as he blandly assures David: "Years don't tell much in our firm, Master Copperfield, except in raising up the umble, namely, mother and self—and in developing," he added, as an afterthought, "the beautiful, namely, Miss Agnes" (518). The only positive outcome of David's meeting with the Wickfields and Heep is his being told of a possible employment opportunity. His old master, Dr. Strong, is now retired, living in London and in need of a secretary. David wastes no time in immediately mailing the doctor a letter announcing his interest in the position and his desire to see him in person about it the next day.

Uppermost in David's mind is the need to assist his aunt in her difficulty. Even though, as we have seen, his growing distaste for the proctor's profession has made this renunciation a bit easier, David's decision to cancel his articles stems mainly from his almost filial devotion to his aunt and her welfare. He expresses his feelings succinctly but eloquently as follows:

> *What I had to do, was to show my aunt that her past goodness had not been thrown away on an insensible, ungrateful object. What I had to do was to turn the painful discipline of my younger days to account, by going to work with a resolute and steady heart.* (520)

Nowhere is David's growth as a human being highlighted so starkly as in this simple resolution. The boy Aunt Betsey took in, comforted, and raised in accord with English ethical standards has become a man who manifests the best in the national character. He is anything but an "insensible, ungrateful object," a description more suited to the likes of Steerforth or Heep; he is a man following the path of Bunyan's pilgrim, even if the path now seems to be taking him back to privations and sacrifices he thought he had put behind him. No matter, though, because David is prepared to take a detour on the way to personal advancement so that one most dear to him can retrieve her situation. For however long this takes, he will give up "yearnings after gallant greys" (520) and other appurtenances of gentility Julien Sorel acquired, however briefly. He will henceforth take responsibility for the welfare of Aunt Betsey, Mr. Dick, and anyone connected closely to them, repaying these extraordinarily generous benefactors as a grateful gentleman should.

He will begin by accepting Dr. Strong's offer of employment in "morning and evening work" (524) related to the dictionary the doctor has been compiling so long, just like Mr. Dick with his memorial and Mr. Micawber in his unending pursuit of a position matching his talents. David also resolves to learn shorthand, so he can become a proficient recorder of parliamentary speeches and debates, thereby earning extra income and helping his aunt even more. Mr. Dick will contribute as well. Tommy Traddles arranges for him to copy legal documents, a task Mr. Dick discharges admirably "from the moment of his being usefully employed" (529). Here in microcosm is the self-reliant English middle class responding to adversity not with despair or resignation or criminal schemes, but with renewed emphasis on productive labor, performed by all concerned for the good of one who has nobly served the interests of her loved ones but now must depend on their good offices for survival. This is how those who view society as a great family respond to the distresses of their brothers and sisters. The parson of *The Canterbury Tales* preaches the brotherhood of all humanity and stresses that when one person suffers, everyone suffers with him or her. The worst sin is indifference to others, as illustrated by one Jack Maldon, a relative of Dr. Strong through marriage. In David's hearing, with lazy callousness and cynicism, Maldon dismisses reports of murder, hunger, and discontent in the daily paper as unworthy of his notice or concern, because such calamities are always occurring somewhere. Far be it from him to suffer empathetically with any of these poor unknowns or lift a finger to alleviate any circumstance that may be contributing to their afflictions.

In sharp contrast to Maldon is Mr. Micawber, who has finally been given what seems like an opportunity that will engage his talents, at least initially, so that he can "rise, ultimately, to the top of the tree" (533). The fact that the new position requires Micawber to assist none other than Uriah Heep, "a man of remarkable shrewdness" (532), who "has not fixed the positive enumeration at too high a figure, but . . . has made a great deal . . . contingent on the value of [Micawber's] services" (532), gives David some pause. But he rejoices in his first landlord's good fortune and watches happily as Micawber solemnly places "an I O U in the hands of Traddles," (536) to cover all the family's debt that good man has backed in recent months. This is comical as ever, but it is consistent with the gratitude and sense of honor that guides Micawber, who cannot let Traddles' decency go unrewarded. Traddles' brotherly kindness has saved the Micawbers, who expect soon to be able to respond in the same spirit and make their benefactor whole. The wheels are in motion now for eccentrics like Dick and Micawber to prove their unsuspected worth and for David to embrace the duties his magnanimity will demand.

Buoyed by his aunt's unwavering care and concern and by Peggotty's resolve to give him her last penny should his newly straitened circumstances so require, David begins resolutely on the path of austerity, even considering dieting as a good way to limit outlays for food. He also decides to inform Dora right from the start that she will be "engaged to a poor man" (541), but that "a crust well-earned was sweeter far than a feast inherited" (540), a perfect summation of English principle. Dora, however, is uncomprehending: "Oh, yes, but I don't want to hear any more about crusts!" said Dora, "And Jip [her pet] must have a mutton-chop every day at twelve, or he'll die!" (540)

In the true English way, David is reassuring: "Perseverance and strength of character will enable us to bear much worse things" (541). Dora, however, professes to have "no strength at all" (541). This encounter presages many more between the couple that will end the same way. David's blind love prevents him from confronting until too late the practical difficulties a union of opposing types can bring. Dora's stubborn refusal to face hard facts and her equally childish confidence that somehow everything will work out well are unalterable character traits. David's powers of persuasion come up against Dora's adamantine rejection of adult responsibilities and wifely duties. She will be a dependent rather than a "helpmeet." Becoming desperate, David asks Miss Mills, Dora's bosom companion, to intercede for him and stress to his bride-to-be the importance of her taking interest in "the accounts, the housekeeping, and the Cookery Book" (543). Miss Mills responds with philosophic resignation, referring to Dora as if she were a sprite from *A Midsummer Night's Dream*: "The suggestion is not appropriate to our Dora. Our dearest Dora is a favorite child of nature. She is a thing of light and airiness and joy" (543). And so things stand.

As if David's situation is not vexing enough, he is called to account by Mr. Spenlow, who is outraged by love letters David has written to his daughter and that Miss Murdstone has so obligingly shared with him:

> *When I take a gentleman to my house, no matter whether he is nineteen, twenty-nine, or ninety, I take him there in a spirit of confidence. If he abuses my confidence, he commits a dishonourable action, Mr. Copperfield.* (550)

Mr. Spenlow suspects David's motives, wondering if Dora's inheritance is motivating the young man's interest. David is disturbed by this insinuation and stoutly proclaims he loves Dora "to idolatry" and that such love is "above all earthly considerations" (551), which is true enough, as we have seen. Mr. Spenlow walks away to confront his daughter, and as he does so, David is reminded of someone ready to throw off this earthly coil: "He was so peaceful and resigned—clearly had his affairs in such perfect train, and so systematically wound up—that he was a man to feel touched in the contemplation of" (553).

The reality is far different. Mr. Spenlow does, indeed, leave this life abruptly, falling from his coach as he is riding home the next day and dying instantly. But his affairs are in anything but "perfect train." A will cannot be located, and the proctors are so confused about assets versus debts that they cannot initially "make out what he owed, or what he had paid, or of what he died possessed" (559). David learns that there might not be "a thousand pounds left" (559) after everything is sorted through. Now, David's blinders begin falling away as he realizes that a feckless father has raised a daughter in his own image. Notwithstanding, his love abides, and his loyalty and devotion to Dora continue to be unshakeable. David will "love, honor, and cherish" Dora all the days of their life together, but he will do so with the rueful knowledge that his wife will always be a sweet little songstress rather than a life companion willing and able to share marital burdens equally.

The sudden death of Mr. Spenlow, the discovery that he has died intestate, and the realization that his obligations in all likelihood will leave his daughter without any significant inheritance, weigh heavily on David as he stays with and comforts Dora through her hardest days. Once all the loose ends have been tied up, he receives permission from Dr. Strong to take some time off, which David will use to clear his head and to confer with Agnes Wickfield, his "ever present help in time of trouble." He travels to Canterbury and without delay calls upon Agnes at her apartment in the Wickfield and Heep home and office. David is worried that Mr. Spenlow's two elderly sisters, who ironically have had little contact with their aloof brother since his marriage, might speak unfavorably of David to Dora while they are with her in his absence. He asks Agnes for advice, and she responds sensibly as ever, recommending that David call upon the sisters and explain all that has occurred *vis a vis* Mr. Spenlow, Dora, and himself. While David hesitates and raises objections, Agnes ends the discussion in her usual way by invoking David's obligation to act as his conscience and character demand: "Perhaps it would be better only to consider whether it is right to do this, and, if it is, to do it" (569). The path dictated by simple virtue is clear, and David's doubts vanish. He will request in writing that the sisters meet with him and hear him out.

This is the only relief he experiences at Wickfield and Heep. David also meets Micawber there, now busily employed as Heep's assistant and still sanguine despite the pedestrian character of the work Heep assigns and the fact that Micawber has to "labour under the pressure of pecuniary embarrassments," compelling "the drawing of stipendiary emoluments, before those emoluments are strictly due and payable" (564). David suspects that Heep allows such advances like a payday lender does today, at usurious interest that will make the sums impossible to cover later. Micawber soldiers on in his florid way, but David senses that life with Heep has made his friend more guarded and less candid with him than ever before:

> . . . *I clearly perceived that there was something interposed between him and me, since he had come into his new functions, which prevented our getting at each other as we used to do, and quite altered the character of our intercourse.* (566)

Nothing has changed with the Heeps and Mr. Wickfield, however. Uriah and his mother, as always, are both deferential to "Master Copperfield" but intensely concerned about any private contact he may have with Agnes. Actually, David and Agnes cannot enjoy much private time at all, since Mrs. Heep, the spy in chief, manages to stay near them constantly, pretending to knit but observing the two intently with her "evil eye" (571). After David's frustration boils over and he complains, Uriah answers candidly but characteristically that "we [his mother and he] must really take care that we're not pushed to the wall by them as isn't umble. All stratagems are fair in love, sir" (572). David responds bluntly that in her purity and virtue, Agnes lives in a different moral universe than Heep and that any love match between the two is inconceivable. Uriah then opens up as he never has before, recounting how his mother and father and he had been brought up in charitable institutions where the admonition to be humble was drilled into all three from day one. His father and mother took the lesson to heart, consciously putting themselves down so that those above them would not feel challenged; they got on by staying down. Uriah has done so too, as he reminds David how years ago he had refused David's offer to teach him Latin, because learning the language of scholars and *savants* would not be appropriate for one like him. Uriah concludes chillingly, "I am very umble to the present moment, Master Copperfield, but I've got a little power!" (574). If that "little power" can bring about a union with Agnes, there is no telling how far the man and his mother will go as their debilitating origins fade from memory.

David now understands better from whence Uriah Heep's burning ambitions have arisen:

> *And he said all this . . . that I might understand he was resolved to recompense himself by using his power. I had never doubted his meanness, his craft and malice, but I fully comprehended now, for the first time, what a base, unrelenting, and revengeful spirit, must have been engendered by this early, and this long, suppression.* (574–75)

David may understand now where Uriah is coming from, but he cannot bring himself to act in accord with the charity of the old French adage: *"Tout comprendre c'est tout pardoner,"* and forgive the man's resentments and designs, knowing how his path in life has been so twisted. David still detests Heep and is tempted to "knock him down" (575) as, later at dinner, in disgust, he watches him looking longingly at Agnes.

Mr. Wickfield makes things worse. During dinner, Uriah keeps proposing toasts, which soon have an impact on his partner. Mr. Wickfield launches into a painful monologue, blaming himself and his "weak indulgence" (577) for the mess that he and Agnes find themselves in; he recognizes that Uriah has become a "millstone" (578), but given his weakness, Wickfield cannot do much about him. The night ends with Heep's assuring David that he will continue to be "useful" (579) to his compliant partner and that he can be patient while his intrigues mature and his "pear" (580) ripens. David is heartsick, begging Agnes not to give herself to such a man out of "a mistaken sense of duty" (579) to her father.

The visit has been trying, indeed, but it has given David insight. He sees clearly that Heep has woven something like a spider's nest in the Wickfield household, trapping Mr. Wickfield first by ensnaring him in dependency and coming close to capturing Agnes by exploiting her devotion to her father. While the background and circumstances compelling Uriah and his mother to act as they do are clearer to him now, David's recognition of the evil impulses that drive the Heeps forces him to contemplate something like an apocalyptic final combat between himself as St. George and the dragon he understands well but still despises and fears. As we shall see, however, nothing as dramatic as this transpires, thanks to Mr. Micawber's due diligence.

After returning to London, David is surprised to run into Mr. Peggotty one cold and snowy evening as the latter rests on the steps of a city church. True to his word and true to the knightly code he does not realize he is following, Daniel Peggotty has made his way through parts of France, Switzerland, and Germany in search of his niece, tracking down every possible sighting but so far coming up empty: "Some said heer, some said theer. I traveled heer, and I travelled theer, but I found no Em'ly, and I travelled home" (585). All he has is a moving letter, which David reads to him. In her loneliness and misery, Em'ly begs word of her uncle "never to be seen in this world by my eyes again" (586). Mr. Peggotty also shows David bank notes included with Em'ly's letter and from previous communications. Steerforth has evidently been trying in his usual way to "make things right" by funneling cash to the Peggotty household. Daniel is indignant; his austere code has no place for bribes masquerading as gifts. He swears to David that he will, if necessary, return from the dead and set everyone straight if Steerforth or anyone ever suspects him of having touched this cursed cache:

> *If I was to die, and it was lost, or stole, or elseways made away with, and it was never know'd by him but*

> *what I'd took it, I believe the t'other wureld wouldn't hold me! I believe I must come back.* (588)

David inquires about Ham. Mr. Peggotty emphasizes the young man's disdain for personal safety or care: "When a man's wanted for rough sarvice in rough weather, he's theer. When there's hard duty to be done with danger in it, he steps for'ard afore all his mates" (587). Ham has responded to desertion by extending himself for others, as noble a reaction as can be imagined. In contrast to Mrs. Steerforth and Rosa Dartle, who stay locked up and aloof, indifferent to everything except the wounds that their self-absorption makes worse, Ham has put self aside in his determination to redeem his hard days without Em'ly through sacrifice. This is excessive, always a danger in English culture, but it is heroically so, just like Daniel Peggotty's quest. It will ultimately cost him his life as he makes a desperate attempt to save a stranger stranded on a sinking ship during one of the fiercest storms ever to strike Yarmouth. Ham's rescue attempt will fail, but his selflessness will achieve something far greater: reconciliation and redemption.

David meanwhile starts recouping his position *vis-à-vis* Dora by making a positive impression on her two aunts, who now have charge of her. Aunt Lavinia and Aunt Clarissa are lovable eccentrics who deal with David a lot like their brother and Jorkins did; each plays a prescribed role masterfully, deferring to the other whenever a subject outside her comfort zone is raised. David patiently plays along in their conversational ping pong, eventually winning permission to come to their home several times a week, in company with his aunt if he wishes. David is delighted. The visits go well, and all participants are pleased. One fact, however, remains unalterable: Dora will not prepare herself to manage a household. The aunts are no help in this regard, for they persist in treating her "like a pretty toy or plaything," (603). To David, indeed, there is little difference between the way they treat Dora and the way Dora treats Jip. The man who loves Dora with all his soul determinedly persists with his cookery book and expense accounting, but even he gives up after repeated failures, admitting that he too is falling "into the general fault" and making Dora "a plaything too" (604).

If Dora remains irredeemably immature, David is becoming just the opposite. He cannot do enough for or bear enough responsibility toward those he loves. He describes his thinking and work habits at this point in his life in terms that the sturdy English character instantly recognizes and commends:

> *I have never believed it possible that any natural or improved ability can claim immunity from the companionship of the steady, plain, hard-working qualities, and hope to gain its end. There is no such thing as such fulfillment on this earth.* (605–06)

Looking back later from the heights of literary fame and success, David avers that he could not have achieved much of anything "without the habits of punctuality, order, and diligence, without the determination to concentrate . . . on one object at a time, no matter how quickly its successor should come upon its heels" (605). Here he is decidedly different from Steerforth, who cares little for industrious labor and who never stays focused on "one object at a time," whether it be a task, a dalliance, or a friendship. He is also different from Uriah Heep, who, at least on the surface, seems dogged, diligent, and determined but who in practice uses his skills and aptitudes only to acquire power over others. He is driven by resentment, while David is moved by good will. To Steerforth, "Davy's" Boy Scout virtues are indicative of innocence, and to Heep, "Master" Copperfield's character is too naïve and unreal, most likely a mask hiding hostile designs. In reality, however, only David, who is younger than both, is behaving like a mature, balanced, responsible, and honorable adult.

Heep does his best to disarm the man he has always judged his rival when he next meets Agnes, Mr. Wickfield, and David at Doctor Strong's residence in London. On an earlier occasion, Heep had expressed doubts to David about the fidelity of the doctor's young wife, Annie. A relative of hers, the aforementioned Jack Maldon, whom David considers irresponsible, has returned from service in India, Heep suggests, only to be near Annie. As David balks at this insinuation, Uriah responds dismissively, "I'm astonished at that, Master Copperfield, you being usually so quick!" (608), as if David is pretending not to see the obvious out of an exaggerated loyalty to the Strongs. David feels his usual indignation over Uriah's "odious behavior" (608) but says nothing more. This silence does not signify agreement by any means, but Uriah will soon misrepresent it as consent.

David comes upon a visibly troubled Doctor Strong, together with Mr. Wickfield and Uriah, in the doctor's study. With "an obtrusive show of compassionate zeal in his voice and manner," Uriah tells David he has "called Doctor Strong's attention to the goings-on of Mrs. Strong" (613). The doctor has taken this hard, fearing that he "may have unwittingly ensnared that lady into an unhappy marriage" and blaming himself for the "aspersions" on her character he has just heard (616). He reacts, in other words, exactly as Mr. Wickfield did when he blamed himself for the professional irregularities and errors in judgment Uriah supposedly discovered. Both he and David are gentlemen through and through forced to deal with a scoundrel through and through. Uriah is not content to libel Annie alone; he makes David complicit: "But since we have got so far, I ought to take the liberty of mentioning that Copperfield has noticed it too" (616). David is appalled; his doubts about Maldon, however, have betrayed him as "the confession of my old misgivings and remembrances was too plainly written in my face to be overlooked" (616). The doctor tries to retrieve the situation with a ringing endorsement of his wife's honor, insisting that "the dear lady's name never must be coupled with a word, a breath of doubt" (618), but the damage has been done. Allowing as he has Heep's web to wrap around him as well, "Master" David has been anything but masterful.

It is clear that Mr. Micawber is being lured into a similar trap. His wife sends David a plaintive letter, describing her husband as "entirely changed" since becoming associated with Heep; "He is reserved. He is secret. His life is a mystery to the partner of his joys and sorrows" (623). Moreover, living expenses "are obtained from him with great difficulty" (624). Micawber is, as his wife ceaselessly attests, a man of parts needing only opportunity to demonstrate his talents. Heep has afforded him such an opportunity but only at great cost and peril. As his careful accounting of debts and payment schedules indicates, under what appears to be indifference to responsibility, Micawber is a man of principle. Unlike Harold Skimpole in *Bleak House*, who has no interest in fulfilling monetary obligations and who readily exploits to his benefit the kindness of friends whom he never intends to repay, Micawber takes seriously the iron-hard rules of finance and never argues that a legitimate debt need not be satisfied. In the performance of his duties at the firm, however, he has undoubtedly come upon evidence of his employer's schemes, distortions, deceptions, and ruses, all designed ultimately to disgrace his partner and ruin clients like David's Aunt Betsey. Micawber is torn between the need to earn a living and pay back Heep's numerous cash advances and the compelling duty to heed the imperatives of conscience and expose the villainies he sees. The situation is complicated by Heep's two-faced *modus operandi.* He can, with some maneuvering, make white look black and then make it seem as if the perpetrator of the fraud is Micawber himself! The man of principle can be painted as a secret embezzler. Who would not be "entirely changed" as he strives daily to bear calmly and prudently a weight such as this?

Nevertheless, despite the trials and tribulations the likes of Steerforth and Heep have occasioned, David, now twenty-one and having "come legally to man's estate" (625), can assess his situation with satisfaction and optimism. For one thing, he has "tamed that savage stenographic mystery" (625), enabling him to record parliamentary debates on a regular basis. This work is remunerative but dispiriting; as with the goings-on at Doctors' Commons, he is forced to document "predictions that never come to pass, professions that are never fulfilled, explanations that are only meant to mystify" (625). He is repelled by everyday political life's focus on words as a substitute for efficacious action. But words will be David's salvation. In addition to recording meaningless political chatter, he has "taken with fear and trembling to authorship" (625). David is composing original stories for a magazine that pays to publish his submissions. He now has to use four fingers to calculate his income. David's success arises from the application of talent in sturdy, serious, and regular exertions. The Protestant ethic has no more shining exemplar.

Happiness overflows for David. The Spenlow aunts have consented to his marriage to Dora, which takes place soon after. All goes swimmingly, an apt image for the young groom who does all he is supposed to do, including taking out a license, reciting his vows, signing the register, and enjoying a repast, as if in a "dream, a flustered, happy, hurried dream" (627).

Prosaic reality sets in when the celebrations end, the guests return home, and husband and wife are left alone to begin married life together. It is a rocky beginning for two individuals moving in opposite directions. Like Bunyan's pilgrim, David is moving forward, facing a multitude of challenges with mature judgment and unremitting effort; Dora, by contrast, is moving hardly at all, content to remain a charming "child-wife" as she plays with her dog and sings lighthearted French *chansons* in the evening to entertain her "Doady." David finds her impenetrable; every suggestion he makes to facilitate household management Dora dismisses with airy indifference and comments like "No, no! please!" . . . "don't be a naughty Blue Beard! Don't be serious! (634). If David persists, his wife breaks down: "She was so pathetic in her sobbing and bewailing, that I felt as if I had said I don't know what to hurt her" (636). Aunt Betsey advises him to make moderate headway in small steps because "Rome was not built in a day, nor in a year" (637), and Dora is "a very tender little blossom, and the wind must be gentle with her" (636).

A dinner one evening with Traddles illustrates the couple's divisions. David is embarrassed by the liberties Dora allows Jip to take, including walking "about the table-cloth during dinner" (640), and by Dora's disorderly habits, such as placing "skirmishing plates upon the floor" and scattering the castors all around (640). When Dora serves oysters, Traddles' favorite dish, as an opening course, the diners are frustrated by their hostess's failure to open them. The main dish, mutton and capers, is undercooked, and only some "cold bacon in the larder" (641) prevents a total social catastrophe. Dora promises to improve, but her efforts prove inadequate. She is and will remain Doady's "child-wife" (642).

David resigns himself to loneliness: "Thus it was that I took upon myself the toils and cares of our life, and had no partner in them" (645). He remains in love with and committed to Dora in spite of everything, however, as one does to a beloved but ill-trained pet, and never contemplates separation or infidelity. In accord with the moral norms of English culture and society, David recognizes that the vows he has made rule, no matter how misguided or deluded he might have been when he pronounced them. In contrast to Madame Bovary, for instance, who reacts to marital incompatibility with adulterous affairs, David stays loyal and faithful, just as incapable of blaming Dora for any deficiencies as Doctor Strong is of blaming his young wife for any alleged waywardness.

Since Uriah Heep's accusations concerning Annie Strong were made in the doctor's presence, relations between this husband and wife, on the surface so ill-matched in age and education, have been strained. Nevertheless, with true gentlemanly courtesy, the doctor has taken responsibility for whatever discontent his wife may have felt and has given her the benefit of doubting the truth of any rumors concerning her fidelity. His devotion is confirmed when, shortly after the dramatic episode with Heep, Doctor Strong makes out his will, granting Annie "all unconditionally" (654). This bequest means little to Mrs. Strong, who has "never thought of any worldly gain" (658) her marriage might bring, but it is of immense importance to her mother, a grasping, egocentric conniver who is overjoyed that "the dear creature [Doctor Strong] has signed, sealed, and delivered, and his mind's at rest" (654).

Her joy will be short-lived. Mr. Dick, who has been enjoying excellent rapport with both the doctor and Annie, intervenes at this point to end the couple's estrangement. Reminiscent of the time he told Aunt Betsey that the best thing she could do when young David, orphaned and in need, showed up at her cottage, would be to "put him to bed," Mr. Dick, in the most direct but unforced way, brings husband and wife together in the presence of Anne's mother, Aunt Betsey, and David, and invites them to talk. Annie immediately falls to her knees at the doctor's feet in supplication. This humility, so characteristic of the Christian helpmeet, brings a reproach from her mother. Annie's riposte is memorable: "Waste no words on me, for my appeal is to my husband, and even you are nothing here" (655). This effectively puts that self-important pretender in her place, denying her influence in her daughter's affairs now and ever after.

A long dialogue between husband and wife ensues. Annie reviews the history of their relations, everywhere emphasizing the benefits the doctor has provided her since childhood: "He stored my mind with its first treasures, and stamped his character upon them all" (657). Her gratitude and love have been uppermost in her life with her husband ever since, she insists, and, in an outpouring of sentiment, closes with this ringing declaration:

> *Oh, hold me to your heart, my husband! Never cast me out! Do not think or speak of disparity between us, for there is none, except in all my many imperfections. Every succeeding year I have known this better, as I have esteemed you more and more. Oh, take me to your heart, my husband, for my love was founded on a rock, and it endures.* (661)

Here is the English moral ideal upheld and justified: A marital bond is founded on mutual trust and mutual commitment. Differences in age, temperament, education, class, financial circumstances, and so on cannot of themselves break apart a conjugal union where husband and wife give themselves completely to each other. The doctor and Annie give "all unconditionally" and, in so doing, become "one body," indivisible and impregnable.

In profound appreciation for all he has done, Aunt Betsey kisses Mr. Dick, whose powers she has repeatedly invoked. He is like one of the "little ones" in the Gospels, whose very simplicity make them apt receptacles for revelations hidden from "the wise and learned" (Matthew, 11:25). This reaffirmation of the Strongs' marital commitment signals the beginning of a change in the narrative's momentum. Mr. Dick's guilelessness has undone one of Heep's intrigues, showing that that master manipulator's plots can be foiled. Looking ahead, we will soon learn that Mr. Peggotty's dogged pursuit of Em'ly will eventually defeat Steerforth and Littimer, so practiced in exploitation and hypocrisy, while Mr. Micawber, harassed and made dependent by Heep, will courageously confront his oppressor and expose his sharp practice. David, too, once condemned to live as a child laborer, will also emerge triumphant as he disables the carefully crafted strategies the Heeps have devised to capture Agnes Wickfield and climb the social ladder. King David displaced and disposed of Uriah the Hittite in his passionate pursuit of Bathsheba; even if the parallel is inexact and strained, Master Copperfield will likewise displace humble Uriah in the Wickfield household.

The unraveling continues. One evening, on the way back from a walk, as he pauses before the Steerforth home, now looking like a house of the dead, David is surprised to be summoned inside. He is greeted there by Rosa Dartle and Steerforth's manservant, Littimer. Rosa asks if David knows of Em'ly's whereabouts, for "she has run away" (664). David knows nothing of this, so Rosa, with "vaunting cruelty" distorting her features more than ever, interjects, "If she is not found, perhaps she never will be found. She may be dead!" (664). Littimer then tells what he observed of the couple's last days together. To Rosa's disgust, he describes Em'ly fondly, emphasizing how quickly she learned to speak the languages of the various European peoples among whom the trio traveled and that "she wouldn't have been known for the same country-person" (665). Em'ly was popular wherever they journeyed: "What with her dress, what with the air and sun, what with being made so much of, what with this, that, and the other, her merits really attracted general notice" (665). In other words, Em'ly made great strides in her ambition to become a lady.

Steerforth, however, apparently took little notice of this transformation in "the boatman's daughter" (667), focusing instead on the difficulty of coping with her mood swings. In reality, of course, Steerforth had lost interest in Em'ly and was once again feeling a "restless" and narcissistic urge to change his life's circumstances. One day he left Em'ly with Littimer and then just disappeared for a time. Before this, as noted previously, in compensation for the misery he had caused both, and, like an autocratic master, Steerforth had offered his paramour to his lackey as a marriage partner. Littimer presents himself now as a wonderful "catch," calling himself "a very respectable person, who was fully prepared to overlook the past, and who was, at least, as good as anybody the young woman could have aspired to in a regular way, her connections being very common" (666). To Littimer's astonishment, Em'ly showed no interest in the "very respectable" alternative partner Steerforth had so generously provided for her. Like her uncle, who indignantly rejected Steerforth's cash, Em'ly not only spurned Littimer's proposal, she did so furiously, leaving the man in fear for his life, until she too managed to escape. After Steerforth returned and heard about all that had happened, instead of thanking his faithful companion for all he had tried to do to help him, he subjected the footman to reproaches and insults. His long relationship with "Mr. James" thereupon ended on the spot, and Littimer is "at present out of employment" (668). The man's fate may have been cruel, but David is not sympathetic; he knows Littimer's willingness to assist his amoral master in escapades that were anything but respectable makes him less a victim and more of an unfortunate casualty in the debacle that has befallen both men.

Mrs. Steerforth appears once Littimer has left, still stubbornly proud, obstinate, and suffering acutely in her loneliness. She insists that she and Rosa sincerely wish to have Em'ly found safe but mainly so that her "son may be saved from again falling into the snares of a designing enemy" (670). A scene of extraordinary power and poignancy then follows. Mrs. Steerforth tells David she has heard that the young writer is "beginning to be famous" (671). With all his gifts, privileges, and connections, her son is in disgrace and nowhere to be found, while David's star is ascending. The contrast is bitter, but in a final exchange, Mrs. Steerforth rises above her misery to strike just the right note:

> *"You have no mother?"—in a softened voice.*
> *"No."*
> *"It is a pity," she returned. "She would have been proud of you. Good night!" (671)*

The fact that Em'ly has left Steerforth and Littimer and has been forced, as a result, to make her way alone in a foreign land changes the landscape for David and Mr. Peggotty. It is only natural that Em'ly should try to work her way back to her native country, in particular, London, since transport to the British capital would be readily available in any European port. David and Daniel Peggotty return to London, therefore, with their hopes high. There they will be aided in their efforts by Martha, the Yarmouth native whom Em'ly befriended when most of the populace considered her disreputable. Living as a prostitute, Martha knows the dark side of the city and its ugly alleys and byways. David and Mr. Peggotty meet her in a neighborhood "as oppressive, sad, and solitary by night, as any about London" (676). It is near the Thames River, whose currents offer a means of permanent escape for the despairing young woman the two come upon. Her old acquaintances intervene to ward off any such catastrophe, seeing in Martha's desperation something similar to what Em'ly could be contemplating.

Martha responds with surprise and resolve as the two searchers explain who they are and whom they are seeking. Martha's self-loathing vanishes once she realizes they are asking for her help in locating Em'ly. Purpose is introduced to a life heretofore detestable, "a living disgrace to everyone" (680). With the same sturdy devotion as Daniel Peggotty has shown, Martha promises to do all in her power to aid the search for Em'ly, who gave "such kind help" (679) to her when it was most needed. Her statement of commitment to the two men's cause could have been uttered by Joan of Arc:

> *She lifted up her eyes, and solemnly declared that she would devote herself to this task, fervently and faithfully. That she would never waver in it, never be diverted from it, never relinquish it while there was any chance of hope.* (682)

Martha, the rejected one, proves herself noble. Her generous embrace of a duty that in no way is required of her is in marked contrast, once more, to Mrs. Steerforth's icy immobility. In an instant, Martha rejoins the human family, becoming a willing participant in a quest that opens up the possibility of redemption through selfless service. She joins Mr. Dick in finding purpose through such service. And like Dick and Daniel Peggotty, she grandly refuses all compensation. Her reward for the trust David and Daniel place in her is beyond anything money can bring. She marvels at the transformation they have wrought: "I am to be trusted, for the first time in a long while, with my miserable life, on account of what you have given me to try for. I know no more, and I can say no more" (683).

David and Mr. Peggotty realize that Martha is more than her lifestyle. She is honorable, grateful for kindnesses done to her, and capable of steady and loyal commitment in the right cause. She is worthy of all their trust. Mr. Peggotty understands that the young woman who was formerly an outcast, even in his usually forgiving eyes, has become potentially the most valuable link between his niece, now also in disgrace, and himself. She has value beyond usefulness, however; Martha is a fellow sufferer, needing love and respect as much as anyone else. Daniel Peggotty's natural goodness and charity are deepened through this recognition of mutual sorrow. David senses, "a new and thoughtful compassion in him that I was at no loss to interpret" (683). David and he have learned from experience that underneath differences in class, education, profession, and other externals, men and women of good will are as one and must recognize each other as brothers and sisters. In so doing, David and Mr. Peggotty model English moral sensitivity at its finest.

David is called upon to show a like sensitivity in the most intimate experiences of his life. Even though the challenges presented by Mr. Peggotty's quest, his aunt's finances, Mr. Wickfield's decline, Heep's endless manipulations, and the Strongs' marriage have been and continue to be extremely taxing, they pale before the stubborn reality of Dora's helplessness. David is becoming more and more successful, having published a novel to wide acclaim and winning plaudits in literary circles in England and abroad. True to his very English character, he accepts acclaim modestly, saying "the more praise I got, the more I tried to deserve" (686). Given his talent, however, he puts modesty aside in his home life as he makes a herculean effort to lift Dora to a new level of responsibility and capability. He will strive to "form Dora's mind" (690). And so begins a sequence of what David regards as helpful interventions, akin to those made by earnest social workers trying to change addictive behaviors. Thus, he quotes Shakespeare to Dora (who considers the Bard "a terrible fellow"), shares "scraps of useful information, or sound opinion" with her, and enlists Traddles to reinforce the "practical wisdom" (691) David dispenses freely. He continues in this way, despite Dora's lack of receptivity, "even for months" (691). Finally, however, he admits the obvious as "it began to occur to me that perhaps Dora's mind was already formed" (691). He abandons his ambitious project, buys "a pretty pair of ear-rings for her, and a collar for Jip," and resolves to make himself "agreeable" (691). Dora will be Dora, and David must live with this realization. His determination to "accept what he cannot change" and to do so without rancor, in accordance with the moral standards he has assimilated, is expressed eloquently in this statement:

> *It remained for me to adapt myself to Dora, to share with her what I could, and be happy, to bear on my own shoulders what I must, and be still happy. This was the discipline to which I tried to bring my heart, when I began to think.* (694)

This is mature acceptance of responsibility. Dora and her father, Steerforth and his mother, Heep and his mother, and the Murdstone siblings are all alike in resisting growth, enlightenment, or change of any sort. They are or will be at sixty what they were at twenty. David is the polar opposite: he has made his way successfully in the world by learning from the world and by adapting to the human comedy in all its diversity. He has learned that not everyone is like himself or is amenable to his good offices or influence. Nevertheless, so long as such people have done him kindnesses or, like Dora, depend on his care, the teachings of Chaucer's parson that have formed the English character require that all these, rich or poor, young or old, learned or simple, prominent or obscure, receive his unwavering love and respect.

One of these is Wilkins Micawber, who has been imprisoned for debt and spent a good part of his adult life improvident and in need of constant assistance. Members of his wife's family dismiss him as a hopeless failure and avoid occasions when they may be in contact with him. Micawber has taken advantage of good-hearted friends, like David and Traddles, so often, there is little likelihood they will ever be "made whole." David knows all this only too well, but he also knows that Micawber treated him with care and consideration in the worst days of his young life, when he boarded with the family while toiling at the blacking factory. He also remembers how Mr. Micawber exemplified the gentility he so longed to acquire, the only adult of his young acquaintance who did so. These facts outweigh the negatives, just as Steerforth's friendship and protection at Creakle's school outweigh what has happened since. David cannot remain anything but steadfast in his loyalty to the Micawbers, and, with Traddles, stands ready to help the man now laboring under the oppression of Uriah Heep.

Micawber began his work at Wickfield and Heep optimistically, thinking Uriah one of the best of men. His experience over time, however, has been disillusioning. Heep has treated him cruelly, saying at one point that without his favor, Micawber would "probably be a mountebank about the country, swallowing a sword-blade, and eating the devouring element" (706). For Micawber, the "only starry spot in a miserable existence" (703) is Agnes Wickfield, pure and selfless but always vulnerable to Heep's plotting. Micawber's life has become a *via crucis*, as he alienates his wife and children and suffers unending mental anguish and pangs of conscience in furthering Heep's designs. Thus, when he sends an emotional appeal to David and Traddles, begging that they "condescend to meet" him and "renew . . . past relations of the olden time" (698), the two readily agree.

The meeting is inconclusive until the three stop to see David's aunt. Mr. Dick is also present and realizes immediately that Micawber is in distress. He acts accordingly:

> *[Mr. Dick] was by nature so exceedingly compassionate of anyone who seemed to be ill at ease, and was so quick to find any such person out, that he shook hands with Mr. Micawber at least half-a-dozen times in five minutes. To Mr. Micawber, in his trouble, this warmth, on the part of a stranger, was so extremely touching, that he could only say, on the occasion of each successive shake, "My dear sir, you overpower me!"* (705)

Dick's magic works again. Micawber at last can unburden himself:

> *What is the matter, gentlemen? What is not the matter? Villainy is the matter, baseness is the matter, deception, fraud, conspiracy, are the matter, and the name of the whole atrocious mass is—HEEP!* (707)

He follows this with a passionate outburst, promising to expose the "interminable cheat, and liar . . . the—transcendent and immortal hypocrite and perjurer—Heep!" (708) Though sputtering almost incoherently and causing all who watch him to worry that he will collapse, Micawber manages to invite David, Traddles, Aunt Betsey, and Dick to what he promises to be a decisive meeting with Heep in a Canterbury hotel one week later. His denunciation of Heep on this occasion will be an "act of reparation" (709) for the way Micawber has until now remained silent about Heep's corruption and suffered so in consequence.

Here again one who is, apparently, all talk and no action will soon show courage, skill, and moral resolve as he goes head-to-head with a cunning rascal. In the process, Micawber will do what David never has: he will expose and silence the devious manipulator once and for all.

Another long-suffering but patient man, the most determined character David has ever known, will be granted his reward. Through the efforts of Martha, Emily (as she will be referred to in this encounter) has been found and given shelter in a London rooming house. The "strong assurance" (710) Daniel Peggotty has exhibited throughout his quest, regardless of failures and disappointments, will be justified. David writes about his friend's steadfast and virtuous character in terms reminiscent of Agnes:

> *. . . there was something so religious in it, so affectingly expressive of its anchor being in the purest depths of his fine nature, that the respect and honor in which I held him were exalted every day.* (710)

Before her uncle arrives at her shelter, however, Emily must endure a withering denunciation from Rosa Dartle, who has never met her but has discovered her whereabouts through Littimer. David arrives just as Rosa begins to speak. Since the room is dark, he listens unobserved and says nothing. Most of what Rosa venomously spews forth he has already heard, more or less in the same words and with the same fire in Miss Dartle's eyes. To Emily, though, this eruption of passionate hatred is a new agony. Rosa accuses her of being nothing other than a gold digger and flirt, "a bold, flaunting, practised companion of persons like James Steerforth" (714), a classic instance of blaming the victim by blackening her character. When Emily asks for "some compassion" lest she "die mad" (715), her unwelcome guest responds with cold contempt: "It would be no great penance," said Rosa Dartle, "for your crimes" (715). An ironic miscommunication follows. Rosa asks Emily if she ever thinks of the house she has "laid waste" (715). Emily responds with profound grief, lamenting the misery she has caused her uncle and all the good people left behind. Rosa Dartle, of course, cannot care less about "these earth-worms" (715), who, she is sure, have been amply compensated for their troubles. The only broken home she is referring to is the Steerforth home, and the only inhabitant of that home whose suffering she cares about is herself. As Emily insists she loved Steerforth and left with him because she thought he loved her, Rosa cannot contain herself. She flails at Emily "with clenched hand" (716), screaming incredulously, as if this woman has blasphemed. David knows of Rosa's unrequited love for James Steerforth, but even he recoils from her sadistic retort: "If I could order it to be done, I would have this girl whipped to death" (717). She ends by advising Emily basically to disappear, to go back to Yarmouth and live out her sad life in obscurity, sustaining herself with memories of "James Steerforth's tenderness" and his incredible generosity in offering her as "his gift" to Littimer (718). If memories do not avail, she should at last marry "the serving man" and "be happy in his condescension" (718). Should neither of these options prove practical, Emily ought simply to find a way to take her "flight to heaven," for there are many "doorways and dust-heaps for such deaths and such despair" (718).

At the start of Rosa's screed, Emily senses that the wounds Steerforth's scorned lover was beginning to inflict had to be borne: "I have deserved this," said Emily, "but it's dreadful" (714–15). Rosa's lies, insinuations, threats, and condemnations are painfully purgative. They give harsh expression to the pangs of conscience Emily's upbringing and her virtue have imposed. She has allowed romantic fantasy and ambition to lure her off the "right paths" a Christian pilgrim must follow. The sorrow Rosa's attack calls forth is the sorrow a repentant sinner feels when he or she becomes conscious of and ashamed of the transgressions that have created so much pain for oneself and others. This is necessary, as Chaucer's parson stresses, for any contrition to be sincere and for any forgiveness to follow.

It is clear that Em'ly's contrition is indeed sincere, because once Daniel Peggotty finally arrives, the atmosphere and mood change dramatically. His embrace and his words are life-renewing for the swooning penitent: "I thank my Heav'nly Father as my dream's come true! I thank Him heartily for having guided of me, in His own ways, to my darling" (719). Now, only light and peace prevail, as Em'ly is welcomed back into her family and into the community of all those who, in spite of lapses, strive to follow the ways of the Lord.

Mr. Peggotty visits David to bring him up to date on Em'ly's condition and on the circumstances of her rescue. It turns out that the "kindness of strangers" in Europe was vital in enabling Em'ly to cope with Steerforth's desertion. As she wandered distraught on a foreign beach one day, she became slightly unhinged, imagining herself at home in Yarmouth, calling out for Mr. Peggotty and the others to turn away when she passed, unworthy as she was to be seen by respectable people. A woman whom she had spoken with before and who had befriended Em'ly noticed her distress. Though poor, she "found space" for her friend (722) in her small cottage, comforted her, and, once she recovered, helped Em'ly depart for France. Mr. Peggotty cannot recount something so uplifting without emotion: "He was more affected by this act of kindness, than I have ever seen him affected by anything since the night she went away" (721–722), says David. Mr. Peggotty's sympathies are enlarged, as, first with Martha and now with a complete stranger in a foreign land, he realizes that the human comedy includes men and women of natural virtue in all classes and in all places. Em'ly eventually makes her way back to England, but "fear of not being forgiv" (724) has led her to London rather than Yarmouth. In London, "Martha, trew to her promise, saved her," and arranged the reunion with her uncle, who, she assured Em'ly, "loved her, and forgive her" (724).

Mr. Peggotty then tells David, "There's mighty countries, fur from heer. Our future life lays over the sea" (725). This statement is momentous for many reasons, the most important being Daniel Peggotty's realization that he and Em'ly can cross the ocean and begin life anew where "no one can't reproach my darling in Australia" (725). In so doing, they will continue their pilgrims' progress as they reproduce the life experience of John Bunyan's co-religionists, the seventeenth century Dissenters who willingly risked all on a dangerous North Atlantic crossing so that they could live and worship together in their own communities in a new Promised Land. By leaving England permanently, Em'ly will also fulfill in a totally unexpected way Rosa Dartle's injunction to avoid in the future all proximity to the Steerforth establishment. That episode is over, but in her new surroundings Em'ly will not be pining for her lover or living on memories, like the wretched Miss Havisham in *Great Expectations*. She will, instead, join countless English-speaking migrants in making a new and better life for herself, one characterized, above all, by service to others. Mr. Peggotty, too, will sever any remaining connection to Steerforth and his mother by returning all the funds sent to him, decisively repudiating the notion that somehow money can cure all wrongs and confirming the Gospel's mandate to "lay up treasure in heaven."

One who will not be leaving for Australia is Ham Peggotty. He will remain at home to live out the rest of his days separated from Em'ly but performing acts of charity and self-sacrifice akin to hers, only on a grander scale. He will never marry, he assures David, but though he cannot live in happy domesticity, he is neither bitter nor angry. Like all the Peggotty clan, Ham, in his own way, embraces Em'ly and confirms his loyalty and love. In their rugged eloquence and touching sincerity, his parting words to David are profoundly moving:

> *But if you, being so full of learning, Mas'r Davy, could think of anything to say as might bring her to believe I wasn't greatly hurt, still loving of her, and mourning for her, anything as might bring her to believe as I was not tired of my life, and yet was hoping fur to see her without blame, wheer the wicked cease from troubling and the weary are at rest—anything as would ease her sorrowful mind . . . I should ask of you to say that—with my prayers for her—that was so dear.* (733)

This chivalric devotion and generosity of spirit are beyond anything David has experienced in his interactions with the likes of Steerforth and company. Ham is speaking from a moral height reached only by those, like Chaucer's parson and Bunyan's pilgrim, who have suffered mightily but can still forgive and still love.

The reconciliation between Em'ly and her family is followed immediately by another reconciliation, this one a more impersonal but no less important resolution of badly mixed up legal and financial affairs. As by previous arrangement, Mr. Micawber now meets in Canterbury with David, his aunt, Mr. Dick, Agnes, and Traddles, who has secured Mr. Wickfield's power of attorney. Like a commanding maestro, Micawber is prepared for a culminating confrontation with his employer, during which he will lay out a carefully documented explanation of all the "treasons, stratagems, and spoils" Uriah Heep has perpetrated over the years to blackmail Mr. Wickfield and defraud the firm's investors. This will be Micawber's finest hour, an occasion that will bring out talent and conviction fully equal to Mrs. Micawber's high estimate of her husband's capabilities. From the start, the man who characterizes himself with studied theatricality as "unworthy to be regarded in any other light but as a Waif and Stray upon the shore of human nature" (739), takes charge of the impending duel with Heep. He asks his friends to allow him to direct what is about to occur, and when David expresses "perfect confidence" in him, Micawber quickly drops all pretense of self-abnegation, affirming that David's "confidence is not, at the existing juncture, ill-bestowed" (740). This tone he will maintain throughout the upcoming encounter, showing all the skill and careful review of evidence of a seasoned prosecutor.

Heep knows something is badly amiss when Micawber and company arrive in his office unexpectedly and demanding they be heard without delay. He is alternately fawning or threatening as he senses a "conspiracy" (743) is afoot. He tries to bully Micawber, whom he orders back to work, and to "counterplot" David, whom he derides as "always a puppy with a proud stomach" and whom he accuses of envying Heep's "rise" (743). He threatens Agnes as well: "Miss Wickfield, if you have any love for your father, you had better not join that gang. I'll ruin him if you do" (743). Since "ruining" Mr. Wickfield through slander, falsification, and forgery has been Heep's *modus operandi* ever since becoming his partner, this add-on has little impact now. In fact, nothing Heep says or does will have any effect. Micawber remains "immoveable" while David tells all present that Heep will be "brought to bay" (743), as he recognizes the man's desperation like an experienced boxer does a weakening opponent. Heep is surrounded, with no means of extrication, a plebeian counterpart to Richard III looking everywhere for a horse. The only effect of his flailings is to underline his essential nature. As he rudely silences his mother, at his side as always, David witnesses a transformation. Now, "with his mask off" (744), Heep becomes almost satanic:

> *The suddenness with which he dropped it [the mask], when he perceived that it was useless to him, the malice, insolence, and hatred he revealed, the leer with which he exulted, even at this moment, in the evil he had done— all this time being desperate too, and at his wits' end for*

> *the means of getting the better of us—though perfectly consistent with the experience I had of him, at first took even me by surprise, who had known him so long, and disliked him so heartily.* (744)

Micawber quickly seizes his opportunity to take center stage. He has compiled a detailed account of Heep's malpractice, and, just as he did with his grandiloquent petition in the debtors' prison, he launches into a lengthy indictment of "the Forger and the Cheat" (746). At these words, Uriah lunges at Micawber, only to be slapped on the hand with a ruler his former clerk has brought with him just in case something untoward should flare up. For David and Traddles, with their memories of Creakle's cruelty, this blow seems like justice long overdue, because, for once, the guilty party is being punished. For Heep and his mother, however, the crack of the ruler and the obvious pain it inflicts evoke the school where both were taught to be "umble" and where any who resisted such abasement were dealt with harshly. It is as if Uriah's "rise," so carefully calculated and steady, has been abruptly halted and reversed. The dominant partner in Wickfield and Heep has quickly been reduced to a delinquent urchin who must be reminded of his status. Uriah's mother cannot help reproaching her son for being too uppity: "I can't see you running into danger, through carrying your head so high. Better be umble, as you always was" (751). Such a rebuke from his mother, in these circumstances and with his "betters" listening, must be more painful and humiliating than the slap of the ruler. The man whose resentment of his upbringing is an abiding wound is being told to behave again like a workhouse boy, the very source of this resentment. He has been put back in his place.

Micawber continues. He notes Heep's salary advances and the improper practices demanded of him in return. As a man of honor, he laments how his "services were constantly called into requisition for the falsification of business" (747) and the humiliation of Mr. Wickfield. Heep has "obtained Mr. W's signature . . . to documents of importance, representing them to be other documents of no importance" (748). He has also "induced Mr. W to empower him to draw out, thus, one particular sum of trust money . . . and employed it to meet pretended business charges and deficiencies which were either already provided for, or had never really existed" (748). This money Aunt Betsey recognizes as hers. Heep has also forged a bond for the trust money, falsely stating that he had lent the sum to Mr. Wickfield to save his partner from "dishonor, though really the sum was never advanced by him, and has long been replaced" (750).

These and similar webs of deceit have enmeshed Mr. Wickfield to such a degree that the man who should have been mentor and guide to his aspiring former clerk has become Heep's pawn, as has Micawber, who has had to keep assisting in corruption to maintain his position. Now that all this has been finally exposed, corrective action can be taken. Micawber concludes his performance like a tragic hero, bravely awaiting society's vengeance for his complicity in what has been done. Agnes, though, is "weeping, half-joyfully, half-sorrowfully" (752), as she hears her father vindicated and his reputation restored. Traddles orders Heep to place himself under the equivalent of house arrest, and David summarizes the lessons the victim should derive from his painful experience in words Chaucer's parson might have used: "It may be profitable to you to reflect, in future, that there never were greed and cunning in the world yet, that did not do too much, and over-reach themselves. It is as certain as death" (755). Once again, the *via media* has been violated and catastrophe has ensued.

David also accords Mr. Micawber an extraordinary accolade. He looks back once more to the old days, when Micawber, in an act of *noblesse oblige*, took him under his roof and made David a part of his large family. Though those days were hard and David suffered cruelly in the company of the urchins he had to work with, he realizes that without his privations, he and Mr. Micawber might never have met. Since this would have been a disaster and Heep might never have been exposed, David is "devoutly thankful for the miseries of my younger days which had brought me to the knowledge of Mr. Micawber" (756). David's "miseries" have served as the catalyst without which justice could not have been done. He has discovered meaning and necessity in what others would consider pointless suffering and in so doing has grown in moral understanding and in character.

As David, Traddles, Aunt Betsey, and the Micawbers relax after the "explosion" (736) with Heep, David's aunt makes a suggestion that will have a life-changing impact. She asks the Micawbers if going abroad might be to their advantage. Illustrating again how, at this point in the novel, the separate plot strands are coming together, Aunt Betsey mentions the plan Daniel Peggotty has devised for a new life in Australia and wonders if the Micawber family would consider joining him and his on their voyage. She also offers to assist the Micawbers in raising the necessary capital. Micawber accepts this offer only on condition that any money Aunt Betsey advances be classified as a loan, which he will repay at "five percent interest per annum" (758). She readily agrees. Mrs. Micawber gives her consent only on condition that Australia provide "a reasonable opening for his [Micawber's] talents to develop themselves—that would be amply sufficient—and find their own expansion" (758). In earlier days, such concerns would be subjects for comedy, but after his handling of Heep, they are not so funny. Micawber senses that "something of an extraordinary nature will turn up on that shore" (759) and resolves to try his fortune with his family in the land of the kangaroo.

There is more here than a travel plan. This decision to join Daniel Peggotty, Em'ly, and the others culminates the Micawbers' endless search for stability and security. Like the Peggottys, they have "fought the good fight" in their native land and now are in a situation reminiscent of Bunyan's faithful ones, who at the end of their earthly journey can approach the kingdom of heaven in company with the "saved." The pilgrims have to wade through water to reach that blessed shore, water that cleanses and purifies. The emigrants will also cross waters that will symbolically wipe away all traces of former sorrow and degradation, as well as wash away sins like Micawber's chronic indebtedness and his participation in Heep's criminal schemes and Em'ly's abandonment of her family and friends. These families will not be "crossing over" into paradise, but they will be entering an environment that will be welcoming and open. They will be "resurrected" as they establish new identities and new ways of life. All this will occur because they have tried, like Bunyan's Faithful, to follow the path of virtue no matter the cost. In the greatest challenges, Daniel Peggotty and Wilkins Micawber have stayed the course and triumphed without ever forsaking the "generosity of spirit" that has made every encounter they have had with their fellows an occasion for sharing and caring. Of Micawber, Traddles says, "he is a most untiring man when he works for other people" (770). The same is true, even more obviously, of Daniel Peggotty. These two have prevailed over a seducer and an exploiter through courageous determination to redress wrongs. For this, they will thrive in a new world whose citizens will hold them in high esteem ever afterwards.

David's life journey has now reached a crossroads. His professional successes have earned him recognition and reward but have not turned him away from virtuous and selfless devotion to those he loves. His wife, Dora, has presented challenges in everyday living that he has tried to help her overcome, to no avail. David has accepted the fact that his wife will be less of a companion and helpmeet and more like a perpetual child bride who is too delicate and too fickle to discharge capably her share of household responsibilities and duties. This recognition, however, does not lead David to castigate Dora over her failings and break her spirit, as Murdstone did with his mother and his succeeding wife. David's love is less romantic as the days of his married life proceed, but it is no less real.

Fate now intervenes to change the narrative radically. Dora becomes ill, so ill she is bedridden most of the day. She and her "Doady" try to put the best face on things, though both realize that a full recovery is unlikely. As Dora declines, she asks to see Agnes Wickfield, that embodiment of care, concern, and affection. She and David then enjoy a last conversation. As David assures her of his love, Dora reflects on what might have happened had she not contracted her fatal illness. With a clear-sightedness that perhaps only impending death can bring, she is utterly honest and perceptive:

> *I was very happy, very. But as years went on, my dear boy would have wearied of his child-wife. She would have been less and less a companion for him. He would have been more and more sensible of what was wanting in his home. She wouldn't have improved. It is better as it is.* (762)

In the company of Agnes, whom, we learn later, she asks to marry David after she has passed on, Dora leaves her "Doady" and her beloved Jip forever. David will recover, but Jip cannot. He dies of a broken heart as soon as he senses his mistress's passing.

This is, admittedly, an overly sentimental episode, almost too Victorian for contemporary readers to bear. It also smacks of authorial contrivance, a *deus ex machina* solution to an intractable complication. Sentimentality undoubtedly is present, culminating with Jip's simultaneous death. But Franklin D. Roosevelt's Fala reportedly went more than a little berserk when his master died suddenly in Warm Springs, Georgia. Then, too, in the midst of Dora's wrenching last hours, she reveals insights about her husband and their life together that are perfectly accurate; she does not leave this earth clueless as a child but as a young woman grown suddenly mature. Her generous concern for her husband and his needs, as well as her appreciation of Agnes's character, prompts a final request that no pampered and selfish child-bride could ever make. Dora understands at the end that she probably was "too young" (762) for marriage and not prepared to become overnight a sensible and down-to-earth English spouse, ready to take charge of her husband and household. Her death evokes tender sentiment but also a realization that character is destiny. Dora could not change her ways; neither could her father take charge of his affairs, nor her aunts get over slights inflicted long ago. With a maturity gained through experience and the vicissitudes of a rich and eventful life, David has put the "miseries" of his past in perspective and has gone on. Dora's life ends with tragic awareness and self-understanding that have come too late to matter.

As for her death replicating the "god from the machine" contrivance of the Greek stage, that may well be, but Dickens is hardly alone in resorting to such a device to free his protagonist of entanglements. *David Copperfield* is a novel of education. The focus is how experience deepens David's understanding and forms his character. Life with Dora has taught him the folly of romantic excess, while at the same time toughening his will and forcing him to accept realities that cannot be altered. He realizes, as does Dora on her deathbed, that the couple are ill-matched and cannot bond as one flesh. They would have had to live not as life partners but as separate individuals had Dora not passed on. David learns from this episode how important compatibility is in married life and how impossible it is to create such if the potential is not present to begin with. English culture has recognized the fact that some marriages cannot succeed and, unlike Catholic Europe, has accepted the necessity of divorce if a husband and wife fail to connect as a reasonably happy, mutually supportive, and productive pair. Dora and David's conjugal union probably would have been dissolved in time. Dickens avoids such an eventuality by terminating the marriage through death, but not before the couple reach a degree of understanding about their situation that will give David priceless insight and guide his thinking in succeeding years. Death will take away any possibility that Dora will use her experience to make a better life; her last hours, however, go far to redeem her profitless earlier years.

Dora's death is, therefore, meaningful, just as David's boyhood miseries have been. This is hardly the case in another novel with a comparable intervention. That most sophisticated master of language and analyst of character, Vladimir Nabokov, resorts to a sudden and most unlikely dramatic incident in

Lolita to free his protagonist, Humbert, from his wife's fury. As she rushes toward the mailbox across the street with an incriminating letter about her husband's pedophilia, Charlotte is struck in the street by a speeding auto and dies instantly, with the letter still in hand. Humbert thereupon tears up the letter, buries his wife, settles accounts, and begins a continent-wide *hegira* with the real love of his life, his fourteen-year-old stepdaughter. All this Humbert does with cold calculation and detachment, consigning his wife to oblivion and feeling only relief after her death. He takes away nothing of any value from this catastrophe, continuing instead his manipulation of a young victim, who soon becomes as cold and detached as he is.

David emerges from his trial sobered and wiser but, thanks to Agnes Wickfield's ministrations, still whole and intact. He remembers how as a boarder in the Wickfield home he had elevated Agnes to a saintly level, linking her to "the stained-glass window in the church" (765). True to this dignity, throughout Dora's last hours, Agnes has been a calming and consoling presence, even to the very end as Dora expires "on her bosom with a smile" (765). For David, she has been like "a sacred presence" in that "lonely house" (765). Given her virtue and her unwavering faith, David could hardly have given way to anger, bitterness, despair, or denunciation of divine will, as so many who have suffered the loss of one so young frequently do. Instead, he absorbs his grief and channels his energy into good works, as Chaucer's parson would have recommended. Thus, when his aunt realizes that the funds she had invested with Wickfield and Heep have been found, David agrees with her wholeheartedly in dispensing a portion to Micawber, albeit with restraint, to finance the family's voyage and to cover any obligations still remaining from Heep's salary advances to his clerk in past days.

Aunt Betsey, the soul of decency and charity despite her gruffness, pays David the ultimate tribute, commending him not only for his consideration of the Micawbers' needs now, but also for his unflinching support during all the time she had believed her investment lost: "I wanted to see how you would come out of the trial, Trot, and you came out nobly—persevering, self-reliant, self-denying!" (772). David has so thoroughly absorbed the moral code inculcated in British culture he can act in accordance with its mandates without hesitation or doubt. Unlike the self-inflating Julien Sorel, who for a short while was "the biggest dandy in Paris," and unlike Steerforth, whose charm and wit conceal heartlessness, David models the gentlemanly ideal in the best sense.

A final trauma awaits David. After returning from a period of rest and renewal abroad, he decides to visit Yarmouth one more time before the Peggotty clan leaves England for good. He is eager to deliver in person Emily's (she is no longer "Little") last communication to Ham. This is a brief but heartfelt farewell, expressing her gratitude for and her devotion to her once-betrothed and ending: "Now, my dear, my friend, good-bye forever in this world. In another world, if I am forgiven, I may wake a child and come to you. All thanks and blessings. Farewell evermore" (781). Though Ham's wounds can never fully heal, Em'ly's words provide balm. Like David, he has responded to loss by performing extraordinary service; where there is need, he assists without thought of obstacle or recompense. He loses himself in embracing others. This willingness to go the extra mile in any emergency makes Ham disregard risks or possible harm. He can be reckless and disdain danger because the man is beyond caring about this life. The focus of his last letter to Emily is like the conclusion of hers to him; both look to the life of the world to come, "where every tear will be wiped away."

For Ham, that world lies on the horizon. On the way to Yarmouth, David sees dark skies and feels winds so strong, his coach's horses can "scarcely face" (782) their fury. A storm of biblical proportions is building. It will be remembered later by all in Yarmouth "as the greatest ever known to blow upon that coast" (784). This is an apocalyptic climax for the novel and for Ham and Steerforth, who reappears now after a long absence. The storm not only will sweep away men and materiel; it will also make all things new for its victims by making irrelevant hurts, slights, resentments, disappointments, and soul-destroying conduct in any whom its cleansing solvent touches. The flood that only Noah and the ark's creatures survived left nothing of the old world in its wake. Noah and his descendants had to start anew once the rainbow announced God's reconciliation with mankind and the earth. The Yarmouth flood will have a similar impact, not for all mankind but for two individuals trapped in its destructive path.

David rushes to the shore at the height of the storm, his "whole frame thrilled with objectless and unintelligible fear" (785). His apprehension is justified: "A schooner, from Spain or Portugal, laden with fruit and wine" (787) is breaking apart before his eyes. Only "one active figure with long curling hair, conspicuous among the rest" hangs on as the sea batters the vessel and "sends men, spars, casks, planks, bulwarks, heaps of such toys, into the boiling surge" (787). That person's situation is desperate. Ham Peggotty knows this and knows that only he has the courage and skill to attempt a rescue. All on shore try to hold him back, to no avail. He wades into the maelstrom with ropes and tackle, intent on saving the stranger. The doomed one is dashing in the face of death as he waves his "singular red cap" (789), with *sangfroid* fearlessness. This is, of course, Steerforth, who might as well have been on stage. Ham and he come very close to meeting. Ham is "so near that with one more of his vigorous strokes he would be clinging" (790) to the ship and to Steerforth. The two who have been so opposite in life, the one so favored and the other so ill-used, come close to a lifesaving embrace and to a reconciliation of opposites. In this extremity, social class, education, wit, manners, style, all the externals, mean nothing. These two "in peril on the sea" are one in their need to save and to be saved. They are two human beings united in common struggle and focused on bare survival. The man whom Steerforth held in contempt is his sole hope. Ham has never gotten over Steerforth's betrayal, but that is all history now, having no bearing on his conduct. They are together as two worlds meet in mutual need and two human beings extend their arms out to each other in supplication and hope. They are brothers, Chaucer's parson would have said, as all men are regardless of circumstances of birth. Here is biblical teaching acted out in a biblical setting.

The moment when the two might actually have escaped their doom passes in an instant. The rescue fails, and the two perish, probably without ever realizing who the other was. They have come, nevertheless, as close to reconciliation as their life circumstances could allow. Now David performs a last service for the man whose friendship and patronage saved him from the wrath of Creakle. He always has thought of Steerforth at his best, and so he will do whatever obsequies are appropriate. Although all in Yarmouth know what Steerforth has done, the seamen too put aside resentments as they render their fellow sailor honors reminiscent of those accorded Prince Hamlet in death:

> *They brought a hand-bier, and laid him on it, and covered him with a flag, and took him up and bore him on toward the houses. All the men who carried him had known him, and gone sailing with him, and seen him merry and bold.* (791)

Out of respect for the man he wronged, their neighbor and friend, they will not however lay Steerforth's body, even temporarily, in the cottage where Ham already rests: "They felt as if it were not right to lay him down in the same quiet room" (791). David understands, so he takes charge of the body, arranges for its transfer to London, and faces up to "the hard duty of preparing his mother to receive it" (790), a duty he knows only he can discharge because he alone remains loyal to the memory of one who once meant everything to him and to her.

David's final encounter with Mrs. Steerforth and Rosa Dartle is just as painful as his previous meetings with them have been. Mrs. Steerforth does not suspect the news he is bringing, but Rosa senses that David is a "bearer of evil tidings" (793). He tells them what has occurred as gently and compassionately as possible. At one point, Mrs. Steerforth asks if her son is ill and if David has seen him. David cannot bear to tell her the harsh truth, so he says only that James Steerforth is "very ill" (793). Mrs. Steerforth then asks, "Are you reconciled?" (793). David cannot answer one way or the other. He is certainly reconciled to the memory of Steerforth at his best, which David's lasting gratitude demands, but in view of "the ruins of the home he had wronged" (790), there can be no pardoning of his conduct toward the Peggottys. David finds himself close to Mrs. Steerforth in this respect, whose home has also been "wronged"; neither can imagine, however, the dramatic last moments of Steerforth's and Ham's lives. The one most wronged sacrificed his life in a hopeless attempt to save his worst enemy from certain death. Here was played out a transcendent act of charity and forgiveness that dwarfs all else.

The truth soon comes out. Mrs. Steerforth "sat like a stone figure" (794), immobilized now more than ever by the need to wall off the tumultuous emotions that yielding to grief would unleash and that her pride would be ashamed to reveal. Rosa, however, is under no such restraint; true to her passionate nature, she lets loose a torrent of invective, allying her sorrow to her frustrated love, her resentment of Mrs. Steerforth's rigidity, her hopelessness now that "James" will never appear again, and her uncontrollable anger at David for having first brought his friend to Emily's home. Rosa cannot stop harping on how her devotion could have accommodated James Steerforth's restless spirit: "I could have loved him and asked no return. If I had been his wife, I could have been the slave of his caprices for a word of love a year" (795). She concludes with a parting shot at David: "A curse upon you!" she said, looking round at me, with a mingled expression of rage and grief. "It was in an evil hour that you ever came here! A curse upon you! Go!" (796)

Mrs. Steerforth breaks down under this barrage, like one who has been beaten so badly he or she simply crumbles. Rosa attempts to revive her prostrate mistress, suddenly showing care and concern for one she has served so long, but like Littimer with such mixed emotions. This is Mrs. Steerforth's final agony. She will never recover from her shock over her son's premature death and Rosa's wild verbal assault. David's last moment with her is like taking leave of a corpse: "I lifted up the leaden hand, and held it to my heart, and all the world seemed death and silence, broken only by his mother's moaning" (797).

Steerforth's death, in company with Ham, and Mrs. Steerforth's collapse form the climax of the novel's final section; despite the emotional power of these scenes, they reveal little that is unexpected. Steerforth departs this life with death-defying bravado, as if the monstrous storm were just like Creakle or Mr. Mell writ large. To the last, Steerforth acts as if no force can knock the golden boy off his perch. On the sinking ship, he defies death like the English public-school recruits in World War I, who faced overwhelming firepower with a dash and *panache* learned on the football field. Steerforth is still the confident boy David so admired; unlike David, however, who has become a man of character through sorrow and stress, Steerforth has not grown or changed, has not moved to another level and faced soberly the possibilities of tragedy life affords. His mother and Rosa, likewise, are stuck in the roles they have been acting out since David first entered their lives. The two have nothing more to offer than soul-destroying resentment and irreconcilable anger over what seems like divine betrayal.

By novel's end, since only he has moved forward and grown in spirit, that family connection is just burdensome to David. The gloom, doom, and calcification that have overtaken the Steerforth household leave a powerful impression on him. In an attempt to put the emotional turmoil of the past days behind him, David escapes England for a time and roams about continental Europe, hoping for a renewal of energy and strength in a foreign environment. In so doing, he retraces the steps of Steerforth and Emily, as well as Daniel Peggotty, although not consciously so. In the beginning, the depth of his sorrow makes this sojourn dispiriting; as he tours old Europe's many places of interest, David is too melancholy to take much notice. "Listlessness to everything but brooding sorrow" (808) oppresses him, as if he were still with Mrs. Steerforth. Rather than visit famous sites, David starts to seek relief in solitary rambles through the countryside, like Wordsworth and Coleridge, who found inspiration in England's Lake Country and like Byron's Childe Harold, who finds in Nature mystic communion impossible to experience in conventional society:

There is a pleasure in the pathless woods,
There is a rapture on the lonely shore,
There is society where none intrudes,
By the deep Sea, and music in its roar:
I love not Man the less, but Nature more,
From these our interviews, in which I steal
From all I may be, or have been before,
To mingle with the Universe, and feel
What I can ne'er express, yet can not all conceal.
"Childe Harold's Pilgrimage, A Romaunt"
(Canto the Fourth, CLXXVIII)

In a bucolic Swiss valley one evening, David is struck by the stupendous majesty of snow-covered mountains, springs, forests, and pastures. In this setting, he finally feels a degree of peace and allows himself to relax. As he does so, all the emotion and sentiment he has kept bottled up are at last released. The effect is cathartic: "All at once, in this serenity, great Nature spoke to me, and soothed me to lay down my weary head upon the grass, and weep as I had not wept yet, since Dora died!" (809)

The life-giving renewal "great Nature" provides is a staple of Romanticism in general, but especially of English culture. As far back as Shakespeare, who set *As You Like It* and *A Midsummer Night's Dream* in natural settings that stimulate romance and magic, the English have responded to nature as passionately as the French have to beauty and the Germans to the transcendent. Wordsworth believes he can "see into the life of things" through immersion in nature, while Keats and Shelley are lifted out of depression and pessimism by a nightingale's song or a west wind's force. The great composer Frederick Delius captures the complex natural sights and sounds of Florida, as well as the simple joy one feels on hearing the first birdsong in spring. Lesser composers like George Butterworth and Arnold Bax leave indelible imprints of a river's rhythmic flow or the grim majesty of icy winterscapes. In *"The Scholar Gypsy,"* Matthew Arnold even goes so far as to make the hermit's life in the wild an appropriate means for a former Oxford scholar to enjoy continual inspiration, since no human contacts or entanglements can interfere with his communing with nature. The lifting of David's sorrow and despair through nature's intervention is firmly within this very English tradition.

As he reflects on his situation, David opens a packet of letters he had brought with him. One is from Agnes Wickfield, whose advice he has always sought and followed. She asks David to "turn affliction into good" (810) by continuing to work. She is sure the severe trials he has endured ultimately will lead him to new depths of understanding and empathy that will enable him to produce the great masterpieces destiny has "reserved" for him (810). All the while, she assures David, she will be his consolation and support, providing day to day what "great Nature" gives in exalted moments.

The renewal he has sought becomes almost like an emotional resurrection as David returns to his Alpine village, makes numerous friends, resumes his writing, and regains his health. Only one regret remains. As he looks back on misjudgments and opportunities lost, David is convinced he has given up all possibility of marrying Agnes: "The time was past. I had let it go by, and had deservedly lost her" (812). He will not let this bitter truth haunt the rest of his life, though. David has seen what distortions of character unrequited love has caused in Rosa Dartle's life, and he will not be victimized this way. Instead, he will accept manfully and try even to embrace his fate like the ancients, making having loved and lost yet another character-building episode: "I endeavored to convert what might have been between myself and Agnes, into a means of making me more self-denying, more resolved, more conscious of myself, and my defects and errors" (813). On this note of stern Christian fortitude, he ends his sojourn abroad and returns to England ready to resume his career.

In sharp contrast to David's struggle are the joyous anticipation and optimism of the Micawbers and the Peggottys. Her husband's triumph over Heep has made Mrs. Micawber, in particular, positively giddy. Her much put-upon faith in Micawber's capability and mastery has been vindicated by "the latent power" (803) he summoned up in public combat with his oppressor. She is now more than ever convinced he will stand out in like fashion in Australia and take the new country by storm. His meteoric ascent will be noticed back home: "Can I be so weak as to imagine that Mr. Micawber, wielding the rod of talent and power in Australia, will be nothing in England?" (804). Impossible to imagine. Among those who will be forced to take notice are the members of Mrs. Micawber's family, who, true to form, have not appeared to see them off.

More subdued, as always, are Daniel Peggotty and Emily. Daniel sets sail after a characteristically selfless final act. He welcomes Martha, Emily's savior, as a traveling companion, thereby guaranteeing her return to conventional society and bringing his niece a life-long friend. David is deeply affected by this act of kindness, averring that "if ever I have loved and honoured any man, I loved and honoured that man in my soul" (806). Seeing Emily leaning on her uncle's shoulder as the ship departs, he offers a quasi-scriptural injunction: "Aye, Emily, beautiful and drooping, cling to him with the utmost trust of thy bruised heart, for he has clung to thee, with all the might of his great love" (807).

David's sabbatical in Europe has helped him come to terms with the loss of his child-wife, Dora, his childhood friend, Steerforth, and, in all probability, his dearest friend, Agnes, who, he is sure, will marry someone else. He is resigned to loneliness once again as he arrives in London to visit with Traddles, who is laboring diligently to move ahead in the legal profession. Traddles greets him affectionately and informs David he is now married to his beloved Sophy. With Sophy have come her sisters, eager to have "a peep at London" (818). So many guests are crowding into the small apartment Traddles and his wife share that the newlyweds are forced into a "little room in the roof" (820) for the time being. Clearly, the sisters are trying the kind-heartedness and generosity of their hosts, but Sophy and Traddles are not bothered by this. They delight in their company, joining in games and such with zest and good spirits. David cannot help entering into this atmosphere of perfect domestic bliss and, for awhile at least, he stops thinking about his own situation. Of Traddles and Sophy, he cannot say enough:

> *But their self-forgetfulness charmed me. Their pride in these girls, and their submission of themselves to all their whims, was the pleasantest little testimony to their own worth I could have desired to see.* (823)

In contrast to the happy home life of his friends is the household of Mr. and Miss Murdstone. David learns from Mr. Chillip, the doctor/undertaker who had long ago buried his mother and whom he encounters unexpectedly at his London hotel, that Mr. Murdstone has married again. The new wife is "a young lady . . . with a very good little property, poor thing" (827). Murdstone and his sister, apparently, have wasted little time in exercising "firmness" so that, like David's mother, the young wife's "spirit has been entirely broken since her marriage" and "the brother and sister between them have nearly reduced her to a state of imbecility" (827-28). This domestic cruelty is justified by religion, which Mr. Chillip does not recognize as that taught by Jesus of Nazareth but as some aberrant strain generated by Murdstone's egotism: "Mr. Murdstone sets up an image of himself and calls it the Divine Nature" (828). Between the Traddles' selflessness and the Murdstones' self-absorption lies an impassable moral gulf. These back-to-back dichotomous portraits throw into high relief the beauty of charity lived out in service to others and the horror of life-crushing malice intent on the enslavement of others.

David resolves finally to visit Agnes. Before leaving for Canterbury, he asks his aunt if she is aware of "any lover" (831) in Agnes's life, almost as if David wishes to foreclose once and for all any hope of his ever being with her. Aunt Betsey thinks Agnes "has an attachment" (831) but declines to elaborate. The truth, of course, is that Agnes loves David as his aunt's soulful gaze and warm embrace suggest. David, however, is too certain his "sister" (832) loves another to react to these signals.

Arriving at the Wickfields' home, David notes approvingly: "Everything was as it used to be, in the happy time" (832). This is grounds for hope since "in the happy time," Agnes and he were close. Though his head tells him it is illogical to continue to imagine Agnes and he can ever marry, David responds to his heart's longing and treasures every positive sign. When he and Agnes meet, he learns she has restored the old décor deliberately, and he is cheered by her words: "I have found a pleasure," returned Agnes, smiling, "while you have been absent, in keeping everything as it used to be when we were children. For we were very happy then, I think" (834). Agnes also says nothing about an "attachment," only blushing briefly as David alludes to such. Perfectly in character, she returns to her major concern as she reminds David of his ethical obligations now that he is a well-known author: "Your growing reputation and success enlarge your power of doing good" (837). The conversation ends as David reiterates his respect for Agnes: "You will always be my solace and resource as you have always been" (837). Although Agnes plays gently on her piano "some of the old airs" (836) and cannot take her eyes off David, he does not pick up on any of this. He, instead, takes leave of Agnes, imagining how, like Ham and Emily, they may become as one in the next life, where David "might yet love her with a love unknown on earth" (838).

A "love unknown on earth," however, is not at all what Agnes and David are about to experience. With his feet firmly planted on this earth's soil, his imagination cleansed of emotional excess and fantasy, and his career settled and flourishing, David pays a second visit to Canterbury, this time determined to learn the identity of the life partner Agnes must by now have chosen. His aunt has become more explicit, assuring David that Agnes is serious and predicting that she will soon be married. David expects to offer Agnes his sincere congratulations and to continue to rely on her chaste friendship, support, and good counsel as before. Their dialogue, however, moves quickly in a different direction once David tells Agnes he has heard "that there is someone on whom you have bestowed the treasure of your love" (854). Agnes reacts with sudden emotion, bursting into tears and moving away from David. This unexpected response is enough to arouse in the hopeless suitor a glimmer of new hope: "[Agnes's tears] awakened something in me, bringing promise to my heart" (854). Daring not to hope too much lest he be let down harshly, David declares nobly:

> *"If you have any lingering thought that I could envy the happiness you will confer, that I could not resign you to a dearer protector, of your own choosing, that I could not, from my removed place, be a contented witness of your joy, dismiss it . . . There is no alloy of self in what I feel for you"* (854–55).

But the "alloy of self" is precisely what Agnes desires above all. For a brief moment, she falters, telling David things are not as he believes and that she has a "secret" (855) that cannot be revealed. She has misinterpreted David's renunciation, thinking it was prompted by lack of feeling for her. She starts to move away. David, though, is encouraged by what has just happened; he feels "new-born hope" that he may one day call Agnes "something more than Sister" (855). This is followed by tears that make David even more hopeful. He finally says what he had wanted to say for so long but had let his fears stifle him: "I went away, dear Agnes, loving you. I stayed away, loving you. I returned home, loving you!" (856). Agnes then reveals her secret: "I have loved you all my life" (856). As if this were not reason enough for the two to become one, Agnes informs David that as she attended Dora on her deathbed, the Little Blossom had made "a last request . . . and left a last charge": "That only

I would occupy this vacant place" (858). David and Agnes are married "within a fortnight" (858).

David's life has reached fulfillment. He has gone to Canterbury one final time, not to pray at the shrine of a long-dead saint but to meet and love a living saint, who will become the perfect English wife and helpmeet: kind, sensible, devoted, and virtuous. David's pilgrimage will be lifelong, but the formative experience chronicled in *David Copperfield* culminates when he marries Agnes, ending the novel as Shakespeare ends his romantic comedies, with a wedding. On the way to this joyous event, David has gained knowledge, experience, depth, and wisdom as he coped with a range of characters and narratives just as representative of the human comedy as those of Chaucer's merry band. Throughout, he has striven to remain faithful to the moral code preached by the parson and lived out by Bunyan's Christian and Faithful, prototypes of David and Agnes. They will spend the rest of their lives as a contented couple and will model for their children an unbreakable conjugal union.

Though tragedy at times casts great gloom over the lives of David and many of the characters he is engaged with, *David Copperfield* is not a tragic tale like *The Red and the Black*. The gloom is permanent for some, such as Rosa Dartle and Mrs. Steerforth, who cannot move past the ruin of James Steerforth's promising life, and for the Murdstones, who, like grifters today, live only to exploit naïve young women who come under their fatal spell. These are, however, exceptional; they are living warnings about what can befall persons who act contrary to common sense and common decency, the guiding lights of English conduct. They can bruise the Christian pilgrim, but so long as he or she stays on right paths, the bruises will heal.

David's bruises have been numerous, especially in his interactions with those like Creakle, Heep, and Littimer, who have played key roles in some of his life's most painful episodes. Ironically, he and Traddles meet all three, together, one last time. They discover that, despite the passage of time and the impact of life experience, these characters, like the restored Bourbons, have "learned nothing and forgotten nothing." Creakle has managed to earn an appointment as director of a prison operating under a system designed to rehabilitate reprobates. The methods used, however, involve prolonged isolation and exhortation, creating an atmosphere where loneliness, boredom, and fear of reprisal produce zombie-like inmates, who resemble the brainwashed hostages in terrorist detention camps. In his new position, Creakle has stopped beating those under him but, characteristically, continues to inflict psychological torment on his charges. He also cannot help making exceptions, as he did with Steerforth.

Like Steerforth, two see through Creakle's system to gain advantage. One is Uriah Heep, whom David and Traddles recognize immediately when they visit the prison. Heep is introduced proudly as "Number Twenty-Seven" (844), a model of obedience and piety. In reality, he is the same Uriah, mouthing platitudes, writhing in humility, and quietly burning with the urge for vengeance. He has had to revert to what he was as a youth, the workhouse boy, who gets on by dissembling and hiding resentments carefully. When not under official observation, his gaze remains "villainous" (848). The second model prisoner is "Number Twenty-Eight" (844), who turns out to be Steerforth's manservant, Littimer. In prison, he exhibits the same deference and propriety he showed his master; adding some pious phrases to his customary polite speech is not difficult, so he too seems regenerate. Littimer is serving time because he was found to have "robbed a young master of two hundred fifty pounds in money and valuables, the night before they were going abroad" (849), which sheds some new light for David on Littimer's relationship with Steerforth. David can only conclude that, like sinners in Dante's *Inferno*, Heep and Littimer are "perfectly consistent and unchanged" (850) in their current domicile, where they cannot do anyone any further harm but, likewise, cannot ever achieve anything like emancipation from either their past or their dark selves.

These are in marked contrast to those who have renewed their lives, aided by changed circumstances and by their innate virtues and gifts, finally allowed expression. Ten years after his marriage to Agnes and the emigrants' departure, David learns during a visit home by Mr. Peggotty that Mr. Micawber has indeed risen to "the top of the tree," becoming a magistrate in Australia and being feted by his fellow citizens as a man of distinction. Though he is still florid and grandiloquent, he now applies these verbal adornments to good effect, much as a lawyer does when he appeals in the grand manner for a client. His words, too, radiate sincerity and credibility, coming as they do from one who has "been there" but, against all probability, risen above every trial and challenge to emerge whole and become the man he always imagined himself to be. He knows others have done much to bring about this transformation. In a newspaper Mr. Peggotty has brought back from Port Middlebay, David reads a tribute Mr. Micawber has offered him, ostensibly on behalf of a grateful public, who treasure his uplifting tales, but really in gratitude and appreciation for what his "friend and companion" (865) has done for and meant to him. This is a man who realizes that without the "amazing grace" of David's good will and Aunt Betsey's largesse he would have perished long ago, "unwept, unhonored, and unsung."

Since their arrival in Australia, Mr. Peggotty and his charges have "allus thrived" (860) in their new setting, putting talent and experience to good use in a land where solitude compels every inhabitant to be as charitable and hospitable as the Peggottys. Martha has married, her husband well aware of her past but not letting that mar the prospects of the present. Em'ly has not married, choosing like Ham to overcome loss by living for others. Daniel Peggotty's portrait of Em'ly in action is music to David's ears:

> *Cheerful along with me, retired when others is by, fond of going any distance fur to teach a child, or fur to tend a sick person, or fur to do some kindness tow'rds a young girl's wedding . . . liked by young and old, sowt out by all that has any trouble. That's Em'ly.* (862)

They may be from different social circles and from different levels of education, but in their selflessness, Em'ly and Agnes are more faithful to the imperatives of English morality than any others in the novel. They redeem the human comedy and make this long story end happily, as comedy should.

RUSSIA

Leo Tolstoy
War and Peace

INTRODUCTION

In comparison to England, France, and Germany, which share a common background as components of the Roman Empire since the time of Julius Caesar, Russia has been integrally connected to Western Europe only since the late seventeenth century, when Tsar Peter I guided his nation into the orbit of European politics and culture quite as dramatically and decisively as Caesar did Britain, Germany, and Gaul centuries before. Prior to Peter, Russians had viewed their Western neighbors with suspicion and fear, and with good reason. Poles and Germans, in particular, had mounted numerous incursions into Russian territory since the late Middle Ages, viewing the immense Eastern nation as a source of plunder rather than as a respected partner. Even in the reign of Peter, King Charles XII of Sweden, intent on conquest, confidently led an invading force into the heart of northwestern Russia, only to be repelled by the tsar's armies at Poltava in 1709.

The roots of this mutual hostility lay in the distant past. Russia became a Christian nation in the late tenth century, long after the establishment of the faith in the Mediterranean basin and the rest of Europe. In contrast to the Western nations, however, which professed the Catholic faith as interpreted, practiced, and organized in accordance with the Church of Rome, Prince Vladimir of Kievan Rus, around whom the nascent Russian state had coalesced, embraced Orthodox Christianity, as professed by the subjects of the Byzantine Empire and as interpreted, practiced, and organized in accordance with the Church of Constantinople, capital of what remained of the Roman Empire. These two main branches of Christianity differed then and still do in theology, liturgy, church law, and ecclesiastical governance. Though they were still technically unified in the prince's time, adherents of each body considered only themselves to be members of the "true church," dismissing the counter-party's claims on all contested issues as fundamentally false. When, in 1054, the Pope of Rome, Patriarch of the West, and the Archbishop of Constantinople, Patriarch of the East, made this division a formal reality by excommunicating each other, they created a wall of separation between Christians that has never been removed.

Prince Vladimir's conversion and the adoption of Orthodoxy by his people is said to have been prompted by a report from emissaries he sent to Constantinople to observe the liturgical rites performed in *Hagia Sophia,* the magnificent cathedral built by the Emperor Justinian in the sixth century. According to legend, the Russian guests were so awed by the artistic decoration they saw everywhere in the massive church and by the beautifully sung liturgy celebrated at the altar directly under the gigantic mosaic of Christ, the Divine Judge and Ruler, that took up the entire dome above, they could hardly contain their admiration.

In this tale lie many of the themes emphasized not just in church life in Russia but in the larger culture as well. The Byzantine Empire that upheld and nourished the Orthodox faith proclaimed itself the successor of the Empire of the Caesars, which had disappeared in the West when the last Emperor in Rome was deposed in 476. In reality, however, the Byzantine Empire was more like the successor of the Seleucid and Ptolemaic kingdoms that were carved out of the territory in the eastern Mediterranean conquered by Alexander the Great. Constantinople may have been the organizational center of the empire and the church, but the political and theological teachings underpinning state and church owed more to Asiatic than to European influences. With the culture and prestige of Rome declining steadily under barbarian pressure in the early Christian era, the Eastern Empire and church came to reflect more and more the thought patterns of long-established Middle Eastern traditions. Scholars in the patriarchal cities of Alexandria, Antioch, and Jerusalem contributed numerous commentaries on and interpretations of Scripture in these centuries. These contributions were later collected and distributed as definitive works of the Greek Fathers of the Church and became immensely important in the development of Orthodox thinking. Men such as Origen, of Alexandria, Cyril, of Jerusalem, Ignatius, of Antioch, and Basil, of Caesarea, gave Orthodoxy a decidedly "eastern" cast.

The founder of what eventually became monasticism, the hermit Anthony, lived out his life of solitary prayer and fasting in the Egyptian desert, modeling for all who followed him later the austere life style this discipline imposes. Even though he wrote in Latin and served as a Catholic bishop, St. Augustine stands high in the roster of Orthodox guides. He was born in North Africa, where he would later end his days as Bishop of Hippo, and educated first in Carthage, a center for Manichean teachers, who stressed the dichotomy between children of the light and children of darkness, a distinction Orthodox believers could easily graft onto Christianity, particularly when having to deal with recreant Westerners and aggressive Moslem enemies. Augustine also emphasizes the majesty and omnipotence of the Godhead, his gift to mankind of his son, who eventually becomes Lord of the Universe and by whom weak and dependent sinners are given the grace that enables them to accept the true faith and be saved. Augustine dwells on the disabling effects of the original sin of Adam and how utterly necessary baptism is to wipe the believer's spiritual slate clean and enable him or her to resist temptation henceforward. Salvation comes from God, as revealed in the Bible, and not from any enlightenment man by himself can achieve.

The Western Church, of course, absorbed all of these teachings as well but made a great effort to reconcile them with the best in pagan thought. Ironically, the impact of the writings of the Greek philosopher Aristotle, whom Dante calls "the master of them that know," was stronger in the West than in the Byzantine world. Herculean efforts were made in places like the University of Paris to harmonize Aristotle's assertions, all based on rational analysis, with the teachings of the Bible, all based on God's revelation. Thomas Aquinas is the best known of these scholastic philosophers and theologians, sifting through arguments like a Roman lawyer to show how biblical statements do not necessarily conflict with Aristotle's writings, something Augustine, for instance, never would have accepted. The Orthodox Church largely agreed with Augustine and paid little attention to Aquinas and company. Indeed, with the conclusion of the seventh ecumenical council, convened at Nicaea in 787, Orthodoxy essentially reached fulfillment in its understanding of Christian faith and morality. It would propagate its teachings from this time forward as dogmatic truths admitting of no deviation and no need for further development. The faith Prince Vladimir professed in the tenth century was and would remain essentially the same faith Tsar Nicholas II and his family, the last of the prince's successors, professed until their deaths in 1917.

What characterizes the faith of Russians? One element is the grandeur of God, which the magnificently decorated Orthodox churches throughout the country suggest visually and which the solemn sonorities of the liturgy suggest aurally. The Orthodox gaze is otherworldly; in the Divine Liturgy, one of the invocations before Holy Communion highlights this perspective vividly: "Let us who here mystically represent the cherubim put aside all earthly cares." Those in attendance, in other words, are lifted by faith to the precincts of heaven, to partake with the angels and saints in the celestial banquet. Mystical transcendence is a path to the divine open to all believers, not just men and women living in monastic seclusion. In *War and Peace*, for instance, Prince Andrei undergoes several out-of-body experiences, one of which occurs after he is wounded and lies helpless on the battlefield at Austerlitz. This moment of transcendent exaltation is life-altering, confirming for this irreligious man of action the reality of God and the beauty of all creation.

Among the devout faithful, adherence to Orthodox teachings and traditional practices is vital. Like the Orthodox Jews, who demand strict fidelity to the law, Russian clergy and laity are scrupulous in observance of traditional Orthodox liturgical and sacramental rites, days of fast and abstinence, church decoration and icon artistry, and so on. Any attempt to modernize ancient practices is considered misguided and deviant. When the Patriarch of Moscow, Photius, ventured into this no man's land in the seventeenth century by mandating changes in the wording of some liturgical prayers, he provoked a schism. Thousands of his "faithful" denounced his actions as virtually heretical and repudiated his leadership. They became known as "Old Believers" and over the centuries continued to remain separated from the official church. Even something many would consider a neutral option can arouse passionate feelings. Dostoevsky's Father Zossima in *The Brothers Karamatzov*, for instance, is regarded by his followers as a living saint, but when he dies and his body starts to decay as a saint's should not, those who disliked him intensely in life for accepting the title and status of "elder" gloat in spiteful joy. To them, "elder" is an innovation that true believers can never permit.

Within the population, those most attached to the faith and most focused on living under its guidance are the simple people, the less educated, the less worldly or fashionable, the less powerful. Those who appear most successful in the eyes of the world are in reality the most endangered spiritually. They are chasers after false political or economic gods, seduced by the lure of the foreign and the exotic, forever hungering for wealth or power, and always striving to climb the social ladder, only to fall backward like Sisyphus. These must be saved through purifying contact with the poor, who almost alone have preserved and practice the faith in humble obedience to the Gospel. Dostoevsky's Elder Zossima makes this point in a visionary oration:

> *But God will save His people, for Russia is great in her humility. I dream of seeing, and seem to see clearly already, our future. It will come to pass, that even the most corrupt of our rich will end by being ashamed of his riches before the poor, and the poor, seeing his*

> *humility, will understand and give way before him, and will respond joyfully and kindly to his honourable shame.* (*The Brothers Karamatzov.* Trans. Constance Garnett. New York: Vintage Books, 1955, p. 379)

This Christianity is distinctive. It differs from the French understanding, which lays great stress on the ability of human reason to advance one's access to even the most sublime truths. It differs from the English approach, which makes virtuous living the hallmark of faith in action. It differs from the German conception of man as capable of reaching the most exalted levels through assertion of will and intellect. It differs from the American preference for the Bible alone as the guide to salvation and for individual choice in denomination. Russian Orthodoxy stresses humanity's weakness and dependence, conditions affecting the rich and powerful just like the poor. The Orthodox believer accepts this reality in meekness and humble resignation to all life may bring, led, supported, and nourished by the tenets, teachings, and practices of the "old time religion."

Even in the most difficult historical circumstances, Orthodoxy remained the most important formative influence in Russian culture. After the Mongols under Genghis Khan marched westward from their Central Asian homeland and conquered Kievan Rus in the thirteenth century, the princes of Moscow, far to the east, gradually took on the role of political leadership for "Great Russia," that is Russia minus the western territories of Byelorussia and Ukraine. These princes gained a measure of freedom and independence from the Mongols by accommodation—that is, by publicly acknowledging and acting out ceremonially on specified occasions their theoretical subservience to the Golden Horde. This ritual humiliation gave Moscow's leaders the space and liberty necessary to build the Russian state. The metropolitan of the Orthodox Church aided this process when he transferred his patriarchal see from Vladimir to Moscow in 1326, giving new stature to the city. "Holy Moscow" henceforth would be the center of the church, governing all the clergy spread throughout the country and defending the national faith.

For the next two centuries, the church flourished as never before, with monasteries opening up around the city and accruing large properties, with icon painters like the monk Andrei Rublev creating masterpieces, and with devout leaders like Dmitri Donskoy finding the strength to begin standing up to the Mongols and defeating them in battle. Holy Moscow ascended to even greater heights when Prince Ivan III married Zoe Palaeologina, niece of the last Byzantine emperor, in 1472, nineteen years after the Turks captured Constantinople and abolished the empire. In the eyes of devout Russians, this marriage was providential, allowing Moscow to become the successor to Rome itself as well as to Constantinople. As the "Third Rome," Moscow would take the lead in protecting and propagating the true faith and bringing all neighboring Russian jurisdictions, and eventually all of Russian Orthodoxy, within its control. Under the Byzantine double eagle, appropriated by Prince Ivan to serve as Russia's emblem, Moscow's seat of political and ecclesiastical administration, the fortified Kremlin, with its palaces, cathedrals, and staterooms, was like a nucleus around which the city grew in concentric circles and the nation coalesced.

By the beginning of the seventeenth century, despite the crimes of rulers like Ivan IV, first to call himself tsar and known ever after as "the Terrible," and despite the need to repel invaders from west and east, Muscovite Russia solidified itself as an independent state. Trade with neighbors to the west and south increased, and foreign merchants and agents, and their non-Orthodox ideas and belief systems, became so numerous in Moscow that special quarters had to be designated for them, the better to shield native Russians from the contamination contact with such people might bring. This expedient illustrates well the xenophobia Russians have displayed throughout history, combining a conviction that their faith and ways are superior to all others with a fear of what might happen if foreigners strongly challenge both.

With the Romanov accession in 1614, a dynasty was born that would rule Russia for the next 300 years. Some of the Romanovs, like Tsar Alexis I, who ruled for thirty years, showed keen interest in advancing Russian artistic and technical achievements and even welcomed the contributions foreign craftsmen made to this effort. On the whole, however, and over time, something like ossification began to afflict Muscovite life, especially in the Kremlin. Court ceremonial laid great emphasis on formality, correctness, rigid adherence to protocol, awe-inspiring royal spectacle, just as the medieval Byzantine state did. Courtiers acted and dressed alike, wearing loose-fitting, long-sleeved, floor-length robes and sporting beards. Wives and daughters lived in convent-like isolation in their own precincts of the Kremlin, where they spent their days praying and fashioning elaborate embroideries and handicrafts. Bishops and priests performed liturgical rites with punctilious regard for proper form and careful attention to established rubrics; following everything to the letter so strictly led to services whose predictability made them more routine than inspirational. In government circles and, by extension, in the nation at large, ambition and individual initiative at all levels were discouraged. The autocratic tsar made all the important decisions on his own; the church taught and lived by the Orthodox tradition, which resisted any evolution or development; and the common people largely followed the ways of life of past generations.

Gazing into this stagnant political, religious, economic, and cultural pool, Tsar Peter I, Alexis's youngest son, after his rise to power in 1696, determined to "make waves." The cumulative impact of his many reforms amounted to nothing short of a revolution, comparable to Henry VIII's separation from Rome and Napoleon's assault on the old order throughout Europe. Over the span of his twenty nine-year reign, Russia changed its orientation, turning away from Asiatic influences from the east and south and welcoming Western European art, science, technology, and philosophy. Time-worn Muscovite practices and traditions were either abolished or altered radically. Court ceremonial was simplified, with multiple bowings and lengthy proclamations eliminated; the long beards so prized by courtiers and civil servants were shaved, sometimes by Peter himself, and their flowing robes of office were replaced by short jackets and trousers, outfits more appropriate for sustained work; and women were liberated from the isolation and marginality that had made their lives so strained in Muscovite times.

Peter did not just issue orders and decrees. He also showed by example how he wanted his countrymen and women to unleash their creativity and exercise their skills through purposeful labor. The tsar did not disdain to be taught carpentry and shipbuilding by the artisans he befriended when he toured Western Europe right after his coronation. A small boat he helped build is treasured today as the first vessel of the Russian Navy. Peter set up schools on the Western model and sent promising students to Europe to learn from masters in engineering, navigation, art, and science. The tsar also invited European architects, designers, actors, musicians, sculptors, and painters to work in Russia, drawing this inward-looking and conservative society more and more into the Western cultural orbit.

Peter's transformational advances and innovations were made permanently visible in the new capital city the tsar ordered built in northwest Russia, at the mouth of the Neva River, with access to the Baltic Sea and all points west. Like Alexander the Great, who laid out the design for Alexandria, the port city the Greek conquerors built in Egypt beginning in 331 BC, Peter, who also would be designated "the Great," personally chose the site for his new capital and port and drew up its architectural plan. Overcoming all obstacles nature, weather, and terrain presented, Peter and his European master builders, with the invaluable help of a multinational small army of workers (many of them forced laborers), constructed in just seven years the city of St Petersburg in a place where no settlement had stood before.

When the sophisticated French observer, the Marquis de Custine, visited St Petersburg in his travels through Russia in the nineteenth century, he was highly critical of the city's European-inspired architectural styles and designs, believing them out of place in the rugged Russian north. But this is exactly what Peter intended. He was determined to make his "Window on the West" as recognizably European as any continental city and to be as different from Moscow as possible. Whereas Moscow had mostly wooden structures, given the vast forests of the Russian heartland, St Petersburg's government buildings, palaces, and churches are mostly stone and brick. The gardens were originally laid out in French-inspired geometric patterns, only to be rearranged in a more English style years later. Though the churches are typically Russian because they have to be, their brightly gilded domes and cupolas and richly decorated interiors evoke in their own ways something like European baroque splendor. Public buildings have characteristically French or Italian columns and spires and palaces are decorated and furnished with European finery. The famous equestrian statue of Peter the Great that Pushkin meditated upon in *"The Bronze Horseman"* could easily have found a home in Rome or Vienna, but not Moscow.

Peter's city and its legacy, therefore, are highly ambiguous. In his poem, Pushkin at first rhapsodizes over St. Petersburg, speaking with admiration about its architecture, promenades, and all the foreign vessels crowding its port. The rest of the work, however, tells the story of a poor government clerk trying hard to rise in the civil service so he can marry and eke out a decent life for his family. The flood of 1824 makes all these aspirations hopeless, as the clerk's mother and fiancée are swept to their deaths, causing the bereft young man to lose all interest in life. In one dramatic scene, he stands at the base of the statue known to all as *The Bronze Horseman*. Peter on horseback faces and seems to defy the elements that have just combined to take away the poor man's loved ones and leave him bereft. He hisses a curse toward the man who dragooned laborers as poor and oppressed as he to build what now seems an artificial and crushing metropolis that offends nature by maintaining itself in an environment inhospitable to human settlement. The statue then comes suddenly to life, and Peter on horseback pursues the fleeing clerk down the Nevsky Prospect, as if the all-powerful tsar senses in the clerk's ravings a threat to himself and his city. The haunted man escapes, only to become a homeless vagrant living on others' charity. He is found dead at the end in the flooded-out ruins of the habitation his mother and fiancée once called home.

In Andrei Bely's early twentieth-century novel, *Petersburg*, poor students are in the vanguard of radical socialism, threatening far more seriously than a lone clerk the ruling classes ensconced in the mansions and ornate government palaces of the capital. One of these is a prominent senator, who strives to create in his work and personal life, formal, orderly, and geometrically clean and clear constructs, almost as if he is channeling the Petersburg ideal into everyday living. He fears and tries to keep distant the masses, many of them non-Russian, who fill the Petersburg streets wearing native dress and babbling with thick accents. But the senator's protective web is like the capital's flood walls, useless in a serious storm. An apocalypse is looming whose effects will be worse than any flood, as all that Peter and his successors conceived and built will soon be wiped away. The senator's own home, in fact, harbors danger. His only son, a scholar and philosopher, is a secret agent of the coming chaos. Though attached loosely to "the Party," he has, nonetheless, accepted responsibility for an ultimate act of rebellion: the assassination of his father. This patricide will prefigure the wholesale overthrow of the paternal tsarist monarchy and all its henchmen that will occur afterwards. A bomb hidden in a sardine tin goes off in the home the two share, but the senator survives. His chastened son quickly escapes the city and spends the rest of his days abroad tormented by guilt.

This novel is a literary equivalent of Ravel's *La Valse,* in which the elegant rhythms of Viennese orchestral dances, like the geometric patterns of Petersburg, are gradually drowned out by sounds suggesting marching and cannon fire, as the chaos unleashed by World War I tears apart the delicate fabric holding monarchies and empires together throughout Central and Eastern Europe. In St. Petersburg, a revolution will begin in 1917 that will generate a wave of revolutionary violence, bringing terror and torment throughout the vast and polyglot Russian Empire. It will topple the tsar and a governing class grown too weak and fearful, like Bely's senator, to resist. One of its consequences will be the end of Peter's city as the seat of government. Moscow will be restored to its old eminence, and the Window on the West will close.

The differences between the two capitals are not just stylistic. Over time, the two cities became symbols of competing political and cultural interests. Moscow grew to prominence as the Third Rome, the patriarchal see of Russian Orthodoxy; the repository of native Russian arts, customs, and habits; and the custodian of the nation's soul, with its stubborn survival under the Mongol yoke and then its brave defiance of the oppressors, as well as European invaders. St. Petersburg became identified with aristocracy and bureaucracy, the place aspiring civil servants or military officials had to go to make their mark; with Western-inspired theatrical and musical productions and *soirees* where French was spoken more often than Russian; and with European influence in general, which in so many ways clashed with native thinking. *War and Peace* reflects the tensions between the two cities vividly, tensions that would lead later in the nineteenth century to the formation of two competing interest groups: the Westernizers, reflecting St. Petersburg's sympathies, and the Slavophiles, firmly grounded in Moscow's tried and true Russian ways.

Under this overarching dichotomy, *War and Peace* highlights thematic variations that emerge through the decisions and deeds of the great historical actors in the invasion of 1812 and the experiences of Tolstoy's fictional characters, whose peregrinations define the Russian political, social, and cultural identity. Among the historical figures, the Emperor Napoleon and Tsar Aleksandr I are entirely different in personality and philosophy. Napoleon is invariably confident, sure of himself, incapable of self-doubt, and determined to prevail no matter how challenged. As a son of the French Revolution, he is guided by practical reason and calculation, not by any religious convictions. His troops largely share these values, seeing in

Russia opportunities for enrichment and recognition, as well as for the spreading of revolutionary concepts.

Tsar Aleksandr, by contrast, is more of a medieval monarch, an autocrat ruling by divine right and in partnership with the Orthodox Church, whose unchanging teachings and traditions guide his actions. He is young and without much experience in war and politics; Aleksandr is emotional, generous, innocent, an "angel" among hardened men. He is the guardian of his people, their protector, their father. The great majority of his sons and daughters see in him a role model for all. They perform extraordinary feats of valor and endurance in the duress the invasion brings, giving up homes and possessions, burning crops and poisoning wells, remaining steadfast and united through all the displacements of war. Following the lead of the tsar, who refuses to come to terms with Napoleon so long as he and his troops remain in Russia, the people ignore all attempts by the occupiers to procure food or goods through normal commerce. They come together as members of a national family firmly resolved to resist at all costs. Their sons and brothers in military service, particularly the poor, display a similar spirit when they at last make their stand near Moscow. With a miracle-working icon carried to the field, and with their commander in chief and all his subordinates kneeling before it in humble devotion, the Russian Orthodox army stays together and stands its ground, inflicting serious damage. Though the Russian forces cannot mount a counterattack, their retreat is not a defeat. The heretofore invincible *Grande Armee* has been weakened severely, and its so-called victory is pyrrhic. Holy Moscow has to be sacrificed too, lest the infidel invaders, who engage in looting and plundering on a grand scale once inside the city's walls, find occupation comfortable. The fires that devour so much of the old capital, most of them deliberately set at the direction of Governor-General Rostopchin, have the desired impact. The enemy troops are forced to vacate the city just as the Russian winter approaches. They begin a long journey back to Europe, a journey the great majority will not live to complete. This is an outcome military strategy and firepower cannot prevent; Russia's survival has been decreed by the Almighty, whose will is absolute and immutable. On this point, there is universal agreement within Russia, as everyone from Tsar Aleksandr down to the poorest peasant kneels in thanksgiving as liberation dawns.

"War" and "Peace" is exactly what this novel combining fiction, history, and philosophy is about. The war is Napoleon's invasion of Russia in 1812, culminating in the Battle of Borodino, near Moscow, and the French occupation of and then retreat from the ancient Russian capital; the peace is the life experience of a number of aristocratic families coping with all the challenges and opportunities life brings normally and taking on the extraordinary pressures of wartime in characteristic ways. These families are the Bezukhovs, the Bolkonskys, the Rostovs, the Kuragins, and the Drubetskoys. Each family's members resemble each other in personality, lifestyle, and value system. They are, in addition, representative of one or the other element of the St. Petersburg/Moscow pairing, with the Kuragins and the Drubetskoys embodying Petersburg perspectives and points of view and the Rostovs, the Bolkonskys, and the Bezukhovs those of Moscow.

The Bezukhov "family," for most of the novel, consists of only one man. Pierre Bezukhov is the illegitimate son of Count Kiril Vladimirovich Bezukhov, one of Russia's richest men. In the beginning of the novel, the count is on his deathbed. When he passes, his "bastard son," Pierre, inherits the bulk of his fortune, something that shocks polite society. Pierre has traveled and studied in Western Europe and been exposed to the revolutionary concepts and ideals of the French Revolution, now espoused by Emperor Napoleon Bonaparte. Shortly after his return to Russia, Pierre attends a *soiree* in St. Petersburg that includes many titled guests. He upsets this gilded company by openly praising some of the reforms and proposals Napoleon has introduced in the territories he and his forces have overwhelmed, compelling their dynastic rulers to yield powers and privileges enjoyed for centuries. This is characteristic of Pierre, who is not attuned to conventional opinion and not afraid to speak his mind, no matter how his words will be received. He is a "seeker," searching for meaning and purpose and finding inspiration in unexpected places and among people far removed from aristocratic circles.

His life's journey is not a back-and-forth transit between St. Petersburg and Moscow, with a few brief stops at various estates. Pierre makes his way deeper and deeper into the Russian heartland, becoming less and less "cosmopolitan" and more and more "Russian" as the events of 1812 draw him into the vortex of a life and death struggle. He participates in the Battle of Borodino as a civilian observer embedded within an artillery unit that takes heavy enemy fire. In Moscow during the occupation, he is arrested by the French as an incendiary and narrowly escapes execution. While imprisoned, he meets a stout-hearted peasant whose folk wisdom and good cheer help him endure captivity. This simple man's influence connects Pierre more firmly to his native country's heritage. The cumulative impact of all he has seen and felt causes the man who once lauded Napoleon's achievements, and dabbled at times with Freemasonry, philanthropy, enlightened estate administration, and liberal politics, to find fulfillment and identity finally as a *paterfamilias*, content to uphold traditional Russian family values and raise his children accordingly.

The Bolkonsky family members, at least on the surface, appear similar. A crotchety patriarch, Prince Nikolai Andreyevich Bolkonsky, lives at Bald Hills, his country estate outside Moscow, with his daughter, Princess Marya, and a French-born housekeeper and clever flirt, Mademoiselle Bourienne. The old prince is a scoffer who has no use for politicians, military officials, religious zealots, and fellow nobles, particularly those wishing to make marital arrangements involving his daughter. Indeed, in one memorable scene, when he is informed that the head of a prominent family will be visiting him very soon, he orders his steward to clear away the snow near the main house to be sure his guest can navigate the grounds easily. Later on, however, he learns that this guest will be Prince Vasily Sergeyevich Kuragin, for whom he does not care, and that Prince Vasily will be bringing his son with him, an eligible but dissolute bachelor. Prince Nikolai is outraged and immediately demands that all the snow be put back.

Prince Nikolai's only son, Prince Andrei Nikolaiyevich, shares many of these same qualities. He does not suffer fools gladly, he sees through others' pretensions, and he is a harsh realist. But he and Princess Marya, the sister who is devoted to him, share interests that go well beyond practical affairs. Because his background and heritage almost compel Prince Andrei to assume a leadership role in some branch of state service, the prince makes demands on himself. He strives to embody and manifest the ideals of honor, selfless service, and patriotism that men of his class were expected to uphold but rarely did. His experience trying to live in accord with high principles is decidedly mixed. In civilian life, he meets influential officials, like Speransky, the reformer who believes "rational" approaches to bureaucracy and privilege will create efficient and effective government. The prince is at first attracted to such an approach but soon loses interest as he realizes Speransky and company are just as obsessed with advancement and favor as the old guard they are trying to displace.

His military service brings similar disillusionment. As an aide to Supreme Commander Marshall Mikhail Ilarionovich Kutusov, Prince Andrei meets high-ranking officers, attends strategy sessions, studies detailed plans, and receives invitations to important social events. Far from feeling comfortable amid all this polish and glitter, however, Prince Andrei is mostly repelled by what he sees and hears. He is realistic enough about the fog of war to know that the most detailed planning can never guide actions that are inherently random. As a proud soldier who prefers action to observation, Prince Andrei is disgusted by the intrigue and self-promotion he encounters at all levels. Society balls are nothing but huge distractions in times of war. Like Pierre, the civilian, Prince Andrei, the soldier, casts aside ideas, possibilities, and personalities that do not impress or inspire him.

As the mist lifts on the field at Austerlitz, for instance, and the Russian troops realize that instead of retreating, which the

Austro-Russian leadership expects, the French are attacking with great force and compelling the Russians to fall back, Prince Andrei rallies his comrades and, waving the regimental flag, leads a brave countercharge. His warrior's spirit will not let him stay out of harm's way at such a critical juncture. But the French momentum is too powerful to stall. The prince is wounded and falls to the ground. Lying motionless and helpless, he looks up to the sky, where the heavens dwell, and feels something like mystical enlightenment. He transcends mundane cares and preoccupations in a realization that in life, the plain, the simple, the natural, and the ordinary are what really matter and that sacrifice is more ennobling than any worldly gain.

Prince Andrei will have more moments of insight and inspiration as the novel proceeds, all tending toward a heightening awareness of possibility and purpose. He recovers from his wounds, suffers through the death of his wife after child birth, falls in love with a young woman of admirable naturalness and guilelessness, is made to endure an attempted seduction and kidnaping of his fiancée, suffers another wound during the Battle of Borodino, and dies muttering words of love and forgiveness that reveal a profound acceptance of the divinely ordained necessity of sacrifice that has formed his life. This acceptance allows him to join in spirit his sister, Princess Marya, a person of rock-hard faith. Ironically, she, who has had to cope with a harsh parent, with the loneliness of country living, and with the hopelessness only prayer can relieve, will meet and marry a man as upright as her brother, will raise her nephew, the prince's son, and will find fulfillment and happiness in the role of dutiful wife and mother enshrined in Russian tradition. Her sacrifices will lead to contentment in this life, while those of her brother will liberate him spiritually from this life.

The Rostov family is different from the Bezukhov and Bolkonsky clans. Instead of a dying patriarch leaving a fortune to a son only the tsar can legitimize or an irascible old man tormenting family members and associates through arbitrary will or caprice, the Rostov family is led by Count Ilya Andreyevich, an exemplar of generosity and good will. His wife, Countess

Natalya, more practical than her sometimes improvident husband and given to fits of worry about household finances, is nevertheless just as kind and considerate as he whenever family members or friends show need. Their children, Count Nikolai and Countess Natasha, are high-spirited romantics, responding to challenges with ardor and *joie de vivre*. Unlike Pierre and Prince Andrei, who are older and bookish, Nikolai and Natasha let their instincts guide decisions and judgments. Nikolai, for instance, enters military service thinking only of how he can perform bravely and selflessly in battle. He does, in fact, do so at Austerlitz, exposing himself to injury or death while moving far ahead of his cavalry group as French advance units approach through the mists. He is wounded but survives. Like his parents, Nikolai also strives to assist fellow soldiers in need, going so far in one instance as to appear at the tsar's headquarters and plead for a pardon for a fellow officer who, without authorization, has taken provisions from a commissary to feed his hungry men.

As the novel proceeds, Nikola's pride and passion are brought more and more under control and channeled toward worthy ends, as in the memorable encounter he has in 1812 with the serfs who are holding up Princess Marya Bolkonskaya's departure from property that is about to be overrun by French invaders. Nikolai courageously faces and, in true Russian patriarchal fashion, imperiously rebukes the recalcitrant peasants, who, also in true Russian fashion, respond in meek submission to his assertion of authority. He eventually marries the princess, whose wealth keeps the Rostov properties from being sold, and devotes his days to careful cultivation and productive use of all the land his father never could manage properly. Nikolai becomes a local leader, proud and respected but not popular with his peers, who see him as too idiosyncratic and aloof. He is like a true aristocrat of the antebellum American South, who scorns arrogance or cruelty in his treatment of laborers, encouraging all by his dedication, liberality, and sense of justice.

Natasha's life follows a similar arc. Her debut in St. Petersburg at a grand ball graced by the tsar's presence is wildly successful. Her elegant style, her dancing, her innocent charm, all earn her plaudits. But too much praise is perilous. Natasha becomes too vain and self-absorbed, to the detriment of the simplicity and naturalness that have formed her character and that have captivated Prince Andrei Bolkonsky, for one, now her fiancé. Natasha gets caught up in the intrigues and jealousies of society, almost being victimized by manipulative and amoral character assassins, as in *Les Liaisons Dangereuses*. This phase culminates in an attempted elopement, foiled only by the timely intervention of friends and retainers. Shame, sorrow, and illness ensue, as Natasha undergoes a purgatorial cleansing. The falseness and vanity that led her nearly to disaster melt away finally and, with Pierre Bezhukov's indispensable ministrations, she recovers her true spirit and identity. After Prince Andrei's death, Pierre becomes her husband. As children are born, Natasha discharges the duties of wife and mother with mature dignity. The most "natural" character does what comes to a Russian woman most naturally.

Pierre, Natasha, Nikolai, Prince Andrei, and Princess Marya gain depth of understanding through their life experience. If in their younger days they have "chased after false gods," such as glorified liberalism, Freemasonry, military renown, utopian social reform, or romantic or religious excess, as adults they have "come down where [they] ought to be," in the words of the old American Shaker hymn. They have become custodians and models of all that is best in Russian culture, including the ennobling power of sacrifice freely given, the importance of the natural and the simple, the danger posed by blind striving for social distinction or power or wealth, the almost superhuman strength brought by immersion in the spirit of the nation, and, most significantly for what occurs in 1812, acceptance of destiny as the guiding force in one's personal life and in the life of nations and distrust of any who believe human reason and intellect can somehow overcome or alter what is divinely ordained.

The experiences and insights of these characters are not matched by others of their acquaintance. The Drubetskoys and the Kuragins go through life wearing blinders. They are focused entirely on self-advancement through the acquisition of influence, money, or the favor of others. The anxious search for meaning and purpose in life that Pierre and Andrei pursue, the urge for distinction that motivates Nikolai, and the beauty of lives lived in service to others that Princess Marya and Natasha try to manifest, are absent in the carefully calculated careerism of Boris Drubetskoy and his mother and in the frenetic search for personal advantage and recognition that Prince Vasily Kuragin, his sons, and his daughter engage in ceaselessly. From Book I, where Princess Anna Drubetskaya seeks to jump-start the military career of her son by "talking to the right people," as when she appears uninvited at the home of Count Bezukhov as he lies dying and tries to curry the favor of the count's relatives, particularly Pierre, his legatee, to the end of the novel, when Boris has wangled his way up the ladder, thereby earning distinction without having endured the rigors of combat, mother and son connive their way through life shamelessly. Prince Vasily is no different, as he too upsets the Bezukhov household by searching all over for an alternate will that he is sure is on premise at the same time the count is receiving the last sacrament, to the end when he is last seen in St. Petersburg "strutting his stuff" obnoxiously. In between, his useless son, Anatol, plays at matchmaking, first under his father's prompting but to no avail, with Princess Marya, and then on his own, aided by a notorious confederate, with Natasha, when she is at her most vulnerable and with whom he tries and fails to elope. Princess Elena does not bother with melodramatic schemes or intrigues; she simply relies on her sexual attractions to advance steadily in society, first through marriage to Pierre, whom she studiously ignores after their wedding, and then through various liaisons. Just before her death, she converts to Catholicism in order that the inconvenience of being married to two husbands simultaneously can be relieved through a papal annulment. Elena's success in society, where she unaccountably acquires a reputation for wit and intellect, augments the vanity and narcissism that impel her every word and deed. She is happiest when she can be admired, as at the opera, or when she can "guide" a neophyte into society's whirl, as she does briefly and almost disastrously with Natasha.

These characters are disconnected from their native culture, people, and history as they go from one *soiree* and one lavish ball to another, search out ways to exploit the wealth or the naivete of those easily led, praise important people in public and then tear them down in private, and in general graft themselves like parasites onto the body of Mother Russia, the great majority of whose people do not speak French, do not live in or visit St. Petersburg, and do not go out at night because they labor all day. The Drubetskoys and the Kuragins are like the "rootless cosmopolitans" Stalin and his goons would denounce as aliens in the next century: as such, they would have come to terms with Napoleon in a heartbeat had he marched to the gates of St. Petersburg rather than to Moscow.

In addition to the family members whose interactions constitute the bulk of Tolstoy's narrative, a rich supporting cast of characters populate the novel. There is, for instance, Dolokhov, a soulless adventurer who ruins whatever or whomever he touches. He resembles Steerforth in his egotism, his devotion to his mother, and his need to excel by bringing others down, especially those who have befriended him. He is the archetypal outlier, the one irredeemable character in the entire novel. As noted above, a totally different personality inspires Pierre as he languishes in French captivity. A fellow prisoner, Platon Karatayev, is a resourceful peasant who makes the best of his situation, keeping busy with simple but necessary chores and projects and all the while employing folk wisdom, childlike faith, and brotherly kindness to rise above privation and despair. Pierre recognizes in Karatayev the resilience and strength of the Russian people, the same spirit that animates the troops at Borodino as they refuse to break or surrender under the pressure of steady attack. Denisov is one of these soldiers, a man of principle who overcomes wounds and military timeservers to lead those entrusted to him honorably and conscientiously. He is Nikolai Rostov's mentor, teaching him by example how a soldier should behave, not only in action but in every circumstance or situation. Among the many women who play key background roles is Sonya, a live-in cousin and confidante of Natasha, who loves Nikolai but whose dowryless condition makes their marriage improbable. Sonya accepts what was not meant to be with the quiet resignation the women of Russia are schooled to exhibit when destiny disappoints.

Destiny commands not only in the lives of individuals but in the life of a nation. Tolstoy is firmly in the Orthodox tradition when he makes not just Sonya accept her situation without rancor but also when he makes the fate of his country in 1812 equally dependent on how the Russian people accept and act out their destined roles. This theme is the overarching philosophical construct that places people and events in a recognizable context. Very few understand this basic truth. Among the historical personages who figure prominently in the chapters devoted to political and military history, only one, Russia's supreme commander, Marshall Kutusov, has a clear grasp of the basic truth that men alone cannot guide or govern the actions that play out on a grand scale when armies clash. This wise leader lets time and space largely determine the war's outcome. He knows that the allied invaders, all of whom are Europeans, have had little experience marching and maneuvering in a territory as large as Russia, nor have they faced anything as daunting as the Russian winter, a force of nature capable of stopping any human enterprise in its tracks. Kutusov, therefore, limits the occasions when pitched battles need to be fought, making only one major defensive stand, at Borodino, under pressure from Tsar Aleksandr and his staff. He prefers to maneuver and evade, deceiving Napoleon into thinking he is conquering territory and frightening his foe. This strategy leads to the regrettable outcome of Moscow's capture, an endgame that ends nothing. In reality, Napoleon's long march has depleted essential supplies and exhausted men and animals, the "scorched earth" tactics of the Russian peasantry have made foraging useless, and the surrender of the capital has resulted only in widespread looting, a breakdown in military discipline, and burned-out buildings. After a time, the conqueror has no choice but to sue for peace, as the conquered normally do. This is Kutusov's moment of triumph. He promises to pass on Napoleon's proposal for terms to the tsar but knows Aleksandr, true to his word, will agree to no armistice so long as enemy troops remain in Russian territory. The *Grande Armee*, therefore, must begin a long march in the opposite direction, enduring guerilla raids, foul weather, hunger, disease, and desertion every mile of their *via crucis*. Kutusov will win what has become a war of maneuver and skirmish, and though the tsar and his staff in comfortable St. Petersburg keep pressing for a major annihilating engagement, nothing of the sort is required. Wise employment of time and space has already brought victory.

Kutusov, however, is the exception. His fellow commanders, many of whom are non-Russian, see the all-encompassing war plan as the essential element for success in battle, and from Austerlitz on, they work incessantly on perfecting such schemes. But these conceptions have too many moving parts, any one of which can go awry and reduce the whole organic machinery to breakdown. Plans also mislead because they are drawn up prior to engagement, with objectives and timetables that are built on estimates and presumptions. As hostilities begin, though, the unexpected can occur; in real time, individual units may fall apart in panic and retreat haphazardly, thereby throwing follow-up units into disorder. On the field, officers receive reports that are already inaccurate, because between the time a report is issued and the time it is read, the situation has altered, sometimes appreciably.

Tolstoy rejects the optimistic Western concept of strategic planning as a controlling factor in mass conflict. Military science does not win battles. They are won because the martial ardor or "spirit" of one combatant prevails over that of an opponent. In 1812, the Russians are defending home and hearth, while, with the exception of the Poles, who see Napoleon as their nation's liberator, the allied invaders are being driven to battle by nothing other than imperial ambition. The Battle of Borodino, as a result, becomes for the French a victory without consequence and Moscow just a place to be looted. Though

Kutusov's forces have withdrawn, they are still threatening. The Russian defenses during the battle have been formidable, as Pierre sees during his time with an artillery brigade that has maintained fire throughout the battle, even under intense pressure, and he marvels at the indomitable spirit of the fighting men, who courageously accept death or injury rather than capitulation. This inner strength is something military planning cannot gauge, but it trumps strategy.

Napoleon's tactical genius is an irrelevance on this vast battleground. His original orders are vague and in conflict with the realities of the field and the troops' respective lines. The orders he issues as the fighting continues have little impact on the outcome, and toward the end of the day, he cannot gamble on a final Waterloo-like surge by his elite Old Guard, because he has no confidence this can win the day, and if it fails, he will be left in the middle of Russia with no reserve force to resist a Russian counterattack. The greatest military commander and army in the world have been checkmated by a commander and an army of mostly peasant recruits who defy Western-inspired rules of engagement.

They are not the only Russians who defy logic. As Napoleon arrives at the outskirts of Moscow, he sends staff officers into the city to bring the "boyars" outside the walls under safe conduct for a conference with him. He plans to offer these leaders the most magnanimous terms, grant the most generous benefits to peasant farmers and urban craftsmen, and support the most liberal political reforms, making Russia a nation of proud citizens rather than humble serfs. In the German states, Napoleon had created the Confederation of the Rhine and abolished the Holy Roman Empire, and in Italy he had broken the power of the local nobility and the church. Why should he not do something similar in Russia? He cannot do anything of the sort because the Russian people will not allow a foreigner to dictate terms to them. No boyars can be found to offer Napoleon their capital city, and, in later weeks, as he issues proclamation upon proclamation, he is met with the same indifference. The Russians will let Moscow burn rather than come to an understanding with someone they regard as an alien despot.

It is not, however, nationalism alone that motivates the Russian people. Napoleon and his invaders are bringing with them ideas and concepts that differ fundamentally from all those the Russians hold dear. The French emperor is the successor of a monarchy disestablished by revolution; this unheard-of infamy unites Russians of all regions, classes, professions, and ages in solidarity against a man and his invading force espousing a philosophy that somehow dispenses with royalty. Tsar Aleksandr I's deep faith, high-mindedness, and guilelessness make him the polar opposite of the shrewd opportunist who is attacking Mother Russia. Napoleon also embodies the spirit of the Enlightenment as he downplays religion, exalts human reason as the best interpreter of man's place in the world, scorns the wisdom of the past, and regards tradition as a burden that must be cast off. The Russian people in 1812 still retain their Orthodox faith, so grounded in the nation's history and tradition and so powerful as a unifying force. As the armies take their positions at Borodino, Kutusov pauses as the Icon of Smolensk is carried with solemn reverence to the field. The commander in chief kneels before the miracle-working image of the Holy Virgin, and, with tears flowing, kisses this revered representation of maternal solicitude. Nothing illustrates the great divide between the two sides as this pious moment. Russia is still religious, still confident that God is with the troops, called by the pundit Bilibin, "the Orthodox Russian Army." Julien Sorel typifies the post-revolutionary Frenchman as he participates in religious ceremonies without faith. Kutusov and most of his countrymen, by contrast, perform their devotions with the sincerity of true believers.

The French Revolution has made governing through the people's representatives rather than through a ruler's autocratic will popular and preferred. Russians do not respond to this imperative as wholeheartedly as Western Europeans and Americans. Indeed, when Pierre speaks during a consultation about the need for his fellow nobles to join him in offering the tsar advice rather than just listening to his commands, acting, in other words, more like citizens rather than subjects, he is shouted down. In the same spirit, as Nikolai confronts recalcitrant peasants blocking Princess Marya's flight to safety from the advancing French, he slaps one he perceives to be the group's leader and, in authoritarian fashion, intimidates the others into acquiescence. Russia will remain firmly royalist and authoritarian until the Revolution of 1917. Even this cataclysmic upheaval did not change political attitudes or behavior very much. The tsar was replaced by leaders whose ruthlessness and tyranny far exceeded anything the old regime imposed. Even today, with Communism only a memory, authoritarian leadership is apparent at all levels and in all of what used to be the Union of Soviet Socialist Republics.

In sum, the Russian character is fundamentally different from what we associate with the West. Peter the Great's reforms brought Western influences, styles, architecture, science, and technology to a Russia still attached to medieval customs and thinking, but they did not substantially alter the Orthodox, Asiatic, and traditional Russian ways. As we review *War and Peace* book by book, we will see time and again how important these ways are and how they define and direct this very distinctive national culture.

The novel is divided into four books and an epilogue. Within these overall divisions are individual parts. Book I has three parts; Book II, the longest section, has five; Book III has three; Book IV has four; and the epilogue has two parts. The novel begins with a social gathering in St. Petersburg, and it ends with a family gathering at an estate outside Moscow. Even though the principal characters in *War and Peace* move frequently between St. Petersburg, in Russia's northwest, and Moscow, in the east, and to various points in between, the main trajectory is away from St. Petersburg and toward Moscow. This movement reenforces the theme; as Pierre, Natasha, Nikolai, and company are compelled by Napoleon's advance to retreat further and further into the Russian heartland, they recognize and embrace their Russian identity. They discover who they are, what they believe and value, what is true and genuine and what is false, what is native and natural and what is foreign and artificial. The catalyst for all this self-discovery is Napoleon and his multinational invading force, who cross the Niemen River, in Lithuania, in June 1812 to become the largest, best-equipped, best-led, and most-experienced hostile army to have entered Russia in over a century. These invaders are collectively the "other," the successors to all those Western aggressors striving to occupy and rule Mother Russia since the Teutonic Knights marched against Aleksandr Nevsky in the thirteenth century. In fleeing from Napoleon's troops, Pierre and the others are fleeing not just from military conquest but also from the heavy overlay of Western influence that has been assimilated into Russian culture since the time of Peter the Great. These influences are most apparent in St. Petersburg, the city Tsar Peter laid out and had built to resemble a European capital. They are diminished in Moscow, still distinguished by the cupolas of the Orthodox churches and cathedrals, the wooden palaces of the local nobility, the covered market places and walkways where vendors ply their wares, and the grim fortress of the Kremlin, behind whose walls state and church officialdom conduct business in protected isolation.

Napoleon and his troops pay little attention to St. Petersburg, as if they realize the new capital is not the nation's nucleus. Their objective is Moscow and their program is inspired by the French Revolution. The emperor who took the unprecedented step of abolishing the centuries-old Holy Roman Empire and arrogating to himself and his *imperium* the old empire's power and prestige could very well do the same in Russia, making the tsar a puppet and marginalizing the Orthodox Church. He would conclusively finish what Peter only started, a process that could deprive Russia of any distinctive national identity. This supreme threat galvanizes the Russian resistance, making compromise, negotiation, appeasement, or surrender impossible and awakening in Pierre Bezukhov, and to a lesser extent in Prince Andrei, Count Nikolai, Princess Marya, and Natasha, an awareness of themselves as Russians to the core.

BOOK I

PART ONE

Book I, Part One, of *War and Peace* begins in 1805 at a St. Petersburg gathering of prominent socialites in the home of Anna Pavlovna Scherer, "lady-in-waiting and confidante to the Empress Marya Fyodorovna" (*War and Peace*, trans. Ann Dunnigan. New York: New American Library, 1968, p. 29). The event is a *soiree,* modeled on the salon evenings so cherished by Parisian high society. The conversation revolves around the burning political issues of the day, as well as smaller matters bearing on the needs or aspirations of individual participants. The key political concern is Napoleon Bonaparte's relentless assault on noble fiefdoms in the territories he controls. Anna Pavlovna's only hope for a counterweight to this relentless assault on long-established sovereignties is Tsar Aleksandr I, who is "so virtuous and noble that God will not forsake him, and he will fulfill his mission and crush the Hydra of revolution, which has become more dreadful than ever in the person of this assassin and miscreant" (31). As noted earlier, this encomium is typical of those that follow throughout the novel. The tsar is revered by noble and peasant alike as a uniquely just autocrat, whose idealism and sincerity contrast starkly with the ruthless calculation of a usurper like Bonaparte. This grandson of Catherine the Great, raised to be her successor, resembles in many ways the sixteenth century Holy Roman Emperor Charles V, another ruler of a vast empire compelled to engage in conflicts with France, the Ottoman Turks, the pope, and Protestant dissidents, when all he really wished to do was purify and promote the Catholic faith. Aleksandr was also animated by religious zeal, ending his reign like Charles, in quasi-monastic retirement.

Anna Pavlovna's sentiments are not shared by a young guest who arrives early. Pierre Bezukhov, the illegitimate son of one of Russia's wealthiest men, shocks the company by speaking favorably of Napoleon: "What's important is the rights of man, emancipation from prejudice, equality of citizenship, and all these Napoleon has retained in full force" (47). Pierre is in "bad form" but, having imbibed revolutionary principles and ideals during study in Europe and unconcerned about the restraints social conventions impose at an event like this, he speaks his mind. What he reveals is a young person's eagerness to read the signs of the times and take a position on people and events making an impact on his world, regardless of the displeasure he may cause in doing so. With the exception of Prince Andrei Bolkonsky, who stands up for the excitable younger man and deflects some of the hostile commentary of the other listeners, the rest of the company are dismissive. For Pierre, Prince Andrei is now and will remain ever after a "model of perfection" (57), with his strong will and soldierly devotion to duty. Pierre will continue to confide in the prince and seek his aid and approval as he tries to chart a life course consistent with high principle and noble idealism.

Some of the guests are preoccupied with more mundane matters. Princess Anna Mikhailovna Drubetskaya asks Prince Vasily Kuragin to use his influence "to procure an appointment to the Guards for her only son" (43). The prince is at first reluctant to agree, realizing in his self-centered way "that if he interceded on behalf of everyone who appealed to him, he would soon be unable to ask anything for himself" (43). He does, however, make an exception for Boris Drubetskoy, the first of many favors this ambitious young man will enjoy as he climbs the social and military ladder.

Two of Prince Vasily's children are present as well, Princess Elena and Prince Ippolit. Elena is a "classic beauty" (39), whose narcissism is evident as she listens to a long-winded guest:

> *The whole time the story was being told, she sat erect, gazing now and then at her beautiful round arm resting lightly on the table, or at her even more beautiful*

bosom, on which she readjusted a diamond necklace. (39)

Prince Ippolit resembles his sister in looks, but his face is "overcast by an idiotic and invariably peevish, conceited expression, and whenever he tries to tell a story, he leaves his listeners wondering whether his tale is "very clever or very stupid" (39). Elena and Ippolit, as well as the other son, Prince Anatoly, are self-seeking, profligate, and without talent or drive, exploiting others and using their father's connections, and nothing else, to move ahead.

This *soiree* is characteristic of St. Petersburg life. It is an occasion for people of means and influence to meet others like themselves and use the opportunities such encounters present for personal advantage. The Russian upper classes have embraced the French model wholeheartedly, just as they have the opera, the ballet, and the academy. The Kuragins, Princess Drubetskaya, Anna Pavlovna, and the like are *habitués*, expert at attracting and then manipulating important contacts during such evenings. Prince Andrei is of the same social circle but exceptional in his discomfort with all the hypocrisy and deceit these evenings encourage. He offers Pierre a rueful assessment, sounding like Rousseau: "Drawing rooms, gossip, balls, vanity, frivolity—there you have the enchanted circle from which I am unable to escape" (57). For this prince, not just *soirees,* but all the other St. Petersburg offerings, including bureaucracy, corruption, favoritism, political chicanery, and power-brokering, are likewise alien.

Pierre will eventually share these sentiments, but not just yet. Later that night, and contrary to Prince Andre's admonitions, Pierre attends a party given by Prince Anatol Kuragin, known for "dissipation, debauchery, and all the rest" (58). In attendance is Dolokhov, "an officer of the Semyonovsky Regiment, a notorious gambler and duelist" (60). In such company, the guileless Pierre is vulnerable, particularly with alcohol flowing liberally. Dolokhov's behavior goads Pierre to extremes. With characteristic daring and contempt for caution, the officer sits out on "a sloping ledge" outside a window high above a street "without holding on to anything" (61). While perched so perilously, he drinks "a whole bottle of rum without taking the bottle" (61) from his mouth. He does so without falling, eliciting loud commendation. Pierre insists on following suit but is dissuaded by the other guests. He contents himself with "dancing around the room" (63) with a bear, a performance Anna Pavlovna and her set would hardly have expected from the serious young exponent of revolutionary upheaval but which Dolokhov has a way of provoking. Later on, both he and Dolokhov will go completely overboard by tying a policeman "back to back to the bear" and then throwing both "into the Moika Canal" (67). For this offense to law enforcement, Dolokhov is "reduced to the ranks" and Pierre is sent in exile "to Moscow" (66). This is the first time in the novel Dolokhov's company leads to trouble for another, but it is certainly not the last.

Dolokhov combines wit, charm, intellect, and charisma to achieve ends that cause nothing but misery for those close to him. He is guided by opportunism detached from moral principle or restraint. His is a type that recurs in Russian literature, the gifted youth who attracts others but is too egocentric and self-assured for his own good. Turgenev's Bazarov in *Fathers and Sons* is a more benign variant, espousing a bloodless scientism that leads to the repudiation of all traditions and authorities, one of the first manifestations of nihilism in Russian literature. His rudeness and sense of superiority are off-putting, but Bazarov is not as lethal as Dolokhov. He, too, survives a duel and falls in love, both of which experiences are foreign to his character as a detached observer of human folly. Bazarov also dies young, before his nihilism can cause any serious damage to others.

Dostoevsky's nihilists, Nikolai Stavrogin and Peter Verkhovensky, of *The Possessed*, are far more sinister. Stavrogin is also the only child of a mother who adores him and is just as spoiled as Steerforth and Dolokhov. He becomes a leader in a revolutionary cell whose motley crew of eccentrics and misfits commit random acts of violence for no other purpose than to stir up trouble in their provincial surroundings. Peter Verkhovensky is the neglected son of an aging intellectual who once flirted with radical theories and groups but has mellowed considerably as he has grown older. Verkhovensky's father admires Mrs. Stavrogin, who is well-connected and strong-willed. His son hero-worships Nikolai in the same way. This spoiled youth, however, is as mercurial as Dolokhov, picking fights for no reason and leaving a number of adoring young women alone and abandoned in his wake. Like Alyosha Karamazov, Nikolai seeks the counsel of an old monk known for his spiritual insight, and lets the holy man read a long self-analysis that culminates in Nikolai's describing his rape of a young girl. This meeting, though, does not lead to any conversion, and soon the cell members are preparing more crime. Peter manages to convince the band that a former associate is an informant who must be executed before he can expose every one of them. Nikolai plays no direct role in any of this, but, like Dolokhov, he is the catalyst for the murder that follows. Verkhovensky flees, but Stavrogin returns to his mother's home, where he has been living comfortably. Tormented by what he has done himself over the years and what he has inspired associates like Peter and the cell members to do, Nikolai Stavrogin, in total despair, hangs himself in his bedroom. For Dostoevsky, such a grisly end is pre-ordained when people abandon their Russian faith, embrace ideas and theories alien to their nation, and betray their birthright.

While Dolokhov's and Pierre's shenanigans are running their course, Count Kiril Vladimirovch, Pierre's father, lies on his deathbed in Moscow. Pierre's banishment brings son and father together for the last time. Count Kiril has lived a life so amoral he has "lost count of his children" (67). Pierre is regarded as his father's favorite and is rumored to be his sole heir. This alarms Prince Vasily Kuragin, a cousin of Count Kiril, who is sure a will exists naming him a benefactor. "Forty thousand serfs—and millions" (67) are at stake. Anna Mikhailovna Drubetskaya is also an interested party, laying great stress on the fact that Count Kiril is her "mother's second cousin" as well as

"Borya's godfather (67). She is very much in need now of any assistance since, thanks to Prince Vasily's intervention, the tsar has transferred her son to the Semyonovsky Regiment. This transfer, however, brings with it a large expense because Boris must purchase a special new uniform, in addition to regular military gear, compelling Anna Mikhailovna once again to beg Prince Vasily to plead her cause to Count Kiril.

All of this information is revealed during conversations at a dinner party in the Moscow home of the Rostovs, Anna Mikhailovna's "rich relations" (64). This dinner is being given to celebrate "the name day of the mother and younger daughter, both of whom were called Natalya" (64). Despite the inordinate attention given to the gossip surrounding Pierre Bezukhov's distress and his father's sufferings, the atmosphere here is more welcoming and kind-hearted than in the Petersburg *soiree.* Count Rostov clearly enjoys being the generous host and, notwithstanding her discomfort with some of the gossipy guests, his wife also performs her role with courtesy and grace. This party is enlivened by the presence of teenaged children, most notably Natasha Rostova, "not pretty but full of life" (69) and her brother Nicolai, eager to follow Boris into military service but for different reasons; Nicolai is an ardent patriot who believes he is "not suited to anything but the army" (71) in this time of unprecedented challenge. Nicolai is a "short, curly headed young man with an open expression" (70); in contrast to Boris, who has the social graces of the St. Petersburg *haute monde*, Nicolai is ill at ease with the ballet-like formalities of the higher-ups. He and Natasha are most comfortable in more casual situations, where their eager, youthful spirits can be given free expression. They are, in other words, at home in the "natural" surroundings of Russia outside the capital cities. Only Vera, Natasha's older sister, has the style to thrive in society; in total contrast to the rest of the household, she is beautiful, vain, and egocentric, making her a perfect match for one of the St. Petersburg set, preferably Boris Drubetskoy.

Boris and his mother, however, have more immediate concerns. As we have already learned, Anna Mikhailovna does not have the wherewithal to equip her son properly with the uniform and accessories a member of the prestigious Semyonovsky Guards must have. Though she has asked Prince Vasily to intercede for her with the dying Count Kiril, she decides a personal plea might best reenforce whatever the prince has said or will try to say. Mother and son, therefore, leave the Rostovs peremptorily to present themselves to the count. Boris participates reluctantly, embarrassed as his mother pulls out all the stops, her eyes taking "on an expression of deep sorrow" (81) while she commiserates with Prince Vasily and Count Kiril's niece, neither of whom desires her company. She infuriates the latter when Anna Mikhailovna promises to help the family "nurse" her "uncle" (83), implying an extended stay. As it turns out, the count is "in a dreadful state" (88), recognizing no one, so there is no point to Anna Mikhailovna's offer of help. She withdraws without having attained her object, but remains hopeful that the count's genuine will, which "will tell everything" (88), can be found. Boris is puzzled as to why his mother expects anything at all from a man her son does "not regard as a relative of his" (87). Anna Mikhailovna can only respond lamely, "He is so rich, and we are so poor" (88). Here is the aristocratic sense of entitlement being acted out brazenly: Anna Mikhailovna has a noble title and a son in need; she is, therefore, deserving of a portion of his godfather's vast riches, period, even if said godfather hardly ever paid her son the slightest interest.

The princess's importunate gestures and sorrowful mien have yielded nothing, but she and her son are saved anyway. With a magnanimity worthy of any *grande dame*, Countess Rostova lends the princess the money Boris needs. She does this because she and Anna Mikhailovna have "been friends from childhood" (90). Here, in cameo, is the Rostov family character standing out brilliantly. It is "natural" for longtime friends to help each other in times of stress, regardless of costs or sacrifice. This is solidarity in action, a solidarity that will extend beyond just personal friends as Russia's people become a national family in opposition to the invasion of 1812. Pierre will feel the same solidarity in the midst of the peasant artillery brigade he is with on the field at Borodino; Prince Andrei will be moved by the same sense of charity for all as he forgives on his deathbed those who have wronged him; and Nikolai and Natasha will emulate her mother's solicitude for those in distress in a variety of circumstances and situations all through the rest of the novel.

No signs of the sweetness and light permeating the Rostov household are apparent in Count Kiril Bezukhov's quarters. Prince Vasily remains there most of the evening. He is still convinced a will nullifying Pierre's bequest is in the home, and he is determined to find it. Time is growing short. As the prince tries to ingratiate himself with one of the cousins taking care of the count, the governor-general of Moscow pays a last visit, and Orthodox priests begin a ritual anointing of the dying man. Performing this "awesome sacrament" (105) is a clear signal death is near. If the count dies and no other will is produced, Prince Vasily knows that the will he cannot accept as authentic will leave the count's "direct heirs" [he and the cousins] (108) nothing and the bastard son, Pierre, everything. He also knows that the count has prepared a petition to the tsar, asking the emperor to declare unilaterally that Pierre is legitimate. The prince will do anything to forestall such an outcome, even to destroying both documents if they are found with the count's papers. Prince Vasily cannot bear the thought that dreamy Pierre will become "Count Bezukhov" and "inherit everything" (109). His cousin, the princess, shares his disgust, blaming all this misfortune on "the base, the vile," people like Anna Mikhailovna, whose "intrigues" (110) turned the count against his household. She then reveals to the prince that the papers he wants to burn are "in the inlaid portfolio [the count] keeps under his pillow" (111).

Before he can react to this news, Prince Vasily comes face to face with Pierre, just arrived, and accompanied by the ubiquitous Princess Anna Mikhailovna. Count Kiril's niece slams the door in her face, but Countess Anna is not deterred. Despite having just received Countess Rostova's loan, she is continuing in her single-minded pursuit of worldly gain, now allying herself with the putative heir, assuring him she has loved him like "a son from the first" and will "not forget" to watch over his "interests" (112). Pierre is still unworldly and passive, letting himself for now be guided by this "efficient Petersburg lady" (113). He is so innocent that Pierre is baffled by the way the others in the room adjacent to his father's bedroom direct "awestruck and even obsequious glances at him" (114) as he enters. Anna leads him into the bedroom for a final moment with Count Kiril. His father looks "directly at him, but with a gaze the intent and significance of which no man could have fathomed" (118). They retain eye contact for several minutes, until the count's facial muscles start to "twitch" (118) and he makes a "hoarse, indistinct sound" (119), as if suffering a stroke. Shortly thereafter, "he is no more" (122).

Prince Vasily's face is also twitching as he tries to absorb the magnitude of what is about to occur. Despite his best efforts, no copy of a second will has been discovered. Even a battle royal between Anna Mikhailovna and the count's niece, who engage in an unseemly back-and-forth struggle to possess a document that may be what they need, ends in disappointment. The two titled ladies have fought like schoolgirls for a prize that turns out to be "just a paper that has been forgotten" (121). The "real will" (121), naming Pierre as sole beneficiary, is in the count's desk and will have to be produced in front of witnesses. True to form, the totally trusting Pierre "falls fast asleep, his head on his arm" (123) in the midst of all this commotion. When he awakens, he has to listen to Anna Mikhailovna, who has accepted the inevitable and moved ahead to be the first to remind him that "Uncle promised . . . only the day before yesterday not to forget Boris, but there wasn't time. I hope, *mon cher ami*, that you will carry out your father's wish" (123). Prince Vasily will adopt a similar strategy in the weeks ahead, using every opportunity to exploit Pierre's naivete and dependence to enrich himself and members of his family.

Nothing like the intrigue and conflict in the Bezukhov household is evident at the Bald Hills estate of Prince Nikolai

Andreyevich Bolkonsky, a *paterfamilias* like Prince Vasily and Count Rostov but very different in personality and character. Prince Nikolai is not young, but he has "the tough, indomitable vigor of hardy old age" (125), preferring productive work to the endless socializing and scheming of the drawing room. He is more like the young Peter the Great, who, in his tours of Europe, would gather up his tools in the morning and then spend an entire day with workmen who would teach him the intricacies of whatever craft he would wish to master. Prince Nikolai is equally conscientious about having close at hand whatever might be needed for a project:

> *The enormous study was full of things that were obviously in constant use: a large table covered with books and plans, tall bookcases with keys in their glass doors, another table high enough to write on when standing, on which there was an open exercise book, a lathe with tools ranged beside it, a scattering of shavings; all these bespoke a continuous, varied, and orderly activity.* (125)

The prince is practical and down to earth, more like an Enlightenment philosopher in his scorn for "idleness and superstition" (124) than a typical Orthodox believer. He has one daughter, Princess Marya, whom he tutors in mathematics and science in the hope she will grow to be more like him, but whose ardent piety makes such a possibility unlikely. Prince Andrei, his only son, shares many of his father's convictions, but though he is not conventionally religious, he has a deeply spiritual side that keeps him immune to pettiness and time-serving mediocrity. Like his sister, he is capable of mystic flights and an awareness of transcendence. He is, by nature and choice, a loner.

Prince Andrei is married to Princess Lisa, now expecting, whom his sister describes as "an absolute child, a winsome, merry child" (142), but like David Copperfield and Dora, the prince and his childlike wife are hardly compatible. Princess

Marya senses this, and, moved by piety and charity, begs her brother, despite his weak faith, to ask God to grant him the "love" he does "not feel" (145). Prince Andrei is noncommittal, but as he prepares to leave Bald Hills and begin military service, he promises to "never take off" the "holy image" (144) his sister has given him, as if at least to maintain the appearance of a strong faith. Prince Nikolai also knows his son and his wife are not close. He, however, offers no religious articles for solace, only "tough love," as "looking straight into his face with eyes so keen that it seemed they could see through a man," father tells son, "there's no getting unmarried now" (147). He assures Prince Andrei he will assist his daughter-in-law through her delivery while he is away, and gives him a letter for Marshall Kutusov, the Russian commander with whom Prince Nikolai once served. The letter asks Kutusov to "make use of [Andrei] in the right places" (147). These "right places" are not cushy staff postings far from danger, such as Boris Drubetskoy always desires, but assignments that will compel Prince Andrei to confront and prevail over his enemies in mortal combat. The old prince and his son embrace the knightly ideal, demanding and expecting courage and sacrifice. Prince Nikolai's parting words make this expectation explicit: "But if I learn that you have not conducted yourself like the son of Nikolai Bolkonsky, I shall be—ashamed" (147). The power and resonance of that final word are not lost on either father or son; the old prince is in tears, along with Princess Marya, as Prince Andrei leaves for the front.

PART TWO

As Part Two begins, the scene shifts. We leave the homes and estates of the aristocratic families introduced in part one to spend considerable time with the officers and the troops deploying against Napoleon's advancing forces. It is October 1805, and the rival armies are converging in Austria. Russian troops under the newly appointed commander in chief, Mikhail Ilarionovich Kutusov, are allied with the Austrian Imperial

Army so that maximum legitimist power may be brought to bear to repel the Corsican upstart.

Though the setting is entirely different, the gossip, self-seeking, and intrigue among the titled few in part one are matched by similar discord and in-fighting within the military leadership tasked with preparing plans and strategies to defeat a commander and an army that up to this point, have not lost a major land engagement. The Russo-Austrian coalition, however, is not a union of like-minded equals. Kutusov's very Russian appreciation of essentials, such as provisions, water, health of men and animals, weather, terrain, and, above all, contingency, is in contrast to the Austrian leaders' meticulous planning, leading to overconfidence and a refusal to let any of the realities of combat upset their faith in the science of war, whose abstract principles they believe they have mastered. This divide between Russian and European approaches to military strategy and tactics will be highlighted again and again as the novel proceeds. One instance highlights the disconnect. A member of the "*Hofkriegsrat* from Vienna" arrives at Kutusov's headquarters with orders for the Russians to "move with dispatch to join the army of the Archduke Ferdinand and General Mack" (151), the principal Austrian commanders. Kutusov is aware of the "wretched condition in which the troops had arrived from Russia" (151) and is reluctant to force march these ragged, hungry, and fatigued men to the Austrian lines. To emphasize their need for rest, he stages a review of one of the Russian regiments, insisting that the contingent parade past him and his Austrian counterparts in "exactly the same condition in which it had been marching—in greatcoats and with packs, and without any preparation whatsoever" (150). This decision throws the regimental officers into a tizzy, since they had already ordered their soldiers to change to dress uniforms and are made to feel almost like society *doyens* who demand that all guests arrive in gowns and tuxedos at an event whose hosts prefer plain dress. They manage, nevertheless, to get everyone changed in time. The regimental commander behaves toward Kutusov exactly as a corporate department head does toward a feared CEO:

> *From the manner in which the regimental commander saluted Kutusov, obsequiously standing at attention with his eyes glued on him, and from the way he could hardly control his quivering movements as, leaning forward, he followed the generals and trotted up at every word or gesture of the Commander in Chief, it was clear that his duties as a subordinate were executed with even greater delight than his duties as a commanding officer.* (154)

Such deference, however, is out of place with Kutusov, because this commander is anything but a martinet. During the review, he is informal, relaxed, and almost playful, chatting amiably, for instance, with a trooper he remembers from previous service with him. He also meets Dolokhov, now just another enlisted man but eager to restore his position. Kutusov admonishes him to do his duty and assures Dolokhov he will not forget him. Dolokhov exhibits no anxiety or fear in Kutusov's presence; his "clear blue eyes gazed at the Commander in Chief . . . boldly . . . ; their expression seemed to tear aside the veil of convention that placed so great a distance between a commander in chief and a private" (156). This brave and talented soldier is capable of extraordinary feats but is too moody to be relied upon. His captain describes him in words that accurately portray Dolokhov's character as a member of the regiment, as well as a civilian: "One day he's sensible, intelligent, good-natured and the next day he's a wild beast" (157).

Afterwards, Kutusov tries to relax for a time in his private quarters with Prince Andrei Bolkonsky, now his adjutant, and the Austrian officer. Disturbing rumors have been spreading regarding the fate of Austrian General Mack's army. With a combination of flattery and forced optimism, Kutusov expresses confidence that Mack's troops "have by now won a decisive victory, and are no longer in need of our aid" (161); he says this knowing full well the opposite is probably true, and his forces will be more in need than ever if Vienna is to be saved. Prince Andrei is clearly in his element at the commander in chief's side. Gone is the dyspepsia of a man ill at ease in polite society and in domestic circles: "In the expression of his face, his gestures, his walk, there was scarcely a trace of his former affectation, lassitude, and indolence …" (162). Kutusov values him highly, writing to his father, "I consider myself fortunate to have such a subordinate" (163).

The repose and *bonhomie* of this little group are soon disturbed as one of *War and Peace's* most dramatic scenes unfolds. "A tall Austrian General, his head bound with a black handkerchief "(163) and wearing an Imperial decoration, enters Kutusov's headquarters. His words are shattering: "You see before you the unfortunate Mack" (164), and all present know what has occurred. Prince Andrei cannot "help feeling a thrill of joy at the thought of arrogant Austria's humiliation" (164), but with his clear grasp of the consequences of Mack's defeat at Ulm, he prepares for action. When a fellow Russian officer makes a joke about the news, the prince responds as only a noble warrior can: "Forty thousand men massacred, our ally's army destroyed, and you find this a cause for jesting . . . Only a *street urchin* would amuse himself in such a way" (166).

Prince Andrei is not the only aristocratic soldier whose sensitive pride provokes indignation. Nikolai Rostov flares up immediately when a quartermaster, whom he regards as obnoxious despite his superior rank, admits to pilfering some money from the quarters Nikolai shares with his friend and comrade, Denisov. The matter can end quickly and satisfactorily if, as Denisov advises, Nikolai simply apologize to the regiment's commander for his loss of composure in front of a superior officer and thereby protect "the honor of the regiment" (175). But Nikolai cannot "go and apologize like a little boy asking for forgiveness" (176), and, if forced to do so, will demand "satisfaction" (a duel with pistols) from his colonel, something unheard of in the army.

He is saved from further entanglements only when the regiment is called forward following Mack's defeat. Both Prince Andrei's outrage and Count Nikolai's resolution derive from the same code of masculine honor that these strong gentlemen uphold in word and deed. This is a pan-European code, to be sure, but in a Russia still untouched by revolutionary fervor, still led by an autocratic ruler who relies on the nobility for support and still hierarchical in class structure and governance, the need for men like Prince Andrei and Count Nikolai to embody and model ideals of virtue and conduct their ancestors would all recognize is well understood. This is another reason the *haute monde* opposes Bonapartism; an adventurer like this man and his people's army cannot be allowed to overturn in the rest of Europe all that is good and admirable in the old regimes.

The usurper, however, is making steady progress. After the Austrian defeat at Ulm, only Kutusov's mostly Russian force opposes Napoleon's advance toward Vienna. But having just arrived from domestic duty in their homeland, these troops are not battle-hardened. Among the cavalry, for example, anxiety is apparent: "On every face, from Denisov's to the bugler's, there appeared around the mouth and chin the same lines of conflict, nervousness, and excitement" (185). Nikolai, however, is exhilarated, like "a schoolboy called up before a large audience for an examination in which he is confident he will distinguish himself" (185). Far from dreading impending combat, he is "filled with a dread of not measuring up to the hussars" (188), like a rookie ballplayer making his debut on the same field as his seasoned teammates. He is tested when the regimental commander orders a key bridge to be burned and sends most of his command to execute the order. With grapeshot whizzing by and stretcher bearers in sight, Nikolai experiences fear for the first time: "And the fear of death and of the stretchers and a love of the sun and of life—all merged into a single sensation of sickening anxiety" (191). This shames him, but no one faults Nikolai for being human, least of all the colonel, who cannot wait to report that "I the bridge have burned!" and though two of his men have been wounded and one *"killed outright,"* such losses are "not worth mentioning" (192). All that is important is the glory that will attach to Colonel Bodyansky's name from now on.

A series of engagements ensues as Kutusov's force of approximately 35,000 men begin to engage Napoleon's much larger *Grande Armee*. The Russians fight with spirit, but they are so outnumbered and so in need of essential supplies, they cannot help falling back in the face of a superior foe. "The defense of Vienna could no longer be thought of," and Kutusov's sole desire is "to effect a junction with the forces that were advancing from Russia, without losing his army as Mack had done at Ulm" (192). An opportunity to counterattack the French and slow their push forward presents itself after Kutusov's army crosses the Danube River. A French division has also made the crossing, but in so doing has become separated from the main body of French troops still on the other side. Given their vulnerability, Kutusov orders an attack. The Russians win a clear victory, capturing "banners, cannons, and two enemy generals" (193).

Such an outcome finally gives the allied powers something to celebrate. Kutusov dispatches Prince Andrei as a courier to Brunn, where the Austrian minister of war awaits news of the encounter. The prince is happy to carry out this assignment, "enjoying the feelings of a man who has at last begun to attain a long-desired happiness" (193). His meeting with the minister later in the evening, however, dims some of this joy. The atmosphere is more bureaucratic than military, and the minister shows little interest in his guest. When he reads Kutusov's report, he highlights the fact that an Austrian general serving with the Russians has been killed in the action and the defeated French commander has somehow escaped capture. The victory seems tainted, and Prince Andrei leaves the meeting feeling "that all the interest and happiness the victory had afforded him had now been left in the indifferent hands of the Minister of War" (196). What the prince does not suspect because he is incapable of pettiness or jealousy, is the simple fact that a Russian victory, however minor, coming shortly after Austria's debacle at Ulm may suggest to the minister that Austrian deficiencies and shortcomings are responsible for the empire's plight, not the genius of Napoleon or the valor of his troops. If Russian arms could roll up a division, why could not Austrian arms have done something similar? In 1942, Russia's Josef Stalin met with Britain's Winston Churchill, his ally against Nazi Germany. He displayed on this occasion the kind of crudity Prince Andrei would have considered beneath contempt. The Russians at the time were doing very well in combat against the German invaders, in contrast to the British, who had retreated in France and were being pressed hard in North Africa. Stalin drove home this disparity, telling Churchill the British had to show more courage and resolve in combat and stop being so timid and weak. A British bullet could disable or kill a Nazi attacker just as effectively as a Russian round could. Why were the British not firing more of them? Churchill responded to such taunting with gentlemanly restraint, undoubtedly feeling as divided as the minister of war in Prince Andre's presence.

Prince Andrei's mood does not improve as the day wears on. He is staying in Brunn "with his friend, Bilibin, a Russian diplomat" (196). Bilibin is witty and talented, valued "for his skill in conversing and dealing with those in the highest spheres" (197). He takes great care with formal papers, "preparing a circular, a memorandum, or report, expertly, incisively, elegantly" (197). Bilibin resembles the staff officers Prince Andrei dislikes, since they also are immersed in a world of papers and plans too far removed from actual combat. But though Bilibin has never smelled gunpowder, his diplomatic experience has afforded him strategic insight; he can speak and write about a battle and assess its significance better than most combat veterans, who know only what has occurred in their sector. The perceptive diplomat throws cold water on the recent engagement, telling Prince Andrei, "your victory [was] somewhat less than victorious" (198) and wondering, like the Austrian war minister, how the Russians let the French commander slip away. The prince begs to differ; he emphasizes to Bilibin, as he would to a punctilious staff officer, that "not everything happens as one expects, or with the orderliness of a parade" (198). He is exasperated that "Kutusov alone at last wins a victory, breaks the spell of the French and the Minister of War is not even interested in learning the details" (199).

Bilibin then moves from the battle to the politico/military "big picture." He points out with clear logic that the war minister cannot get very excited over what was basically a brief holding action that put one enemy division out of commission but had no serious effect on Napoleon's relentless advance toward the Hapsburg capital. In fact, the French emperor is, at the moment Bilibin and Prince Andrei are speaking, "at Schonbrunn" (199), the residence of "His Most August Majesty, Emperor and King Franz" (198-99). Bilibin concludes curtly, "So, you see, your victory is not a matter for very great rejoicing, and you can hardly be received as a savior" (199). In all probability, says the diplomat, whose grasp of such matters is firm, right now "there are negotiations with France and plans for peace, a secret peace, separately concluded" (201). The prince goes to bed upset by all he has heard, especially the possibility of a separate peace, an act he regards as a betrayal of Russia. That night, in recompence, he dreams vividly, reliving the Battle of Krems and experiencing "tenfold the joy of living, as he had not done since he was a child" (201).

This stimulating dream gives Prince Andrei a brief interlude of martial ardor in an otherwise oppressive time in Brunn. The morning after finds the prince "in full-dress uniform" (201) and ready for an audience with Emperor Franz. As he waits to be summoned, he relaxes briefly in Bilibin's study. There he meets Prince Ippolit Kuragin, "a secretary at the embassy" (201-02) and a few other staffers. These gentlemen, "rich, gay young men" are part of "a special set with Bilibin, their leader, called *les notres*, our people" (202). The major concerns of "our people" are "interests relating to high society, to certain women, and the official side of the service" (202). The warrior prince is clearly not a good candidate for membership in such a group, even were he younger and unattached. He politely declines Bilibin's offer to "do the honors of Brunn" (203) with him. Andrei is a soldier eager to do whatever his nation requires, not a dilettante playing all day with papers and endlessly scheming for promotions, honors, invitations, and assignations. The prince lives in a moral universe inaccessible to such people.

Prince Andrei's day becomes progressively worse. His meeting with Emperor Franz is brief and unsatisfactory. Bilibin warns the prince that the emperor "has a passion for giving audiences, but doesn't like talking himself—and can't as you will see" (203). Andrei sees exactly that. As he approaches the emperor at a "levee," he notices that His Majesty looks "confused … as if not knowing what to say" (204). During their interview, the emperor asks Prince Andrei a number of questions about the engagement at Krems but says little in response. On the important matter of fodder for the horses, the prince begins with "fodder has not been supplied to the extent –" (205) but then is interrupted as Emperor Franz changes the subject. This is clearly a monarch who cannot or will not take decisive action to address urgent concerns. He reigns but does not rule, leaving, like King Louis XVI, all decisions on the most serious national issues to his ministers. It is no wonder that an ambitious upstart like Napoleon, who has faced every challenge confidently and resolved contentious disputes authoritatively, could take the measure of a monarch like Franz fairly easily.

Despite the lack of substance in his discussions with the emperor, the prince is feted throughout the day and Kutusov is "awarded the Grand Cross of Maria Theresa" (205), all of which lets Emperor Franz revel in royal display. But outside this charmed circle of pomp and privilege, danger is fast approaching. The French are solidifying their hold on the capital and are now bearing down on Brunn. Bilibin tries to persuade Prince Andrei to escape capture by leaving the town with him and his group immediately. This would mean not returning to Kutusov's headquarters for the duration of the emergency. In this exchange, the value systems of each man come into sharp focus. Bilibin tells the prince, "Your duty is to take care of yourself" (208), expressing concisely the indifference he and his set feel for any ideal other than self-preservation or self-advancement. Prince Andrei responds in terms Bilibin cannot fathom: "I am going in order to save the army" (208). For the supple diplomat, these words come from "a hero" (208), a species he considers virtually extinct. For Prince Andrei, returning to Kutusov's side and doing all he can to save the army is his soldierly duty, what he promised his father he would always discharge; he is not delusional because he knows in his soul that a soldier burning to excel as a leader of men can work wonders in even the most desperate circumstances.

The circumstances are trying indeed. The Russian army is "moving with great haste and in the greatest possible disorder" (209) to avoid being overrun. When he arrives on the scene, Prince Andrei is appalled, likening the fleeing masses to "a mob" (211). He tracks down the commander in chief, whom he meets exiting a conference with his subordinates. To one, in particular, Prince Bagration, Kutusov is almost fatherly. With tears in his eyes, the devout old general makes the sign of the cross over Bagration's bent head and offers his cheek for a parting kiss. No one in Napoleon's army, from the emperor down through the ranks, ever does anything comparable in *War and Peace*. The French, for the most part, are aggressively anti-Christian, heirs of the 1789 Revolution's hostility toward the old regime's state church and all its works. Little of this iconoclasm has penetrated Russia, however, so that even though skeptics and scoffers can be found in any unit, the great majority of officers and men of what Bilibin calls "our dear Russian Orthodox Army" (210) make all the familiar ritual gestures with simple faith and piety.

Kutusov and Bagration indeed need something like divine assistance to save themselves and their army from total defeat. Napoleon's "army of one hundred and fifty thousand" (214) is "advancing by forced marches" (215) to cut off the retreat of Kutusov's "exhausted army of forty thousand men" (214). If that occurs, the Russians will suffer the same fate as the Austrians at Ulm. It is therefore imperative that "Bagration's advance guard of four thousand men" (215) set up a defensive position along Kutusov's line of retreat before the French arrive and "fight a delaying action for as long as possible" (215). Since Bagration's small detachment is no match for Napoleon's large force, especially with its exhausted troops being rushed into position, the likelihood of any delaying action succeeding is slim. But what occurs next is in the nature of an "answer to prayers." Prince Murat, the dashing commander of Napoleon's cavalry, decides that a battle with Bagration's little detachment, which he believes is "Kutusov's whole army" (215) might be inadvisable. He uses craft and guile to persuade Kutusov and Bagration to stand down temporarily, a tactic that worked earlier outside Vienna when an Austrian commander allowed a critical bridge to be taken without a shot being fired. "In the hope of completely crushing this army" (215), Murat proposes a truce of three days to allow Napoleon's separated units to converge. He assures Bagration that he is making this offer "to avoid unnecessary bloodshed" (216), especially at a time when peace negotiations are already underway. Bagration confers with Kutusov, who quickly agrees to accept Murat's terms in order to buy time. In three days, he can get a head start in moving the troops, supply train, and animals to safety, all the while leaving Bagration's detachment in place to maintain the fiction that the Russians are holding their positions and to take the brunt of the inevitable attack later.

Napoleon, though, has other ideas. He is livid over Murat's insubordinate presumption that he could unilaterally grant an enemy a truce. He orders the prince in writing, "Break the armistice at once and march on the enemy." (216). Meanwhile, Bagration's men are "cheerfully building campfires, warming and drying themselves, cooking their gruel for the first time in three days" (217) and quite unaware of what is in store. Kutusov allows Prince Andrei to join Bagration's staff, praising him as "a favored and trusted adjutant;" in response, upon meeting him, Bagration accords the prince "marked respect and consideration ..." (217). This appointment means Prince Andrei will be in harm's way once the armistice concludes, but this is exactly where he wants to be. The prince quickly begins surveying the Russian emplacements, including an artillery battery commanded by a "thin, dirty little artillery officer" (218) named Tushin and decides to propose some changes in the disposition of troops and guns once he returns to headquarters. He never gets back, however, because the attack now begins, with the rival artillery batteries exchanging fire and the advancing French infantry discharging their muskets. The ensuing battle emphasizes the futility of command and control by officers and the unpredictable impact individual groupings can generate through their independent decisions and actions. Prince Andrei, for instance, is ready, willing, and eager, hoping somewhat theatrically that this battle will be for him what Toulon was for the young Napoleon. For the soldiers in their battle lines, the excitement of actual combat, after seemingly endless marching and preparation, is energizing: "Awesome and joyous!" the face of every officer and soldier seemed to say." (225).

For those in command, the unfolding battle presents more confusion than clarity. Prince Bagration appears sure of himself, nodding his head approvingly when informed of events, as if "everything that took place and was reported to him was exactly what he had foreseen" (226). In reality, the battle is proceeding without much influence from the higher-ups. Bagration rarely gives orders, and when he does, they cannot be obeyed because the ebb and flow of the conflict alters the realities on the field so quickly. Bagration's calm demeanor is more significant than any of his commands; subordinates and staff are inspired and become more confident as they observe their imperturbable leader. Not so the regimental commanders, however. The fog of war makes their situation akin to the blind leading the blind. A colonel, for instance, informs Bagration that his regiment had been attacked by French cavalry, had suffered severe losses, but had "repulsed" (230) the enemy. But the truth is "he did not know what had happened during that half hour to the troops entrusted to him and could not have said with certainty whether the attack had been repulsed or his regiment had been routed" (230). In another sector, obduracy impedes necessary cooperation as two officers argue over how and where to place their adjoining commands so as to maximize their firepower. Even though their troops "were by no means ready for an engagement" and the French were closing in, these two gentlemen could not get past "discussions the sole aim of which was to insult each other" (234).

The battle descends into a chaotic series of disconnected incidents and actions that defy any attempts at coordination. Small units and sometimes individual soldiers take matters into their own hands. Cavalryman Nikolai Rostov, for instance, exhilarated by the thrill of approaching combat, charges the enemy impetuously, moving ahead of his comrades. He is wounded and unhorsed before he reaches the attackers. Lying on the ground, he sees a Frenchman on foot coming near. Nikolai panics, gets up quickly, and, despite his injuries, hurries away into the woods as energetically as he had ridden ahead a moment before, feeling like "a hare fleeing from the hounds" (237). Whole formations do much the same thing, ignoring officers' shouts and threats. Others, by contrast, maintain order and discipline. A group of Russian sharpshooters, among whom Dolokhov serves, surprises an advancing French unit that stumbles upon the well-hidden riflemen. Dolokhov is "the first to seize a surrendering officer by the collar" (239), earning his commander's commendation and, he hopes, his restoration as an officer. His courageous act may be valorous, but it is not disinterested. This is not the case with Tushin and the gunners in his artillery battery. Though exposed to deadly fire in an untenable position, they continue to stay in place and shoot off rounds. The French do not understand this, not being able to "conceive of the temerity of anyone continuing to fire from completely unprotected cannons" (240). The battery commander is oblivious; "Tushin experienced not the slightest disagreeable sense of fear, and the thought that he might be killed or seriously wounded did not enter his head" (241). Here is a man risking his life not out of any desire for glory or for promotion but in humble service to duty. His example inspires everyone else, who keep shooting despite terrible losses "still as cheerful and high-spirited as ever" (241). Only a direct order from Prince Andrei, on the scene still, forces Tushin and his team to retreat.

This engagement prefigures the Battle of Borodino in 1812, where, on a much larger scale, Russian batteries will keep firing in the midst of intense bombardment, and small groups or individuals will stand firm or splinter apart in disorder, all as circumstances and inner resolve dictate. Officers' plans and commands, particularly those of Napoleon himself, quickly become irrelevant as thousands of men act in idiosyncratic ways, making "real time" situations totally different from what had been anticipated in map rooms hours ago or even on the field moments before. What determines the outcomes of battles involving masses of individual soldiers is an indefinable spirit, a transcendent power conferred by destiny, which makes those so favored advance or resist bravely, while those denied flee in terror as bullets start to fly. The French think soldiers should behave rationally and, when cut off or surrounded, surrender or run to safety. The Russians of 1812 are still Orthodox believers, sure that Almighty God is with them as they defend their nation and faith and that God will either shield them or demand their sacrifice; each soldier's fate is something he has no control over and must welcome no matter what is decreed.

The Asiatic influence in Russia's early centuries also plays a role in later military experience. Genghis Khan, for instance, decreed that in any of his Mongol "platoons" of ten men each, the surrender of a single man would necessitate the execution of the remaining nine. As late as the twentieth century, intimidation of this sort still ruled in the Soviet Army of World War II, although not in published terms. The German invaders in 1941 expressed sentiments similar to those of Napoleon's troops: they could not understand why men would persist in hopeless defensive combat from positions that would soon be overrun or obliterated. Most of the Russians they captured were either taken by surprise and had no choice except to surrender or were trapped without arms or ammunition or were disabled by wounds in exposed open areas completely surrounded by their foes. Those in this category who survived the war and were repatriated after the Western allies took over the Nazi POW camps suffered a fate in their home country as terrible as that of the innocents in the Mongol platoons. At the order of Josef Stalin, of Georgian descent, these freed prisoners were summarily shot as deserters.

The thinking that animates such policies has no connection to the rational rules of engagement guiding Western military operations. It is firmly grounded in the medieval political and religious traditions that over the centuries have formed the way Russians view the world. As noted earlier, the individual in Russia does not control or create his or her destiny. What happens in one's life is willed by the all-powerful triune God of Orthodox believers, who, in their most famous invocation, the *Trisagion*, three times pray and plead "Holy God, mighty God, holy and immortal, have mercy on us." The individual man or woman is a tiny part of a much bigger whole, whether it be a family, an army, a church, a nation, or all of these. He or she has no identity or freedom outside collectives like these. The proper attitude is a willingness to act in ways that enhance the larger bodies, either by heroic leadership, as Prince Andrei manifests, or by death-defying endurance, as Tushin demonstrates. Whether called upon to lead, like Kutusov, or to sacrifice, like Princess Marya, the best posture is humble acceptance of God's plan. Trying to change the divine decree is always useless, and any assertion of autonomy is akin to the rebellion of Lucifer. This is the "resignation" preached by Orthodoxy, which is best understood as an embrace of fate (*amor fati*) rather than a passive submission to the inevitable. Therefore, if God decides that a member of the Russian Orthodox Army must die while defending a position, he must bravely make this supreme sacrifice. This one member is less significant than the body of which he is a part. His death is to be mourned, but it may have been necessary to preserve the army. Surrender is worse than death because in surrendering, a soldier shows that he places more value on his own life than on the welfare of his nation. He allows an enemy to take control of his life, acting less like a patriot and more like an alien. For such conduct, there can be no forgiveness.

Most of those taking part in the holding action against the French understand all of this instinctively and act accordingly. They do what seems like the impossible, delaying the enemy advance just long enough to keep their retreating comrades from being overtaken. Not everyone sees clearly how this outcome was achieved. The officers and staff who spend much of the battle in the dark on exactly what was happening where and when continue to let false assumptions and misinformation cloud their judgments in the battle's aftermath. Thus, in spite of his endurance, his example, and his humane concern for the men in his command and the wounded all around, Tushin finds himself summoned to Prince Bagration's headquarters to answer a charge. He is accused of abandoning a gun, a clear indication that the prince and his staff have been so removed from the action and are so ignorant of what actually occurred around Tushin's battery, they believe exactly the opposite of what is true. Fortunately, Prince Andrei is present. He knows the facts and offers a ringing endorsement of Tushin's conduct that silences everyone else. He tells Prince Bagration and his subordinates that as the fighting raged around Tushin's battery, Prince Andrei "found two thirds of his men and horses killed, two guns, destroyed, and no covering force whatsoever" (249). He continues, asserting that "we owe today's success chiefly to the action of that battery and the heroic endurance of Captain Tushin and his company" (249). Tushin's courage is matched by that of his fellow warrior, Prince Andrei, who dares to "speak truth to power" to save a comrade. Here is genuine leadership on display in an environment totally different from the battlefield but one where a casualty can occur just as easily from "friendly fire."

PART THREE

Part three of book one takes us back to St. Petersburg where self-seeking and hypocrisy play a far greater role in the lives of the upper classes than do military virtues. Prince Vasily Kuragin, a man who has "a rare gift for seizing just the right moment to make use of people" (252), wakes up one morning and decides that Pierre Bezukhov, now one of Russia's richest men, would make a perfect husband for his daughter, Princess Elena. Not incidentally, such a union could also secure for the prince a "forty thousand ruble" (251) loan, which he needs to cover previous debts. Once this resolution is made, Prince Vasily proceeds like a master manipulator, fussing over Pierre like a doting uncle, advising his charge, for instance, to enter government service so Prince Vasily can procure a diplomatic post for him and thereby incur Pierre's gratitude, and so forth. Though ostensibly preoccupied by business affairs, the prince will "not let Pierre slip out of his hands" (253). His efforts are made easier by Pierre's stubborn innocence, which compels him to believe "in the sincerity of those around him" (253). Soon, society gossip begins to link Pierre and Elena, a circumstance about which Pierre is ambivalent, fearing that "an obligation were being imposed on him that he could not fulfill, and at the same time pleased him as a delightful idea" (255). At one of Anna Pavlovna's *soirees* "at the beginning of the winter of 1805–6" (255), Pierre and Elena meet. Pierre is attracted immediately, with Elena's sensual appeal irresistibly drawing him to her:

> *He was aware of the warmth of her body, the scent of her perfume, and heard the creak of her corset as she breathed. Instead of the marble beauty constituting a whole with her dress, he saw and felt the complete allure of her body, concealed only by her garments. And having once seen this, he could not see her otherwise . . .* (257)

Pierre is helpless to resist Princess Elena's allure and incapable of responding to her attractions except through marriage. Despite anxiety that "for some reason it [marrying Elena] would be wrong . . . he knew that it was to be" (257). Pierre is aware of rumors regarding Elena's possibly incestuous relations with her brother Anatol but is equally aware that in just about everyone's mind, he and the Princess Kuragina are already linked. Putting doubts and moral misgivings aside, "in another part of his mind, her image rose in all its feminine beauty" (259), and Pierre lets sexual attraction lead him into the spider's web woven by Elena and her father.

Pierre's fatalism results from surrender to what seems inevitable, as well as from the guilt sexual ardor creates in a sensitive nature like Pierre's:

> *Pierre was one of those people who are strong only when they feel that they are absolutely pure and since the day that he had been overpowered by a feeling of desire while bending over the snuffbox at Anna Pavlovna's, an unconscious sense of the guilt of that passion paralyzed his will.* (260–61)

Before Pierre realizes quite what has happened, Prince Vasily celebrates with characteristic insincerity the *fait accompli* his scheming has brought about: "I loved your father . . . and she will make you a good wife . . . God bless you!" (266). Elena seals the deal when she and Pierre are alone for a moment. She asks him to remove his glasses; then, as he bends to kiss his betrothed's hand, "with a precipitant, brutal movement of her head, she intercepted his lips and met them with her own." (266). Pierre is "shocked by the change in her face, by its unpleasantly abandoned expression" (266). This raw sensuality reveals Princess Elena's character: she is a bold enchantress willing to use sexuality to achieve selfish ends. This behavior is totally contrary to the native Russian ideal of a wife choosing to sacrifice for and defer to her husband. The princess has been corrupted by the cosmopolitan Petersburg society in which she has been raised. Not only does she speak French by preference, she also mimics French manners and style, becoming a Russian version of Mademoiselle Bourienne, who runs rings around old Prince Bolkonsky. Elena's world is the *salon* and the *boudoir*; she gains an undeserved reputation for wit and intellect in the one arena and, with more justification, for sexual philandering in the other. As the novel proceeds, Elena's amoral character plumbs new depths of decadence. After Pierre finally ends their sham marriage, she dies alone, childless, heavily in debt, and on the verge of leaving the church of her birth.

Perhaps emboldened by his easy win with Pierre and, of course, quite ignorant of the ugly future his matchmaking will bring about, Prince Vasily moves from his daughter's nuptials to his son's prospects. On the pretext of going on a "tour of inspection" (267) of some properties near the Bald Hills home Prince Nikolai Bolkonsky shares with his daughter, his daughter-in-law, and his lady-in-waiting, Prince Vasily asks if he and his son Anatol may call upon the prince at the conclusion of their inspections. Since "old Bolkonsky had always had a poor opinion of Prince Vasily's character" (267), these visitors are not exactly welcome. As the old prince learns that the real "purpose of the visit" (267) is to introduce Prince Anatol to his daughter, with the object of securing for this dandy the hand of Princess Marya Bolkonskaya, Prince Nikolai feels nothing but "hostile contempt" (267) for these callers. As referenced earlier, this contempt leads to one of the great exchanges in *War and Peace*. On the morning Prince Vasily and his son are to arrive, old Bolkonsky looks outside and sees his steward Alpatych and some workmen clearing away the snow in front of the main house, so that the distinguished "minister" (268) and his son may drive in unimpeded. The Prince is outraged: "For me there are no ministers" (268) and orders Alpatych and his "scoundrels" to "shovel the snow back on the road" (268). So much for making the way easier for a father and son who are coming to stir up trouble in the household.

With such a start, it is hard to see how this visit can succeed, and it will not. As it proceeds, things go from bad to worse. Prince Anatol makes little effort to ingratiate himself with the Bolkonskys. He is as egocentric as his sister: "He regarded his entire life as one continual round of amusement, which someone or other was for some reason obliged to provide for him" (270). His view of marriage also is as utilitarian as his sister's. Princess Marya is not a great beauty, and her piety would certainly be too much for this Petersburg man of the world; nevertheless, "why not marry her if she has so much money?" (270). For her part, Princess Marya fantasizes about a husband who is "a strong, masterful man," (273), and with whom she would happily bear children, the most characteristically Russian feminine aspiration. Before going down to meet the Kuragins, she prays before a "large icon of the Savior." (274). She desires "family happiness and children" (274), and though like Pierre she is drawn to "earthly love" (274), she suffers the same guilt as he whenever sexually aroused. The princess ends her prayer affirming total acceptance of "the will of God, without whose decree not so much as a hair of man's head can fall" (274). In these few lines, Princess Marya reveals all the virtues of the perfect Russian wife and mother, virtues to which the totally selfish Anatol and Elena give little heed. No serious observer of Princess Marya and Prince Anatol could ever imagine these two married to each other.

Nevertheless, the princess experiences something akin to Pierre's powerful response to Elena at first sight; as she enters the room where he is seated with his father, Princess Marya is immediately stunned by Prince Anatol's glittering figure, momentarily blinded by his undeniable "beauty" (275). But beauty is all the prince has; with "his composure and unalterable self-assurance" (275), he feels no need to speak or do anything except allow the others present to gaze at him in admiration. His "unruffled silence" (275) is broken not by any words to or from Princess Marya, but by Mademoiselle Bourienne, who finds Prince Anatol as attractive as any "Russian prince" (280) she has fantasized about but never met and engages in witty and charming exchanges with both Prince Vasily and Anatol. She is joined by the "little Princess" (276), Prince Andrei's wife, who does not let pregnancy keep her from enjoying a conversation with such a guest. The self-effacing Princess Marya is the least involved in these dialogues, despite being at the center of Prince Vasily's scheme. As her father enters, she has to endure greater humiliation. Noticing that his daughter has a new hairstyle, Prince Nikolai crudely chastises her, demanding that she never again change her customary "way of dress" (278) without his prior permission. Then, for good measure, he follows this with a cruel insult to his daughter-in-law, commenting "there is no need for her to disfigure herself—she's ugly enough as it is" (278). The old prince is not monstrous so much as apprehensive; he cannot imagine living "without Princess Marya, little as he seemed to value her" (277). In any case, having to consent to a union with young Kuragin is a worst-case scenario Prince Nikolai can hardly endure. At one point, Prince Anatol cannot remember the army unit he is attached to and laughs about this. The old prince's spit-and-polish military pride is so offended by this attitude that he ends the conversation abruptly and puts off any talk about a betrothal to the next day.

The next morning, the already slim possibility that Princess Marya and Prince Anatol might be betrothed vanishes altogether. At the precise moment Princess Marya walks by the conservatory, Prince Anatol is "embracing the Frenchwoman [Mademoiselle Bourienne] and whispering in her ear" (285). What she sees quickly confirms the suspicions her father had voiced earlier: "He will take you with your dowry, and grab Mademoiselle Bourienne into the bargain. She will be the wife, while you—" (285). Anatol gets over his embarrassment easily: "Anatol, with an amused smile, bowed to Princess Marya, as if inviting her to laugh at this novel incident, and then, with a shrug of his shoulders, went to the door leading to his rooms" (285).

Princess Marya does not react to this incident as one might expect. Instead of furiously denouncing Mademoiselle Bourienne and appealing to her father to dismiss her from his service, she tries to comfort the astonished woman, "looking with tender love and compassion at Mademoiselle Bourienne's pretty little face" (286). The Frenchwoman then expresses in one pithy sentence the essential difference between their respective cultures: "You, who are so pure, can never understand being carried away by passion" (286). For the French, passion is irresistible, the means by which lovers experience an ecstasy beyond anything else this life can offer; for the Russians, being carried away by passion is perilous because it can lead easily to moral ruin. Princess Marya may admire her suitor's "beauty," but such admiration cannot form the basis for anything solid and lasting. Prince Vasily's proposal she firmly and definitively rejects afterwards: "I thank you for the honor, but I shall never be your son's wife" (286). She resolves to "find happiness in love and self-sacrifice" and to help "make poor Amelie [Mademoiselle Bourienne] happy" (287) by working to bring her and Anatol together. This is saintly renunciation carried to the highest degree of charity. It is Moscow's feminine ideal made brilliantly real in direct contrast to Petersburg's moral emptiness (Anatol and his father) and France's exaltation of passion (Mademoiselle Bourienne).

Moscow's sincerity and naturalness are highlighted again as news of Count Nikolai arrives at the Rostov home. Anna Mikhailovna is present when a letter from Nikolai is delivered to Count Rostov. As the family members gather to hear how Nikolai is faring, they learn from Princess Drubetskaya, who has, in her commanding Petersburg way, coolly absorbed the letter's content before anyone else—namely, that the ardent patriot of the household has been injured. The women and girls react emotionally, with Sonya, in particular, "instantly turning white" (288). Only Petya, too young and too much like his brother, senses something positive in this news: "I'm very glad, really very glad, that my brother has distinguished himself so. You're all blubberers! You don't understand!" (289). Encouraged by the fact that Nikolai's wound is not mortal and that he is now an officer, Sonya declares her undying love for Nikolai once more, promising that "no matter what might happen to him or to me, I could never cease loving him—as long as I live" (289). As matters turn out, she will keep this promise but will have to love Nikolai in a manner and in circumstances far different from those she imagines now. Natasha reacts to the news in her own way. She conjures up memories of "Nikolenka" (289) easily but cannot remember much of anything about Boris Drubetskoy, her supposed soulmate. This is probably because in contrast to Natasha, who is above all genuine, Boris has become a true Petersburg gentleman, groomed by his mother to be all show with little substance. He comes in handy at this point, however. Characteristically, Anna Mikhailovna has pulled strings to guarantee that her letters to Boris go directly to "the Grand Duke Konstantin Pavlovich" (292), his commander, who passes them on quickly. The Rostovs now make use of the same channel, sending through Boris letters, as well as gifts and money, to their newly commissioned Count Nikolai Rostov.

Boris and Nikolai meet shortly after. The scene is Olmutz, where the Russian and Austrian emperors are preparing to confer and conduct a grand military review even as Napoleon threatens. Boris and his friend Berg, two peas from the same pod, are "sitting in the immaculate quarters assigned to them, playing chess" (294), as if they are expecting Nikolai in an elite private club. Nikolai arrives, eager not so much to play chess but to share with them his experience in the field. Wearing "his mud-stained riding breeches' (294), Nikolai seems like a visitor from another planet; his first words to the two staff officers are telling: "Oh, you damned peacocks! Fresh and clean as if you'd just come from a fete—not like us poor devils in the line" (294). Boris asks how Nikolai has been doing and if he has been "under fire already" (295). Nikolai points to his bandaged arm and to his St. George Cross in reply. Berg makes no comment on Nikolai's wound or decoration; instead, with typical Petersburg insouciance, he describes his and Boris's very different "splendid campaign":

> *You know, His Imperial Highness rode with our regiment most of the time, so that we had every comfort and convenience. What receptions we had in Poland, what dinners and balls! I can't tell you! And the Tsarevich was very gracious to all our officers.* (295)

To Nikolai, whatever Berg and Boris have been doing can hardly qualify as a "campaign." The atmosphere becomes tense. As Berg takes exception to Nikolai's receiving so much money from his family while he and Boris have had to "scrape along" (295) on their meager pay, Nikolai flares up angrily and dismisses Berg rudely. He regrets his outburst, but what is clear is that Count Nikolai Rostov has had to grow up overnight, becoming through combat a tougher, more rugged, and battle-tested military professional. A man like he cannot appreciate or abide the effete lifestyle of staff officers like Boris and Berg, nor grasp what is important to them. In his mail from home is a "letter of recommendation to Bagration," secured "on Anna Mikhailovna's advice" (296). Nikolai throws it to the floor, horrifying Boris, who rushes to recover it, warning Nikolai not to discard something that "might be very useful" (296). But Nikolai has no interest in using a letter like this to try to become, for instance, an adjutant, which he calls "a lackey's job" (296). But then he has to listen while Boris confesses that "he should very much like to be made an adjutant, and not remain at the front" (296). After all, combat service is dirty, dangerous, exhausting, and with masses of men taking part in operations, largely invisible. Plodding along day in and day out and then risking everything when the enemy is met is not exactly the way to achieve "as brilliant a career . . . as possible" (296). Nikolai is dumbfounded by this point of view: "He looked intently and inquiringly into his friend's face, as if trying in vain to find the answer to some question" (297).

But if Boris is too frank in admitting that careerism guides his decision-making, Nikolai is less than frank or forthcoming as he describes what he did at the Battle of Schongraben. He does not recount with scrupulous accuracy the episode that led to his being injured. He does, instead, what "men who have taken part in battles generally do" (298): Nikolai describes the action as he would have wished it "to have been" (298). He, therefore, never mentions that "he had fallen from his horse, sprained his arm, and then had run from a Frenchman into the woods as fast as his legs would carry him" (298). While Nikolai is speaking, Prince Andrei Bolkonsky arrives and immediately registers displeasure as he listens. Nikolai senses the older man's disapproval, especially when the prince alludes to the "many stories" (299) he has heard concerning the Schongraben engagement. Nikolai insists that his story, like those of other participants in the action, "has some weight" (299) since he was actually there. He ends by implying irritably that Prince Andrei is just another one of "those fine fellows on the staff, who are rewarded for doing nothing" (299), obviously not realizing that Prince Andrei was also on the field and under fire at Schongraben.

The prince keeps his self-control and, with stern fatherly concern, invites both Boris and Nikolai to his quarters after the next day's review. Prince Andrei has risen above the staff officer/combat officer divide. In his mature understanding and appreciation of the values both groups bring to military affairs, he tries to bridge the gulf between Petersburg's stress on order and ceremony and Moscow's eager embrace of service and sacrifice. He will soon reconcile these opposites in his own person by leaving the security of headquarters and plunging into the danger zone of battle with clear acceptance of the mortal peril he will face as a leader of men. Prince Andrei has a date with destiny on the field at Austerlitz.

Before this clash between the Austro-Russian allied armies and Napoleon's *Grand Armee* takes place, the Austrian and Russian emperors, as well as their heirs, conduct a joint review of their combined forces at Olmutz. Nikolai is present and in awe as Emperor Aleksandr comes near. To this ardent patriot, the emperor is more than a head of state; he is practically a demi-god, an embodiment in his youth and innocence of the national spirit at its best, as was made clear at the Petersburg *soiree* that begins the novel. Nikolai is swept away: "One word from that man, he felt, and this huge mass (including the insignificant grain that was himself) would go through fire and water, commit crimes, die, or perform deeds of the greatest heroism" (302). The tsar is not a military officer or strategist like his rival Napoleon; he is a man of peace compelled by circumstances to take on the awkward cast of a warrior. Nikolai and the thousands of cheering comrades all around therefore will go above and beyond all normal limits to defeat the enemy and preserve their leader's health, maintain his sovereignty, and manifest his power. Nikolai feels "an even stronger access of love for his sovereign" as he sees the great man smile affably "in front of the Pavlograd regiment" (303). The French, too, admire their emperor, but somehow "love" does not seem an appropriate term for their relationship to him. Combat-hardened troops respect a commander whom they regard as exceptionally capable and will cheer him enthusiastically in appreciation of his and their successes on the battlefield. But the schoolboy hero worship of Nikolai and the other young Russians called to the colors is over the top, more like the attachment of devout believers to a young prelate whom they wish to guide and protect from the slings and arrows of the faithless. This quasi-religious emotion Nikolai experiences is so uplifting he puts aside all thought of challenging Prince Andrei, whom he sees in the emperor's suite: "At a time of such love, rapture, and self-sacrifice, what do any of our quarrels and insults matter?" (304). The tsar may be an autocrat, but to the Russian Orthodox Army, this does not denote oppression or tyranny. He is the Little Father, the divinely appointed master of all, and all must submit fully and willingly to his paternal authority.

Very different emotions motivate Boris Drubetskoy. Boris's focus is not on the tsar as the majestic leader whom all must obey and protect; if Boris thinks of the tsar, he does so as one who wishes to be favored by the autocrat. He goes to Olmutz mainly to see if Prince Andrei or someone else with influence can secure for Boris "the best possible post, preferably that of adjutant to an important personage" (305). He is, in truth, more like an ambitious civil servant, looking always for the best-paying and least-demanding sinecure, rather than a soldier eager to do battle. As soon as he arrives in Olmutz in "his dashing guardsman's uniform" (305), though he knows hardly anyone in the emperor's entourage except Prince Andrei, he is, notwithstanding, consumed by a "desire to belong to that higher world "(305). As he encounters Prince Andrei, he notices something that a man raised in Petersburg society recognizes quickly. Boris sees the prince listening with barely concealed impatience to a report from "an old Russian general with many decorations" (306). Once he spies Boris waiting to speak to him, Prince Andrei, who is only a captain, abruptly breaks free of the general, whom he asks to "be so good as to wait" (306), and becomes totally involved with Boris. For Boris, this behavior is eye-opening at the moment but altogether familiar. Prince Andrei obviously is following an "unwritten code" (306) that allows him to keep a senior officer cooling his heels while he chats with a lieutenant. Boris's intuition comes from his Petersburg experience in the drawing room, where masters in the art of advancing themselves professionally learn exactly how to engage influential people in the language and style of those in the know that produces results that cannot be obtained "through the prescribed regulations" (306). Julien Sorel would have understood this clearly, an analogue to the maneuverings and stratagems which enable him to keep his head above water in the seminary at Besancon.

The prince agrees to assist Boris, magnanimously going out of his way "to guide a young man and help him to attain worldly success" (307). The two call upon General Dolgorukov, who is returning from a council of war, where against the advice of the "old generals, Kutusov and Schwartzenberg, it had been decided to advance without delay and give battle to Bonaparte" (308). Dolgorukov is brimming with confidence, just like the Austrians before the Battle of Ulm. He tells Prince Andrei and Boris in French:

> *No, my dear fellow, it would be impossible to devise more advantageous circumstances than those we are in now. The combination of Austrian precision and Russian valor—what more could you want?* (309)

As he hurries away, General Dolgorukov promises Prince Andrei to do what he can for "this charming young man" (310). Boris is entranced by his proximity "to the higher powers" (310) and by Prince Andrei's skillful intervention. The prince then establishes his mastery of the unwritten code once more as he deliberately stands in the way of "a short man in civilian dress with a shrewd face and a sharp prominent jaw" (310). He turns out to be the Russian minister of foreign affairs, whom Andrei finds "distasteful" (310). He laments the fact that "such men as he . . . decide the fate of nations" (310). Prince Andrei's moral repugnance makes no impression on Boris. Being in the rarefied heights among men "who decide the fate of nations," however badly, would be for him the summit of his career. Nikolai Rostov may be prepared to perform any sacrifice for the tsar, while Boris is prepared to use all the means at hand to make the tsar serve him.

Nikolai sees the tsar once again the next day after a skirmish in which "an entire French squadron" (311) had been captured.

This "brilliant victory" (311) brings Tsar Aleksandr and his retinue to the field. The emperor pauses briefly in the midst of the reserve of the Pavlograd Regiment, among whom is Nikolai. Though disappointed by his failure to engage the French directly, Nikolai is now "completely caught up in the feeling of joy that sprang from the nearness of the Tsar, which itself compensated him for the day he had lost" (313). Once more, Nikolai sees how Aleksandr's face glows with "innocent youthfulness," reminding him of "the playfulness of a fourteen-year-old boy while still being the face of a majestic emperor" (313). The tsar's is the face of Russia. Though the Russian state dates back to the tenth century, in 1805 this nation is still a newcomer on the pan-European stage. The French, the Spanish, the British, the Austrians, the Poles, and the Germans have been in various stages of conflict since the Middle Ages. The abrupt entrance into European history of Peter the Great's Russia dates back only to the late seventeenth century. His vast country had been basically *terra incognita* before then, not having any connection to some of the great upheavals of Western Europe, such as the Hundred Years War, the Reformation and Counter-Reformation, the Scientific Revolution, and, lately, the Enlightenment and the French Revolution. Russia is still walled off from any impact these momentous events have had in Western history. It is, in many ways, like Japan before the arrival of Admiral Perry. Tsar Aleksandr exercises a quasi-priestly autocratic rule, as if he and his people are still living in the time of Justinian. They are "innocents" in that little of what has occurred in Europe since medieval times has penetrated Russia deeply and caused its leaders and people to move past feudal beliefs and customs. Now, however, the West and everything it stands for is, in Napoleon and his multi-national force near the Russian border, a menacing presence to a ruler and a people unprepared to deal with political, philosophical, or religious heterodoxy.

As the tsar moves among the troops, he lingers over a soldier lying "prostrate, his bare hair covered with blood" (314). The young ruler's "eyes fill with tears" (314) as he takes in this painful scene. In contrast to Napoleon and other battle-hardened officers, who are long past agonizing over the wounded, the emperor is one with his people in grieving over one victim openly and sincerely, as anyone unaccustomed to the dark side of war would. Nikolai is carried away again, toasting the tsar, "that good, enchanting, and great man" (314), as he would a beloved family member or friend. In this regard, he is totally in accord with his comrades since "nine tenths of the men in the Russian army at that time were in love, though less ecstatically, with their Tsar and the glory of Russian arms" (315).

In the following days, as the Austrians and Russians prepare to meet Napoleon's advance, the mood at the joint headquarters, with some important exceptions, is mostly optimistic and confident. General Dolgorukov, for instance, is positive Napoleon does not wish to risk an all-out attack on an allied army that far exceeds his in numbers of troops. He has also recently met Napoleon in person, sent by the tsar to determine if the peace overtures he has sent to Aleksandr are sincere. For Dolgorukov, the very fact that such communications were received is decisive. As he tells Prince Andrei, "If he were not afraid of an engagement, what reason did he have to ask for that interview, to open negotiations and, above all, to retreat when a retreat is so contrary to his method of conducting war?" (318). Prince Andrei is not as sanguine. Dolgorukov's conclusions are based not on actual military intelligence but on assumptions that could prove false. Prince Andrei is also uneasy with the war plan drawn up by the Austrian General Weyrother, since it too is grounded on the premise that Napoleon's forces are too weak to do anything except engage in a defensive struggle.

To make the upcoming conflict even more ominous, General Kutusov, in overall command, is likewise skeptical. He tells Prince Andrei frankly: "I think the battle will be lost" (319). Kutusov's wide experience has made him place little faith in meticulously drawn-up plans like Weyrother's. He knows that an enemy rarely conducts operations in ways that can be predicted or confidently assumed. Such factors as landscape, roadways, bridges, lines of communication, fatigue among troops and animals, and countless other contingencies play decisive roles as combat begins, making plans devised far from and well before battle almost useless.

At a meeting the evening before the expected encounter with the French, General Weyrother reviews his complex plan with General Kutusov and all the column commanders, a multinational group that includes German, French, Polish, Austrian, and Russian officers. Most of the officers say little even if they have misgivings; one who does speak, however, makes a telling point. Count Langeron is an *émigré* noble from the south of France who is offended by Weyrother's "military vanity" ((322). He states bluntly that "Bonaparte might easily attack instead of being attacked and thereby render the entire disposition worthless" (322-323). General Weyrother dismisses this possibility, insisting without accurate information that Napoleon has only "forty thousand men at most" and that indications from his encampment suggest he is preparing to retreat, "which is the only thing we have to fear" (323)—that is, he will slip away from the allied army's grasp. This is Austrian arrogance at its purest, assessments inspired by logic and military science and fortified by excessive self-assurance. But it is too late to rethink or revise any of the plan's elements. General Kutusov, who has been dozing off during the briefing, cuts off further discussion, saying simply: "Gentlemen, the disposition for tomorrow—or rather for today, for it is past midnight—cannot be altered now . . . You have heard it, and we shall all do our duty" (323). Supremely practical as always, he ends by stressing that "before a battle, there is nothing more important . . . than a good night's sleep" (323).

Despite all he has seen and heard during the conference to arouse anxiety, Prince Andrei's fighting spirit is excited by the possibilities the upcoming clash may bring. He is eager to excel, to stand out, to save the day, and, above all, to win glory: "I cannot be blamed for wanting that, for wanting nothing but that, and living for that alone" (324). He will, indeed, have his moments of glorious action as the Battle of Austerlitz unfolds, but the outcome for the Russians and for Prince Andrei himself will be anything but favorable. The main reason is that early in the morning of November 19, Napoleon is doing exactly what Count Langeron highlighted during the war council: he is moving thousands of troops into position for attack. Nikolai Rostov and the hussars under General Bagration sense this as they hear "the prolonged shouting of thousands of voices" and cries of "*Vive L'Empereur*" (327) as the enemy advances. Nikolai is as stimulated by the approaching clash as Prince Andrei, except that he dreams not of winning personal glory but of performing valorously in service to the tsar. General Dolgorukov, stubbornly sure Napoleon is withdrawing, insists to Bagration the noise all are hearing is a deception to cover the French retreat. Even when Nikolai rides back to the two generals to report he has heard shots coming from the fog ahead, Dolgorukov sticks to his conviction, saying the French must be leaving pickets in their rear to maintain the fiction that they are about to attack. Here is a textbook example of how reality, as revealed to the senses, cannot be believed because it gets in the way of a fixed idea. The heavy fog enveloping the area is both literally and metaphorically the fog of war, creating confusion and uncertainty at every level.

The fog upsets the initial deployment of the Russian troops. Soldiers cannot see "either the place to which they were going or the one they were leaving" (331), a perilous blindness that makes them prey to a surprise attack. All through the marching columns, the same difficulties are felt. Soon, everyone is forced to halt, as if stuck in a traffic gridlock. The Russians fear "a dangerous muddle" (332) has been created by the Austrian column guides, who, they are convinced, "don't know themselves what they are doing" (333). To make matters positively threatening, the French are not "ten versts away" and retreating, but "nearby in the fog belt" (334) and advancing. A tsunami is about to strike the allied columns. Napoleon and his marshalls stand on a hill overlooking the valley through which the Russian troops are groping their way. The French commanders are above the fog, which is beginning to break, and have a good view of their enemy's movements. They await only Napoleon's order to commence hostilities. Napoleon is focused on the Pratzen Heights, which he judges "the key to the position" (334), and down which columns of Russians are pouring into the valley below. As the sun begins breaking through, and "the fields and the mist" become "bathed in its dazzling light" (335), the emperor, like a character in grand opera, waves a glove, signaling to his marshalls that an attack against the heights should begin.

Occupying the Pratzen Heights at this critical juncture are Commander in Chief Kutusov and his suite. Kutusov is anything but confident. His anxiety apparent in the "worn and irascible" (336) manner he projects, Kutusov responds to his stress by lashing out, berating one regimental commander for incautiously filing his troops through narrow village streets where they cannot spread out and form battle lines if attacked. The commander is not worried, though, because he too believes the enemy is "still a long way off" (337) and withdrawing. Kutusov sends Prince Andrei to one of the divisions moving through the valley to remind its commander to post sharpshooters in front so that the French cannot suddenly appear without warning. This commander is astounded by the reminder, since he also believes the French "could not be less than ten versts away" (337). Kutusov realizes that in the fog misinformation can be deadly if it is transmitted and accepted without verification all through the ranks. Better to prepare for any eventuality, even the most unlikely, than to stay attached to only one possibility no matter what. At this point, the Emperors Franz and Aleksandr arrive. The tsar is irritated that Kutusov seems to be "waiting" (339) rather than hurrying his troops into position for attack. The emperor rather pedantically points out to the most experienced of his generals that the army is not "on parade" (339), where nothing can start until all participants are assembled and in line. Kutusov concurs but with a different conclusion: "That is just why I do not begin, Sire, because we are not on parade" (339). The tsar continues to show disapproval, so Kutusov defers as he must and orders more troops into position.

In the lead are the "gallant Apsherons" (340), a confident and seasoned regiment. They expect to occupy a village and then move on ahead to meet the French later. But like all the other Russians in not expecting any action soon, the unprepared Apsherons will be face-to-face with the French attack formations in just a few seconds. Unless they can be stopped immediately and arranged in defensive lines, they will be overrun. The scene about to be played out is visible from the heights where Kutusov and his staff officers watch in horror. One of the officers cannot help shouting, "Brothers, it is all up!" (342). This is all it takes to precipitate a panicked rout. Officers cannot "check this mob" (342) of soldiers running for their lives all around them; if they try to, they are swept away themselves. Even Kutusov himself is wounded, and "with his staff diminished by more than half" (342) can do little except bark out orders that cannot be obeyed.

One member of the staff tries to take matters into his own hands. Prince Andrei cannot bear to see Russians behaving like frightened children, losing all discipline and spirit. When he sees an officer drop his regiment's standard as he flees, a shameful act, the prince picks it up and begins waving it, hoping to rally soldiers to follow him in a charge against the French. Before any of this can transpire, however, Prince Andrei is staggered by a powerful blow, "as though one of the soldiers near him had bludgeoned him on the head with all his might" (344). His wound causes him to lose consciousness, and he falls to the ground. He awakens after the fighting in his sector has concluded, with only the moans of other wounded men breaking the silence. Prostrate and helpless, Prince Andrei stares at the "lofty, infinite heavens" (344) and experiences a kind of revelation, persuading him that "all is vanity, all is delusion, except those infinite heavens" (344). This moment of transcendence resembles the out-of-body ecstasies of Dostoevsky's epileptics. Prince Myshkin, for instance, is described thus:

> *His mind and his heart were flooded with extraordinary light; all his uneasiness, all his doubts, all his anxieties were relieved at once; they were all merged in a lofty calm, full of serene, harmonious joy and*

hope. (*The Idiot.* Trans. Constance Garnett, New York: Bantam Books, 1958, p. 218.)

Prince Andrei lies seriously wounded but is at peace with himself and at one with the universe. He will have more moments of special insight and mystic awareness as his life proceeds and will eventually join his sister, Princess Marya, in spiritual sensitivity.

On the other side of the Russian deployment, Prince Bagration, unaware of what has been happening on the opposite flank and "wishing to avert the responsibility" (344) of making a decision that could have adverse consequences, hesitates to take any action. He tells Dolgorukov, instead, that he will send a courier to the commander in chief to ask for orders, ignoring the fact that this will take a long time and will immobilize his force indefinitely. Since, however, he and Dolgorukov are still sure the French are far away, a delay does not seem unwise. Count Nikolai Rostov will be his emissary. Nikolai, of course, welcomes this opportunity to be of special service, even though his will be a long and dangerous trek. As he begins, he runs into a "mass of cavalry in dazzling white uniforms, mounted on black horses, and trotting straight toward him and across his path" (346), preparing to charge the French cavalry. This sight is reminiscent of the moment in Gogol's *"Taras Bulba,"* when the magnificently arrayed Polish knights ride out from their castle to meet the Cossack invaders. Nikolai sees the beginning of the "brilliant charge of the Horse Guards that amazed even the French" (347). Brilliant it may be, but this charge ends in disaster, with "only eighteen" (347) coming back alive. Futility and despair are evident everywhere behind the Russian lines. Nikolai hears only of defeat and disorder whenever he speaks to retreating soldiers and learns that confusion has been so extreme that, at one point, Russian and Austrian allies have been "firing at one another" (349). Though "the idea of defeat and flight" (349) cannot be entertained, Nikolai can hardly deny that something awful has occurred as he sees "French cannon and French troops . . . on the very spot where he had been told to look for the Commander in Chief" (349).

What is illustrated in these chapters once again is the power of war's imponderables to overwhelm the most ingenious human constructs. The notion that plans and orders can guide multitudes and achieve desired results regardless of circumstances that are inherently unpredictable is disproven by what occurs at Austerlitz. Napoleon acts in ways that the allied planning staff cannot conceive. He moves ahead when the staff say military science demands that he should retreat, and even when the evidence becomes overwhelming that he and his troops are advancing early in the morning, the commanders find reasons to deny or explain away the obvious. His troops, as a result, begin to engage the Russian forward units when they are supposed to be still a long distance away. Such an astounding development leads to something like a train wreck, with all the Russian forces following behind the advance guard piling up on each other like railroad cars crashing and running off the tracks. Individual officers and soldiers succumb to panic and fear, causing widespread breakdowns and making coordination and cohesion impossible.

Although the Austro-Russian high command fails in this instance to take into consideration unconventional possibilities, they are not the only military professionals to do so. At Borodino in 1812, Napoleon himself will do much the same thing, and, later on, marooned in Moscow, he will try to negotiate his way out of dangerous isolation despite the refusal of the tsar, contrary to normal diplomatic practice, to accept his overtures. The inspiration for most of these miscalculations is the Western world's exaggerated faith in reason and science; doctors, lawyers, clergy, teachers, and military leaders in the West are taught laws and principles that govern their professions and that create predictable outcomes. In the Russian mindset, however, molded by Orthodoxy and autocracy, man is puny, weak, and dependent. His destiny is not brought about by his own free choices or universal laws of nature but by divine will. Rather than trying to control fate, the Russian aligns himself with it. Throughout Russian history, powerful invaders have tried and failed to conquer Mother Russia because the sheer size of this nation makes even the largest armies seem helpless as they cross endless plains, move through trackless forests, try to ford wide rivers, and deal with extremes of weather. Russian military history illustrates over and over how strategic retreat, improvisation, surprise, and sacrifice can throw out of whack the most carefully calculated master plans. In 1812, this Muscovite tenacity will prevail over Western-inspired logic and reason, and Kutusov will come into his own.

Before that climactic defense of the homeland and Napoleon's humiliating retreat, the agonies of defeat at Austerlitz must be borne. Nikolai Rostov's journey has exposed him to despairing soldiers moving listlessly to the rear, sure "that the battle was lost" (351). He also hears a rumor that the tsar has been wounded and rushed to a field hospital for treatment. Nikolai responds to this possibility with characteristically Russian self-abnegation: "If the Tsar is wounded, should I try to save myself?" (351). Then, in a scarcely to be believed coincidence, as he mingles among the retiring troops, Nikolai stumbles upon both the tsar and the emperor of Austria, strangely alone alongside a creek. Nikolai is astonished and abashed. At first, he is tempted to approach His August Majesty and ask for "orders to the right flank" (352) as per his instructions, but since "it is four o'clock in the afternoon and the battle is lost" (352), further orders are pointless. Nikolai's awe in the presence of the autocrat makes him too timid to move or speak. He sees that the tsar is not physically hurt but is emotionally distraught over what has just occurred. Nikolai also notices tears flowing from the beloved emperor's eyes, and he cannot keep from shedding his own "tears of pity for the Tsar" (353). Here in cameo is a moment of genuine connection and empathy, with ruler and soldier coming together as two young men joined in common sorrow.

Tsar Aleksandr's tears would be flowing more abundantly had he witnessed what Nikolai sees shortly afterwards. The retreating Russians are still being harassed by cannon fire, so all are eager to escape beyond range as quickly as possible.

In their anxiety and haste, the soldiers, along with horses and wagons, jam the path leading to the "Augest dam" (354), whose narrow walkway cannot be accessed because of the congestion. Desperate to get across the frozen "millpond" (354) under the dam, men see Dolokhov recklessly "leaping over the ice, which cracked under him" (355), and exhorting others to follow. Many do so, but more ice begins to crack as a heavy cannon is being dragged across. The result is horrifying:

> *The ice, which had held under the men on foot, caved in; a huge fragment with about forty men on it gave way, casting some of them forward, some back, and they drowned one another as they fell into the water.* (355)

This is the nadir for both Nikolai and his compatriots.

Prince Andrei has avoided all such scenes of tragedy because since the beginning of the battle, he has lain on the Pratzen heights moving in and out of consciousness. During these hours he has experienced something akin to Job's overwhelming sense of the grandeur of creation and the pettiness of mundane human concerns, such as why good and upright people must suffer. As the prince lies motionless but attuned to the metaphysical insights he has been granted, he hears someone speaking French and coming near. In a coincidence like Nikolai's with the tsar, he is astounded that Napoleon himself is standing over him and speaking in admiration of the way Bolkonsky has died, tightly gripping the regimental standard. Prince Andrei's reaction to this is nothing like Nikolai's to the tsar, however. The prince has been transported to a realm where political and military affairs mean next to nothing, so the emperor's words are like "the buzzing of a fly" (357).

When he realizes that Prince Andrei is still living, Napoleon orders him carried to a French aid station for immediate treatment, a magnanimous gesture that Andrei hopes will "bring him back to life, which seemed to him so beautiful now that he understood it differently" (357). Though the French emperor has been chivalrous, Andrei continues to hold him and "all the interests that engrossed Napoleon" (358) in contempt, so alien were they when matched to his vision. Thus Napoleon's "greatness" is nothing in comparison to "the greatness of something incomprehensible but all-important!" (359), such as Andrei has experienced on the field. Napoleon is the quintessential post-revolutionary man of action—bold, confident, relentless, and sure, fearing neither God nor any enemy, focused solely on his cause. He brings to war all the best in leadership, expertise, weaponry, and highly trained and motivated forces. He believes in the irresistible strength and spirit of his arms, supporting his determination to remake societies and cultures through the force of his will and the transformative power of the ideals espoused by the French Revolution.

Prince Andrei, like the Russian nation, finds all of this impious, presumptuous, and contrary to nature. He knows that "what was taking place between his soul and that lofty, infinite sky with the clouds sailing over it" (357) trumps anything that a foreign prince, however high-minded or enlightened, could ever bring to Russia. The Russian soul has been formed over centuries by the Orthodox Church and the monarchy and by the Asiatic influences of invaders like the Mongols and the Tartars. These ideals exalt meekness rather than pride, sacrifice rather than acquisition, submission rather than striving, destiny rather than independence, faith rather than science, and tradition rather than innovation. The vast territory of Russia, surpassing that of all of the European nations combined, its punishing weather and topography, its huge population and armies, and its strictly graded hierarchies in state, church, and the military, all constitute an overwhelmingly formidable series of obstacles to conquest and to the propagation of liberty, equality, and fraternity. Russia is something like an earthly analogue to the transcendent realm Prince Andrei has been allowed to enter. Just as the prince judges Napoleon's exertions futile and irrelevant, so too in 1812, a pan-European invading force of seven hundred thousand might seem overpowering to any Western observer, but on the endless grasslands and in the deep forests of Russia, it melts into insignificance.

BOOK II

PART ONE

Following the Battle of Austerlitz, while an armistice is declared and peace talks begin, the Russian Army stands down for a time as the dead are buried, the wounded are sent to hospitals, and the survivors are granted leave. One of these survivors is Count Nikolai Rostov, who has earned a commendation and a promotion and, early in 1806, been given permission to visit his family in Moscow. This visit comes as a complete surprise to the Rostov family, each of whom is delighted to see Nikolai and his friend, Vaska Denisov, who joins Nikolai at the family home. One of the family's retainers, the footman Prokofy, exclaims upon seeing Nikolai arrive, "Can it be? The little lamb!" (364). But "little lamb" hardly describes Nikolai these days. His experience with the regiment and his participation in mortal combat has made him, as his sister Natasha realizes, "a grown-up man now" (367). Sonya, whom Nikolai has promised to marry, sees this change in him as well, and, with characteristic selflessness, reiterates that Nikolai is free to marry anyone else. Though Nikolai assures Sonya "he would never cease loving her, for it was impossible not to love her" (370), his love is now more like that for a sister than a future spouse.

Nikolai is so "grown-up" he has "acquired a trotter of his own, very stylish riding breeches such as had not yet been seen in Moscow, boots of the latest fashion with extremely pointed toes and little silver spurs" (371), accoutrements making him resemble, at least to the eye, Julien Sorel in Paris. Also, like the sexually aggressive Julien, this "lieutenant of hussars," his love for Sonya notwithstanding, enjoys the company of "a lady on one of the boulevards whom he visited of an evening" (371). In fact, and not surprisingly, Nikolai does "not grow closer to

Sonya" (371) during his stay in Moscow. He has developed other interests: "The races, the English Club, carousing with Denisov, and visiting a certain house—all that was another matter, and quite the proper thing for a dashing young hussar" (371). Nikolai at this juncture can better understand, though never identify with, Berg and Boris, who, his mother informs Count Ilya, "is now on the staff!" (373), in a post of eminence and perfect safety.

All this time, Count Ilya is busy with the arrangements for "a banquet at the English Club in honor of Prince Bagration" (371), whom Moscow's social elite consider a hero for his actions in "the Schongraben engagement and in the retreat from Austerlitz, where he alone had withdrawn his column in good order, repelling an enemy force twice his number during an entire day" (375). There is no mention of Bagration's hesitation to order an attack on the French approaching his front at Austerlitz, largely out of fear of making the wrong decision. The Muscovites, however, need someone to elevate as a "way of showing dislike and disapproval of Kutusov," whom they denounce as "the court weathercock and an old satyr" (375). To thicken the fog that obscures and distorts the realities of the battle in its aftermath just as it did the realities of the actual battle, Berg is reported to have gone forward with his sword in his left hand "when wounded in the right hand" (375), while of Prince Andrei, who led a charge and whom all believe died at Austerlitz, "nothing was said" (375). From misperceptions and misrepresentations such as these are reputations made and reputations destroyed.

The banquet goes well at the start as the guest of honor enters "modestly and awkwardly" (378) and enduring as best he can the crush of club members and notables straining "to get a look at Bagration over one another's shoulders as if he were some rare beast" (378). Count Ilya Rostov's meticulous planning of the banquet's many courses and dishes pays off handsomely, with all in attendance acclaiming their excellence. Soon the toasts begin. "To the health of our Sovereign, the Emperor!" (380) Count Ilya exclaims, raising high his glass of champagne. Thunderous applause and shouts greet this toast, with Nikolai's "ecstatic voice" clearly audible "above all three hundred voices" (380). A patriotic hymn follows. A second toast is then proposed in honor "of the hero of our last campaign, Prince Pyotor Ivanovich Bagration!" (380). This time a chorus sings a cantata specially composed for the occasion. More and more toasts are offered, and glasses are smashed. This is Russian celebration in all its theatrical excess. Count Ilya keeps welling up with tears as the acclamations continue. He is in his element here, so happy all are pleased with his work, and like a *grand seigneur* playing his part to perfection, he basks in the glow of approval coming from all corners.

The festivities are marred, however, by an incident having nothing to do with Count Ilya Rostov, Prince Bagration, the tsar, or Austerlitz. Among the guests at the English Club are Dolokhov, "now reinstated and once more an officer in the Semyonovski Regiment" (376), and Pierre Bezukhov, "fashionably dressed but looking melancholy and depressed" (376). Pierre's gloomy mood is due, at least in part, to a letter he had received earlier in the day. The anonymous note said, among other things, "that his [Pierre's] spectacles were not of much use to him and that his wife's liaison with Dolokhov was a secret to no one but himself" (381). It is highly likely Dolokhov himself wrote the letter in an effort at self-promotion and to make Pierre's humiliation even more acute. This man's chameleon character, infected by a malignant narcissism, in its "moments of cruelty" (381) has caused many who have helped and befriended Dolokhov to suffer like Pierre. Pierre refuses to credit the letter's assertions but avoids looking at Dolokhov's "handsome, insolent eyes" (381) for fear of "something terrible and monstrous rising in his soul" (381) and causing him to lose self-control.

But Dolokhov's bullying is obstreperous. He approaches Pierre, offering this toast: "To the health of beautiful women . . . and their lovers" (382). Pierre drinks without pleasure. Then, as a footman hands Pierre a copy of the cantata composed in Bagration's honor, Dolokhov rips it from his hand, as if Pierre were an unworthy child. This public insult enrages Pierre, just as Dolokhov intended ("Ah, this is what I like") (383). Pierre immediately challenges his tormentor to a duel, ignoring in his anger the fact that Dolokhov is a military officer who has been trained in marksmanship and Pierre is a civilian who has never fired a pistol. At the moment he issues his challenge, Pierre also decides to separate from his wife, the real cause of this misery: "He abhorred her and was severed from her forever" (383). With stunning abruptness, the novel's most dramatic scene so far puts Pierre in mortal danger, ends his loveless marriage, and elevates Dolokhov to a status he could scarcely have attained without extreme behavior. The cocky rogue is confident and murderously cold, telling Nikolai Rostov that one should approach a duel "with the firm intention of killing your opponent as swiftly and surely as possible, then everything will be all right" (383).

The next day the duelists and their seconds arrive at the designated site prepared to do as custom prescribes. Pierre's second tries to mediate, insisting "there are not sufficient grounds for this affair, or for blood to be shed over it" (384). Pierre admits his actions were "terribly stupid" (384) but cannot apologize. Dolokhov, in any case, is not interested in apologies. Both men move to their respective places, Pierre all the while trying to familiarize himself with the pistol, a weapon "he had never had . . . in his hands before—a fact he was unwilling to confess" (384). This affair does not bode well for one of Russia's richest men.

As he moves toward Pierre, Dolokhov is intimidating, with "his clear, sparkling blue eyes peering into his opponent's face" (385). Pierre, by contrast, cannot even keep his balance on the path, since he must walk with his right arm extended to keep from accidentally shooting himself. Impatient and fearful that the longer he delays the more likely Dolokhov, with his military training, will fire first and with deadly precision, Pierre shoots almost without aiming. Incredibly, the round strikes Dolokhov's left side, knocking him to the ground. Though badly hurt, Dolokhov will not drop his pistol as Pierre, "hardly able to restrain his sobs," (386) rushes toward him, contrary to accepted practice. Dolokhov tries desperately to steady himself as he kneels in the snow and aims at Pierre, standing before him "defenseless . . . his legs and arms spread wide, his broad chest directly facing him" (386). Pierre is smiling, not maliciously but "sorrowfully" (386), as if in firing his pistol, he has committed a crime. Dolokhov manages to fire, but despite having a perfect target in front of him, misses Pierre. This is as improbable as Pierre's accuracy.

Nikolai Rostov, his second, attends to Dolokhov in his agony and is struck by "the totally altered and unexpectedly exalted, tender expression on Dolokhov's face" (387). But this expression is not due to a glimpse of heavenly glory, such as Prince Andrei beheld on the field at Austerlitz. Dolokhov is uncharacteristically sentimental because "he lived with his mother, who, if she were to see him dying, would not survive it" (387). Here is James Steerforth's clone, a "bullying, brawling" version living "in Moscow with an old mother and a hunchback sister," toward each of whom Dolokhov is "the most affectionate of sons and brothers" (387).

Dolokhov will recover but will not be changed in character after this brush with death. Far from becoming kinder or gentler, he will remain his same viperish self, taking particular pleasure in wounding members of the Rostov family. Nikolai will be stung one night when he makes the mistake of joining the duelist at cards, whose secrets Dolokhov has mastered. His former second will go home in shame and self-recrimination after losing a small fortune. Dolokhov will also assist Anatoly Kuragin as he tries to elope with Natasha Rostova, whose cousin, Sonya, had earlier rejected Dolokhov's proposal of marriage. They do not succeed, but Natasha suffers greatly afterwards. In 1812, Dolokhov will stand out as a daring but cruel leader of guerilla-style raids on vulnerable French units retreating from Moscow. On one such raid, Petya, Nicolai's younger brother, joins him, in defiance of his commander's order. This venture ends tragically for Petya, too young and too in awe of Dolokhov to stay back in safety. This is a man whose charisma attracts many into his circle, but the attraction is toxic. None who get close to him can escape harm.

Pierre, by contrast, will indeed be a changed man after this duel. He will become forceful, assertive, less aloof, less timid, or sensitive to a fault. He will take charge of his life, confront his faithless wife with a decisiveness and command that Elena has never seen before, and begin to grow in spirit and strength. He will become like his nation, gathering strength for the trial 1812 will bring, and the bonds formed during this life-and-death struggle will grow deeper and deeper among himself and families like the Bolkonskys and the Rostovs, as well as with strangers, who, in solidarity with Pierre, will act as if they were his brothers and sisters.

At first, Pierre suffers after the duel, blaming himself for what has occurred and ascribing all the trouble with Dolokhov to the fact that he had married Countess Elena "without loving her" (388). He remembers his uneasiness at the prospect of marrying Elena, when he "knew she was a depraved woman" (389) but was too weak to resist the social pressures driving their union. This self-accusing tone changes abruptly, however, as soon as he comes face to face with Elena in his father's study. The countess is her usual self, haughty and openly scornful, as she castigates Pierre for believing malicious rumors and provoking a totally unnecessary confrontation with Dolokhov. She ascribes his actions to jealousy, praising his antagonist as "a better man . . . in every way" (391) while firmly denying any intimacies with Dolokhov. She goes on in this vein, even telling him "there are not many wives with a husband such as you who would not have taken lovers" (391).

Pierre finally acknowledges the obvious and says quietly: "We had better separate" (391). Elena agrees, provided Pierre provide her with "a fortune" (391) to go away. This is too much. The man who has been listening to his wife's abuses with apparent passivity now allows all his pent-up fury to be released. He picks up a "marble top of a table with a strength he did not know he had" (391), and moves threateningly toward Elena, now visibly frightened. He orders her out "in a voice so terrifying that the whole house heard it with horror" (391). For almost the first time, Pierre feels the reserves of power and passion he is capable of arousing. This is unnerving but necessary if he is to overcome the indifference and apathy others have exploited to make decisions for him. Shortly after this climactic meeting, Pierre has given Elena "a power of attorney for the control of all of his estates in Great Russia, which constituted the larger part of his property . . . and gone away to Petersburg alone" (392). Far from surrendering to Elena's demands, Pierre's gesture actually transfers oppressive business concerns to the countess, while at the same time effectively shutting her out of his life. He will use this freedom to grow spiritually as he begins a soul-searching quest for authenticity and identity.

Prince Andrei has already had a spiritual awakening that has made Napoleon's presence a matter of little interest. At Bald Hills, though, the family knows nothing of this, since no definite word on Prince Andrei's fate or whereabouts has been received. Kutusov himself confirms in a letter to Prince Nikolai that his son "fell . . . at the head of a regiment, a standard in his hands, like a hero worthy of his father and his fatherland" (392), which certainly proves the prince's valor and makes his father proud. But though Prince Andrei "fell," it cannot be said with certainty that he died in action, because his name is not on the list of dead Russian officers the French have given Kutusov. Despite this omission, the old prince is sure his son has been "killed" (393), and so informs Princess Marya. The princess's profound faith allows her to accept this news without despair and to cling to the hope that in the duress of war, her brother had "repented of his unbelief" (393) in time to enter "the realm of eternal peace and blessedness" (393). Prince Nikolai is too skeptical to entertain such sentiments and refuses "to hope" (394). Instead, he orders a "monument" (395) placed in the garden in Andrei's memory, though no corpse is buried beneath. Marya keeps praying, preferring to believe "no news is good news" and shielding the "little Princess," her brother's wife, from hearing any of her father-in-law's grim conclusions while she is preparing to give birth.

What occurs next is as improbable as Prince Andrei's encounter with Napoleon or Nikolai's with the tsar. As the little

Princess goes into labor with "a childish fear of the physical suffering that lay before her" (395) and with only a midwife in attendance until a doctor arrives from Moscow, the household is suddenly turned upside down. Princess Marya is told that someone is "driving up the avenue . . . with lanterns—it must be the doctor" (398). As she comes out to greet the gentleman, who "does not know Russian" (398), she hears another "voice that seemed familiar—saying something" (398). Princess Marya thinks it sounds like her brother's, but "that would be too extraordinary!" (398). Extraordinary or not, the voice is indeed Prince Andrei's, who has come with the doctor. The man last seen being carried from the battlefield to a French infirmary, where it was expected he would soon die, now steps into his home "in a fur coat . . . pale and thin, his face altered by a strangely softened and anxious expression" (398). As they absorb this incredible moment, the Bolkonsky family and all their retainers feel exactly as the family of Lazarus must have felt when Jesus brought his friend out of the tomb alive and well.

The prince has not only survived; his experience of transcendence has made him more sensitive, more charitable, and more loving than he ever was before Austerlitz. The first words he utters to his wife are "my darling," words he has never spoken to her before, and then "God is merciful" (399), the same expression his devout sister had used earlier when the little Princess had begun her labor. These sentiments are not characteristic of Prince Andrei, whose relationship with his wife has not been particularly romantic and whose faith in God has not been as deep or as unquestioned as his sister's. They mark the beginning of a new phase in this man's life journey, in which all human endeavors and aspirations will be assessed under the aspect of eternity. For now, mercy is needed more than ever. The little Princess suffers through a very difficult birth, emitting "piteous, helpless, animal moans" (400) throughout, similar to those of men seriously wounded in battle. The baby is born at last, but his mother does not live long enough to hear the "wail of an infant" (400). Andrei is alternately overjoyed that he has a son and heir, Prince Nikolai Andreyevich, but torn by sorrow and by the fear that in impregnating his wife, he has been "guilty of a wrong he could neither rectify nor forget" (401).

This couple resembles David Copperfield and Dora, the one growing in spirit and humanity day by day, and the other stubbornly remaining childlike and dependent. Prince Andrei and the "little" Princess also have been moving in opposite directions. The one has been given a glimpse of the divine and will live differently as a result, while the other has been taken from this life altogether by the same power whose mercy has brought an end to her travails. Russian culture does not see any dichotomy between these two outcomes since both involve sacrifice, and whether the sacrifice be renunciation of worldly attainments, as with Andrei, or the renunciation of life itself, as with his wife, the willing acceptance by each of what he or she cannot change is all that matters. As noted earlier, Orthodox tradition lays great emphasis on this resignation to the inevitable and on how what seems tragic can actually be a sign of grace. Thus, Prince Andrei's heroic charge results in a wound that brings spiritual regeneration, and his wife's death in childbirth brings forth a new life that will be her legacy. Prince Andrei's life will go on, but it will include challenges and pain at every juncture. The prince will suffer more wounds, not only in body but in his turbulent emotional life; he will endure disappointment and disillusionment in political, military, and business affairs; and he will live to forgive the man who tried to kidnap the only woman he will have loved since the little Princess's passing. He will become the embodiment of noble acceptance and renunciation, a Russian knight born to leave behind money, power, romance, heroism, and all the other idols a fallen world holds dear, in favor of unconditional charity.

The same can never be said of the other wounded man who also has cheated death but has undergone no serious spiritual awakening. Having learned next to nothing from his near-death experience, Dolokhov continues to behave as the spoiled son of a doting mother, who refers to him as a "lofty, angelic soul," one "too pure of heart for the corrupt society of our day" (401–2). In reality, of course, he is too self-centered to care about others in the way a "lofty, angelic soul," such as Alyosha Karamazov would; he refers to the majority of men and women he encounters as beneath notice: "I pay attention to them only insofar as they are useful or harmful to me" (402). He counts Nikolai Rostov among his "two or three friends" (402), but his treatment of him after his recovery is malevolent. Nikolai at first defends Dolokhov, especially with Natasha, who dislikes him almost on sight. Nikolai remonstrates with her: "You have to understand what a soul that Dolokhov has. You should see him with his mother—what a heart!" (403). Nikolai has not yet had enough worldly experience to see through hypocrisy and conceit; he still believes everyone is like himself deep down inside, innocent until proven guilty.

Nikolai's encomiums prove ironic in the short time Dolokhov frequents the Rostov household. He quickly falls in love with Sonya, or so everyone thinks as they see the two together often. Dolokhov knows Sonya is betrothed to Nikolai but acts as a suitor, nonetheless. Nikolai tries to deny what is plainly evident to Natasha, for instance, and continues spending "the greater part of his time away from home, at dinners, parties, and balls" (404). Such activity detaches Nikolai from both Sonya and Dolokhov, who soon exploits his opportunity by proposing to Sonya. He is chagrined by her firm refusal. At an awkward dinner afterwards, Nikolai notices new tensions between Dolokhov and Sonya. When Nikolai asks if his friend will be attending a popular holiday ball, Dolokhov replies noncommittally, at the same time giving "Nikolai just such a look as he had given Pierre at the Club banquet" (405). This is ominous, as it suggests Dolokhov is not going to accept Sonya's rejection graciously.

Nikolai tells Sonya later that he would have made no objection if she had accepted Dolokhov's offer of marriage. This, however, would have been impossible since her love for Nikolai is too deep, too sincere, and too necessary for her well-being. Should he marry someone else, says Sonya, that will not matter, because she will always love Nikolai, even if "as a brother" and will "want nothing more" (407).

As the holiday season nears conclusion, Natasha and Sonya look forward to the annual ball given by Vogel, the most popular dance teacher in Moscow. With the prettiest girls and the most handsome young gentlemen in the city all together in one place, the event is always so wonderful the two cousins are rapturous in anticipation:

> *Sonya had whirled about so that the maid could hardly get her hair braided before she left home, and now was radiant with impetuous joy. Natasha, no less proud of her first long dress and of being at a real ball, was even happier. Both girls wore white muslin dresses with pink ribbons.* (408)

The highlight of the evening, nevertheless, is not the sort of romantic excitements that one might expect in a ballroom filled with young people dressed to the nines and in the first stages of adolescent sexual awakening. As the best student in Vogel's school, Natasha is free to begin the night's festivities by choosing to dance with anyone on the floor. Prodded by her brother, she picks Vasily Denisov, Nikolai's best friend in the regiment but someone much older than she. Denisov turns out to be an excellent choice, nevertheless, as the two glide and turn about in a dashing mazurka. Vasily cannot help being attracted to his beautiful and talented partner and will not "leave her for the rest of the evening" (408), undoubtedly upsetting other potential suitors, many of high rank, in attendance. Natasha, though, is too enchanted by the intoxicating atmosphere, the swirl, and the aura of the holiday ball to pay too much attention to one man, especially a military officer, whatever his virtues might be: "She was not in love with anyone in particular, but in love with everyone" (408).

Nikolai Rostov experiences something considerably less delightful two days after the ball. Before returning to his regiment, Dolokhov invites Nikolai to a "farewell supper" at "the English Hotel" (410). Nikolai arrives while Dolokhov and several guests are playing cards. As soon as he notices Nikolai, Dolokhov greets him with a "cold, lucent gaze, as if he had long been expected" (410), like Mephistopheles fixing Doctor Faustus in his chilly sights. Nikolai is uncomfortable right away, fearing that Dolokhov, "as if bored with everyday life," has a need "to escape from it by some strange and for the most part evil act" (411). Dolokhov quickly invites Nikolai to "put up a stake" (410), and as the latter hesitates, goads him into participation by asking if he is "afraid" (411) to take his chances with him, a taunt similar to what so enraged Pierre at Bagration's banquet. Nikolai has brought little money to the Club, but Dolokhov is reassuring, stressing his "trust" (411) in Nikolai's honor. Play begins, and Nikolai promptly loses "ten cards running" (411). The only way to recover these losses is to keep playing, a dangerously addictive and expensive response. With his skills at cards and the practices he has perfected as a well-known "sharper" (412), Dolokhov overwhelms Nikolai, whose losses mount to eight hundred rubles. Since his father had given him two thousand rubles prior to this night and had advised his son to be "economical" (412) with that sum to make it last until spring, Nikolai feels he must cut his losses immediately in a one-card draw. He places all his hopes on a "seven of hearts with a torn corner" (412), a telltale detail. He loses again, not surprisingly, and sees his debt increase to sixteen hundred rubles. His descent into "the abyss of some unknown, undefined misery" (412) does not end until he is down forty-three thousand rubles, an impossible sum to repay.

Nikolai is ashamed, not only because of how he has hurt his father but also because he realizes he has been like putty in Dolokhov's hands, "those hands that he loved and hated, held him in their power" (413). Those hands are ugly. Dolokhov does not just take terrible advantage of a "friend" out of avarice; he also hurts the man Sonya loves out of revengeful malice. He mocks Nikolai in his agony, pointedly quoting the adage, "Lucky in love, unlucky at cards" (415). He demands his money peremptorily. Nikolai promises to have it the next day, not knowing at all how he will acquire such a sum. He leaves the English Hotel utterly despondent.

Nikolai's distress is real and apparent to those in the Rostov household who, upon his return, take note of his mournful air and downcast gaze. His gloom is in marked contrast to the spirit of the season, as mirth and joy pervade the home. The after-effects of Vogel's ball, particularly "the poetic atmosphere of love," are lingering "around Sonya and Natasha, like the air before a thunderstorm" (416), a perfect metaphor for growing sexual awareness. Nikolai cannot share in the girls' happiness until Natasha begins to sing. As she performs an operatic aria with her "untrained voice," Natasha sends Nikolai into another realm, where "all that misery, and money, and Dolokhov, and malice, and honor—it's all nothing" (419). In its "virginal purity" (418) and naturalness, Natasha's singing lifts Nikolai like the nightingale and the Grecian urn do John Keats. Both can affirm that "truth is beauty and beauty truth," and that is all they "need to know" (*"Ode on a Grecian Urn,"* lines 49–50). As Natasha hits the highest note, Nikolai cannot help harmonizing with her in a lower register. While he sings, he becomes conscious of being moved by "something best" in his "soul," rising to embrace a reality "apart from everything else in the world, and above everything in the world" (419). Nikolai joins Prince Andrei in experiencing through beauty a transcendence that makes all else in this life insignificant. Once again, the mysticism that is so embedded in the Russian spirit allows Nikolai to "put aside all earthly cares" and keep from being crushed by his misfortune.

Nikolai's meeting with his father follows. It is brief but emotional. The old count, as usual, is charitable and empathetic, agreeing that a catastrophe like his son's occurs as a part of maturation ("Happens to everyone . . . yes, happens to everyone" (420)) and agrees to help raise the necessary funds. Nikolai kisses his father's hand in gratitude as he begs forgiveness. It is impossible to imagine a more considerate or sensitive response to a son who has erred so badly; it is almost as saintly as it is paternal, suggesting comparison with the Gospel's parable of the prodigal son. It is as if Nikolai is still in that ideal realm where only charity and love prevail.

The denouement to the dramatic events Natasha, Sonya, and Nikolai have just lived through is blessedly uneventful. Denisov has been so entranced by Natasha he proposes to her before his leave ends. Natasha is sure she is "not in love with him" (421) as a husband to be, so she politely refuses, taking care to assure Denisov she will always "love [him] as a friend" (421). The countess coolly reprimands Vasily Dmitritch for asking her young daughter to marry him without first broaching the matter with her. This intervention has a calming effect and lowers the emotional temperature in the household considerably. Nikolai pays Dolokhov in full, though the count requires time and expends a great deal of effort to raise the large amount needed. Sonya stands by Nikolai as faithfully as ever, paying no attention to Nikolai's fear that he is "unworthy of her" (422). Denisov and he return to their regiment "at the end of November" (422), allowing everyone else to return to a much more placid routine.

PART TWO

After his tempestuous separation from his wife, Pierre leaves for Petersburg to seek some rest and relief. During the journey, he is preoccupied by metaphysical questions and concerns, trying to put into perspective the harsh realities of his nearly fatal duel and the end of his marriage. While in this rather distracted state, he meets a fellow traveler, who immediately impresses Pierre with "his austere, intelligent, penetrating expression" (425). This gentleman knows what has occurred recently, since Moscow society has spread word of Pierre's "misfortune" (426) far and wide. He addresses Pierre paternally: "You are young, I am old. I should like to help you as far as it lies in my power" (426). This help will not rest on friendship or good will but on something far more profound. His new acquaintance is a Mason, as Pierre realizes when he sees his "ring with its death's head—a Masonic symbol" (427). As such, he feels compelled to offer spiritual support and guidance, exactly what Pierre is looking for at this point in his life.

A dialogue ensues, with Pierre declaring in a tone of regret that he does not believe in God, making him more like the French revolutionaries than his fellow countrymen. The Mason takes this skepticism as a challenge. He insists that God is real and in intimate touch with all humanity: "You do not know Him, but He is here, He is in me, He is in my words, He is in thee, and even in those blasphemous words thou hast just uttered" (428). Pierre is so impressed by the Mason's firm convictions and "by the tone of sincerity and authority in the vibrant voice" (429) of his companion that he experiences a complete change of heart, assenting to the powerful certainty "radiating from his [the Mason's] whole being" (429). Pierre becomes a believer all at once, basking in a "joyous feeling of solace, regeneration, and return to life" (429), like one swept away by the zealotry of an American revivalist.

The belief that animates his new guide is anything but skin-deep. The God whom the Mason invokes is not apprehended by reason or science; this omnipotent divinity must be approached and felt through "life" (429). The life a Mason strives to lead needs to be purified and "made perfect" (429) through faith. Because the "purest essence we may wish to imbibe" cannot enter "an impure vessel" (429), Pierre should begin a regimen of self-mortification. By this means, he can atone for his many sins, such as not applying his wealth is ways that could alleviate the sufferings of his "tens of thousands of serfs"; not choosing "a post in the service" where he "might be of use to others"; not helping Elena "find the path of truth"; and not sparing Dolokhov, who had, after all, simply "offended" (430). Pierre is aghast after hearing this indictment, convinced he has been living "a contemptible, dissolute life" (430). He begs his friend to help him "be what you would have me be" (431) by teaching and guiding him. His interlocutor promises that in Petersburg "such measure of aid as it is in the power of our Order to give will be afforded" (431) Pierre, and leaves him with a note of introduction to one of the city chapter's leading members.

Pierre learns later that his patron is Josef Alekseyevich Bazdaev, a well-known member of the order. This man's generous and serious commitment to a stranger's regeneration inspires Pierre to do all he can to be like Bazdaev. Pierre senses that a new chapter is opening in his life, one that will allow him to embrace "a blissful, irreproachable, virtuous future" in the company of "a brotherhood of men united in the aim of supporting one another in the path of virtue" (431). He aspires to transform himself into a seeker of the highest wisdom and virtue, like one of the ancient Gnostics, privileged to intuit the essence of divinity through study, faith, charity, and purified understanding.

In his ardor, though, Pierre is not fully cognizant of the implications his idealism brings. In challenging Dolokhov and standing up to his manipulative wife, Pierre had shown himself how strong and forthright he could be. For a brief time, he had revealed an independent, forceful personality, not allowing himself to be toyed with or ruled by others. The man who had let Prince Vasily rearrange his finances and choose his wife has emerged healthy and whole from his recent crises. His conversation with Bazdaev, however, has brought to light aspects of his life experience that diminish the satisfaction the aftermath of the duel and the separation has brought him. His failures and omissions have to be purged, never to reappear. This radical moral surgery cannot be accomplished without the guidance and support of the Masonic fraternity—that is, without others' intervention in his thinking, acting, and behaving. Pierre will be like a new member of Alcoholics Anonymous, surrendering his or her freedom and will to others and letting them monitor his decision-making to facilitate the achievement of organizational goals. In other words, Pierre will once more allow himself to be led, and even though he values the Masonic tenets and aspirations highly, this surrender of individual autonomy is more of a step backward than a way forward.

Count Willarski, a Polish nobleman whom Pierre has met socially, sponsors his entrance into the brotherhood and invites Pierre to undergo an initiation ritual that combines elements of

Christian penitential rites and the vowed life with references to practices members of ancient pagan cults utilized to access sacred knowledge or *lumina.* At the start, Pierre's eyes are covered and his hair tied back painfully while he awaits a knock at the door, as if he is symbolically preparing to leave darkness and the clutches of sin and "at last set out on that path of regeneration and the actively virtuous life of which he had been dreaming ever since his meeting with Josef Alekseyevich" (433). After hearing the knock, Pierre enters a room whose only illumination comes from a candle "burning inside . . . a human skull with its apertures and teeth" (433). The candle lights up a Testament opened to the first words of St. John's Gospel: "In the beginning was the Word and the Word was with God" (433); Pierre also sees an open "coffin with bones in it" (433).

The atmosphere is decidedly spooky, but Pierre is not phased: "Hoping to enter on an entirely new life, absolutely unlike the old one, he expected everything to be extraordinary, even more extraordinary than what he was seeing" (433). A man designated as the "Rhetor" (434) now appears. Pierre knows him also, and this makes him self-conscious, as if meeting an acquaintance in a place he thought private. The Rhetor quizzes him like an abbot would a postulant entering a religious order, wondering about his motives (desire for "regeneration"), his religious faith ("considered it erroneous and did not pursue it"), his willingness to persist in Masonry ("You seek truth for the purpose of observing its laws in your life . . . do you not? Yes, yes." (434–35)), and so forth.

All this is distinctively Masonic, but the ritual evokes traditional Christian practices so often that it is not totally foreign to one raised like Pierre in the Orthodox Church. What the Rhetor mentions next, however, is different. He informs Pierre of "the principal aim of our order," which is "the preservation and bequeathing to posterity of a certain solemn mystery . . . which has come down to us from the most ancient times, actually from the first man, a mystery upon which perhaps the fate of mankind depends" (435). Only the spiritually elect can expect to be enlightened about something so profoundly important. The Masons, therefore, must "reform their hearts" through "long and sedulous self-purification" so that they will be "capable of receiving it [the mystery]" and thereby "improve the whole human race" (435). The Rhetor then leaves to give Pierre time to "think on these things" (435).

This mystery is not the Christian Incarnation nor the Gospel teachings, since the apostles and their successors received and passed on knowledge of these gifts to all the baptized. The "solemn mystery" of the Masonic Order is rather akin to the oracles spoken at Delphi or the Eleusinian mysteries vouchsafed to pagan Greek priests, or the manifestations of Isis and Osiris, or the prophecies of Mithras. The Masons are offering Pierre a path to this *gnosis* or divine knowledge, a path blocked to those outside the order, whose conventional Christian faith and practice are insufficient to merit such a revelation. The prospect of "improving humanity" through propagation of everything the order teaches, inspires Pierre, who envisions himself as a missionary to and counselor of "debauched and unfortunate people" (435), whose lives he can transform.

The Rhetor continues by enumerating the seven virtues Pierre should strive not only to understand but to model in his life. Pierre accepts this challenge with the zeal of a new convert. He pronounces himself "ready for everything" (436), feeling "only too glad to be delivered from his own free will and to submit to those who knew the indubitable truth" (436). He is then presented with the garments of the order and exhorted to "seek blessedness not in passions but in your heart" (437).

As the initiation goes on, Pierre suffers a momentary unease, as if he has been drawn into something he will later be "ashamed to remember" (439). The anxiety passes, but it is a telling clue as to how his connection to the order will evolve over the coming years. Now, though, he agrees to "prostrate himself at the gates of the Temple" (439) and receive "a white leather apron, . . . a trowel and three pairs of gloves " (440). Such items evoke the origins of the Masonic lodges in the European Middle Ages. During the centuries when great cathedrals, palaces, and fortifications were constructed, certain masons alone had solved the "mystery" of how to shape and secure the keystone that completes the construction of an arch. This secret they jealously guarded, fearing that any sharing would make their services as master builders less valuable. In other words, all the high-minded aims of the current brotherhood and its special connection to a salvific "mystery" derive from all too human self-interest.

Another aspect of Masonry becomes apparent as Pierre looks up to see a number of his "brothers" seated before him and dressed in the same fashion as he. He recognizes many by sight, all of them part of the city's social and intellectual elite. The Masons are, in reality, a self-anointed group of *cognoscenti*, sure of their status in the order and in society as a whole. Though Pierre prefers to think of these men as "only brothers," one of whom solemnly reminds all present of "the necessity of humility" (441), these are hardly the sort of people who would be likely to join Pierre in ministering to those less fortunate.

Pierre, nonetheless, is hardly conscious of this disconnect between the Masonic ideals of service and support and its members' lives of privilege. He has gone through his initiation as if in a hypnotic trance, and his conviction that the ceremony has signaled that he "was completely changed and had left behind his former habits and way of life" (441) is too strong to be questioned. As a result, he fails to acknowledge that he has gone through a quasi-religious conversion experience under the powerful influence of men of distinction largely separated from their countrymen and women, not only socially and intellectually but spiritually. This fact makes all the more fantastic a proposal drawn up by Mikhail Speransky, at one time Tsar Alexander I's closest advisor and confidant and a man Prince Andrei will get to know and work with later in the novel. Speransky was the son of a village priest and always deplored what he saw as the backwardness and ignorance of the Orthodox clergy nationwide. His proposal was to entrust the education of Orthodox seminarians to the Masons, whose intellectual, cultural, and social celebrity would bring to these cloistered young men a worldly sophistication they would need to acquire if they were ever to rise above the shortcomings of their mostly rural backgrounds. The Masons could become for Russia's seminaries what the Jesuits were for those in Western Europe, role models of intellect and influence for the aspiring lower classes. Apart from the fact that the Masons and their "mystery" are not recognizably Orthodox, this proposal, if implemented, could not possibly have succeeded since the elite could not ever be comfortable with peasants' sons, men they would despise outside the seminaries' walls. If Julien Sorel regarded his fellow seminarians in Besancon as hopeless rubes, Pierre's brothers could not be expected to feel otherwise about their charges.

Pierre begins his new life in the brotherhood with an invigorating dedication and ambition. Shortly after his initiation, Prince Vasily, Elena's father, calls upon Pierre unexpectedly. The prince is eager to reconcile his daughter and Pierre, worrying that the separation will compromise both the prince and Elena "in the eyes of society and even of the Court" (442). He reminds Pierre that "the Dowager Empress is taking a keen interest in the whole affair" (442), a development that socialites like the prince and his family fear and that can come back to haunt even a loner like Pierre, especially if he needs help from important people. Prince Vasily, of course, is most concerned about the financial impact a possible divorce may have on himself and his profligate family, so the sooner he can get Pierre to patch things up with Elena, the better. Pierre is "so used to submitting to Prince Vasily's manner of nonchalant self-assurance" (442), he has to resist the tendency just to go along with whatever the prince desires. His initiation, however, at least for the time, has armored him with new principles that strengthen his will to resist Prince Vasily's coaxing. With "an enraged expression on his face that recalled his father" (443) and which so frightened Elena, Pierre shows his father-in-law the door without agreeing to any of his requests. He then prepares to leave St. Petersburg, letting talk of the duel and his separation subside and move to his estates in the south, where he will strive to apply humane and enlightened practices to improve the lives of the serfs.

Petersburg society has largely given up on Pierre at this juncture anyway, considering him "that absurd young man . . . ruined by the depraved ideas of the age" (444), the same judgment first pronounced by Anna Pavlovna and company at the novel's beginning. Little else has changed in Anna's world either. The grand hostess continues to bring together the most prominent guests at her *soirees* and strives always to find "some new and interesting person" (444) she can introduce as a special attraction. At one such gathering, none other than Boris Drubetskoy is the favored invitee. Boris is steadily rising in military circles as he follows the "unwritten code," which makes "success" depend on "the faculty of getting along with those who confer the rewards" (445). His strategy has lately gotten him appointed "aide-de-camp to a very important personage" (444). On this evening, in the midst of introductions and greetings and in the constant chatter about the implications of Napoleon's recent victories in Prussia, Boris suddenly finds himself seated next to "the beautiful Ellen, who several times met the glances of the handsome young aide-de camp with a smile" (446). She wastes no time in small talk, insisting that Boris visit her privately on "Tuesday, between eight and nine" (447). The woman whom Prince Vasily, in his meeting with Pierre, characterized as "as innocent . . . as Christ before the Jews" (442) obviously considers seduction compatible with innocence. For his part, in true Petersburg fashion, Boris pays no attention to innocence nor to the fact that Countess Elena is still married to Pierre. He savors the distinction of being "an intimate in the Countess Bezukhova's house" (449), where sexual favors can lead to social, political, and/or military favors through the operation of the unwritten code, giving a beautiful woman access to the right people at any time.

While his wife is thus occupied, Pierre begins his work among the serfs in the province of Kiev, "taking with him full directions, which he had set down for his own guidance, as to what he should do on his estates" (457–58). He begins by laying out a progressive plan "to liberate his serfs" (458). As Pierre's plan is unveiled, the chief steward and his assistants learn just how "enlightened" his program is for the Russian heartland in the early nineteenth century. To wit, serfs "were not to be overburdened with labor . . . women with children were not to be sent to work . . . punishments were to be admonitory rather than corporal; and . . . hospitals, schools, and asylums were to be established on all the estates" (458). These goals cannot be achieved singlehandedly; Pierre needs the help of the chief steward, in particular, whose long experience in managing the estates can compensate for his master's lack of practical business skills and perseverance.

Such a partnership seems to be working out well as the implementation process starts, but this is only on the surface. The chief and his associates are not happy about any changes that might reduce their power, income, security, or independence. They go through the motions of complying with Pierre's wishes, but in truth nothing really changes. The hard facts of serfdom stubbornly resist Pierre's interventions. All that the idealistic young Mason sees as progressive innovations to be celebrated come with crippling drawbacks hidden from him:

> *He did not know that since by his orders nursing mothers were no longer sent to work on his land they did even harder work on their own plot of ground. He did not know that the priest who met him with the cross oppressed the peasants with his exactions, and that the pupils gathered around him had been yielded up to him with tears and redeemed with large sums of money by their parents. He did not know that the brick buildings being raised according to plan were built by serfs whose corvee was thus increased, having been reduced only on paper. He did not know that where the steward had pointed out to him in the account books that the serfs' quitrent had been reduced by a third their corvee had been increased by half.* (461)

Clearly, the chief steward has orchestrated a complete triumph for himself and everyone else holding privileged positions in the management of the estates. The steward has taken full advantage of the naïve young man, playing “with him as with a toy” (461), and in every way forcing Pierre’s serfs “to give in money and labor just what other people’s serfs gave—that is to say, all that could be got out of them” (461).

This devastating denouement highlights the difficulty reformers of all stripes face as they work to change minds and hearts in entrenched systems and patterns of thought built up over centuries. New principles developed by scholars and intellectuals and promoted by elites like the Masons cannot take root within cultures dominated by traditional thinking and authorities unless, through herculean effort, the value such transformative principles create can be experienced in day-to-day living. The ingrained suspicion that makes Russian peasant culture, and the country as a whole, react against any fundamental changes in social, religious, or political life, particularly those inspired by foreigners, is too strong to be eradicated by impositions from on high, as everyone from the Masons, the liberals like Speransky, the Bolsheviks, and the post-Communist advocates of democracy eventually realize.

Pierre suffers in this experience the fate of the military commanders in *War and Peace*. He thinks his plans are so rational and scientifically justified they will be adopted with enthusiasm and will carry the peasants to new heights of knowledge and achievement. But plans and schemes go awry when situations on the ground do not correspond to the outlines developed in abstraction. Mistakes are made, orders are not carried out, fear replaces dogged determination, and focus and confidence are lost. Troops in battle can perform just as badly as the peasant masses when their officers or stewards fail to lead, temporize, or waver in their commitment to the cause. Halfhearted or deceptive efforts ensue, making it impossible to accomplish missions. Thus, Pierre has been walked through a series of Potemkin-like charades and falsities devised only to humor him. He accepts deference and commendations afterwards like Prince Bagration, who also thinks his vague and confusing orders and leadership had a decisive impact on the "victory" at Schongraben and the retreat from Austerlitz, when in fact whatever good came out of both enterprises owed everything to the valor and stubborn defense of individual soldiers giving their all.

Despite the fact that Pierre's estate managers have given their all only to efforts to sabotage his reforms and life among his peasants remains as hard as ever, Pierre maintains his blissful ignorance and is so happy after his sojourn in the south, he decides to pay a visit to Prince Andrei, whom he has not seen in years and with whom he is eager to share some of his enlightened thinking. They meet at the prince's "recently acquired estate," which is actually "a small, newly built lodge," modest, functional, and "scrupulously clean" (462). Pierre is struck by Prince Andrei's "dull and lifeless" (463) eyes, suggesting that the trials caused by his battle wounds and the loss of his wife have taken a toll. He senses that it would be "somehow unseemly to speak of his enthusiasms, dreams, hopes of happiness, in Prince Andrei's presence" (463). Pierre, though, is so determined to show his friend that he [Pierre] is "now a quite different and better person than he had been in Petersburg" (463), he presses on anyway. He describes "what had been done on his estates" (464), carefully minimizing his personal role, perhaps in deference to Prince Andrei's listlessness. The prince listens but offers little praise, seeming to regard Pierre's exertions as "an old familiar story" (464) of youthful enthusiasm carried to extraordinary lengths. The dialogue becomes increasingly strained. It turns out that Prince Andrei also has adopted "a new outlook" (465), one very much opposed to Pierre's selfless idealism. He wishes now to live only for himself, abjuring the heroism a love of "glory" demands, a love that "entirely ruined" (465) Prince Andrei's life. Like someone determined to cure an addiction, he wishes no longer to return to regular military service and will be content to assist his father in organizing the local militia. The prince will, in addition, renounce society, politics, and friendships, preferring like Rousseau to live simply and quietly in his new lodge, managing the day-to-day affairs of the estate and its workers.

Pierre is sure Prince Andrei is heading in the wrong direction. He asks why it is wrong to introduce his peasants to "the comforting belief in a future life, retribution, recompense, and consolation" (466) in accord with Masonic teachings. Pierre also questions why anyone could object to his addressing the peasants' everyday needs. Is it, again, wrong-headed to provide, as he has, "a doctor, a hospital, an asylum for the aged?" (466) and the like. He cannot help regarding the changes in thinking and living among his peasants as gifts freely and generously bestowed through his mediation and owing to his Masonic enlightenment.

Prince Andrei does not know that Pierre has been deluded into thinking all he has described has actually occurred, but from the tenor and tone of his response, he might suspect that his friend has been carried away by his plans and projects, for he vigorously disputes the value and usefulness of everything Pierre has done. Like a defender of American slavery taking on the arguments of an abolitionist, Prince Andrei questions how the benefits Pierre has brought can be enjoyed by someone who reacts only to "animal happiness" (467). Endowing such a creature with "moral needs" (466) is not possible because unlike aristocrats like Pierre, Prince Andrei, and the brethren of the Masonic Order, the peasant has neither the intellect nor spiritual sensitivity to feel these needs. Force-feeding the peasant formal education and other "gifts" is akin to throwing good seed on barren ground. The peasant needs "physical labor," just as Pierre and his peers need "mental activity" (467). Reversing these needs is hopeless; Prince Andrei fears he "should die within a week" if he had to perform the exhausting physical labor of a peasant, and he is sure the peasant would simply "go to the tavern or fall ill" if he were deprived of his "plowing and mowing" and made to sit through school lectures (467).

The prince is jaded and contemptuous to an extreme degree, but he is more in tune with the grim realities of peasant life than Pierre ever could be. He ends the discussion by dismissing Pierre's most noble aspiration, his desire once and for all to liberate his serfs immediately and unconditionally. Prince

Andrei thinks this proposal can lead to nothing except further oppression. Suddenly relieving so many men and women of bondage will be so disorienting that the majority will soon find themselves unable to maintain life and limb. Many will be sent to Siberia as criminals and vagrants, there to live once again "the same brutish life" (469) Pierre's emancipation is supposed to end. Liberating the serfs helps only the "morally ravaged serf-owners" (469), whose exercise of absolute power over others will thereby be curbed. Pierre, then, winds up saving the souls of his fellow masters while making the peasants' lot worse, an outcome directly opposed to his original intention. Appalled by all he has had to hear, Pierre can only exclaim in horror, "No, no, a thousand times no! I shall never agree with you" (469).

As history will show, both Pierre's and Prince Andrei's aspirations and doubts will be borne out. The serfs all over Russia will be freed by imperial decree, not by the sainted Aleksandr I but by a successor in 1863, but the aftermath will be problematical. Certain former serfs will take advantage of their new status to acquire land and become relatively prosperous. But many of these better-off *kulaks* will be subjects of envy and resentment among those whose poverty and dependence remain severe despite their freedoms. These conflicts and tensions will come to a head in the early years of the Communist regime and particularly in the rich farming territories of Ukraine. There, the local party apparatus, prompted by the authorities in Moscow, will attempt to turn back the clock and reverse the advances made since liberation. The unpopular *kulaks* will be compelled to return their properties to and become employees of the state. They will be forced back like everyone else to hard labor for meager pay and will see no way to rise above the beaten-down condition they thought they had permanently escaped. Those who dare to resist this virtual re-enslavement will be sent to Siberian *gulags*, where life will be "nasty, brutish, and short." Those who will submit in resignation will face starvation, as the Communist dictator Josef Stalin and his henchmen divert Ukraine's abundant harvests to other uses. To this day, relations between Ukraine, now independent, and Russia, its menacing neighbor, continue to be antagonistic.

Although Prince Andrei's cold refusal to approve his visitor's solicitude for his serfs is disillusioning, Pierre cannot let matters rest. On their way to the Bolkonsky estate at Bald Hills, Pierre tries once more to show the prince "the true light, and . . . come to his aid, to enlighten and uplift him" (469) by expounding more of his brotherhood's key concepts. He explains that Freemasonry is basically "Christianity freed from the fetters of state and church, a teaching of fraternity, equality, love" (470). Prince Andrei should realize he is "a part of that vast, indivisible chain, the beginning of which is hidden in heaven" (470) and the end of which is veiled in immortality. In reply, Prince Andrei reveals that the source of his discontent is something so personal, abstract arguments cannot avail. He is in mourning for the death of his young wife and, like one of Dostoevsky's conscience-stricken souls, still burdened by guilt over a fatal wrong he believes he has done to her and failed to "expiate" (471). Since her passing, the prince has been "left facing that abyss, looking down into it" (471–72). where loneliness and despair reign.

Pierre can relate to this. He faced much the same emptiness after his duel and separation and was roused back to purposeful living only by his becoming a Mason. Pierre thus exhorts his grieving friend to rise above his immobilizing fear and guilt by recognizing that "we must live, we must love" not only today but "forever, there, in the Whole" (472). These words finally touch Prince Andrei deeply, recalling as they do the time he lay wounded on the field at Austerlitz and was lifted out of misery and despair only by gazing at the majestic heavens in mystic rapture. He feels aroused in spirit as "something that had long been slumbering in him, something that was best in him, suddenly awoke, joyous and youthful, in his soul" (472). Despite all their disagreements earlier, Pierre's ministrations now have succeeded in bringing this strong and dedicated officer back from the depths, renewing his energies, and jolting his return to the active life he had all but abandoned. To all appearances, the prince continues "to live in the same way," but "inwardly a new life began for him" (472) following Pierre's bracing visit. Later, Princess Marya will confide her anxieties about her brother's condition to Pierre, concluding "he needs activity, and this quiet, regular life is very harmful to him" (477). She is exactly right but does not know that the antidote to Prince Andrei's apathy has already been administered.

Nikolai Rostov, by contrast, hardly has to think at all. On duty with the Pavlograd Regiment, he takes comfort in the comradeship of his fellow hussars and in the fact that the regiment is a "home as unalterably dear and precious as his parental home" (479). Though he realizes military service leaves him "divested of his liberty and riveted to a single, narrow, inflexible frame," Count Nikolai assumes "his proper place" (479) without discomfort or complaint. He appreciates the reality that on duty, life is "clear and simple," and so long as he does what is "clearly, distinctly, and definitely commanded" (479), he can incur no blame. Nikolai resolves to become "an absolutely first-rate comrade and officer—in other words, an altogether splendid man, a thing that seemed so difficult out in the *world* but so possible in the regiment" (480). He also pledges to "repay his gambling loss to his parents within five years" (480), thereby regaining his self-respect and wiping away the one blemish still staining his honor.

Nikolai's high standards affect more than personal or family issues. On one occasion, in a search for supplies for troops that are not being properly nourished, Nikolai discovers in a deserted village "an elderly Pole and his daughter with an infant in arms" (482). Since they are too weak to move away on their own, the gallant young count invites them to stay "in his own quarters" (482) while they recover their strength. An officer later teases Nikolai about his selfless deed, suggesting he should introduce him and his comrades "to the pretty little Polish woman he had rescued" (482). Nikolai finds such words and implications insulting and berates the officer, almost to the point of provoking a duel. Only Denisov's intervention defuses the situation. Like all the Rostovs, Nikolai acts in the most natural way when it comes to assisting anyone in distress, responding to the requirements of *noblesse oblige* to comfort the weak, shelter the homeless, and protect the helpless.

Nikolai's gesture and his eagerness to defend his honor and his *amour propre* earn him respect, particularly from Denisov, who soon does something that seems as if he has been inspired by Nikolai's example. One day as he scouts the countryside for food sources, he runs into a supply train filled with enough rations to feed his troops for quite some time. Though they have no permission to do so, Denisov and his mounted comrades impulsively divert the wagons directly toward his regiment's encampment, all the while arguing with the infantry commander of the train about whose men need the provisions most. Such behavior amounts to theft in the eyes of the quartermaster, and a court-martial must follow. Denisov is told that he will be "lucky if the matter ended in his being degraded to the ranks" (486). Before these proceedings can get underway, however, Denisov is wounded "in the fleshy part of the leg" (487) during a skirmish. He then does what no one in the regiment ever does voluntarily for fear of suffering even more: he enters the hospital.

Nikolai visits there during an armistice following the battle at Friedland. The sights, sounds, and smells are overpowering. When Nikolai asks about Denisov, the doctor is sure he is dead, just like Prince Andrei should have been at the French infirmary. Undeterred, Nikolai moves toward the officers' ward despite a warning that he could contract a communicable disease just by entering. Nikolai proceeds fearlessly, nevertheless, encountering some men whose wounds have made them unconscious and therefore immune to pain; others, showing "thin yellow faces" stare directly at him "with the same expression of hope for help, reproach, and envy of another's health"; and one man begging for water so piteously, Nikolai, appearing like "a hospital official" (489), demands that an orderly bring him some immediately. This scene is set in 1806. Over fifty years later, American poet Walt Whitman will have similar experiences while visiting and tending to the wounded in Washington's hospitals during the

Civil War. The helplessness and indignation he will feel while doing so is conveyed in poetry of profound depth of feeling. The following excerpt from "The Wound Dresser" could have been written by Tolstoy, so little has changed:

> *I dress a wound in the side, deep, deep,*
> *But a day or two more, for see the frame all wasted and sinking,*
> *And the yellow-blue countenance see.*
> *I dress the perforated shoulder, the foot with the bullet-wound,*
> *Cleanse the one with a gnawing and putrid gangrene, so sickening, so offensive,*
> *While the attendant stands behind aside me holding the tray and pail.*
> *I am faithful, I do not give out.*
> *The fractur'd thigh, the knee, the wound in the abdomen,*
> *These and more I dress with impassive hand, (yet deep in my breast a fire, a burning flame.)*
> (*"The Wound Dresser,"* 3, lines 18–31).

In spite of steady progress in medical science, the wounded Whitman tries to comfort are just as agonized, abandoned, desperate for companionship or aid, and haunted by fear of impending death, as the Russian men Nikolai meets. One of these is Denisov, who is not in mortal danger but is far from the high-spirited man of action Nikolai knows so well. Although his wound was supposed to be "slight" and "six weeks had passed since he received it" (491), it has not been healing as expected. Rostov's friend, in consequence, does not display his "habitual swagger and exuberance" (491). He is not interested in hearing about "the regiment" or "that other, free life that was going on outside the hospital" (492). In his loneliness, Denisov exhibits symptoms of monomania, focusing exclusively on his court-martial and on the response he has drafted to the latest communication from the commission managing the affair. A fellow patient recommends that Denisov go over the heads of the commissioners by asking the tsar for a pardon. Denisov's "inflexible will and passionate integrity" (493) make him recoil from asking for a pardon for an offense he believes he has not committed. Later in the evening, however, as Nikolai is preparing to leave, Denisov breaks down and asks his friend to do whatever he can to get his petition, specially composed by a legal advisor, into the tsar's hands. He makes this request without enthusiasm and "with a painfully unnatural smile" (493). Denisov's strong spirit has been wounded as well.

Nikolai follows through. He secures permission to leave his regiment and join the Russian officers and staff members accompanying Tsar Aleksandr to his historic face to face meeting with Napoleon at Tilsit, on the Niemen River, the same river Napoleon and his army of six hundred thousand will cross in 1812 to begin their invasion of Russia. Boris Drubetskoy also has pulled strings to be made part of the "suite appointed for duty in Tilsit" (494). Boris, of course, sees this appointment as yet another step up the ladder he has been climbing since he began his military service. As always, he still thinks "success in the service" (494) consists mainly in being present at important moments and with important people. He has become so proficient in getting himself sent to events like the Tilsit conference, that Boris has "become known . . . accepted" (494) in the highest circles. In these circles, opinion has changed radically since the defeat of the Austro-Russian alliance. Napoleon and his troops have been "transformed from foes into friends" (495), so much so that on the evening of the conference, Boris and his associates host French officers at dinner in their quarters.

Count Nikolai Rostov calls upon Boris at the same time, not aware that the French have been invited. Upon seeing these members of the enemy's army he had so recently fought, laughing and relaxing among their Russian hosts, "a hostility he always experienced at the sight of the enemy, seized him" (495). Boris senses that Nikolai will be an uncongenial guest and shows brief annoyance. Nikolai tries to apologize for crashing this private affair and moves to leave: "I've come at a bad time, it seems. I shouldn't have come but for a matter of business" (495). Boris immediately recovers his composure and insists Nikolai join the gathering, extending "both hands" (496) as he leads him inside. Tolstoy adds this supremely apropos observation: "His eyes, gazing steadily and serenely at Rostov, appeared to be veiled, screened as it were by the blue spectacles of social life" (496). The "blue spectacles" are blinders, carefully set to keep everything except what is advantageous to Boris's ambitions out of view.

Despite, or maybe because of, Boris's welcoming gesture, Nikolai is uncomfortable, clearly in the role of "odd man out." He says little and keeps trying to excuse himself. Finally, he manages to get Boris alone for a time; Nikolai quickly explains what has happened to Denisov and ends by asking if Boris "through his general . . . could and would intercede with the tsar on Denisov's behalf and get the petition for pardon to him" (496). The blinders are busy processing this appeal out of the blue and finding reasons not to cooperate. Boris realizes right away that by getting involved in Denisov's affair, he could become associated with an impropriety, since back-channel contacts, especially at the highest levels, are considered irregular. He recommends that Nikolai take the matter up with the corps commander, who can follow normal procedures in passing the petition through to Tsar Aleksandr. In other words, Boris will not get involved. Nikolai is indignant. Here again the stark contrasts between a man of simple decency and generosity of spirit, who will not think twice about doing all in his power to help a friend in distress, and the coldly calculating egotist, who will lift a finger for another only if by so doing he will gain something for himself, are evident. Boris ends by promising to do what he can, the classic brush-off, and rejoins his group. Nikolai stays alone in Boris's small bedroom, refusing supper and any further contact with the others.

The next day, Nikolai takes matters into his own hands. Concluding that normal relations between Boris and him are now broken, he resolves to enter the tsar's private quarters and deliver the petition himself, an act of bold self-assertion. Upon arrival, however, he is quickly rebuffed by a valet, shocked by Lieutenant Count Rostov's "effrontery" (499). Leaving the quarters, though, he has the good fortune of running into an officer "who had won the Tsar's special favor during the recent campaign, and who had formerly commanded the division in which Rostov was serving" (500). This man is no Boris. He agrees to carry the letter to the tsar personally, and because the emperor and his entourage are passing by at the same moment, he can do so immediately. The tsar listens as Nikolai's friend describes Denisov's situation "at some length" (500). This extraordinary effort, nevertheless, fails. The man whom Nikolai regards as an angel on earth is immoveable, displaying no magnanimity and insisting loudly and firmly that "the law is mightier than I" (501) as he mounts his horse.

While this reaction hurts Nikolai, it does not cause him to question the Tsar's judgment or doubt the monarch's sense of justice. Even when, during a joint French and Russian military review, Tsar Aleksandr yields to the prompting of the commander of the Preobrazhensky Regiment and chooses an enlisted man completely unknown to the autocrat to receive from Napoleon himself the Legion of Merit as the "bravest" (502) of the tsar's soldiers, Nikolai refuses to question the propriety of his hero's arbitrarily approving an award for one stranger while curtly rejecting a well-reasoned and supported plea of another. He suppresses the "strange thoughts" (504) that such contradictory actions inspire, and instead Nikolai ends his stay in Tilsit by publicly endorsing the prerogatives of absolute monarchy.

That evening, Count Nikolai is enjoying a dinner given by the Preobrazhensky Regiment in honor of their "bravest" member when he hears an officer "saying that it was mortifying to look at the French" (504), so recently their sworn enemies. Even though he said much the same thing at Boris's dinner party, now, after his emotional response to Tsar Aleksandr's appearance with his regiment, Nikolai interprets these words as a critique of the autocrat's leadership and remonstrates loudly. With the contents of several bottles of wine swirling in his system, Nikolai repeats the time-worn argument dutiful subordinates make to any who commit *lese-majesté*: "How can you judge the Tsar's actions? What right have we to discuss them? We cannot understand the aims or actions of the Tsar!" (504). To drive the point home, Nikolai emphasizes the impact of such critical inquiry across the whole spectrum of order and settled belief: "Once we begin sitting in judgment and arguing about everything, there'll be nothing left. That way we'll soon be saying there is no God-nothing!" (505). Indeed, it is only a matter of time before Dostoevsky's Ivan Karamazov will draw out the implications of such thinking and conclude that "if there is no God, then everything is permitted." As soon as the divinely appointed monarch is treated as a mere mortal, autocracy's foundation is threatened, as are its companions in the Russian state's triad, orthodoxy and nationality. The three stand or fall together, so, like the Tories in Britain and the Catholic conservatives in France, Nikolai and his titled fellows will continue instinctively to rally behind the lawful and established order, crushing any who show even the slightest skepticism about the powers that be.

PART THREE

At one time, Prince Andrei Bolkonsky's independent cast of mind might have led him to become such a dissenter, but now he is too detached from all such concerns to stake out personal positions. He has been brought back from despair through Pierre's intervention, but he is still far from serious involvement in political and social affairs. The prince continues, at least, to follow court news and keep track of who is up and who is down in "Petersburg, the very vortex of life" (507), but preoccupied as he is by estate management, he is more observer than participant in the larger world outside. He does, however, institute liberal reforms at home along the same lines as Pierre, and with better results, thanks to his "practical perseverance . . . which, without fuss or exertion on his part, gave impetus to any enterprise" (506). Thus, the serfs on one of his estates have been "converted to free agricultural workers", and on another "a trained midwife was engaged at his expense to assist the peasant women in childbirth and a priest was paid a salary to teach the children of the peasants and household serfs to read and write" (507). Prince Andrei, nonetheless, feels little sense of accomplishment by so doing, nor does he take pleasure in much of anything. Touring his "Ryazan estates" in springtime, for example, he fails to respond to the renewal of nature the season brings. His melancholy is oppressive: "Always the same and always a delusion! There is no spring, no sunshine, and no happiness" (508). His indifference is numbing, causing the prince to be "disturbed by nothing, desiring nothing" (509).

Prince Andrei's passivity is disturbed decisively soon after. As part of his effort to help his father organize the local militia, the prince is obliged to call upon Count Ilya Rostov, the marshall of the nobility in the Ryazan region, who is spending the spring months in his estate at Otradnoe. As his coach approaches the estate's main building, Prince Andrei notices a group of teenaged girls frolicking in the sunshine on the road ahead. He is drawn to their gaiety, youth, charm, and innocence. One of the girls stands out, "a strikingly slender, black-eyed girl in a yellow print dress with a white pocket handkerchief tied around her head, from under which escaped loose locks of hair" (509). This is Natasha Rostova at her high-spirited best, embracing the day and deriving maximum pleasure from all that a spring morning in the country can offer. Prince Andrei's gloomy and mournful cast is in such contrast to this girl's zest for living, he feels "a sudden pang" (509), as if his own heart is aching to participate in the happy scene playing out in front of him.

Though the business that has brought Prince Andrei to Otradnoe is quickly concluded, Count Ilya insists that his distinguished guest stay the night. Put up in a room just below the one occupied by Natasha and Sonya, the prince finds it hard to sleep. The girls are staring out of their window, wide awake, voluble, and enchanted by "the moon and its light and the shadows" (510), whose romantic associations they clearly sense. Their awakening eroticism resonates within Prince

Andrei, as he experiences "an unexpected turmoil of youthful thoughts and hopes, contrary to the whole tenor of his life" (511) and so magical that the prince, a man of such deep and wide acquaintance with the vagaries of life, cannot understand what has happened to him.

Magical or not, whatever has happened has had a profound impact. On the way back to Ryazan, Prince Andrei looks for a gnarled old oak he had spotted days before and whose apparent world-weariness he had shared. He finds it soon enough but is surprised this day to see "young leaves" sprouting "through the rough century-old bark" (512). This striking change does the trick. Even though he had made a similar resolution in response to Pierre's pleading the previous year, Prince Andrei, who is all of thirty-one, now definitively decides that he cannot stay walled off from normal living any longer. His vital forces must once again be awakened, and the company of others must be welcomed. The prince knows that it is essential not only for himself but for his family and even for Mother Russia, that he once again take "an active part in life" and apply renewed energy and effort "to work of some kind" (513). He has to do the opposite of Candide; instead of retiring to his own garden and leaving the chaos, injustice, superstition, and foolishness of worldly life behind, Prince Andrei will reenter the din and whirl of engagement and once more do his best to combat all the ills he will encounter in so doing. Here we see how the power of vibrant young people, particularly nubile females like Natasha and Sonya just coming of age, can work life-enhancing wonders in a man still young enough to feel the pull of desire and the need for love. Combined with Pierre's more abstract and theoretical exhortations, the emotional uplift Prince Andrei has received is irresistible.

Prince Andrei's return to purposeful activity in Petersburg does not begin auspiciously. As a "gentleman-in-waiting" (514), to Tsar Aleksandr, the prince attends a royal reception shortly after arriving in the capital. He is immediately taken aback on this occasion by the tsar's "cold, elusive glance" (514) and refusal to engage in any conversation, confirming that Prince

Andrei is not in good graces in the small world of the court. He hears that His Majesty is displeased by "Bolkonsky's not having served since 1805" (514), another consequence of the prince's prolonged isolation. In an effort to regain trust and improve military administration, Prince Andrei, through an intermediary, presents a "memorandum on army regulations to the Tsar" (515), who in turn passes it down for review by Count Arakcheyev, the minister of war. The count asks to meet with Prince Andrei shortly afterwards. On his arrival, the prince is forced to join a host of nervous petitioners crowding the minister's anteroom and endure the humiliation of waiting to be called in turn. When he finally gains admittance, Prince Andrei is greeted brusquely and has to listen in silence as the minister dismisses his work with a quickly jotted marginal note: "unsound inasmuch as imitation copied from french (sic) military code and needlessly departs from articles of war" (516). Arakcheyev, however, does open a door slightly as he informs Prince Andrei he will recommend that the prince be appointed "without salary" (517) to the Committee on Army Regulations. This may not amount to anything serious or substantive, but it will keep the prince occupied and may lead to other opportunities for service later.

Despite this rough introduction to Petersburg's high officialdom, Prince Andrei is not discouraged. He soon takes interest in the liberal wing of the court's administration and in the reforms being advocated by Count Mikhail Mikhailovich Speransky, the "Secretary of State, the Tsar's informant, his companion at Erfurt, where he had more than once met and talked with Napoleon" (519). The prince meets this dynamo for the first time in an informal setting at the home of a friend. He senses immediately that Speransky is a man of culture and fine manners, utterly unlike Arakcheyev or the court flunkies:

> *In the society in which Prince Andrei lived, he had never seen such calm and self-assurance as was manifest in this man's awkward, stolid movements; he had never seen so resolute yet gentle an expression as that in those half-closed, rather moist eyes, or so steadfast if*

> *meaningless a smile; nor had he ever heard such a soft, smooth, urbane voice.* (519)

At the close of the evening, the count and the prince separate themselves from the company to confer in private. Speransky clearly has been briefed on Prince Andrei's recent activities, praising, in particular, his liberation of the Ryazan serfs ("a first instance, of which it is desirable that there should be many more") (520), and the prince's reluctance to condemn "the new decree concerning courtiers' ranks" (520), which so many of his titled peers oppose. Prince Andrei is grateful for these words, the first positive comments about his views he has heard in the capital, but he feels compelled to offer qualifications. He upholds, for instance, the antique notion of "*l'honneur*" he has derived from his father. The prince asserts that "certain rights and privileges of the nobility [are] a means of maintaining" (521) honor's preeminent role in the conduct of affairs of state. This strikes a raw nerve. The man whose father was a village priest and who was created a count only through royal decree insists that honor is not a "court or class privilege" (521) and that sons and daughters from the countryside can embody its principles just as well, especially if they are tutored in assimilating these principles by acknowledged masters like the Masons, something Speransky advocates. The tension between those born to power and privilege and those aspiring to such, which is turning Western Europe upside down even as these two speak, is highlighted once again. The prince is an "enlightened" member of the nobility, but he cannot completely discard the preconceptions of superiority his birth brings, while Speransky, a count by accident, cannot completely discard the sense of grievance he shares with those born poor.

Nevertheless, the two men of contrasting upbringings part amicably, with Speransky asking Prince Andrei to call upon him again in a few days to learn more about the bureaucratic appointment. The prince feels, almost in spite of himself, some attraction to the country's leading exponent of liberalism and some sympathy with his views. This meeting is reminiscent of

Pierre's with the Mason Bazdaev. In both cases, men of means and pedigree come under the spell of men whose powerful convictions penetrate the closed-off comfort zone erected by privilege and preferment. Count Pierre and Prince Andrei realize that something other than custom and tradition must undergird effective leadership and that an openness to new concepts and new exponents is vital, lest atrophy cause steady erosion of power and influence within their circles.

Just as Pierre believes that Bazdaev and his peers embody the ideals of Masonry, and as such consider it their duty to propagate these high principles and values in society as a whole, so in Speransky, Prince Andrei sees "the ideal of an entirely rational and virtuous man" (522), one who will through example and education awaken, first among Russia's ossified, entrenched interests and then within the peasants and artisans, an acceptance of new values and perspectives. He quickly is drawn into Speransky's orbit by a sense of kinship, which the minister encourages; he speaks to the prince as if only the two of them are "capable of understanding all the folly of the rest of the world and the wisdom and profundity of one's own ideas" (523). Speransky is not a revolutionary, but he is clearly a son of the European Enlightenment, which inspired much of the French Revolution's program. His mindset is not Orthodox or mystical but Cartesian, for he "found a rational explanation for all the phenomena of life, recognized as valid only what was logical, and was capable of applying the standard of reason to everything" (523).

In the capital built by Peter the Great, Speransky and his close advisors are striving to extend in a Russia still dominated by stubborn political, economic, and ecclesiastical vested interests, the same types of reforms and transitions Tsar Peter first applied in all these spheres over a century before. Speransky's ideas are best characterized as Western, including as they do the gradual abolition of serfdom and promotion of free agricultural labor and personal property, free elementary education for all, the removal of all impediments to the rise of talented individuals in the ranks of state and church, and a welcoming response to some of the innovations inspired by the democratic revolutions in the United States and France. In Prince Andrei's eyes, the very fact that Speransky could rise above the poverty and backwardness of his origins and become such a role model for all others like him (the majority of the country), makes the prince "cherish his sentiment for him the more and unconsciously to strengthen it" (524) as the first minister tries to deal with an ambivalent Tsar Aleksandr and duel with recalcitrant nobility and clergy, who cling to the old ways. In one respect, the two differ: Bolkonsky is forever in doubt about his purpose in life, always introspective, soul-searching and anxious about matters of conscience, while Speransky apparently never does anything similar, such as, for instance, wonder whether for most Russians his rationalism "might not be utter nonsense" (524). Despite this character divide, Prince Andrei is happy to work with the man who seems to be guiding his nation down right paths. Soon he becomes not only a member of the Committee on Army Regulations but also "chairman of a section of the Commission for the Revision of the Legal Code" (524), a body that "had existed for 150 years, had cost millions, and had done nothing … except had stuck labels" (524) on various sections of the compendium. The prince has his work cut out for him.

In another part of Petersburg, Pierre Bezukhov is embarking on a project both Speransky and Prince Andrei would find congenial. In the eyes of the idealistic young Masonic recruit, who is still trying to find his way in the brotherhood, his peers in the Petersburg lodge are not setting the right example. They are not living out their vows in ways that inspire a man like Pierre. Their charitable giving, for instance, is "niggardly and irregular" (525). Many are far from embracing the "Masonic vow in which each Brother promised to bestow all his goods on his neighbor" (526). Others are serious and scrupulous but "exclusively occupied with the mystical science of the Order" (526), too unworldly, in other words, to have any real impact in the here and now. A "majority" of brothers are functionaries, concentrating only on performing "external forms and rituals" and paying little attention to the "content or significance"

(526) of what they are acting out. A large group of mostly newer members have joined the order "simply for the sake of associating with the many wealthy young Brothers in the Lodge" (526) and using such connections to advance purely personal interests, not Masonic goals. Clearly, this body needs reinvigorating and renewal, and with all the zeal and drive of a recent convert, Pierre takes it upon himself to lead this effort.

He feels well prepared for this task. During a sojourn abroad, Pierre has made contact with "highly placed persons" in the order, has been "initiated into many mysteries" and been "elevated to a high degree" (527). He returns to Petersburg determined to share with his brothers all that he has learned and experienced. His reputation now is such that a special meeting is called for all to hear him speak. On this occasion, Pierre goes all out to light a fire under his complacent colleagues. He touches on the need to "act" so that "the honest man may obtain his eternal reward even in this world" (527) and even envisions the brotherhood taking the lead in establishing "a form of government with universal sovereignty" spread over the whole world to bring about the "triumph of virtue over vice," and thereby realize the "aim of Christianity itself" (528). Pierre concludes with an exhortation to missionary service: "As soon as we have a certain number of worthy men in every state, each in turn training two others and all being closely united, everything will be possible for our Order, which in secret has already accomplished so much for mankind" (528).

This extraordinary appeal is not greeted with approval or even polite applause. Instead, Pierre's powerful words are received with "coldness" (528); he has rocked the boat to such a degree, it may sink. Many of the brothers fear that Pierre's critique threatens their preferred style of Masonic commitment, demanding that they do far more than they are prepared to to make their membership sincere. Those who are comfortable with the status quo react with fury to just the slightest questioning of their motivations or life choices. Though they are highly educated and cultured and profess the most exalted ideals, the brothers are no different from any others in entrenched positions within organizations who regard criticism as an attack. Pierre has to contend with "the endless variety of men's minds, which prevents a truth from ever appearing the same to any two persons" (528). The grand master chides Pierre for his "love of strife" and states categorically that his "proposal" (528) cannot be entertained. The man who has tried so hard to move a mountain leaves the meeting like a lover scorned and spends the next several days immobilized by depression.

While Pierre broods, others in his world grant him no respite from pleadings or admonitions. He receives a letter from Countess Elena imploring him to reconcile with her. Shortly thereafter, one of his Masonic brothers visits and coincidentally reminds him of his obligation to pardon a penitent. Pierre's mother-in-law then begs him to see her, undoubtedly to reinforce her daughter's plea. In his distracted state, he is hardly in the right frame of mind to make rational decisions on a matter as serious as the state of his marriage, so he quickly packs a bag and leaves for Moscow. There he can talk with Josef Alekeyevich Bazdaev, his mentor and trusted guide on all matters moral, spiritual, and Masonic.

Brother Josef is ill, but he still manages to spend a great deal of time with and offer much advice to Pierre, which the latter records in detail in a journal Josef has recommended he keep. Brother Josef, too, is disturbed by the tenor and direction of Pierre's reforming proposal to the Petersburg lodge. He reminds his protégé of the paramount importance of "reformation and purification of oneself" (530) and the folly of making grand plans for the enlightenment of all mankind when one is "setting an example of depravity and abomination" (530). This hits home, and Pierre is chastened. He admits he "ought not to refuse a suppliant" (531), and even if this means humiliation and pain, he forgives Elena, who has never stopped professing her innocence, and invites her to resume living with him. Their conjugal union, however, will have "only a spiritual aim" (531), a requirement that may be appropriate for Pierre's "reformation and purification" but can only lead to more infidelity on the part of his beautiful and sensual wife. In the space of a few weeks, Pierre has turned 180 degrees, going from a reforming leader of his Petersburg lodge to a self-accusing *isolato*, pulled every which way by others. He is back to square one, almost as if he welcomes dependence and ineffectuality as necessary purgatives.

As these resolutions play out, Elena continues doing what she does best: charming all in high society who vie for her attention and favor. The countess soon earns a reputation for depth of intellect, something no degree of self-abnegation can convince Pierre to take seriously. Whenever guests at a *soiree* praise his wife's wit and insight, Pierre is incredulous: "Elena Vasilyevna Bezukhova could say the most banal and stupid things, yet people continued to go into raptures over the least remark she made and to discover some profound meaning in it of which she herself had no inkling" (532). As Elena struts her stuff like a starlet and begins seeing Boris Drubetskoy regularly again, Pierre suffers in the eyes of society. He is regarded as "the rather blind and absurd husband of a celebrated wife, a clever crank, who did nothing, harmed no one, and was an excellent, good-natured fellow" (533). Pierre is going backwards, turning himself into a caricature of what he used to be and in an excess of self-sacrifice and personal renewal, accepting the status of a nonentity.

Prompted by Bazdayev, however, Pierre is much more focused on his spiritual life than he is on society gossip. His diary entries from this period call to mind St. Augustine's *Confessions*. Pierre is trying through heroic striving to reach the heights of perfection scaled only by a few. In an excess of charity, he goes so far as to sponsor Boris Drubetskoy for membership in the Petersburg lodge. He is still tormented by "evil thoughts of him" and quite sure that Boris has joined the order only "to be intimate and in favor with the members of our Lodge" (535), who can do him many services; nevertheless, Pierre suppresses all doubts and misgivings and guides Boris through the initiation ceremony like a proud godfather. Later on, Boris rewards his patron by sharing some details of "adventures" (536) he has enjoyed recently; though Elena is not mentioned, Boris's tastelessness infuriates Pierre, and the two argue. Pierre once again blames himself for the scene, admitting to an all too human "contempt for him" (536). He prays for relief also from "these dogs—the passions" (536) whose urges will not abate. His celibate union with Elena is a source of continual turmoil, exacerbating Pierre's need for sexual contact outside marriage but provoking Josef Alekseyevich to remind him "that a wife ought not to be deprived of a husband's embraces" (537). Pierre records a dream he has, in which Josef shows him original drawings representing "the love adventures of the soul with its beloved" (537). But Pierre's soul is not as engaged as is his body, which responds strongly to "the maiden portrayed in the Song of Songs" (537) and similar drawings. Try as he would, Pierre cannot overcome his desires, though he knows his "lewdness" (538) is causing him to approach an abyss that will swallow him up. The conflict between flesh and spirit in Pierre's introspection is exhausting, forcing him always to fall from the heights he is desperate to reach. His herculean efforts do not yet bring the regeneration he had hoped to experience in himself and inspire among the members of the Petersburg lodge. Pierre is floundering.

A very different scene is playing out in the Rostovs' home, one that has hardly any spiritual connection. Boris Drubetskoy's friend and fellow staff officer, Berg, has decided that the time has come to fulfill a promise he had made years before, when he had noticed Vera Rostova enter a theater and had told a comrade that "that girl shall be my wife" (539). If this seems like something from a romance novel, it is just about the only hint of romance in Berg's life. Like Boris, Berg is a careerist, carefully cultivating those who can advance his interests. He is also very good at self-promotion, turning a minor wound at Austerlitz into a nearly crippling injury, and "in the Finnish War" picking up a piece of a spent grenade that had killed a man nearby, an act that had somehow saved the life of his "Commander in Chief" (539). Berg has played up these exploits so cleverly that he has earned decorations, which he proudly wears as "a Captain in the Guards" and has been given "some special, lucrative posts in Petersburg" (539).

The Rostovs are not exactly honored by this proposal from "the son of an obscure Livonian gentleman" (539), but they see no alternative to giving their consent, since Vera is now twenty-four and without other prospects. There is no hint of passion or charm in this engagement. Berg is looking at the upcoming marriage in strictly practical terms, calculating that "with her little fortune and my careful habits" (540), the couple can do fine. It helps that Vera is beautiful, has a "sensible character," and is "nice," unlike her "not very pleasant" sister, Natasha, but these are not as important as "her connections and some means" (540). The Rostovs celebrate the betrothal as prescribed by custom but without much enthusiasm. The count is concerned about Vera's dowry. The properties he had designated for such expenses when both Vera and Natasha were born either have already been sold or will be soon. Indeed, the family is in St. Petersburg when Berg proposes only because Count Ilya is looking "for a government post" (538) that will relieve some of his chronic financial stress.

Berg waits until just a few days before the wedding to confront the count and demand to know the amount of Vera's dowry. Count Rostov resorts to generalities but assures the "businesslike" young man he "will be quite satisfied" (541). This is not good enough; the future son-in-law has the temerity to ask for an exact amount and to have a portion of the total "in advance" lest he be "obliged to renounce the marriage" (541). The man who had insisted he would not be "marrying for money" (540) now flatly insists on at least "twenty thousand in cash" (541) up front. The count wants the unseemly haggling to end, so he consents and, for good measure, throws in "a note for eighty thousand" (541) as well, without giving any indication of how he will cover this note. This extortionate arrangement is sealed with a kiss between the two gentlemen.

This is pure Petersburg back and forth. Like papal Rome in the Renaissance, everything in Russia's capital is for sale. If Count Ilya is looking for appointment in a department of government, he must make contact with the right people and be prepared to offer the right fee for services. If he accepts a marriage proposal offered to his daughter by a man bent on social and professional advancement, he must come up with an acceptable dowry somewhere somehow. With his experience winning military awards and cushy postings, Berg is a past master of the art of the deal. The Rostovs, however, are not born and bred in this milieu. They are regarded as "provincials" (538) by the haughty Petersburg elite, and as such are almost the equivalent of lambs ready for slaughter. They are also unabashedly direct, natural, sincere, and generous in all their dealings with family and friends; in other words, they are exactly opposite to those like the Kuragins, who are perpetually exploitative. Significantly, Berg is least comfortable with Natasha Rostova, whose high spirits and guilelessness reflect the Rostovs at their best but go against the grain of this schemer's Petersburg character.

Boris Drubetskoy is cut from the same cloth. Four years before he had rashly promised Natasha that he would someday marry her. Nowadays, whenever this subject is raised in the household, Natasha quickly dismisses any such possibility as "childish nonsense not worth talking about and long forgotten" (541). Nevertheless, she still feels it is possible that at the time, Boris sincerely made "a solemn, binding promise" (542) to her, and she is eager to see him in Petersburg. Like Berg, though, Boris is not moved by vows but by careful calculation, and on a matter of great importance, like marriage, the calculations must show how well a wife like Natasha can promote Boris's interests. His preliminary estimate is not encouraging. He is making steady progress up the military and social ladder, so a future wife, ideally, should be someone like an unmarried Countess Elena Bezukhova, who moves easily in the highest circles and knows everyone who is anyone.

Boris's reasoning is Petersburg perfect except for one missing element. What Boris is not prepared for and what no bloodless analysis can anticipate is the effect Natasha has on him when he sees her for the first time in many years:

> *Boris remembered Natasha as the little girl he had known four years before in a short dress, with flashing*

> *black eyes under her curls, and a hilarious, childish laugh; he was confused when a quite different Natasha appeared, and his surprise and admiration were apparent.* (542)

For once, Boris is forced to acknowledge the power of genuine feeling and attraction as Natasha's beauty and charm draw him in. He resolves not to "yield to this feeling because to marry her—a girl without a fortune—would be to ruin his career" (543), a catastrophe beyond measure. His resolution is hard to keep, however, since he finds himself becoming "more and more entangled" (543) at the same time he is struggling to break free of Natasha. The ease with which romance and sexual attraction can upset the best laid plans is never more evident; like Pierre Bezukhov trying to come to terms with his sexuality, Boris is "in a fog" (543) and unable to take decisive action.

Countess Rostova comes to his rescue by intervening forcefully. She reproaches her daughter for encouraging Boris's attention and interest. With the sturdy common sense of women her age, who can see with jaundiced eyes the whim and caprice of youthful imaginings, the countess knows Natasha has "completely turned [Boris's] head" (545). This her daughter must try to stop immediately: "Because he is young, because he is poor, because he is a relation . . . because . . . you do not really love him" (545). Natasha protests at first but soon accepts her mother's points, particularly the last one. She admits Boris can be "very sweet, really very sweet," but in her eyes "he's narrow, like the dining-room clock . . . you know, gray—pale gray" (546). Pierre Bezukhov, on the other hand, "is blue—dark blue and red, and foursquare" (546). These metaphors say more than a thousand words, highlighting the one-dimensional dullness of the careerist and the bright clarity and sturdy reliability of the seeker, respectively. Natasha's sharp insights and imagery flow from her unclouded perceptions and her naturalness; she never lets ideas get in the way of the facts that are so apparent. The countess ends the romantic ballet the two young people have been playing at by summoning Boris for a private chat, after which "he gave up visiting the Rostovs" (547). Boris's one experience of emotional ardor ends abruptly, but his career and his marital prospects are preserved.

Natasha moves on. Shortly after this episode with Boris, she makes a strong impression in a very public arena by attending a glittering ball in Petersburg given by "an old grandee of Catherine's day" (547) and including the royal family and members of the diplomatic corps among the guests. Sonya and Natasha prepare for this great event carefully, choosing to wear "white tulle over pink silk slips, with roses on their bodices," having their hair perfectly coiffed "*a la grecque*," and showing "openwork silk stockings and white satin slippers with bows" (548) under their skirts. Most of these choices are influenced by Marya Ignateyevna Peronskaya, "a friend and relative of the Countess," brought in "as a guide to her country cousins in Petersburg high society" (548). Everything possible must be done to make Natasha's and Sonya's entrances into Petersburg society successful.

The girls' fussing and fixing has taken so long the Rostov party arrives later than most of the other guests. With so many eyes staring at her, many of them critically, Natasha is extremely tense as she enters the ballroom, "her pulse beating a hundred to the minute" (551), but this nervousness actually enhances her attractions, because her complexion colors and her eyes brighten. As the hostess greets Natasha, she offers "something more than her usual smile . . . perhaps reminded of the golden irretrievable days of girlhood and her own first ball" (552). As everyone starts to gather around the entry in anticipation of the royal couple's entrance, Natasha relaxes slightly, conscious that "she is making a good impression on those who had noticed her" (552). Madame Peronskaya lightens the atmosphere as well by pointing out some of the socialites and well-known guests within view and characterizing each with a pithy phrase. Thus, Countess Bezukhova is "the Queen of Petersburg;" her husband is "the great Freemason;" the French Ambassador, Caulaincourt, "might be a king;" and Prince Andrei Bolkonsky is “all the rage now . . . hand in glove with Speransky; they’re working on some project or other.” (552–53).

Tsar Aleksandr, his wife and family, and a retinue of “ambassadors, ministers, and various generals” (554) appear finally to great acclaim, and the dancing begins. Natasha experiences a momentary dread as she searches for a partner and no one comes forward, causing her to feel that she, her mother, and Sonya are “standing in the depths of a forest, of no interest, of no use to anyone” (555). But, at last, Pierre stops by, with Prince Andrei at his side. The prince remembers Natasha from the night at Otradnoe when he could not sleep and took great delight in young Natasha’s and Sonya’s laughter, stargazing, and innocent night thoughts. He immediately asks her to dance, and the two glide along the floor effortlessly, in the same way Natasha and Denisov did at her Moscow debut. Natasha’s response to the prince, “one of the best dancers of his day” (556), is however more positive and enthusiastic than her somewhat lukewarm feelings toward Denisov.

Throughout the opening waltz, Natasha’s “little feet in their satin dancing slippers moved swiftly, lightly, as if they had wings, and her face beamed with ecstatic happiness” (556–57). Prince Andrei is likewise enchanted. Natasha’s gaiety and charm go “to his head like wine” (557), and he again feels “animated and rejuvenated” (557) like he did in the forest after his transfigured night at the Rostovs’ estate. He cannot take his eyes off her as she dances with many young men, noting with pleasure “the joyous radiance of her eyes and smile” and the “shy grace” (558) she exhibits. She is not as womanly and curvaceous as Countess Elena, but this is to her advantage. Elena Bezukhova’s beauty is too familiar and too tarnished by affectation and conceit to be of any further interest; to Prince Andrei, she is like damaged goods, “coated with a lacquer left by the thousands of eyes that had glanced over her body” (557). The “superabundance of her own happiness” (559) takes possession of Natasha, compelling her to spread her joy everywhere; she takes particular notice of Pierre, whose “downcast, unhappy face” (559) radiates gloom, something that should be impossible on this occasion. "In Natasha's eyes all the people at the ball were good, kind, splendid people, loving one another and incapable of offending one another, so they ought to be happy" (559). Natasha's "un-Petersburg like" (559) *joie de vivre* begins now to manifest itself in a wider circle than family and friends. She is coming out in such a way as to make everyone and everything in her orbit the better for her presence.

Natasha's naturalness casts a spell over Prince Andrei that will not go away. It is especially strong in its sharp contrast to the Petersburg posturing and hypocrisy that the prince must endure as he discharges official duties and interacts with Speransky and his circle socially. Shortly after the ball, he attends a dinner at Minister Speransky's residence "with just a few friends" (560). Although Speransky is clearly cultivating the prince with this invitation, Andrei's interest in political reforms is fading. In comparison to what he has seen and admired in Natasha, the dreary routine of state service and bureaucracy is anything but stimulating. While waiting to dine, Prince Andrei listens to a report on the tsar's statement at "the opening of the State Council, an event he had awaited with such impatience and to which he had attached so much importance, and was amazed now that it was an accomplished fact it not only left him unmoved but seemed less than insignificant" (560). None of the controversial governance issues that Petersburg's political class are obsessing over can engage Prince Andrei any longer, and he wonders how their resolution can make him "any happier, any better" (560). The disillusionment that had caused him to withdraw from society previously is now returning. His dark mood makes him less receptive than ever to Speransky and his associates. As the dinner drags on, Prince Andrei becomes increasingly critical about everything and everyone. Speransky's "shrill, ringing laughter" is not appropriate in "a statesman" (561); the other guests appear to be competing with each other in jokes and witticisms that extend "good-humored ridicule" toward Russian "officialdom" (561); and the "gaiety" these people try to exude appears "forced and mirthless" (562) to the saturnine prince.

At home later, Prince Andrei casts a cold eye on all he has witnessed and done "in Petersburg the last four months" (563), seeing a great deal of wasted labor, disappointed hopes, indifferent leadership, and endless obstruction in all his efforts to promote positive change. Petersburg is a world unto itself, concerned only about forms and titles, rules and privileges, ranks and perquisites, access and influence; this closed-off capital has little connection with Mother Russia, just as Pierre's Masonic lodge has hardly anything to do with the nation's Orthodox faithful. The firm reliance on custom and tradition that characterizes church and society in the heartland is beginning to look to Prince Andrei more and more normal and natural than all the confusing reforms advocated by Speransky and his supercilious associates. Both he and Pierre are finding less and less sustenance in so-called enlightened company.

These sentiments are reinforced when Prince Andrei visits the Rostovs the next day. He is greeted so warmly by the count, whose "hospitality and good nature" (564) are the opposite of typical Petersburg insincerity, that Andrei agrees to stay the entire day and night. All the while, he takes every opportunity to gaze almost in awe at Natasha, a "remarkably poetic, enchanting girl . . . bubbling with life" (564). At his request, she sings and performs with such heartfelt emotion that the prince actually feels "choked by tears, a thing he would not have believed possible for him" (564). At night, he stays awake as he did at Otradnoe, and once more responds to what he can only call his "soul . . . so full of a new and joyful sensation" (565). He begins "making happy plans for the future" and resolves to "live and be happy" (565) with simple responsibilities, like taking charge of his son's education, completing his military service commitment, and traveling. This renewed energy and forward momentum are inspired by his love for Natasha and all the soul-stirring qualities she possesses, a love of which he will soon become conscious.

Another social event follows, a *soiree* carefully planned and choreographed by Colonel Adolf Berg and his wife, Vera. This small gathering is nothing like the Rostovs' informal dinner.

Berg is in character. The gathering has only one purpose: to "cultivate the acquaintance of people above one, that being the only real satisfaction of having friends" (566). Because she "considered such people as the Bergs beneath her" (566), Countess Elena has turned down their invitation, but Pierre has accepted, as have the Rostovs, Prince Andrei, Boris Drubetskoy, and Berg's commander, Count Ilya Andreyevich. In the Bergs' eyes, this roster alone makes the party successful, because any one of these worthies can be called upon later to help Colonel Berg in some way or other whenever the next "vacancy to be made a regimental commander" (566) opens up. The man who "reckoned his life not by years but by promotions" (566) could not be happier. Berg has drawn Vera into his way of thinking as well; she agrees with her husband, but not her family, that postponing children is to the couple's advantage at present, since "we must live for society" (567)

The *soiree* proceeds amicably, with no spirited arguments, no gaffes or conversational blunders, and no unacceptable fashion statements. In reality, this event adheres to script so strictly, it resembles every other similar assembly "as two peas in a pod, with the same talk, tea, and lighted candles" (568). Conforming to established standards and not allowing spontaneity or originality to rock the Bergs' boat is exactly what host and hostess desire. They see nothing to fret about, even if the stilted, false, and empty conversations all around them are devoid of interest or significance. They are happy that "in the little drawing room where it was impossible to sit down without destroying the symmetry, neatness, and order" (567) the Bergs have contrived, all guests have been on their best behavior.

One guest, however, is clearly uncomfortable in this setting. Natasha Rostova sits in silence, looking "positively plain" and reacting with "benign indifference to everything about her" (568). The Bergs' preferences and priorities are obviously not hers. Only the arrival of Prince Andrei relieves her boredom. The two delight in each other's presence, as Vera soon realizes. The older sister takes the prince aside, and with feline malice, highlights potentially damaging features in Natasha's background and upbringing, proving that she has assimilated well the Petersburg style of her husband. Prince Andrei learns from Vera that Natasha may be fickle, since "no one has been more courted than she" (570); that she and Boris Drubetskoy once felt "a childish love" (570) for one another, and so on. There is just enough suggestion in these observations to give the prince pause. He decides that the time is fast approaching when he must speak frankly to Natasha about what he has been hearing but also, more importantly, what he has been feeling about her.

"Everything was, in fact, just like it was everywhere else" (568) at this evening with the Bergs, so frankness of any sort is not to be tolerated. It is an occasion for display, for currying favor, for gaining notice, and for advancing certain interests. At a typical Rostov gathering, every guest is welcomed warmly, regardless of his or her rank, influence, power, or potential for future use. All are treated as friends, even scheming relations like Anna Mikhailovna Drubetskaya. The stark divide between Petersburg, the center of cosmopolitan living and European influence, and the vast countryside surrounding the ancient capital, Moscow, where native traditions still rule, cannot be more marked than in the opposing lifestyles of the Bergs, Kuragins, Drubetskoys, and the Rostovs. Prince Andrei and Pierre are not quite separated from Petersburg yet, but both are becoming more and more disheartened by what they are experiencing in the capital's drawing rooms, fraternal lodges, government bureaus, and political power centers.

Natasha and the Rostov household are aware of the prince's interest and, with "a feeling of awed anticipation, as if something of great moment were about to take place" (571), await the result. Prince Andrei is quickly losing all doubt as to his future, as Natasha's enchantments continue to arouse his feelings. Natasha, too, senses that destiny is playing a hand in this mutual attraction, which she believes began the moment she first laid eyes on the prince on the road to Otradnoe: "It is clearly fate that everything has led up to this" (572).

Pierre, by contrast, is growing more and more isolated and depressed. Appointed "a gentleman-in-waiting" to Tsar

Alexander, he is required to attend court functions more regularly, a duty that inspires "dark thoughts of the vanity of all things human" (573). Despite the Masonic Brothers' coldness toward him, Pierre persists on his path toward moral purification, "in the hope of warding off the evil spirit threatening him" (573). But day-to-day concerns and responsibilities, even including works of charity and benevolence, seem to Pierre "insignificant in comparison to eternity" (573). He is in the same situation as Prince Andrei after his wounds at Austerlitz, questioning how to go on living as before after an experience of transcendence. He feels no better as he listens to the prince rhapsodize over his new love: "I cannot help loving the light; I cannot be blamed for that" (575). Romantic attachments, too, cannot answer Pierre's yearnings.

Prince Andrei's plans and expectations, however, hit a roadblock almost immediately. With his usual self-absorption, Prince Nikolai Andreyevich, who must consent to his son's marriage, cannot give his blessing just yet: "He could not comprehend how anyone could wish to alter his life, introduce anything new into it, when his own was so near its end" (575). He advises his son to "put it off for a year" (575), so that the depth and sincerity of Prince Andrei's love for Natasha and hers for him can be tested. Although this appears to be sensible advice on the surface, in reality the old prince is hoping his son's "feelings or those of his prospective bride would not stand the test of a year or that he, the old Prince, would die before then" (576). Despite his father's suspect motives, Prince Andrei plays the part of dutiful son, nevertheless, and agrees to "defer his marriage for a year" (576). The prince then informs Countess Rostova of his intentions and his father's stipulation. Both she and her husband give their consent and agree to the one-year delay. The countess, though, is not entirely comfortable with this suitor: "She wished to love him as a son, but felt that he was a stranger, a man who inspired fear in her" (578). A military officer and widower with a crotchety old father, a pious sister, and a young child, is not exactly the ideal mate for her high-spirited daughter. Natasha, too, feels some trepidation at the prospect of marrying a man much older than she but is too swept away by her emotions to hesitate. While she is not happy about postponing the wedding for so long a time, she cannot help agreeing to this too: "No, no, I'll do anything," she said, instantly checking her tears. "I am so happy" (580).

Notwithstanding, other indications suggest that Natasha's engagement to Prince Andrei is not being arranged or viewed normally. There is, for instance, no "betrothal ceremony," and the engagement is "not announced" (581). The prince binds himself to Natasha but grants her "complete freedom" (581) in the ensuing year, and even agrees that though they are affianced, "if after six months, she [Natasha] felt that she did not love him, she would have a perfect right to refuse him" (581). As if all this were not enough, Prince Andrei also informs Natasha that "his son would not live with them" after their marriage because the prince "cannot take him away from his grandfather" (582). All in all, these numerous conditions make the engagement seem more like a modern American prenuptial agreement rather than an early nineteenth-century Russian Orthodox betrothal. Natasha's reaction to these decidedly unusual terms is mixed. She does not doubt her love for Prince Andrei, but she is not quite lost in admiration for him as before. After the prince leaves Petersburg, she appears disoriented and preoccupied but remains dry-eyed. When her spirits revive after a time, she experiences a "change in her moral physiognomy, as a child's face changes after a long illness" (583). The comparison to a "long illness" is ominous.

Upon his return to Bald Hills, Prince Andrei does not at first reveal to his sister anything of what has transpired in Petersburg, on the pretext that "she might ask his father to give his consent and, without attaining her object, irritate him and have to bear the brunt of his displeasure" (587). But this solicitude is misplaced, since Princess Marya endures her father's moody outbursts and sarcasms almost daily. The prince's reticence is, in fact, one more sign that his engagement is troubled. Meanwhile, the princess soldiers on, taking comfort in her religion and delighting in mothering her little nephew. Prince Nikolai wastes no opportunity to ridicule his daughter's twin devotions, sounding off frequently on “the superstitiousness of old maids or the pampering and spoiling of children” (584). Marya bears these cruelties stoically, modeling the ideal Orthodox woman’s resignation to and acceptance of her lot. Her outlook is one of almost apostolic charity: “For all the complex laws of mankind were summed up in the one clear and simple law of love and self-sacrifice, laid down for us by Him who in His love had suffered for all mankind, though He Himself was—God” (584). If God Incarnate embraced sacrifice, the dutiful Marya must as well.

But while her father’s rants are familiar and predictable (and more tolerable in consequence), Prince Andrei’s possible engagement is altogether different. The princess has heard rumors of “her brother’s betrothal to the little Rostova” (586) but has dismissed them as undoubtedly false. She believes the prince is still too grieved over the death of his wife to “ever marry again” and “let another fill her place and be a stepmother to our little angel” (586). He also would never marry Natasha, who is “not at all the sort of girl” (586) Prince Andrei would find attractive. This is all perfectly reasonable and perfectly wrong. Princess Marya receives the incredible news of Andrei’s engagement in an “unexpected letter” full of “rapturous love for his betrothed” (587). She ascribes his foolish actions to “the shortsightedness of men who seek enjoyment and happiness here on earth: toiling, suffering, struggling, and doing harm to one another in their pursuit of that impossible, illusory, sinful happiness” (588). In contrast to these, “who are corrupting their souls, their immortal souls, to attain some boon that endures but an instant” (588), are the pure “God’s folk—the pilgrims and deranged wayfarers” (588), who work their way through the countryside, teaching and preaching Gospel values by example and depending for sustenance and support on the kindness of strangers like the princess. She briefly considers joining them, given everything that is happening, and has already fashioned for herself “a complete outfit of a pilgrim” (589). Such an escape is not possible, let alone desirable, however, since her duties to her father and nephew must take precedence. Princess Marya does not need to perform extraordinary acts of penitence or self-mortification to bring her closer to her savior. Coping with her daily trials, now magnified by Prince Andrei's revelations, is more than enough to bear.

PART FOUR

Nikolai Rostov is another who is duty-bound to go where he is needed and do what he must, no matter how hard or uncongenial the tasks. Though he has become comfortably ensconced in the Pavlograd Regiment as the commander of a squadron "that had been Denisov's" (590), he realizes that family responsibilities rise above any personal or professional interests. Therefore, when Nikolai learns that his father's financial affairs are once again in disorder and that his assistance is required to stabilize matters, he cannot hesitate. Leaving a world "protected from all the entanglements of life" (591) and parting from comrades who he knows would do anything he asked is very painful; nevertheless, Nikolai requests and is granted temporary leave of his unit, so that he can return home and prevent those he loves from being "left beggars" (591).

Upon arriving at Otradnoe, Nikolai notices immediately a change in the familiar tempo and good spirits of the household. He is not used to the "uneasiness and occasional disagreement" now evident among the Rostovs and compounding the strain caused by "the wretched state of their affairs" (592). Like everyone else who has not seen Natasha for some time, Nikolai too marvels at how his sister has changed in the interim, projecting "such dignity" (593) as becomes a princess. But the calm and serenity she radiates are not at all typical of "a girl in love and parted from her betrothed" (593). He hears that his mother has "doubts about the marriage" (593), doubts similar to the uneasiness he is beginning to feel. Although Prince Andrei and Natasha profess total commitment to each other, members of both their families are clearly uneasy about the appropriateness of their union. A mature man rich in experience, particularly painful experience, is preparing to marry a girl only just embarking on the course of adult life. For such a couple, there is hardly any basis for shared companionship. This fact casts a worrisome shadow over what is about to transpire.

This shadow is not Nikolai's immediate challenge, however. Stabilizing the Rostovs' finances is why he has been called home, and he accepts this charge with gusto. He begins by confronting the Rostovs' steward, Mitenka, and, with growing suspicion, demanding an "*accounting of everything*" (594). But Nikolai's aggressive and accusing approach immediately backfires, as his father patiently explains that Mitenka's apparent chicanery is due to his employment of accounting principles unfamiliar to the young soldier. Once again, Count Ilya's reluctance to cause a trusted retainer pain and embarrassment overrules any attempt to clear up irregularities or modify existing practices. Nikolai comes up against the same mindset that caused Pierre Bezukhov so much trouble as he attempted to institute reforms in the management of his estates. The steward or estate manager as corrupt and self-serving functionary is a stock figure in Russian literature. As early as Gogol, the type had become recognizable in the operation of the vast network of agricultural enterprises countrywide:

> *The manager appeared. He was about forty, clean-shaven, wore a frockcoat, and apparently led a very quiet life because his face had a sort of puffy look while his yellowish complexion and narrowed eyes indicated that he knew too much about the charms of featherbeds and comforters. It was possible to tell right away that he had reached his position in the same way as had so many of his colleagues: first he was just a house boy who could read and write, then he had married some house-keeper, a favorite of his mistress, had himself become a steward to start with, and after that, a manager. And once a manager, he acted, of course, like all managers: he was chummy with the better-off villagers while squeezing the life juice out of the poorer ones; and in the morning he woke up around nine and took it easy until*

> *the samovar was brought in and he was served his tea.* (*Dead Souls.* Trans. Andrew R. McAndrew, New York: New American Library, 1961, p. 40)

Nikolai is sure Mitenka is "a scoundrel and a thief" but in deference to his father agrees to "say no more to him" (595). Later, Nikolai will encounter a body of recalcitrant peasants interfering with Princess Marya's attempts to leave her country estate south of Moscow before the French invaders arrive. Perhaps reflecting on this unhappy experience with Mitenka, Count Nikolai will deal with their leaders harshly, showing none of his father's restraint as, with authoritarian firmness, he awes the peasants into meek submission and allows the princess to make her escape. Nonetheless, Nikolai too is a Rostov. His mother shows him a promissory note signed by Boris Drubetskoy's mother, probably from the time she had had no means to outfit her newly enlisted son properly. The debt has never been paid. For a family scrambling desperately for added income, payment of this note should be demanded immediately. Nikolai, however, in a gesture worthy of a *grand seigneur*, tears it up, causing his mother "to shed tears of joy" (596). He explains that while he does not really like Anna Mikhailovna or Boris, "they were our friends and poor" (596) when the borrowing occurred and deserve relief these many years later. Father, mother, and son display the same Rostov magnanimity in all its glory. They are motivated by charity and love in their thinking and decision-making, even if in practical affairs these virtues can lead to loss and exploitation. The resolution of Count Ilya's difficulties will have to wait.

Eager to devote his time and energy to something resulting in tangible accomplishment, Nikolai welcomes the opportunity to lead a hunting party that will run after the wolves in Count Rostov's preserve at Otradnoe. Nikolai is "carried away by that irresistible passion for the chase which makes a man forget all previous intentions, as a lover forgets everything in the presence of his mistress" (597). The party includes Natasha and Petya, both of whom insist on taking part despite Nikolai's fear that his inexperienced siblings will be more hindrance than help. It includes Count Ilya as well, who is present mainly as an observer and admirer of his older son, who "understands all the fine points so well" (602). This shared experience is more than sport. For Nikolai, it is a rite of passage, marking his acceptance of adult responsibilities and his willingness to engage in activities that his male peers regard as sacred duties. This is, after all, a blood sport, one that connects Nikolai to his earliest ancestors, who had to hunt to keep their families nourished. Though procuring meat is not the real object of the hunt in the nineteenth century, the chase goes on because men need contact with the natural world and its harshness, so they can assimilate the same rugged mastery of challenges and threats in their contemporary world as the ancients did in theirs.

The huntsmen are rough and ready, the very opposite of French-speaking cosmopolitans detached from soil and countryside. They know they must run down and eventually kill their prey, a wolf, who will be pursued mercilessly by hounds, horses, and humans. Nikolai admits "it is a sin to ask this," but he prays, nevertheless, that his hound may "get his teeth in his [the wolf's] throat and finish him off" (604), knowing all the while that the strategy, anticipation, and quick action of the party have no other purpose than to achieve this brutal outcome.

On this occasion, Nikolai and his dog, Karai, prevail. The wolf they are chasing appears to have evaded entrapment, but a hound Nikolai does not recognize cuts across the animal's path and knocks the wolf off balance. The unknown hound suffers the wolf's wrath and, "with a fierce yelp, fell with its head thrust to the ground, bleeding from a gash in its side" (606). This interlude, however, allows Karai and the other dogs to overtake the wolf and overwhelm her. The scene is sickening, but Nikolai is exhilarated:

> *That instant when Nikolai saw the wolf in the gully struggling with the dogs, saw her gray coat and outstretched hindleg under them, her head with ears laid*

> *back in terror and gasping (Karai had her by the throat), was the happiest moment of his life.* (606)

Here is played out the time-worn Darwinian struggle that ends in the survival of the fittest. This same struggle will be recreated several years hence when Napoleon's *Grande Armee* marches into Russia, intent on defeating the country's armies, capturing its ancient capital, imposing terms of capitulation reflecting enlightened principles, and returning home in triumph. Napoleon's troops do, indeed, give battle at Borodino and force a Russian retreat, enter Moscow unimpeded, and from the city send out emissaries to begin peace negotiations. Nothing, however, goes as expected afterwards. The captured city is virtually empty, its boyars and residents having left their homes and most of their possessions behind rather than submit to foreign rule. Moscow's mostly wooden structures are being destroyed by rapidly spreading fires, depriving the French of shelter, and outside the city, peasants everywhere are plowing their crops under rather than allowing the enemy food and forage. Tsar Aleksandr bans any negotiation while foreigners remain on Russian soil, leaving the "triumphant" French and their allies with nothing to show for all their herculean striving and effort. They have no choice but to march back to where they came from, but with no peace accord, they are harassed constantly by Cossack marauders and have to endure hunger, cold, and disease all the while. Individual members of this once magnificent military command suffer like Nikolai's prey, eventually beaten down man after man, their bodies left to lie ignominiously on what seems like another planet, unknown and unlamented. Nikolai's success in the hunt presages in microcosm that of Mother Russia itself, in whose heart and culture he is beginning now to thrive.

Natasha Rostova shares in the excitement as well. While she takes no active part in chasing down wolves or rabbits, she imbibes the heady vibrations given off as animals are hotly pursued by men and beasts. This is the same earthy, quasi-primitive world of the fields and forests that draws Nikolai and his party into a kind of communion with his ancestors and heritage. In this environment, moving to rhythms of its own, nature overwhelms the delicate constructs of civilization. Natasha's response to all she sees, hears, and feels in these places is very different from her emotions at her coming-out ball in St. Petersburg. At that event, she performed brilliantly but with stylized formality, careful to execute steps and patterns as prescribed and to move and interact with a partner as the dancing masters would expect. In the rough country around Otradnoe, very little is laid out to be followed, so Natasha can do and act as she wishes, freed from the rules and conventions imposed by society.

Toward the end of the day, as she watches a hare being run down and killed by her uncle's dog, Natasha yields to the emotional power the grisly scene excites, just as Nikolai did while seeing the wolf mangled. Neither brother nor sister is cruel or insensitive; rather, each is responding instinctively to humankind's primordial need to subdue nature and its creatures, lest they overwhelm settled life. The rather sheltered and very feminine "girly girl" who has been raised in a proper household, suddenly discovers in herself a capacity to rejoice in humanity's sovereign sway over the raw forces threatening all that people treasure. As the hunters and their animals, fatigued by the chase but savoring the results, take in what has occurred, they hear from Natasha "an ecstatic shriek so shrill that everyone's ears tingled" (614). This is Natasha responding viscerally to conquest, exulting in the skill and courage of the animals and their handlers, and identifying with the men like Nikolai and the relative called "Uncle" in their sportsmen's victory. Her cry is "ecstatic," like that of Mlle. de la Mole when Julien Sorel waves an ancestral sword over her head, and she experiences the sexual excitement this act of masculine assertion arouses in her.

Later that evening, at Uncle's cottage, with its rustic simplicity, plain food, and native dress and entertainment, Natasha continues to revel in the timeless delights of family life in the provinces, from which in cosmopolitan settings she has been separated. Like Nikolai, she is growing more aware of her

Russianness in a place like this, enjoying "Uncle's mushrooms, honey, and liqueurs," listening in rapture to the "absolutely enchanting" (618) balalaika played by a retainer, and to Uncle's guitar rendition of a well-known song. At Uncle's invitation, Natasha then begins to dance: "The moment she struck her pose and smiled that proud, triumphant knowing smile, the fear that had at first seized Nikolai and the others that she might not do the right thing passed, and they were already admiring her" (620). Natasha's "so perfect, so absolutely perfect" (620) performance comes naturally; she is so in touch with her Russian traditions at the cottage that she can almost visualize exactly how native dancers must have moved and gestured in this setting centuries before. As she leaves for home, Natasha's enchantment is so strong that she wonders if her brothers and she are driving through the darkness to arrive "not at Otradnoe but in fairyland" (621).

This magical interlude serves for a time to give Nikolai and Natasha welcome relief from the hard realities facing them and their parents, but upon their return, they have no choice except to face these pressures once more. The countess concludes that the best, and maybe the only, solution to her husband's chronic improvidence is "for Nikolai to marry a wealthy heiress" (623). She even has chosen a candidate, Julie Karagina, "the daughter of fine, upright parents . . . and heiress to a large fortune" (623). Nikolai is not enthusiastic about marrying for such a reason and remonstrates with his mother, who insists his "happiness" (624) is her sole object. Nikolai, though, still believes that his happiness lies with "the dowerless Sonya" (624), whom his mother cannot help acknowledging as "so meek, so good, so devotedly grateful to her benefactors and so faithfully, constantly, and unselfishly in love with Nikolai" (624-625). Despite Nikolai's pledge to "sacrifice everything" (624) for the countess, she cannot yet bring herself to demand that he immediately renounce Sonya, regardless of how his attachment to her impacts the Rostov family.

Natasha's engagement to Prince Andrei, whom the countess and Nikolai are both uneasy about, is still far from concluding.

This leaves the young woman who has just experienced such stimulation in the countryside to suffer "fits of depression against which she was unable to contend" (625). She longs to see her betrothed, stuck in Rome now and battling complications from his wounds, and paces about the house aimlessly in his absence, looking for something to rouse her spirits. Natasha is too full of life, however, to remain immobilized. One evening during the holiday season, at her mother's request, she agrees to sing for the family the countess's favorite song. "Since it was a long time since she had sung" (632), no one knows quite what to expect. What they hear is nothing short of spectacular. Count Ilya is mesmerized, Nikolai is fascinated, the Countess is in tears, and Dimmler, the harpist, is effusive in his praise: "That is a European talent; she has nothing to learn: that tenderness, sweetness, power" (632).

The "European talent" of Natasha, though clearly evident, cannot suppress the native Russian element in her makeup, awakened so strongly by her sojourn in Uncle's cottage. One night, mummers call at the Rostovs' residence to offer holiday entertainment. Natasha and the other young people in the household join the group in various guises. This, too, is in the tradition of Russian Christmas/New Year's folkdom and festivities, as the celebrants in their costumes break down barriers, eschew formalities, release inhibitions, and laugh their way through every visit. Natasha transforms herself into "a hussar," like her brother, while Sonya turns into "a Circassian, with burnt cork eyebrows and mustache" (633). They and their companions then travel to a neighboring estate of a widow "with a family of children of all ages and their tutors and governesses" (633). The sleigh ride to this home is like a jaunt through a mysterious realm, with the darkness and the snow obscuring familiar sights and guideposts. To Nikolai, who is driving a troika, "with his short, shaggy black wheeler" (634), the experience is one of continual wonderment, as he tries to keep the mummers in sight and stay on track in an atmosphere like a ballet stage setting. As they approach their destination, the company might as well be in fairyland. Once inside, the mummers radiate theatrical charm, dancing and cavorting effortlessly and in harmony, all the while fascinating the children. Nikolai and Sonya grow ever closer as they kiss each other on the lips. Like Natasha at the cottage, Nikolai is "breathing, not air, but the vital force of eternal youth and joy" (640). The setting and the costumes show everyone in a new light. Nikolai finds in Natasha "something singular, something bewitchingly sweet" (641) and Sonya, with her mustache and burnt cork, is "beyond all doubt his happy, loving, future wife" (642). This is the apogee of eternal youth and all its wondrous possibilities.

Such bliss is once again an interlude only. Back home, the countess flatly refuses to consent to her son's marriage to Sonya. This rebuff drives Nikolai to distraction and elicits guilt-ridden sympathy from his father, who realizes "that if his affairs had not been in disorder no better wife for Nikolai than Sonya could have been wished for, and that no one but himself, with his Mitenka and his incorrigible bad habits, was to blame for the state of their finances" (644). This self-accusation is characteristic of all the Rostovs, who, with typical Russian loyalty to family and friends, suffer keenly when any of them fail to fulfill their obligations to others. By contrast, the St. Petersburg born and bred Kuragins, led by Princess Elena, feel responsible only to themselves, and therefore never worry about not helping others in need. Sonya accepts her fate, whatever it may be, since "self-sacrifice was her most cherished ideal" (645), but whether she has to sacrifice Nikolai alone or the whole Rostov family, now in such straitened circumstances, is not clear. Before any final or fatal breach opens up within the family, however, Nikolai ends his leave, and the Rostovs prepare to divest themselves of certain assets, an expedient they have resorted to before. These family tensions take their toll on Natasha as well. Her loneliness and gloom, so happily dissipated by the holidays and the mummers' frolics, return, and she sounds the same sad note as before: "The thought that the best time of her life, which might have been spent in loving him [Prince Andrei], was being wasted and of no use to anyone, fretted her continually" (646).

PART FIVE

Pierre Bezukhov is not in much better shape than Natasha. In St. Petersburg, nothing is very appealing: "Only the shell of life remained: his house, a brilliant wife who now enjoyed the favors of a very important personage, an acquaintance with all Petersburg, and his court service with its tedious formalities" (647). He returns to Moscow and his spirits revive, at least initially, because Moscow seems so quiet and natural in comparison to the artificialities, falseness, and endless politicking and intriguing at the capital. In Moscow society, Pierre is popular and esteemed as "the nicest, kindest, most intelligent, genial, and generous of eccentrics, an absent-minded, warmhearted Russian of the old school" (648). But this admirable man still lacks purpose. At his age, he is ashamed to be living the lazy, monotonous life of a "retired gentleman-in-waiting" (649). Pierre reflects bitterly on the irony of this fate and of how he had had such lofty ambitions and had undertaken so many generous and progressive initiatives in the seven years since his return to Russia, only now to be sinking into apathy and alcoholism. The hypocrisies attached to family life, religion, Freemasonry, politics, estate management, and the like seem intractable, causing "every sphere of activity" and every collective endeavor to be stained by "evil and duplicity" (650). Most days, Pierre is too pained by world weariness to rouse himself to productive labor.

Some of what makes Pierre despair is evident in other parts of the city. Also in Moscow at this time are Prince Nikolai Andreich and his household. The prince has earned the distinction of being "the center of the Moscow opposition to the government" (652). He has been anointed such largely because he is regarded as an exemplar of traditional ways and lifestyles. His "old-fashioned coat and powdered wig," his "laconic and scathing criticisms of the present," his "antiquated house" (652), and his pious daughter, make him the very antithesis of Speransky and his modernizers. The old prince seems the embodiment of sturdy Russian character, provoking "in all his visitors alike a feeling of respectful esteem" (652). This stature is, in its own way, a product of the emphasis on externals that has propelled Countess Elena to the center of elite social life. Prince Nikolai, in reality, is a petty tyrant at home, with his coquettish live-in lady friend and his mercilessly abused daughter, whose faith alone keeps her stable and compels her to forgive her father again and again. The countess is a great beauty whose narcissism recognizes no boundaries, rules, or disciplines, and whose marriage to Pierre is a source of amusement in her circles. These two acquire prominence because others judge only by appearances, thereby allowing "the evil and falsity of life" (650) to perpetuate falsity and intensify Pierre's misery.

On his name day, Prince Nikolai is visited by distinguished political and civic leaders of the city, all eager to express congratulations and best wishes to one they regard as a role model. Among these worthies, the conversation is typical of what one hears when grouchy old men reflect on current conditions. Each point anyone raises illustrates how matters are "going from bad to worse" (657). Thus, the depredations of Napoleon against the pope and the Duke of Oldenburg and the insolence the new French ambassador has displayed in the tsar's presence during a recent military review, highlight the lack of respect for titled authority characteristic of the current age. The French are so depraved that Prince Nikolai goes so far as to ban a prominent *émigré* doctor from his presence because he knows a "spy" (656) when he sees one. He also recommends that the Russian government sever ties with Austria and the German principalities to focus on the nation's true "political interests . . . all in the east" (659). The prince is sure that if the western frontier is defended by armed troops and policy toward France is "firm," Napoleon will "never again dare to cross the Russian border, as he did in 1807" (659), an assessment that events, of course, will disprove in just a few years. This hostility toward France and all it stands for echoes the remarks made at Anna Pavlovna's *soiree* at the beginning of the novel and underlines exactly how the old order in Europe has been unhinged by the repercussions set off by the French Revolution.

Among Prince Nikolai's guests is Count Rostopchin, the governor-general of Moscow, who will play so pivotal a role during Napoleon's occupation of the capital in 1812. He makes a telling point in response to Prince Nikolai's Francophobia. Reflecting on the prince's determination to repel any French incursion into Russia, the count asks how Russians can possibly combat the French, who are and have been since Peter the Great's day "our teachers, our divinities . . . The French are our gods, and Paris is our Kingdom of Heaven" (659). The privileged company to whom Rostopchin is speaking may find his words regrettable but can hardly disagree about French influence. They and their children have been raised in households where French was spoken more often than Russian and have been schooled by masters well acquainted with and eager to propagate French-inspired art, literature, architecture, music, and dance. But elites like theirs, with decidedly ambiguous connections to native Russian culture, are a minority of the population. In the crisis of 1812, as we will see, the resistance of what Bilibin calls "the Russian Orthodox Army" (210) will be rugged, brave, and determined. The troops will be greatly aided by the civilians, who, with virtually universal accord, will refuse to deal with the French invaders in any respect. Peasants will choose to burn their crops and even their homes rather than provide anything of value to the enemy. Count Rostopchin and his aristocratic peers are no different. They will watch as Moscow burns rather than come to agreement with Napoleon for the capital's surrender. Blood and soil will prove more powerful in shaping national policy than any shared appreciation for the values of European high culture.

All of this political back and forth is of little interest to Princess Marya. She is more concerned about whether her father's guests know, to her shame and embarrassment, how hostile the "loving despot" (653) habitually is to her. The princess's distraction causes her to miss "the marked attention and gallantry shown her all during dinner by Boris Drubetskoy," on leave in Moscow and "that day paying his third visit to the house" (660). He is in the city "with the object of marrying an heiress" (661), as Pierre Bezukhov wryly observes. Pierre informs the princess that Boris, who has been similarly attentive to Countess Elena, albeit for sex alone, is now paying calls on Julie Karagina, as well as Princess Marya, two of the city's most eligible heiresses. The princess blurts out candidly that "there are moments when I would marry anyone!" (661), if only to escape the painful life she is leading at home. Love is not part of this calculation, as it is for her brother, so smitten by Natasha Rostova. The princess asks Pierre "what sort of girl is she?" (662). Pierre demurs, admitting only that Natasha is "fascinating" (662), not just to Prince Andrei but to him too, although he cannot explain why. Princess Marya declares she does "so want to love her" (663), and putting her own needs and desires last, promptly forgets about Boris.

This is for the best, since Boris realizes he can make a stronger impression on Julie Karagina than on Princess Marya. Julie is "very wealthy" but at age twenty-seven "decidedly plain" (663). Nevertheless, she believes herself "far more attractive than ever before" (663) and welcomes the many men who pay her visits and enjoy the hospitality of her home. What Julie does not realize or cannot accept is that most of her male guests look at her "not as a marriageable girl but as a sexless acquaintance" (663). Julie reinforces this conclusion by an affectation of sadness, sorrow, and melancholy, rather like Dora's friend, Julia Mills, in *David Copperfield*. Still, even though Julie says she expects "solace only *in the beyond*" (664), she remains quite aware of the power of her wealth to bring her a suitable mate in this life.

Such a match is imminent. With his ingrained calculation and ingratiating manner, Boris Drubetskoy has decided that a marriage to Julie will bring many benefits, so he begins seriously courting her. He knows time is short, with his leave ending soon, and that if he does not act decisively, he will have wasted his time in Moscow and given up all hope of becoming master of Julie's "Penza and Nizhni Novgorod estates" (665). With his mother's strong encouragement, Boris wins over Julie by describing "his early disappointments in life" (664) and sympathizing with her perpetual sadness, like a soul brother. He hesitates briefly as he is overcome by "a feeling of horror at renouncing the possibility of real love" (665), as he had with Natasha. Anna Mikhailovna thereupon puts an end to this dithering by informing her son that Anatol Kuragin has been ordered to Moscow by his father "for the purpose of marrying him to Julie" (666). She has pressed the right button because, love or no love, Boris cannot allow "that blockhead" (666) to make a mess of Julie Karagina's business affairs. He proposes and is accepted. What follows is exactly what is to be expected: "The engaged couple, with no further allusions to trees that shed gloom and melancholy upon them, laid plans for a sumptuous establishment in Petersburg, paid calls, and made every preparation for a brilliant wedding" (667).

Things do not go as swimmingly for Natasha Rostova. The Rostovs, minus the countess, "still unwell and unable to travel" (667), journey back to Moscow after the holidays. Since their "house in Moscow had not been heated all winter" (667), they arrange to stay with Marya Dmitrievna, the imperious relative who guided Natasha through her coming-out ball in Petersburg and who now takes it upon herself to prepare "her favorite" (669) for her upcoming nuptials. She takes care of Natasha's trousseau first, earning a discount through shrewd bargaining. Marya Dmitrievna then arranges a visit for the next day to nearby Bald Hills, where Prince Nikolai and his family agree to welcome Natasha and Count Ilya. Her mentor advises Natasha to use "wits and . . . warm heart" in coping with the moody old prince and his daughter and "all will be well" (669). Natasha accepts this good advice but does not really think that in her betrothed's home she will face any challenges requiring such resourcefulness. She is in a romantic daze, quite content to let Mme. Dmitrievna offer her help and even take charge of matters not directly affecting her love for Prince Andrei, a love "so apart from all human affairs . . . [and] beyond anyone's understanding" (670).

This transcendent love will be tested the next day. Natasha approaches her visit to Bald Hills with joyous anticipation.

"They can't help liking me" (670) is her confident expectation. It turns out they can. As soon as she lays eyes on Natasha, Princess Marya, usually the soul of kindness, becomes uncharacteristically censorious, thinking her future sister-in-law appears "too fashionably dressed, vain, and frivolously gay" (671). Despite her desire "to so want to love" Natasha, as she confided to Pierre, the princess has been in fact "prejudiced against her" from the start, envious of "her beauty, youth, and happiness" (671) and resentful that Natasha has won her beloved brother's heart. But Natasha is too guileless and too much in love to be sensitive to such dynamics and preconceptions. Prince Nikolai Andreich makes matters worse by entering the drawing room wearing "a white night cap and dressing gown" (672) and protesting repeatedly his ignorance of the Rostovs' visit. Princess Marya's embarrassment cancels out her initial displeasure as she strives to stave off disaster by claiming she is glad her brother has "found happiness" (673) with Natasha, who is too affected by the preceding scenes to respond warmly to the princess's soothing words. Nothing can rescue the occasion, so the visit ends coldly. Natasha blames herself for the fiasco, even though she cannot discover in her words and demeanor any offense to dignity or hospitality.

The following night, Natasha goes to the opera, albeit unwillingly. As if to compensate for the harshness of the day before, she forces herself to take pleasure being in public and in society's eyes. Sensing "how pretty, how very pretty she" (674) is, she enjoys "having hundreds of eyes looking at her bare arms and neck" (675). The sexuality that blossomed during the hunt and in the cottage at Otradnoe is aroused again in a very different context. Also at the performance are three individuals who will, in their own way, appeal to Natasha's subterranean urges and desires with devastating effect. "In the very center of the front row, leaning back against the orchestra rail" and wearing "Persian dress" (676), Dolokhov is preening, basking in the attention he is drawing. Present as well is "a tall, beautiful woman with a tremendous plait of hair and a deep *décolletage* displaying her plump white shoulder and neck" (677). This is

Countess Elena Bezukhova, who takes an immediate interest in Natasha. With her feelings having recently been deeply hurt and her husband-to-be ill and far away, Natasha is now very vulnerable. She is getting drawn into a world where men and women are always performing, as if perpetually on stage, and where polished words and gestures, elaborate dress, and endless display mask falsity, exploitation, greed, and menace. This is not Uncle's cottage in the heartland.

As the opera commences, the antics and labored efforts of the singers on stage strike Natasha as "blatantly false and unnatural" (678), a far cry from the artless simplicity and naturalness of her singing. Nevertheless, the spell of the performers and the equally extreme behavior of audience members like Elena, who is "looking positively undressed" (678) as she feels the eyes of so many on her, Natasha starts to respond to all this sensuous excess, to the point of being in "a state of intoxication" (679). In this condition, she encounters Anatol Kuragin, "so good-looking" (679), who is with Dolokhov, and compliments Natasha. During the intermission, both men stare intently at the Rostovs' box; Natasha is sure they are talking about her and allows herself to enjoy being admired. She turns so they can "see her profile," which she knows is "her best angle" (680). The "intoxication" is taking effect and overcoming normal scruple and restraint. Natasha seems unconcerned about her display of vanity or by the fact that two notoriously lecherous men are showing great interest in a woman betrothed to another. She notes that Anatol, in particular, seems "so captivated by her and it did not occur to her that there could be anything wrong in it" (681). Adding to the emotional swirl is Elena, who invites Natasha to share her box "so that they might become better acquainted" (681).

This invitation leads to complications almost immediately. Anatol Kuragin, Elena's brother, enters the box right after Natasha has seated herself and begins a conversation with her. Though Anatol shows "nothing formidable" in manliness or intellect, and his manner is "artless, good-natured, and jolly" (683), the encounter is anything but casual. Coming to her senses, Natasha realizes that Anatol is "fascinated by her," while at the same time she recognizes that the "barrier of decorum" (683), which has hitherto kept Natasha safely distanced from other men, is breaking down with Anatol sitting so close to her in the small theater box. In these confined quarters, she wonders if she is being "more intimate" (683) with Anatol in a few minutes than she has ever been with any other man, Prince Andrei included. Natasha tries but fails to suppress the attraction she is clearly feeling, and sitting near "the half-naked Elena with her proud, serene smile" (685), who seems in her comfortable self-display to sanction any illicit attraction, Natasha falls "completely under the spell of the world" (684) she now has entered. The simple and natural ways of everyday existence seem flat and dull in comparison to the excitement and hormonal arousal she is experiencing. At home later on and musing on all that has occurred, Natasha cannot help admitting that "the former purity of her love for Prince Andrei" (685) has been stained.

Anatol is in Moscow, as Boris's mother observed sarcastically, because he has been living the life of a spoiled rich boy in St. Petersburg, a life his father can no longer endure or support. He is under orders to "make a good match" (686) in Moscow such as Boris has. Unknown to anyone but "his closest friends" (686), however, is the fact that Anatol is already married. In Poland two years before, a "Polish landowner of small means had forced Anatol to marry his daughter" (686). Since such a marriage could not advance the Kuragin family's interests, Anatol bought his way out of the compact but never bothered to make the separation legal. He is, in consequence, still married.

This means nothing to him. Anatol joins Dolokhov's circle in Moscow, drinking heavily and consorting with "gypsy girls and French actresses" (686). He is cut from the same mold as Steerforth, "incapable of considering what the gratification of his desires entailed for others" and drawn only to "pleasure and women" (687). Even the supreme rake Dolokhov counsels him against any involvement with Natasha, reminding him that he has "already been caught once" (688) and does not need a second scandal.

This advice falls on deaf ears, not only because Anatol is enchanted by Natasha but also because his sister, Countess Elena, is actively engaged in matchmaking. The countess goes out of her way to call on the Rostovs shortly after the opera and invite Natasha and her father to a recital at her home that will be given by a well-known French actress. Natasha is flattered: "She felt happy, as if she were blossoming under the praise of this charming Countess Bezukhova, who formerly had seemed so grand and unapproachable" (690). The countess also informs Natasha that her brother "is madly, quite madly in love" with her and makes light of her engagement, assuring Natasha that her fiancé would approve of her going "into society" rather than "die of boredom in his absence" (690). One final statement highlights how swiftly and fully Natasha has fallen under the amoral wizardry of the countess and her acquaintances: "And once more, under Elena's influence, what had seemed terrible became simple and natural" (690). Against the advice of Marya Dmitrievna, Natasha agrees to accompany her father and Sonya to the countess's home to hear "Mademoiselle Georges" (689) that evening.

At the recital, Natasha is once more lured into the orbit of society, theatricality and falsity, despite her best attempts to stay grounded. By contrast, Count Ilya is made uncomfortable by the company as soon as he arrives, noticing that many of Elena's guests are "men and women notorious for the freedom of their conduct" (691). The guest artist, Mademoiselle Georges, adds to the count's discomfort by performing a soliloquy from *Phedre*, "the subject of which was her [Phedre's] guilty passion for her son" (692). The moral ambiguity of setting and guests is undeniable. Rather than being put on her guard, though, Natasha surrenders to the hypnotic glamor of "that strange and senseless world . . . a world in which it was impossible to know what was good or bad, what was reasonable or senseless" (692). Anatol, who is happy to live in such a world, is brazen. He mouths French compliments, clings to Natasha tightly as they dance, gazes into her eyes, and, when they are alone declares openly, "I am madly in love with you," even though Natasha has just told him, "I am betrothed and love another" (693). The encounter is so intense it upsets her later as she lay in bed, grappling with powerful and conflicting emotions. She ends the day without any firm conclusion or resolve, only trying to rationalize: "What am I to do if I love them both?" (694)

Being so strongly influenced by the Kuragins and accepting so uncritically the worldly vision and values they model, Natasha is hardly able to focus on her relations with the Bolkonskys. Marya Dmitrievna has returned to Bald Hills in an effort to repair the damage done previously. Though Prince Nikolai shouts at her, the redoubtable Marya does manage to procure an apologetic letter from Princess Marya. With her gracious and generous spirit restored, the princess assures Natasha that she loves her "as the one chosen by her brother" and that despite his outbursts and excesses, her father also is "good and magnanimous, and will come to love the woman who makes his son happy" (695). Such a peace offering should allow Natasha to feel some relief and added confidence that her marriage to Prince Andrei will indeed take place as expected. But this will not be the case, because Natasha has received a second letter as well, which commands all of her attention. This is "a passionate love letter composed for Anatol by Dolokhov" (696). In it, Anatol pleads for Natasha's love, which he must have "or die," (696) and pledges ominously that once she says "Yes," he will "spirit her away and carry her to the ends of the earth" (697). He also comments vaguely about the Rostovs never allowing her to marry him "for secret reasons" (697) that he will reveal to her later. The "secret" he alludes to is indeed a deal breaker: Anatol is still legally married.

Such conflicting pressures are too much for Natasha. Instead of taking some time to evaluate her situation and make some carefully reasoned decisions and choices, Natasha yields to impulse. Anatol's ardor has carried her away and pushed the Bolkonskys out of her life. Her new suitor is young, handsome, sexually charged, of good family (or so she thinks), and, most importantly, physically present. Letting passion and impulse rule, Natasha burns her bridges by replying to Princess Marya in unmistakable terms. She announces that she is "availing herself of Prince Andrei's magnanimity in giving her complete freedom when he went abroad" (700) and allowing her to cancel their engagement if she felt she must. Although Prince Andrei is *sans peur et sans reproche*, Natasha has concluded that she cannot "be her brother's wife" (700), and therefore terminates their engagement. While this drama is playing out privately, Sonya discovers Anatol's letter in another part of the residence. She is horrified that Natasha may be succumbing to his blandishments. She notices how her cousin seems to be "in a strange, unnatural state, making irrelevant replies to questions, beginning sentences she did not finish, and laughing at everything" (701). Sonya fears Natasha may actually "run away with him!" (701), an act that will shatter her family and turn Natasha into a pariah. Sonya thereupon resolves to stay awake every night to guard Natasha's room, stop her if she tries to leave, and "not let the family be disgraced" (702).

Sonya's instincts are right. Dolokhov has drawn up a careful plan for Anatol's abduction of Natasha. It involves racing the couple away from Moscow in the middle of the night to a small village, where a "defrocked priest" (702) will be waiting to perform a marriage ceremony. Post horses will be harnessed to a waiting carriage that will then take the newlyweds across the Russian border. Once they are settled outside the country, no one will ever suspect that the marriage of Anatol and Natasha is invalid, so no reference to her husband's other marriage need ever to be made. As Dolokhov explains all the details of this quasi-military operation to Anatol, he takes great pleasure in toying with the man's feelings and playing with his dull-witted companion as if he were a house pet. Dolokhov also relishes the chance to take revenge on the Rostovs and Sonya, in particular, whom he has never forgiven for rejecting his proposal. Pain and shame, he knows, will linger long after the drama of elopement ends.

Dolokhov and Anatol, however, have not taken into account a wild card that will undo their caper right at the start. Marya Dmitrievna, who fears no one and takes charge whenever a crisis threatens, has also read Anatol's letter and seen Sonya "weeping in the corridor" (709). On the very night Dolokhov has designated for his adventure, she has locked Natasha in her room and ordered her footman, an imposing figure, to bring any unwanted visitors to Marya. As Anatol approaches the home's entrance, he is surprised by the footman, who immediately grapples with him. Anatol breaks free, but the plan has to be abandoned, lest the plotters be captured and brought before Marya. In her fury, the *grande dame* turns on Natasha, denouncing the girl she once called her "favorite" for conducting herself "like the lowest hussy" (710) and allowing herself to be duped by "a scoundrel, a good-for-nothing" (711). Natasha cannot bear what has transpired and sobs "with the desperation of those who bewail a misfortune they feel they have brought on themselves" (711). Shame and guilt overwhelm her as she falls into apathy and depression that will persist for weeks, alienate her from the rest of the family, and resist every medical intervention.

This scene is played out near the halfway point of the novel, approximately the same point as Steerforth's abduction of Lil Em'ly in *David Copperfield*. The dynamics are similar. In each novel, a high-spirited and charming young woman engaged to a man of sturdy virtue is swept away by someone from what seems like an alluring alternate universe. Natasha is rescued at the last minute, while Em'ly is forced to spend years in a companionship that keeps deteriorating until she finally abandons her paramour and eventually makes her way back to England. She spends the rest of her days atoning for her catastrophic decision by living selflessly for others. Natasha eventually will recover and pull her life back together, but, like Em'ly, she will never marry the man to whom she was betrothed and will also exhibit extraordinary charity to those displaced by invasion and war. In *War and Peace,* as emphasized so often, the conflict between St. Petersburg and Moscow is a central theme, and it underlies the drama leading to Natasha's near Petersburg elopement.

Anatol's appearance at Marya Dmitrievna's home is the culmination of a series of challenges to Natasha's innocence and natural virtue, all stemming from the foreign-dominated Petersburg influence that clashes with native Russian thinking and traditions throughout the novel. The falsity and immorality portrayed as glamorous on the stage by mostly non-Russian performers, the posturing and preening of audience members concerned only about impressions, the pretentious exhibition given by Mademoiselle Georges, Elena's insinuations and encouragement of licentious behaviors, Anatol's lies, and Dolokhov's cruelty all have played on Natasha's conscience, creating distortions in her thinking and arousing the sexuality that, at her age, is becoming more and more urgent. At her best, Natasha responds to what is healthy, natural, and exhilarating in Russian tradition, as she demonstrated during the hunt and at Uncle's cottage. She is a pure vessel deserving to be loved and treasured by one like herself. But Anatol, Dolokhov, Elena, and the like are not the society she needs; they have been corrupted by cosmopolitan influences that have had a devastating effect on their personalities, habits, and values. They are more Parisian than Russian, more like the drawing room *habitués* whose superficial wit and charm so annoyed Rousseau, and worlds away from the down-to-earth men and women of the heartland, like the Rostovs, the Bolkonskys, and Marya Dmitrievna, who are without pretense. These will prevail ultimately, not only in their individual life experiences, but also in the epic trial that will soon unfold and see the entire nation threatened not by a few cosmopolites but by armed, aggressive invaders bent not on influence but on conquest.

At Marya Dmitrievna's urgent request, Pierre Bezukhov appears at her home immediately after the fracas. He is appalled by the tale of woe he hears and astonished that the "deeply loved and hitherto winsome Natasha Rostova, should give up Bolkonsky for that fool Anatol" (714). Natasha remains coldly aloof, not out of pride or resentment but because she has been numbed by "despair, shame, and humiliation, and that it was not her fault that her face happened to express calm dignity and severity" (714). Pierre then adds to the weight of her sorrow by informing Natasha of Anatol's prior marriage. He leaves her "unable to speak" and wishing only to be "alone" (716).

Pierre soon learns that some of Moscow's upper-class gossips are already talking about "Kuragin's abduction of the little Rostova" (717), and this infuriates him. After searching for Anatol throughout the city to no avail, he confronts him directly in, of all places, his own home, whence Anatol has gone in search of aid and succor from Elena. The two men have a tense encounter, nearly ending in a challenge. Pierre reads the riot act to Anatol, who puts on the air of one so sensitive to harshness of tone he cannot bear Pierre's denunciations. Pierre cares little for Anatol's posturing, berating him over and over and concluding quite correctly that his brother-in-law is "ruining a whole life for the sake of amusing" (719) himself. If amusement is all he desires, says Pierre with brutal frankness, he should go to women like Elena—that is, to courtesans. As Anatol rises to leave, Pierre notices his smile, the same "base, craven" smile he knows "so well in his wife" (719) and which he finds repulsive. Pierre finally dismisses the whole Kuragin clan as a "vile, heartless breed" (719), incapable of anything good or generous. Anatol leaves for Petersburg the next day, unwilling to risk any further trouble.

In the midst of all this anger and sorrow, Prince Andrei arrives at Bald Hills. He is informed about most of what has occurred and reads Natasha's letter. He reacts without visible emotion, although, as Princess Marya notes, her brother's "pride will not let him express his feelings" (720). He confers with his father and a visiting magnate about politics instead. The news that Minister Speransky has been exiled for some trumped-up offense is the main topic of conversation. Prince Andrei sums up his reaction in words that reflect his nobility of character: "Personally, I do not like and have never liked Speransky, but I do like justice" (721). This is not exactly true, since the prince, at least initially, was impressed by the logical and rational approach Speransky took toward all contested issues and by his courageous advocacy of reform in the face of the political elite's opposition. Only when he is joined by Pierre and the two move away from the others can the talk return to Natasha and Anatol. Prince Andrei's nobility of character is not displayed when this new subject is discussed. He seems to Pierre as dyspeptic as Prince Nikolai, reacting to news of Natasha's illness "with a disagreeably cold, malicious smile that reminded one of his father," and laughing "unpleasantly" (722) when told of Anatol's marriage. The same coldness marks Prince Andrei's last word on the matter. He compels Pierre, on pain of losing the prince's friendship, to promise "never" to allude to "this whole affair" (723) in Prince Andrei's presence ever again. Both Prince Nikolai and Princess Marya appear relieved that the engagement is irretrievably broken and that the marriage which has caused so much anxiety in both families will not take place.

Pierre sees Natasha once more. This time no reproaches toward or expressions of disappointment in the victim are voiced; Pierre extends almost paternal "pity, tenderness, and love" (725) to his thoroughly abased friend, who actually swallowed a non-fatal dose of arsenic when hearing of Anatol's marriage. Natasha's conscience torments her as she reflects on the "wrong" (724) done to Prince Andrei and the humiliation her conduct has brought to family and friends. Pierre is moved by this sincere contrition, and his affection for Natasha, always latent, is aroused. His is not an erotic attraction but a need to comfort and restore a deeply wounded girl, on the verge of entering adulthood but not yet able to cope with powerful emotional upheaval by herself. From this moment until Natasha recovers fully, Pierre will take on the role of guide and exemplar, showing unfailing kindness and concern as he gently walks this precious lady back to normal physical and psychological health. This mission is exhilarating, allowing Pierre to make real the high ideals of personal conduct he has always striven to achieve, as well as to accept the native Russian obligation of gentlemen like himself to assist those who have fallen, no matter how onerous the task may turn out to be.

Returning to his home (rather than the club) at the end of this memorable day, he feels that his soul has been "raised" to exalted "heights" (726), and a new sense of purpose has been entrusted to him. From his carriage, Pierre looks to the heavens and sees the "huge, brilliant comet of the year 1812" (726) lighting up the night sky. To him, this phenomenon portends "a new life" (726), one characterized by devotion to, service for, and gentle love toward a radiant spirit who must one day be his life partner.

BOOK III

PART ONE

The comet Pierre sees and considers a sign of hope for himself and Natasha is interpreted differently by most of his countrymen. To them, this "comet of the year 1812" is a divinely inspired warning that "all kinds of horrors and the end of the world" (726) will arrive in the year ahead. The two projections are not mutually opposed. As events transpire, "all kinds of horrors" will in fact be visited upon the Russian people as Napoleon Bonaparte leads a gigantic military force toward Moscow, bringing death and destruction of every sort, including his own army's annihilation, in its wake. But out of all this suffering, the "new life" Pierre envisions will also emerge, as he overcomes captivity, humiliation, isolation, and the threat of summary execution, while Natasha redeems herself by caring for and transporting the wounded, including Prince Andrei, to safety, leaving behind her home and possessions without regret. Eventually, these two star-crossed lovers will begin a long and happy life together as husband, wife, father, and mother, a life purified by and strengthened through adversity. For the Russian people as a whole, the same fiery trial will lead to innumerable "resurrections" of a similar sort. Like Pierre and Natasha, the nation will survive and, like Abraham Lincoln's federal union, will "bind up its wounds" and thrive once again.

Book III begins with a reflection on the causes of the conflagration about to begin. The conventional explanations laid out in textbooks and highlighting such factors as "the wrongs inflicted on the Duke of Oldenburg, the nonobservance of the Continental system, the ambition of Napoleon, the firmness of Aleksandr, the mistakes of the diplomats, and so on" (729) are hardly adequate to explain why in 1812 "millions of Christian men killed and tortured one another" (730) mercilessly. Nor can the war be the result of the discrete decisions of leaders, such as Napoleon and Aleksandr, because, however eminent their status, these men lack the power to impel millions of diverse individuals to act together to pursue vague objectives through means that in civic life are deemed criminal and in spiritual life earn damnation. For so many to be so affected by the "will" of so few, "the concurrence of innumerable circumstances was required, without any one of which the event could not have taken place" (731). For millions to act in some sort of concert, a higher power has to be invoked, whether it be called God, destiny, or history. This higher power "uses every moment of the life of kings for its own ends" (732). Although most men and women think they act freely in their decision-making, they deceive themselves. Once an action is decided upon and performed, it "becomes irrevocable and belongs to history, in which it has not a free but a predetermined significance" (731–32). When it comes to history and its guiding force, everyone from peasant to king "serves as an instrument for the accomplishment of the historical, social ends of mankind" (732). The war between Russia and France (more accurately Western Europe, since troops of numerous Western nations take part) is therefore a cataclysmic event that occurs because it has to. This fundamental truth makes the actions and dictates of "so-called great men" (733) anything but free:

> *Every act of theirs that seems to them an act of their own free will is, in the historical sense, not free at all, but is connected with the whole course of history and determined from eternity.* (773)

This conviction that man is not a free agent but only an instrument of a mysterious higher power, whatever it may be called, is profoundly Russian. In contrast to their counterparts in the West, Russian writers and thinkers always stress man's dependence, his weakness, his limitations, and his need for guidance from above. In the history of Europe, successive developments since the Renaissance have made man an independent actor, a being who freely makes decisions affecting his/her future, a creative spirit who makes a life determined by himself or herself. For Russians raised in the Orthodox tradition and with memories of Mongol and Tartar domination, such thinking is presumptuous, prideful, and dangerous. It makes men and women of the West too sure, too impetuous, too eager to challenge obstacles and overstep bounds. For Russians, the ideal is acceptance of one's condition and situation, resignation to what cannot be helped or changed. No matter how oppressive or difficult, one's life experience is God-given; it must be endured bravely, even joyfully, rather than in opposition or lamentation. Princess Marya exemplifies this spirit, with her quiet resolve to accept her father's denunciations and insults with Christian resignation and no recrimination. Pierre, too, after dabbling with revolutionary ideas, Freemasonry's tenets, and the reform of his estates and the uplifting of his peasants, all of these inspired by European example, will realize that he must embrace his Russian identity and become one with his countrymen in their great struggle against Napoleon's invaders. He is liberated by this self-understanding, even to the point of facing with dignity and courage the possibility of being hauled before a French firing squad to be executed.

The very opposite spirit is evident in Napoleon Bonaparte. The man who crowned himself emperor is not one to dwell on his dependence or weakness. On the contrary, as he prepares with his mighty force to cross the Niemen River and enter Russian territory, he is perfectly confident that even though his advance is "contrary alike to strategic and diplomatic considerations" (734), it will succeed. He shows no fear, anxiety, or self-doubt. Instead, he is caught up and seduced by the adulation his presence inspires, not just among the French contingent but among the allies as well. None are more fervent than the Poles, whose passionate desire to free their proud country from Russian control, makes them perform acts of reckless daring to impress the man they see as their nation's savior. As the army waits to cross the Niemen, for instance, Polish uhlans are told to look for a ford to make this passage easier. Their colonel offers, instead, to swim across the river with his men, a gesture that does not make any practical sense but highlights the extremes fervent men in arms will go to prove their mettle. The result is tragic, as forty men drown in this doomed effort. Rather than being court-martialed, however, the colonel is later rewarded when Napoleon enrolls him in the Legion of Honor.

This urge to overcome limitations and exceed normal bounds, culminating in the "glory" of victorious battle against a powerful foe, infects Napoleon as fatally as it does the Poles. Throughout the campaign, he relies too much on his own judgment, resisting advice and assuming conflict "on the steppes of Asia" (734) will be the same as war in the middle of Europe. He thus expects to fight and win a decisive battle early, perhaps near the frontiers, compel the tsar to ask for terms, and then move on in triumph to capture Moscow. All the rules governing the conduct of war in Europe will prevail in Russia as well, with a conquered people submitting to military rule, trading with and victualing the occupiers, carving up their empire as the victors dictate, and in effect allowing themselves and their nation to become a part of the French imperium.

None of these rational and orderly processes will be followed in the coming campaign. There will be no decisive battle until Borodino, on the outskirts of the capital. The battle will not end in capitulation, however, because the Russians do not admit defeat. Their army will conduct a strategic retreat and let the enemy enter Moscow. No delegation of leading officials will greet the conquerors or offer them keys or regalia in tribute. Napoleon and his troops will enter a deserted city, which will cause a breakdown of military discipline as soldiers turn into pirates and thieves in their lust for booty. Soon, fires will break out in widely separated neighborhoods, some of them spontaneous but many deliberately set. No ordinary Russians in or outside the city will accept Napoleon's offers to purchase food or other items at fair prices. In desperation, Napoleon has to send a delegation to the Russian commander's headquarters, in essence to beg his foes to lay down their arms and agree to peace terms. This initiative goes nowhere, since Tsar Aleksandr has rejected any negotiations so long as the enemy occupies Russian territory. As the cold weather begins to set in, Napoleon has no choice but to order a retreat back across the large area he and his troops have already crossed in conditions that will worsen steadily and take a terrible toll on men and animals. General Kutusov will not exploit his enemy's vulnerability with any further attacks. Mother Nature and Cossack marauders will assure the enemy's destruction at no further cost in men or materiel. Napoleon's "genius" will prove helpless to avert this totally unforeseen but inevitable endgame.

None of what will transpire over several months, of course, can be known, or even imagined, at the outset of the campaign, but early on, hints of what may occur are apparent. Tsar Aleksandr I reacts to the news of Napoleon's invasion on June 13, 1812, "in the agitated tone of one who has been personally affronted " (739). He receives word of the enemy's crossing of the Niemen River and their advance into Russian territory while attending a ball given by his aides in Vilna, part of Russian Poland. The tsar has been vacillating at this outpost for some time, showing no interest in military preparations, refusing to appoint a commander in chief for his three armies, and apparently trusting in God alone to arrange matters between the two empires satisfactorily. Aleksandr does, however, make a statement in response to Napoleon's "aggression" (740) that will have a lasting impact on how the invaders will fare. He declares in "an order to the troops" that he can "never make peace so long as a single armed Frenchman remained on Russian soil" (739). In other words, unless Napoleon, the tsar's "*frére*," immediately turns his force around and moves back across the Niemen, he will face the prospect of a punishing, exhausting, and costly war of attrition in Russia that will go on no matter how many battles Napoleon's army wins, how many cities are destroyed, how many peasants starve, or how many blandishments the invaders offer. Of Napoleon's former opponents, only the Spanish have taken a stance like the tsar's and as the 1812 campaign commences, guerrilla units in their nation have been tying down and actively combating through ambush and surprise thousands of French troops for many months.

Tsar Aleksandr attempts to reason with Napoleon before events spin out of control. He sends a trusted associate, Balashev, to deliver a letter to the French emperor personally, and to repeat in his presence the tsar's directive not even to begin discussing terms "so long as a single armed foe" (740) is in Russia. Balashev is met first by the dashing cavalry commander, Murat, on whom Napoleon has bestowed the title "King of Naples" (742) for no apparent reason. Murat plays his role superbly, assuming a royal air, with "his scarlet embroidered cloak, his plumes, and glittering jewels" (744). He extends elaborate courtesies to the Russian envoy and assures him of his eagerness to see the two emperors "settle the matter between them" (743) expeditiously. Murat, however, cannot help referring to the tsar as an "aggressor" (743) for having had the temerity to ask in public that Napoleon "withdraw his troops from Prussia . . . thereby offering an affront to the dignity of France" (743). If it is thought something of this nature hardly constitutes sufficient grounds for a massive invasion, French history says otherwise. As alluded to earlier, in the seventeenth century, King Louis XIV invaded the Netherlands after being similarly affronted. This initiative ended in failure and a humiliating retreat, a cautionary tale for the present company.

Murat sends Balashev to Marshall Davout, Napoleon's rough adjutant. Davout is anything but courteous, as he demands peremptorily to see Balashev's credentials and his dispatch. When Balashev responds that he has been ordered by Aleksandr to deliver the dispatch only to Napoleon himself, Davout is dismissive: "Your Emperor's orders are obeyed in your army," … "but here you must do as you're told" (745). Balashev then has to wait four days before Napoleon condescends to receive him. The French now are in Vilna, and Napoleon makes it a point to meet Balashev "in the very house from which Aleksandr had dispatched him on his mission" (746).

The conversation begins amicably, with the emperor insisting, "I do not and did not desire war," . . . "but it has been forced upon me" (747). This is actually correct, but in a sense Napoleon does not realize. Tolstoy has explained earlier that human will or judgment is not a determinant in how events play out. Napoleon has been "forced" to attack Russia not because Tsar Aleksandr said or did something aggressive or provocative, but because the imperatives of history have decreed such. Balashev is no philosopher, so he tries to make just the points the tsar instructed him to stress in reply to Napoleon. The envoy, though, is made uncomfortable by the emperor's steady gaze and cannot concentrate on what he is saying. As he tries to communicate Aleksandr's momentous declaration, he alters his emperor's words at the end to "on condition that the French army retires beyond the Niemen" (748). The tsar's original statement is so ominous because it threatens war without end while the French are in Russia; Balashev's change includes the possibility of a negotiated settlement while the French are still present, provided they agree to leave Russia by a certain date. At this point, however, verbal subtleties are immaterial. To the emperor of the French, the tsar's message is highly insulting: "Such demands to retreat beyond the Oder and the Vistula may be made to a Prince of Baden, but not to me!" (749). Once again, *amour propre* dictates policy.

The rest of the interview yields no breakthroughs. Napoleon cannot stop talking, trying hard to prove how foolish and mistaken his "*frére*" the tsar has been and how "splendid a reign" he "*might have had*" (752) had Alexander worked in tandem with Napoleon. The French emperor is clearly carried away by his power and position, sounding more autocratic than the autocrat opposing him and sure he holds all the winning cards in the great match portending. He rattles off the names of Aleksandr's principal commanders, most of them non-Russian, and finds fault with each; he then notes that his allies, particularly the Poles, who "fight like lions" (752), are far more valiant than Russia's, ignoring the fact that Aleksandr also has Polish contingents. Napoleon's praise of the Poles also sounds odd after the episode at the Niemen, when forty of those "lions" lost their lives in a suicidal attempt to swim to the other side. Real lions are far more circumspect. Balashev listens to Napoleon's monologue politely, realizing that the emperor is "in that state of irritation when a man has to talk and talk, simply to prove to himself that he is in the right" (751). The envoy comports himself with dignity and sensitivity, almost like the kind relative of a man speaking incessantly in a drunken rage over real and imagined grievances. The encounter ends, finally, with no meeting of the minds.

Balashev, however, enjoys one last opportunity to engage in dialogue with the emperor of France. Wholly unexpectedly, he is invited to dinner that evening with Napoleon and a few courtiers, a rare honor indeed. On this occasion, the emperor is affable and friendly at first, still basking in the glow of the reception he had received riding through Vilna earlier, where he was "rapturously greeted and followed by crowds of people" (753). The atmosphere changes quickly, however, as Napoleon returns to the themes of the previous conversation, and "convinced that it was impossible for him to make a mistake" (753), resumes in a badgering tone a listing of the tsar's errors that compelled the current intervention. But in the midst of Napoleon's verbal assault, Balashev finally finds his voice and repels brilliantly Napoleon's barbed comments on Russian culture and history at least twice. The first is his rejoinder to Napoleon's dismissive remark about how Moscow's "large number of monasteries and churches is always a sign of the backwardness of a people" (754). In Europe, says the emperor, nothing like such a superabundance of churches and monastic houses can be found. The philosophers of the Enlightenment and the revolutionaries of 1789 are channeled in words like these. Balashev begs to differ, noting correctly that Spain boasts "a great many churches and monasteries" (754). For the French in 1812, Spain is anything but backward; it is, instead, a source of endless trouble, as a combined force of British regulars and Spanish guerrillas for several years has been inflicting numerous defeats on the armies of the client king installed by Napoleon, his brother Joseph. The reference is also eerily prophetic because Napoleon's retreat from Moscow five months later will be afflicted in much the same way by marauding Cossacks, who will employ similar tactics. Neither Napoleon nor his guests react to this retort, but when, upon his return, Balashev repeats his words in the tsar's court, they are "highly appreciated" (754).

The second riposte is even more telling. The conversation turns to the towns through which the direct road to Moscow passes. Balashev observes that like Rome, "all roads lead to Moscow, and "among them the road through *Poltava*, which Charles XII chose" (754). At Poltava, Sweden's King Charles XII, hitherto considered invincible, suffered a crippling defeat in 1709 at the hands of Peter the Great, bringing his invasion of Russia to an abrupt end. The parallel will turn out to be exact, since another commander hitherto considered invincible will end a similar invasion after winning a pyrrhic victory that will lead to nothing except humiliating retreat. The meeting concludes with Napoleon, oblivious to the impending trials, bidding Balashev farewell. He tweaks the envoy's ear as he rises to depart, a gesture regarded by the French guests as a mark of favor but in this context more like a headmaster's reproof. Napoleon then hands Balashev his formal reply to Tsar Aleksandr's letter, the first of a series that will go unanswered.

This dialogue is illustrative. Balashev says little but demonstrates great insight when he does speak, just like his countrymen, who will fail to block Napoleon's march toward Moscow until they give battle at Borodino. There the hitherto mute Russian Orthodox Army speaks volumes as it stubbornly resists the powerful French advances all along the line of battle. By day's end, the invader holds the field while his adversary retreats in good order, but the French and their allies have been severely hurt. As he speaks with Balashev, however, Napoleon shows no anxiety about what is to come. He is voluble, confident, arrogant, and obsessively critical of the tsar. He is too sure, convinced that the Russian conflict will conclude like all his other campaigns, with a decisive victory that will lead to capitulation and his dictating terms. In this regard, he resembles

Agamemnon and Oedipus, who make decisions that accelerate the tragic downfall that destiny has decreed for each.

Decades after 1812, Leo Tolstoy insisted on this truth repeatedly, highlighting the necessity of Napoleon's doom and his inability to do anything other than what would eventually lead to his and his army's failure. The fear that Napoleon was moving with headstrong unconcern into a war that he could not avoid because of his *hubris* but could not successfully manage and end was shared not only by Tolstoy but by at least one of Napoleon's closest advisers. His former Ambassador to Russia, Armand de Caulaincourt, served Napoleon as Master of the Horse during the run-up to the invasion, the campaign that culminated in Borodino and the capture of Moscow, the failure to negotiate terms, the retreat and its horrors, and the flight back to Paris. Caulaincourt kept a journal of his observations over the months these events transpired, being careful to report accurately conversations he had with the emperor, advice he offered based on his experience in Russia and how it was received, decisions made and their consequences, and reflections on what was occurring and why. His notes were finally collected and published in 1935. Given the title *With Napoleon in Russia*, they constitute a striking confirmation of Tolstoy's central thesis: Napoleon was captive to "the irresistible course of fatality that was drawing him forward" (New York: William Morrow and Company, Inc., 1935, p. 34) and could no more resist the immolation awaiting him than he could cease to breathe. His pride and his conviction that his army could not be defeated led Napoleon to throw the dice in a vast and inhospitable territory defended by men and women prepared to sacrifice all to save their nation.

Tsar Aleksandr personifies his people's resolve. Renowned for his gentleness and kindness, he turns out to be immoveable in his resistance to the greatest military leader and the greatest military organization of his time. He and his people prevail not through strategy, shrewd diplomacy, or exceptional skill, but by perseverance, endurance, faith, and the certain knowledge that Mother Russia, the largest land mass on earth, would absorb and then exhaust and devour the impudent foreigners daring to violate her beloved space and assail her sons and daughters.

Away from the military encampments, life goes on as usual in the balmy summer of 1812. Prince Andrei searches for Anatol Kuragin, but that cowardly opportunist has used his family's connections to gain a quick transfer to Moldavia, as far away as possible from Moscow. The prince has also received a new military appointment; he will become a "duty general" (757) on the staff of Kutusov, who commanded the Russian army at Austerlitz, the scene of Prince Andrei's mystic communion with the heavens. Since Kutusov is presently commanding the Russian troops in Turkey, Anatol is actually not too far away. The prince seethes over what this amoral fop has dared to do and thinks only of revenge. He knows if he meets Kuragin, he will "be as unable to resist challenging him as a starving man to resist pouncing on food" (757). Nothing of the sort will occur, however, because as soon as news of Napoleon's invasion reaches Kutusov, he promptly releases Prince Andrei, whose exceptional performance of all assigned duties makes him too conscientious for the general who so values flexibility and freedom to maneuver. Kutusov sends him on "a mission to Barclay de Tolly" (758), who leads the western army, with whom the prince will remain through the rest of the campaign.

On the way to his new posting, Prince Andrei stops at Bald Hills. There he finds everything as it always has been. His father continues to torment his daughter; the princess refuses to assign any responsibility to Prince Nikolai, reminding her brother "that misfortunes come from God and . . . men are never to blame" (761); and Mademoiselle Bourienne is the "same self-satisfied, coquettish young woman, enjoying every moment of her life and full of bright hopes for the future" (758). Only Nikolushka has changed, now a young boy showing personality and spirit in "this enchanted, sleeping castle" (758). Barely after his arrival, Prince Andrei manages to offend his father by commenting critically on his obvious fondness for Mademoiselle Bourienne and his inveterate hostility to his daughter. The old man takes all this as evidence brother and sister have joined forces against him. In his fury, he lashes out at Andrei: "Out—get out! Never let me set eyes on you again!" (760). The prince refrains from responding in kind; in comparison to what he has recently had to endure, this is a trifle. His emotional wounds have led him to wall himself off from strong feeling. Like Natasha, he moves about the estate as if numb, with not even his son, "the sturdy little boy, curly-headed like his mother" (760), stimulating any strong reaction. At one point, Prince Andrei sits Nikolushka on his knee and tells him "the story of Bluebeard" (760), but this has no follow-up. As he takes leave of everyone, he goes through the motions of farewell and no more. Domestic affairs, emotional hurts, the need for revenge, all these are decidedly secondary now that Prince Andrei is on his way to the war front.

What Prince Andrei experiences at the western army's command center is anything but reassuring. He finds that this vital force is not a single body under one head. It is rather a diverse grouping divided among three separate armies, each led by its own commander, whose authority does not extend beyond his one command. Tsar Aleksandr is with the combined armies, but he does not wield supreme power since he is not a military professional. His presence and his wishes, of course, must be respected, so in a limited way, the tsar is "in control of the armies" (763). This control, however, is mediated by the men who constitute, whether formally or informally, his personal staff, a varied contingent made up of military officials, civic leaders, courtiers, family members, and foreign dignitaries. Most of these, as well as aides and strategists attached to each of the armies, hold strong opinions about how the enemy must be handled, and they clash repeatedly as rival schemes are advanced and debated.

Ever since the miscalculations of the Austro-Russian command at Austerlitz resulted in overall military defeat and Prince Andrei's own battle wounds, the prince has placed little confidence in strategic plans. He now believes like Kutusov "that everything depends on the way unexpected movements of the enemy, which cannot possibly be foreseen, are met and by whom the whole operation is directed" (763). What he sees at headquarters is so disturbing because plans are again being crafted continually and are being propounded with dogmatic certitude, while no theater commander who can reconcile and meld the contrasting approaches is visible in the tsar's suite. Prince Andrei counts nine distinct factions or parties advocating competing strategies. Some argue that a Fabian conception is best, with the Russian forces withdrawing "into the depths of the country" (764) to make the enemy steadily lengthen his lines of communication, wearing out men and animals all the while. Others, mostly native Russian officers, argue for the opposite option: only a determined resistance from the very start can "beat the enemy, keep him out of Russia, and not let the army lose heart" (765). Another faction advocates a negotiated settlement "as soon as possible" (765).

Adherents of particular generals insist that nothing can succeed if their favorite is not made supreme commander. In the tsar's entourage, the same assertion is made, with the tsar himself the preferred candidate, the only personage with the prestige and charisma to "lead his troops, who, by this alone, would be roused to the highest pitch of enthusiasm" (766). Another group disagrees, arguing that the tsar needs to separate himself from operations because his presence in whatever capacity brings "that indefinite, fortuitous, fluctuating instability of relations which may be expedient at Court, but which is pernicious to an army" (767-68). A very large body, the largest one, in fact, "numbering ninety-nine to every one of the others" (766), offers no strategic vision nor supports any specific commander; this majority is focused on only "one supremely important thing: the greatest possible profit and pleasure for themselves" (766). These are those who are "angling for rubles, decorations, and promotions" and, like time-servers and lackeys everywhere, will support any proposal earning "imperial favor," thereby enlisting "the whole drone population of the army" (767), at least until the tsar changes his mind.

With so many holding such a variety of opinions, politicking, infighting, backstabbing, and sabotage are inevitable, particularly when the key decision-maker is so aloof. Prince Andrei observes the play of all these forces shortly after his arrival at Vilna. The tsar invites the prince to his quarters so he can be briefed on the recently concluded war with Turkey. Before the interview can take place, a council of the tsar's advisors convenes. This is not "a council of war but a council as it were to elucidate certain questions for the Tsar personally" (769), a mechanism, in other words, that can advance certain views and/ or reject others. Prince Andrei is allowed to stay as the proceedings begin. The key participant is the German military theoretician, Pfuhl, who has designed a "fortified camp" (768) at Drissa to block the enemy's progress; it is "regarded as a *chef d'aeuvre* of tactical science" (769), but many in attendance who have toured the camp are skeptical. One Colonel Michaud, who has accompanied the tsar on his latest visit to the camp, describes it as an "absurdity and the ruin of the Russian army" (769). This sets the stage for confrontation. Pfuhl is altogether convinced that his design is perfect and resists every objection. He shows the same characteristics Prince Andrei saw in the Austro-German commanders prior to Austerlitz. Pfuhl is "one of those inordinately, unshakably self-assured men—self-assured to the point of martyrdom, as only a German can be, because only a German bases his self-assurance on an abstract idea: science, that is, the supposed knowledge of absolute truth" (770). This basis gives the planner overweening confidence, making Pfuhl "more inflexible and repellent . . . because he imagines that he knows the truth, science, which is his own invention but which for him is absolute truth" (770–71).

These words were written before the unification of Germany in 1870 and before the great conflicts of World Wars I and II, but they characterize Austro-German military thinking in these later years exactly. The confidence Pfuhl exhibits is the same as that of the Austrian High Command in 1914, who persuaded a doting Emperor Franz Josef to agree to war with Serbia, a nation whose military capabilities they scorned and whose defeat they expected quickly. The same confidence compelled the kaiser of Germany to give Austria the famous "blank check" guarantee of support, regardless of what the polyglot Hapsburg Empire might do. Confidence in the superiority of German arms and German military planning made Kaiser Wilhelm's Imperial General Staff believe that their master plan for defeating France and Great Britain in the west could guide the complex movement of men, animals, and equipment day by day, no matter the circumstances on the ground at any given time. The science of war dictated that this Schlieffen plan, if followed precisely, could not fail to bring about the victory its timetable guaranteed. Adolf Hitler, too, dismissed all anxieties about invading the Soviet Union in 1941, exactly as Napoleon did in 1812. His three-pronged assault was designed to bring about the capture of the key cities of Leningrad (formerly St. Petersburg) in the north and Moscow in the center of Russia, as well as secure for the German war machine a steady supply of oil from the Caucasus region in the south. All of these confident plans and assumptions proved wrong. While the Austro-German forces in both world wars enjoyed many tactical successes, strategic objectives were never achieved, and final victory never attained. Faith in the power of science proved fatal, as the realities of space, topography, weather, and human fallibility overrode the formulae of the theoreticians.

Prince Andrei is well aware of how the unknown and the unanticipated can render useless the most conscientious planning. As a Russian, "he does not believe in the possibility of knowing anything fully" (770), since such pretensions make ordinary mortals think they can be like gods, the most dangerous of sins. He also has had the bitter experience of Austerlitz, which has convinced him "that there was not and could not be a science of war, and consequently no such thing as military genius" (775). What happens in battle is the result not of well-laid plans that treat human beings as passengers on a plane, all seated alike in their proper places and obeying their pilot's instructions; in war every soldier's behavior is unpredictable, every unit leader is subject to the doubt and confusion of the "fog of war," and every deviation from the planners' script is a pretext for further alterations, all of which make the original scheme obsolete.

As the members of the council continue to debate, Pfuhl becomes even more rigid, insisting that not adhering faithfully to every intricacy of his defensive plan and construct will lead to disaster. Though he stands his ground under the barrage of criticisms and questions, Pfuhl realizes, as do the others, that his "downfall" (774) is taking shape and his grand concept will never be approved or revived. Prince Andrei feels a degree of respect for the man, now that his critics are leaving him "visibly in despair" (774). He knows these men are not attacking Pfuhl because they fear his proposals will hurt the defense of Russia, but mainly because they are clearly self-interested and eager to push aside a rival for influence. For Prince Andrei, councils like these are largely academic and, as such, have almost no real impact on a battle's outcome. He consoles himself with this simple truth: The success of a military action "depends . . . on the man in the ranks who shouts 'we are lost!' or 'Hurrah!' And only in the ranks can one serve with the assurance of being useful" (776).

The next day, Prince Andrei asks Tsar Aleksandr "for permission to serve with the army" (776), leaving councils, planning, and administration behind, at least for a time. In so doing, the prince joins his comrade-in-arms, Count Nikolai Rostov, who is at the front. Nikolai is a patriot, so when his parents ask that he "retire from the army and return home" (776) immediately to assist Natasha in her recovery, he demurs. Nikolai cannot let his comrades down, since they are all members of the larger family known as the regiment. He also cannot "put personal happiness before love and duty to the fatherland" (777) in a time of national crisis. On a less high-minded note, like his comrades, Nikolai is "infected with the exhilaration and excitement that always attend the commencement of a war" (777). He is eager to engage the enemy and overpower him.

He does not have long to wait. After a few pleasant days during the Russian retreat from Vilna, Nikolai's cavalry regiment is ordered forward early one morning. Riding "four abreast" (784), they hear "the sound of guns ahead" (785). As they form for attack, the hussars listen to the distinctive "whistling and whining" of bullets "flying from the front" (786). For Nikolai, the firing is not frightening but "pleasurable and exhilarating" (786). He suggests to a captain that the regiment charge the enemy, as if the opposing force were like hunters' prey. Before the officer can give a command, "without reflecting or considering, as he did when hunting" (787), Nikolai gallops ahead, with the rest of the squadron falling in behind. Instinct and adrenalin rule. While the French dragoons are beating a hasty retreat, Nikolai makes one horseman his personal target. As he overtakes this rider, Nikolai's horse collides with the enemy's; in the ensuing confusion, Nikolai strikes the Frenchman with his saber, wounding him slightly. His victim falls to the ground "from the shock to his horse and from fright" (787). But the sight of his "prey" in distress causes "all Rostov's fervor" (787) to fade. The basic humanity that is essential to the Rostov character overtakes all martial ardor as Nikolai sees the "pale, mud-spattered face" (787) of his foe, whose looks are "not at all hostile or suited to the battlefield" (788). The man quickly surrenders before Nikolai can do him any more harm.

For his "gallant action" (788), Nikolai Rostov is recommended for the St. George Cross, a singular honor, and will earn a subsequent promotion. His feelings about what he has done, however, are still so mixed, Nikolai can take neither pride nor satisfaction in these awards. The warrior and patriot cannot get over a "vague, disagreeable feeling of moral queasiness" (788). He has nearly killed a fellow human being, a man with "the most simple, familiar kind of face" (788), hardly the mien of someone bent on conquest. Though an officer, the French cavalryman is actually "boyish . . . with light blue eyes and a dimple in the chin" (787-88). The words of World War I poet Wilfred Owen are appropriate: "For his teeth seem for laughing round an apple." (*"Arms and the Boy,"* III, 1.) Nikolai is horrified that he has come close to killing someone who is like him in every way, except his uniform. He joins Prince Andrei in undergoing a life-changing experience on the field of battle, an experience that will affect Nikolai not only for the rest of the war but also for the rest of his days.

Nikolai's sister undergoes nothing quite as dramatic, but she too will begin to make her way back to normal living thanks to the efforts of friends and family members who patiently guide her recovery. At first, Natasha's doctors take charge. They treat her with a variety of standard medications and therapies, most of which have no effect. The doctors are like the military "scientists" who plan campaigns with such minute care, all the while neglecting the obvious fact that every combatant is an individual who will act in battle not as programmed but as conditions, pressures, and the fog of war dictate. The same is true of Natasha; her illness is a phenomenon peculiar to her, "a new complex malady unknown to medicine—not a disease of the lungs, liver, skin, heart, nerves, and so on, as described in medical books, but a disease consisting of one of the innumerable combinations of the disorders of these organs" (790), with moral and psychological dimensions added in. Natasha has no choice except to go along with all the doctors advise, but she does not take long to realize that "no medicine could do her any good and that it was all nonsense" (791).

She begins recovering only as her "grief" starts to fade, "submerged under the impressions of daily life" (792), and by Pierre's ministrations. Because he is still married, Natasha has no inkling that "their relations could lead to love on her part," though Pierre once admitted to her "that if he were free, he would have been on his knees asking for her hand and her love" (793). Natasha acknowledges Pierre's care and concern and knows no one can be "more tender, more discreet, and at the same time serious than" (793) he; she stops short, however, of expressing any stronger affection. At the same time, in an intervention of a different character, a neighbor persuades Natasha to "fast and prepare to take Holy Communion" (793). Natasha readily accepts the duties this preparation entails, "going to church every day for a whole week and not once missing Vespers, Matins, and Mass" (794). By the time she receives the sacrament, she feels spiritually renewed and overjoyed. Natasha has given herself so fully to the prayer life of the church during her preparations, she is able afterwards, for the first time since the onset of her illness, to believe in "the possibility of redemption from sin, of a new, pure life, and of happiness" (794). When her doctor visits after her reception of communion on "that blessed Sunday" (795), he notices the change in his patient immediately. In his ignorance of all that has occurred, the doctor proclaims with immense self-satisfaction and dramatic irony: "This last medicine has done wonders for her. She's picked up enormously" (795).

The new medicine continues to work its wonders. Natasha joins her family and "the Moscow notables" (796) the following Sunday for Divine Liturgy at a fashionable chapel. Here she is distressed to hear others speaking about her and mentioning only "what had happened to her" (796). Natasha's conviction that her formerly "wicked" (796) ways have been banished by "her recent purity of heart" (797) inclines her to refrain from any judgmental conclusion or response. Instead, she enters fully and emotionally into the service, devoutly following the celebrant's lead and becoming less and less self-absorbed; she conscientiously prays for Denisov, Prince Andrei, her family, her family's "enemies," (797), even Anatol, at appropriate points in the invocations.

About halfway through the liturgy, something unexpected occurs that changes the atmosphere entirely. The priest suspends the prescribed ritual, leaves the altar, kneels before the royal doors of the icon screen, and begins to read a special prayer for the nation just released by the Holy Synod of the Orthodox Church. The prayer has a kind of baroque eloquence, as, in typical Orthodox style, it overflows with biblical references, pleas, citations of individuals, and confident assurances of final triumph. The priest begs God that the "foe confounding thy land" and "the lawless men" (798) joining him be overpowered, as were the godless tribes defeated by Moses, Gideon, and David, an apt comparison since most of the French invaders have imbibed the atheism spawned by the 1789 Revolution. The synod's prayer asks the Lord to preserve Russia's "humble people" and not allow the enemy of the faith to "overthrow Thy kingdom, to destroy Thy fair Jerusalem, to defile Thy temples, to overthrow Thine altars, and to profane our sanctuaries" (798).

The priest prays for "Emperor Aleksandr Pavlovich," invoking his "uprightness and meekness" (798). He implores God not to allow "the scepter of the wicked" to decide "the destiny of those whom thou hast sanctified" (799). Instead, let Him "smite our enemies and swiftly annihilate them beneath the feet of thy faithful" (799).

This language is appropriate to a war between competing faiths. The French and their hired allies are depicted as dangerous revolutionaries bent on nothing less than the abolition of the monarchy and the church and the dechristianization of Holy Russia. They must be resisted and expelled so that the damage inflicted on the Eldest Daughter of the Church, monarchical France, may not be extended to Orthodoxy's largest kingdom. No quarter can be asked for or given in such a clash of rival world views. For the Russian people, the choice is victory or death, with no compromise or accommodation possible. This determination will animate the tsar and his countrymen all through the coming months and will justify every sacrifice that will have to be made. In an irony that no one in Russia in 1812 could ever have foreseen, just over a century later, most of Western Europe and the United States would take the same militant stance toward another force of godless revolutionaries, the Communists, led and inspired by none other than tsarist Russia's successor state, the Soviet Union. As the synod's prayer concludes, only Natasha manages to rise above chauvinist zeal. With truly universal charity, she silently dissents from the synod's condemnations. She extends an ecumenical embrace, asking God "to forgive them all, and her too, and to grant them all, peace and happiness" (800).

Pierre Bezukhov is not so magnanimous. Although his love for Natasha is deep and genuine, he does not yet share her charity and her selflessness. He is restless and eager to make some kind of impact in a world where dramatic collisions and larger-than-life characters are making insupportable "that spellbound, petty sphere of Moscow habits" (802) chaining him to dull routine. Pierre is now drawn to esoteric practices, such as numerology, leading him to identify Napoleon as the "beast prophesied in the Apocalypse" (801); he then manipulates the calculations to give himself "exactly six hundred and sixty-six" (802), the sign of the Antichrist in the Apocalypse. Pierre cannot help concluding "that his part in the great affair of putting a limit to the power of the beast that spoke great and blasphemous things had been predestined from eternity," so all he need do is "wait for what was bound to come to pass" (803). His gifts of intellect and moral seriousness are leading in this instance to something like delusions of grandeur.

Seeing Natasha shortly afterwards brings Pierre back down to earth. She has recovered so well since her immersion in religion she considers singing again, something Pierre encourages. Natasha is so delighted with him and so grateful for all he has done to help her, she cannot stop praising him: "Anyone kinder, more magnanimous, better than you I have never known" (805). During dinner at the Rostovs', Pierre listens to Shinshin, a special guest, whose gossipy commentary on current affairs and Moscow society leaves him cold. Moscow's social life is what he is trying to escape from, not become even more drawn toward. Natasha alone provides relief. Following dinner, Sonya reads aloud Tsar Aleksandr's recently published appeal to Moscow and "its illustrious nobility" (807). Count Ilya Rostov is so moved by its power and sincerity, he pledges total commitment to the national cause: "Let our Sovereign but say the word and we'll sacrifice everything, begrudge nothing" (808). Between the count's ardor and Natasha's sweetness, Pierre is emotionally aroused. Apocalyptic fantasies are forgotten as Pierre accepts the fact that he is now a suitor in the Rostov home and that his marriage is no longer binding. He wants to declare his love for Natasha immediately but, like a blushing teen, cannot speak the words. Embarrassed and in inner turmoil, he leaves quickly, kissing Natasha's hand and vowing "not to go to the Rostovs' anymore" (809).

While Natasha and Pierre are performing their delicate lovers' dance, the Rostovs' younger son, Petya, is yielding to an irresistible urge to begin military service. Although his parents refuse to consent to any such thing, Petya, nonetheless, impulsively leaves home to join the crowd waiting to greet the tsar as he enters Moscow. With boyish naivete, he believes he might be able to persuade "a gentleman-in-waiting" (810) to carry his petition to join the army directly to the tsar, who he is sure will grant it without hesitation. In this aspiration, Petya resembles his older brother, who was likewise sure the tsar would pardon Denisov as soon as the particulars of his plight became known to him. Once they see Tsar Aleksandr in the flesh, the onlookers' acclamations are worshipful, as if their "Father! Angel! Our Master!" (811) were another David, whose intimate contact with the divine will guarantee Russia's victory over the demonic aggressor, Napoleon Bonaparte. Since the crowd is so large and he is some distance away from the royal procession, Petya gives up any attempt to communicate with the godlike autocrat, particularly when he is almost crushed by the surging multitude. Instead, Petya concludes: "If he could just see him, he would be happy!" (812)

He does see him finally as the tsar emerges on a balcony, carrying a half-eaten biscuit and waving to everyone as if offering a benediction. He then orders that more biscuits be brought out, which he throws out to the people below, who scramble for them as if they were the consecrated bread of communion. Petya participates in this quasi-sacramental banquet, eagerly snatching a biscuit from an elderly woman too weak to resist, all the while cheering and shouting "in a voice that was now hoarse" (814). Once again, Petya mimics his older brother, Nikolai, who acclaimed the tsar in exactly the same adulatory style whenever he was visible. The next day, Count Ilya Andreich yields to his son's importunings and goes out among his influential contacts to see how he can "arrange for Petya to serve where there would be the least danger" (814).

The devotion of the crowd in Kremlin Square is matched by members of the Moscow nobility, summoned for a personal audience with Tsar Aleksandr in the Sloboda Palace to discuss how best these notables can contribute to the defense of the motherland. Pierre is among them, excited by some words in the emperor's appeal indicating Aleksandr is planning "a consultation with his people" (815). By so doing, the tsar will act more like an elected leader responsible to his citizens rather than a divine right monarch answerable only to God. For Pierre, who has imbibed the spirit of the French Revolution during his travels in Europe, this "consultation" marks an extraordinary departure from customary practice. But for the majority of titled heads gathered for the meeting, no such implication is acknowledged. They rival Petya in their deference to the supreme authority. Pierre, notwithstanding, insists on speaking, arguing that the "Emperor himself would hardly be pleased to find in us merely owners of serfs whom we are willing to turn over to him, and cannon fodder, which we are willing to make of ourselves instead of obtaining from us any co-co-counsel" (817). He ends by proposing that the assembly request information on the state of the army and its position *vis-à-vis* the enemy. His listeners react with fury. They insist that the nobility "have no right to question the Emperor," that this is "no time for deliberation," and all must "follow our Father the Tsar!" (818) in defense of the nation. Pierre turns into the *bete noire* in this august company, feeling the same sense of outraged rejection as he had when he advocated for fundamental reforms in the Petersburg Masonic Lodge. No matter how hard he tries to explain his views, he is shouted down. No tennis court oaths will be taken here. The tsar is and will remain autocrat of all Russia.

Tsar Aleksandr may rule officially as an absolute monarch, but his is not an authoritarian personality. As he begins to speak to the Assembly of the Nobility, he does so "in a trembling voice," which Pierre finds "pleasantly human" (821). He speaks "with emotion" (821), commending the nobles for their commitment to "sacrifice ten serfs in every thousand, fully equipped" (820)) for campaigning, and, like the most grateful of masters, thanking these wealthy Muscovites for doing more for Russia than he could ever expect. The tsar says much the same thing to the merchants assembled in an adjoining room and weeps openly as they too offer the nation all that they have: "Our lives and our property—take both, Your Majesty" (821).

Observing these very moving scenes, Pierre regrets having made "his speech with its constitutional tenor" and looks for "an opportunity to make amends for it" (821). His amends take the form of an extraordinary gift to Russia. To prove his devotion to the tsar and his love for his endangered country, Pierre pledges to "provide and maintain a thousand men" (821) for the duration of the war. He cannot help himself, as he gets swept up like everyone else in the excitement and fervor of the moment. The tsar is more like a "priest—king" than a conventional statesman; though he is not a priest, he has the aura and the paternal grace of one ordained to serve God's people, along with the full political authority of one chosen by God to govern these same people. The nobles and the merchants respond so zealously and generously because they cannot deny or even question a father's pleas, especially when this royal father is such an angelic being.

PART TWO

All of this activity is occurring because the tsar and many of his advisors are convinced that Napoleon must be stopped as close to the border as possible. Aleksandr will be upset later, for instance, upon learning that Smolensk, a large city in western Russia, has been "taken and burned without a pitched battle having been fought before its walls" (824). The pain and suffering this destruction will bring to the city will be felt, to a degree, by all Russians. But from the perspective of history, nothing can be more advantageous to the defenders than the French Army's steady advance into the nation's heartland. The deeper their penetration into a hostile and unforgiving territory, the weaker the invader's forces must become. Men and animals suffer constant fatigue; lines of communication have to be extended; summer is giving way to fall, bringing cold, snow, and impassable roads; so once battle is finally joined at Borodino, outside Moscow, the French and their allies are hardly in the best of shape. This battle rages for most of one day, and though they outnumber the Russians, who eventually withdraw, the attackers suffer severe casualties, making their "victory" hollow. What is left of the army makes its way to the capital like a boxer leading in points and apparently strong but in reality so staggered by the previous round he is just trying to stay upright to the end of his match.

Napoleon and Aleksandr are compelled by the fate that has brought the two into mortal combat to do what they have to do to achieve the end already decided, even if appearances seem to be suggesting otherwise. Even though Aleksandr has wanted to give battle early, his commanders never could agree on either the best place for their troops to stand, or whether they should mount a full-scale counteroffensive or take a defensive position around a fortified encampment. The Russians, as a result, keep retreating, but retreat turns out to be the "one thing that could save Russia " (823). Napoleon keeps moving forward, convinced that he is not being attacked because the enemy fears him but sure that when they are forced to give battle, he will win decisively, enter Moscow, and dictate terms to the tsar, exactly as he has done in previous conflicts. This thinking and this course of action, of course, will achieve only the opposite, ending with the destruction of the *Grande Armee* and the beginning of the end of the Napoleonic *Imperium*. Like the principal characters in a tragic drama, Napoleon, Aleksandr, and the military movers and shakers are the unwitting instruments of God's will: "Providence compelled all those men, striving for the attainment of their own personal ends, to combine in the accomplishment of a prodigious result, of which not one of them . . . had the slightest expectation" (823).

Only the tsar and his commanders are making decisions on strategy and troop movements. Even influential nobles like Prince Nikolai Bolkonsky know little about what is occurring at the front. The old prince is, therefore, utterly unprepared for what his son writes in his latest letter to his father. Prince Andrei informs the household that the French are nearing Smolensk, which means they could be approaching Bald Hills in less than a week. It is imperative that preparations for an evacuation to a safer place begin immediately. Prince Nicholai, nevertheless, temporizes. Instead of acting quickly, the old man with so many ailments, so many resentments, so many prejudices, and so many reasons to turn a blind eye to all that is occurring in real time, walls off the present and its perils. He waxes nostalgic, remembering the glorious days in the reign of Catherine the Great, when "as a young general without a wrinkle on his ruddy face" (833) on campaign in Austria, the prince was brought into the headquarters of the court favorite, Potemkin, with whom he discussed military affairs, and with the Mother Empress, who smiled and spoke kindly to him during "her gracious reception" (833) of the overawed guest, who now can only cry out "Ah, soon, soon, to return to those days and have done with the present! Soon, soon, may they leave me in peace!" (834)

Princess Marya is not taking refuge in such reminiscences. On the advice of her nephew's tutor, Desalles, she dispatches her steward to Smolensk, where he is ordered to deliver a letter to the provincial governor himself, "asking him to let her know the state of affairs and the extent of the danger to which Bald Hills was exposed" (834). The steward, Alpatych, does as directed. The governor, in response, gives him a letter he has recently received from none other than Barclay de Tolly, commander of one of the Russian armies marching to defend his province. The letter is reassuring. With a self-confidence typical of non-native commanders, Barclay tells the governor not to worry, because he and General Bagration, commander of a second army, are preparing to unite and thereby overwhelm the enemy. The governor should "reassure the inhabitants of Smolensk, for those defended by two such dauntless armies may feel confident that victory will be theirs" (838). Alpatych leaves, only to find himself in range of an artillery barrage from "a hundred and thirty guns which Napoleon had ordered up" (839) while he and the provincial governor were meeting. Far from "feeling confident that victory will be theirs," the people of Smolensk are running about in terror, desperately seeking cover from the shelling, which is causing fires to break out everywhere. A crowd rushes to the cathedral "to fetch the wonder-working icon of Smolensk" (841), as if at this critical time divine protection is all that can save them. In a coincidence comparable to his battlefield meeting with Napoleon at Austerlitz, Prince Andrei runs into Alpatych in the burning city. He hurriedly writes out an urgent message to be given to Princess Marya: "Smolensk has surrendered. Bald Hills will be occupied by the enemy within a week. Leave for Moscow at once" (843). So much for the efforts of Barclay, Bagration, and their "dauntless armies."

Prince Andrei is in command of a regiment whose line of march in the retreat from Smolensk brings them near "the avenue leading to Bald Hills." (844). The prince is devoted to this regiment, and the troops under his command are devoted to him, calling him "our Prince" and noting how "solicitous" he is "for his men and officers" (845). These men are a source of inspiration and motivation, which Prince Andrei badly needs during another humiliating retreat. He, of course, is equally devoted to his family and to his "beloved Bald Hills, which he had built and peopled, to be plundered" (845). Even though his father, sister, and son have left the estate and are on the way to safety in Moscow, leaving him "nothing to do at Bald Hills," the prince still wishes to stop at his home now that he is nearby, even if this will "aggravate his own sufferings" (845). Upon arrival, he meets only Alpatych and some of the peasants. They are all respectful and a little awed, with the steward stooping and "kissing his young master's knee" (846). Alpatych fills him in on the family's departure and assures Prince Andrei he will remain at his post no matter what transpires. With typical Orthodox acceptance of his fate, the old man affirms with simple eloquence, "He is my refuge; His will be done!" (847). They part, never to set eyes on each other again.

As these events unfold and the enemy moves closer and closer to Moscow, life in St Petersburg, where "form predominates" (850), goes on as before. In this city is the distillation of all things foreign, such as the French language, the social rivalries, grand balls, ballet, and, above all, court maneuvering, in-fighting, and intrigue. The capital is more cosmopolitan than anywhere else in Russia, "distinct from village, country, provincial, or even Moscow life" (850). In their tight little circles, notables talk endlessly about the war, the key players, and the tsar's decisions, manifesting a range of opinions and predilections. In the competing *salons* of Anna Pavlovna and Elena Bezukhova, for instance, attitudes toward Napoleon and the French differ greatly. "None but the most inveterate legitimists among the French were received in Anna Pavlovna's *salon*, and patriotic views were expressed to the effect that one ought not to go to the French theater, that to maintain the French troupe was costing the government as much as a whole army corps" (850). In the latter, "the war in general was regarded as a series of formal demonstrations, which would very soon end in peace" (851), like a theatrical production. Among Elena's jaded set, "the patriotic fervor of Moscow" is considered bad form and "the subject of ironical and very witty if circumspect raillery" (851).

"Circumspect" also describes Prince Vasily Kuragin, who moves artfully between both establishments, offering supposedly informed commentary on all things political and military. Dissatisfaction with Barclay de Tolly is now widespread, having percolated up from the field generals to the tsar's court. Discussions about who should succeed him and bring Russia decisive victory take place in both *salons*. The name of the new chief of the militia, Mikhail Ilarionovich Kutusov, is raised as a possibility. Prince Vasily, however, with his "in the know" conceit, dismisses Kutusov out of hand as one who could not possibly "please His Majesty" (852), citing his age, his infirmities, and his dubious morals as serious impediments for the young and virtuous monarch. Nevertheless, shortly after Prince Vasily's comments, the Tsar grants Kutusov "the title of Prince" and when a special royal commission concludes that "a divisive command" has to be unified under one overall commander and that Kutusov is the group's choice to fill this post, the tsar puts his reservations aside and confers the appointment on "the very oldest general in Russia" (852). With the wind from the seat of power not just blowing but howling in the opposite direction, Prince Vasily does a quick about face. With perfect insouciance, he extols the appointment of Kutusov: "I am so pleased, so delighted" (852-53), calling him "a second autocrat" and mendaciously insisting that "our Sovereign has always esteemed him highly" (853). This is Petersburg insincerity in its most brazen form, denouncing someone in public one day and exalting him the next, all because of the outsize impact the All Highest and his retainers have on every aspect of the capital's life and on all who need to be on the right terms with both.

The *Grande Armee* meanwhile is proceeding steadily toward Holy Moscow, "*la capitale asiatique de ce grand empire*" (855). This exotic Eurasian city gives "Napoleon's imagination no rest" (855), as if it were the embodiment of something conjured up in an Oriental saga. Despite his dangerously extended communications and his troops' weariness, he is like Alexander the Great in Persia, irresistibly drawn to the east. He now orders a "direct advance on Moscow" (855), an advance that is not to be impeded by Russian defenders, who "owing to innumerable combinations of circumstances" (855), cannot assemble in force to block the French. The emperor learns at this juncture that Kutusov has been made commander in chief; this is a man known among French officers as "shrewd" (855), a quality the new commander will quickly exhibit to deadly effect. Napoleon also has an unusual encounter with a captured Cossack, who warns him that unless he compels the Russians to fight a battle soon, he and his troops will have to deal with "a long-drawn-out affair" (856). Though the emperor does not take him seriously, this illiterate peasant's grasp of strategic realities is unerring and prophetic.

While all this is taking place on the march, drama has been unfolding at Bald Hills. As Prince Andrei approaches the property, at the last moment before his family's planned departure and with an old man's willfulness and contrariness, Prince Nikolai announces he will never leave his estate; instead, he puts on his old uniform and "wearing all his Orders," prepares "to visit the Commander in Chief" (858) to inform him of his intention to defend his home to the end, whether supported by Kutusov's troops or not. But the prince does not get very far. His peasants bring him back, weak and stumbling, to Princess Marya with "his formerly stern and determined expression" transformed into "one of timidity and submission" (858). That night he suffers a stroke and loses consciousness. He is then taken to Prince Andrei's former home at Bogucharovo, where Prince Nikolai lingers for several weeks. Princess Marya attends to her father without respite, but to her dismay and shame, she finds herself sometimes "*wishing* to see some indication of the approaching end" (859). She also is feeling a kind of liberation as she gazes upon her dying father, looking "like a disfigured corpse" (859). The princess's long-suppressed "personal hopes and desires" revive, as "the world of earthly, arduous, free activity" starts to intrude upon "the spiritual world in which till now she had been confined and in which her greatest comfort had been prayer" (859). The princess, in other words, is starting to reenter everyday life, where she can once more respond to normal desires and interests (including the need to love), take pleasure in society, and make religious duties and prayer an aspect of her life rather than its totality. She is experiencing the same kind of uplift as her depressed, recently widowed brother did when he heard Natasha's laughter and felt her charm.

Prince Nikolai's last moments are powerful and moving. As he struggles to speak, Princess Marya senses that her father's "soul is in pain" (861). Her instincts are correct; the prince wants desperately to speak tenderly to one he has tormented for so long. He finally manages, in tears, to offer her thanks and to beg forgiveness "for all the . . ." (862). Like a priest hearing a penitent's last confession and forgiving him or her now and forever, Princess Marya opens up to her father the possibility of redemption. While his retainer Tikhon wipes away Prince Nikolai's tears, the dying man mumbles a few more words, this time about Russia, the war, and his son. His final words to the princess are "Put on your white dress, I like it" (863), as if by donning something close to a wedding dress, she can celebrate his passing, not mourn it, and begin a chapter in life altogether different from the one just ending. The princess reproaches herself for what she considers her wayward thoughts and impulses prior to her father's gentle end, but the fact is, she is becoming emotionally and temperamentally prepared to return to a world she hardly knows.

Her preparations for departure to Moscow create more stress, something Princess Marya has had quite enough of but cannot avoid. The princess and her party have not had many dealings with Bogucharovo's peasants, who remain "primitive" despite her brother's efforts to introduce reforms, such as "building hospitals, schools, and reducing the peasants' quitrent" (865). These peasants are also credulous, believing, for instance, the most fantastic tales about French liberality, while at the same time doubting the sincerity of their masters, no matter how reasonable their wishes are.

Knowing the invaders are coming closer, Alpatych has to deal with this difficult band and somehow persuade them to aid in the family's evacuation and then leave the endangered area themselves. He begins with the village elder, ordering him "to collect carts to move the Princess's luggage from Bogucharovo" (867). The elder vacillates because villagers have "decided not to move but to wait" (867). The peasants have been too influenced by French leaflets distributed all over the steppe region that promise fair and humane treatment to all who stay in their homes; one peasant has even received "a hundred rubles in notes (he did not know they were counterfeit) paid to him in advance for hay." (867). This undercurrent makes Alpatych's task very challenging. He reiterates his demand to the elder, insisting he "stop all this nonsense and get the carts ready" (869). The elder agrees, only to have the villagers balk once again. Enraged, Alpatych rushes to the authorities, leaving the princess caught between a hostile army and an uncooperative community. We see here in microcosm how the social and civic order prevailing in Russia for centuries is starting to show cracks and stresses. Peasants who have been conditioned from childhood only to work and to obey, are beginning to think and make decisions on their own. This phenomenon is by no means widespread yet, but it will develop enough momentum in the decades to come to bring serfdom to an end in Russia at almost the same time slavery is abolished in the United States.

But in 1812, at Bogucherovo, an obdurate group of peasants was not supposed to be listened to; the instigators had to be dealt with firmly and law and order had to be maintained lest further damage be done. Princess Marya, however, does not follow these rules. She has spent her life dealing kindly and charitably with a moody tyrant, letting prayer and Scripture guide her response to Prince Nikolai's tantrums. Her instincts are maternal, and she is by nature warm, loving, and giving. Thus, when the village elder tells her that "what horses we had have been taken by the army or have died" (873), making it impossible for her to travel, the princess does not suspect that he may be dissembling. He then exclaims that "we may die of hunger ourselves!" (873), upsetting Princess Marya to such a degree she makes an unprecedented move. She orders that all the grain in Bogucharovo being held for the Bolkonsky household be allocated immediately to the hungry peasants: "Distribute it all. I give this order in my brother's name, and tell them what is ours is theirs" (874). The elder cannot believe his ears. Authoritarian rule is giving way to Christian charity in Russia in 1812. He asks to be discharged, knowing his lying will be exposed if the grain is given out. He also knows that the peasants will judge Princess Marya's gesture harshly. They will consider what she is doing as prompted by fear and weakness and, in consequence, will extort even more. Nothing good, in other words, can come from this act.

The princess is informed that the peasants have gathered at the granary, undoubtedly because word of her donation has spread, and that they wish to see her. The village elder wants no further dealings with the peasants and begs Princess Marya to send them away. She refuses and walks out to meet them, channeling the strength and courage of her father and brother and the faith that can move mountains. She is in a situation similar to that of Marie Antoinette, who, with her husband, bravely stood on the balcony of the palace at Versailles in 1790 and faced down an angry mob of Parisians demanding bread. Princess Marya does more than stare; she speaks eloquently and kindly to the peasants, repeating her offer of grain, emphasizing the danger they all are in as the French approach and insisting they follow her to safety in Moscow. The response to her generous and sincere appeal is what the elder has expected. She is met with mute silence at first, but soon some individuals in the crowd loudly dissent, refusing the grain and demanding that everyone remain in Bogucherovo no matter what the princess does or wishes. This stubbornness pervades the assembly, who adopt a posture of "angry resolve" (876). It gets worse. One peasant throws Marya's words back at her, twisting their clear meaning into something exactly opposite. This proposal is all a trick, he screams; what Marya really wants is for the peasants "to follow her into slavery," because once they leave the security of their homes, which the French have promised not to disturb, the defenseless peasants will have no choice but to "go into bondage" (877) just to stay alive. Seeing that she cannot overcome such extreme suspicion, Princess Marya gives up and turns away.

She has encountered the dark side of Russia's peasant masses. Having been suppressed so long and having seen no scheme for advancement or liberation work in their favor, the peasants of Bogucharovo see every proposition from their masters as a well-disguised scheme that will only bind them even more firmly to poverty, toil, and servitude. Just as they refused to participate in Prince Andrei's plans for improving their lives and those of their families, and just as they undermined Pierre's reforms, seemingly so popular and successful on the surface, by allowing the managers to sabotage good faith undertakings, so too Marya's peasants turn her sincere gestures of concern, motivated solely by charity, into malevolent deceptions.

In Russia in 1812, customary thinking and practices still rule, not only among the peasantry but throughout the civil, political, and military order. Speransky's fall proves that structural change in the governing circles provokes immoveable resistance; Pierre's experience at the Assembly of the Notables shows that even the most modest recommendations for consensual policy-making within the highest circles are intolerable; Prince Vasily's 180-degree turn regarding General Kutusov's fitness is one small instance of the autocrat's supreme control of individual consciences; and the confusion in the Russian high command over how to stop Napoleon's march highlights the inability of the most experienced and most senior commanders to act independently of court interference. Russia is a nation where authoritarian traditions distort and choke personal and social development in countless ways.

Princess Marya's predicament is getting worse. The peasants have dug in strongly, now demanding outrageously that the princess remain with them, so they can "serve her as before and obey her in everything" (882). To emphasize their resolve to stay in place and keep the Bolkonsky family immobile, they prepare to "unharness the horses" (882) that the village elder said had either died or been commandeered. They are, in essence, overpowering their mistress, like the Paris mob did when they forced their king and queen to abandon Versailles and reside in Paris under house arrest until their executions. A fate like this is avoided, however, because at this critical juncture, Count Nikolai Rostov and an aide arrive quite by chance and are instantly informed about the princess's plight. Nikolai takes charge immediately, not only as an officer but also as "a man of her own class" (882). He assures the princess that "no one shall dare to cause any unpleasantness" so long as she allows him to serve as her "escort" (883). Princess Marya is overcome with emotion at this providential intervention. Touched by Nikolai's aristocratic "delicacy" (883), she speaks to him in French and places herself under his protection. For his part, Count Nikolai "sees sweetness and nobility in her features and expression" (882). A refined lady who has had to deal with "coarse peasants" (881) for several days responds powerfully to a man of her own class seemingly dropped from the skies to save her. The attraction is intense and mutual.

This interlude is like something out of a Viennese operetta, where everything stops as a handsome stranger suddenly appears to straighten out the mess the princess is in, leading the two to fall instantly in love. As for the "mess," Nikolai follows the Russian playbook in bringing the peasants under control.

Charity and magnanimity are replaced by a man in uniform's authoritarian assertion. He starts by peremptorily knocking one of the spokesmen to the ground with a "powerful blow" (885) to the head for failing to remove his hat in Nikolai's presence. As the man continues to "argue," Nikolai orders him bound and taken away, which two of the peasants do "obediently" (885). These actions have the desired effect. The crowd disperses quickly enough, with one member wondering out loud how they had had the temerity "to talk to the gentry" (885) so disrespectfully. Soon the erstwhile "Brigands!" and "Traitors!" (885) are loading the family's possessions into carts for transport to Moscow. Nikolai invites none of the peasants to follow, their insolence toward Princess Marya causing them to forfeit any opportunity to escape the enemy. The princess is smitten by this "man of lofty, noble soul, capable of understanding her position and her grief" (887), while at the same time her cavalier is already thinking of marrying the fine lady, who has everything his family could wish for in a wife. Only his promise to Sonya disturbs Nikolai's reveries.

Count Nikolai has performed admirably as a gentleman and a knightly protector of a defenseless maiden, but his fantasies of domestic harmony and bliss must yield for now to the realities of war. He has to rejoin his regiment and continue dutifully to do his small part to repel the invader. Others of his acquaintance are engaged in similar efforts. In the small world the principals in *War and Peace* inhabit, coincidental encounters occur frequently. At the commander in chief's headquarters, one of these takes place now. Prince Andrei Bolkonsky has been ordered to report in person to "His Serene Highness, as everyone now called Kutusov" (888). By chance he meets another guest there, "Lieutenant Colonel Denisov, better known as Vaska" (889), who was last seen trying to avoid court-martial. The prince remembers hearing about Denisov as one who had "proposed to a little girl of fifteen without realizing what he was doing" (889); the prince knows this girl well, having proposed to Natasha Rostova himself not too long ago. Denisov is at headquarters to present to Kutusov "the plan of campaign he had devised while serving at the outposts during the retreat" (889). It is simple and logical: with the enemy so overextended, "instead of, or simultaneously with, a frontal attack to block the advance of the French, attacks should be made on their line of communication" (889–90).

But Denisov's exertions have been in vain. His scheme "for the welfare of the fatherland" (891) will not be given a hearing, even if Kutusov invites Denisov to brief him. This is because the old general has no patience with "intellect and knowledge" (893), having seen at Austerlitz and elsewhere how useless the most detailed plans become as soon as battle is joined and matters do not fall into place as expected. His Serene Highness lets "his age and experience of life" (893) guide his actions, and these are telling him that at this point it is not necessary to attack the French anywhere. All the Russian troops need do is pull back as the enemy moves deeper and deeper into Russia. The land and the weather will do the rest. When he is asked to approve "a document pertaining to payment for standing oats mown down by soldiers" (893), for instance, Kutusov refuses indignantly, emphasizing that "I do not order it, I do not permit it, but neither can I enforce punishment for it. It cannot be helped" (893). What is left unsaid is that every source of food and forage not consumed by Russian soldiers or civilians will be commandeered by the French to feed their own troops and animals. Such discoveries will only give the enemy a continuing lease on life and prolong the campaign. The more barren fields the French march through, the more hunger they will suffer, until, in desperation, like the Turks he defeated in Romania, they will have to "eat horseflesh" (896). Kutusov's grim prophecy will come true in ways even more grisly than he imagines. According to Caulaincourt's memoir, during some of the worst days of the retreat from Moscow, the French "lived on grilled horseflesh alone. Horses that fell in their tracks were carved up while still alive" (191).

Prince Andrei hears the commander in chief expand on these themes and related subjects during their private meeting. His Serene Highness has sent for the prince because he has admired him ever since he observed his gallant charge at Austerlitz. Kutusov asks Prince Andrei if he is interested in joining his staff, but he almost knows in advance the offer will be refused. He can find someone else since officers who want to do administrative work are "plentiful," but "men" like Prince Andrei, who can lead by example and bring out the best in those they command, are "scarce" (895). The prince, however, should not be too eager for combat just yet. Regarding the current campaign, Kutusov stresses his central point: "Everything comes to him who knows how to wait" (895). This simple statement is Kutusov's entire strategic plan. He will not fight useless battles or waste precious manpower if "patience and time" (896) will conquer anyway. Prince Andrei is a warrior, but Kutusov's approach is reassuring. He leaves the meeting certain that the commander in chief intuits "the inevitable course of events; he can see them and grasp their significance" (897), content to let the iron laws of nature work their course.

As His Serene Highness patiently awaits the enemy's self-destruction, the people of Moscow show little disposition to let events govern their conduct. Their responses to the crisis range from serious preparation for national defense to largely symbolic patriotic gestures. Thus, Pierre and many of his fellow nobles, on the one hand, personally recruit, pay for, outfit, and, in some cases, lead regiments consisting of their own peasants, while on the other hand, Julie Drubetskaya and some of her society friends take a vow to "speak only Russian" (899), as if somehow this renunciation of a language many know better than Russian will help the war effort. Despite the assurances of Rostopchin, governor-general of the capital, that "the villain will not set foot in Moscow" (901), a large number of civilians, particularly propertied women, are so eager to get out of harm's way, they are abandoning their homes and fleeing east with only minimal baggage. Rostopchin puts the best face on this exodus by expressing joy that with "ladies and merchants" wives . . . leaving the city," in large numbers, those remaining will experience "less panic and less gossip" (901) to cause trouble. One of these loyal Muscovites, Pierre Bezukhov is still in his

Moscow residence and not anxious or concerned, even if the regiment he is raising will cost him one of his estates. He senses that matters are coming to a head and is willing to make his contribution to the nation's defense without misgivings.

Pierre's calm, however, is soon shattered. On a drive through the city, he witnesses a shocking scene. A mob is watching with approval as a French cook, "accused of being a spy" (904), is flogged. The cook is so hurt and so humiliated by this savage attack he cannot hold back tears. This brutality is far different from some women pledging not to speak the enemy's language. Now a citizen of the city who happens not to be a native Russian, is being abused simply on the strength of hearsay or rumor. This is one of several acts of violence against innocents that will be perpetrated by vigilantes, and even official law enforcement, as the pressure on the capital intensifies and the hunt for scapegoats grows unchecked. Pierre is "choked with emotion" (904) as he sees the cook's ordeal unfold. His instinct for justice and his natural magnanimity recoil from the crowd's sadistic glee. He decides immediately that rather than endure any more gruesome spectacles in the days ahead, he will leave for the army and take a direct part in the nation's struggle against the invaders. Pierre has already sacrificed property and peasants; he will now offer everything else, including "comfort, wealth, even life itself" (905) in Russia's desperate hours.

Pierre's journey takes him into the vortex created by the impending meeting of two great armies. The Battle of Borodino will be the one significant military engagement of the Russian campaign. Though, as stated previously, the commander in chief would like nothing better than to see Napoleon and his troops burn themselves out marching all over Russia and battling constant hunger, fatigue, and cold, Tsar Aleksandr and his high command in St. Petersburg insist that Kutusov give battle at some point to defend Moscow. The battle will cost Napoleon one-fourth of his army, one-third of Kutusov's force, and, shortly after, the ancient capital, Moscow itself. Such appalling human and civic losses should lead to some settlement or truce, but the "ten hours" (911) of battle at Borodino will result in nothing of the sort. Kutusov's smaller army has to withdraw from the field, leaving the way open for the French to capture Moscow. This development, however, simply prolongs the strategic retreat the Russians have been engaged in since Kutusov's appointment and leaves Napoleon and his men immobilized in an empty city.

As the emperor continues to put out feelers for a negotiation of terms and the tsar continues to resist every invitation to confer, precious weeks will go by, leaving the occupiers more and more isolated. When the *Grande Armee* finally begins its retreat, no resolution of the conflict will have been agreed upon, so the French and their allies will be hopelessly vulnerable to the elements and to the Cossack marauders, who will harass their march mercilessly. Though "Napoleon's historians themselves tell us that from Smolensk onward he wished to stop," and though he "had not received a single reply to his repeated declarations of a wish to negotiate" (907), the emperor and his men are in an awful predicament as winter sets in only because Napoleon would not and could not do as reason dictated in the summer of 1812 and abort the mission before it would be too late. Compelled like Oedipus to act in ways that assure his destruction, Napoleon had to keep moving forward. The all-powerful destiny that the Russian people submit to with resigned acceptance but which the French, formed by the Enlightenment, think they can control, proves irresistible.

Pierre Bezukhov arrives at what will be the field of battle on August 25, 1812. As he makes his way to the army's encampment, he runs into scores of wounded and badly shaken soldiers who have barely survived the Battle of the Schevardino Redoubt, which has taken place the previous evening. The loss of the redoubt has forced the Russians to abandon a fortified position that was supposed to anchor their left flank, causing the whole center of gravity for the opposed armies to shift. Instead of meeting the main French assault on their right, where some defenses have been erected, the Russians will have to do so on their over-extended left, on an open field that gives them no cover. These unprotected lines will be subject to murderous artillery and musket fire, the effect of which could induce panic and withdrawal among some units. Only the bravest, most determined, and most loyal will be able to hold their ground, and how many of these will live to do so cannot be calculated or predicted.

Pierre, of course, knows nothing of these tactical concerns, but as he observes and speaks to the battered men walking past him and staring "with frank, childlike curiosity at Pierre's white hat and green swallow-tailed coat" (912), so incongruous in that setting, the man who has spent countless hours searching for meaning and purpose begins to comprehend at long last what his soul has been craving. Speaking with a doctor who is certain the impending combat will overwhelm the Russian Army's medical personnel and facilities, Pierre marvels at how, nevertheless, the troops are preparing to give battle fearlessly and valiantly, even if, like ancient gladiators, many will be maimed or killed that day: "The cavalry go into battle, meet the wounded on their way, give them a wink as they pass, and never for a moment think of what awaits them" (914). It is not just dashing cavalrymen showing such *sangfroid*; "peasants of the militia wearing white shirts and caps with crosses on them" (914) are laboriously putting up earthworks, as if, with God's mercy, these protective barriers will stop bullets and muffle the effect of projectiles, saving countless men from injury or death. Pierre remembers a remark one of the wounded had made earlier: "They mean to throw the whole nation against them" (914). Pierre is one of "the whole nation." As the great battle unfolds on the twenty-sixth, he will become one with the masses of humanity of all classes who, on this field, will demonstrate courage, strength, endurance, and good cheer in the midst of mortal peril; many will die in place, hopelessly outnumbered and outgunned, rather than commit the sacrilege of surrender or retreat, because Mother Russia and Holy Moscow demand their sacrifice. Pierre will live, but after experiencing the power of his nation's embrace, he will live ever after as a Russian patriot, a man no longer set apart from his brothers and sisters by wealth, education, or position. His identity will be established and confirmed in fire and fury.

Part of this identity is the Russian Orthodox Church. It is to Russia what the Roman Catholic Church was to monarchical France, the Eldest Daughter of the Church. This connection between church and nation has been broken as a result of the French Revolution. Although Napoleon has negotiated a concordat with the Vatican affirming Catholicism as "the religion of France" and giving priests and nuns important responsibilities in education, marriage, and family life, the former connection to the state has not been restored. Napoleon himself is openly scornful of religion in general, as he revealed during his discussions with Balashev, and has no respect for the prerogatives of even the highest clergy, as he demonstrated in Notre Dame Cathedral on December 2, 1804, when he snatched the crown of Charlemagne from the hands of Pope Pius VII and arrogantly placed it on his own head, as if he were a priest-king needing no one else to ratify his rule. Most of his suite, most of his officers, and a great number of his common soldiers share the post-revolutionary contempt for the ancient faith, equating religious profession with ignorance and superstition.

Russia has largely escaped such a contagion. Although Pierre and many of his better educated and more cosmopolitan peers in the aristocracy are not conventionally religious, they know how integral the Orthodox faith is to Russia, shaping much of its history and guiding the lives of the majority of its people, particularly the devout peasants, who pray before the icons in their homes and village churches faithfully. On the day before the great battle, therefore, Pierre is not surprised by a scene playing out before him on the field outside the town of Borodino. In solemn procession on ground that will soon be stained by blood, soldiers, priests, deacons, and choristers are carrying a treasured icon, the Smolensk Mother of God, brought out of that burning city earlier and now accompanying the army wherever it goes, like an Orthodox equivalent of the Ark of the Covenant. All those whom the icon passes bare their heads, kneel, bow reverently, cross themselves, and join in the fervent prayer of the clergy and choir: "Save from calamity thy servants, O Mother of God . . . For to Thee under God we all flee as to an everlasting bulwark and protection" (918). As alluded to earlier, among the group Pierre is watching is none other than His Serene Highness himself, Mikhail Ilarionovich Kutusov, who kneels and bows in exactly the same way as everyone else, ending with this gesture: "At last he rose, put out his lips in a naïve, childlike way, and kissed the icon, and again bowed down and touched the ground with his hand" (919). The contrast between the two opposing commanders, one so full of himself and so ostentatiously impious and the other so humble and so sincere in his simple faith, cannot be more striking.

The contrast between the commander in chief and some of his own staff is also sharp. As the icon procession moves on, Pierre is greeted by Boris Drubetskoy, who is, of course, "elegantly dressed, with just a suggestion of the campaigner" (919). Boris is aware that the greatest struggle of the war will commence the following morning, but as a staff officer far removed from the battle lines, he has little anxiety about being among the killed, wounded, or captured. Thus, while Kutusov tearfully prays for divine aid in the coming clash, Boris, the quintessential careerist, focuses on the battle's aftermath. He is in "a state of nervous exhilaration all that day" (921) over the possibility of winning "important rewards" (921) once the shooting stops. Unlike the peasant laborers or the officers and men preparing for action who had so impressed Pierre earlier and whose "expression of excitement" concerns "universal questions of life and death" (921), Boris and his compeers are shamelessly self-centered in their preoccupation with "questions of personal success" (921), which could be achieved regardless of how Mother Russia might fare. Pierre's old nemesis, Dolokhov, also appears out of the blue. He is in characteristic form, presenting himself to Kutusov with brazen temerity and reminding His Serene Highness with theatrical bravado that if he "has need of a man who doesn't mind risking his skin" (921), he should summon Dolokhov immediately. He is equally self-centered, seeing the upcoming conflict not as mortal combat for the salvation of Russia but as a stage for self-display. The reckless and amoral adventurer then embraces Pierre, whom he once tried to kill, and "with tears in his eyes" apologizes to him "for the misunderstanding that occurred between" (922) the two in the past, confirming his contrition with a kiss. Dolokhov then exits the stage like a gracious cavalier.

Prince Andrei Bolkonsky is in an entirely different frame of mind. He is like the soldiers of the line in contemplating the "possibility of death" (925), but, as he does so, he falls back into a despairing contempt for all of life's vanities and deceptions, a contempt he has felt off and on since Austerlitz. In the evening before what may be the last day of his life, the prince looks back on "three great sorrows" (926) that have marked his time on earth thus far. From the perspective of the battlefield and "in the cold white light of the morning" that will soon be "dawning" (926), the landscape of memory looks bleak. Prince Andrei's romance with Natasha Rostova, sorrow one, seems a hopeless dream, something that "ideal love" (926) inspired and real life doomed. The second sorrow is the death of his father, who "built Bald Hills, and thought it was his place, his land, his air, his peasants" (926). Today it has been overrun by foreigners who are "unaware of his existence" (926), a monument to futility. The third sorrow, the French invasion, will probably result in his death in action, after which enemy litter bearers may very well take him by the "head and heels" and throw him "into a hole" (926) with all the other corpses, where he will turn back into the dust from which he was made. It is no wonder that as Pierre arrives at Prince Andrei's shed for a visit, his friend greets him with an expression "more than cold—it was positively hostile" (927).

The conversation that follows begins with gloom and pessimism. Prince Andrei is curt and laconic as Pierre discusses the army's positions, which he has toured the day before in the company of General Bennigsen. The prince is dismissive: "Success never has and never will depend on position or equipment or even on numbers—least of all on position" (930). War is not like a game of chess, where every move can be thought over interminably and where every piece has a fixed value; the prince stresses that "in war a battalion is sometimes stronger than a division, and sometimes weaker than a company" (929). Everything depends on "the feeling that is . . . in every soldier" (930). As he makes this point, Prince Andrei grows more animated. The will to win cannot be calculated or assumed in advance, so the chance that a particular tactical maneuver may succeed can never be estimated with certainty. The German officers attached to the Russian army continually disregard this basic fact. They believe in the overriding mastery conferred by a carefully drawn-up plan assessing all possible contingencies. But at Austerlitz such a plan led only to failure, as Napoleon made unexpected moves, creating unforeseen contingencies, and the men in the ranks, the Russians in particular, concluded early on that the battle had been lost, despite the fact that French losses "were almost equal" (930) to those of the Austrians and Russians. Likewise, in the upcoming battle, it will not be the planners or the officers deciding the outcome, but the thousands bearing the brunt of combat, whose innumerable and incalculable individual decisions on whether to stand firm or retreat, whether to die in place or surrender, whether to advance against withering fire or run for cover, and so forth, will determine victory or defeat. Prince Andrei is heartened by this fact and his outlook brightens. He ends with a ringing declaration that in its own way reenforces what Pierre has been thinking all along. The prince affirms in no uncertain terms "that whatever happens, and whatever mess those at the top may make, we shall win tomorrow's battle" (930) precisely because the invaders are defiling foreign soil and the Russians are fighting for home and hearth.

This emotional response makes a strong impression on his civilian guest. It culminates all that Pierre has been experiencing in his contacts with the troops and during his tour of the front:

> *Now he understood the whole meaning and importance of this war and of the impending battle. All he had seen that day, ... appeared to him in a new light. He understood that suppressed ... heat of patriotism in all these men he had seen, and it explained to him the*

composure and ostensible lightheartedness with which they faced death. (932)

Prince Andrei ends the conversation with a grim meditation on the singularity of war and how the law of the jungle should guide combatants, with no sides taking prisoners and no "chivalry" (932) impeding mutual slaughter. Such harshness, however, will have the salutary effect of forcing nations to resort to war "only when it was worth going to certain death, as now" (932). The prince takes leave of his friend with an embrace and a kiss. Pierre cannot decide whether his expression is "angry or tender," but he does know "this is our last meeting" (933).

On the other side of the field, the emperor of the French is anything but anxious. As he awaits the test of arms he has been anticipating for so long, Napoleon is brimming with confidence, assuring a courtier newly arrived from Paris that he will see Moscow "in three days" and taking delight in a just delivered portrait of his son, "the child whom for some reason everyone called the King of Rome" (936). The troops of the Old Guard, Napoleon's personal detachment, in "rapturous cries" (937) acclaim the emperor and his heir, as if the continuity of the Bonaparte dynasty is an established fact. Napoleon ends the evening by issuing a grandiloquent "order of the day to the army" (938) that concludes with an echo of Henry V's exhortation to the knights at Agincourt: "May it be said of each of you: He was in the great battle at the gates of Moscow" (938). What Napoleon and most of his hearers do not expect is that after "the great battle" has ended, for one-quarter of the men who fought at Borodino, these commendations will be heard *in absentia*, for their bodies will have been interred in mass graves hundreds of miles from their homes.

The Battle of Borodino begins at dawn on August 26, 1812. Napoleon already has issued orders that, in theory, should guide the movements of the French and their allies all across the broad line of battle. In reality, however, as Tolstoy carefully considers each segment of Napoleon's plan, this is not the case. Despite his supposed military genius, Napoleon gives commands for four distinct attacks and marches that, for one reason or another, do not achieve the desired results. Problems arise right at the start, after the emperor has placed batteries of artillery at certain locations in preparation for bombarding the Russian batteries arrayed on the opposite side. The firing by "one hundred and two guns" (940) begins at daybreak but fails to do much damage, because "from the spots designated by Napoleon, the projectiles did not carry to the Russian works" (940). Therefore, like General Lee on the last day of the Battle of Gettysburg, the emperor will have to send columns of unprotected foot soldiers into an inferno of cannon and musket fire that should have been neutralized early. Napoleon's second and third orders affect the advances of separate infantry divisions. One is supposed to "turn the Russian left flank" while another, in the center, must move "through the wood to take the first entrenchment" (941). But well before these objectives are even in sight, difficult terrain and determined Russian defenders block the advances in both sectors. The fourth order directs a column to "take the village (Borodino)" (941) and then join accompanying forces to capture the redoubt dominating the heights above the town. The redoubt is not taken for the same reason the preceding objectives are not met: the Russians engage the enemy early in cramped surroundings and stand firm, holding their ground though outnumbered and outgunned, with an obstinacy and tenacity the French cannot break. As these attacks and counterattacks ebb and flow, Napoleon ceases to direct events. Stationed well behind the battle lines and blinded by the smoke produced by so much firing, he is in no position to issue follow-up commands. He mostly receives messages requesting reinforcements, which he is reluctant to authorize since he resists pouring every soldier he has into what seems like a meat grinder devouring men, animals, and materiel indiscriminately.

But neither the impracticality of Napoleon's directives nor his remoteness is to blame for the battle's character and contour. As Tolstoy stresses throughout *War and Peace*, mortal human beings do not control their destinies. He reiterates this fundamental Russian truth in his dissection of the course of action at Borodino, emphasizing "that the course of world events is predetermined from on high, and depends on the coincidence of the wills of all who participate in those events and that the influence of a Napoleon on the course of such events is purely superficial and imaginary" (942). The "coincidence of the wills" of all the soldiers who fight in the battle is the determining factor: "At the battle of Borodino Napoleon did not fire a shot and did not kill anyone. All that was done by the soldiers" who fought "by their own volition" (943). Napoleon plays a part laid out for him by destiny. He acts out the role of commander, creating the illusion that he is the grand master of the bloody chess match playing out in front of him. Every move in this match, however, is decided by "the wills of hundreds of thousands of men" (943) acting on their own and making split-second decisions without guidance or influence from anyone in authority.

The "coincidence of the wills" of many individuals is an abstraction. To understand at the micro level what this concept entails, one must be among some of the thousands and observe firsthand how they respond to what is happening all around them. This is what Pierre does as the conflict begins. At first, he is "spellbound by the beauty of the scene" as the "slanting rays of the bright sun" create in the clouds of smoke swirling above the firing "a rosy, golden light streaked with long dark shadows" (948). These dreamy aesthetic impressions may temporarily obscure the horrors such weaponry causes, but as he tours the lines in the company of a staff officer he knows, Pierre is quickly jolted back to earth, especially by the sight of "wounded men, frantically staggering along or being carried on stretchers" (951). This is only the beginning. Still acting as an observer of rather than a participant in the action, Pierre climbs up a barely fortified knoll, which will later become famous as the "Knoll Battery or Rayevsky's Redoubt," an entrenchment for artillery that will be recognized later as "the most important point of the battle" (952). Around this position, "tens of thousands" (952) will contend, as first the French overrun the Russian defenses and then the Russians counterattack and drive them back, much like the back-and forth struggle of the French and Germans to capture or hold Fort Douamont at Verdun in 1916.

Pierre, of course, cannot imagine how dramatic and how perilous the hours ahead will be as he moves among the Russian troops manning the batteries on the knoll. Though he is a civilian, and with his corpulence and elegant attire a rather exotic one, Pierre wins the affection and respect of these rough-and-ready men, who refer to him as "our gentleman" (953). With the firing growing more intense as the morning proceeds and with causalities mounting, the men in the redoubt realize they are in danger, but they remain "cheerful" (954), nonetheless. They react to bombardment and to the loss of comrades in the most unexpected way, with "heightened" (955) exhilaration. But this is not the exhilaration of carefree *joie de vivre*; it is rather the byproduct of fierce determination and resolve, an intensification of the patriotic fervor that animates all the Russian people in their herculean effort to expel those who are despoiling the motherland:

> *Lightning flashes of a hidden, blazing fire, like those of an approaching thunder cloud, flamed in the faces of the men (as if to counteract what was happening) with increasing brightness and frequency. Pierre did not look out at the battlefield, and was not concerned to know what was going on there; he was wholly absorbed in contemplating this fire that burned ever more brightly, and which he felt was burning in his own soul too.* (955)

The urge to contribute to this collective effort to retain the redoubt inspires Pierre to do something beyond just encouraging the troops. When the batteries start to run low on ammunition, he impulsively volunteers to run to the storage wagons in the rear and bring back the "grapeshot" (956) needed for close combat. In doing so, he bonds more deeply with his brave comrades, who continue to stand their ground indomitably. Pierre's "baptism by fire" occurs as he nears the powder wagon.

An enemy artillery round strikes this wagon, and "a violent concussion" (957) knocks Pierre to the ground. He survives, like Prince Andrei at Austerlitz, but is too stunned, disoriented, and terrified to do anything except run back to the battery empty-handed. His wounds are those of a combatant, one of that "whole nation" throwing itself against the invaders. From this time on, Pierre will no longer agonize over life's purpose or meaning. He will find purpose and meaning aplenty in doing his part, first to liberate and then, later, take his rightful place in the life of his homeland.

Returning to the knoll, Pierre runs headlong into a French officer, one of the attackers who has penetrated the redoubt's defenses. Though the civilian is unarmed and injured and the officer has a sword, Pierre summons up his reserves of strength and willpower that always have enabled him to subdue an antagonist regardless of circumstances. He quickly overcomes the officer, while a Russian countercharge regains control of the position. Pierre's elation, however, is tempered as he gazes about, realizing that "of that little family circle that had accepted him as one of themselves not one was left" (958). All have perished without leaving their posts.

Pierre's comrades are not alone in their heroic endurance. As the battle rages, Napoleon and his staff sense that this engagement will not end in decisive victory—that is, the rout of the enemy—but will instead drag on for eight more bloody hours with immense loss of life and no clear result. For the exasperated French, the hard fact is that unlike all previous foes, the Russians are not breaking under pressure, not surrendering even when surrounded, not fleeing the field in panic, not yielding when overrun but regrouping and continuing to attack, thereby tying up and wearing down the *Grande Armee*. This battle of attrition is grinding up units, leading Napoleon, for the first time in his career as a military commander, to contemplate the possibility of defeat: "In previous battles he had considered only the chances of success; now a multitude of possible disasters suggested themselves, and he anticipated them all" (965). He is compelled by his circumstances to hold back his reserves for possible use later. Thus, when a general late in the afternoon proposes "to lead the Old Guard into attack," Napoleon replies with stark and uncharacteristic apprehension, "At eight hundred leagues from France, I do not intend to have my Guard destroyed!" (966)

On the other side, Kutusov is content to issue only a few general instructions and then await the outcome. His vast experience has taught him that "it is impossible for one man to direct hundreds of thousands of men struggling with death" (967), so he refrains from any useless command interference, trusting in "that intangible force called the spirit of the army, and he took cognizance of that force and guided it insofar as it lay in his power" (967). His trust is justified. As the French attacks peter out and darkness draws near, Kutusov is convinced the great battle has been won, since the Russians all along the front have repelled attack after attack. They have fought their enemy to a standstill and can claim to have won by not losing. The commander in chief is so sure of this that when General de Tolly sends his adjutant to Kutusov with this report: "All points of our position are in the hands of the enemy and they cannot be driven back . . .; the men are running away and it is impossible to stop them" (969), His Serene Highness is anything but serene. He refuses to credit the emissary's report: "The enemy has been repulsed on the left, and defeated on the right flank" (969). Kutusov then announces his "firm intention to attack the enemy tomorrow" (969), just as Napoleon fears. This optimism and resolve invigorate the troops, who hear his order of the day gratefully. To "the exhausted and unnerved men" (970) of Borodino, Kutusov's willingness to continue the epic effort to liberate Russia is confirmation of their achievement in halting the French all along the battlefront and creating the conditions for decisive triumph the next day. With characteristic humility and faith, the commander in chief concludes this day by thanking God and his "brave army" (969) for all that has occurred, crossing himself and sobbing unashamedly as he prays.

One, however, who cannot feel rewarded by Kutusov's order of the day is Prince Andrei Bolkonsky. In his second major battle, he suffers another serious injury when an artillery projectile explodes near him, causing a severe wound to his abdomen. The prince is carried to a crowded aid station, where a medic dresses his wound as best he can. In his helplessness and pain, Prince Andrei has been asking himself questions very similar to those existential inquiries that he has tried to answer over a lifetime: "But isn't it all the same now?" he thought, "And what will it be like there . . . and what has it been here?" (975). After he was hit at Austerlitz, Prince Andrei felt himself being uplifted to a heavenly realm where only love and mercy reign. Now lying on a table at the station and hearing the cries and moans of so many comrades, the prince experiences something like a gift from God once again. Looking about, he recognizes "a miserable, sobbing, feeble man whose leg had just been amputated" (978). This is none other than Prince Anatol Kuragin, the spoiled rogue who tried to abduct his fiancée and with whom he once longed to fight a duel. At this moment, however, as Prince Andrei sees Anatol staring at him "in confusion through tears that filled his swollen eyes" (978), all thoughts of vengeance vanish. Andrei responds to a fellow sufferer, a man like him, whom war's arbitrary fate is condemning to a life of weakness and dependence. The man whose striking looks and proud stature once commanded everyone's attention, has become in an instant a doddering old man, who will spend whatever days he may have left being led by another and moving about with aching deliberation. Prince Andrei is moved by charity, the greatest of the theological virtues, as he contemplates this human ruin and is able through the grace of God to understand how "love for our brothers, for those who love us and for those who hate us, love for our enemies" (978) is what finally matters. This realization unites him with Princess Marya, whose life of devoted service and humble acceptance of trial and sorrow exemplifies the self-abnegation at the heart of Russian Christianity. The prince knows that his wound is probably mortal, but he bravely will offer up his life for his nation and accept without bitterness whatever injuries people like Anatol and Natasha have inflicted upon him and whatever other disappointments his life has brought, secure and at peace in the knowledge that he has "fought the good fight" and "kept the faith."

In the evening of August 26, 1812, Napoleon Bonaparte is morose. Even though by any reasonable standard he has won at Borodino, the Russians have absorbed the loss of "*one half* of their army" (983) and continue to menace his position with the possibility of a counteroffensive the following day. Allied casualties are not as severe as those of the Russians, but they are more damaging since the Imperial Army cannot be reinforced so far from its bases in Western Europe. All that this most resourceful commander can do is dig in and await developments as he prepares to "fulfill the cruel, grievous, harsh, and inhuman role that was predestined for him" (980). What Napoleon cannot admit is the fact that a people he despises as ignorant and superstitious have come away from the field with "a moral victory—one that convinces the enemy of the moral superiority of its foe and of its own moral impotence" (984). In much the same way, in December 1941, Adolf Hitler's invading army was thrown back within sight of Moscow when fresh Russian troops, brought to the front from Siberia, mounted a surprise counterattack. This so unnerved the Nazis, who thought the Russian campaign was going to culminate in victory very soon, that even though they and their allies managed to regroup, they never again would be able to summon the energy, courage, or spirit a conquering force must have to conclude a protracted conflict. The endgame took another four years to unfold, but it was apparent as the snow began to fall in the autumn of 1941 that the Soviet Union was going to prevail. The same phenomenon will guarantee the triumph of the Russians in 1812. The "mortal wound" (984) received at Borodino will doom the *Grande Armee* from that day forward.

PART THREE

Kutusov's order to his troops to prepare to attack the enemy the day after the battle (August 27) turns out to have been based on false assumptions. Shortly after issuing it, the commander in chief receives reports of "unheard of losses, of the loss of half the army" (989), so he quickly concludes, like Napoleon, that he cannot risk the consequences of a second day of carnage, especially a day on which his army must attack and expose so many men to the deadly defensive fire his troops inflicted on the French on the twenty-sixth. Consequently, "despite the strength of feeling that had arisen in all ranks" (989) only a day earlier, Kutusov orders a strategic withdrawal beyond the capital, in effect handing Moscow to the invaders. In doing so, Kutusov, the supreme professional, yields to the inescapable realities confronting him. In a matter of a few hours, he has learned enough about his army's condition to upset previous calculations and cancel the attack that was supposed to end the war with a decisive Russian victory. Because no man can "at any moment be in a position to consider the total impact of the event that is occurring" (990), Kutusov has to rescind his previous directive and leave Holy Moscow naked to its enemies, an act for which no Russian commander at any time in history could ever bear responsibility.

As he and his staff reach Moscow's outskirts, Kutusov has to meet face to face with a distinguished delegation of officers and civic officials, who gather around their commander in chief as an informal "council of war" (992). He listens uncomfortably to the opinions expressed by speaker after speaker regarding the army's position, the possibility of withstanding a siege, the poor communication between His Serene Highness and the city's leaders that has led to widespread confusion, and so on; he even finds himself "on the spot" within his command as fellow officers, notably Benningsen, maneuver to make Kutusov's military decisions the cause of "the crime of abandoning Moscow" (993). Such talk and such insinuations muddy the waters but produce no realistic alternative strategy. The fact is, "all the officers of the high command" (992–93) consider a battle before the gates of Moscow "hopeless" (993), so no last-ditch effort to save the city can be entertained. Relying on his colleagues' recommendations and his "own judgment, be it good or bad" (994), Kutusov leaves the Muscovites with no grounds for hope that their city might be saved. The commander in chief ends this consultation, and a subsequent one with his suite, by giving the "order to retreat" (996), something he does with a heavy heart but in the certainty that the "present deliberations could not alter the inevitable course of events, and that Moscow was in effect already abandoned" (996). His last words on this occasion echo sentiments he has expressed throughout the campaign, to wit, that the French and their allies "shall eat horseflesh yet, like the Turks!" (997), an eventuality he now looks upon as unavoidable, just like the abandonment of Moscow.

The people of the capital respond to the approaching danger very much like the people of Smolensk and every small town or village in the invaders' path did. In accord with an "underlying (latent) patriotism" which "is present in the soul of every Russian" (998), the wealthy lock up their properties and flee with only a few retainers and possessions, while the poorer classes scavenge over what is left, a rather idiosyncratic expression of patriotism. The governor-general of Moscow, Count Rostopchin, denounces those who go away but to no avail. He spends precious hours giving contradictory orders and drowning in confusion, not realizing the "significance of what was happening" (999), like one of Tolstoy's ineffectual generals trying to direct a battle raging in many places out of sight and hidden by smoke. He is, in desperation, "trying with his puny hand now to speed, now to stem the tide of the prodigious, popular torrent that was bearing him along with it" (1000). The city's civic authorities join the rest of the population in retreating like the army, but, in so doing, all these together unknowingly will bring about "that momentous event . . . which will remain forever the supreme glory of the Russian people" (999).

Moscow's abandonment, indeed, is the "momentous event" that will save Russia. Napoleon and his army will enter a municipality resembling an ancient ruin; soon, fires will be breaking out in widely separated districts, because "a great city of wooden buildings deserted by its inhabitants must inevitably be burned down" (999). The emperor will try to normalize the occupation by promising amnesty to his enemies, assuring artisans and peasants fair market prices for their goods and crops, and making magnanimity his guiding principle, but none of his high-minded proposals will have any impact. The Russians regard loss and deprivation as less oppressive than living "under the control of the French" (998), so they will pay no attention to Napoleon's blandishments. Sitting alone in the ghostly Kremlin is like being in an echo chamber, where silence is broken only by the emperor's own words reverberating over and over. Reduced to a dependence on his defeated foe's cooperation to extricate himself and his army from imminent catastrophe, Napoleon will send Jacques Lauriston, a former ambassador to Russia, to Kutusov's headquarters to begin peace negotiations. His Serene Highness will receive Lauriston politely and agree to consult with the tsar on the French proposals, but he knows nothing will come of this overture and that the beginning of the end of the French occupation is at hand. In his helplessness, Napoleon has sent through Lauriston an aggrieved plea from a supposed conqueror, who believes he has checkmated an opponent legitimately and should be recognized as the chess game's winner. Napoleon does not understand that his adversary is proceeding according to a wholly different set of rules. Even though the French will have attained their primary objective by capturing the Russian capital, nothing really will change. Moscow will become a profound liability, since a surrender will not follow the city's loss; the enemy's forces will still actively resist; the French will lose freedom of movement as their troops idle away precious weeks; and the war will go on.

While all of this drama is occurring in and around Moscow, with the enemy at the gates, properties and possessions left willy-nilly, and thousands fleeing for their lives, Countess Elena Bezukhova and her society friends in St. Petersburg remain comfortably ensconced, aloof, and absorbed in private affairs. The countess's "affairs," in particular. are creating complications. In Pierre's absence, she has been enjoying the company of an elderly but well-connected gentleman as well as the attentions of a young foreign prince. She needs somehow "to preserve her intimate relations with two men without offending either of them" (1000). Thus, while Pierre has been standing tall with his battery mates at Borodino, ready, if so destined, to die for Russia, his wife has been scheming to betray both. Not only is she openly unfaithful to her husband; in her eagerness to find a solution to the tensions of her compromised love life, the countess is willing to renounce her membership in the Russian Orthodox Church, under whose icons the army is fighting to save Mother Russia. Following the counsels of French Jesuit priests, Elena is "received into the true Catholic Church," whose spiritual leader, the pope himself, will "soon be apprised of her case and send her a certain document" (1002). In the meantime, she will ask Pierre for a divorce, which, in her egotism, she is sure he will agree to readily. Once this is granted, the countess can, as Bilibin advises, "marry the old Count," making "his last days happy" (1005); once he is dead, "as the widow of a great lord" (1005), she can marry the young lover with the blessing of her new church and the two can live happily ever after.

In Dostoevsky's novel, *The Possessed,* his dissection of the socialist/atheistic revolutionary forces that in the late nineteenth century were recruiting disillusioned young people from throughout the nation, Shatov, a former revolutionary turned believer, reminds Stavrogin, a former believer turned revolutionary, of what the latter once asserted so strongly: "One who is not Russian Orthodox cannot be a Russian" (Trans. Andrew McAndrew, New York: The New American Library, 1962, p. 235), but the countess is so far removed from sentiments like these she is virtually deracinated.

Here is illustrated ethical indifference on a grand scale, with representatives of a great world religion allowing themselves to be manipulated by a privileged narcissist into justifying blatant immorality and with almost every prominent voice in Petersburg society acquiescing in the countess's farcical behavior for "fear of betraying one's stupidity and lack of *savoire faire*" (1004). Only Marya Dmitrievna dissents, describing Elena's conduct as identical to what is "done in all the brothels!" (1004) But since this outspoken lady is "regarded as something of a buffoon" (1004) in cosmopolitan Petersburg, no one pays much attention to her. This episode is in microcosm Petersburg at its most cynical, where black is really white and where what matters most is not adherence to accepted principles and practices but simply that which facilitates pleasure and freedom. The sacrifice and patriotism of Moscow and the heartland do not resonate in the personal and social lives of Petersburg's elite. These individuals occupy a parallel universe outside the Russian orbit, one in which nothing matches the rest of the country.

Pierre Bezukhov is with "the rest of the country," and he is inspired and uplifted by what his brothers and sisters together have managed to achieve. After the battle, he leaves the redoubt for the last time, marveling still at its indomitable defenders, the bodies of most of whom have been carried to the rear for anonymous burial in mass graves. Over time, their decaying flesh and bones will become part of the nation's soil, nurturing new life for Mother Russia. For the present, Pierre walks on the ground so recently fought over with unparalleled fury and, as night falls, tries to rest for a time in peace and quiet under the stars. He is soon awakened by "three soldiers . . . dragging some brushwood after them" (1008) and preparing to cook a simple meal over a fire. They are kind and courteous to the "nobleman" (1008), immediately seeing through Pierre's attempts to "minimize as far as possible his social position in order to be closer and more comprehensible to the soldiers" (1008), something his wife and her privileged company would never do. The men share their meal with him, and Pierre finds it in his harsh conditions "more delicious than anything he had ever eaten" (1008). His companions then go out of their way to guide him to "Mozhaisk in the pitch-dark" (1009), where Pierre somehow finds his groom and takes leave of his new friends with gratitude and admiration. Reflecting on his experience at the battle and its aftermath later, he dwells on "the soldiers, those who had been at the battery, those who had given him food, and those who had prayed before the icon," remaining "steadfast and strong" (1010) to the end. He also dreams of hearing a voice praising the "simplicity" of the common recruits: "*They* do not talk but act" (1011). The voice counsels Pierre not to let "fear" guide his actions, as he believes it did during the battle: "Man can have dominion over nothing so long as he fears death, but he who fears it not, possesses all. If there were no suffering, man would not know his limitations, would not know himself" (1011). Pierre is acquiring truth through suffering, as Aeschylus taught centuries before and as Russia collectively has just learned. He is gradually throwing off "the superfluous, the diabolical, the whole burden of this outer man" (1010) to become a vessel receptive to and radiating for all the wisdom that comes to the simple and the fearless through suffering. As his wife and the circles among whom she moves wander farther and farther away from the Russian nation's people, traditions, customs, and values, Pierre is absorbing and embracing these with renewed fervor.

Pierre's suffering is not inflicted exclusively by war. Almost as soon as he arrives in Moscow, Pierre is summoned by the governor-general of the city, Count Rostopchin himself. Their meeting is brief and tense. Rostopchin addresses Pierre as "the great warrior" (1016), more in sarcasm than commendation. He also tells him he has heard of Pierre's "prowess" (1016), a totally inappropriate term for a civilian who clumsily and fearfully did whatever he could to assist truly brave men of prowess at the battery. Changing the subject abruptly, the count asks Pierre if he is "a Mason" (1016). Pierre admits he is, whereupon Rostopchin advises him to "break off relations" with his brothers in the lodge, lest he suffer the same fate as Speransky and his associates, "who, under the guise of erecting the Temple of Solomon, have tried to ruin the temple of their fatherland" (1016). He admonishes Pierre "as a father would do" (1016), insisting that he "clear out as soon as possible" (1017) and ending the interview with an allusion to Countess Elena's consultations with "the holy fathers of the Society of Jesus" (1017). In making these points, Rostopchin is doing Pierre a favor. The atmosphere in Moscow is becoming too oppressive; everyone who does not toe the patriotic line without question or doubt is under suspicion. Already a tradesman has been imprisoned for circulating a proclamation about the defense of Moscow that the governor-general considers treasonous. Since Pierre has accepted papers from the "Director of our Post Office" (1016), whom Rostopchin believes colluded with the tradesman, he likewise could be culpable in something similar. After all, Pierre is, by his own admission, a Mason, whom xenophobic patriots associate with the West, and his wife is consorting with French Jesuits, betraying, by so doing, the national church. If he remains in the city, Pierre will have to walk on egg shells, keeping a low profile and saying little.

Pierre leaves Count Rostopchin's study "glowering with rage and more angry than he had ever been known to look before" (1017). He reaches home, only to be greeted in the evening by "eight different people" (1017), all of them wishing to talk about entirely different subjects. Pierre responds listlessly to their questions and concerns, saying whatever is necessary to conclude each conversation quickly. Thoroughly fatigued, he reads his wife's letter asking for a divorce with the same disinterest, as if this issue were someone else's to decide. The next morning, more guests arrive, as well as a police official sent by Rostopchin to see if Pierre has left the capital yet. Realizing that he cannot spend any more time on business affairs or household management and that the higher calling of sacrifice for and commitment to Russia must absorb all his attention from now on, Pierre sneaks out his home's back door, taking with him nothing of value and leaving his retainers to organize matters as best they can. The man who has been told to let go of "the superfluous, the diabolical, the whole burden of the outer man" (1010) now must include the Masonic lodge, his household, his social and business circle, and his wife, more estranged than ever, in these categories. He is being stripped of all that can distract him, becoming through this purgation more simple and more human than he could ever be otherwise.

In another part of Moscow, a different mood prevails. The Rostovs are preparing to leave the city too, but given Count Ilya's "inveterate carelessness" (1019), they cannot do so expeditiously. The countess does not mind waiting, though, since her younger son, Petya, will soon arrive to bid everyone in the household farewell before joining the regiment Pierre has been raising. She believes, like most mothers, she can keep her impetuous boy soldier "under her wing" (1019) while he is in proximity and can continue to try to use whatever influence she and her husband can summon "to have him assigned to serve where there would be no possibility of his taking part in a battle" (1019). Upon his arrival, Petya senses this intention and reacts "coldly" (1019) to his mother's solicitude. He spends most of his time at home with Natasha, "for whom he had aways had a brotherly affection that was very special and almost lover-like" (1019). The countess accepts this unpleasantness with good grace, particularly now that it appears Nikolai Rostov and Princess Marya Bolkonskaya will soon be engaged, something she welcomes happily as a gift to the Rostovs from "the hand of Providence" (1021). Sonya knows that such a match offers "the only possibility of mending the Rostovs' fortunes" (1021), so despite her bitter disappointment, she soldiers on, throwing herself into managing the "sorting and packing of the household goods" (1021). Petya and Natasha pay little attention to the impending danger and contribute almost nothing to the family's efforts to gather and secure what needs to be taken away. More like spoiled children than responsible young adults, Petya takes delight in his status as "a fine young man" while Natasha basks in the glow of her brother's "adoration," which acts as "the lubricant necessary for keeping the wheels of her mechanism running smoothly" (1021). These two are also energized by the excitement the activities all around them are causing; in such a whirl, boredom and melancholy have no place. Health and vigor allow the Rostovs to rise above the city's travail and face the hard times ahead without undue anxiety.

Natasha also is engaged in separating herself from her old life, just as Pierre has been, although with far less awareness. As she sits "on the floor in her dismantled room," looking over items from her past "strewn about her," she finds an "old ball dress, the very one (now out of fashion) which she had worn to her first ball in Petersburg" (1022). She loses herself briefly in memories of that special night but is quickly brought back to the present as a wagon conveying a number of wounded soldiers passes the Rostov home. She impulsively asks their commander if some of his men might stay in the house, since the family will soon be leaving. He readily agrees, and from this point on, sibling adoration, ball gowns, and happy memories will cease to matter for Natasha. She will become, like Pierre, a dedicated and ever-present help for those who, through no fault of their own, are in desperate straits. Petya, too, gets over his nonchalance, goes out with a friend to try to obtain a transfer to a unit in active service, and prepares to obtain weapons at the Kremlin, with which he expects to help defend the city as the French attack.

The night before the Rostovs' departure, after Sonya and Natasha have directed the packing of only the most valuable or necessary family possessions, leaving behind a varied pile of *bric a brac*, a valet attending one of the wounded inquires about the possibility of housing yet one more man in the Rostovs' home. With a doctor and two enlisted men escorting the sufferer's calash, the household staff conclude that the wounded officer "must be a very important person" (1027). The valet explains that they cannot keep traveling to the man's own Moscow home because it is too far away and deserted and the officer's condition is deteriorating. The Rostovs' domestic servant, taking his lead from Natasha, invites the victim to stay with them since more room will soon be available. As they carry the man inside, however, one retainer, Maura Kuzminishna, experiences the shock of recognition. The wounded officer is none other than Prince Andrei Bolkonsky, once the fiancé of Natasha Rostova.

This is hardly a stroke of unalloyed good fortune for the prince, despite the comforts afforded by "the Rostovs' staid, old-fashioned house" (1028). The wounded already there know that they will be helpless once the family departs and that they could well face mass execution by the French occupiers if a triage crisis develops in the city. Several begin to implore the

Rostovs to allow them small spaces in one or more of "the thirty peasant carts that had come in from their country estates" (1029). Count Ilya Rostov, the soul of generosity, at first agrees to take one wounded officer; immediately, others begin begging for the same consideration. Soon, the count is ordering crates to be unpacked and items like pictures and ornamental decorations be discarded to create more spaces in the carts, which are beginning to resemble lifeboats. Seeing what her husband is doing, the countess objects strongly: "Say what you like, it's the government's business to look after the wounded" (1031), but to no avail. Natasha intervenes forcefully at this point, serving as the voice for all that is best in the Rostovs' character as she remonstrates with her mother and stresses that all the possessions being left behind are not as valuable as a human life. The Countess relents, murmuring in delight, "the chicks are teaching the hen" (1034). The chicks are also thorough:

> *But once the work of unloading had begun there was no stopping it. It seemed not to matter whether all or only half of the things were left behind. Cases full of china, bronzes, pictures, and mirrors that had been so carefully packed the night before now lay strewn about the yard, and still they sought and managed to find it possible to take out this or that and let the men have yet another wagon.* (1035)

Here, Natasha and her family perform an act comparable to Pierre's sacrifice as he leaves his Moscow residence for the last time: they strip away the baggage that is weighing them down and free themselves to offer aid and comfort unimpeded wherever they can. They become more and more authentically themselves, laying bare the "souls of the just," an inscription that should be prominently displayed on the Rostovs' coat of arms.

Their leave-taking is emotional, as each member of the family crosses himself or herself in front of the icons and embraces the household's servants, who will stay behind. Their long caravan of wagons moves out at last; most of the conveyances carry wounded soldiers, including Prince Andrei and men from a neighboring home, rather than family possessions. They depart while the Russian Army is retreating beyond the capital, making its occupation a foregone conclusion. Pierre is not among these men, women, and children desperate to leave a doomed home. Though he is no longer in his residence, he is still in Moscow, lingering in the home of his former Masonic mentor and guide, Josef Bazdeyev. While there, Pierre spends a great deal of time brooding in his friend's library, ignoring the impending danger and turning over in his mind all that has happened in so short a time. Far from feeling renewed in mind and heart, as he did after Borodino, Pierre is listless and apathetic, acting more like a prisoner awaiting sentencing, with "everything . . . at an end, in chaos, falling to pieces, and . . . no escape from the situation" (1041).

Outside the walls, Napoleon and his troops, unimpeded since the battle, arrive at the gates of Moscow on September 2, 1812. Beautiful late summer weather enhances the city's magnificent architecture, more native Russian and Asiatic than the Western-inspired styles of St. Petersburg. Napoleon gazes in admiration at the colorful domes, vaults, and minarets in their "Oriental beauty that lay before him for the first time" (1045). He resolves to treat with respect and charity the people who have erected such awe-inspiring edifices; he will "spare" Holy Moscow and "her golden domes and crosses sparkling and quivering in the sunlight" (1046). At the same time, however, he will become for the Muscovites and their compatriots throughout Russia a new Moses: "From the heights of the Kremlin . . . I will give them just laws, teach them the meaning of true civilization, and make generations of boyars remember their conqueror with love" (1046). Dazzled by this prospect, the emperor sends out a "brilliant suite of adjutants . . . to fetch the boyars" (1046), and as he awaits what he expects to be a large delegation, he goes over the speech he will make and fantasizes how at assemblies in the palace of the tsars, Russian and French dignitaries in the weeks ahead will mingle freely in concord and with common purpose. Napoleon will "shower his bounty" (1046) liberally, especially on Moscow's numerous charitable institutions, which he will endow in his mother's name.

These ambitious goals and aspirations are destined never to be realized. The deputation that is supposed to gather the boyars does not find a single one. Except for "mobs of drunken men" (1047), the city is mostly empty. No one, however, including top subordinates, has the courage to so inform Napoleon because such a reversal of normal formalities may subject "His Majesty . . . to *le ridicule*" (1047). In truth, nonetheless, Moscow has refused to follow the script laid out by the European choreographers of the art of war. If a capital city finds itself unable to resist capture and occupation by an enemy, its civic leaders have no choice except to surrender and ask for terms. Ever since medieval times, dignitaries from cities throughout Western Europe have solemnly approached their conquerors outside the gates with keys and ceremonial swords and other regalia, bowing in deference and with grave courtesy acknowledging their defeat and swearing fealty to their new masters. Titian's *"The Surrender at Breda"* vividly portrays such a scene in the Thirty Years War. But Napoleon in 1812 is in a Eurasian capital, where such rituals are not common and where death is preferable to capitulation. Moscow's abandonment is the equivalent of a death sentence for the city, now "empty as a queenless dying hive is empty" (1049) and soon to be on fire. Napoleon contemplates this emptiness with astonishment, as it slowly dawns on him that he has entered a *terra incognita* where all previous experience is irrelevant, and no existing guides or models can chart a course he may follow with confidence in the outcome.

Although the city is practically deserted as Napoleon prepares to enter, in the days before, confusion and disorder have been rampant. In addition to the city's residents walking or riding out of every neighborhood, columns of Russian soldiers have had to move through Moscow to reach bridges outside the capital leading to safety. But as the bridges fill with slow-moving civilians pushing and pulling their heavy loads over the long spans, the military units have been forced to halt. When these delays multiply, a number of impatient soldiers break away from their places, enter the many shops and trading areas near the Kremlin, and begin looting freely. Their loads of plundered goods, food, and beverages create even more difficulties as horses and wagons strain to transport the added weight. Groups of drunken laborers and artisans, left to their own devices by the fleeing gentry and merchants, mill about as well, provoking tensions as tempers rise and altercations ensue. Even the chief of police is reluctant to have his men intervene in such violent and potentially deadly affairs. The impotence of legally constituted authority is sensed by all, and an "every man for himself" syndrome starts to develop, causing more breakdown.

The highest authority, Governor-General Rostopchin, is the epitome of ineffectuality. He fears that the so-called rabble remaining in Moscow after the troops file away will become more and more of a threat to public order, but he does not have "the slightest understanding of the people he supposed himself to be governing, all his patriotic sentiments notwithstanding" (1061). Rabble or not, they need and want law and order to prevail. Rostopchin tries to promote positive thinking in the capital by sending out broadsheets emphasizing solidarity and unity; most, however, pay little attention to such exhortations, especially since events playing out before their eyes contradict Rostopchin's words. Though he has been informed early that Moscow cannot be defended and Kutusov's army is retreating past the city, the governor-general stays in denial, doing nothing to prepare for this eventuality and leaving everyone from high officials to the poorest laborers to fend for themselves. In the midst of this unprecedented crisis, the man who has long considered himself "indispensable" to civic and political harmony acts like a ship's captain in a powerful storm or like a military commander in the midst of a battle not proceeding according to plan; each is "suddenly reduced" from the one in charge to "a useless, insignificant, feeble man" (1063).

Rostopchin cannot bear what is occurring, nor can he accept marginalization. In his desperation to reassert legitimate authority, he loses sight of exactly what this entails. As his sense of balance and his self-control are strained by duress, and as the departure of the troops leaves him with little back-up, Rostopchin yields to fear. Feeling pressured by a restive crowd gathered outside his residence, he deflects their interest away from himself by inciting them to act as vigilantes and execute "the villain who has brought about the ruin of Moscow" (1065). This is the young man, Vereshchagin, arrested days before for distributing allegedly seditious pamphlets, read by, among others, Pierre Bezukhov. How one obscure man's writings could bring about a great capital's downfall is not explained, but the crowd does not wait for anything more to be said. Rostopchin has aroused a mob's blood lust, and nothing now can prevent the awful *denouement*. The governor-general orders the prisoner released to the savage horde and thereby saves himself at the expense of honor and integrity. Law enforcement is complicit, with constables watching impassively while the scapegoat is beaten to death in minutes. Dragging the victim's mangled body across the courtyard afterwards, the police are not gentle, hurrying away as "the gory, begrimed, half-shaven head on the long neck turned from side to side as it trailed along the ground" (1068). The count suffers guilt, shame, and remorse later, but suppresses all these painful emotions as authority figures in similar straits always do: "But I did not do it on my own account. I had to act that way . . . The mob, the traitor . . . public welfare" (1071).

The French arrive in the capital shortly thereafter "in good order" (1074). This order, however, disintegrates rapidly once the soldiers stand down and begin exploring the city. Soon they are breaking into the boarded-up homes of wealthy Muscovites like the Rostovs, who, as we have seen, in their haste to escape and save as many wounded soldiers as possible, have had to leave numerous valuables behind. The sight of all this booty, plus the inebriating effects of the wine and vodka discovered in most of these domiciles, turns the French troopers into "marauders" (1074), no different from the Russian plunderers just recently departed. The French invaders will remain in

Moscow five more weeks, during which they will cease to be an "army" (1074)—that is, a disciplined body guided by rules and principles and responsive to superiors' commands. They will have been transformed, instead, into a lawless gang of criminals, ignoring order after order banning all thievery. Indeed, as the officers see what the men are taking from the city's empty houses and businesses, many commanders allow themselves to be "drawn into doing the same" (1075). When finally the troops are ordered to leave the city and begin their long march home, what would be a challenging retreat in even ideal conditions will turn into an agonizing *via crucis*, made worse by the enormous loads of stolen property and merchandise each man tries to carry back with him. In his greed, the individual looter resembles "a monkey that puts its paw into the narrow neck of a jug, and having seized a handful of nuts, will not open its fist for fear of losing its booty, thereby bringing about its own undoing" (1074). Only later on, as the French slowly make their way back to Vilna, will the "undoing" caused by their behavior set in: animals will break under their extra burdens, items will be left all over the countryside, and Cossack guerillas will take for themselves whatever they find when a horse falls or a soldier cannot move any further.

Even before the disastrous retreat, the French occupiers have more to handle than stolen goods. Owing to the enormous supply of wood in the vast Russian forests, Moscow in 1812 is filled with mostly wooden structures. These buildings are threatened by "soldiers who smoke pipes, make campfires of Senate chairs in the Senate Square, and cook themselves meals twice a day" (1076). Though any "abandoned city built of wood and occupied by a foreign army!" (1076) is vulnerable to random fires no matter how carefully people behave, in Moscow, beginning on the evening of September 16, flare-ups occur in widely separated parts of the city almost simultaneously, straining men and resources severely. Although Tolstoy is reluctant in the novel to indict Governor-General Rostopchin for instigating and orchestrating the burning of the capital, we know from Caulaincourt's *Memoirs* that the count played the key role in this catastrophic destruction. Many of the arsonists caught in the act of setting fires testified that they had been recruited by the governor-general himself and were acting in concert with others to maximize the flames' impact; in addition, Caulaincourt was shown special "inflammable fuses, all made in the same fashion and placed in different public and private buildings" (121) throughout the city to serve as primary accelerants. Moscow's fires cause more than haphazard damage; they devour so much habitable space, provisions, water, and human energy as to make life for the occupiers increasingly difficult. All of this loss and misery results from the wholly unprecedented and, to the French, wholly irrational Russian preference for sacrifice rather than surrender. The capital's "citizens, instead of receiving the French with the bread and salt of hospitality and the keys to the city, abandoned her" (1076).

One of those still in the city understands why the people of Moscow are casting away property and possessions and refusing to deal with the French in any way. Pierre Bezukhov has been holed up in Josif Alekseyevich Bazdeyev's home for days, ostensibly to organize and catalogue his friend's library but really "to escape the intricate tangle of life's demands" (1077). He does little in his solitude except meditate on the recent past, especially Borodino, where heroic peasant soldiers' "truth, simplicity, and strength" made a lasting impression on him and contrasted so markedly with "his own insignificance and falseness" (1077). In his eagerness to match the selfless commitment of men like these, Pierre decides to do something equally courageous: he will by himself "put an end to the misery of all Europe" (1078) by assassinating Napoleon in Moscow. Though such a deed will result in his own execution, Pierre is determined to follow through regardless. As he turns over this resolution, Pierre recognizes "two equally strong feelings" (1078) impelling him to this act. The statement of purpose that he puts together is as eloquent and succinct a description of the Russian character as anything in *War and Peace* or elsewhere:

> *The first was the feeling that sacrifice and suffering were required of him in view of the common calamity, the same feeling that had impelled him to go to Mozhaisk on the twenty-fifth and from there into the very thick of the battle, and that had now made him run away from home, giving up his accustomed luxury and comforts to sleep in his clothes on a hard sofa and eat the same food as Gerasim. The other was that vague and typically Russian contempt for everything conventional, artificial, and human—for everything the majority of men regard as the world's highest good. Pierre had first experienced that strange and fascinating feeling in the Sloboda Palace, when he had suddenly felt that wealth and power and life—all that men strive to attain and preserve—were worth, if anything at all, only the joy of renouncing them.* (1078)

Prince Andrei Bolkonsky has reached similar conclusions throughout his adult life, rejecting plans and proposals from those on high seduced by delusions of power and control, turning his back on society and all its frivolous pursuits, liberating his serfs, preferring active military service to safe staff work, and forgiving his fiancée and the man who almost abducted her. The Rostovs embody this same spirit in a less dramatic form as they put other people's needs above business affairs, take in and transport wounded troops to safety, leave possessions behind, and accept willingly the vicissitudes life presents. By contrast, the Kuragins and the Drubetskoys exhibit little interest in self—sacrifice or renunciation. From the beginning of the novel to its end, they remain the same: cold, grasping, eager for honors, emoluments, influence, status, convinced that success lies in social standing and that marriage, children, friendships, and faith are like malleable commodities that can be twisted into any shape bringing ease and comfort. These are the Petersburg values, the non—native distortions of the "truth, simplicity, and strength" animating the patriots of the heartland as they give everything they have to resist an invader threatening all that Russia stands for and cherishes.

Pierre's resolution is sincere, and as the novel proceeds, its spirit grows stronger while he faces challenge after challenge; for the moment, however, murdering Napoleon in a theatrical display, a la John Wilkes Booth, is an aspiration that lasts less than a day. As Pierre is preparing to exit Bazdeyev's home, two French soldiers, one an officer, the other an orderly, appear at the doorway, asking about rooms and accommodations. As they converse with the house servant, Bazdeyev's eccentric brother, Makar Alekseyevich, suddenly shows up, clearly drunk and brandishing a pistol. Pierre lunges at him, but the pistol goes off anyway "with a deafening report, and all were enveloped in a cloud of smoke" (1082). The French officer, Captain Ramballe, rushes to Pierre, lauding him as his savior and insisting he is really "a Frenchman!" (1082). The two spend hours together, engaging in pleasant conversation, dining, and, to a degree, developing a bond. The fact that Pierre speaks French and that he has spent a few years in Paris highlights the commonalities the two "enemies" share. Their camaraderie banishes Pierre's "former dark thoughts of vengeance, assassination and self-sacrifice," making them disappear "like dust by contact with the first person he met" (1088). Simple humanity makes dramas demanding heroic self-assertion unnecessary. He and the captain end their time together swapping stories of romance and seduction, with Pierre describing his love for Natasha as too spiritual to be consummated and Ramballe dismissing this purity as "moonshine" (1092). The moon, in fact, is shining as Pierre leaves, and the comet "connected in Pierre's mind with his love" (1092), is also clearly visible in the night sky. So, too, is "a small remote fire in the huge city" (1092).

That "small remote fire" soon spawns successors. While the departing citizens and retreating troops look on helplessly from the city's outskirts, they see more and more fires sprouting and "blazing in the distance" (1094). At first, they try to believe the fires are in neighboring towns, particularly "Little Mytishchy" (1094), which the Cossacks are known to have set ablaze. The reality that "Mother Moscow the white" (1094) is burning is resisted since such a horror is too much to bear, but no one can deny that some of the city's distinctive districts are identifiable in the inferno. "The wind and this dry weather" (1094) aggravate the situation, and the absence of a fire corps makes extinguishing the blazes quickly almost impossible. Count Rostov weeps when he hears of and looks out at all the fires, and Sonya is in despair as she sees what seems like "all Moscow . . . burning" (1095). Throughout this awful time, one of the wounded being transported by the Rostovs moans constantly, lending a mournful background accompaniment to the tragic happenings playing out before everyone's eyes.

One member of the Rostov party, however, is less concerned about Moscow's travail than she is about a certain officer lying in one of the family's conveyances. She has learned to her astonishment that this seriously wounded warrior is Prince Andrei Bolkonsky, the man she once loved so much and betrayed so thoughtlessly. As she approaches the prince, "lying with his arms stretched out on the coverlet, looking just as she had always seen him" (1098), Natasha drops to her knees at his bedside, unable to speak. She does not realize that her former fiancé has moved far beyond any desire for vengeance and cannot squander any precious moments on pointless recriminations. Natasha is, as a result, deeply touched as Prince Andrei extends his hand to her with chivalrous grace and smiles benignantly. From this point on, the balm of reconciliation and forgiveness will reunite the doomed man and the woman whose love he has reclaimed.

Another quasi-mystical experience has illuminated for Prince Andrei the path of noble renunciation he has been following and will continue to follow until his death. Just as at Austerlitz and at the Rostovs' with Natasha, the prince, prostrate and immobilized by what will turn out to be mortal wounds, has been given a taste of heavenly joy: "A happiness that lay beyond material forces, outside the material, external influences on man—a happiness of the soul alone, the happiness of loving!" (1101). Such love "is the very essence of the soul and

. . . requires no object" (1102). It is an all-encompassing power which embraces family, friends, neighbors, and enemies alike, a divinely inspired beneficence that enables one to achieve a nearly inconceivable serenity, accepting with gratitude and charity whatever life brings. This exalted consciousness permits Prince Andrei to put aside Natasha's guilt and proclaim with perfect sincerity, "I love you more—better than before" (1103). For the rest of the journey, Natasha remains at this transfigured man's side, showing "fortitude" (1104), as she comforts and is comforted by the dying man.

While the Rostovs continue their journey away from the burning capital, Pierre stays put, still trying to rouse in himself the resolution to assassinate Napoleon, even though for a man like him, honorable, sensitive, conscientious, and generous, such a deed is an impossibility. Wandering through the familiar neighborhoods of the great city, Pierre comes upon an emergency that forces him to respond quickly and fully and to call upon resources of courage and strength equal to any the murder of the conqueror might require. With her meager possessions piled nearby, a mother sits weeping because her youngest daughter is missing, possibly trapped in the burning building she and the rest of her family have barely escaped. Without a moment's hesitation, Pierre offers to help find and rescue the girl. He now feels "young, cheerful, resolute, and agile" (1109) as purposeful action beckons. He sees French soldiers nearby, engaged in their usual looting. Pierre ignores their crimes and tries to persuade them to help the search. They agree, so for a brief moment Pierre's experience with Captain Ramballe is repeated, with enemies behaving like brothers to the rescue, intent on saving one of war's innocent victims. A Frenchman soon spots the "little three-year-old girl in a pink frock" lying safe and sound "under a garden seat" (1110). He leaves her with Pierre, reaffirming in passing: "Must be human, we're all mortal, you know" (1110). Pierre is overjoyed but almost loses the "sickly, scrofulous-looking child" (1110), who is clearly afraid of him and tries to run away. When he finally grabs hold of her, Pierre feels some revulsion, as if he is "touching some nasty little animal" (1110). The wealthy nobleman and the poor child are more alien to each other than are the French trooper and the Russian civilian.

Pierre's finicky discomfort will be transformed into something like righteous indignation in a few minutes. While making his way back to the place where he had left the child's family, Pierre notices that the marauding French are continuing to take whatever they can from the mostly deserted neighborhood's homes and shops. Some of the thieves are crossing normal lines of decency and respect in their cupidity. Pierre leaves the young girl with a "pock-marked peasant woman" (1114) for safekeeping and confronts two French soldiers behaving like criminals. One is forcing an old Armenian to pull off and hand over the new boots he is wearing, while the other is staring lasciviously at the man's daughter, who seems "the perfection of Oriental beauty, with her black, sharply arched eyebrows and the extraordinary loveliness of her long, delicately tinted, expressionless face" (1111). Pierre's energetic efforts to rescue the child have called up reserves of bodily strength that make him an intimidating presence, and the "transport of rage" (1113) he experiences at the sight of the father and daughter being abused makes him unconscious of risk. Pierre challenges the Frenchman who is beginning to assault the beautiful daughter, beating him mercilessly as onlookers cheer. A patrol of uhlans appears before he can inflict serious injuries, and Pierre is arrested immediately. The officer in charge, on the basis of no evidence except the fires themselves, decides Pierre "looks very much like an incendiary" (1114), a charge that could very well lead to the man's execution. Watching him being taken away, the peasant woman with the rescued child asks what she should do. In his "elation" (1114) at seeing the child, Pierre blurts out to his captors, "She is bringing me my little daughter, whom I have just rescued from the flames" (1114). He has, in effect, adopted the child who seemed more animal than human moments before. Pierre has transcended the barriers of social class once again to embrace a commoner, as he had done with the peasant soldiers at the Borodino redoubt. He is becoming more and more humane and energized through his immersion in the chaotic world of his people, with whom he is one in spirit. In comparison to this identification with the masses, no other distinctions matter.

BOOK IV

PART ONE

While Moscow is being bled white by abandonment, occupation, pillage, and fire, life in the other capital, St. Petersburg, is going on as usual, "with the same receptions, and balls, the same French theater, the same Court interests, the same factions and intrigues in the service" (1117). At a *soiree* given by Anna Pavlovna "on the very day of the Battle of Borodino" (1117), for instance, the hostess and guests display little anxiety about the fate of the army or Holy Moscow. The "news of the day" (1118) concerns the precarious health of Countess Bezukhova, whose conjugal complications are well known to everyone present. She is reportedly suffering from "*angina pectoris*" (1118), pain in the chest brought about by "the difficulty of marrying two husbands at the same time" (1118). She is being treated by an Italian doctor using a "new and unusual method" (1118). Petersburg society considers this "Italian Cure" (1118) to be not a new medication but shorthand for the casuistry of the Jesuit priests, who have been advising and counseling the countess for some time and have arranged for her to convert to Catholicism and receive a papal dispensation to regularize her marital status. The countess's difficulties are fodder for witty commentary and nothing more. Her father, Prince Vasily, is in attendance, but he is focused more on a public reading he has been asked to present rather than on Countess Elena's health or happiness. The Orthodox Metropolitan has composed a letter to accompany his "sending to the Tsar the icon of Holy Saint Sergei" (1118). This letter is "considered a model of ecclesiastical and patriotic eloquence" (1118), exactly the kind of document Prince Vasily relishes, since his theatrical "wail" or "lament" makes each word even more powerful. The irony of the father of a woman publicly renouncing the national church, being asked to read a ruling prelate's message is not noted in the assembly. The prince performs his role as expected, even though his listeners are not sure what to make of his rendition since the letter's strained eloquence makes it hard to follow. It ends, however, with a powerful evocation that carries the audience away:

> *Let the bold and insolent Goliath from the borders of France encompass the Russian realms with deadly horrors; humble faith, the sling of the Russian David, shall be swift to smite his head in his bloodthirsty arrogance.* (1120)

Everyone applauds vigorously, with acclamations like "*Quelle force! Quelle style!*" (1120) resounding as Prince Vasily takes his bows.

This is Petersburg society in the midst of bloody and unprecedented conflict taking pleasure in word play and theatricality. Like Boris Drubetskoy and Berg, they are distant observers of rather than participants in the life and death struggle against Napoleon. They have not suffered the wounds of a man like Prince Andrei, have not been changed from an eager adolescent to a grizzled adult almost overnight as Nikolai Rostov has, have not been brought from profound sorrow to selfless care and concern for all the war's victims like Natasha Rostova, and have not witnessed or been inspired by the sacrifices of so many ordinary men and women as Pierre Bezukhov has. The Petersburg aristocrats are frozen in accepted ways of thinking and acting. The war is an occasion for display and cleverness, not at all a life-transforming trauma. More attention is paid to Countess Bezukhova than to Borodino and Moscow combined.

Shortly after Anna Petrovna's gathering, word that the countess has died suddenly spreads throughout the city. She has apparently suffered a seizure brought on by an overdose of the new medication her celebrated physician has been prescribing. The Jesuits' Italian cure has been effective shock therapy for soul and spirit, while the doctor's medicine has had the opposite effect on the body of Countess Elena. The capital's notables echo each other in lamenting the loss of this fixture on the social circuit, whose wit and charm had so impressed everyone except "that wretched profligate Pierre" (1122).

The big picture is obscured in Petersburg, even in the highest circles of government and the military. A message sent by Kutusov to the High Command right after the Battle of Borodino but before the Russian retreat beyond Moscow gives assurance, widespread at the time, that the French have been stopped and the Russians are preparing to counterattack. All sing Kutusov's praises in response, including Prince Vasily, who once openly scorned him. Then, subsequent information changes things drastically. Rostopchin venomously informs the tsar that Moscow has been abandoned without a battle. Public opinion quickly turns against Kutusov, now regarded as the equivalent of a traitor, "a blind, depraved old man" (1122), who never should have been given command of the army. The tsar immediately dispatches an envoy with a note demanding to know why Kutusov has made "this grievous decision" (1123). His Serene Highness is put into the same position as Union General George Gordon Meade will be in just over fifty years later during the American Civil War. After three days of bloody fighting ending July 4, 1863, engaging most of Meade's Army of the Potomac, his forces held the field at Gettysburg, effectively blunting Confederate General Robert E. Lee's invasion of the North. General Meade did not retreat afterwards like Kutusov, but he did not counterattack either, letting the remnants of Lee's army withdraw unopposed. The joy Washington's elite felt when they learned of Meade's victory turned into hostility and scorn as soon as it became known that the commander had failed to follow up his success. President Abraham Lincoln was among these critics. In both instances, the defeat of an invading enemy, at great cost in men, animals, and materiel, is somehow tarnished if it does not result in instant capitulation.

Lincoln eventually accepted the reality that Gettysburg was more like the beginning of the end of the Confederate rebellion rather than the end itself. Tsar Aleksandr, too, recovers his spirits once Kutusov's messenger meets with him and reviews what has happened after Borodino. As he hears of Moscow's plight and of the widespread destruction the fires have caused, the tsar is at first crestfallen. His confidence returns, however, as he and the envoy carry on a high-sounding dialogue that resembles an operatic duet, with each speaker adding something more to augment the other's sentiments. The tsar asks, for example, about the condition of the army; his interlocutor tells him in the best Petersburg style: "They are burning with impatience to go into battle again" and "their only fear is lest Your Majesty . . . should be persuaded to make peace" (1125). This sends Aleksandr to rhetorical heights as he vows "to go and eat potatoes with the meanest of my peasants" (1125) if the herculean struggle he, his "beloved nobility," and "his worthy peasants" (1125) are engaging in to expel the invader does not succeed. This resolve so moves Kutusov's envoy, a foreigner named Michaud, that he feels "transported" and assures the tsar solemnly: "Your Majesty has at this moment endorsed the glory of the nation and the salvation of Europe!" (1126). If the right words could ensure victory, Petersburg's flowery contribution would be decisive.

Such powerful resolutions and commitments may move hearts and minds in the capital, but they do not resonate in the provinces, where only day-to-day concerns matter. The retreating troops basically have put Moscow out of mind; like men and women who are trying to make a perilous situation bearable and who have no sense of their role in history, they are "all thinking about their pay, their next quarters, Matryoshka the canteen woman, and the like" (1127). Among these soldiers is Count Nikolai Rostov, ordered to Voronezh to "obtain remounts for the division" (1127). At Voronezh, filled with wealthy Moscow exiles and provincial notables, Nikolai cuts a grand figure, becoming a "universal favorite" (1129) with his good looks, cavalry uniform, military decorations, and expert dancing. Young women openly flirt with him while their mothers and grandmothers scheme to arrange marriages for him and their eligible kinswomen. Nikolai revels in these attentions, even going so far as to carry on extended conversations with "a plump, pretty little blue-eyed blonde, the wife of one of the provincial officials" (1130). Before anything further occurs, however, Nikolai learns that none other than Princess Marya Bolkonskaya is also "in Voronezh with her aunt" (1131). Arrangements are quickly made for the two to meet again. Nikolai is torn every which way, feeling a "sensation of shyness and even of fear" (1132) as he recalls the woman he once rescued but, at the same time, remembers his promise to Sonya, which still weighs on his conscience. Nevertheless, he is exhilarated by the prospect of seeing again the wealthy heiress his mother and other relatives consider the best possible match for Count Rostov and his family. Princess Marya, too, is aroused by the upcoming meeting with the man she regards as her savior. She is very excited by the possibility of resurrecting "the personal dreams and hopes" (1134) suppressed for most of her life and last brought to the surface at the time Nikolai had first appeared on the scene. But she feels uneasy as she senses how assiduously others are working to bring her and Nikolai together, something that seems like "an insult both to her and to her father's memory" (1135).

When the two at last reunite, however, the doubts and hesitations affecting both Nikolai and Princess Marya vanish altogether. The princess greets Nikolai "with shining eyes," perfect grace, and a voice that strikes "a new, deep, womanly note" (1135). Mademoiselle Bourienne, "an accomplished coquette" (1135), observes all this with knowing eyes. Princess Marya is experiencing sexual excitement as she gazes at Nikolai's "dear, loved" face (1136), but Nikolai does not respond in the same way. He recognizes "a being before him . . . utterly different from and better than anyone he had met before, and, above all, better than himself" (1136). The princess's virtue and goodness radiate in "those luminous eyes, in the delicate smile, and in every feature of her gentle face" (1136). Then, as Nikolai pauses to bend down and play with her nephew, Princess Marya decides definitively that he is the man she will marry, while Nikolai welcomes the same happy fate "irresistibly carrying him away" (1137). Married life with this woman whose "singular moral beauty" (1139) captivates him is still too much to imagine now, but suddenly all the charms and delights of his former carefree life and the ladies he had been drawn to disappear as Nikolai listens to the urgings of his heart, mind, and soul and accepts what is inevitable.

Nikolai begins praying, which he rarely does, and his prayer is very specific: he asks God to release him from his promise to Sonya. This commitment only guarantees mutual misery, he reasons, because "nothing but unhappiness can come from marrying Sonya. Entanglements, grief for Mamma . . . business difficulties . . . muddles, terrible muddles" (1140). As the count prays and weeps before the icon, what seems like a providential intervention occurs dramatically. A letter from Sonya arrives. With profound self-sacrifice, his cousin releases Nikolai from their engagement, recognizing that her insistence that the two marry will bring "sorrow or discord" to the Rostov family and will deny Nikolai the "happiness" (1141) he deserves. But these words do not actually reflect Sonya's thinking. Even though "sacrifice for others" is "second nature" (1142) for Sonya, and even though the countess has been pressuring her for some time to allow her son to marry "an heiress" (1142), Sonya cannot just fade away. She is experiencing something beyond "placid love" for Nikolai; "a passionate feeling" is being aroused, overpowering "principle, virtue, or religion" (1043). Sonya is encouraged when Prince Andrei appears among the wounded, thinking that Natasha still loves him and that their marrying is a good possibility. If this occurs, "owing to the kinship that would exist between them" (1143), Nikolai and Princess Marya could not marry. Such a scenario seems to her altogether plausible, giving Sonya genuine hope that her marriage to Nikolai is meant to be. Therefore, as the countess virtually begs Sonya to write to Nikolai, she finally agrees, confident that "the renewal of Natasha's relations with Prince Andrei would prevent Nikolai from marrying Princess Marya" (1145) no matter what concessions her letter might contain. Sonya's supreme self-sacrifice is really not what Pierre's seems, so "blissfully aware of performing a magnanimous deed" (1145), Sonya composes a letter that she is sure will mean nothing. In calculating as she does, however, Sonya neglects a pertinent fact: Prince Andrei Bolkonsky is a dying man.

Pierre Bezukhov is not yet *in extremis*, but his situation in Moscow is perilous indeed. After being apprehended in a neighborhood where fires are breaking out all over, he is imprisoned with a number of other "suspicious characters" (1146). They are all "men of the lowest class" who stay apart from the heavy-set bespectacled "gentleman" (1146), who speaks French. Not even in extreme circumstances do the rigid social barriers of eighteenth-century Russia break down. Pierre's sophistication, however, will serve him well. At first, as he is taken before a military tribunal and interrogated, Pierre answers the questions truthfully but soon realizes that "truth" is not the object of the panel's probe. The questions are designed "to lead to the desired end, namely, a conviction" (1147). Since the defendant's replies do not correspond to what the tribunal needs, they are discounted. An exasperated Pierre ends by refusing to identify himself, a decision the chief interrogator pronounces "bad, very bad" (1147).

Pierre is then brought before Marshall Davout, the Duke of Eckmuhl, one of Napoleon's chief associates and "a man notorious for his cruelty" (1150). By this time, Pierre is sure he is doomed, seeing himself as "an insignificant chip fallen between the wheels of a machine whose mechanism he did not understand but which worked smoothly" (1149). What occurs next, though, is exactly the opposite of what he is expecting. As Davout questions him in "Prince Shcherbatov's house, where he [Pierre] had often been a guest" (1149), and as Pierre responds candidly in French, carefully observing the proprieties by addressing Davout as "Monseigneur" (1150), and expressing hurt feelings when he, a gentleman, is accused of lying, the two men establish "human relations" (1150). They are no longer conqueror or conquered, French or Russian, captor or prisoner; they are "brothers," two men of the same class whose common culture and breeding could, in different circumstances, lead to concord and mutual pleasure, very much like the friendship that develops between the aristocratic French officer Boldieu, and his German captor, Von Rauffenstein, in Jean Renoir's *La Grande Illusion.*

Pierre's sophistication has rescued him, but he is not told so officially. He is still "sixth" (1152) on the list of the condemned and must walk with the others to the place of execution. In horror, he watches as each one of the five ahead of him is brought to the stake, tied, blindfolded, shot to death, and thrown into "a freshly dug pit" (1152), where his bones will mingle with the remains of strangers. These helpless victims die not knowing what they have done to deserve such punishment and begging "with the same mute appeal for protection in their eyes" (1153) for a rescue that never comes. Everyone taking part in this slaughter views the proceedings as sickening. Unlike the mob who beat the pamphleteer to death at the urging of Rostopchin, the French commanders and shooters do their duty as they have to, but "on the face of every French soldier and officer without exception," Pierre sees "the same consternation, horror, and conflict" (1153) he feels himself. As the soldiers hurriedly throw the fifth and last body into the burial pit, even though it still shows signs of life, they act "like criminals who must hide the traces of their crime as quickly as possible" (1154). Pierre has been spared, almost as if only he should be allowed to live to testify to what seems like a satanic ritual murder, in which five men have been chosen at random to be sacrificed in order that the hellfire devouring Moscow may cease.

Pierre learns afterwards that he has been "pardoned" but will still have to endure confinement in "a barracks for prisoners of war" (1155). Imprisonment may be better than execution; nevertheless, for Pierre, who has just gone through a shattering experience that has robbed him of any "faith in the right ordering of the universe, in humanity, in his own soul, and in God" (1156), prison seems more like being buried alive. At this lowest point in his life, however, Pierre receives what amounts to a new dispensation. He encounters a fellow prisoner, almost providentially, who will lift him out of despair and give him cause to embrace his world once more. A peasant, Platon Karateyev, greets Pierre in a sing-song voice that radiates "simplicity and kindliness" (1157). This man is making the best of his situation, keeping his corner of the barracks "well-ordered" and gladly sharing "several baked potatoes" (1157) with Pierre, whom he has never laid eyes on before. He soon draws the newcomer into a conversation that brings the two closer despite their class differences, and, with liberal doses of folk wisdom and shrewd commentary, begins to bring Pierre out of his despair and into a renewed acceptance of and resignation to his fate. Platon should be anything but cheerful considering how he was forced into the army after being caught taking some wood from a neighbor's copse, but he is not at all bitter over being thus singled out, since he understands now that his service is a "blessing" (1159); had Platon not committed his "sin" (1159), his younger brother, the father of five, probably would have been drafted in his place, causing immense disruption at home. This man's charity makes the greatest misery one more opportunity for sharing and sacrifice. He warns Pierre about trying too hard to keep and control all that is good rather than cooperating with one's destiny for the good of all:

> *Fate has its reasons. But we are always judging: "That's not right, that is wrong ..." Our happiness, my friend, is like water in a dragnet: pull—it expands, take it out—it's empty. That's how it is.* (1160)

The man whose spiritual strivings have led him to liberalism, Freemasonry, cabbalistic calculations, and stargazing is reduced to awed admiration as he is and will continue to be touched by the profoundly human, earthy, good-natured, and life-enhancing presence of this simple man. Pierre feels "the world that had been shattered . . . beginning to rise again in his soul, but with a new beauty, and on new, unshakeable foundations" (1160).

Platon Karateyev is the "personification of everything Russian, kindly, and round" (1161). While his rotund appearance reminds no one of Adonis, Platon's stamina and strength are extraordinary, allowing him to work ceaselessly. He is the proverbial "jack of all trades," knowing instinctively "how to do everything not very well but not very badly either" (1162). Platon's joy in living inspires him to sing without self-consciousness, "like a bird" (1162). At night, he talks freely, repeating "folk sayings which taken out of context seem to have so little meaning, yet when aptly applied acquire the significance of profound wisdom" (1162). Platon is "on affectionate terms with everything life" presents; he gives undifferentiated love, placing "the French" on equal footing with "his comrades" (1163) as he strives to live harmoniously with all in his orbit. Above all, Platon is not conscious of individuality; his life lacks any "meaning as a separate entity . . . [but] only as a part of a whole of which he was at all times conscious" (1163).

This awareness of oneself as one unit in an immense mass of humanity is deeply embedded in the Russian character, formed over the centuries by life on the endless plains in the company of peasant work gangs needing the cooperation and support of each other to complete the myriad tasks of agricultural labor in season and out. Unlike Julien Sorel, who is conscious always of how alien others are and how he must strive to separate himself from those who would hinder his success or deny his pleasures; and unlike David Copperfield, who moves through life purposefully and virtuously, staying focused on personal achievement and emotional fulfillment within the context of moral duty; and unlike Huckleberry Finn, for whom adult society offers little besides crime, cruelty, hypocrisy, exploitation, and entrapment, Platon Karateyev opens his arms wide to welcome all that destiny has arranged, not questioning, disputing, or trying to defy whatever has been fated to occur or whoever must cross his path. Platon is tied to his nation, guided by its faith and its traditions, especially as these find expression in simple prayers and pithy maxims and at home in his native fields, forests, rivers, and villages. Pierre's quest for identity is leading to a similar acceptance of his place in this same world and of the duties a man in his station ought to perform. Once his captors depart the capital and he is eventually freed by Russian partisans ranging through the countryside, Pierre is ready to take on, without doubt or equivocation, the responsibilities his rank, family, education, and talent set before him. Platon, his peasant guide, has made all this clear and inevitable.

Pierre is not the only character experiencing an enhanced awareness of his place in life. Princess Marya has found love, and it has taken possession of her "whole soul" (1164). Upon learning that her brother is staying with the Rostovs, the extraordinary coincidence stimulates her to extraordinary effort. She and her household companions undertake a long and difficult journey to Yaroslavl, following a roundabout way to avoid traveling through the occupied capital. All the while, the princess shows "courage and energy," letting no difficulty "deter her" (1164). She and her party finally reach the Rostovs' residence, where, after brief introductions, the princess hurries toward her brother's room. As she comes near, she meets Natasha, whom she initially disliked, "all but running into the room" (1167). The princess sees in her urgency the same love and concern for Prince Andrei she herself feels, making Natasha a "true comrade in grief, and consequently a friend" (1167). They are reconciled immediately, with Natasha selflessly yielding to a "passionate desire to give herself entirely to helping" (1167) the prince and the princess in every way.

Prince Andrei's condition is grave, and he is grateful for his sister's visit. But his manner is off-putting; his gaze is "turned not outward, but rather into himself," and he speaks "in a voice as even and aloof as his gaze" (1169). This is so unsettling that Marya can hardly respond. The prince, however, is not ill-tempered but rather absorbed in "that alienation from all things earthly that is so terrible to one who is alive" (1170). He is already beyond the mundane and the transitory concerns of everyday living, "indifferent because something of far greater importance" (1170) has drawn his "spirit to the Eternal and Unfathomable, whose presence so palpably hovered over the dying man" (1172). The prince's son, Nikolushka, "with fear in his eyes" (1171), is brought to him. The father the little boy hardly knows kisses him but cannot manage to say or do anything more. Marya weeps as she watches this awkward and painful scene.

This disturbing encounter with his sister and his son is provoked by an internal conflict Prince Andrei has been suffering through ever since his rescue by the Rostovs. He struggles with his love for Natasha, revived so strongly by her constant presence and care, and his acceptance of impending death, which draws him more deeply into transcendent regions, where earthly attachments are unimportant. His love for Natasha, nonetheless, persists, keeping him tied to this world and to one particular being, while his awareness of love as the unifying and binding principle that keeps all elements in the universe moving together in harmony, draws him toward the infinite and the eternal, the glorious realm he will enter "as a particle of love" (1175) upon dying. As he experiences these competing desires, the prince reflects ruefully on the irony of his situation: "Can fate have brought us together so strangely only for me to die?" (1174). Natasha, of course, encourages him to retain his connection to her and to this life, insisting near the end that the prince will emerge from this trial renewed and restored. He tries to agree: "How good it would be!" (1175), and kisses his beloved's hand. This intense moment, however, is Prince Andrei's last attempt to keep hope for this life alive. He drifts into a deep sleep and dreams he is talking with many different people about mostly "trivial" matters and that "all this is of no consequence" in comparison to "other, more serious concerns" (1175). The people leave, but the door to his room must be locked. The prince tries manfully to get to the door quickly, but "his legs do not move" (1175). He struggles to lean against it to keep "death" (1176) from entering. His efforts are "superhuman" but "unavailing" (1176). Death takes hold.

This is a dream from which he awakens. This awakening from impending death, however, brings enlightenment and revelation through a sublimely comforting mystical visitation:

> *And his soul was suddenly suffused with light, and the veil concealing the unknown was lifted from before*

> *his soul's vision. He felt as if powers that till then had been confined within him were liberated, and from then on, that strange lightness did not leave him again.* (1176)

Natasha and Marya are with him hour by hour. They sense that what they are doing to comfort the prince is useless and that their ministrations are focused only "on their most immediate memory of him—his body" (1176), since Andrei's spirit has already departed this earth. His last conscious act is to consent to Princess Marya's prompting and embrace his son one last time. Like before, however, he offers Nikolushka a kiss but nothing more. Prince Andrei dies as he must, sacrificing life itself in his nation's service. This supreme sacrifice culminates a series of renunciations that have punctuated his whole life experience. The prince has sacrificed social position, political prominence, military influence, romantic love, paternal care, and so much else that the overwhelming majority of his friends and colleagues consider vital to happiness. But happiness in the conventional sense has never been granted to this outlier personality. Like Pierre, Prince Andrei has been a lifelong "seeker," who has moved from one interest or enthusiasm to another without finding lasting satisfaction or significance in any one of these. Beginning on the field at Austerlitz, where the seriously wounded prince lay after leading a brave charge, and, intermittently, all through his later years and finally on his deathbed, Prince Andrei has experienced graced moments of insight and enlightenment that have caused him to cease "chasing after false gods," such as wealth, power, popularity, sexual excess, charm, wit, and so on. He has been brought time and time again to accept and embrace the necessity of sacrifice, a letting go that brings fulfillment. The self-giving that has guided Prince Andrei's inner life keeps unlocking reserves of love, forgiveness, and serene acceptance of divine will that enable him to find meaning and wisdom through renunciation. Though born to wealth and social distinction and gifted with the strength of character that welcomes challenges, the prince goes through life showing, in his own way, the same characteristically Russian meekness and resignation at key moments as his pious sister. In so doing, Prince Andrei models a nobility and generosity of spirit that Russian culture values most highly, as he joyously lays down everything, including life itself, in order that others may not perish.

PART TWO

Prince Andrei's death comes at almost the same time as the fortunes of war are beginning to change. Kutusov's retreat has ended at Tarutino, where supplies are abundant. The French in and around Moscow are inactive, with their plundering having rendered the majority of troops incapable of mounting any concerted offensive action against the Russians, who are now "out of sight, out of mind." Kutusov, alone among the Russian commanders, understands that the best strategy for defeating the French is to continue to do nothing, because soon winter's furies and the emptying of Moscow's remaining supplies and provisions will compel the enemy to begin a long retreat to its bases in Vilna and Warsaw. Napoleon still has hopes that he can cajole the peasants in the countryside outside the capital to sell him enough food to sustain the army, particularly since he is offering to pay handsomely for what they provide, albeit in counterfeit Russian notes. Nevertheless, as noted before, he decides at the end of October to send an emissary to Kutusov, Count Lauriston, a former French Ambassador to Russia, who will, in effect, sue for peace. Tolstoy calls this desperate and humiliating action, "the moan of that wounded beast, the French Army" (1182). Though he is, on the surface, the conqueror of Russia, Napoleon is, in reality, in a much more dangerous situation than his Russian counterpart. The Russians can "snatch victory from the jaws of defeat" simply by waiting. Napoleon needs the cooperation of the Russian people, its political and military leadership, and the weather to extricate himself and his army from their deteriorating position. As circumstances play out, he will get no cooperation. Kutusov tells Lauriston, "I should be cursed by posterity if I were regarded as the initiator of a settlement of any sort whatsoever" (1182); the peasants ignore his appeals; and the weather turns cold and stormy early.

The leadership in Petersburg, however, is not inclined to wait patiently for the invaders to self-destruct. The High Command, led by the tsar and including commanders put into the shade by Kutusov and eager to retain their eminence, insist that His Serene Highness mount an attack against Murat's cavalry, encamped in a forest outside Moscow and vulnerable to a flank movement. Kutusov resists mightily but cannot prevail. He issues orders reluctantly for what he regards as a "useless and harmful" attack (1185). Plans are quickly drawn up and dispositions laid out, with the German strategist Toll taking a lead role as he did at Austerlitz. But just as at Austerlitz, nothing works out as prescribed. In an egregious example of comic-opera blundering, a key Russian commander and his subordinates are attending a ball the night before the attack and receive orders too late to make the required dispositions by the next morning. It is even alleged that this man has made himself unavailable deliberately, so that a rival officer will be placed in jeopardy and suffer the consequences. These consequences are soon being felt early in the day as Kutusov approaches the area where forces ought to be in place but clearly are not. He flies into a rage and begins abusing any officer within earshot. The result is a postponement of the expected attack to the next day, enraging Kutusov even more, because he has felt all along that the proposed action will produce nothing except a waste of precious men and resources like at Austerlitz, yet still he has to go through with it no matter how badly preparations have been muddled.

The action begins the following morning. This time fortune seems to be shining on the Russians. With the aid of a deserter who knows Murat's whereabouts, two Cossack regiments are designated to accompany the deserter in a lightning raid to capture the king of Naples and his suite. The regiments achieve surprise and quickly capture "fifteen hundred prisoners and thirty-eight guns" (1191). They do not, however, exploit their success since the Cossack cavalrymen immediately engage in plunder, stealing "horses, saddles, horsecloths, and the like" (1191). Their officers demand that the men cease and continue in pursuit of Murat. The Cossacks are too busy doing what they most like to do to pay any heed, another instance where spot decisions by common soldiers rather than orders from above determine the outcome of battles. The same thing is happening in every sector. Columns wind up in places they are supposed to bypass; line officers give more orders and start blaming each other for the confusion; ordinary soldiers lose heart and with minds of their own begin "a reverse movement" (1192) that soon degenerates into a rout. A few finally get to the desired ground, "too late to be of any use but just in time to be fired upon" (1193).

Though the Battle of Tarutino produces only small military gains, and though the Russians' performance is anything but brilliant, the action Kutusov wanted to avoid does resonate psychologically for both sides. Tolstoy stresses how in this case less has generated so much more:

> *With a minimum of effort, with insignificant losses in the midst of utter confusion, the most important results of the whole campaign were achieved: the transition was made from retreat to advance, the weakness of the French was exposed, and a shock administered which was all that was needed to put Napoleon's army to flight.* (1195)

"Flight" is the correct term. Despite his best efforts to conclude an armistice and negotiate terms from strength and despite his benevolent despot's appeals to the peasants and craftsmen of the region, Napoleon has languished in Moscow for weeks, all his initiatives having been rebuffed. When, therefore, he receives news of the engagement at Tarutino, under the guise of organizing an expedition from Moscow "to punish the Russians" (1202), the emperor issues, instead, an order for full withdrawal. The *Grande Armee* is now, to cite Tolstoy's favorite comparison, "a wounded beast which feels that its death is imminent and does not know what it is doing" (1203), so any possibility of engaging the enemy in force is out of the question. The troops want only to make their way back to safety alive and with their booty. But this enormous movement of men, beasts, prisoners, and materiel shows all the deficiencies haste and improvisation bring. The French follow the worst route, suffer mounting casualties as marauding Cossacks harass them, lose most of their stolen valuables and precious animals, and slowly and steadily disintegrate as an organized fighting machine. For Tolstoy, once more, the retreat from Moscow resembles "the spasmodic movements and death throes of a mortally wounded animal" (1203). This "wounded animal" is supposedly being guided and supported by its peerless master, but though Napoleon sends out orders and advisories incessantly, they have little impact on what is transpiring. Hunger, fatigue, cold, and fear combine to create an inertia at all levels that compels movement but resists awareness or direction. With his ineffectual words and gestures, the Emperor Napoleon is like "a child, who holding onto the straps inside a carriage, imagines that he is driving the vehicle" (1203).

Unlike the beaten and bedraggled soldiers of France, Pierre Bezukhov is experiencing renewal and reinvigoration in captivity. In addition to Platon's inspiring presence, Pierre has derived numerous benefits from the austere regimen he follows daily. He loses weight, making his "massive, powerful" (1204) frame muscular rather than stout. The same is true of his demeanor; his eyes radiate "resolute calm and an alert readiness such as they had never had before" and "his former slackness" has been "replaced by an energetic readiness for action and resistance" (1204). His captors treat Pierre respectfully as "a man with education" who "speaks French" (1205). Pierre does not exactly collaborate with the enemy, but he is gentlemanly and rational, helping, for instance, to avert bloodshed after a fight breaks out between some prisoners and their guards. Members of both groupings intermingle out of shared necessity. Over time, mutual bonds develop, with particular needs driving captive and captor together to address them. On one occasion, responding to Pierre's wordless encouragement, Platon knits a new shirt for one of the guards, "a thin, shallow, ragged French soldier" (1206). The soldier returns any leftover pieces of fabric, which Karateyev then uses to "make fine leg rags" (1207) for his mates. Simple humanity keeps the two sides together in their common plight, overcoming the artificial hostilities that should separate them completely.

Pierre bears his "position not only lightly but joyfully" (1208), allowing him to attain "the serenity and content for which he had long striven in vain" (1208). His lifelong quest for such is being fulfilled in ways and circumstances he could not conceive previously. Pierre's odyssey of the mind and soul over many years, and the various blind alleys he had traveled through, are culminating in a revelatory prison experience whose impact is more like that of a monastic retreat:

> *In the course of his life, he had sought in various ways for that peace of mind, that inner harmony, which had so impressed him in the soldiers at the battle of Borodino. He had sought it in philanthropy, in Freemasonry, in the dissipations of society, in wine, in heroic feats of self-sacrifice, and in romantic love for Natasha; he had sought it by reasoning—and all these quests and endeavors had failed him. And now, without thinking about it, he had found that peace and inner harmony only through the horror of death, through privation, and through what he perceived in Karateyev.* (1208)

This perspective brings Pierre insights that at first blush seem counter-intuitive, but upon examination, prove correct. One of these is as follows:

> *The satisfaction of his needs—good food, cleanliness, and freedom—now that he was deprived of all these things, seemed to Pierre to constitute perfect happiness; and the choice of occupation, that is, of a way of life, now that that choice was circumscribed, seemed to*

> *him so easy that he forgot that a superfluity of the comforts of life destroys all joy in satisfying one's needs, while great freedom in the choice of occupation—such freedom as his education, wealth, and social position had given him—is just what makes the choice of occupation insolubly difficult and destroys the need and even the possibility of having an occupation.* (1209)

In other words, wealth, power, and social position are actually heavy burdens when it comes to understanding and appreciating basic needs and one's life work; too many choices create too many options, the effect of which is to make every possibility viable and no possibility natural and inevitable. In captivity, Pierre realizes that only one possibility can be chosen; he must continue to use all of his education and sophistication to keep himself and his fellow prisoners healthy and safe. Since he gives the impression of being "a somewhat mysterious and superior being" (1210), he has no choice except to exercise the leadership role he has been born to assume.

This task will become more challenging once the retreat from Moscow gets underway. The soldiers who had been so thoughtful and kind while with their captives in one place become like martinets as the masses of men and animals exit the security of the capital and face the hazards of open country. In their anxiety and sensitivity, the guards now obey "that mysterious, obdurate force" (1211) that suppresses normal human feeling. Pierre senses that the atmosphere going forward will be tense, interactions with the authorities will be minimal, and favors or considerations will be restricted. An "every man for himself" spirit will pervade the body henceforth, so "to address entreaties or exhortations to those" who have become little more than "tools" of this inhuman force is "useless" (1211). He can "only wait and endure" (1211). As the prisoners mingle with the rest of the French Army, delays, accidents, roadblocks, and the like slow everyone down, causing arguments and fights to break out everywhere as impatient men and frightened animals try to cope. The *Grande Armee* is no more than a mob striving to keep one step ahead of catastrophe. The prisoners have to bear this brutal gang's oppression, manifesting itself starkly in the meat ration issued right at the start of the long march: "horseflesh" (1216).

As the retreating columns move into open country, some elements become separated. The Russian guerillas shadowing the French report that a detachment has been spotted in an exposed position and ought to be attacked. Kutusov reluctantly agrees to engage but sends only a small force. He has no interest in a major encounter, remembering well the confusion at Tarutino. Before the Russians can move into action, however, word is received that the main body of the French Army has reunited with the troops previously exposed, and the small Russian contingent is now inadequate for what would have to be a major undertaking. A messenger is dispatched to Kutusov's headquarters to report these developments and receive new orders.

Kutusov is awakened and briefed in detail. With staff officers surrounding him, ready to draw up once again a comprehensive plan for overwhelming the French, His Serene Highness, who has said repeatedly: "Patience and time are my two valiant warriors" (1223), considers all that the messenger has reported as confirmation that "his heart's sole desire" is being fulfilled, and "the destruction of the French" (1225) is at hand. In one of the most moving scenes in the novel, the old general orders his suite to stay silent as he turns to the icons he, like all devout Orthodox believers, has set up in his quarters. The supreme commander then offers up this heartfelt thanksgiving through tears: "Lord, my Creator, Thou hast heard our prayer . . . Russia is saved. I thank Thee, Lord!" (1225).

Kutusov is so sure that the French no longer pose any threat because their retreat shows no sign of being a redeployment in preparation for further aggressive action. It is, instead, a desperate effort "to get away as quickly as possible" (1227). Tolstoy emphasizes this point by repeatedly highlighting the French Army's woeful condition. Far from marching toward further conflict with Kutusov's troops, everyone, including

Napoleon, is striving only to escape "as quickly as possible from the hopeless position that they were all, if but dimly, aware of" (1226). Kutusov knows this and realizes the French are already defeated; he tries to restrain his subordinates, therefore, who are hungry for action mainly because they would like to "distinguish themselves" (1229). Any attempt to win glory through unnecessary risk-taking just postpones the inevitable. The soundness of Kutusov's thinking is reinforced after two generals, without Kutusov's knowledge or permission, engage two enemy corps near Vyazma. The French succeed in "closing ranks at the threat of danger," and the Russians, who march into battle to "music and the beating of drums" (1230), suffer grievous casualties. The attack has no appreciable effect on the retreat, which proceeds as before toward Smolensk. Kutusov deplores such murderous folly since "one third of their [the French] army has melted away" (1229) already and every day more become casualties, but his common-sense analysis makes little impression on those who believe only military victories win wars, and the only way to win such victories is through mortal combat. Men die and suffer terrible wounds for no purpose whenever military leaders refuse to think "out of the box."

PART THREE

Napoleon is one of these military leaders wearing blinders. He mounts an invasion of Russia confident that what will transpire there, both on the battlefield and in settlement negotiations, will correspond to standard military and diplomatic protocols and processes. But from the very start, what actually occurs is contrary to every conventional principle. The Russian defenders, for varying reasons, do not give battle either at the frontiers or farther inland; they retreat deeper and deeper into the country, requiring the French to extend their lines of communication and to wear themselves down with endless marching. Important Russian towns and cities are left defenseless, but instead of surrendering to the unopposed enemy and begging for lenient terms, the civic leaders in places like Smolensk encourage their citizens to flee, leaving nothing of value behind and watching impassively as fire devours everything in sight. Finally, at Borodino, the Russians fight a defensive battle, bravely standing up to the French attackers and obstinately refusing to surrender or run; the French suffer more casualties than in any previous conflict and, by the end of the day, are preparing for a counterattack from an outnumbered enemy who will not admit defeat. Such an attack, however, proves impossible to organize, given the logistical difficulties involved, so Kutusov orders further retreat, leaving Moscow unprotected. If he had followed the rules Napoleon believes govern the conduct of war everywhere, Kutusov should have surrendered and negotiated terms favorable to his troops and to the capital. The accepted wisdom is clear: "An army suffers a defeat, and at once a people loses its rights in proportion to the magnitude of the defeat, and if its army suffers complete defeat, the nation is completely subjugated" (1231). Kutusov's retreat and his abandonment of Moscow are, in Napoleon's eyes, unmistakable evidence of complete defeat. Yet no terms are requested, and no armistice is declared. The capital's citizens leave *en masse*, no boyars walk out to greet the conqueror on his arrival, and fires soon break out in widely separated parts of the city. Moscow burns like Smolensk.

Napoleon is stuck in a city more Asiatic in design and custom than it is European and among a people similarly foreign in thinking and behavior. No one from the tsar down to the meanest peasant will acknowledge or accept the enemy's victory. Aleksandr will not negotiate until the French retire beyond the Niemen River and the peasants will burn their hay rather than sell it, so there will be "no forage for the horses and cattle" (1232) as the French stay marooned in Moscow. The effect of this isolation on the invaders is toxic. The French troops, led by the elite Old Guard, quickly debase themselves, repeatedly violating orders and stealing anything and everything they find valuable, mocking the notion that they are bringing civilized Western European values and ways of thinking to backward Russia. Napoleon, meanwhile, is in an alternate universe. Tolstoy uses a brilliant analogy to highlight his distress. The emperor may be likened to a duelist fighting "in accordance with all the rules of the art of fencing" (1233). His opponent, however, "realizing he has been wounded . . . flings down his sword, seizes the first cudgel that comes to hand and starts brandishing it" (1233). The combat becomes chaotic and unequal, since Napoleon and the French have to battle not only an army but a whole people, who inflict "blow after blow till the feeling of outrage and vengeance in the soul yields to contempt and compassion" (1234).

The cudgel is also wielded most effectively by Russian irregulars, who "disperse and make isolated attacks, instantly fleeing when attacked by superior forces and then attacking again when the opportunity presents itself" (1234). In 1812, the masters of what has come to be known as "guerrilla warfare" (1234) are the Cossacks, those superb horsemen who wreak havoc on the exhausted French infantry in surprise attacks day and night, unimpeded by any opposing cavalry because the invaders have lost so many horses. The Cossacks have the same "spirit" that animated the Russian regulars at Borodino and that Prince Andrei Bolkonsky embodied and Pierre Bezukhov so admired. This eagerness to take on the enemy even if outnumbered, and in defeating him appropriate his belongings as spoils, enables the Cossacks to inflict significant damage while coming away unscathed. The retreating French are so intimidated and disoriented by the monumental obstacles they have to overcome to reach safety that they do not dare divide into smaller, nimbler, and flexible units. They move as one body to be sure of protection and support among each other. But such a body is too slow moving, too prone to accident and delay, too encumbered by the sheer weight of its compressed thousands, to react effectively to the guerillas' swift strikes. They concentrate on the body's flanks and rear, picking off or capturing scores who are most exposed or least mobile. These exploits are so intoxicating to the Cossacks that they ramp up the power and intensity of their body blows, striking "at the French without orders and without having to be forced to expose themselves to hardship and danger" (1236). These bands destroy "the *Grande Armee* by degrees" (1237) as it lurches across the bare steppes of Mother Russia.

One of these irregular bands is commanded by Denisov, while a "small band operating in Denisov's vicinity" (1237) is led by Dolokhov. A young man Denisov has known since childhood soon joins his group; Petya Rostov has been given a commission and is a staffer at a regimental headquarters. In this capacity, he delivers a message to Denisov, who, playing the role of wise guardian, lets Petya become part of his unit. Like Nikolai Rostov at the beginning of his service, Petya is eager to see action, and, with the French in full-scale retreat, the only possibility of engaging in combat is with a band of raiders like Denisov's. The danger an inexperienced youth like Petya faces is downplayed in the adolescent's mind as he grasps at "any opportunity to do something heroic," (1248) and thereby affirm his courage and manhood. In his desire to take part in such "heroic exploits" (1248) Petya ignores his former commander's explicit instructions. Before Petya left with his message to Denisov, knowing how impetuous the young man could be, his general had told him not "to take part in any engagement whatever that Denisov might be planning" (1249). This order Petya considers inappropriate, since it could compel him to "desert" his new comrades "at a critical moment" (1249). He, therefore, never lets Denisov know of the general's stipulation.

The situation becomes more complicated when Dolokhov arrives to take his part in an upcoming initiative. Denisov is contemplating an attack on a French transport convoy his troops have been scouting for days. The attack must come the next evening, lest a nearby detachment of the regular Russian army beat Denisov to the punch. Dolokhov's well-known aggressiveness makes him and his band ideal for this "'hit and run" operation. The man known as a chameleon is the same now as he was earlier, dressed like "the most punctilious Guards officer," complete with "the order of St. George in his buttonhole" (1252), but underneath this dashing façade still as cold, cruel, and sinister as ever.

As Petya watches, Dolokhov immediately tries to persuade Denisov to execute a young French drummer boy captured earlier, a boy to whom Petya has been kind and considerate. Responding like a disciple of Prince Andrei, Denisov will not consider "sullying . . . the honor of a soldier" (1253) by such an act, however inconvenient maintaining this prisoner may be. Dolokhov demurs, but then he insists that if the upcoming attack on the French transport unit is to succeed, he must be allowed to reconnoiter the enemy's position first, taking note of "what troops they are, and their numbers" (1252). Dolokhov needs someone to accompany him on this dangerous mission, so that he can keep in touch with and inform Denisov of his findings without leaving his position. Petya volunteers instantly. Denisov tries to dissuade him, but Petya is so affected by Dolokhov's charisma, he insists on participating. Against his better judgment, Denisov relents, and so the youngest member of the Rostov family and the cousin of the girl who once turned down Dolokhov's marriage proposal, thereby inflicting on him humiliation that has never been forgotten, places himself in Dolokhov's company, naively trusting that the great man's skill will be sufficient to keep him out of harm's way. Petya does not know that over time practically everyone who has gotten close to Dolokhov has been burned in some way by the radioactive attraction/repulsion he has always exuded. The die is cast for a terrible denouement.

At first, all goes incredibly well. With nerves of steel and a panache that elicits Petya's admiration, Dolokhov approaches a French encampment in darkness and begins boldly questioning the men he meets there, asking in unaccented French about troop strength, prisoners, and so forth in the units his and Denisov's band will soon attack. He even goes so far as to suggest that their Russian prisoners, among whom is Pierre Bezukhov, must be burdensome, since "dragging their carcasses along with one" (1256) expends resources and energy. It would surely be "better to shoot the swine" (1256), says the man whose reputation for cruelty is well-known to his comrades. In this instance, however, he goes far beyond any norms in suggesting that fellow Russians be targeted. Undoubtedly, Dolokhov is looking for a pretext to execute French prisoners, something he can claim to be doing as payback for the enemy's initial violations. If Dolokhov's "law of the jungle" approach prevails on both sides, the French retreat will become a death march for anyone caught by an antagonist. Petya is too impressed by how Dolokhov has brought off his imposture to worry about atrocities. He cannot wait for the morning, when battle will commence.

As dawn approaches, Petya is in a state of nervous excitement, enraptured by the awesome setting, so reminiscent of the sylvan world in which the ghosts and dragons of myth perform their lethal magic; as he dozes and dreams, Petya hears again and again the strains of a solemn hymn, played first on instruments and then sung by a choir of mixed voices. In his excitement, he cannot conceive of the possibility that the hymn may be a portent, a threnody for the repose of his young soul.

As the engagement is about to start, Denisov admonishes Petya to "obey" him and "not plunge into anything" (1262). Dolokhov also cautions the youngster not to get too far ahead: "Wait for the infantry!" (1263). None of this sensible advice sinks in though. Petya is too eager to excel, too sure he will flourish on the field as his brother did when, in his first action, Nikolai charged ahead of his company to meet the enemy in close combat and prevail. But this romantic self-image will yield to the harsh realities of conflict sooner and more decisively than anyone can imagine. As the surprised French contingent responds with chaotic fire, Petya is unhorsed by a wound to the head that proves fatal. He dies in the arms of a grieving Denisov. Dolokhov reacts ambiguously, repeating the words "done for" (1263-64) several times, as if this conclusion had not been apparent as soon as Petya fell. He also takes no French prisoners, a savage revenge for Petya's death and an open affront to Denisov's respect for the rules of conduct toward captured troops. He prefigures Dostoevsky's Nikolai Stavrogin, the nihilist revolutionary who radiates charm and sex appeal while coldly arranging the murders of rivals and innocents, and Andrei Bely's Nikolai Appolonovich, a Senator's son whose dilletante embrace of revolutionary principles leads him to attempt an assassination of his father in support of the world-shattering cause.

With the captured French convoy are Pierre Bezukhov and a large number of Russian prisoners, most in tears and delirious with joy to be among their fellow countrymen at long last. Pierre is still serene and confident despite having had to endure miserable conditions during most of the retreat and despite having lost the inspiring companionship of Platon Karatayev, who has not survived the long march. Since Platon had been a beacon of simple humanity and stoic peasant resourcefulness, his deteriorating condition in the last days was difficult for Pierre to bear. He could not go near him in his suffering, which Platon accepted almost cheerfully, because Pierre feared an encounter with mortality could weaken the sturdy resolve to persevere and ultimately flourish that had been motivating him to overcome all adversity. He has continued to hold fast to the counterintuitive conclusion he had reached earlier, namely, "that all unhappiness arises not from privation but from excess" (1266). Apart from the state of his "bare, lacerated, scabby feet" (1266), Pierre has been conscious of no crippling pain, cold, hunger, anxiety, or despair as the retreat has proceeded. Even the feet cause just temporary discomfort because he is "without pain" (1266-67) when he walks and aches only when he rests. Pierre has been able to summon "the full strength of man's vitality" (1267) to overcome daily challenges and has allowed whatever "joyful and comforting thoughts, memories, and fantasies" (1267) coming to him at rest, to pull him through oppression and hardship.

Like Platon, Pierre has embraced the peculiarly Russian understanding of "resignation," a welcoming acceptance of whatever fate metes out, along with an invigorating gratitude that one can live, love, and provide in the midst of trials. Pierre remembers a story Platon told just before his death. It is a folk tale about injustice, betrayal, and baseless condemnation being overcome by forgiveness and magnanimity. Platon has lived an entire lifetime according to such dictates. The "expression of serene exaltation" (1271) accompanying the tale's end stayed with the wise peasant up to the moment a French guard's bullet ended Platon's suffering. Pierre later muses, "To love life is to love God. Harder and more blessed than all else is to love this life in one's sufferings, in undeserved sufferings" (1272). He remembers Karateyev, above all, as a man who modeled this truth, but Pierre himself is fast approaching the same serenity in the midst of tribulations, a mystic awareness akin to the final illumination of that other great spirit, Prince Andrei Bolkonsky.

Meanwhile, the French Army, now moving across the open spaces of western Russia like desperate refugees, is deteriorating steadily under ever mounting pressure from the weather, the Cossacks, the lack of food and clean water, and the conditions of transport. While the emperor and his senior officers ride by in carriages, with their pack trains full of booty close behind, the soldiers walk toward almost certain death, since nothing they do can alter the terrible calculus mandating a certain number of corpses per mile. Napoleon and the marshalls cling to the formalities as they issue orders demanding that the troops maintain discipline and march in formation in well-defined columns, but these orders have little effect. Each man has only one object, survival, and pursues this obsessively. As they stagger toward the western border and presumed safety, individual commands separate themselves from the main body, each one trying to outmaneuver the harassing Russians through night marches, circuitous routes, and dangerous side tracks into dense forests. As they move, they embrace Darwinian principles, abandoning everything and everyone, including comrades, standing in the way of their quest for survival. French mastery of the art of war gives way to instinctual animal urges that have no place for rational calculation, companionship, or any other civilized habits. Toward the end of the long trek, Napoleon himself behaves in a wholly unprecedented and unprofessional manner. He commits an unheard-of desertion of his troops in a frantic effort to reach Polish territory and sanctuary as soon as possible. To all those who later on exempt Napoleon from blame for exhibiting this "ultimate degree of baseness" (1279), excusing his actions as necessary to save the great man's life and ensure his continued leadership and rule, Tolstoy is unsympathetic. The Russian soul resonates in the author's eloquent verdict on all such conduct:

> *For us, with the standard of good and evil given to us by Christ, there is nothing for which we have no standard. And there is no greatness where there is not simplicity, goodness, and truth.* (1279)

The retreat of the French liberates Mother Russia. As it proceeds, the proud force that began the invasion is reduced to "one hundredth part of the original army" (1281), as costly an outcome as any in military history. The Russians have fared better, but they too have suffered severe losses over the long trek athwart the enemy's flanks. In fact, "fifty thousand men" will have been "left in hospitals and in graves" (1283) by the time the pursuit ceases. All of this has occurred because implacable fate decreed that Napoleon and his allies should attack Russia, a nation hitherto friendly and amenable to French influence. The invaders expected to fight and win a critical battle or two as they had in Germany, Austria, and Italy, ending with the surrender of the Russian army, the conversion of the Russian nation from foe to ally, and the introduction of Western political, social, and economic principles throughout the tsar's territory. Just as in 1806, the Holy Roman Empire of the German Nation, with its numerous jurisdictions and political and ecclesiastical units, became almost overnight the Confederation of the Rhine, uniting all these disparate entities under a common legal code, so too in 1812, the Russian Empire could be transformed into something similar, with Aleksandr I becoming a constitutional monarch rather than an autocrat.

Nothing in this conception ever came close to being realized, largely because Russia did not follow the playbook governing the behavior of defeated powers in Western Europe. Fate brought Napoleon into armed conflict with an outlier, a nation formed and guided by mostly Eastern influences. These dictate a response to invasion very different from what Napoleon and his marshalls could ever have anticipated. The tsar does not negotiate an armistice, let alone a surrender agreement, despite the fact that the French are occupying his ancient capital; the capital's residents mostly flee rather than live under foreign command, rejecting all opportunities for enrichment and preferment the French could provide; the peasants and artisans likewise refuse to deal with the invaders, even if the French offer to pay highly for food or goods; Kutusov snatches victory from defeat by allowing nature's elements and marauding guerrillas to destroy the *Grande Armee* as decisively as his soldiers could; and these strategies and calculations teach the French the bitter truth that war in Eurasia is not like a chess match, where the right moves guarantee success, but more like the endless feuding of rival gangs, where random violence never ends, no quarter is given by either side, and no lasting compromise or peace agreement is possible. The experience of Napoleon and his allies confirms that "truth is only learned by suffering it," as Aeschylus declared centuries before. And suffering of epic dimensions has been shared by all in this inter-continental clash of civilizations playing out over six months in 1812.

PART FOUR

The departure of the French allows the Russian people to start putting their lives back together again. Among those attempting to recover from the sorrows and displacements of war are Princess Marya Bolkonskaya and Natasha Rostova, both of whom not only must restore properties and reestablish normal routines but also move out of the dark shadows of mourning and misery left in the wake of Prince Andrei's death. Princess Marya has duties that must be performed regardless of her moods, so she begins "to emerge from that world of solitary contemplation in which she had lived till then" (1286) to bring the household's accounts up to date, resume her nephew's studies, and prepare for the family's return to Moscow. Natasha, however, still lingers in the past, striving zealously to connect in mystic communion with the prince, who she is sure is still tied to her and this life. On one occasion, she senses his almost palpable presence and remembers a conversation in which Prince Andrei offered this admonition: "One thing would be awful . . . to bind oneself forever to a suffering man. It would be everlasting torture" (1287). Natasha draws an unusual conclusion from these words, believing that "to suffer with [Prince Andrei] is the greatest happiness for me" (1288).

Harsh mundane realities, nevertheless, break through Natasha's detachment. She is suddenly drawn back into her family's orbit the day she hears her father trying to choke back "convulsive, anguished sobs that distorted his soft, round face," all the while murmuring "Pe-Petya" (1289) and imploring Natasha to hurry to her mother's room. The horrific news of Petya's death ruptures the cord binding Natasha to spiritual realms. She feels "an instantaneous release from the constraint . . . cutting her off from life" (1289). Her immediate task is to try to comfort her mother, who is "beating her head against the wall" and "refusing to believe that she could live when her beloved boy was killed in the bloom of life" (1290). Natasha finds purpose in this life once more since she is best equipped to "keep her mother from insane despair" (1291). In this effort, she is joined by Princess Marya, the two becoming "united . . . still more closely" (1291–92) as they cope with all that has just occurred. The memory of Prince Andrei starts to fade, and to the astonishment of former fiancée and beloved sister, they are "gradually forgetting him" (1293). Despite their current challenges, Natasha and Princess Marya are recovering a "belief in life and its enjoyment" (1293). The bond developing between these two soul sisters is "one of those tender, passionate friendships that exist only between women" (1292). Together they will embrace life and all its possibilities for love, joy, happiness, and fulfillment, and in so doing they will strive to help others, particularly in the Rostov household, to do the same.

The death of Petya, which has devastated the Rostov family and has galvanized Natasha and Princess Marya to renewed life commitments, is more than a tragic byproduct of war. It is a sacrifice that should never have been made, the outcome of one young man's recklessness and one body of irregulars' lust for conquest and booty. Had Dolokhov and Denisov simply bypassed the opportunity to surprise a non-threatening French detachment, nothing significant would have been lost. The enemy still would be moving west and losing men daily to hunger, disease, the elements, and desertion. "Patience and time," Kutusov's preferred weapons, eventually would have brought about the same results as the raid, without any deaths like Petya's to have to absorb. The liberation of Russian prisoners, including Pierre, an entirely fortuitous benefit, would not have occurred as it did, but the probability of these men being released anyway to lighten the burden on supplies is high.

Kutusov's strategy of restraint and watchful pursuit ultimately succeeds, but it prevails in spite of its practical wisdom. Some of his more aggressive field commanders, acting just like Petya, cannot resist the lure of glory, earned, in their eyes, only through battle. At Krasnoe, ambitious generals come upon and attack "Napoleon himself with sixteen thousand men," notwithstanding "Kutusov's efforts to avoid this disastrous encounter and to preserve his troops" (1295). The action nets "twenty-six thousand prisoners, several hundred cannons, and some sort of stick which was promptly dubbed 'a marshall's baton' ..." (1296) but not Napoleon. The hungry and exhausted Russian troops are forced, as a result, to care for enormous additional numbers of men and tons of heavy equipment, making their shadowing of the main French body much more arduous. This is one of several pointless victories Kutusov has to endure as the retreat goes on.

The unnecessary bloodletting occurs because Kutusov`s perspicacity is neither understood nor appreciated. He suffers as one "of those rare and always solitary men who, discerning the will of Providence, subordinate their personal will to it. The hatred and contempt of the crowd punishes these men for their percipience of higher laws" (1297). The "purity and power of his own national feeling" (1299) also inspires this son of the Russian blood and soil. It accounts for his matchless grasp of the realities of conflict in the immensity of Russia, whose endless plains, impenetrable forests, vast rivers and countless streams, and dangerously extreme weather, make European-style warfare, stressing maneuver, coordination, and rigid concentration of masses of soldiers in parallel lines, impossible to execute. Nature frustrates such ballet-like pattern and precision at every turn. The fact that Napoleon and the *Grande Armee* have to march through most of Russia before finally fighting a major battle near Moscow attests to the difficulty terrain and space present to both armies as they seek just the right positions for attack or defense. Even when battle is joined at Borodino, nothing goes as planned, casualties are immense, and neither side can claim victory.

Kutusov is one with his troops and the Russian people as a whole. He cares nothing for glory or medals, gives no attention to his reputation, and risks defying the highest authorities if such must be done to save lives. He is a commander in chief who directs "all his powers not to killing and destroying men, but to saving and taking pity on them" (1300). Consequently, while many of his subordinate commanders work against him and defame him in court circles, his troops love him. On one occasion during the retreat, as French prisoners pass by and captured standards are piled before him as tokens of victory, Kutusov pauses to address the Preobrazensky Regiment, an elite body. His words are heartfelt and extraordinary. Kutusov reflects on the campaign, promising a conclusion soon and much-needed relief: "We'll see our visitors off and then we'll rest" (1302). He points to the prisoners: "It's hard for you, but still you are here at home, whereas they—you see what they have come to . . . Worse off than the lowest beggars." (1302). The supreme commander ends magnanimously, asking for humane treatment of the defeated enemy since "now we can afford to be compassionate. They're human too." (1302). But, to the delight of his audience, he cannot resist a last jibe: "When all's said and done, who asked them to come here? Serves them right, the—!" (1302). The effect is powerful as the regiment breaks into "joyous, prolonged cheering" (1302), and Kutusov fights back tears. His remarks could have been made by Platon Karatayev, so perfectly do they reflect the Russian spirit at its best.

The ordinary soldiers largely share Kutusov's feelings. Despite weather, fatigue, irregular provisioning, worn boots, ragged uniforms, and so on, the Russian Army maintains its pursuit of the rapidly retreating French, minimizing contact, taking into captivity any who fall behind, and allowing their own "physically and morally weak" (1305) comrades to melt away. What remains is "the flower of the army" (1305), men who work willingly together to keep warm, erect makeshift shelters, and encourage each other. They are also as considerate toward the vanquished foe as their commander. One night, Captain Ramballe, whom Pierre befriended in Moscow, and his orderly wander into a Russian encampment after leaving their hiding place in a forest. The Russians treat them with kindness and sympathy, laying "a greatcoat on the ground for the sick men" and offering "both of them gruel and vodka" (1309). Ramballe is too weak to walk, so he is transported to a warm hut "on the crossed arms of two soldiers" (1310), all the while crying out his thanks. His orderly, Morel, remains with the group and soon begins singing old French songs, which his captors very much enjoy, as well as men from neighboring emplacements. One of the Russian soldiers expresses the entire body's sentiments: "They're men like ourselves" (1311), and as such must be accorded all the hospitable care customarily granted to strangers in distress.

No such care is given to the man whose restraint and realism have guided and inspired these soldiers. The wise men advising Tsar Aleksandr in the safety and comfort of St. Petersburg are convinced that Kutusov has squandered too many opportunities to cut off the fleeing French and thereby either annihilate or capture the whole lot. They have continually prepared detailed plans for intercepting the enemy, only to see Kutusov ignore or reject them on the grounds that plans devised far away from the theater of conflict cannot be implemented as directed in real time and in constantly changing conditions. The tsar, however, is persuaded that Kutusov's assessments are erroneous. After the remaining French and allied troops have made a harrowing crossing of the Berezina River and escaped Russia, Aleksandr takes the extraordinary step of joining the Russian Army himself and, for all intents and purposes, leaving Kutusov without authority. The old general realizes his usefulness is no longer appreciated, so "his day was over, his part was played, and his supposed power was no more" (1314).

His end comes swiftly. Kutusov greets the sovereign with proper deference as Tsar Alexander arrives in Vilna with his suite. The tsar immediately embraces the victor of 1812, compelling the emotional commander to sob, but when the two are alone in private, the tsar expresses his displeasure over the conduct of the campaign, highlighting particularly his "dissatisfaction at the slowness of the pursuit of the enemy" (1316). Kutusov listens in silence, knowing that he will quickly be relieved of command due to his "infirmity and impaired health" (1317). After receiving "the Order of St. George, First Class," (1316) a medallion he at first does not recognize, and after the tsar has "honored" Kutusov by attending "a banquet and ball" (1316) given in the commander's name, the old general leaves the stage, never to return. Having completed his mission as best he knew how, he faces the inevitable: "Nothing remained for the representative of the national war but to die. And he died" (1318).

Pierre Bezukhov, by contrast, is very much alive, having been actually strengthened by the privations of captivity and liberated by his wife's death, which he learns of only after his rescue. He is ready at long last to become all that he should be, rejoicing in the prospect: "I am going to live. Ah, how splendid!" (1319). Pierre is also released from the torment of continually searching for "the aim of life," having attained in his duress "faith in a living, perpetually manifest God" (1320). This God has been revealed to him through his interactions with Karateyev as "greater, more infinite, and unfathomable than in the Architect of the Universe that the Freemasons acknowledged." (1320). Pierre's deity is more like the incarnate God of the New Testament, who does not dwell in unapproachable transcendence. Pierre admits to having been deluded for a long time by "European life, politics, Masonry, philosophy, and philanthropy" (1320) into imagining that only in the midst of "distance" (1320) could God be approached. He realizes now that "a mental telescope" (1320) is unnecessary in one's interaction with the God who became man; the "God without whose will not one hair of a man's head falls" is always near in "the ever-changing, eternally great, unfathomable, and infinite life around him" (1320). This "simple answer" (1320) to his endless questioning will govern Pierre's life ever after. These insights and realizations, however, do not turn Pierre into a narrow-minded credulous zealot but rather make him going forward a man happy in his world who will welcome any opportunity to offer through his "sympathy for others" some of the "joy of life" (1321) he feels almost all the time.

The change in Pierre is apparent to all who deal with him, including his servants, who like the fact that their master is "more simple" (1322) and thus more agreeable and more approachable. Likewise, Pierre's "old Masonic acquaintance, Count Willarski" (1323), who values the company of "a man of his circle" (1323) and eagerly shares with Pierre all the "military, administrative, political, and Masonic interests" (1323) he is absorbed in for the betterment of mankind. Pierre does not argue with, much less condemn, Willarski for his vain pursuits. He has come to accept "the legitimate individuality of every man's views" (1323), leaving it to his God to enlighten men like the count. Pierre's "center of gravity" (1324) is making him more adept at addressing practical concerns as well, particularly finances, which he usually left others to sort out. He decides, in consequence, to rebuild his house in Moscow and pay his late wife's considerable debts, neither of which he has to do but chooses to, so that the ruins inflicted by the invaders can be cleared away and the pain Countess Elena inflicted can be assuaged through forgiveness.

On the way to Moscow to begin these tasks, Pierre is again inspired by the fortitude and spirit the Russian people continue to show as they work to put back together all that the war has shattered. He marvels at the "strength" which "this whole, original, unique people" (1325) are displaying everywhere. What Pierre has experienced as one individual, a rebirth that has intensified his identification with Russia, the nation itself has undergone in spirit, so that its people can as one strive without ceasing to bring about the rebirth of Mother Russia. They do so most energetically in Moscow, whose "intangible yet powerful and indestructible" (1326) animating spirit keeps the heart of the capital beating strongly no matter the devastation. After some plundering by Cossacks and neighboring peasants, the authorities soon restore law and order, allowing enterprising people, including "householders, clergy, officials of high and low rank, tradesmen, artisans, peasants" (1327) to make the city hum with purposeful activity. Since "many hands make for light work," restoring and rebuilding Moscow is less an onerous burden than a joyful collective effort in which cooperation prevails over competition. Pierre is determined to participate in this effort with renewed energy and interest, now that he appreciates and feels the power immersion in life can generate.

Soon after his arrival in the capital, Pierre makes it a point to call on Princess Marya. He has not yet been able to express his sympathies to her in person, having learned of Prince Andrei's death only after Pierre's captivity had ended. Their meeting is cordial but a bit strained. The princess is with a companion dressed in mourning, whom Pierre does not immediately recognize. As the conversation proceeds, he mentions the "strange coincidence" (1330) of Prince Andrei's spending his last days with the Rostovs. This causes a stir. The lady in black`s "intent, friendly, quizzical gaze" (1330) is striking. Suddenly Pierre realizes he is face to face with none other than Natasha Rostova, whosc "stern, thin, pale face that looks so much older" (1330) he finds irresistibly appealing. He is overcome by emotion at this moment, unable to suppress the love welling up inside. Natasha today is not the Natasha he remembers, with a "face whose eyes had always shown with a suppressed smile of the joy of life" (1331). All she has had to endure has made the eyes that Pierre now gazes upon seem "intent, kind, and full of mournful inquiry" (1331). Suffering has made Pierre stronger and inspired him with a zest for life lived in the moment and in the midst of all; suffering has matured Natasha, making her youthful *joie de vivre* less evident and casting a "mournful" shadow over her womanly complexion. Her beauty is as riveting as ever, but it is the beauty of a woman challenged by adversity. The two are ready for a life together as adults, firmly grounded in their families, their land, culture, traditions, and faith, and responsive to their overpowering need to express love not only to each other but to everyone in their orbit. Theirs will be a union nurtured over time and through powerful experience by destiny itself.

The meeting is prolonged, as Natasha describes her culminating reconciliation with Prince Andrei, sharing not only with Pierre but Princess Marya "all that she had lived through during those three weeks of their journey and their stay in Yaroslavl" (1332). The effect for Natasha is cathartic, since at long last she can release herself from the emotional ambivalences that have been inhibiting her for too long. Pierre also opens up as the three dine together. He insists that though he has lost "two millions in Moscow," he is now "three times richer" because he has gained "freedom" (1334) from all concern about money. Pierre also laments the sad circumstances of his wife's death "without friends, without consolation!" and describes "the horrors and sufferings he had witnessed" (1335) while a prisoner. Natasha listens intently, their bond becoming so strong she can understand even what he cannot put into words. As Pierre talks about Karatayev and his vital influence, he feels "that rare pleasure men know when women are listening to them" and senses that Natasha is "divining the secret import of all Pierre's spiritual travail" (1336). As Princess Marya watches the two and listens, she understands quickly that a serious relationship is developing and rejoices over "the possibility of love and happiness between Natasha and Pierre"

(1336–37). The evening concludes with Pierre reiterating to Natasha that neither he nor she should "be blamed for being alive and wanting to live" (1337). Reflecting on everything she has heard and how positive and purifying the encounter has been for her, as well as for Princess Marya, Natasha marvels over how Pierre has "somehow grown so clean and smooth and fresh—as if he had just come out of a bath . . . Out of a moral bath" (1338).

She is exactly right. Pierre's cleansing has made him know, love, appreciate, and assist everyone around him; his dreamy aloofness and his constant chasing after sublime truths have given way to a determined absorption in the life and affairs of this world. Later, as he goes over at home everything occurring earlier, he remembers that he is supposed to leave for Petersburg the next morning. He has been so preoccupied, though, by his yearning for Natasha and the need "to do everything" (1339) to win her consent to marriage that he cannot even remember why he should be in Petersburg. This scene is about more than travel plans; it is emblematic of the transformation in values Pierre has been reaching for throughout the novel and has finally achieved. Petersburg is like Versailles, the place where the social and political elite gather; where wit, style, show, and masquerade are more prized than sincerity and frankness; where the Kuragins, the Drubetskoys, and the salon devotees connive endlessly for social distinction and self-advancement; and where a family like the Rostovs is looked down upon as naïve and backward. Moscow is different. The ancient capital is just beginning to return to normal after extraordinary destruction and suffering; this is where the soul of Mother Russia resides, weakened but still pure and undefiled. Pierre has shared this soul's trials, having suffered much and now so eager to help restore his people's strength and vitality. Pierre will nurture his connection to Moscow from this point on, making his home in the heartland, venturing into Petersburg only when necessary, turning his back on the false gods the cosmopolitan city has made into idols.

This time, nevertheless, Pierre will still go to Petersburg, largely because Princess Marya, whose aid in firming up his engagement to Natasha he desperately needs, advises him to do so. The princess is sure Natasha is strongly attracted to Pierre, and, if she does not already, will in time grow to love him without condition or doubt. But matters of the heart cannot be forced or rushed, as the unhappy experience of Natasha and her brother shows. Furthermore, Pierre and Natasha are not exactly a "natural" pairing. Pierre is honorable but is older and has had to endure a marriage that only the death of Countess Elena freed him from, while Natasha is barely over the guilt and shame her near elopement with a notorious rake and her fiancé's death have caused. Pierre is also ardent, living through "a period of madness" (1344) and unable to "imagine life without" Natasha (1342); by contrast, Natasha, even if clearly smitten, is more cautious, surely in response to what occurred previously. Pierre could use a time out to compose himself and steady his emotions, hence the Petersburg sojourn, while Natasha has to consider alone and in private all the dimensions and possible drawbacks of marrying a man who has become indifferent to wealth and power and identifies mostly with the poor and the simple.

Natasha's deliberations do not really alter the basic conviction she arrived at almost as soon as she parted from Pierre on the night they met for the first time since his release from captivity. Their talk that evening as they dined made such a lasting impression on Natasha, she cannot resist his proposal. Everything Pierre experienced in the occupied capital, including his rescue of a stranger's child and his agonizing witness to executions, and all he had had to endure as a prisoner caught up in the French retreat, has made him not only stronger in body and spirit but also more human and more connected to everyday life and ordinary people. The purgatorial purification he has undergone, "just exactly as if he had come out of a bath" (1345) has given him wisdom and serenity, charity and compassion. As a result, Pierre can offer unconditional love and loyalty, making it inevitable that the two should become one flesh. Natasha responds to "the life force and the hope of happiness" (1345) welling up within her. With Pierre as her guide and unfailing support, Natasha is ready to embrace life and explore all its possibilities, especially conjugal love, motherhood, and domestic responsibilities. Princess Marya lets go of the past as she pardons "Natasha for her joy" (1346) and welcomes her successor suitor warmly. Natasha's happiness extends beyond her personal situation, as she assures the princess both will be happy when she marries Pierre and Marya marries Nikolai. Though the princess asks her not to mention this other marriage possibility to anyone, Marya is deeply affected by her words.

EPILOGUE

PART ONE

War and Peace concludes with Tolstoy's final judgment on all that has occurred, not only in 1812 but through its aftermath, as the key players, Napoleon and Aleksandr I, leave the stage. In the years leading up to the invasion of 1812, Napoleon has foreclosed on numerous opportunities to consolidate and retain power; these opportunities have arisen largely by chance and have been grasped sometimes wittingly but more times through a combination of forces and events over which the emperor has had no influence. Despite, or perhaps because of, the fortuitous elements affecting the military and political successes he has enjoyed over the approximately ten years it has taken him to reach the pinnacle of power in 1812, Napoleon has ceased thinking in normal, rational ways, having become afflicted instead with an "insane self-deification" (1358): "*Chance*, millions of *chances*, give him power, and all men, as if by agreement, collaborate to confirm that power" (1358). This power coalesces around the ideals of the French Revolution, which stimulate a great movement taking shape in France and advancing steadily eastward. In all the territories Napoleon's forces conquer, ancient forms and traditional orders give way to new structures embodying liberal principles. The French draw more and more foreign troops into their movement as "the crowned heads of Europe" (1358) offer Napoleon support, highlighting like vassals "their insignificance before him" (1359). This amalgamation process culminates in 1811 when "the group of men that has formed in France unites into one enormous mass with the peoples of Central Europe" (1358). Napoleon Bonaparte, child of chance, is now ready to play "his formidable role" (1359) in leading a multinational army of six hundred thousand soldiers on what is regarded as a final campaign to subdue Tsarist Russia, universally condemned in the West as poor, feudal, superstitious, and resigned to tyranny.

Over the span of a few months, everything changes dramatically. Russian resistance takes the form of self-sacrifice, denying the invader everything of value, including food, water, shelter, and collaborative relations, and thereby weakening the allied onslaught. Napoleon and his forces are stuck in unknown territory, as the Russians persist in behaving in unexpected ways. In the only major battle, at the village of Borodino, the French force the retreat of the Russian Army and their abandonment of Moscow, but this victory proves hollow. Occupying the ancient capital gives the invaders a degree of prestige and a mountainous load of booty, but no armistice, no terms, no acknowledgement of defeat, and certainly no adoption of Western ideals in politics, religion, or culture. The man whose hubris has compelled him to overreach drastically has no choice except to order an ignominious retreat, which turns into an endless trial. The movement from west to east is reversed for good. As the remnants of the *Grande Armee* stagger into Lithuania and Poland, they are shadowed by the Russian Orthodox Army, firmly loyal to the autocratic tsar, and now poised to lead a countermovement from east to west that redirects the peoples of Central Europe against Napoleon and his liberators. Russian absolutism keeps the old ways in place wherever its army goes. The badly hurt French cannot stem the Russian tide. "Paris, the ultimate goal, is reached. The Napoleonic government and army are destroyed" (1359). Despite a brief resurgence after his escape from Elba, Napoleon's "role is played out" and, like his great antagonist, Kutusov, "he will not be wanted anymore" (1360).

Aleksandr I stands highest among the dynastic monarchs quickly restored after the war. This eminence he neither desires nor values. In a gesture similar to that of the sixteenth-century Emperor Charles V, on whose empire "the sun never set," the tsar "suddenly recognizes the insignificance of that illusory power" (1361) and walks away from active governance. He devotes the rest of his days to prayer and sacrifice, as if, like Napoleon and Kutusov, he has done what he had to do and now must let others guide the ship of state. Before this retirement, Aleksandr had forced the Congress of Vienna to adopt the Gospels, not human reason, as their guideposts in statecraft, a concession the unworldly autocrat considers sufficient to bring peace and concord back to war-ravaged Europe. For the rest, the tsar, in very Russian deference, places his trust in destiny, whose "ultimate purpose is beyond our comprehension" (1362), and turns his back once and for all on the human comedy. His detachment is total. Russia goes with him into reaction, becoming a bulwark of order and tradition continent-wide until the catastrophe of 1914.

One more scene in the domestic denouement of the novel remains. After Pierre and Natasha marry, Count Ilya Andreyevich falls into a depression that worsens rapidly. He senses that death is imminent and makes it a point to ask "forgiveness of his wife and absent son for having dissipated their fortune—that being the chief sin on his conscience" (1363). He passes away "peacefully" a short while after receiving "communion and the final anointing" (1363). It then turns out that the count's "chief sin" will have a crushing effect on his survivors: his debts are "double the value of the estate" (1363). After resigning his commission, Nikolai leaves Paris and returns home to confront this challenge. Consistent with his strong and honorable character, he immediately rejects any suggestion that he renounce his inheritance and walk away from the debts. The man whose youthful exploitation by Dolokhov resulted in staggering gambling debts that his father generously covered, will not "slur" Count Ilya's "memory" (1363) by such an action. With Pierre's help, he pays a portion of the debts and goes into government service to earn enough to discharge the remainder, all the while fending off creditors, who are "merciless" in their determination to make "the guiltless young heir" (1364) pay in full.

In their newly straitened circumstances, the countess, Sonya, and Nikolai move "to a small house in one of the poorer quarters"

(1364) of Moscow. While such a transition is a sensible course of action, Countess Natalya cannot reconcile herself to such a drastic lifestyle change and continually spends as before. Sonya provides invaluable service at this stage by artfully keeping the household books in balance, while cutting other expenses to the bone to satisfy her aunt's proclivities. Nikolai knows he is "irredeemably indebted to Sonya" (1364-65) for such extraordinary care and concern, but he still cannot feel any renewal of the love he once felt for her. Paradoxically, "the more he appreciated her the less he loved her" (1365). He stands firm in maintaining that the engagement the two once agreed to has been voluntarily abrogated by Sonya, and he is, consequently, free to marry anyone. His financial situation, however, limits his choices, since he has been "incurring small debts as a result of complying with his mother's demands" (1365). Nikolai accepts these realities with characteristic Russian resignation, taking "a grim and melancholy satisfaction in so doing" (1365).

Princess Marya visits Moscow soon after and hears "the town gossip," to the effect that Nikolai Rostov is "sacrificing himself for his mother" (1365). The woman who lived for years under a similar obligation to a difficult parent regards this news as "a joyous confirmation of her love for him" (1365-66) and of their deep compatibility. Several weeks later, on the pretext of offering comfort to the still grieving countess, Princess Marya calls on the Rostovs. Nikolai meets her first but is anything but cordial in his greeting; his "cold, constrained, and proud expression she had never seen before" (1366) forecloses any possibility of a friendly exchange. Once the princess leaves, he speaks irritably about having to show interest "in these fine ladies and their civilities!" (1366). In reality, Nikolai's pride keeps standing in the way of an alliance with someone as wealthy as the princess because he is determined to repay his family's entire debt by himself.

Fortunately, Princess Marya's long experience with male *amour propre* leads her to conclude wisely that Nikolai's coldness does not reflect his real feelings toward her but is a mask to conceal feelings he does not want to deal with yet. At the constant urging of his mother, that most practical of matchmakers, Nikolai returns the princess's call soon enough. Once again, the encounter begins badly. He talks freely of his mother's health and his time at war, but only out of an obligation to be civil. He rises to leave after about ten minutes. This time, Princess Marya reacts coldly, wondering if the man she loves is so imprisoned by emotional strains he will never return. At last, however, Nikolai pauses, realizing in his naturally kind and sensitive way that the princess needs reassurance. He allows himself to speak more frankly, recalling the confrontation at Bogucharovo, where he behaved so masterfully, and admitting that he "would give a great deal to bring back that time" (1368) when the princess overflowed with gratitude and admiration. Today, though, their relationship has undergone a major reversal. Princess Marya capsulizes all the strains and tensions pithily: "He is poor now, and I am rich . . . Yes, that is the only reason" (1369). Count Nikolai's coldness hides his shame over these circumstances. But underneath the princess sees "his noble, resolute, self-sacrificing soul as well" (1369) that draws her to him in love beyond measure. The two are now "on the same page" as they gaze into each other's eyes and understand instantly that "what had seemed impossible, and remote suddenly became possible, inevitable, and very near" (1369). Like Pierre and Natasha, they marry as soon as they can.

Nikolai and Marya, along with Countess Rostova and Sonya, take up residence at Bald Hills, where the princess spent so many years caring for and enduring her very mercurial father. Here Nikolai plunges into estate management with enthusiasm and good sense. He quickly pays his remaining debts, as well as Pierre's loan, and is making such progress that soon he is "negotiating to buy back his ancestral home, Otradnoe—that being a long-cherished dream" (1370). He enjoys exceptional success because he keeps to the age-old traditions and practices that guide the cycle of plowing, planting, and reaping, being very careful to forswear "innovations" (1370), a characteristically Russian aversion. He also takes great pains to understand and treat with respect "the peasants who worked the land"

(1370). Like Pierre in his interactions with Platon Karateyev, Nikolai appreciates the skills and folk wisdom his peasants have acquired over so many generations of agricultural labor; though he is their master, he often behaves more like their student, "learning from them their methods, their way of speech, their opinions of what was good and bad" (1370). Nikolai becomes "akin to them," (1370), showing no partiality or bias and demanding only that his orders be carried out as assigned. As a result, he rarely has "to be hard on or punish" nor does he have "to make things easy for or reward" (1371) someone on a whim. Nikolai follows an inner standard that over time has solidified into something "firm and inflexible in his soul" (1371). He manages like Denisov commanded, conscientiously and reasonably, earning the acclaim of the peasants just as his friend did of the men in his regiment. His methods bring many rewards, as "few landowners had their crops sown and harvested as early and as profitably as Nikolai" (1371).

Nikolai takes to his work in the fields with so much gusto he sometimes disturbs his wife, who cannot understand how her husband can devote so many hours to labors among the peasants, work she considers "remote and alien" (1371). But this work, which 90 percent of the Russian people perform in some form, gives Nikolai the joy of fulfillment. Through it, he can respond to the urges and aspirations of his soul, that native soul first awakened during the hunt at Otradnoe. Nikolai is with simple men and women, who live intimately with the natural world and know more than the most sophisticated when it comes to elemental realities, like soil, seeds, fertilizer, sun, and rain. His time in the fields and among the peasants in the open air is so invigorating, Nikolai is almost always "brisk and cheerful" (1371), no matter how hard his day may be. Like Pierre, he has been rejuvenated by his immersion in the life around him. The man who always preferred the life of an officer of the line rather than that of an officer attached to headquarters, is in his element, facing and overcoming with his stewards and laborers every challenge nature presents to men, animals, and plants year-round. His peasants are happy to work side by side with him because they know he will be magnanimous and fair in all his dealings with them. After Nikolai's death years later, they cannot help speaking of him with awe, holding the "memory of his administration . . . in reverence" (1372).

Nikolai also displays sensitivity. He has always had a quick temper and is by no means averse to fighting, as Princess Marya's recalcitrant peasants discovered in 1812. One day he confronts "the village elder from Bogucharovo, the man who had replaced Dron when he died and who was accused of various instances of fraud and negligence" (1373). Almost immediately, "the sound of cries and blows" (1373) is heard by, among others, Marya, now by marriage a countess. Later, at lunch with his wife, Nikolai complains that the elder had been drunk and deserved to be punished. The countess begins weeping, wordlessly reprimanding her husband for cruelty and abuse of power. The count is taken aback, since disciplining estate workers harshly if called for, he has accepted as "a matter of course since childhood" (1373), even if resorted to rarely. As he reflects on what has occurred, however, Nikolai admits that his wife is probably right and that he has "long been sinning against himself" (1373) by indulging his temper and flailing away with his fists. He promises the countess solemnly that such behavior will not recur, a promise that, with only occasional exceptions, he keeps. Nikolai's growth as a man of conscience and honor endears him to his wife and family, but it does not make him popular with "the gentry of the province," who consider him either "proud" or "a fool" (1374). In this regard, he resembles both Prince Andrei and Pierre, both of whose independence and outspokenness frequently provoked the same jealousies and dislikes.

Nikolai also does his best to comfort Sonya, taking upon himself all blame for their separation and begging his wife to be kind to her. The countess tries, but she just cannot warm up to this permanent guest, who has "attached herself not so much to the people as to the home" (1375) at Bald Hills. Natasha describes Sonya as "a *sterile flower*" (1375), a very apt phrase combining beauty and sweetness with an inability to blossom and reproduce. Sonya accepts this hard truth with the same self-sacrificing resignation Countess Marya knows so well but cannot bring herself to admire in another. Thus, though Sonya does all she is required to do and more, her efforts earn "scant thanks" (1375). She is indispensable yet irrecoverably damaged.

Nikolai and Pierre, meanwhile, in their respective households, enjoy a large measure of domestic bliss, supported always by their exceptional spouses. Although Nikolai can be abrupt and sometimes neglectful, Countess Marya bears the sharp swings of her husband's moodiness well enough. She is happy as a wife and mother, happier than she ever thought possible. Seeing her husband playing with their young children, and in so doing forgetting everything else, is, for Marya, the height of satisfaction. On one such occasion, after an exhausted and irritable Nikolai has gone to bed early, he is awakened by his little daughter, whose presence cheers him up instantly. The countess delights in this heartening encounter and wonders how it could be "possible to be so happy" (1381). Countess Marya performs her conjugal and maternal duties naturally, fulfilling them without complaint and embracing wholeheartedly the traditional Russian woman's role. She bears children joyfully and raises them with love but also with careful instruction in religion, morality, courtesy, and charity. Count Nikolai, in turn, assumes the patriarchal duties of an estate owner, deferring to his wife in regard to home life, but reserving to himself most decisions affecting crops, peasants, finances, and political involvements.

Natasha and Pierre enjoy a similarly symbiotic relationship. Her marriage to Pierre has matured Natasha almost overnight. With "three daughters and a son" (1381) to take care of and a prominent husband to keep contented, Natasha finds herself wholly absorbed in her family, a condition universally applauded in her culture. Concerning abstract issues like "women's rights, the relations of husband and wife, their freedom and rights" (1387), just beginning to emerge in her time, Natasha is mostly indifferent, preferring to fulfill her daily responsibilities in their customary ways rather than argue about new styles of thinking.

She has grown into "a strong, handsome, fruitful woman," having left behind "the slender, ebullient Natasha of former days" (1381). She no longer sings, takes little interest in society, and does not try to charm or excite romantic feelings in her husband. The bond with Pierre transcends all these superficialities; to the mature Natasha it is "as firm as the bond between her own soul and body" (1383). She demands from Pierre the same devotion to home and family she gives; in return, "he had only to express a wish" (1385) and Natasha would respond. Her commitment influences Pierre positively, confirming him in the conviction that his marriage is life-affirming and surpassing in importance everything else. He is now rooted in a "circumscribed" but supremely fulfilling "way of life . . . determined once and for all till death, and that to change it was not in his power" (1391). Theirs is a rock-solid relationship, one that in real life decades later Tsar Nicholas II and Tsarina Alexandra will embody for all the world to admire and, in its tragic ending, to mourn to this day.

The two households may be firmly grounded as far as marriage and family are concerned, but their members, particularly the men, are different in personality and temperament, leading sometimes to disagreement, particularly on sensitive or controversial issues of the day. After Pierre returns from a lengthy sojourn in Petersburg, much against his will, he is drawn into a discussion about politics with Nikolai Rostov and his old friend, Denisov, now retired with the rank of general. Pierre reports with strong disapproval the virtual abdication of Tsar Aleksandr I, who has chosen to live a retired life centered on prayer and mysticism. The tsar has left the management of affairs of state to Count Alexey Arakcheyev, a military strong man intent on crushing any manifestation of independent thought, and Prince Aleksandr Golitsyn, a minister of education equally hostile to anything that might provoke political unrest. Pierre denounces such reactionaries as "men of no faith and no conscience, who slash and stifle everything" (1399). He fears something on the order of the French Revolution will arise in Russia in response to such repression, which will bring on "a general catastrophe" (1399). This why in Petersburg he has met with fellow aristocrats of a secret society, not the Masonic lodge, but a "Society of true conservatives—a Society of gentlemen in the full meaning of the word," who are ready to "join hands solely for the common welfare and general security" (1400), especially in times of social upheaval. Pierre is acting in defense of traditional Russian values and structures and calling upon "gentlemen," who are part of the ruling class, to stand up for their status and independence, against despotic pretenders on the one hand and radical extremists on the other. He is accepting his position in society and acting purposefully to maintain it.

Nikolai Rostov is doing much the same thing in his own way, but as soon as he hears the words "secret society" he becomes agitated. The former hussar cannot help associating such a group, no matter its composition or principles, with anti-government sympathies. He opposes Pierre's idealistic leanings instinctively, telling him with dramatic emphasis how law and order must be maintained:

> *You are my best friend, as you know, but if you formed a secret society against the government—whatever it may be—I know it is my duty to obey the government. And if Arakcheyev ordered me to lead a squadron against you and cut you down—I should not hesitate for a second, but should do it.* (1401)

This is so powerful that only a stunned silence follows, with Natasha finally asking for calm and coming to her husband's aid. The conversation resumes more cordially, but wounds and hurt feelings linger.

This discord occurs near the end of part one of the epilogue, which concludes the story of Pierre and Natasha, Nikolai and Marya, and their families. It provokes in the four major players reactions that highlight the strongest elements in their characters. Though he has become a *paterfamilias* and is happiest when with Natasha and their children, Pierre still cannot resist the possibilities of "an idea whose time has come," or what passes for one. Over the span of the novel, he has flirted with numerous ideals, only to find each inadequate, impractical, false, corrupt, or ultimately empty. The new "society of the just" is not much different from his former enthusiasms, particularly in its appeal to individual assertion, which Pierre can seldom resist. As he and Natasha talk about the conflict with Nikolai, Pierre hears again the siren song that once led him to take seriously the notion of his single-handedly assassinating Napoleon in Moscow in broad daylight. This time he imagines being "chosen to give a new direction to the whole of Russian society and to the whole world" through his union of "honest men" (1409). The fantasy briefly lights up Pierre's imagination in spite of the fact that just prior to his outburst he had admitted to Natasha that Platon Karateyev, the embodiment of simplicity, folk wisdom, and self-sacrifice, would have paid no attention to aspirations like these; the man who was "always anxious to find seemliness, peace, and happiness in everything" (1408) would have counseled Pierre to focus on family life rather than joust with windmills.

This family life owes much to Natasha. She has welcomed with enthusiasm the duties and obligations Russian tradition has laid down for wives and mothers. Her love for Pierre is genuine, deep, and the source of fulfillment in its tenderness and of new life in its conjugal fruitfulness. Her depth of love has generated the same response in Pierre, who so overflows with affection he seems to be Natasha's plaything. But these are not newlyweds; Natasha rejects the notion that a marriage's "greatest happiness" comes "at the beginning" (1409). As she prepares to nurse her baby and sees how "their little son" so closely resembles Pierre, she decides "now is much the best" (1409). Natasha is wholly absorbed in her numerous responsibilities as household manager and mother of young children; while she respects Pierre's need for intellectual and political stimulation and the company of like-minded citizens, Natasha remains rooted in hearth and home.

Family life is just as appealing to Princess Marya. Her children with Nikolai and her stepson, Nikolenka, are for her practically the whole world. Nevertheless, she is different from

Natasha in her deep spirituality. This is a resource she considers indispensable and one of the main reasons her husband admires her. Like a conscientious teacher and guide, Countess Marya keeps a diary recording her efforts to raise their children to be well-mannered, sensitive, and virtuous. Every evening she takes stock of the progress the children have made that day "with marks . . . showing how they behaved" (1403). Nikolai is awed by "this constant and untiring spiritual effort, the sole aim of which was the children's moral welfare" (1403). As with Pierre, the countess needs the stimulation her ardent spiritual strivings provide. She knows there is a "happiness, unattainable in this life" (1381) and different in kind from the happiness of family life. The countess yearns to experience it; "her spirit was ever aspiring to the infinite, the eternal, the absolute and, therefore, could never be at peace" (1406). What Prince Andrei felt on the field at Austerlitz and in certain special times afterwards, Marya reaches for in ordinary moments over a lifetime. Unlike the prince, she does not commune with the Almighty in these moments, but she is granted what her brother sorely missed: the inexpressible joys of marital oneness and family solidarity. These joys are more down to earth and palpable than the mystic glories of spiritual ascent, but they are gifts of immeasurable value to one like Marya, who never expected to be so favored in her lifetime. She will let death determine how "the infinite, the eternal, the absolute" will manifest themselves in the afterlife.

Countess Maria's happiness owes as much to her husband's character and strength as Pierre's does to Natasha's sturdy support. Both Marya and Pierre have been seekers after truth and perfect virtue, and both have known disappointment in their high-minded quests. Nikolai and Natasha, however, are attached firmly to this world's possibilities and potential. They observe their church holidays and name days faithfully, but they feel no compulsion to move beyond standard observances or aspire to contact with the divine. The ecstatic emotions that overtook Nikolai and Natasha during the hunt at Otradnoe and afterwards have brought more than enough sustenance to these children of the earth. It is no accident or coincidence that as the narrative of the families ends, Nikolai has set his sights on purchasing the magical estate which generated all of that life-enhancing experience. Marya does not share her husband's attachments to soil and heritage, nor does Nikolai really want her more involved with him in this rural arena. Nikolai has mastered the largely masculine challenges of sowing and reaping and of managing peasants and animals exactly as he once did the exigencies of mortal combat.

The count is not one-dimensional, however, or content to do no more than required to prosper as a landowner. He takes time each evening to read and reflect, not only on day-to-day concerns but on the larger political and cultural issues affecting his way of life. Unlike Pierre, though, he has little interest in ideas, especially in the abstract, and considers debate and discussion more of a "pastime" (1407) than a necessary pursuit. While Pierre is absorbed in Russian statecraft and key personalities in the capital, Nikolai admits that "what goes on there [Petersburg]" is of no interest to him and he could care less whether "Arakcheyev is a villain, and all the rest of it?" (1404). His is a much more practical and pragmatic nature, constantly calculating costs and benefits, income and expense, planting and harvesting, all of which demand concentration and careful planning. To Nikolai, Pierre is the closest of friends but "always was a dreamer, and always will be" (1404), just as Marya will never give up trying "to accomplish the impossible—in this life to love her husband, her children, Nikolenka, and all her fellow creatures, as Christ loved mankind" (1405-06). Natasha and Nikolai, as a result, see their responsibilities as similar, hers to keep the "dreamer" and his to keep the "mystic" firmly grounded in the mundane family life that sustains them all.

One member of the next generation is already moving in a direction his elders well understand. Prince Andrei's son, Nikolenka, makes a very brief but very revealing appearance at the end of part one. He is depicted awakening from a dream during which he is sure his late father has shown him affection and "approval" (1410). Though Nikolenka admires Pierre and vows to study so that he can strive for truth like his uncle, he knows even at a young age that scholarly pursuits will be only preparatory to actions and deeds. These stronger aspirations will place Nikolenka squarely within the framework of his father's life and legacy. The youngster gives voice to his imaginings in memorable terms: "I ask God for only one thing: that something will happen to me such as happened to the men in Plutarch, and I will do as they did. I will do better" (1410).

He invokes finally the one man he considers *sans peure and sans reproche*: "Oh Father, Father! Yes, I will do something that even *he* would be satisfied with" (1411).

On this note of ardor and longing, part one concludes. A son and heir wants nothing more than to be worthy of the Bolkonsky name, the same thing Prince Nikolai asked of his son the night Prince Andrei left Bald Hills to join his regiment. Compared to fulfilling these unconditional imperatives of filial duty, accolades, honors, wealth, power, and the like fade into insignificance.

PART TWO

Part two is a long meditation on historical change. It lays out the theoretical foundation of many of *War and Peace's* overarching themes, including the illusion of heroic genius as a mover of events, the forces that impel individuals to act together in solidarity in the face of danger, the myth of free will, and the impenetrable mystery of historical causation. Tolstoy challenges conventional historians, particularly those mostly European thinkers who believe they can explain through reasoned analysis and argument exactly how and why certain events take place as they do. These writers enjoy the benefit of hindsight, knowing well which of many possibilities in history have been realized as a result of certain actions and how such realizations appear as inevitabilities from the perspective of time and distance. The confident rationalism underlying such thinking is to history what confident military planning is to battle; adherents of both schools believe that their designs and constructs explain how and why the movements of thousands have brought victories or defeats in actual combat. Tolstoy argues against all these pseudo-scientific approaches to understanding how events play out, insisting that human beings act and occurrences transpire in ways no one can predict beforehand or understand fully afterwards. The processes that lead to a battle can be described, but why certain individual actors in the ensemble do what they do involves "spirit" more than any mundane factors.

A famous battle in American history provides evidence for such an assertion. At Gettysburg, on July 3, 1863, Confederate General Robert E. Lee ordered a frontal attack on the center of Union General George Gordon Meade's battle line. As the Confederate columns marched forward, one brigade on the extreme left of the advancing lines suddenly broke formation and abandoned the field. This brigade included many combat veterans who had performed well in previous engagements. It was the only unit in the attacking body of nearly ten thousand that behaved this way. To Tolstoy, such an event shows how the most careful planning can go awry. Something "spooked" a few of the men, whose desertion of their comrades led others to follow suit, until the brigade's entire complement melted away. Why members of this particular unit acted as they did while all the others stayed on course cannot be answered fully or explained satisfactorily. Panic can overtake even the bravest men, especially when they are under intense fire and are seeing fellow soldiers falling all around them. Nevertheless, though the same fire was felt and the same casualties witnessed by all along the march, no other contingent gave way.

If it is difficult to know how individual soldiers will react to combat, it is likewise challenging to understand why the masses of men in certain armies succeed in attaining their objectives more or less consistently, even as rival groupings fail in such efforts. In earlier times, focus was placed on leaders like Alexander the Great, Julius Caesar, or Moses, who, it was thought, guided "the life of a people" by accepting the role "Divinity" (1412) chose for them and allowing this supernatural power to lead them and their followers forward to triumph. Modern thinkers reject divine influence but still hold "1) that nations are guided by individual men, and 2) that a goal exists toward which humanity and these nations are moving" (1413). In place of the deity, philosophers from the Enlightenment on highlight what they regard as decisive actions of certain individuals, whose genius and vision compel whole populations to move in synchrony and advance toward the achievement of specific goals. In reality, however, as Tolstoy reviews what happened in Europe after 1789, genius and vision are hard to identify.

The one man who comes closest to directing the great "movement of peoples from west to east" (1413) is, as noted throughout the novel, Napoleon Bonaparte. The arc of his career, nevertheless, shows no clear pattern or trajectory. He makes conquests in Italy at the start, ending feudal practices and traditions in many provinces, but he then crosses the Mediterranean with his army and lands in Egypt. In an environment as inhospitable as this, he and his troops could hardly have expected to spread revolutionary ideals. Except for some precious archaeological discoveries, the Egyptian sojourn brings no gains. He also obsesses over England and Spain, one so liberal and one so medieval, to no apparent end. In Spain, he installs his brother as ruler, exactly the kind of dynastic favor the French Revolution was supposed to have abolished. Moreover, in 1803, he forces the pope to travel to Paris to crown him as the successor of Charlemagne, a rite more appropriate to the Middle Ages than post-revolutionary France. In 1812, not content with presiding over France and a number of vassal states, Napoleon raises an enormous multi-national army to attack Russia, ostensibly to restore Poland and end autocratic rule in the tsar's empire. As Tolstoy lays out in painstaking detail, nothing in Russia goes as planned. Moscow is captured and the Russian army neutralized, but these successes are illusory, with no surrender taking place and no terms for ending hostilities ever even discussed. The conqueror and his badly depleted forces have to stumble back across the length of European Russia, only to be defeated decisively two years later. Napoleon's great antagonist, Tsar Aleksandr, leads a countermovement from east to west, all the while striving to undo the implementation of liberal social and political reforms among peoples that formerly embraced them. A conference is held in Vienna that formally restores the old order throughout Europe, including the Bourbon monarchy. For all intents and purposes, the French Revolution and its impact throughout Europe have been nullified. Napoleon is exiled not once but twice, compelled to spend his last years isolated and without influence. If Napoleon is a genius and a visionary, says Tolstoy, why is his narrative so full of contradictions and his legacy so ambiguous and ephemeral? The "power that moves peoples" (1416) cannot reside in the will of someone like this.

If it is next to impossible to believe that one man's unique genius or vision caused "six hundred thousand men" from different nations, speaking different languages, and animated by different causes to "go to war" (1423) in 1812 against a nation presenting no immediate threat to any of them, what power could have brought such a mammoth undertaking into being? Modern thinkers reject the ancients' belief that God's intervention was responsible, with Napoleon acting as an inspired agent. Physical compulsion is out of the question too, since the men who marched into Russia did so enthusiastically, revealing again and again extraordinary ardor for and commitment to their cause. Moral fervor is also unconvincing, since Napoleon's narcissism and his willingness to jettison revolutionary ideals whenever he had to to advance his ends would undermine any moral authority he might have exerted. Constitutional scholars and lawyers argue that a man like Napoleon expresses "the will of the people" (1424), who have transferred to him the right to exercise power over them. Exactly how this transfer took place in his case, however, is unclear. Did it occur when the Directory gave him executive authority to keep the Paris mobs and, by extension, restive elements throughout the country, under control? Or did Napoleon's coronation as emperor confer upon him the people's collective will? If the former is correct, the follow-up event should not have been necessary. If the coronation actually transferred power, why did Pope Pius VII, specially summoned to preside at the ceremony, not crown the new ruler of the West, as his predecessors had done since the Middle Ages? He did not do so, of course, because Napoleon took the crown from the pontiff's hands and placed it on his own head, thereby delegitimizing the ceremonial conferral.

This judicial conception is too vague, too open to skepticism as to why some rulers exercise their people's power legitimately and why others do not. In an effort to respect the role improvisation and circumstance play in politics, historians of the juridical school contend that "certain of these phenomena are not in essence the regular transferences of the people's will but are accidents, dependent on the craft, the guile, the blundering or weakness of a diplomat, a ruler, or a party leader" (1426). Even in retrospect, however, such "accidents" are not accepted by all those affected by them as just causes for the transfer of power. The same arguments over their legitimacy persist long after the accidents have taken place.

The American Civil War, for instance, resulted from arguments over if and how a state or states originally joined in a federal union could leave the larger body and either become independent or join a new arrangement with like-minded sister states. The states that formed the Confederacy in 1861, after formally seceding from the union built around the provisions of the 1787 Constitution, justified their actions by asserting that the president elected in 1860 and the platform adopted by his victorious party represented a mortal threat to their institutions and way of life. President Abraham Lincoln and his Republican colleagues condemned the secessionists, insisting that what these states did was illegal, since no mechanism for leaving the American union was included in the governing United States Constitution. With no possibility of resolving these fundamental differences through compromise, war between the two groupings broke out in the spring of 1861. Though the war resulted in the dissolution of the Confederacy and the reconstitution of the union, as well as the emancipation of those born into slavery, its resolution opened wounds in the American social and political fabric that have not healed to this day. In civics classes today, the policies followed by Lincoln and his unionist supporters are taught as correct, but many living in the states of the old Confederacy, as well as some disaffected sympathizers elsewhere, deny this ascription altogether, arguing that the victors of 1865 imposed on everyone else in America their own understanding of the law and justice issues that provoked the conflict. For white supremacists and their allies, particularly, Jefferson Davis is a patriot and Abraham Lincoln a tyrant; to citizens who largely approve of the positions taken by the unionists in 1861 and implemented through constitutional amendments, particularly including most members of racial and ethnic minorities, Davis is a traitor and Lincoln a liberator. It is hard to see how such dichotomous interpretations can ever be reconciled, and because they are held with passionate conviction by so many in the opposing sides, the notion that accidents causing a transfer of power from a people can be identified and categorized as legitimate or illegitimate is highly doubtful.

In any case, regardless of how the exercise of power is explained or justified, it must be understood not as a singular proceeding emanating from some leader's fiat but rather as a dynamic, multi-faceted, organic phenomenon created by the confluence of innumerable individual acts. Commands or injunctions from on high, even from one of the stature of Napoleon, do not by themselves effectuate anything. The emperor, like all executives, military or civil, issued countless commands, orders, proclamations, manifestoes, and the like throughout his time in power. A number of these were simply ignored, such as his appeals to the artisans in and around Moscow and the peasants in the countryside to maintain on favorable terms all normal trade relations with the capital's conquerors. Likewise, his order that the boyars meet him at the gates of Moscow to hear him announce generous terms for the cessation of hostilities and the occupation of the city could not be obeyed. No boyars could be produced despite a thorough search of the city, a fact that no one in the search parties wanted to admit to the emperor for fear of humiliating the great man.

As Tolstoy reminds us: "Every command executed is always one of an immense number unexecuted" (1432) for one reason or another. The *post hoc, ergo propter hoc* fallacy comes into play usually later, as analysts argue that what occurred after a command was issued transpired because of the command:

> *Our erroneous idea that an event is caused by the command that precedes it is due to the fact that when the event has taken place, and out of thousands of commands those few that were consistent with the event have been executed, we forget about the others that were not executed because they could not be.* (1432)

Those that are executed require much more than lockstep compliance by all affected by the command. Experience shows that a multitude of subsequent commands by those at every level of responsibility must follow if the commander in chief's directive is to be realized. A supreme commander like Napoleon is at the apex of a pyramid; he issues orders, observes their effect, and awaits the results. His orders are general and lack detail. Subordinates must give their own commands to bring the troops they lead into conformity with the supreme commander's design. Lesser ranking officers in the pyramid must do the same to keep their ranks in line with the guiding plan. All of those at various levels of responsibility, nevertheless, even with the most conscientious care and dedication, must defer to the common soldiers, who form the wide base of the pyramid, when it comes to actual combat. These men engage in "the stabbing, hacking, burning, and pillaging" (1433) that determine a conflict's outcome. They do not give commands, but the circumstances they encounter on the ground and the ebb and flow of the masses of men on both sides dictate whether and how the commands they have been given are carried out.

To illustrate, we return to the Battle of Gettysburg. On the first day of combat, as evening approached, General Lee sent an order to one of his corps commanders, Richard Ewell, to the effect that Ewell and his troops should make every effort to secure the high ground known as Cemetery Ridge, a key strategic position. The order ended with the words "if practicable," giving General Ewell a degree of discretion in how he could proceed. The general examined the territory he and his men would have to advance over to capture the heights; assessed the physical condition of his forces, who had been engaged most of the afternoon; estimated the strength of the enemy occupying and digging in on Cemetery Ridge; and concluded that fulfilling General Lee's command was not a "practicable" option. He halted and made no further effort. Ever since, General Ewell's conduct has been the subject of controversy, as scholars and tacticians have debated the wisdom of his decision. Standing at the apex of command, General Lee could not by himself move his troops to a desired spot. Only with the cooperation by and coordination of all the subordinates affected by the command and then the exertions of all the common soldiers ordered into action could a result such as the supreme commander envisioned be achieved. Lee's inability to bring about this result through personal intervention demonstrates "by the very nature of the case, those who command take the smallest part of the action itself, and that their activity is exclusively directed to commanding" (1434). A commander by himself no more exercises power over those he commands than the driver of a vehicle makes the motor run smoothly. The driver directs; he or she reaches the desired destination only through the systematic operation of the auto's interconnected components.

On the grand scale of history, therefore, this conclusion presents itself:

> *The movement of nations is caused not by power, nor by any intellectual activity, nor even by a combination of the two, as historians have supposed, but by the activity of all the people participating in the event, who always combine in such a way that those who take the largest direct share in the event take the least responsibility, and vice versa.* (1437)

Such a conclusion, however, is disturbing in that it seems to leave no room for the free exercise of personal will or choice. In this conception, Napoleon, Tsar Alexsandr, Kutusov, and all the other prominent figures directing masses of men to do this or that collectively, are acting not as free agents but as instruments of an inscrutable necessity, which compels all, from the so-called leaders to the humblest recruits, to behave in pre-determined ways. They are not making decisions based on rational calculation or scientific analysis, but are simply following the script already prepared for the matter at hand, a script that no individual forethought can alter. The script can require actions that, in retrospect, appear contrary to what common sense would have dictated. For instance, Napoleon, the master strategist and analyst of conditions, plans his retreat from Moscow to follow certain roadways through central Russia. He chooses these routes with the expectation that they will allow his troops to move through his enemy's territory with a minimum of delay and disruption. In reality, his "choices" turn out to have been those least designed to achieve these ends. He and his troops face shortages of food and forage that could have been alleviated had he taken a more southerly course. Likewise, the later disaster at the Berezina River, near the border, where French engineers had to build bridges with astounding speed and skill just to get a portion of their troops and camp followers across the river to safety, could also have been avoided had the leader not taken the route he did.

These and other military catastrophes result not from personal error or miscalculation but from the iron law of necessity under which Napoleon labors. He is destined to fail because the attack on Russia in 1812 is irrational to begin with. It is an example of perilous and senseless overreach, just like the Nazi invasion in the summer of 1941. Napoleon's and Hitler's losses in these forays have to be so decisive as to ensure the end of their respective regimes; Hitler at Stalingrad and Napoleon in Moscow have to do as foolishly as their fate demands to expedite their ultimate collapse. Like Agamemnon and Oedipus in Greek tragedy, under the illusion that they are acting in accord with their best interests, everything they do simply hastens the ends prescribed for them. What holds for Napoleon and company binds everyone else as well. Even though everyone expects the law of gravity, for instance, to operate according to immutable necessity, and so no sane person ever dares to leap from a great height thinking that gravity will not pull him or her to certain death, man still stubbornly resists the conclusion that "his will is subject to laws" (1439) of the same nature. If this were the case, a melancholy realization follows: "He could not live because all man's aspirations, all his impulses of life, are only a striving for greater freedom" (1440).

Nevertheless, actions seem freely chosen only if they are viewed in the abstract. Once a context for an act is drawn out in detail, the degree of freedom someone performing the act enjoys diminishes greatly. The more an observer knows of an individual's upbringing, personality, background, susceptibility to certain influences, biases, fears, ambitions, and so on, the less likely it becomes that in a given situation, the person could not have acted otherwise than he/she actually did. Once again, military history provides evidence for this skeptical view of freedom of choice. In the Korean War in 1950, American General Douglas MacArthur landed troops behind his North Korean foe's line of advance, forcing his enemy to retreat back toward home. The dividing line between North and South Korea is the thirty-eighth parallel of latitude. The general was warned that if he and his troops should cross this border in pursuit and enter his enemy's home territory, he would risk provoking intervention by China, the North's neighbor and fellow communist ally. General MacArthur dismissed all such warnings as alarmist and pressed his advance north. Shortly after American troops entered North Korea, the Chinese attacked them in force, pushing the Americans back, killing and capturing many, and coming dangerously close to annihilating the army that had performed so confidently and well up to this point. General MacArthur saw no way to extricate his men and restore the initiative except to intensify the conflict by attacking the Chinese on the ground and in their mainland with atomic weapons, whose toxic residue could only blight the land and endanger any civilians living near the bombs' targets. This grisly option was rejected by the authorities in Washington, and the general was relieved of command.

Did General MacArthur freely choose to cross the thirty-eighth parallel and exploit his strategic advantages? Weighing all the facts pertinent to his situation and looking back at MacArthur's education, war experience, temperament, and character, one is hard-pressed to see how he could have done otherwise. At West Point Military Academy, the future general was taught that "there is no substitute for victory;" in World War I, as a young brigadier, he took extreme chances in combat, almost taunting the enemy by his bravado and declaring to all who urged caution: "The bullet that will kill MacArthur has not been made;" he habitually referred to himself in the third person, in emulation of Julius Caesar in *The Gallic Wars*; after World War I, as Army chief of staff, MacArthur led an assault on the bonus marchers, war veterans who camped out in Washington's parks while the Congress deliberated on the timing of a bonus promised to them, and in direct violation of President Herbert Hoover's orders, he not only scattered the marchers but also burned out their makeshift camps, effectively terminating their continued presence in the capital; and in World War II, he and his family escaped capture in the Philippines by leaving the islands in a fragile PT Boat, evading the Japanese naval blockade and arriving in Australia unharmed, where he famously stated, "I came through and I shall return." These examples reinforce the portrait of a strong, aggressive, confident military commander, one unhampered by doubt, anxiety, or fear. His decision in Korea was consistent with his character and a lifetime of mostly successful military experience. Halting a promising advance out of fear of a rumored intervention was, for General MacArthur, an impossible choice. He did as he had to do and then had to deal with the consequences, confirming this conclusion:

> *So that if we examine the case of a man whose connection with the external world is very well known,*

> *where the period of time between the action and our judgment of it is very great, and the causes of the action are quite accessible to us, we arrive at a concept of a maximum of necessity and a minimum of free will.* (1447)

This example of a well-known historical actor's decision-making is not an exceptional case. Whether famous or obscure, all men and women live and make decisions on the basis of their relationships to their individual worlds, their perspectives at a particular moment in time, and the influences of their heredity and life experience. Complete freedom is an illusion, since "a being not influenced by the external world, standing outside time, and independent of cause is no longer a man" (1448). Granted, no one can enumerate, consider, and evaluate each of the forces that come into play as a person exercises what he/she believes is freedom of choice. There is, therefore, room for some contingency and some doubt as to how someone will act in a given situation, but as far as history is concerned, what appears to be the result of free choice is "only an expression for the unknown remainder of what we know of the laws of human life" (1451). In the ancient world, disease was regarded in many cases as a divine punishment; leprosy, for instance, which required isolation among the Israelites, was viewed as so severe an affliction that it must have developed in response to its victim's grave sin. As a result of advances in science and medicine, today we know much more about its causes and treatment, so much so that leprosy is now largely eliminated. The bad "choices" its sufferers were supposed to have made are chimerical, because convincing impersonal explanations for leprosy's occurrence have been established. The "unknown remainder" for leprosy has been filled in over time, so everyone knows personal conduct is no longer relevant as a contributing factor in its onset.

The study of history leads one to the realization that far from commanding events, men and women of whatever degree of eminence act in ways largely determined by factors outside individual control. It may be easier to believe that a man like Napoleon forged his own destiny and that his freely chosen actions brought about the results that are chronicled in conventional histories. The theme of *War and Peace*, however, is exactly the opposite: Napoleon thought he was choosing wisely and controlling events, when in reality he was adhering to a pattern of behavior that led inexorably to the tragic outcome foreordained. Tolstoy drives home this very Russian conclusion by asserting at the novel's end that "in history the difficulty of recognizing the subjection of the individual to the laws of space, time, and cause lies in renouncing the spontaneous feeling of independence of one's own personality" (1454–55). Unless such a renunciation occurs and men and women humbly and gratefully acknowledge, accept, and grow to love whatever destiny has decreed for them, they cannot reach any depth of understanding as to why they were put on this earth.

Among the historical characters Tolstoy depicts, only Kutusov has such insight. His realization that the immensity of the Russian heartland and the challenges its topography and elements present to outsiders are the keys to victory, which can be achieved with minimal military engagement; such an understanding sets him apart from the other generals and the tsar, who see mortal combat as the sole means of triumph. Among the civilians who figure in the narrative, the Kuragins and the Drubetskoys are blinded by their preoccupation with wealth and power exclusively; they are too worldly and too addicted to advancement through intrigue and influence to acknowledge any governing destiny in their lives. Dolokhov, too, is impervious to anything like fate guiding his thoughts and actions, even though the sociopathic character he was born with consistently leads him to inflict pain indiscriminately.

The members of the Bezukhov, Rostov, and Bolkonsky clans best exemplify the acceptance Tolstoy prescribes. After half a lifetime of going down blind alleys in his search for meaningful life commitments, Pierre Bezukhov finds fulfillment as a *paterfamilias*, performing the customary duties a man of his education and status should discharge within his own and his extended family, serving, in particular, as a model of dedication and responsibility for the children who surround him. His wife, Natasha, takes similar satisfaction in her maternal and household duties, caring little for personal pursuits or predilections separate from family life. Nikolai Rostov is managing his estates with care and concern, following time-worn agrarian principles and practices, while Countess Marya is conscientiously raising the Rostov children and her brother's son to be honorable and diligent in living out the values both the Rostov and the Bolkonsky families uphold. These exemplary figures accept the responsibilities Russian culture assigns to people of their station, and in so doing embrace the roles destiny has prepared for them as heirs of privilege. They do not try to evade or alter their fates; once they realize what their purpose is, they strive as best as they can to achieve it. Prince Andrei does not assume the same posture; his fate has led him to an early death but has also granted him insights and illuminations that have allowed him to feel and manifest unconditional love. In the best tradition of Russian mysticism, the prince's out-of-body encounters with the divine compel him to forgive his former fiancée and her would be abductor before his own death.

These men and women are more sophisticated in their understanding of their destined places in the life of their communities and nation than the soldiers at Borodino exhibited, but both the aristocrats and the peasants have the same respect for identity. The courage and indomitable will Pierre saw in the peasant defenders of the redoubt's batteries and in Platon Karateyev's cheerful embrace of daily trials and stresses, made easier to bear by the solace of folk wisdom, are the same virtues that helped Pierre survive arrest and deprivation; led Natasha to give of herself totally to alleviate the sufferings of the wounded, including Prince Andrei; fortified Countess Marya throughout a difficult life with her father; inspired Nikolai to honor his father by assuming and then repaying all his debts and restoring his estate; and prepared Prince Andrei to endure with dignity and respond with love to the sorrows brought by his life of sacrifice. For these and all like them in Mother Russia, the words of the old American Shaker hymn, "Simple Gifts," express succinctly their spirit of humble gratitude for God's providential care:

T'is the gift to be simple,
T'is the gift to be free,
T'is the gift to come down
where you ought to be.
And when you find a place just right,
You will be in the valley of love and delight.

GERMANY

Thomas Mann
Doctor Faustus

INTRODUCTION

Unlike France and Great Britain, Germany in ancient times was not conquered by the Romans during their northern European military expeditions. Julius Caesar's legions remained west of the Rhine River during their conquest of Gaul. Later, scattered Roman forays into Germany brought slaves and plunder, but these were isolated endeavors. In 9 AD, however, three battle-ready Roman legions arrived in northwest Germany and began a slow-moving reconnaissance in force within a heavily forested area east of the Rhine. Their presence provoked the tribal leader Arminius to gather a native contingent to shadow the invaders. Since, as a young captive, Arminius had been schooled in Roman strategy and tactics, he was able to assess how best to confront and defeat these legions. He aligned his forces in such ways as to promote ambush, which the heavily armored enemy had little experience defending against, so that when the Germans attacked outside the Teutoburg Forest, the surprised Romans panicked and fled in confusion and disarray. This defeat of the veteran legions was so shocking and so devastating that no further military incursions into the German heartland were attempted. The Emperor Caesar Augustus was forced to recognize the line formed by the Rhine and Danube rivers as the boundary of the Roman Empire in what would become Central Europe. Along the rivers on both sides, Romans and Germans mingled in settlements and carried on trade, but few Romans ventured further inland. As a result, the Latin language, Roman law, and Roman administration never had the impact in Germany that they did in France and Great Britain. Centuries later, in his *Addresses to the German Nation*, the philosopher Fichte attributed the survival of the German language and German culture, and hence the German identity, to the epochal victory of Arminius and the resistance to assimilation it inspired.

Nevertheless, within the empire as a whole and over time, German influence was disproportionately strong. Particularly in the army, German-born officers and commanders were numerous, largely due to their exceptional skills, their aptitude for organization and planning, and their courage and steadfastness in battle. In 451 AD, for instance, a Roman force that included many Germanic personnel, defeated Attila the Hun at Chalons-sur-Marne, thereby preserving most of France and the West from being subjugated to and plundered by marauding Central Asian nomadic tribes.

The Germans also embraced Christianity, as preached and practiced by the Roman Catholic Church. In 800 AD, Pope Sylvester recognized the growing power and importance of the northern European territories by crowning Charlemagne, the Frankish king, emperor of the west, a bold act that pushed the center of gravity in the new empire far to the north and away from the lands bordering the Mediterranean Sea. Charlemagne's realm included Germany in the east, thus bringing Germans, Franks, Lombards, and Belgians together in one giant political entity under the suzerainty of the pope. This unified structure, however, did not succeed Charlemagne. Under his heirs, the empire gradually separated into three distinct divisions. The western portion eventually became France; the eastern portion remained Germany; and the middle strip extending to the Italian border encompassed parts of modern Belgium and the provinces of Alsace, Lorraine, and Burgundy. The German territories eventually coalesced within a federation of largely independent provinces and cities united nominally under an elected emperor who reigned over the "Holy Roman Empire of the German Nation." This body retained its structure and sovereignty through numerous upheavals, multi-national wars, religious disputes, and popular uprisings, until 1806, when Napoleon abolished the empire entirely.

The decentralized character of the Holy Roman Empire, with individual units exercising an independent authority amounting to virtual self-rule, contributed greatly to what would become the most important development in German history since Armimius's defeat of the Romans centuries before. In 1517, Martin Luther, an Augustinian monk and newly minted doctoral degree holder, nailed a hefty document to the door of the castle church in Wittenberg, a small city in northeast Germany where Luther taught Scripture at the local college. The document contained ninety-five theses, propositions concerning a variety of teachings and practices in the contemporary Catholic Church that Luther found questionable at best. His intent was to stimulate academic discussion and debate around these matters, with a view toward ultimate reexamination and reform where necessary. One issue, in particular, drew the monk's scorn. In parts of Germany at this time, specially commissioned clerics were drawing crowds in and outside of churches with fund-raising appeals based on the issuance of indulgences, papal pardons that would lessen a penitent's time in purgatory after death. Ordinarily, indulgences could be earned for oneself or a family member through prayer, good works, fasts, certain devotions, or other approved pious practices. In 1517, however, a different theme was being stressed: if believers made a cash donation to a fund established to defray the costs of the construction of a new St. Peter's Cathedral in Rome, an indulgence remitting time in purgatory would be gained immediately, with no further penitential practice required. Luther was outraged by what he saw as a gross misrepresentation of the nature and necessity of true penitence by agents sanctioned through and working on behalf of the Holy See.

Far from provoking only gentlemanly debate among scholars, however, Luther's powerful pronouncements unleashed a wave of pent-up resentment and criticism among members of all social and political classes in Germany. Over the succeeding months, churches were invaded and despoiled, clergy were harassed, ecclesiastical lands were overrun, and many students, seminarians, and priests were radicalized. The authorities reacted harshly, subjecting known reformers to instant execution upon capture and trying mostly in vain to suppress all pamphlets and publications advocating heterodox views. For Luther himself and his closest followers, matters came to a head in 1520, when the pope condemned a number of Luther's propositions as contrary to established doctrine and teaching. At this critical juncture, Elector Frederick of Saxony, later referred to as "the Wise," exercised his prerogative as the governing executive in Wittenberg to intervene on Luther's behalf. Rather than having Luther arrested, the elector persuaded Charles V, the Holy Roman Emperor, to allow his subject to appear for a hearing under a guarantee of safe conduct at the Diet of Worms the following year. The emperor agreed, but Luther's associates were immediately apprehensive. Almost a century before, the Bohemian reformer, Jan Hus, who had also questioned the efficacy of indulgences, was invited by political and church leaders to appear before them at the Council of Constance to explain his views. He, too, was issued a safe conduct pass by King Sigismund of Germany and Hungary. At this meeting, Hus was acquitted of heretical teachings on certain issues, but on others, amounting to capital offenses, he could be spared the death penalty only if he formally recanted his teachings. Hus did not recant, so despite the safe conduct assurance, he was burned to death on July 6, 1415. Such an ominous precedent could not be ignored.

Assured by the elector, however, and buoyed by his profound faith and trust in God, Luther took the emperor at his word and agreed to appear at Worms. This encounter would become one of Western history's most dramatic moments. The contrasts among the participants could not have been greater. Arrayed in elegant robes and wearing all sorts of medals and ornate headgear, on the one hand, were the juridical ruler of the nation, as well as many other places, the emperor Charles, and the princes of the individual states within Germany, and on the other hand, facing all this wealth and power, in simple monk's habit, stood Friar Martin Luther, vowed to poverty, chastity, and obedience. It was David confronting not just one Goliath but a whole roomful of giants. But after a day of reflection and prayer, Martin Luther found enough courage and strength to stand before the glittering assembly on April 17, 1521, and make a statement of conscience in words that would echo through the ages: "Here I stand; I cannot do otherwise; God help me." The stunned gathering watched in amazement as Luther quickly departed with his friends, emphasizing his triumphant moment by thrusting his arms in the air like a victorious jouster. He had entered the lion's den, reaffirmed his principles, and left unharmed.

The Elector Frederick, however, took no further chances. He sent knights the following day to find Luther and bring him to the Wartburg Castle, in Eisenach, for safekeeping. He spent approximately one year there, principally occupied in translating the New Testament into German. Luther survived his early trials and went on to develop further his radically reformed teachings on the Bible, sacramental graces, the priesthood, and ecclesiastical and political governance. With all hope of reconciliation with Rome gone, the Lutheran community formed its own church, laying out and codifying its beliefs within a document called the *Augsburg Confession of 1530*. This statement has guided Lutheran teaching and practice worldwide ever since. With the establishment of Lutheranism as a valid and legal Christian church, and with the addition of Calvinism, a contemporary movement inspired by Haldrych Zwingli and John Calvin, Germany became the first religiously diverse nation in Europe. Over time, individual states became predominantly Catholic, Lutheran, or Calvinist, largely in response to the preferences of their ruling princes. These three bodies were officially recognized, but other groups on the fringes, like Moravians and Pietists, were not. Because they were discriminated against, many adherents of these sects later migrated to parts of the New World, where they could live and worship freely.

Martin Luther is probably the most important and most influential German thinker, theologian, and personality not only of his time but of all time. His religious reforms amounted almost to a new foundation for Christianity, but his impact extended to other spheres as well. He was a trailblazer, for instance, in the presentation of his teachings. Luther differed from the scholastic thinkers of the Middle Ages, such as

Thomas Aquinas, who followed a pattern of exposition and argument that purported to reconcile reason, as exemplified in Aristotle's works and revelation, as contained in the Old and New Testaments. This pattern resembles the proceedings in a Roman law court. A proposition concerning an article of faith is offered as a point to be disputed (i.e., "God does not exist"). Then, as in a court examination by a prosecutor, a number of points are asserted to confirm that the proposition as stated is correct. With the words "sed contra" ("but on the contrary"), the defense makes its case in favor of the article of faith, carefully refuting the arguments made before by use of Aristotle's words and relevant Bible references. Following the refutations, a number of positive arguments are highlighted to confirm the article in question, buttressed again by pagan and Christian sources. For each proposition cited, the conclusion or verdict goes to the defender of the faith, who weaves rational and faith-based elements together to make it appear that every article of faith has both a natural and supernatural justification. Luther laid aside this scholastic procedure, even though for several centuries it had formed the basis for seminary education in most of Catholic Europe and for studies in philosophy per se. For Luther, scholasticism relied too heavily on Aristotle and other pagan thinkers for its proofs, became too engrossed in abstract or metaphysical issues, like the means whereby transubstantiation occurs in the Eucharist, and utilized the Bible mostly as a source of brief and disconnected insights, not holistically, as the living Word of God.

Luther's writings are filled with biblical citations and references, particularly from Paul's Epistles, that illustrate in detail how a certain teaching must be shaped by the exact words of a key passage or passages. He also tries to show how some theological tenets do not flow from or correspond to the clear sense of passages in the Bible adduced in their confirmation. On the subject of transubstantiation, for instance, he basically dismisses the explanation of the action by rejecting the Aristotelian distinction between substance and accident that is its centerpiece, famously insisting that "the Holy Spirit is greater than Aristotle." He defines the Eucharist as the reception of the bread and wine Jesus offered to his disciples at the Last Supper as his body and blood, quoting Paul's words in *1 Corinthians*, and adds little by way of explication.

Over the following centuries, German scholars continued to subject the articles of faith, as well as received knowledge in cognate disciplines like philosophy and history, to serious analysis. German biblical scholars in the nineteenth and twentieth centuries, for example, made important discoveries about the essential teachings of Jesus that highlighted his emphasis on the "Kingdom of God" as an imminent manifestation, an emphasis embraced by the early church as well. Other scholars laid out the different strands of narrative woven into the account of creation in the Book of Genesis, identifying parts of four distinct traditions within the canonical text. Taking their cue from Luther also, who stressed the transcendence of God and the inability of human reason alone to arrive at revealed truth, German secular thinkers such as Kant, Fichte, Hegel, Nietzsche, and Heidegger, also dwelt on the need for humans to rise above empirical realities and strive to access the highest truths revealed by spirit (*Geist*), especially the moral imperatives that must guide conduct. Disagreement among these and other philosophers on various points should not obscure their nearly unanimous insistence on the priority of intuition (analogous to faith) rather than reason in one's striving to reach the realm of the spirit.

With regard to the arts, Luther provided his countrymen similar guidance. The size and splendid decoration of the Catholic churches in Luther's time, particularly the new cathedral of St. Peter taking shape in Rome, did not appeal to the young monk, and not just because of the dubious methods resorted to in fund raising. To Luther, and Protestants generally, these churches are too distracting and too ornate, seducing worshippers with their almost idolatrous excesses and inspiring a piety that elevates the arts over apostolic simplicity. Zealous reformers in the early days of the Lutheran revolt who took over Catholic churches in some towns, immediately painted over elaborate artistic renditions of biblical events and replaced high altars and statuary with plain furnishings. To this day, Lutheran and other Protestant churches are notably austere in regard to visual arts.

The direct opposite, however, occurred in the musical arts. Martin Luther loved music. He sang psalms and hymns devotedly both as a monk and as a reformer and left one powerful composition, *"A Mighty Fortress is Our God,"* that became the anthem of the Reformation. This hymn is based on a Latin chant that Luther adapted and translated into German, thereby doing for liturgical music what he had done in his translation of the New Testament, making key elements of the faith comprehensible to all. In so doing, he was firmly within the German cultural tradition, which since medieval times had promoted musical competitions and festivals of every sort. Indeed, the Wartburg Castle, where Luther stayed in hiding for a year, was the setting for the Meistersingers' contests celebrated later by Richard Wagner. Protestant composers largely followed Luther's lead in presenting their works in German, while their Catholic counterparts kept almost exclusively to the Latin texts. The greatest Lutheran composer, however, Johann Sebastian Bach, produced compositions in both languages. On the one hand, he used classic sixteenth-century German hymns in cantatas and instrumental elaborations that contain sophisticated contrapuntal variations on the simple tunes of masters like Praetorius, Rinkart, and Hassler. On the other hand, in what could be viewed later as ecumenical gestures, Bach created magnificent Latin choral works such as the *Mass in B Minor* and the *Magnificat in D Major*. The level of expertise and mastery German and Austrian composers, instrumentalists, choirs, and soloists achieved in succeeding centuries may not always have reached the heights of Bach, but it was very high, indeed. Catholic and Protestant churches throughout the German-speaking world employed musicians of the highest caliber to ensure that sabbath and holiday worship would be enriched by expert presentation of all that was best in the liturgical repertoire. Outside the churches, composers like Handel, Beethoven, Brahms, Schubert, and Mendelsohn, composed magnificent religious music independently, relying on performances in concert halls and theaters to lift the mind and heart to God.

What distinguishes German music is its complexity. Borrowing from the seventeenth-century Italian and French masters, especially in instrumental compositions like the sinfonia, sonata, concerto, quartet, and quintet, German composers like Bach and Telemann, and Austrians like Haydn and Mozart, perfected a form intermingling themes with variations to create a dynamic and interrelated compositional whole. This style makes a listener concentrate carefully on how a theme is introduced, shaped, contrasted, returned in altered form, and repeated finally in its original version. In Italian and French works of the same type, the degree to which variations subject a theme to complex alterations is lessened in favor of sometimes lush and recurring melody. This format appeals strongly to the emotions, while in Germanic compositions, themes and variations must be absorbed and traced by the intellect.

The upheaval Luther began and the nascent communities he and others established led to conflict between German Protestants and Catholics locally and, in the case of the Thirty Years War of 1618 to 1648, between Protestants and Catholics from most of Europe. This long struggle was fought intermittently all over Germany by troops loyal to the Holy Roman Emperor, who was determined to extirpate Protestantism completely and reestablish Catholicism as the only religion in the nation he theoretically ruled; by troops loyal to the Lutheran and Calvinist principalities, fighting literally for their survival as separate entities; by troops from Sweden, intervening late in the war to save the Protestant cause; and by troops from Denmark and France, dispatched not to defend a particular religion but mainly to annex territory near their borders. Indeed, in the case of Catholic France, dynastic hostility to the likewise Catholic Hapsburg Empire made it necessary for the French to oppose in every way their co-religionists' interests. France even declared war on Catholic Spain in the last years of the conflict. Liberal subsidies of gold but no troops arrived from England to aid the Protestant states, and more gold from Spain's New World territories came to bolster Catholic fortunes. Spanish troops would have been even more welcome to the Catholic emperor, but geography worked against a large-scale Spanish military advance into Germany. Because English and French navies controlled the sea routes from Spain to the Low Countries, Spanish troops could not disembark in Belgian or Dutch ports and then march over the Rhine into northwest Germany. The Spanish could not risk a long Mediterranean expedition for the same reasons; English and French vessels routinely patrolled these waters. The only remaining possibility was to advance a sizeable body of troops under strong naval guard the relatively short distance from Spain to northern Italy. From there, the Spanish could move over the Alps and enter Austrian territory from the west. This expedient could not be employed, however, because a single pass through the Alps, called the Val Telline, was the only feasible route the Spanish troops could take through difficult mountain terrain, and this narrow passage was blocked by the French throughout the war.

By 1648, all combatants realized that the confessional status quo recognized in Germany for over a century could not be altered by force. The Peace of Westphalia ended the war and maintained these divisions, which, at least formally, still govern religious life in Germany. The end of religious warfare, though, did not bring ecumenical convergence. For about the next three centuries, a political and cultural divide separated Protestants and Catholics, which manifested itself in recurring episodes of mutual hostility. In areas predominantly Protestant, largely in Germany's north and east, not just believers but citizens in general displayed seriousness of purpose and a cold certainty about core values and perspectives. They tended to look down on Catholics as backward, almost superstitious, dominated by clergy, and nonchalant about their faith. Some of this prejudice would become starkly evident in the late nineteenth century when Prussian authorities instituted the *Kulturkampf* (Culture War), a countrywide effort to reduce the influence of the

Catholic Church, seen as retrogressive, in education, culture, politics, and family life. Although this non-violent renewal of denominational hostilities did not succeed in fundamentally changing Catholic beliefs or practices, it left lingering tensions. In the eyes of many Protestant Prussians, who, after 1870, would lead a unified Germany, Catholics seemed an alien body, more loyal to the pope than to the kaiser. Prussian state-building demanded loyal and patriotic commitment, something regarded as second nature for Protestants but eliciting more of a pragmatic or provisional response from Catholics. The great nineteenth-century German philosopher Hegel was so impressed by the highly organized bureaucratic apparatus that made Prussian administration almost as strict and efficient as a military command, he apotheosized the Prussian state as the culmination of historical development, the ultimate exemplar of all that previous centuries had contributed to social and political evolution.

German Catholics, concentrated in the northwest and south, perhaps because they sensed how necessary it was to keep from further exciting Protestant enmity, kept a low profile politically and religiously. They looked to the time-honored and more relaxed style of the multinational Hapsburg Empire, the successor to the Holy Roman Empire, for guidance on how to integrate diverse faiths and nationalities harmoniously. Hapsburg Vienna's waltzes, polkas, and festivals contrasted sharply with Berlin's army parades and disciplined habits. German and Austrian Catholics did not usually fret over the flagship tenets of Lutheranism or Calvinism, such as justification by faith or predestination; they tended to internalize traditional ways and practices, performing spiritual duties and following well-established rites and rules carefully enough to feel secure about salvation. The close-knit rural and small-town families of modest means that made up the majority of German-speaking Catholics kept most members loyal to each other and to their common faith.

The monumental task of unifying Germany after the Holy Roman Emperor's failure to do so along religious lines despite thirty years of warfare, fell, as noted above, to Prussia, more precisely Brandenburg-Prussia, a province in northeastern Germany that was built up in the Middle Ages by the Teutonic Knights, a military order that used this territory as a staging ground for raids and expeditions into Slavic lands to the east. The process of bringing so many independent political units together under Prussian leadership took over a century and involved several generations of monarchs from the Hohenzollern dynasty, as well as diplomats, generals, and, above all, strong armies.

Aggressive leadership and daring characterized the Prussian efforts. In 1740, for instance, the year he ascended the throne, the Prussian King Frederick II (later honored as "the Great") brazenly invaded neighboring Silesia, an Austrian rather than a German province. This provocation led to a multi-state and worldwide conflict, the Seven Years' War of 1756–1763. This war was fought in Europe and in North America. In Europe, a coalition consisting of France, Russia, Sweden, and Austria attacked Prussia when Frederick refused to restore Silesia to Austria and bring an end to Prussian expansionism. In North America, Great Britain and France fought a separate war for control of Canada and the American colonies. Frederick was under immense pressure, as his outnumbered troops had to repel attacks on several fronts, but aided by talented generals, he emerged victorious. The British were also successful in the New World, forcing France to cede control of Canadian territory it had governed since the seventeenth century. These results made the two strongest European Protestant powers, Great Britain and Prussia, even stronger and the two major Catholic powers, Austria and France, weaker.

This trend continued into the next century. After the French revolutionaries ended the Bourbon monarchy, Napoleon Bonaparte declared himself emperor of the French in 1804. At the Battle of Austerlitz two years later, as *War and Peace* describes, he decisively defeated a combined Russian and Austrian force assembled to overthrow him, compelling the Holy Roman Emperor Francis I to surrender in humiliation. Napoleon took advantage of this fluid political situation by summarily abolishing the Holy Roman empire, a structure dating back to the successors of Charlemagne, and absorbing its German Catholic provinces into what he termed the Confederation of the Rhine, a nascent national grouping. These actions would become the equivalent of gifts to Prussia. By 1814, Napoleon's own empire was being abolished, and he himself banished into exile. Prussia continued to grow in strength and prestige, defeating Austria one more time at the Battle of Königgrätz in 1866 and France at the Battle of Sedan in 1870. After the French were defeated, Kaiser Wilhelm I was crowned emperor of Germany in the palace of Versailles, and the Second German Reich was born, the First Reich having gone the way of the Byzantine Empire. Ironically, after its defeat in World War I and the abdication of Kaiser Wilhelm II in 1918, Germany would be forced to sign a peace treaty with victorious Allied powers in the same place the Second Reich was created, the palace of Versailles.

But even though political leadership in the German states moved from Vienna to Berlin in the nineteenth century, the ancient Austrian capital still retained cultural leadership contemporaneously. With the Hapsburg emperor and his family, high government and church dignitaries, members of the nobility, and foreign emissaries all residing in or near Vienna, composers and musicians, in particular, from throughout Germany, Austria, Hungary, Bohemia and the Czech lands (all parts of the Holy Roman Empire until 1806) took up residence in the city in search of commissions and appointments. The creative work these artists did would make the period from the mid-eighteenth century to the mid-twentieth century a golden age for Vienna and for music, the art form most congenial to the German spirit. In this regard, Vienna's eminence as a musical capital through this span parallels Rome's eminence as a capital for painters, sculptors, architects, and all the craftsmen associated with them, between the fifteenth and the seventeenth centuries.

As noted earlier, in the eighteenth century, in addition to liturgical masterpieces, Haydn and Mozart made great advances in secular forms, such as symphonies, piano sonatas and concerti, and compositions for various string ensembles. These contributions were developed further by Ludwig van Beethoven, who left Bonn, in the Rhineland, as the eighteenth century was drawing to a close and settled in Vienna. Enjoying the patronage of members of the royal family and other notable benefactors, he would overcome handicaps of every sort through almost four decades to produce a body of works unsurpassed in power and originality. For instance, his innovations in the structure of the symphony made this form far more dramatic, expressive, and emotive. His *Eroica Symphony*, originally dedicated to Napoleon, departs from the classic models by adding a fourth movement and lengthening and intensifying each segment for an orchestra far larger than the classical ensemble. Near the end of his life, Beethoven composed the *Ninth Symphony,* which includes a vocal quartet and large chorus in a final movement that sets to stirring effect Friedrich Shiller's *"Ode to Joy,"* a paean to universal brotherhood. After Beethoven, Franz Schubert, who was a pall bearer at his great predecessor's funeral, and Johannes Brahms, who left northern Germany like Beethoven to make Vienna his home until his death in 1897, made notable contributions in a variety of musical formats. Schubert turned out exceptionally powerful works for solo piano and string ensembles that plumb emotional depths akin to those Beethoven called up in his last compositions, while Brahms offered rich melodic and thematic variations in orchestral, instrumental, and choral works, adhering carefully to classic models.

As the nineteenth century drew to close, two composers brought the Viennese chapter of German musical history to culmination. Gustav Mahler, director of the Vienna Court Opera from 1897 to 1907, and Anton Bruckner, church organist and frequent visitor to Vienna, created numerous and varied works but are probably best known for their symphonies. Each composed nine like Beethoven. Mahler's melded folk themes as well as sophisticated orchestral, vocal, and choral elements into symphonic movements ranging from high-spirited and joyful to solemn and exalting; Bruckner crafted long and sometimes rugged structures that, at their best, evoke the power and grandeur of organ recitals.

A few prominent German composers resisted the call of Vienna and spent most of their careers in their native country. In the mid-nineteenth century, Felix Mendelsohn played an important role in restoring and promoting the music of Bach, a composer who seemed anachronistic in post-revolutionary Europe. In concerts he arranged and conducted, Mendelsohn programmed Bach's great choral works, such as the *St. Matthew Passion* and the *Mass in B Minor,* as well as other compositions, allowing the public to hear again music that is at the soul of German culture. Mendelsohn's own *Reformation Symphony* is set in the same spiritual cosmos in which Bach lived, as it strongly suggests the purposeful determination of the Reformers with references to *"A Mighty Fortress is Our God"* and other hymn-like themes echoing throughout. Robert Schumann's works celebrate festive events, such as grape harvests in the Rhineland and the coming of spring and nature's rebirth; this composer also offers in his *Rhenish Symphony* a solemn orchestral evocation of a service in Cologne Cathedral, Germany's greatest Gothic structure, illustrating again how central religion is in the German consciousness.

Two German composers had a lasting impact on music drama. Richard Wagner brought medieval legends to brilliant life on stage, in the process forcing orchestral players to test the limits of their skills repeatedly and demanding that singers stretch power, range, and control beyond what could normally be achieved. The Wagnerian bass and the Wagnerian soprano were and still are, as a result, a rare and special breed, with only a select few performers over time considered worthy of the roles Wagner laid out. Richard Strauss was younger than Wagner and more cosmopolitan in his inspirations. If Wagner looked mostly to medieval Germany for ideas and tales, Strauss's music radiates more of the Italian-inspired spirit of Mozart's operas. *Der Rosenkavalier*, for instance, with its eighteenth-century setting, its male/female disguises and intrigues, its lush harmonies and vocal ensembles, and its many comic moments, bears comparison to a work like *The Marriage of Figaro*. Strauss also composed imaginative symphonic narratives, such as the tone poem *Till Eulenspiegel*, that renders in colorful variations the "merry pranks" of a happy-go-lucky archetype, and *Also Sprach Zarathustra*, a soaring and visionary musical realization of Friedrich Nietzsche's philosophical exploration of superhuman striving.

Strauss was the last great German composer of serious music, ending a line that can be traced back to the sixteenth century church musicians. It is, therefore, appropriate that his final full-scale orchestral piece, *Metamorphoses for Strings*, should serve as a requiem for all that German musical genius has left to the world. In a series of somber variations on a theme resembling the *"Funeral March"* of Beethoven's *Eroica Symphony,* Strauss mourns the devastation World War II inflicted on his people, their institutions, and their heritage. In the last days of this war, cities like Munich and Dresden, so important in German cultural history, were bombed heavily, badly damaging theaters, opera houses, conservatories, and museums that had supported artistic life for centuries. The German capital, Berlin, was attacked by over a million Russian troops in 1945, many of them eager to avenge in blood the ravages German invaders had perpetrated all over Russia since 1941. Add to these ravages the systematic persecution and slaughter of the Holocaust, and one realizes that Strauss's musical lament is all-encompassing in the range of its sorrow. The sufferings Germans had to endure in 1945, combined with the sufferings Germans had inflicted on so many others throughout the Second World War, are called up and blended in this haunting masterpiece as nowhere else in music.

If the finest German music soars in its power and beauty into the highest realms, lifting the listener to new levels of perception and spiritual experience, German philosophy, through roughly the same mid-eighteenth to mid-twentieth century span, has a similar effect on the intellect. Like many of the composers, these philosophers find inspiration in concepts enunciated in dramatic form in Goethe's *Faust*, which they lay out and organize within systems that purport to explain the nature of the world and man's place and function within it with absolute certitude. Their starting point is the terms of Faust's pact with

Mephistopheles. Just as the God of the Hebrews gives Satan the freedom to torment Job, upright and faithful, by any means, in an effort to make him abandon his God, so in the *"Prologue in Heaven"* that opens *Faus*t, God grants Mephistopheles the power to try and produce the same outcome in the scholar Faust, whom the Lord calls "my servant" (*Faust, Part I*, trans., Bayard Taylor. New York: Washington Square Press, 1964, p. 11). Mephistopheles relishes the opportunity to make Faust submit to his guidance rather than obey "The Ancient's word." (12). Faust is vulnerable because at this point in his life, the aging scholar is restless, skeptical, despairing, sure now that study is unavailing and that "nothing can be known" (13). He is even ready to resort to "magic" (13), the primitive method for accessing nature's secrets and unlocking her might. After some preliminary back-and-forth, Faust agrees to put himself under Mephistopheles' tutelage and control and to allow his soul to endure eternal agony in hell after his death, in exchange for a quasi-divine freedom to know and experience all the possibilities of life and to produce achievements of world-historical importance. Faust also specifies that his earthly life should end and his descent into hell begin at the moment he ceases to "strive" and gives in to the desire to linger and pause in some agreeable place and rest content, even for just a short while:

When thus I hail the moment flying:
"Ah, still delay—thou art so fair!"
Then bind me in thy bonds undying,
My final ruin then declare!
Then let the death bell chime the token,
Then art thou from thy service free!
The clock may stop, the hand be broken,
Then time be finished unto me! (54)

German philosophers likewise emphasize the need to break out of the mundane everyday world and move higher into the metaphysical world of Spirit (*Geist*). From Immanuel Kant reacting in the eighteenth century against the empiricism of

David Hume, to Martin Heidegger speculating on being and time in the twentieth century, German thinkers have been insistent on mankind's need to "strive" like Faust ceaselessly to intuit truth. In the nomenclature of Kant, the world of *phenomena* experienced by the senses must be superseded; the philosopher can do this by entering through rigorous intellectual effort the realm of Spirit, wherein he or she can grasp *noumena*, abstract and eternal absolutes that, once apprehended and embraced, will become the foundation for a virtuous life. Kant terms the instinct to seek moral truths the "categorical imperative." It is like the serious thinker's North Star, a guide that, if followed faithfully, leads invariably to the right life choices. Like Faust, the philosophical seeker of truth must not let complacency or self-satisfaction contradict the realization that only continual striving can bring the soul to a level of moral perfection over the span of a lifetime.

The philosopher Johann Gottlieb Fichte elaborated on these principles, stressing the potentialities that could be unlocked in everyone through universal education. In his *Addresses to the German Nation*, a series of lectures composed and delivered while most Germans chafed under Napoleon's control, Fichte laid out a scheme for educating all his countrymen in the higher thought, so that they could then show everyone else by example how to attain moral excellence. By means of this "national education," a student would be prepared for self-sacrifice and self-achievement and think hardly at all about personal gain. Modeling in their lives the highest standards, the earnest and industrious Germans would inspire in others the urge to become their proteges, for "the German spirit is an eagle, whose mighty body thrusts itself on high and soars on strong and well-practiced wings into the empyrean, that it may rise nearer to the sun whereon it delights to gaze" (*Fifth Address*, trans. R.F. Jones & G.H. Turnbull, New York: Harper Torchbooks, 1968, p. 74).

Georg Wilhelm Friedrich Hegel (1770–1831) echoed these sentiments, albeit without poetic embellishment. A scholar and professor, he published voluminous collections of lecture notes, essays, theoretical speculations, and discursive forays into history and aesthetics. He devised the theory of dialectical interaction between thesis and antithesis leading to synthesis, which Karl Marx later recognized as the prime mover of historical change. Conflict is an important component in German philosophy; without it, the complacency and stagnation dreaded by Faust are inevitable and corrosive. Being then stifles becoming, tradition overpowers innovation, age trumps youth, and staleness pollutes the freshest atmosphere. The operation of Hegel's dialectic keeps man and beast, nature and culture, constantly developing and creating anew. As noted earlier, Hegel saw in the Prussian state a new and unique organism, where all citizens have a role and a status, where duty and teamwork are freely accepted, and where bureaucratic organization systematizes the interactions of the units of government and makes quasi-military order and discipline the guiding principle in all enterprises. The Prussian state apparatus for Hegel was the product of centuries of political development, a work of art that could never be surpassed or superseded, just copied. Both Fichte and Hegel must be regarded as German nationalists but in the best sense only. They saw in Germans a seriousness of purpose, an intellectual orientation, and a moral sensitivity different in kind from the personal qualities of other nationalities. The figure of "German Michael," modest, honest, industrious, and direct, approximates in folk culture what these philosophers were trying to portray in high culture.

Friedrich Nietzsche (1844–1900), by contrast, rejected pretty much the whole of mainstream German philosophy's presumptions and conclusions, particularly its focus on the heights where Spirit dwells and moral certitude is attained. Nietzsche could hardly conceal his contempt for such thinking and for the people who seemed so eager to assimilate its teachings. This self-styled "pure blooded Polish nobleman" with "no drop of bad blood, least of all German" (*Ecce Homo*. Trans., R.J. Hollingdale, New York: Penguin Books, p. 13) flowing in his veins, was clearly an outlier in the nation of his birth and in the life around him. Not surprisingly, as someone who saw himself possessing "in so instinctively pristine a degree" (14) the virtues of self-assertion, courage, knightly grace, and romance that characterized a Polish "*pan*" of the seventeenth century, as portrayed, for instance, by Gogol in *Taras Bulba*, Nietzsche could find little to admire in his homeland. Not even "the young German Kaiser," Wilhelm II, was worthy of the "honor" of being this philosopher's "coachman" (14). Nietzsche argues that one of the main reasons for the absence of greatness in his contemporaries is the pervasive influence of Christian morality, which over the centuries since medieval times had brainwashed European humanity. For him, the virtues inculcated by earnest Christian teaching, humility, selflessness, charity, and self-abnegation, are not ennobling but debilitating. Men and women, says Nietzsche, would be much better and stronger if they did what their instincts and natures dictated, regardless of conventional proprieties. Nietzsche proposes a "revaluation of values," through which the opposite of each of the virtues Christianity upholds is made preferable. For instance, Christians are taught to love their enemies and, if struck, to turn the other cheek. Nietzsche sees nothing to be gained by acting this way. This descendant of hussars admits to being "by nature warlike" (20). Though he spent most of his life in solitary pursuits, he approached his tasks like a jouster, "challenging problems to a duel" (20). Far from shrinking away from or, worse yet, loving away a confrontation with an adversary of whatever type, one should respond to the inner need to strive mightily to overcome the strongest "enemy." Only by so doing, can the breakthroughs and advances Hegel attributed to dialectical clashes in the abstract be achieved in one's own experience. The result confirms an individual's capability and invigorates:

> *The undertaking is to master, not any resistances that happen to present themselves, but those against which one has to bring all one's strength, suppleness, and mastery of weapons—to master equal opponents . . . Equality in face of the enemy—first presupposition of an honest duel.* (20–21)

The passivity and meekness recommended by Christianity do not resonate for such a thinker, nor do any of the other traditional virtues.

Nietzsche also objects to the German philosophical orientation toward idealism and metaphysics, insisting that such a tendency leads only to pointless speculation about the nature and role of Spirit as the world's prime mover. To him, thinkers in this tradition are chasing after phantoms and are no more wired into the nature of things than Luther was when he threw his inkwell at what he was sure was the devil, come to harass and frighten him in the Wartburg Castle. Though most of the German philosophers who preceded Nietzsche were by no means practicing Christians, they still retained, in his view, a mindset formed by the faith of their fathers taught to them as youths. The Spirit they sought connection with could be seen as God by another name, and the moral certainties revealed through spiritual insight were nothing but classical Christian precepts taken out of their biblical context. The spirit/flesh duality these philosophers subscribe to is, for instance, a fundamental element of St. Paul's teachings, as in this excerpt from the Letter to the Romans: "Those who are in the flesh cannot please God. But you are not in the flesh; on the contrary, you are in the Spirit, if only the Spirit of God dwells in you" (Romans 8:8-9).

Nietzsche is a seeker too but not for God or Spirit or moral absolutes. Like Fichte, he wants to teach not just the youth of Germany but the youth of all the world to emancipate themselves from the constraints of conventional wisdom by aspiring to the state of an *Ubermensch*, an exalted creature who uses every means necessary to assert freely his or her uniquely human strengths and abilities. Such people do not strive to live as disembodied souls; for Nietzsche, this condition holds as little attraction as it does for Achilles, who would rather till the soil of earth than rule in the Underworld. The *Ubermensch* is, in his or her own way, pure and undefiled, indifferent to money, prestige, honors, distinction, and every other illusory "good." This magnificent being soars like Fichte's eagle, but does so by following natural propensities since "everything good is instinct—and consequently easy, necessary, and free" (81). Thus, an idealized embodiment of the Polish "*pan*" becomes a master of the universe.

A historical footnote is appropriate at this juncture. Nietzsche's celebration of Polish knighthood focuses too heavily on its superficial glitter and gold. The nobles he admires undoubtedly registered remarkable achievements, including incorporating Lithuania and Ukraine into a Polish Commonwealth that for a time rivaled in power Germany and Russia. This nation's greatest military triumph was of world historical significance. In 1683, a coalition led by King John III Sobieski and his Polish hussars decisively defeated a Turkish invading force laying siege to Vienna, thereby sparing Europe any further Islamic expansion. But while the largest cavalry charge in history undoubtedly captivated the imagination of a man who described himself as "warlike by nature," it was a moment of glory that brought little in the way of lasting benefit to Poland.

Over the next century, the self-assertion Nietzsche regards as the essential attribute of true greatness worked against political progress and stability in the multi-national Polish Commonwealth. Each one of the nobles who served in the nation's Parliament had the right to exercise the "*liberum veto*," a single but critical vote against a proposal for change in the operation of any fundamental legal or administrative procedure that would effectively negate the proposal. This provision made unanimity essential for any legislation with countrywide impact to become law. Because it was virtually impossible to get self-important, touchy, and willful individuals like the members of the Polish governing class to agree on anything of importance, political paralysis set in. Poland's Commonwealth began to fracture over the course of the eighteenth century, as no shared initiatives could be undertaken to address issues. Soon, powerful neighbors saw opportunity in Poland's impotence. Austria, Prussia, and Russia combined in 1772 to divide parts of the Polish-Lithuanian Commonwealth among themselves, a process of dismemberment repeated in 1793 and 1795, after which the proud and heroic nation of Poland ceased to exist. The "noblest of races that the earth has ever possessed" (14) had managed in just over one hundred years to squander all the power and prestige that had built a commonwealth and had prevented a hostile takeover of Christian Europe. Because of this epic failure of national leadership, Friedrich Nietzsche was born a German citizen.

All the important and evolving strains contributing to the formation of German identity and culture outlined in this introductory section are referred to in some fashion in Thomas Mann's *Doctor Faustus*. This novel is the story of a fictional German composer whose lifespan coincides with the history of his nation through a period beginning with confidence and optimism and ending in catastrophe. From Adrian Leverkuhn's birth in 1885, after Germany becomes unified within a Prussian Empire as a result of military triumphs over Austria and France that make her the most dominant and feared continental nation-state, to Adrian's death in 1940, shortly before the full sorrows of defeat, civilian suffering, and unprecedented atrocity and persecution will be revealed and endured by the German people, Adrian Leverkuhn experiences as an individual the same dizzying exaltation and advance accompanied by moral betrayal, shame, and self-loathing that the entire nation does collectively.

By the time of Adrian's birth, the high-minded academic exhortations of Kant, Fichte, and Hegel and the poetic flights of Goethe that have guided Germans to a widely admired social, political, economic, and cultural eminence among bourgeois nations are beginning to lose their power to stimulate and excite their countrymen and women. Nietzsche's hammer blows are having an impact, especially among the young, who increasingly identify with his revaluation of values, whereby every classical and Christian moral principle is turned upside down. The *Ubermensch* gradually becomes not a universal but a strictly German incarnation, increasingly pagan in rejecting kindness, gentleness, and love in favor of ice-cold assertiveness, aggression, and superiority. This being has a will to conquer and subjugate, not to teach or lead by example. The extraordinary impact such incendiary writings have on Adrian Leverkuhn and his people is highlighted by the fact that in World War I, German soldiers will be issued copies of Nietzsche's *Also Sprach Zarathustra*, along with the Bible, so uniquely precious in the life and teachings of Martin Luther and his followers for centuries. In World War II, German soldiers will not have to decide between dichotomous world views laid out in books; they will have already been indoctrinated to become as "hard as Krupp steel," so that when ordered to smite pitilessly all who through race, nationality, mental fitness, sexual orientation, or any other factor project an inferiority or influence inimical to the descendants of Aryans, the soldiers will do so without hesitation. Adrian Leverkuhn will join his nation in a descent to the abyss as he willingly surrenders the values he has been raised to uphold in order to achieve an artistic "breakthrough" orchestrated by Satan.

PART ONE

Thomas Mann's *Doctor Faustus* is a biographical novel as well as a *Bildungsroman*, a story of a protagonist's growth and development from youth to adult maturity. The life of Adrian Leverkuhn, a composer of great gifts, great originality, and great failings, is recounted as a memoir by his friend and admirer, Serenus Zeitblom, PhD. Neither of these characters has life outside Thomas Mann's imagination, but real-life composers, conductors, and musicians appear throughout the novel, set as it is in Europe between the last decades of the nineteenth century and the first half of the twentieth, a period of exceptional creativity and virtuosity in musical composition and performance. The trajectory of this learned and powerful work moves from a time of relative peace and security (1885–1914), to a wholly unexpected and tragic pan-European military struggle that brings immense loss of life, destruction, and revolutionary upheaval; a pause succeeds this cataclysmic war (1918–39), during which time new political structures take shape in Central and Eastern Europe until a worldwide economic collapse allows despotic opportunists to emerge as leaders of totalitarian movements that eventually gain power; the book ends as another war spawned by these extremists engulfs Europe a second time (1939–45), bringing even more suffering and misery than the first installment.

Adrian Leverkuhn's development matches the historical experience, with youth and study occupying the first phase, compositions increasingly original and revolutionary in style and content dominating the second, and failure of health and personal loss leading to harrowing final works in the third. Dr. Zeitblom does not begin his retrospective narrative until 1943, so he is able to refer to contemporary happenings, such as

Germany's desperate attempts to keep from being overwhelmed by enemies approaching the Reich from east and west, in counterpoint with happy memories of growing up in company with his friend Adrian in a largely small-town environment closely tied to traditional habits and ways that seem almost alien in contrast.

The novel is entitled *Doctor Faustus* because the controlling *leit-mo-tiv* in Leverkuhn's spiritual and artistic development is his intimacy with Mephistopheles, making this novel one more variation on the legendary tale of the scholar who dooms himself to eternal torment so he can, in this life, utilize Satan's supernatural powers to achieve a "breakthrough" of some sort that is beyond anything a mortal, no matter how gifted, can produce through his own efforts. This connection is explored in detail twice in *Doctor Faustus*. The first reference occurs about halfway through the novel and consists of a long dialogue between the twenty-one-year-old Adrian, who is visiting Italy, and Satan, who appears in Adrian's rooms one night uninvited and unannounced. Shortly afterwards, Adrian prepares an account of what the two said and agreed to, and it is this document that Zeitblom later gains possession of and reproduces in his book. The second is a final confession from the composer, who has invited friends and colleagues to his home ostensibly to hear excerpts from his latest work, based on the *Apocalypse* of John. They hear, instead, a totally unexpected and soul-baring description of all Adrian has done and what price he must pay for his betrayal of faith, family, and friends. No musical excerpts follow because this *cri de couer* is itself so apocalyptic it provokes a stroke, the effects of which will cause Adrian Leverkuhn to live his last days as a helpless invalid.

Dr. Zeitblom cannot forget this convulsive event and the effect it has had on him. Though his book is begun four years after Adrian's death, his biographer can still invoke the possibility in his prologue that his "unhappy friend [may] now [be] resting—oh, may it be so!—now resting in God" (*Doctor Faustus*, trans., H.T. Lowe-Porter, New York: The Modern Library, p. 3). Almost like Abraham bargaining with God over

Sodom's fate, Zeitblom describes his friend as, after all, "a beloved fellow-creature and musician of genius" (3), whom "fate" (3) ensnared in a diabolical net at a time in his youth when the artist was just beginning to realize his calling. Zeitblom can scarcely imagine the temptations and yearnings that must have compelled his ambitious friend to follow so sinister a path, since the biographer is "by nature wholly moderate . . . of a temper both healthy and humane, addressed to reason and harmony" (3); he is himself "a scholar" and "a son of the Muses" (3), but can boast only modest attainments. Even though, as a cradle Catholic, Zeitblom acknowledges the reality of "daemonic . . . influence upon human life" (4), no supernatural visitations have upset the order and normality of his bourgeois existence. Indeed, the only time he feels pressure from what seem like "the powers of darkness," (i.e., the Nazis), he "unhesitatingly" gives up his teaching position rather than engage in a hopeless "challenge" (4) to or, worse yet, acquiesce as an acolyte of such powers.

Not so the "genius" he has known so well and "loved . . . with tenderness and terror, with compassion and devoted admiration" (5). This friend 's creativity demands entrance to "a radiant sphere" (4), that lofty realm of Spirit the great German composers, philosophers, and writers of genius over the centuries have aspired to reach through concentrated artistic or philosophical exertion. To Leverkuhn, nothing is more important than transcending limitations and being inspired to compose music of hitherto unknown power and profundity; since such musical treasures, in his case, can be crafted only if "the daemonic and irrational" are granted "a disquieting share in this radiant sphere" (4), so be it. Despite the fact such a dalliance with evil and its "sinful and morbid corruption of natural gifts" (4) will forever sully "the musical genius" (4) Adrian possesses, the artist will make such a sacrifice to gain the prize dangled by the tempter. Zeitblom shudders at the thought of Leverkuhn's agreeing to "a horrible bargain" (4) like this for any reason and at first recoils from the "wanton folly" (5) of even approaching so radioactive a subject. His deep friendship and admiration for Adrian, however, who has left him precious "sketches and journals" (5) whose contents should be shared with the world, compel Zeitblom to press on. He will do so even though he knows from a lifetime of experience how Adrian would have reacted to "devotion" (5) like his. He would accept it from him and others "often unconsciously" (6) but still remain aloof. Zeitblom compares Leverkuhn's "absentness to an abyss, into which one's feeling towards him dropped soundless and without a trace" (6). He ends his prologue on an ominous note, as he describes Adrian's "coldness" (6) toward everything and everyone as beyond that of artists and thinkers preoccupied with their work alone and exuding instead "an aura of horror" (6) more suggestive of the netherworld.

Serenus's character, interests, background, and life trajectory are very different. In a chapter offering a brief autobiographical sketch, moderation, order, discipline, and steady application stand out. Zeitblom tells us he was born into "the modest rank of a semi-professional middle class" (7) in 1883. His father "was an apothecary . . . the first in the town [of] Kaisersaschern" (7) on the Saale. This happens to be the same profession practiced by the father of Goethe's Faust, without, however, the deadly consequences some of that man's concoctions produced. Serenus's family is Catholic, even though their hometown lies in "the heart of Lutherland" (8). The young man experiences no conflicts or struggles between his "humanistic attitude in general" and the faith that forms his "inner man" (8), attributing this harmony to his growing up in a place "whose memories and monuments reach back into pre-schismatic times, back into a world of unity in Christ" (8). This sense of being tied in spirit to a long line of sturdy believers, not only in religion but in education and professional life as well, is a strong undercurrent shaping Serenus Zeitblom's development. He attends the local gymnasium in company with Adrian Leverkuhn, who is younger and "two forms below" (8) Serenus.

After the gymnasium, Zeitblom follows a well-trodden path to several universities, where he studies "the classic tongues" (8), as a good humanist should. The classics stimulate in the budding scholar "a lively and loving sense of the beauty and dignity of reason in the human being" (9). Music, however, does not find a place in Serenus's humanism. Its power Zeitblom recognizes, but he hesitates to move beyond his calm comfort zone because he realizes music dwells in "that world of the spirit which one approaches only at one's peril" (9). Better to apply the virtues of "the noble pedagogic world of the mind" than to hazard the potentially anarchic "entrance of the dark and uncanny into the service of the gods" (10). Here is encapsulated the fundamental contrast between the well-balanced scholar and the visionary composer intent on bringing "the dark and uncanny" into prominence in his compositions. After earning his doctorate in philology, Zeitblom settles into a purposeful and regulated life of teaching and scholarship, first at Kaisersaschern in his old school and then in Bavaria. He marries shortly after returning to Kaisersaschern, bewitched by a young woman whose name, Helene, is so suggestive to a classicist. Three children, two boys and one girl, follow. At the time he is beginning his book, 1943, his daughter has married a bank manager and is doing well, while his two sons "serve their Fuhrer, the one in civil life, the other with the armed forces" (10). Knowing their father is immune to Nazi enthusiasms, the Zeitblom sons' "relations . . . with the quiet paternal home must be called anything but intimate" (10).

What we see in Serenus Zeitblom is a well-educated bourgeois incarnation of "German Michael," the modest, hard-working, responsible, reliable, and ethical national archetype. Zeitblom is wary of extremes, comfortable in the faith in which he has been raised, careful to fulfill punctiliously his duties as teacher, husband, parent, and friend, and not at all drawn to anything idiosyncratic, whether in thought or deed. Though not a political or civil official, if he were, he would perform like the solid burgher in one of Germany's larger towns or small cities, for centuries independent and self-governing. Wary of spiritual flights or fantasies, and therefore largely absorbed in practical affairs, Zeitblom is in his dealings with all in his world dependable, helpful, and empathetic. He remains such throughout the novel, the moral norm around whom swirl all manner of deviations and extremes.

If Serenus's way of living is in accord with German respect for law, order, virtue, and precedent, his friend Adrian's is marked by more eccentric influences, particularly from the paternal side. To all appearances, though, the Leverkuhn family embodies the same stolidity and reliability as Zeitblom's. Descended from "superior hand-workers and small farmers" (11), the Leverkuhns have succeeded over time in acquiring a home and property that bespeak a higher degree of social stature and respectability than many of their neighbors enjoy. Their family's homestead, Buchel, includes "a good fifty acres of meadow and ploughed land, with communal rights to the adjoining mixed woodland and a very comfortable wood and frame dwelling-house on a stone foundation" (11). The Zeitbloms and the Leverkuhns have become friends by the time Serenus and Adrian are growing up, so the two boys naturally see much of each other. The Zeitbolms are "town-dwellers" (11) who like nothing better than spending "many a Sunday afternoon in the good time of year at the farm," where Adrian's mother offers delicacies like "the grainy dark bread with fresh butter, the golden honey in the comb, the delicious strawberries in cream, the curds in blue bowls sprinkled with black bread-crumbs and sugar" (12).

In addition to delighting in the pleasures of home and hearth, young Serenus and Adrian spend many hours together in the company of Jonathan Leverkuhn, Adrian's father. Zeitblom remembers him as "a man of the best German type" (12), with features more typical of an earlier age. His long "ash blond" locks, blue eyes, strongly delineated brow and chin, thin nose, and "powerful, browned, and parched, rather freckled hands" (12) would have allowed him to fit in well with Martin Luther's sixteenth-century congregants in nearby Wittenberg. But even though during dark winter evenings, Jonathan Leverkuhn can be seen reading "in a bulky family Bible" containing "prefaces and marginal comments of Dr. Martin Luther" (13), he is multi-dimensional in his scholarly pursuits and interests. Zeitblom records that "to a limited extent and with limited means, he carried on studies in natural science, biology, even perhaps in chemistry and physics" (13). Father Leverkuhn's approach to these disciplines, however, is not that of a trained technician, like Zeitblom's own father, who prepares medicines and compounds according to strict instructions and thinks not at all about original combinations. Leverkuhn is more inclined to "speculate the elements" (13) as he conducts original researches with "a tinge of mysticism" which, in earlier times, "would . . . have been suspect as a leaning to the black arts" (13). The Doctor Faustus of medieval legend, who inspired Christopher Marlowe's sixteenth-century play and later Goethe's long epic drama, dabbles in such "arts" as well. Leverkuhn asks probing questions and reveals mysterious facts about natural phenomena, fascinating both boys, even if at times Adrian laughs about what his father is saying or doing. How, for instance, asks Jonathan Leverkuhn, can the "leaf butterfly" blend so perfectly within foliage that "the hungriest enemy cannot make it out?" (14). And if "the lizards, birds, and spiders, for which surely it is meant for food" (15), cannot see their prey, why has nature permitted this violation of its rules? Then, again, another butterfly "coloured and patterned with unusual gorgeousness" flies about "in perfect security" only because its "secretions" (15) are so revolting any creature trying to devour this butterfly would quickly spit it out. Yet, says Leverkuhn, this same security is enjoyed by other butterflies who look similar and are "perfectly edible" (15). To him, phenomena like these are "matters to be regarded with reverence" (15). Leverkuhn is convinced that mysteries like these cannot be unraveled by reason or conventional experiment; they must be viewed through the lens of "the mystical or an intuitive half-mystical, into which . . . human thinking in pursuit of Nature is almost of necessity led" (17). Only thus can a "breakthrough" in understanding occur.

As Zeitblom looks back on these sessions with Adrian's father and his attempts to intuit the inner "workings" of natural processes, he notes that "the conviction of earlier epochs" was that the speculations and experiments Leverkuhn engages in "had close relations with witchcraft" and could be considered "work of the 'Tempter'" (17). In his own way and without academic preparation, Adrian's father is coming close to embarking on a Faustian quest. Goethe's lonely scholar is considering alchemy and necromancy just before Mephistopheles appears, and, as noted earlier, Faust's father actually dabbled in such practices when he produced deadly remedies for victims of plague that his abashed son had to hand deliver. True to form, Zeitblom calls the old timers' judgment about practices like Leverkuhn's "a decent conviction" (17). The future philologist, therefore, is happy to remain within the bounds of "the high-minded realms of the *humaniora*" and not venture further into matters that "are exclusively Nature's own affair" (20). In the years these sessions with his father are taking place, Adrian too finds them more amusing than revelatory, but by the time he turns twenty-one he will think differently. By then he will go well beyond his father's limitations and will actually give over his body and soul to the "Tempter" to achieve a breakthrough of his own.

Adrian's mother is not mentioned as participating in any of her husband's tutorials with the two boys. This is understandable given Elsbeth Leverkuhn's indifference to matters of the mind. Zeitblom writes of her in almost worshipful terms, nonetheless, recognizing in her feminine virtues and talents of the first order. So taken is Serenus by "the mistress of Buchel" (21) that in later years he could sense how strong her influence over Adrian was and how it shaped aspects of his character: "The reverence with which I speak of her simple, intellectually altogether unassuming person flows from my conviction that the genius of the son owed very much to his mother's vigour and bloom" (21). Elsbeth is a brunette, making her somewhat exotic in Germany, but a "certain sturdiness in the facial structure" (21) confirms her native identity. Even though her figure is "so individual and well-proportioned" (21), Elsbeth prefers "the costume of the region" (21), scorning fashionable city outfits that would make her appear too "ladylike" (21). She also has a warm "mezzo soprano" voice that Serenus considers "the finest thing about her" (22). She never, however, has sung or studied music formally, reinforcing her aversion to anything suggesting personal exceptionality. Zeitblom remembers that no one spoke "more beautifully," and even if nothing musical accompanied her "simplest and most matter-of-fact" statements, his mother's "harmony, was from the first hour Adrian's lullaby" (22). Elsbeth is one with her surroundings, making the most of her life at Buchel and turning her back on the attractions of the great world beyond. She is the loyal and loving helpmeet, a feminine version of German Michael, determined to be her husband's dutiful partner, her children's guide and comfort, and her home life's organizer, decorator, provisioner, and abiding spirit. Zeitblom stresses the impact on Adrian of this "country world of childhood in its simple setting of wood and meadow, pond, and hill" (23). He notes that "the house and its surroundings which Adrian later as a mature man" acquired "bore a most extraordinary likeness and reproduction of his childhood home" (25). This fact makes all the more poignant the writer's reflection on how Adrian's talent, ambition, and Faustian overreach compelled him to leave irretrievably "the vale of innocence" he tried to recreate in that later domicile in order to "mount up to inhospitable, yes, awful heights" (24).

At this point in his narrative, Zeitblom pauses to reflect on current events, specifically the Nazi regime and the war then raging. He admits to wishing for the "downfall" of the Third Reich, which has done such harm to "the decency of the German character" (31). He also touches on, albeit obliquely, a larger significance in the story of Adrian Leverkuhn's ruinous descent. The destiny of Germany can become visible "in the light of a unique and peculiar tragedy" (31), that of his dear friend. Throughout the rest of the novel, Zeitblom will comment periodically on contemporaneous happenings, such as the Allied bombardment of German towns and cities and how these attacks affect him, the developments in France and Russia forcing German retreats, even the possibility that Hitler's V bombs and rockets might actually be as decisive as the Fuhrer imagines, eventually concluding unequivocally that the betrayal of German values the Nazis inspired was just as demoniacal as Adrian's personal betrayal of the same values. He admits now to being "afraid of what is coming" (31), because both Germany's and Adrian's intertwining fates will be so terrible to behold and describe.

Nevertheless, Zeitblom soldiers on despite the difficulty of his project, returning to Adrian's young years and his budding interests. One day a "stable-girl with bosoms that shook as she ran and bare feet caked with dung" introduces Adrian, Serenus, and other children to the singing of "rounds" (27), a pleasant diversion that, without anyone's realizing it, brings the group into "a realm of imitative polyphony," a highly advanced "plane of musical culture" (28–29). Adrian enjoys this activity, and as he enters adolescence starts to experiment with piano improvisations, but he does not yet begin formal training. Family members do not encourage further studies in music since they see in this precocious youth a future scholar, someone who should just naturally bloom into that German archetype, the doctor of philosophy who holds a distinguished university chair. His schoolmaster observes how Adrian reaches "the heights of knowledge" (33) almost effortlessly and recommends that the family enroll him in "high school and the university" (32) without question or delay. Indeed, Adrian never seems to have to work very hard to master the content of his lessons, no matter the subject. In the face of his instructor's spirited explications, he projects a kind of bored certainty that can easily be mistaken for a conceit like James Steerforth's. After teaching Adrian some Latin, Herr Michelson, who fears Adrian's superior attitude is "a danger to the modesty of the heart" (33), abruptly concludes his work at Buchel. Adrian and his family thereupon follow the tutor's advice and make arrangements for Adrian to attend "the Boniface gymnasium, the school of the Brethren of the Common Life" (34), in nearby Kaisersaschern. There, he will be made to feel right at home, since he will stay with "Nicholas Leverkuhn, his father's brother" (34), a native of the town, and will see Serenus Zeitblom, an older Boniface student, as often as he can wish.

Kaisersaschern is near Leipzig, Weimar, Dessau, and Magdeburg, but yields pride of place to none of these well-known centers of burgher civic life and independence. The medium-sized town has "its own historical dignity and importance" (35). It boasts the tomb of Kaiser Otto III, who died in 1002, a cathedral, and many other carefully maintained edifices dating from medieval times that give Kaisersaschern "a sense of continuity with the past" (36). The atmosphere in this evocative setting, however, can conjure up a much less appealing feature of earlier days. Zeitblom mentions how images of "a movement for a children's crusade . . . miracles of the Cross, fantastic and mystical folk movements" (36) and the like could come to mind in Kaisersaschern's byways. In an ominous allusion to what has been happening around him since 1933, Zeitblom admits that "the old folkish layer survives in us all" (38) and can be stirred up even in enlightened times "to all sorts of reactionary evil" (37). Adrian's nine years of study in the gymnasium predate the Nazi era, but the appeal to dark and ferocious instincts Hitler and company will arouse afterwards is the same embrace of dark forces that will capture the brilliant Adrian as fully and terribly as it will the folk.

Adrian's life-altering experience with the Evil One, however, is still far in the future. What is important now as he starts in the gymnasium at age ten has nothing to do with what goes on in the schoolhouse but with what he will discover in his uncle's home. Nicholas Leverkuhn is a skilled string instrument maker. He is well-known and respected throughout the German and, indeed, the international music world. The Leverkuhn instrument collection, built up over years of shrewd purchasing, as well as through the labors of Nicholas and his associates, takes up large spaces in his home. Clients and those with every idiosyncratic musical interest appear frequently, and as they sample the wares, sonorous musical combinations flood the area, "the voices running through the octaves in the most varied colours" (40). For Zeitblom, who at the time plays a viola crafted at Nicholas Leverkuhn's studio, the "whole place afforded a culturally enchanting and alluring sight, stimulating the aural imagination till it effervesced" (40). Adrian, though, is at first indifferent to the sights and sounds of the musical cornucopia he walks through regularly, responding only with commonplaces as Serenus raves about everything he sees and hears. The author remembers how, for whatever reasons, Adrian "hid himself from music: very long, with instinctive persistence, he hid himself from his destiny" (44).

That destiny is, in the view of most who know him, still a scholar's life. In the gymnasium at Kaisersaschern, Adrian excels much as he did at home and again pays little attention to academics: "He obviously looked down on all this that was so easy for him" (44), says Zeitblom. Like his tutor at Buchel, his gymnasium teachers are upset by how blasé Adrian is about "the subject-matter of the lessons, the various branches of study, the purveying of which made up the dignity and the livelihood of the masters" (44). This coolness toward what a scholar will spend his life exploring and expounding baffles them, as well as Serenus. Only when he is engaged in mathematical calculations does Adrian become an enthusiastic learner. Zeitblom, who is not mathematically gifted, records how Adrian once reproached him for not responding to the abstract beauty of mathematical reasoning: "To look at the relations between things must be the best thing, after all. Order is everything" (45). After saying this, Adrian astonishes his friend by referring to St. Paul's Letter to the Romans and how "the powers that be are ordained of God" (45). Zeitblom is thrilled to see Adrian visibly moved by the divinely crafted perfection of mathematical concepts and formulas and by his invocation of God: "He reddened, and I looked at him large-eyed. It turned out that he was religious" (45).

Pure mathematics and pure music are related. Both are about relationships among numbers and notes, and both can be understood and appreciated in the abstract, without realization through the senses. Beethoven, after all, composed some of the greatest music in history after he lost his hearing. As Adrian approaches adolescence, his fascination with mathematics begins to lead him toward a similar fascination with music. Through "his self-taught and secret exploration of the keyboard" (46), Adrian experiments with chordal combinations and variations. His excitement over musical discoveries is so genuine Zeitblom senses "a budding passion—a passion of Adrian's!" (47). This is now so obvious that Serenus wonders how he has missed signs of such a powerful attraction. Uncle Nicholas Leverkuhn is more perceptive. As he listens one day to Adrian playing on an out-of-date harmonium "in the corridor of the family rooms" (46), he recognizes quickly that his nephew is not just diverting himself but that he is "making music" (47). Nicholas transfers the "old box" (47) to Adrian's room so he can improvise whenever he wishes, and then arranges for Adrian to begin piano lessons "twice a week" (48) with Wendell Kretschmar, the local church organist.

This is a critical moment in Adrian's development. As noted above, Serenus is startled when he sees how his friend, the lover of mathematics and abstract thinking, actually shows "passion" while explaining his piano improvisations. This passion, however, is not the sort Marcel Proust, for example, describes. In *Remembrance of Things Past*, music's effect is emotional and sensuous; a delicate filigree of melody in the opening theme of a piece like Franck's *"Sonata for Violin and Piano in A Major,"* for instance, strikes a listener immediately as tender, soft, and caressing. The frankly sexual undertones that are so urgent in the public and private lives of Swann, Albertine, Marcel, and Charlus are brought to the surface through music as well. This is not how Adrian, though a teenager by the time of his musical awakening, reacts to music. His is the characteristically German response: analytical, technical, methodical, and precise. Adrian approaches music the way he does math. He tries to tie parts together, to visualize with the mind's eye how a theme and counter-theme play out and combine, and then seek somehow to communicate these discoveries of the intellect in performance. The emotional impact of themes and variations is subsumed in the German concentration on intellectual apprehension; the excitement felt is not the type that brings tears so much as insight. As Adrian and Kretschmar move through their lessons together, the teacher will demonstrate over and over again how a masterpiece can be built upon the slightest thematic base by stimulating development in complexity through variations both direct and subtle.

Even though young Adrian is not sure of his path in life, his studies are serious preparation for a musical vocation, just as Zeitblom's are for a scholarly vocation. Serenus moves through all the academic hoops on the way to earning his doctorate and beginning to teach, as well as all the personal hoops, such as marriage, fatherhood, and domesticity in good order. Adrian's life course is not as direct. The career as a scholar that many of Adrian's friends and family members expect him to pursue will never be undertaken. Instead, after leaving Kretschmar, Adrian will unexpectedly spend several years as a theology student, like the original Doctor Faustus and, ironically, Friedreich Nietzsche, a Lutheran pastor's son. These interests, however, cannot suppress his musical ambitions, and he will soon move from hearing lectures on the Bible and doctrine to preparation for a career as a composer. He will never marry or have children, compelled instead to sacrifice personal happiness and fulfillment to an overpowering compulsion to create revolutionary compositions that will "break through" and overturn conventional thinking, earning Adrian recognition and acclaim as a visionary artist.

His path may be jagged, but Adrian undoubtedly takes the first steps for a life in music in Wendell Kretschmar's studio. Kretschmar is a highly competent musician and eager lecturer, "gifted with great and urgent riches of thought, passionately addicted to giving out information" (50). In addition to teaching, he gives free concerts of classic organ music that prove very popular with the Kaisersaschern public, as well as free lectures that attract scant interest "because of the all too specialized character of the subjects treated" (50). Another reason the lectures do not have broad appeal is Kretschmar's tendency to stutter, especially when he is most excited, as he often is. Listeners become so distracted at such painful moments they miss whatever points he is trying to make. Drawbacks like these limit the size of his audiences to sometimes a half dozen, but the determined pedagogue is not phased. On one occasion, Adrian and Serenus, regular attendees, gather with a few others to hear Kretschmar speak about Beethoven's *"Piano Sonata in C Minor,"* Op 111. Although the ostensible subject of his talk is why Beethoven writes only two instead of the usual three movements in this sonata, the speaker goes well beyond what might be expected by way of an answer, portraying the work as a heart-rending *cri de couer* of an artist fiercely determined to transcend whatever obstacles his deafness presents by creating music that carries the soul to the world of Spirit the great German philosophers repeatedly invoke. The small-town organist fights back against the limitations his speech difficulties present and manages through sheer grit to lift by his eloquence Adrian, Serenus, and company to the same lofty regions. In the following excerpt, he describes the impact of the second movement, starting from a simple arietta:

> *The theme of this movement goes through a hundred vicissitudes, a hundred worlds of rhythmic contrasts, at length outgrows itself and is finally lost in giddy heights that one might call otherworldly or abstract. And in just that very way Beethoven's art had overgrown itself, risen out of the habitable regions of tradition, even before the startled gaze of human eyes, into spheres of the entirely and utterly and nothing-but personal—an ego painfully isolated in the absolute, isolated too from sense by the loss of his hearing: lonely prince of a realm of spirits . . .* (52)

Kretschmar then plays the "whole composition out of his head" (53), highlighting key moments with shouted commentary and amplifying certain parts by "singing" (54) the music. He ends his talk by answering his initial question. The second movement, like that of Schubert's *Unfinished Symphony,* is climactic. It cannot be followed by anything more. Kretschmar goes even further. With this two-movement masterpiece, sonata form "had fulfilled its destiny, reached its goal, beyond which there was no going, it canceled and resolved itself, it took leave" (55).

This is only one of Wendall Kretschmar's hypnotic presentations. Others follow, such as one linking biographical details of Beethoven's life with the agonies of composition a mighty work like the *Missa Solemnis* imposes. Serenus and Adrian are aroused by the organist's genius, responding to all they hear with "vague and silent reflection upon the new, the far, and the great" (58–59) vistas their teacher projects. These are, once again, glimpses of the world of Spirit, pure and eternal, that the greatest music can open up. Adrian is drawn to these heights and motivated to reach them through a "breakthrough" in musical structure. He insists to Serenus that the "homophone-melodic constitution" (60) that has guided musical development since the Renaissance has reached its culmination, as Kreschmar demonstrated in his lecture on Beethoven's late piano sonata. Adrian wants music to reinvent itself in the present day by returning to "the old contrapuntal polyphone culture" (60) of medieval times. This is progress through restoration, which could then allow a composer like himself to create original works that a contemporary audience could welcome like new wine in old jugs. He even muses to Serenus "that we should have to become very much more barbaric to be capable of culture again" (60). At this point, Adrian is throwing out random observations about cultural transformation and not carefully thought-out propositions. The word "barbaric," though, suggests a youthful interest in Nietzschean concepts, which important segments of German society were taking seriously even then. The barbarism that the Nazis will embody is not a revival of the health and vigor of a young culture that Adrian is thinking of, but a recrudescence of its cruelty and hate, a primitivism more akin to tribalism than to brotherhood and tolerance. Adrian cannot envision anything like what the future will bring to his nation, but he is showing signs, even if faint, of being attracted to ways of thinking about art, culture, and life choices that will ultimately align him with the larger society in rejecting the moral values inculcated over centuries by religion and philosophy and replacing them with a destructive individual or national exaltation more akin to a bestial state.

Kretschmar is more high-minded in his recognition of music's possibilities, acknowledging that this art is "at any moment capable of beginning at the beginning, of discovering itself afresh out of nothing, bare of all knowledge of its past cultural history, and of creating anew" (63). Kretschmar is firmly in the German tradition in seeing in music "a certain inborn lack of the sensuous, yes an anti-sensuality, a sacred tendency to asceticism" (61). As "the most intellectual of all the arts." a point of view shared by Adrian, music makes "hearing, like the other senses . . . the deputy, the instrument, and the receiver of the mind" (61). Kretschmar hypothesizes that it is "music's deepest wish not to be heard at all, nor even seen, nor yet felt; but only . . . in some Beyond, the other side of sense and sentiment, to be perceived and contemplated as pure mind, pure spirit" (61). This is the absolute realm of Spirit where German metaphysicians like Fichte and Hegel place moral truth and composers like Beethoven and Schubert, their contemporaries, strive to access through seraphic harmonies.

Such rhapsodic commentary speaks volumes about Wendell Kretschmar's sincere appreciation of his art's greatest potentialities. Serenus shares this understanding, even if not inclined to elevation of spirit. Adrian reacts to Kretschnar's words and demonstrations more ambiguously, however. He is touched deeply by his teacher's idealism, but still, just as he sometimes did after one of his father's ardent explorations of natural phenomena, Adrian can respond "with mockery and laughter" (67) to Kretschmar as well. He maintains 'an ironic remoteness" (67) during his time in the gymnasium and with Kretschmar that worries Zeitblom, who echoes the concerns many of his teachers raised: "In so young a person as Adrian then was, the presumption of this attitude, it must be admitted is disquieting; it was calculated to cause one concern for his soul" (67). Instead of earnestly striving to reach spiritual heights, in the manner of the great German artists and thinkers, Adrian stays aloof, unwilling to commit to anything outside of himself and secure in his self-absorption. He also likes to turn conventional thinking upside down. An exchange recorded by Zeitblom is illustrative. Adrian asks his friend on one occasion if he thinks "love" is "the strongest emotion" (69). Serenus answers as if this assertion is a self-evident truth. Adrian disagrees. He states that "interest," or "a love from which the animal warmth has been withdrawn" (69) is somehow better. The "interest" Adrian describes is cold, detached, equivocal, and egocentric.

His pupil's attitude and demeanor, notwithstanding, Kretschmar persists in his efforts not just to teach Adrian music and performance but to bring him into intimate familiarity with and appreciation of European high culture's greatest works. This extraordinary teacher and scholar is a "bird of paradise" in provincial Kaisersaschern. He introduces Adrian to Shakespeare and other literary luminaries, as well as to philosophers and historians, making his days with the organist, Adrian Leverkuhn's "earliest contact with greatness" (71). The heavy load of academic and cultural studies a more mature Adrian is pursuing makes Serenus nervous, thinking that his friend may be endangering his health by having to apply himself more diligently than ever. In the best German tradition, Kretschmar demurs, being "a thoroughgoing partisan of impatient youth avid of knowledge, unsparing of its strength" (71) and a man whose own intellectual labors entail "a certain ideal harshness and indifference to the body and its 'health,' which he considered a right philistine, not to say cowardly value" (71). These efforts to move Adrian through the arts, sciences, and humanities, with music in the forefront, remind Serenus of "the education of a young prince" (72), albeit a most amazing prodigy of a young prince. In his final years at the gymnasium, Adrian is so overflowing with ideas, idiosyncratic insights, improvisations at the piano, and highly skilled performances of entire works, Zeitblom imagines "a cataract of musical experience flooding his youthful receptivity" (75). Kretschmar wisely augments his student's solitary hours at the piano and with the study of scores by taking him to concerts and vocal recitals in nearby cities. Once Adrian is moved to tears, uncharacteristically, by a heartbreaking stanza from *"Die Winterreise,"* Schubert's last song-cycle, where the "twilit genius, death-touched" of the composer "lifts to the loftiest expression a certain only half-defined but inescapable destiny of solitude" (77), a destiny that the aloof boy half-intuits as his own. Remarkably, "the lofty humanity and brotherhood of *Fidelio*, with the great overture in C, played before the final scene" (78) also makes a strong impression on the young loner, who has not so far concerned himself much with "humanity and brotherhood" beyond Kretschmar and Serenus. As he prepares to begin university studies in Halle, Adrian has acquired a breadth of knowledge and a widening of perspectives. Serenus knows his friend has made "a great advance in musical knowledge and enthusiastic participation" (79) with Kretschmar and looks ahead with confidence to his furthering a career in music at the University of Halle.

PART TWO

Adrian Leverkuhn, however, surprises Serenus and everyone else by announcing that he will begin university studies not in music but in Halle's Faculty of Theology. For Zeitblom, this choice seems like it comes from out of the blue. But looking back years later, he remembers that in his last term in the gymnasium, Adrian had registered for a class in Hebrew, a free elective, and one which Zeitblom himself, the budding philologist, had not taken. Did this foray into an ancient tongue indicate that Adrian's plans for Halle had been developing early? Hebrew, after all, is a logical entrance point for someone intending to study theology in preparation for "an academic career" (80), a goal similar to Zeitblom's. If this is the case, music and mathematics will soon be relegated to pastimes or hobbies once theology, "the highest and noblest sphere of knowledge, the apex of all thinking" (81), becomes Adrian's principal academic interest. This choice is consistent also with Adrian's susceptibility to moments of transcendent experience great music afforded him when he was with Kretschmar, and which theology can elicit likewise. Adrian's preference also invests him with instant respectability in the eyes of his family and the pious laity in general. Theological studies in seminaries were, as well, the beginning stages for prominent German metaphysicians like Hegel and Heidegger, who later pursued academic careers. Marlowe's Doctor Faustus and Goethe's Faust also spend time as young theology students, though neither continues long nor remains observant.

Nevertheless, Serenus is still uneasy. He knows that even if the choice of theological study makes practical sense for Adrian, his gifted friend has not acted "out of an instinct of spiritual self-discipline" or a desire to acquire an attitude of dependence "through contemplation and knowledge of the other world" (81). Quite the contrary is the case, Zeitblom believes; he thinks Adrian has allowed "pride" (81), the deadliest of the deadly sins, to govern his thinking, almost as if Adrian is being tempted to act and think as if he were God's surrogate. Sharing this concern is the director of the School of the Brethren of the Common Life, Dr. Stoientin. As Adrian is about to take leave of the gymnasium, the director admonishes him:

> *You are a person richly gifted, and you know it—as why should you not? You know too that He above, from whom all comes, gave you your gifts, for to Him you now offer them. You are right: natural merits are God's merits in us, not our own. It is His foe who, fallen through pride himself, would teach us to forget. He is evil to entertain, a roaring lion who goes about seeking whom he may devour. You are among those who have reason to be on guard against his wiles.* (83)

In view of what will occur in a few short years, when Adrian will definitively break with Him who so gifted him and welcome the foe intent on devouring him morally, the director is prescient beyond knowing. Adrian's response to this warning in a conversation with Serenus suggests the prospective theology student is already, to some degree, in the enemy's camp. Adrian denies, for instance, that "native merit" must be accepted gratefully as a free gift of God; instead, Adrian invokes Goethe, from whom the director's terminology comes. He argues that Goethe intends to "divorce from the word 'merit' its moral character and, conversely, to exalt the natural and inborn to a position of extra-moral, aristocratic desert" (84), a perfectly Nietzschean conception in its stress on individual exceptionality. Zeitblom counters that Adrian has misread Goethe but to no avail. As his brilliant friend's days at Kaisersaschern draw to a close, Zeitblom remains deeply ambivalent, not only about Adrian's joining the Faculty of Theology at Halle but also, more seriously, about his moral fitness to engage in such studies.

It is not surprising, therefore, that, at Adrian's urging, Serenus Zeitblom agrees to transfer to the University of Halle, claiming "sufficing intellectual grounds" (87) for the move but realizing clearly that being with Adrian on an almost daily basis will give Serenus opportunity "to watch over him, to have an eye on him from nearby" (86), to be his protector, in other words, in new surroundings. Zeitblom admits that "the theological air" (87) is not congenial, but he has to breathe it if he is to have any impact on Adrian's "life problem, his being and becoming" (87), which matters more to Serenus than his own professional progress. Thus, he attends some of Adrian's classes "as a guest hearer in order to hear what he heard" (90). By and large, Zeitblom is not impressed by what the theologians present. They are trying with little success to respect "the scientific currents of the epoch" while still adhering to "orthodoxy" (89) in framing religious teachings. The resulting clash between current science and traditional doctrine creates "a hybrid half-and-half of science and belief in revelation" (89). Different theological stances try to reconcile these oppositions. Liberalism exalts "moral betterment" and dismisses all else in the Bible or in Christian tradition as "out of date" (89). Zeitblom judges this approach "weak, for its moralism and humanism lack insight into the daemonic character of human existence" (90). The more conservative professors have a keener sense of "the tragic nature of life" (90) but cannot shake off the carapace of old formulations encrusting such valuable teachings. An ominous undercurrent is alluded to in Zeitblom's analyses. He recognizes how the "spirit of the age" affects all who try to keep Christianity relevant and attractive to diverse categories of adherents. That "spirit" includes the Nietzschean emphases on the "non-theoretic, the vital, the will or instinct, in short, the daemonic" (90), which, as noted earlier, many Germans in particular found so congenial as the unified nation continued to grow and prosper at the beginning of the 20th century. The Christian churches were not immune to the effects of such intoxicating forces that challenge reliance on reason, self-control, and sober industry, all virtues of Kaisersaschern, "that corner of German antiquity where we had been brought up" (91).

Adrian is not as excited about these issues as his friend from the philology faculty. Whenever Zeitblom and he talk about "theological problems," Adrian maintains the same detachment as he does on most issues, personal or academic, refusing to fall into "any discussion that would have gone to the root of the matter and have dealt with the problematic position of theology among the sciences" (90–91). The same is true of most of the faculty members and the theology students, who will not take strong positions for or against competing perspectives lest they jeopardize the comfortable sinecures in "State and Church" (91) they now either hold or aspire toward holding. For them, theology is not something to be wrestled with in a life-or-death struggle toward binding truth but a body of core teachings to be accepted as "given" (91). Stendhal's seminarians in Besancon are not much different.

If theological debate leaves Adrian cold or indifferent, the same is not true of classes in philosophy, particularly a course in ancient Greek thinkers taught by "one of the luminaries of the University of Halle" (93), Kolonat Nonnenmacher. In his vivid description of Pythagoras's "Cosmos," understood as "order and harmony, as the interval system of the spheres, sounding beyond the range of the senses" (93), this brilliant teacher elicits in both Adrian and Serenus responses similar to those Kretschmar produced. Since this order is founded upon "the relation of numbers" (93), Adrian's two passions, music and mathematics, rise to the level of pure being, as nature's fundament, from whose numerical foundation "the beautiful, the exact, the moral" (93) emanate harmoniously. Though Pythagoras propounded all of this before the birth of Socrates, his teachings resonate for nineteenth-century German students, since philosophers like Kant, Fichte, and Hegel, through abstract reasoning, intuited moral certainty in the domain of absolute Spirit. Nonnenmacher adds insights into Aristotle, dwelling on "matter as the potential, possible, that presses toward form in order to realize itself" (94). Adrian takes this creative force, Aristotle's "entelechy," and identifies it with the soul, speaking in unusual eloquence about its divinely ordained function: "It is the angel of the individual, the genius of his life, in whose all-knowing guidance it gladly confides" (94).

Then there is Ehrenfried Kumpf, who is considered the "meatiest" professor not only in the Faculty of Theology but "in the whole university" (94) and whom Adrian is so eager to hear, he takes his course out of the normal sequence. This man is "meaty" in more ways than one. Kumpf is "a big, full-bodied, massive man" with "a thundering voice," and a "coarse and hearty good humour, and picturesquely archaic style" (95). Kumpf's "crude heartiness" (95) repels the altogether proper Zeitblom but appeals to Adrian, perhaps because this professor is more of a member of the folk community than the academy. Kumpf is the opposite of Nonnenmacher in that he is "anti-metaphysical, with a position addressed entirely to ethics and theoretic knowledge" (96). He is very much a disciple of Martin Luther, having experienced as a young literary scholar an awakening similar to the young monk's own on the necessity of justification. Kumpf thereupon "embraced the Pauline gospel of sin and justification" (95), turned his back on literature, and became a prototypical "nationalist of the Luther stamp" (96) in belief and culture. He is with Luther and the common people in "being on a very familiar footing with the Devil" (96), who Stump is sure actively distorts our capacity to reason so that we chase after false gods to our peril.

One evening at a family gathering in the professor's home, invited guests Adrian and Serenus see Stumpf act out something very much like Luther's encounter with Satan in the Wartburg Castle. After the professor has talked volubly, eaten and drunk his fill, and sung folk songs, he suddenly points to a dark corner in his dining area and insists the devil is present there. He calls the fiend "the malcontent, the sad, bad guest" who resents everyone's being "merry in God with feasting and song" (97). Instead of throwing an ink well, Kumpf hurls a dinner roll in the direction of the darkness and peremptorily demands that the intruder leave, which, for all anyone knows, he does. As Adrian and Serenus depart Kumpf's home after this episode, the young man who will in the near future be visited by the Evil One and will welcome rather than expel this being, laughs off all he has just observed and seems altogether unaffected by the exhibition.

This atavistic moment is one more instance of the persistence of old fears and ways of thinking among not only the poor and the uneducated but also within the Faculty of Theology. In his whole-hearted embrace of German history and culture, and all entailed therefrom, Stumpf may seem an outlier in early twentieth century Germany. If so, he is not by any means a singularity. There is also his colleague, Privat-docent Eberhard Schleppfuss, whose classes Adrian and Serenus attend throughout the one academic year this lecturer works at Halle. Professor Schleppfuss modernizes the rather crude assertions of Kumpf by turning them into intellectually defensible academic propositions.

Thus, he posits a "daemonic conception of God and the universe . . . illuminated by psychology and thus made acceptable, yes, even attractive to the modern scientific mind" (99). Schleppfuss makes his points clearly and powerfully as he devotes his allotted time to gripping presentations that are "impromptu, well expressed, without effort or break, smooth as though prepared for the press" (99–100). His bold pronouncements demand attention from his mostly young and impressionable listeners, who are forced to respond to highly unconventional ways of thinking. Schleppfuss considers "the vicious to be a necessary and inseparable concomitant of the holy, and the holy a constant satanic temptation, an almost irresistible challenge to violation" (100). Echoing Nietzsche, his contemporary, who stresses the need for the *Ubermensch* to test his mettle by taking on the strongest opponents, Schleppfuss insists that evil must exist not because of some accident or defamation like the fall of Lucifer; it is, on the contrary, a "necessary emanation and inevitable accompaniment of the Holy Existence of God" (100), a dark stain on creation perpetually hounding and confounding humanity. This state of affairs is what it is because God cannot "produce in the creature . . . the incapacity for sin" (100). Doing so would negate the possibility of human beings exercising their free will "to turn away from God" (101). For most men and women separation from God is too terrible to envisage, so they make little or no use of this primal gift, preferring instead to remain firmly in lockstep with received teachings and practices, a condition Nietzsche likens to slavery. Schleppfuss is not so harsh, concluding mildly that the failure to make decisive choices freely produces "a certain existential weakening, a diminution in the intensity of being" (101) in the pious and the virtuous.

Serenus becomes uneasy as the professor elaborates on this theme "somewhat tendentiously, somewhat maliciously" (102). In a striking reference to the time of his "retirement" (102), the years of the Second World War, he becomes emotional: "Certain people should not speak of freedom, reason, humanity; on grounds of scrupulosity, they should leave such words alone" (102). Zeitblom's perspective, however, is one Schleppfuss cannot share. He speaks during a time pre-dating not only the Second World War but also the First World War, a time when Germany is prosperous, optimistic, and at peace. Certainly, there is concern that an armed conflict could erupt, but Germany's leaders, both civil and military, as well as most of its population, are confident that should anything untoward develop, the Kaiser's forces, victorious over Austria-Hungary in 1866 and France in 1870, should prevail no matter the opposition. Besides, no neighboring state would be foolish enough to challenge Germany, so the issue is probably never going to arise. Thus, Schleppfuss can go on and on about sin and evil without the slightest fear his words might be incendiary: "Freedom is a very great thing, the condition of creation, that which prevented God making us proof against falling away from him" (102). Furthermore, without evil, "the universe would not have been complete; therefore, God permitted it, for He was consummate and must therefore will the consummate—not in the sense of the consummately good but in the sense of All-sidedness and reciprocal enlargement of life" (103). St. Augustine himself affirms that "the function of the bad was to make the good stand out more strongly, that it pleased the more and was the more lovely, the more it was compared with the bad" (103).

This approach, which makes evil an almost aesthetic necessity, is too clever, too detached from the actual horrors perpetrated by those acting in the service of evil, to be anything but offensive to one like Zeitblom, whose memoir of Adrian's life experience as it intersects with his nation's crimes against humanity, renders Schleppfuss's antinomies dangerous. The professor even insists that God "had to create the world as it is—namely, saturated with evil—that is to say, to leave it open in part to daemonic influences" (104). Schleppfuss illustrates this realization by dwelling on the role woman has traditionally played in threatening the virtue of young men. This conception of woman as temptress and the devil's instrument was understood well in medieval times, "the classical period of religious rule over the life and spirit of man" (100). Zeitblom remembers a long tale from this period Schleppfuss recounts to his class without disapproval. An unmarried youngster becomes impotent whenever he is with girls or women other than the lady his poverty prevents him from marrying. He confesses his painful plight to a priest, who, against all rules governing the inviolability of the confessional, informs the authorities immediately. They procure an admission of guilt from the lady, who had secured a salve from an "old woman [who] had in fact a compact with the devil" (108). The salve caused the man's impotence, a condition the young lady relished since it prevented the victim from having intercourse with anyone else. Thereupon, "the two witches, the old one and the young, were burned at the stake, one beside the other on the open square" (109). Neither Adrian nor the other theology students seem upset by what Serenus calls "this revolting tale, so characteristic of the tone of Schleppfuss's course" (109). The philology student interprets the tale in the most charitable and rational way, dismissing any "devil's hocus-pocus" and ascribing the lover's troubles simply to "the charm she had for him and the will by which she held him as by a spell against other temptations" (109).

Several points begin to stand out as Zeitblom is moving us through Adrian's theological studies. So far, Adrian has used only the teachings of Pythagoras and Aristotle, as expounded by Kolonat Nonnenmacher, to form an awe-inspiring conception of God the Creator. The master craftsman of the universe and the father-guide of each individual soul is apprehended through pagan philosophy. The two theology professors, both of good repute, do not have anything like Nonnenmacher's positive impact. Stumpf's "old time religion" approach dwells on the influence and virtual omnipresence of Satan, culminating in a bizarre confrontation, which even if it is just play-acting for dramatic effect, leaves Adrian bemused and Serenus embarrassed. The Privat-docent Schleppfuss at first seems more sophisticated and at ease in modernity, but as his lectures proceed, he begins to resemble Stumpf in highlighting God's inability to rid the world of the Tempter and thereby protect humanity from succumbing to the glamor of evil. He goes farther than Stumpf in arguing evil's necessary role in the nature of things as the obverse of goodness, which would be a monochromatic nullity without it. The true grandeur of goodness shows forth brilliantly when humans engage in a battle royal with evil. Schleppfuss finds the best illustrations of such combat in the Middle Ages, when sorcery, superstition, persecution, and witchcraft prevailed. This descent into darkness once again alienates Zeitblom, the humanist scholar, but elicits no discernible condemnation in Adrian. Stumpf and Schleppfuss, however, have planted seeds in the brilliant young man's soul that will blossom into deadly poisons, leading Adrian to decisions that will be permanently scarring in this life and in that of the world to come. On a larger scale, the same witches' brew of daemonic intervention and *volkish* tribalism will infect Germany as the twentieth century proceeds. Jews will replace witches, thoroughly indoctrinated militarists will replace Crusaders, and ideological fanatics will replace inquisitors. But a different cast of characters will not change the outcome of a tragic drama. Adrian and Germany before 1914 are still innocent, still capable of resisting morally corrupting pressures, but the corrosion starting to spread through the classrooms at Halle, however slightly, will become a malignant cancer for individual and nation in the coming years.

Adrian Leverkuhn's life at the university does not begin and end with classroom instruction. He is one of a number of theology students making up the Christian Society Winfried, a fellowship whose seventy members meet periodically in "the smoke-filled private room of Mutze's tavern" (112) for alcohol-free relaxation and discussion, and who, when the weather is good, take long walks together in the neighboring countryside. Even if Adrian is often absent when the Winfried group meets at Mutze's and though his "supposed misanthropy" (112) alienates some members, on "the rare occasions" when he does appear, he is greeted by "shouts" (112) of acclamation. Like Julien Sorel in the seminary at Besancon, Adrian is a *rara avis*, an outlier so detached from and so far ahead of his peers, he seems to be of a different species. During visits to the tavern, Adrian does not socialize; instead, he moves straight to the club room's piano and begins to improvise, as he did with Kretschmar. Serenus, a guest of the society, views this urge to perform as a defensive gesture, as if Adrian needs to find in music a "shelter—actually within himself from a bewildering strangeness into which he had come" (113). The distance between himself and most of his companions is highlighted in an exchange Serenus records. On one evening, "little Probst, a typical student" (113) listening to combinations of notes that he cannot recognize as a familiar theme, asks Adrian what he is playing. "Nothing" (113), he responds, baffling the questioner, who wonders how someone can play "nothing" (113). An observer tells the student, "One can play what does not yet exist" in published form and a third society member ends the dialogue conclusively by reminding his friend that "everything was once nothing . . . and then became something" (113), a sentiment Wendall Kretschmar would share. Thus Adrian's "productive inspiration" (114) is, for these young theologians, analogous to God's creative power, as described in the Book of Genesis. Adrian's exercise takes form as something "coming from above" (114), as if he has access to "divinely existent power" (114), and, as such, cannot be viewed as "one like us" in the minds of the students, who, in their typically German way, exalt music as "an art coming from God" (114).

Along with the tavern visits, the Winfried officers invite their members during holidays or long weekends to participate in excursions throughout the rural areas bordering Halle. Typically, these can last several days and cover many kilometers, so the less hearty members and those not interested in trekking over hiking trails that highlight nature's variety and beauty but are not near towns or settlements, do not take part. Nevertheless, though their numbers may be small and their goals modest (healthy exercise and communal bonding), the Winfried walks are identifiably German, with a pedigree extending back many decades. The Winfried Society derives from the student fraternities that arose in colleges all over Germany in response to exhortations such as Fichte's *Addresses to the German Nation*, rousing German youth to a heightened awareness of national identity and commitment. The most famous manifestation of this new consciousness occurred in October 1817, as representative student groups from throughout the country marched to the Wartburg Castle, in which, three centuries before, Martin Luther was placed in safe keeping after the Diet of Worms. In the year he spent there, Luther translated the New Testament into German, bequeathing to his people the foundational document of their history as a nation. At this historic venue, the students renewed their loyalty to and love for all that was good in the culture, traditions, and values of their still divided homeland. The post-Napoleonic authorities were fearful that such mass meetings could easily get out of control and lead to quasi—revolutionary demonstrations, so they ordered the fraternities to disband. Nevertheless, despite the ban, the Wartburg model would remain for the rest of the century and beyond, a paradigm for all German youth to follow in their eagerness to join together as one body and pledge allegiance to a nation-state they considered uniquely important and destined to lead by example in arts and sciences, religion and morality, knowledge and industry. The fact that under the Nazi regime these noble affirmations and aspirations were degraded into apologies for militarism and conquest, ethnic cleansing and persecution, should not blind us to the power and beauty of their original formulation.

Adrian's ability to conjure complex musical structures out of the barest forms is appreciated by most of the members of the Winfried group, not only because of the wizardry of his variations but also because his fellow students see Adrian as one connected to the primal sources of artistry in music—that is, nature itself. He is seen as one having "relations" with it [music], romantic and devout, like one's relations with nature" (114). In this coupling of music and nature, the members of this society are in accord with the German spirit, which, in the Romantic Movement (circa 1790–1832), opened up new directions for music's development. As noted earlier, at the onset of the nineteenth century, classic musical forms like the sinfonia, the sonata, and the string ensemble evolved from offering pleasant entertainment to making compelling statements of conviction and vision that laid bare the beauty, grandeur, and depth of nature. In the world of royalty, aristocracy, and privilege that the French Revolution challenged, music reinforced, in its adherence to standard forms, the values of order and stability upheld by the governing classes as God-given foundations for harmony and peace within society. Composers and performers attached themselves to aristocratic and ecclesiastical patrons, whom they would not disturb with uncomfortable presentations. After 1789, however, serious musicians like Beethoven in his *Eroica Symphony* rejected the "tried and true" paths that had guided composers before in favor of freedom and originality, enlarging music's appeal by opening new avenues and new vistas. Security and predictability had to yield to experimental and innovative productions, so that at the beginning of the twentieth century, a theology student at the University of Halle could improvise for his fellow students in an exploratory style that, with maturity, would lead to masterpieces uniquely original, even if of disturbing provenance.

This is the background of Adrian's and Serenus's participation in thc Winfried members' regular walking tours through "lovely Thuringia," only "a few hours up the Saale" (114) from Halle. Adrian and Serenus, "in company with a few of the better sort" (114) of the Winfried, find it refreshing to plunge into "the primitive countryside and back to mother earth" (115) for hours or days. This activity awakens in the young men "a feeling of life" (115), a renewed sense of vitality, sensitivity, and possibility, gifts prized by those not yet hemmed in by the duties, restrictions, and debilities brought by age.

These tours also stimulate discussion and dialogue among the travelers as they exchange views on topics of the day with a seriousness and earnestness more typical of debaters than of casual strollers. A high-toned back-and-forth involving Adrian and several other Winfried students is recorded by Serenus. He begins by noting how Adrian disagrees with the other hikers regarding youth's special insight into nature, a core tenet of Romanticism, as illustrated, for instance, in Wordsworth's *"Tintern Abbey"* and his *"Intimations Ode."* Almost in deference to his status as an outlier and to his rationalistic approach to matters under dispute, Adrian asserts, "The young one is by no means so disposed to see and enjoy nature. His eye is directed inwards, mentally conditioned, disinclined to the senses, in my opinion" (116). This challenge provokes a strong response, particularly from Deutschlin, the group's leader. With typical German self-assurance, he asserts almost pridefully: "The idea of youth is a prescriptive right and prerogative of our people, the German people; the others scarcely know it; youth as consciousness of self is as good as unknown to them" (117). He rhapsodizes about the "German spirit, which is young and filled with the future: unripe, if you like" (117) and offers in support the example of Martin Luther, "unripe enough, enough of the people, of the German people, to bring in the new, the purified faith" (116). In Deutschlin's words, the seeds of the nationalism that will bring death and destruction of unparalleled dimensions to most of Europe, are noticeable in hindsight, even though the young patriot cannot imagine these consequences. Adrian, the loner, is immune to such religio-patriotic flights. He states matter-of-factly that it was the many years it took his divided nation to form "a common consciousness, which deludes us into a notion of our uncommon youthfulness" (117).

The discussion continues with Deutschlin invoking a favorite theme of German philosophy. He asks Adrian if he is aware of "German Becoming, of German Wandering, of the eternal migrations of the German soul?" (118). The German, he insists, "is the eternal student, the eternal searcher, among the peoples of the earth" (118), a being, in other words, with Faustian ambitions. That is why German youth has the special vocation of shaking up the status quo, as Luther and company did in the sixteenth century and the Romantics did in the nineteenth century. Deutschlin becomes passionate on this theme:

> *To be young means to be original, to have remained nearer to the sources of life; it means to be able to stand up and shake off the fetters of our outlived civilizations, to dare—where others lack the courage—to plunge again into the elemental.* (118)

Adrian reacts to this as he did to Deutschlin's previous encomium to German youth. He is critical, ironic, even dismissive. His interlocutor, whose name sounds so like *Deutschland*, is exasperated by Adrian's posture, saying he is "too cool to be young, too clever to be religious" (119), too superior too in his aloofness. Adrian even denies the centrality in a believer's life of subjective affirmations of faith, a bedrock conviction of Luther, and, in more secular terms, of German metaphysicians ever since. The church, argues Adrian, must be viewed not as a community of individual souls, but as "a citadel of order" (119) that keeps religious ardor controlled and disciplined, protected against "subjectivist demoralization," which can lead "to a chaos of divine and daemonic powers, to a world of fantastic uncanniness, an ocean of daemony" (119). These words shed light on Adrian's own inner life and the degree to which this theology student already has been introduced to the powers of darkness.

The dialogue continues, with new voices being heard, as these earnest Winfried loyalists try to come to grips with Adrian and with the nature of German character and identity. One speaker dwells on “a myth of doubtful genuineness and not doubtful arrogance: namely, the national, with its romanticism of the warrior type, which is nothing but natural paganism with Christian trimmings” (124), and worries that this conception can be “decisively threatened from the side of the demons” (124). He reminds the assembly that “the word for that [the daemonic] is the instincts” (124), the means by which “seekers” can access Spirit. In its degraded understanding, however, propagated most notably by Nietzsche, “the psychology of instinct” (124) rejects the rational and glorifies the primitive. Since this does not advance either national or individual betterment it is “pure swindle” (124). This speaker has moved logically from Wagnerian archetypes through vulgarizations that lead to self-immolation, and, in so doing, has unwittingly prophesied the eventual destruction of his nation.

Throughout these intellectually sophisticated and highly rhetorical exchanges with the Winfried contingent, Adrian clearly shows little enthusiasm for the cultural ideals his fellow theology students present as self-evident. He does not see any distinctive qualities in German youth or in youth in general; he is not as energized by immersion in nature as the others are; he resists any suggestion of a uniquely German vocation for youthful creative destruction; and he prefers a church that is a bulwark of orthodoxy and discipline, like the Catholic Church of Luther’s time, rather than one that continually advocates the priority of the subjective in the practice of faith. In other words, from a young age, Adrian cannot embrace the accepted teachings the “striving and high purposed youths” (126) of the Winfried brotherhood must assimilate as they move forward in clerical and civil society in future years. Adrian, too, knows he must make steady progress toward his own exalted goal, which differs markedly from his classmates’ aspirations. In Zeitblom’s memoir, Adrian takes on the aspect of “the other, invisibly singled out, who would never forsake the hard route of the mind, would tread it, who knew whither, and whose gaze, whose attitude, never quite resolved in the fraternal” (126).

Given what we have seen so far in regard to Adrian Leverkuhn's studies and his interactions with professors and fellow theology students at the University of Halle, Adrian's decision to cease enrollment in this faculty after three semesters there is hardly surprising. Adrian's focus henceforth will be on musical studies, a change of plan that meets with some reservations among his family, his mother in particular. Frau Elsbeth knows that in Germany, "nobody is put off or embarrassed, uncomfortably impressed, or moved to disrespect or mockery by the fact that a man is a musician" (127), but even so, she is put off by her son's proposed new vocation. While not pinning the blame for her son's U-turn on him alone, Frau Elsbeth is sure Wendall Kretschmar has had a major influence in Adrian's thinking on this matter. The two have not gone their separate ways since Adrian left for Halle; during the summer recess, for instance, which Adrian would spend in Kaisersaschern, he and Kretschmar often took long walks together, enjoying the warmth and engaging in spirited conversation. His mother is uncomfortable with this relationship, fearing perhaps that the organist is supplanting her as the main sounding board in Adrian's decision-making. She is probably justified in her anxieties. Kretschmar is indeed actively encouraging Adrian's movement toward a career in music. He advocates strongly "for the musical calling of his pupil," specifically, "that he should become a composer" (128). Adrian Leverkuhn has, says Kretschmar, "the composer's eye; he bends on music the look of the initiate, not of the vaguely enjoying outsider" (128), so he should not hesitate to apply such gifts professionally. Furthermore, Kretschmar himself is now considering an opportunity to undertake advanced studies in piano and organ in Leipzig, a city rich in German musical history. Should Adrian join him there, Kretschmar is sure his friend can enroll immediately in a conservatory and start making up for lost time.

After additional soul-searching, Adrian decides to follow Kretschmar's advice and begin the rigorous formal training an aspiring classical musician must undergo. He also accepts his tutor's recommendation that he choose composition as his specialty. This choice is the natural career path for one as private and aloof as Adrian Leverkuhn. The possibility of his becoming a piano virtuoso, for instance, cannot be considered because Adrian "had come too late into contact with the instrument" (131), and, in any case, "he was too self-conscious, too proud, too difficult, too solitary, to be a virtuoso" (131). He also rules out a life as a conductor for similar reasons; being "unsocial" (132) by nature, Adrian cannot visualize himself as "a baton-waving, frock-coated prima donna of the orchestra" (131), basking in the glow of strangers' approbation and applause. Adrian will accept a destiny to be spent in mostly cold and solitary labor dedicated to "music herself, the promise and vow to her, the hermetic laboratory, the gold-kitchen: composition" (132).

Indeed, the time is ripe for a man with Adrian's gifts and insights to appear on the musical scene. The personal qualities he has displayed in his life so far, particularly "the eye for the stale and absurd, the early fatigue, the capacity for disgust" (135) that have often alienated his teachers and fellow students, are, says Kretschmar, just what the musical world needs at this time. Adrian's capacity to see through the bombast and persiflage of many post-Wagnerian show pieces brings him into accord with the *Zeitgeist* in experiencing "a collective feeling for the historical exhaustion and vitiation of the means and appliances of art, the boredom with them and the search for new ways" (135). Adrian can serve as the aloof master who can answer "the vital need of art for revolutionary progress and the coming of the new" because he has "the strongest subjective sense of the staleness, fatuity, and emptiness of the means still current" (135). With his friend dizzy now with possibility and drawn almost irresistibly to new surroundings and new creations, Serenus reports the inevitable: "At the beginning of the winter semester, in 1905, Leverkuhn went to Leipzig" (136).

PART THREE

Adrian's move to Leipzig occurs when he is twenty, not quite officially an adult but certainly no longer an adolescent. New vistas are opening up, new people will be coming into Adrian's life, and new styles and experiences will enlarge the Kaisersaschern/Halle provincial world Adrian and Serenus know so well. The two have been together since childhood, but now, at least for a time, they will be going their separate ways. Serenus has to complete a year of mandatory military service in Naumburg, so he can no longer be at Adrian's side "to be near him, to keep watch over him" (137). Serenus is delighted Adrian has chosen a career in music, but at the same time he is anxious: "It made my heart lift up for joy, this decision of his—and at the same time contract with fear" (139). This apprehension has no discernible cause, but just the fact that Adrian will have to navigate alone in a city of strangers makes Zeitblom worry almost like a doting parent, who cannot stop fretting over the worst that can happen to a "manchild" like Adrian in such an environment. As matters develop, this vague uneasiness will be justified.

Adrian notices quickly that Leipzig, a city of seven hundred thousand, is *terra incognita*. In a long, rambling letter to Serenus, written in deliberate "parody of grotesque Halle experiences and the language idiosyncrasies of Ehrenfried Kumpf" (139), Adrian mentions "the common people's . . . devilishly lewd speech" (139), which subjects the "mildly slumbering Thuringian … to a seven-hundred-thousand-man impudence" (139). This much more direct and coarse urban style makes the polite exchanges common in Kaisersaschern seem old-fashioned. Such impudence affects more than language alone, however, as Adrian discovers during his first day in the city. Upon his arrival in Leipzig, Adrian meets a "porter" (140) at the station who claims to be a "guide" (141) for newcomers like himself, showing Adrian the official "brass badge" (141) that licenses his services. Adrian hires the man immediately and asks him to show the young provincial some of the city's interesting places and structures. The guide takes him to "the still standing tower of the Pleissenberg—where Luther held his disputacyon with Eck" (141) and to "the Thomaskirche on account of Johann Sebastian [Bach]" (141). These sights are so stimulating to the wide-eyed young student that despite the supercilious tone of his letter, Adrian senses something like "the pulse of the world beating" (141) within him.

At the end of the day, Adrian asks to be taken to an inn for supper, one "not too dear" (141). The guide chuckles as he takes Adrian "to a house in a little back lane behind the main street" (141) and then quietly disappears after being paid. As the naïve son of Kaisersaschern enters, he is welcomed not by a hostess, but by "a dressed up madame," who shows the guest her "nymphs and daughters of the wilderness" (142), all of them in provocative dress and staring at the prospective client "with expectant eyes, glistening in the light of the chandelier" (142). The confused and thoroughly non-plussed Adrian retreats to the home's piano, "a friend" (142) who has rescued him from staring eyes among the Winfried group on many occasions. While Adrian bangs out whatever comes to mind, one of the women comes up close to him, "a brown wench . . . in a little Spanish jacket, with a big gam, snub nose, almond eyes, an Esmeralda" (*Emeralid* in Spanish) (142). She touches his cheek, which compels Adrian to exit the premises in hasty embarrassment.

He says nothing further about this jarring encounter and ends his letter to Serenus with arch commentary on Romanticism's impact on music, as if the latter is so much more significant to the composer-to-be than a sexual tryst. But the Esmeralda who caressed his smooth cheek will remain in his memory and will, in fact, come to obsess Adrian, whose innocence will vanish at once as he responds to the powerful erotic attraction aroused by this exotic creature.

The reaction of Serenus to Adrian's revelation is anything but casual. Despite their having been together as adolescents, Zeitblom recalls no prior conversations between Adrian and him concerning "the subject of love, of sex, of the flesh" (146). Only "manifestations of passion in the intellectual sphere" (146), such as in music, elicited any response from Adrian, and such a response was "divorced from any personal element" (146). Zeitblom, in fact, admits to never feeling comfortable hearing even impersonal reactions on this subject because they marred his image of Adrian as a pure and lofty being, more fit to be among the angels than with the fallen humanity of earth. Serenus confesses that he "had tasted of the apple" (146) himself, more out of curiosity than desire, but he is sure Adrian had not done the same with any girl or woman. Now, however, that he has been lightly "touched" by one of the "waiting daughters of the wilderness" (147), this man's long repressed sexuality will come to the surface, directly challenging the "purity, chastity, intellectual pride, cool irony" (147) and all the other virtues defining his character before. Zeitblom shudders at what might follow. He knows that Adrian is not attracted to romance or feminine charm, so channeling sexual ardor into marriage with a beloved partner is not likely. Adrian is more like one of the Pythagoreans, a seeker after pure truth whose "proudest intellectuality stands in the most immediate relation of all to the animal, to naked instinct" (147), as if one's profound excursions into spiritual realms are balanced at the opposite end by descents into bestial sensuality. Recreating Adrian's experience on that fateful night in his own imagination, especially his friend's hurried exit from the parlor, Zeitblom reaches only melancholy conclusions:

> *In my eyes, Adrian had not escaped, and only very briefly, certainly, did he feel that he had. His intellectual pride had suffered the trauma of soulless instinct. Adrian was to return to the place whither the betrayer had led him.* (148)

The "betrayer" is not really Adrian's deceiving guide, but, rather, the Arch-Deceiver, who has made use of the man to open up Adrian's "soul" to influences from far below the heights of Spirit.

In the immediate aftermath of Adrian's adventure, however, his reunion with Wendall Kretschmar and the serious and demanding musical studies he undertakes with his old tutor keep Adrian focused, at least for a time. The theology studies Adrian has undertaken have "not weakened his bond with music or been any actual interruption to his preoccupation with it" (149). Instead, they have provided powerful material from the Book of Revelation and cognate literature for musical adaptation. Kretschmar's guiding hand finds a willing follower, as the tutor concentrates first on developing in Adrian a solid understanding of classic forms and techniques, on the assumption that "one must have command over what has been achieved" (151) before he can venture into new possibilities. As noted earlier, Adrian wants to minimize orchestral grandeur, believing that the post-romantic "genre of 'tone-painting,' of 'nature moods' to be fundamentally out of date" (151). Though he is still a young man, Adrian is secure in his judgments and clear-sighted about his artistic direction. His works will be austere and "chilling" (151), foregoing the lush indulgences of Richard Strauss, Mahler, Bruckner, and the like, highlighting rhythm over melody, closer to Stravinsky than to the Austro-German masters. With Kretschmar, he is in the beginning stages of finding his own voice, "when the mechanical studies preliminary to the practice of an art begin to be combined with the first personal, while as yet entirely ephemeral and preparatory plastic efforts" (152) that produce distinctive works.

All of this progress toward mastering his art occurs under Kretschmar's tutelage in, so to speak, the light of day. After hours, a competing urge and aspiration demands acknowledgement, and however hard Adrian resists its lure, he will finally oblige. At the end of his year of military service, Zeitblom reunites with Adrian in Leipzig. Though his friend shows no outward signs of struggle or stress, Serenus judges him to be "a marked man, pierced by the arrow of fate" (153). In the year since he first encountered Esmeralda, who had lightly touched his cheek while Adrian played chords in the brothel, the aspiring composer has battled the constant temptation to return to that place and meet his would-be paramour again, this time for sex. He has managed to resist this "surrender to the naked instinct that had laid its spiteful finger on him" through "a pride of the spirit" (153) that has marked Adrian's aloof and superior character since boyhood. But such resistance can be maintained only for so long; like a teenager who has seen his underaged friends drinking freely and enjoying themselves without guilt, Adrian cannot remain insulated forever from the allure he believes beckons him.

When, however, he at last revisits the scene of his initial meeting with "the 'brown wench' with the big mouth, in the little jacket" (154), he is chagrined upon being told Esmeralda has left the country. Not to be denied, Adrian asks Kretschmar for some time off so that he can attend the Austrian premiere of Richard Strauss' *Salome* in Graz. This takes place in May 1906, shortly after he has celebrated his twenty-first birthday. Whether Adrian actually attended this highly provocative performance, culminating in the sensual dance that gives Salome the head of John the Baptist, Serenus does not know. He does know from his friend's words later that Adrian did locate his Esmeralda in Pressburg, and she still remembered "all that distinguished him from the usual clientele" (154–55). Because of the respect Adrian inspired, the lady tried to persuade him not to engage in sexual relations with her for fear he could contract the venereal disease that was then afflicting her. Zeitblom considers this renunciation "an act of free elevation of soul" (155), rooted in love, and giving Esmeralda something of the same purity, albeit in different circumstances, as Gretchen, the simple, innocent virgin Goethe's Faust deflowers at the instigation of Satan, as well as Esmeralda, the gypsy, who treats Victor Hugo's Hunchback of Notre Dame with kindness and concern.

Adrian, nevertheless, ignores his partner's warnings and her fear for his well-being. Zeitblom cannot decide if his friend was moved by blind love or by darker forces. He wonders years later "what deep, deeply mysterious longing for daemonic conception, for a deathly unchaining of chemical change in his nature was at work, that having been warned he despised the warning and insisted upon possession of this flesh?" (155). In any case, Adrian was so affected by the woman, whom he never saw again that later he carefully arranged note sequences in two of his works, one early and one late, to match the spelling of Esmeralda.

Adrian does not escape the consequences of his boldness. Believing he has become symptomatic, he visits a specialist to determine if he has, indeed, been infected by Esmeralda. The doctor takes no chances, prescribing "a thorough and rather lengthy treatment" even though his patient "was not ailing" (156). After two sessions, Adrian arrives at the physician's rooms for a third, only to discover the specialist "lying on a tufted cushion in an open coffin on two trestles" (157). He consults a second doctor shortly afterwards, "a certain Dr. Zimbalist," who "looked odious" (157), credentials notwithstanding. Adrian once again meets with the doctor twice, but as he mounts the steps to see him for a third consultation, he is astonished once again. Dr. Zimbalist is being walked down the steps by two officials, one of whom is tied to the doctor's wrist by "a bracelet and little chain" (158). All the doctor can do is mutter, "Another time!" (158). Why the man is being hauled away, Adrian does not know then, nor will he ever find out: "But as though frightened off, he never took up the cure after that and went to no other doctor" (158). Zeitblom insists Adrian suffered no symptoms of syphilis afterwards and that the migraines that had afflicted him since he was a young boy were his only health issues extending into adulthood.

There is more to this fortuitous outcome than meets the eye. As all of this drama is playing out, Adrian has just turned twenty-one. In an emotional confession to friends much later in his life, Adrian Leverkuhn, by then a well-known composer of powerful, if highly idiosyncratic, works, admits that he has had dealings with the devil since he was twenty-one, a fact that provides perspective on the happenings described. The devil, he asserts, had targeted Adrian for special attention because the young man had a character and qualities matching well those the most susceptible of his victims also manifested: cold detachment, lofty ambitions, superiority, and a longing to transcend mundane constraints. His turning away from theology and his embrace of musical composition as a career made him even more vulnerable since the challenges to sustained achievement in the arts far exceed those of a cleric or church bureaucrat. The devil's hand, therefore, would push away the doctors and their ineffectual interventions, stop disease in its tracks, and confer on the aspiring master advantages none of his contemporaries could enjoy, while opening up vessels of creativity far beyond those normally accessible.

It may seem extraordinary that a single visit with a prostitute should have so many life-altering consequences. But Adrian's solitary offense is a potent catalyst, setting off reactions on multiple levels. For instance, as noted earlier, German culture was not shaped by Roman influence to the extent that Italy, Spain, France, and even Britain were, and this fact is evident in the German conception of femininity. When Martin Luther explained why he had married a former nun, he did so in an utterly straightforward way. The nun, Katerina Von Bora, had left her convent in response to his movement's rejection of vowed life, so Luther felt somewhat responsible for her situation, which marriage could improve. There could hardly be a less romantic proposal, but this is consistent with German preference and practice through generations. Women whose sexual charms are noteworthy are not as admired or pursued in German tradition as they are in the Latin world. The well-endowed *Marianne* is the French ideal; the German ideal is more like the good wife and mother, whose domestic skills matter more than beauty. Zeitblom marries a woman of sturdy good sense and virtue; Adrian's mother is cut from the same cloth, as is his sister Ursula. These are women who do not find ordinary conjugal life with a less than exceptional partner unendurable, as does Madame Bovary. The German female is not submissive, however; she is strong in body and spirit, a force to be reckoned with, like Brünnhilde or Marlene Dietrich. Later on, Adrian, in his forties, will meet a non-German woman who is talented, desirable, and eligible. He concludes that it is time for him to be married, so, like Luther, he makes his interest known and blithely assumes his proposal will be accepted without condition. But nothing turns out as the still naïve artist expects, whose mother, sister, and best friend's wife match the German ideal so well. Instead of domesticity, tragedy is the outcome.

Adrian's original sin is his pursuit of Esmeralda. This woman is outside the bounds of either innocence or respectability. There is no justification in either Christian teaching or secular middle-class morality for what Adrian is doing. Unable to control passion, he is engaged in the work of the devil, or, as Stumpf would say, the "Divel" or "Debble" (97). Schleppfuss, supposedly more sophisticated, actually went even further in his classes, ascribing to women "the collective concupiscence of the world" (106) and repeating the medieval prejudice that "the whole cult of fleshliness, of slavery to sex, was laid upon the woman" (105). Adrian compounds his guilt by interrupting his studies and actively pursuing Esmeralda, traveling a long distance, and then ignoring her pleas to keep away from her, and yielding to "love" for this ravaged soul. Esmeralda returns his affection "with all the sweetness of her womanhood" (155).

All these factors play a role in deciding Adrian's fate. His "love" is fatal. As his pact with Satan will mandate later, Adrian must renounce love in all its manifestations, such as paternity, friendship, sexual relations, mystic transport. His love for Esmeralda is punished by his contracting her disease. The affliction renders him toxic, as the two doctors trying to treat him find out. They are removed from the scene swiftly and decisively, to be replaced by Satan, who demands unconditional devotion from this point on and will intervene as he does with the doctors whenever Adrian tries to break free from the emotional strait jacket binding him exclusively and forever to this pitiless master. In this regard, Adrian is different from his predecessors, both Marlowe's Doctor Faustus, whom Mephistopheles supplies with abundant sexual partners, and Goethe's Faust, who is much older and involved with only Gretchen, whom he impregnates and shames but who will save him from eternal damnation as his life is ending.

There is a larger dimension to this demonic capture of one person's soul and spirit. The devil has infected the German nation as well. Though it is 1906 and Germany is at peace, the seeds that will sprout later are being planted, however unknowingly. Adrian's experiences within the academy, among his fellow students, and in the towns and cities he passes through, reenforce the transformation of classical German ideals occurring nationwide. The theological luminaries at Halle, for instance, discuss Satan, witches, and medieval superstitions with more interest and care than they do the words and deeds of Jesus of Nazareth, who has become in both liberal and conservative circles a diminished figure, a Jewish preacher of apocalyptic judgment on the one side or a humble teacher of moral truths through homely parables and discourses on the other. The students of the Winfried society renounce alcohol and sexual dalliance only to embrace a militant nationalism, owing more to Nietzsche and his "superman" fantasies than to traditional German theology and philosophy. Townsfolk in pastoral Thuringia, for instance, are capable of behaving like medieval zealots when confronted by human oddity or disability, condemning the victims as somehow responsible for their conditions and denying them charity or concern. Adrian's journey will be replicated by countless Germans, including men and women of the highest culture as well as ordinary citizens. Adrian will go on to create "breakthroughs" in music through innovative techniques and styles, just as German armies in 1914 and 1939 will in military strategy. Both he and they will do so by breaking norms, standards, and conventions guiding conduct for millennia and acting instead under the direction of and in concert with dark forces released by the Arch-Deceiver.

Adrian and Serenus reunite in Leipzig, where the normally solitary composer actually has found companionship among a "group of young intellectuals" (161), who gather at the Café Central regularly. One of these, Rudiger Schildknapp, will play an important role in Adrian's life in the years ahead. He is Silesian and an Anglophile, whose fluency in English enables him to support himself by translating English and American classics into German. For Schildknapp such work is welcome but not fulfilling; he considers himself "a born writer," a poet no less, who should be writing and publishing his own books rather than "being driven by necessity to till another's field (168). He is also handsome and attractive to women but too fickle to settle into a conventional marriage. Zeitblom thinks he shrinks from any commitment "because he saw therein a threat from the possible" (169) that would inevitably limit his options, either real or imagined. Although Adrian laughs often in Schildknapp's company, his first friend Serenus is not amused. He detects in Schildknapp's life style the shallowness of a dilletante and suspects that the real reason he occupies himself with translations is that this duty masks Schildknapp's "lack of a genuine and telling creative impulse" (168). Such a conclusion appears more convincing later when Schildknapp, as he does whenever someone asks him for a service, flatly refuses to prepare a libretto of Shakespeare's *Love's Labour's Lost* for an opera Adrian contemplates composing. In a hugely satisfying turn of the tables, Zeitblom himself eventually furnishes one that fits his friend's conception neatly and allows Adrian to compose a highly original comic romp.

Adrian now is turning out mostly "lieder, short and long songs, even epic fragments" (161), basing these on German translations of medieval Mediterranean poetry, extending even to "the loftiest visions of the *Divina Commedia*" (162), a flight Serenus finds disturbing. For one setting, Adrian chooses Dante's "frightfully stern sequence of verses which speak of the condemnation of innocence and ignorance . . . and the powerlessness of the creatively good before Good in itself" (162). To the humanist scholar, "this rejection of the human in favor of an unattainable absolute foreordination" (162) seems perverse, and Serenus makes known his disapproval. Adrian responds not in words but with a look "peculiar to him" that would appear now and then and was always "painful" (163):

> *Mute, veiled, musing, aloof to the point of offensiveness, full of a chilling melancholy, it ended in a smile with closed lips, not unfriendly, yet mocking, and with that gesture of turning away, so habitual, so long familiar to me.* (163)

It has the coldly shattering effect of a man simultaneously here and many worlds away, caught up in something he cannot control or abandon. Adrian reinforces this impression of cognitive dissonance during Serenus's "Leipzig year" with songs based on poetry of "Verlaine and the beloved William Blake" (165), dwelling on melancholy, madness, suffering, and evil. One terrifying poem by Blake describes "a serpent" who forces itself onto the altar of a shrine "where it vomits its poison out on the bread and on the wine" (166), to the horror of all present. Adrian's setting conveys "with astonishing power" (166) the visceral revulsion this scene provokes. Though Adrian assures Serenus in these frequently upsetting times that the composer will never "have to regret his summons to a musical career" (166), the direction this career is taking is becoming increasingly problematical.

Likewise, in the larger world, where Zeitblom can write in the present tense and with a knowledge and perspective encompassing all the years of Nazism's depredations, only ruin and destruction are evident as the author looks about. The progress of Germany's enemies through 1943–44 makes it impossible to doubt the war's inevitable outcome, just as resuming his account of Adrian's life and work earlier forces Serenus to confess that "the excited state bound up with my subject constantly assimilates itself to that produced by the shattering events of the time" (173) in which he writes. Adrian's consort with the devil, in other words, dovetails with the surrender of an entire Christian nation and culture to demonic influences masquerading "as the heralds and bringers of a world-rejuvenating barbarism, reveling in atrocity" (173). The German people collectively have fallen into the same evil meshes trapping Adrian personally; they and he, says Zeitblom, have turned away from "all that was good, genuine, trusting, and trustworthy in our old Germany" (175). Both have swallowed "a poison draught" and "under its spell . . . committed a superfluity of shameful deeds, which must now be paid for" (175). For Adrian, "fate" will take the form of a hideous reversal, as the soul that once longed to be lifted to artistic heights will be cast into the depths of hell; for Germany, which once preached spiritual exaltation, Zeitblom predicts only oblivion, as "the crimson flames of the death of the gods!" (174) devour "our character, our cause, our hope, our history" (175).

Returning to Adrian in Leipzig, Serenus remembers his worry over what seems like his friend's nihilistic embrace of "the banal, of the no longer permissible," which "threatened to swallow up art itself" (181). Adrian is, at this stage, becoming more focused on what he has been advocating in theory, that is, a return to medieval styles characterized by a "technical primitivism" (181) that practically negates all the musical progress made afterwards. A work exemplifying this tendency is thirteen song settings of poetry by Clemens Brentano. These have, says Serenus, a powerful impact but in a way that contradicts expectations. They incorporate "a glorification of the fundamental, a painfully reminiscent ironic treatment of tonality, of the tempered system, of traditional music itself" (182). Instead of the elementary leading to "the refined and intellectual" (183) as the structure of serious music since the Renaissance demands, Adrian's songs try to free "the simple" (183) from complex patterns initially set down. Serenus waxes poetic on the revelatory effect of such transpositions, as if "spirits in golden barks traverse the heavenly sea" (183). But this liberty is unsettling as well, with Adrian's introducing something like a corrosive foreign element to threaten conventions and forms carefully built up and nurtured over time. In an ominous reference to a meeting recorded in depth later, Serenus notes that his friend "had been instructed one day, or rather one night, from frightful lips, by an awful ally" (181) in the innovations just described. The composer is being drawn ever more deeply into a web of themes and styles fashioned by the enemy of all that radiates order and harmony.

Adrian's susceptibility to patterns of thinking leading to perverse conclusions extends beyond composition. In 1910, he attends the wedding of his sister, Ursula, and Johannes Schneidewein, an optician. Zeitblom is present as well, commenting favorably on the couple as "a pair on whom the eye rested with approval" (185). Adrian, too, speaks well of Ursula's husband, calling him "a sound, clean, honest man" (186) who will be a good mate for his sister. But he then abruptly changes the subject and offends Serenus by characterizing "the domestication of sex, which is evil by nature, into Christian marriage" as "a clever makeshift" (187). Adrian's supercilious tone and assumption of superior insight make him sound like a scoffer, who "by denying the works of God . . . becomes the advocate of nothing" (187). Once again, Serenus detects the Evil One's manipulation behind his friend's scorn: "Who believes in the Devil, already belongs to him" (187). Adrian tries to reassure Serenus by insisting he was only joking; he then goes on, however, in the same hypercritical style to dismiss the Pauline concept of two becoming one flesh as "soothing but nonsensical" and insisting that "love and sensuality are not to be separated" (187). Perhaps because of his memory of the passion he felt for Esmeralda, Adrian ends his denigration of conventional marriage by exalting the sex act per se: "Every sensual act means tenderness, it is a give and take of desire, happiness through making happy, a manifestation of love" (188). Love and marriage, in other words, do not necessarily go together. Zeitblom is "peculiarly upset and bewildered by his words" (188), not only because they seem so wrong for the occasion but also because Serenus himself will soon wed also. Now teaching "in the gymnasium at Kaiersaschern" (185) that both he and Adrian had attended together, the humanist scholar has expectations that are decidedly domestic and customary, highlighting how in marriage "everything is directed towards the foundation of love and tranquility, a fixed and undisturbed happiness" (188). Such calm and serenity are far from the turbulence the solitary artist's concepts have stirred. The two friends leave the subject of how love, marriage, sensuality, and desire interact with probably some relief.

As evening approaches, Serenus and Adrian walk the paths they knew so well as children, marking out sites and recalling activities with mutual pleasure. Nevertheless, tensions surface once again when their conversation moves beyond bucolic memories to the subject of music. The topic of freedom as a stimulus to originality is raised. Adrian cautions that while freedom can stimulate, it inevitably leads artists down well-defined paths, which over time become predictable and, finally, oppressive. Freedom then "begins to lie like a mildew upon talent and to betray traces of sterility" (189). This is an obstacle that orchestral and instrumental composers of the eighteenth and nineteenth centuries faced whenever "the task of organization" (190) constrained their best efforts to make music that would be fresh and interesting but still formally correct. Adrian argues that such care and concern over form stifles the spirit and can be overcome only by recovering the styles and themes of primitive times, as he had begun to do in his Brentano arrangements. The composer speaks of trying to "resolve the magic essence of music into human reason" (193). But for Serenus, such aspirations go too far, and just as the Brentano songs upset him despite their fascinating flights, so too do Adrian's words now. Serenus fears his gifted friend is falling into "a belief in the incomprehensibly and vaguely daemonic," which will "dissolve human reason in magic" (193–194). Adrian is unmoved as he concludes the discussion by reiterating the point that so disturbs his friend: "Reason and magic," said he, "may meet and become one in that which one calls wisdom, initiation; in belief in the stars, in numbers" (194). Such sentiments accord very closely with those of Goethe's Faust prior to his first visit from Mephistopheles.

Zeitblom records these increasingly divisive exchanges as he remembers them and with the added perspective brought by knowledge of Adrian's entire life experience. Since this experience includes more than visionary moral and artistic propositions, at this juncture in his narrative, the author moves to other matters, such as Adrian's living arrangements and friendships after his Leipzig stay. He settles for a time in Munich "as a lodger with the widow of a Senator from Bremen, named Rodde" (194). The Frau Senator has a Bohemian side that never found expression while she performed the duties of a legislator's wife. She now entertains, she says, "in the interests of her daughters but yet largely, as was pretty clear, to enjoy herself and hold court" (196). Daughters Inez and Clarissa are both young and nubile, but they disapprove of their mother's indulging an "unsatisfied humanity" that requires their attendance at evening gatherings with members of the "half-artist world" (196). The two are very different, Clarissa self-consciously eccentric and Inez stiffly proper, but they each befriend Adrian, who stands out within a social set of mostly second-rate artists and intellectuals who work to be charming but seem only odd.

One regular visitor is also much interested in the household's new guest despite Adrian's "utter distaste for society" (199). Rudolph Schwerdtfeger is a violinist of some distinction who values Adrian's advice and judgment on "musical and extra-musical" (199) subjects. He tries to draw out the shy composer and almost forces him to mingle with guests at the Rodde home and other venues. Rudolph projects "a certain cleanness" (199) with his artist's purity, integrity, and simplicity. Though often "blissfully absorbed in flirtation with the other sex" (199) during the Frau Senator's parties, Schwerdtfeger is liked and respected by all, even the hard to please Zeitblom. The violinist embodies the spirit of "Munich of the late Regency, with only four years between it and the war" (203), and the city still relaxed and happy enough to sponsor festivals and carnivals in "the self-indulgent comfort of its ways" (202).

Adrian is able, however, to participate only to a degree in the social swirl and entertainment of the Bavarian capital. The Lutheran from Thuringia cannot fully share in "the Munich joy of life" (204), so "foreign to the soul of a deep, stern nature like his" (202). It is not surprising, therefore, when, on a spring excursion into the countryside, as Adrian rides his bicycle through a village called Pfeiffering, about an hour's drive from Munich, he is immediately attracted to this rural hideaway, with features and structures reminiscent of his old hometown of Kaisersaschern. Stopping at the property of Frau Else Schweigestill for rest and a glass of lemonade, Adrian cannot help discussing with the proprietress the possibility of his renting space in the family's large home, which had formerly been a cloister for monks. Frau Else quickly shows him the abbot's room, once the study of the order's leader, large and comfortably furnished. It would serve the composer well, but Adrian hesitates about making a commitment to a residence still close to the city. He would rather travel "farther away than an hour's journey towards the mountains" (209). In a decision that will have consequences determining how the artist will live the rest of his days, Adrian decides to visit Italy instead. Blissfully unaware of what lies ahead, Adrian Leverkuhn joins Rudiger Schildknapp on this momentous journey.

Adrian and Rudi spend parts of the next two years in Italy, mostly as lodgers in the Manardi house in the Sabine Hills. To all appearances, the two Northern European travelers have landed in just the right place for refreshment and stimulation. Serenus and his wife, Helene, for instance, who visit the pair during the second summer of their sojourn, are entranced by the Italian hospitality, food, and sunshine always at hand. Afternoons are "spent in beautiful walks" (214) through the hill country under the cloudless "classic sky" (214), and evenings bring stimulating conversation and delicious suppers and desserts. The young married couple are moved to "raptures" (214) by all they experience, but their friend is almost indifferent, responding to their excitement with only "a smiling, slightly ironic nod" (214). The "glory of nature's magnificence" (215) and the best in companionship, food, and drink cannot divert the artist from what really matters, "working on his opera" (215). This is the adaptation of Shakespeare's *Love's Labour's*

Lost, for which Serenus has provided a libretto in English. This piece is not at all grand but rather deliberately small scale, "in strict chamber music style . . . ingenious and humoristic, rich in subtle, high-spirited ideas" (217). But as with Adrian's previous works, Zeitblom cannot help feeling ambivalent about the styles his friend exploits. As Adrian plays portions of the work on the out-of-tune piano in his room, Serenus is torn between admiration and doubt. While he is drawn to the "art for artists and connoisseurs" (218) aspect of the opera, Zeitblom fears that it will be judged too pure, too rarefied in its conception to be enjoyable. The down-to-earth humanist cannot envision audiences of music lovers used to rich melody and spectacle responding favorably to a work notably lacking in both. Melancholy mixes with respect in all he hears, almost as if Adrian has created a self-portrait. The gorgeous surroundings and generous friends have not fundamentally altered the self-absorbed character the composer nurtures. As Zeitblom and his wife prepare to return home, Serenus yields to "a certain private feeling of relief" (219), as if the strain of interacting daily with Adrian makes separation welcome. He finds Adrian's life in Italy too closed-in, too lonely, too focused on work, to be healthful or appealing. He, and to a lesser degree Rudi, appear to be like "cloistered monks" (220) in their habits and routines. The happily married Serenus marvels at Adrian's "chastity" and wonders if the composer can be thought of as "a saint" (220). But he quickly rejects the comparison, knowing from their long friendship that Adrian's "abstention from women" (220) is due mostly to the "disinclination, avoidance, reserve, and aloofness" (220) that have formed Adrian's personality and identity since childhood. Although these qualities try the friendship between the two in many ways, they cannot end it. Serenus closes his reflections on his time with Adrian in Italy with philosophic acceptance: "There are people with whom it is not easy to live; but to leave impossible" (220).

PART FOUR

Something else occurred in Italy says Serenus, something that made clearer why the author had been feeling increasingly anxious as he listened to his highly gifted friend speak dismissively about values and ideals the humanist scholar honors and as he detected undertones of eerie mockery in parts of Adrian's latest compositions. Left in a collection of the composer's papers and documents Serenus examined after Adrian's death was a detailed account of a long encounter his friend had had one evening while recovering from a migraine attack. Exactly when this meeting occurred is not certain, and exactly what transpired during that night in Adrian's rooms in Italy is hard to determine. Zeitblom "cannot believe that in the depths of his soul, Adrian himself considered to be actual that which he saw and heard" (221). Notwithstanding, if no "visitor" from the depths of hell in good medieval fashion really appeared to Adrian and conducted a long dialogue with him, culminating in a "compact" signed in blood, "then it is horrible to think," says Serenus, that what the composer later recorded "came out of the afflicted one's own soul" (221). Whatever the truth may be, with his hand shaking, Zeitblom shares the contents of Adrian's manuscript with the world without further comment.

Adrian is sitting alone one evening reading Kierkegaard when he feels "a cutting cold" (223) radiating from the front of his room. He thinks at first his companion, Schildknapp, has returned but soon realizes that "another, smaller than he" (223) is "sitting on the horse-hair sofa" (223) staring at him. This being speaks to Adrian in German, using the informal "thou," as if the two are familiar with each other, and speaking "with an actor's voice and eloquence" (224). Adrian thinks the figure may have been produced by hallucination, given the fact that he has been suffering from migraine attacks. His guest is surprised by such a fantasy and reminds Adrian he should have been "expecting" (225) him since they have had prior communication. The uninvited guest then proudly admits his identity, inviting Adrian to call him "any one . . . among the pet names the peasants give" (225) him, as if the composer and he are on the friendliest of terms. Satan insists he has "delicate and urgent business" (226) that cannot be postponed; he is there "to come to an understanding" (227) with Adrian. Switching to the royal "we," he reviews with his reluctant host the origin and background of his interest in Adrian:

> *Really gifted. That is what we recognized betimes and why from early on we had an eye on you—we saw that your case was definitely worth the trouble, that it was a case of the most favorable situation, whereof with only a little of our fire lighted under it, only a little healing, elation, intoxication, something brilliant could be brought out.* (228)

What Adrian must do is surrender his eternal destiny ("the end is ours . . . that has to be agreed on . . .") (230) in return for the devil's continual creative stimulation throughout a prescribed time span. Satanic assistance will induce "towering flights and illuminations, experiences of uplifting and unfetterings, of freedom, certainty, facility, feeling of power and triumph" (230) that will liberate Adrian from normal restraints and allow him to reach unparalleled heights of inspiration and understanding. It is now time "for express confirmation between us two and a firm contract upon payment against completion" (231). The composer is reminded that four years before, when Adrian was twenty-one, Satan and he first made contact, leading Adrian to Esmeralda, his "French beloved" (229). Things have been moving well since, with the two in tandem and "everything is taking the finest, most exquisite, most promising course, and the bell is now half cast" (231). All that is needed to confirm the union is a signed agreement.

To make his subject's consent more likely, the devil slyly injects the name of one of Adrian's Munich friends, the painter Baptiste Spengler, to illustrate how common daemonic connections are in society. Although Spengler "is no python, in whom we bring sensational deeds to pass" (232), he is still a member in good standing in this far from exclusive club of the outwardly respectable, the same people Nathaniel Hawthorne's Young Goodman Brown observes gathered at night around a bonfire for devil worship deep in the forest. One participant is Brown's own wife, a revelation that the "good man" never gets over. Adrian likewise is shocked by Satan's casual reference to his father, "a shrewd one always wanting to speculate the elements" (235), a passion stoked and channeled through hell's agency. The devil returns to Adrian's climactic sexual encounter with Esmeralda and how his agents enabled the young man's system to suspend the slow ravages of venereal disease while, at the same time, disposing of the doctors standing in the way of his recovery. These interventions bought for Adrian "a whole house-glassful of divil-time, genius time" (234) the composer can draw on for twenty-four years to produce true masterpieces. The fiend even assures Adrian that "what we give to experience, it is the archaic, the primeval, long since has not been tried" (237), which is exactly the artistic element in which the composer of *Love's Labour's Lost* wants to be immersed.

The devil now changes his appearance to resemble an aesthete, "a theoretician and critic, who himself composes, so far as thinking allows him" (238). Adrian "becomes more comfortable in his presence" (238), particularly as Satan speaks positively and at length about "the new music" (238) that so interests the composer. Adrian senses that all this talk has one goal: "to show me that I could avail myself of, nor have, no one other than the devil to kindle me to my work." (240). He cannot, in other words, trust in "a natural harmony, out of which one might create without a thought or any compulsion" (240) from supernatural forces. The devil stresses even more how necessary his participation in Adrian's creative life is, to bring the composer "to giddy heights of self-admiration, and do such things that you will behold them only with shudders of awe" (242). He promises the composer "that toward the end of your hourglass years your sense of your power and splendor" will allow Adrian, like Adam and Eve, to "mount to most triumphant well-being, to a sense of bursting health, to the walk and way of a god" (243). Adrian will feel like Nietzsche's *Ubermensch* as he bestrides the universe free of restraint and beyond good and evil:

> *Not only will you break through the paralyzing difficulties of the time—you will break through time itself, by which I mean the cultural epoch and its cult, and dare to be barbaric, twice barbaric indeed, because of coming after the humane, after all possible root-treatment and bourgeois raffinement.* (243)

The appeal of this intoxicating mixture of artistic breakthrough and transcendence through self-assertion, accompanied by abandonment of stifling cultural and moral inhibitions, is irresistible. Adrian asks his guest about hell, as if even that consequence is worth entertaining in exchange for what the devil has just promised. Satan responds in words that someone without the young composer's compulsion to soar would find terrifying. Hell, he says, is where "everything ends" (244); its utter finality is "unendurable yet to be endured world without end" (245). The devil counts on Adrian's pride to make even this fate no obstacle to his being snared, a pride that he cannot renounce and that makes any form of contrition impossible.

Satan knows now that Adrian is his, noting "that precisely heads of your sort comprise the population of hell" (247). He refers to Adrian again as "an attractive case" with a "quick, arrogant head" (247), the kind susceptible to being turned. Adrian's "vaine glory aspired to the elemental" from his earliest days, but he was "too clever and cold and chaste" (248) to make the necessary leap. Only the ecstasy of sex with Esmeralda, Satan's instrument, brought "the illumination, the aphrodisiacum of the brain" (248) that released the energy necessary to move beyond "cleverness and calculation" (248) and into the realm of genius. Impatient to close the deal, Satan changes appearance once more, becoming again the "cheesy rapscallion in the cap, with the red eyes" (247) Adrian first saw. He is the salesman who has said enough and awaits the result.

Adrian cannot escape. Satan and he have been and must continue to be "in league and business" (248). His master drives home the point, saying "with your blood you have . . . promised yourself to us, and are baptized ours" (248). His "baptismal promises" are stringent. Adrian will be granted a "full XXIV years" of "genius's time" (248) to produce his works, provided he renounce "all living creature, all the Heavenly Host, and all men, for that must be" (248). As Satan's subject, Adrian "maist not love" (248), since love will draw him away from his work, his master, and his destiny. He must remain "cold" throughout his life so "that the fires of creation shall be hot" (249). Adrian will be allowed "extravagant living in return, the only one that suffices a proud soul" (249). Such living, though, will demand "a work-filled eternity of human life" (249) that will keep the composer cold, isolated, and firmly in the grasp of Satan, whose jealous control tolerates no attractions or attachments to others. In this life and in the next, the devil will exclusively "move and manage the fine-created Creature . . . be it in life, soul, flesh, blood, or goods—to all eternity" (249). As the guest departs, he leaves behind "a glacial wave of cold" (249). Adrian feels "a fury of disgust" (249), but this revulsion comes too late. The young man is now and will forever be a prisoner.

"Young man" is important. Goethe's Faust is older and disillusioned, having come to the melancholy conclusion that the studies to which he has devoted his life are not yielding truths or tangible benefits. Faust desires a richer and broader experience and the power to live to the fullest. Adrian is more focused on artistic achievement of paradigm—shattering proportions. He wants to take serious music in a direction fundamentally different from what four centuries of development have produced. The early years of the twentieth century, the time of Adrian's encounter with Satan, are marked by culminating expressions of theme and variations, the organizing principle of sonata form guiding composers' works for solo instrumental and orchestral combinations since the eighteenth century. Under Kretschmar's tutelage, Adrian recognizes early that this classical template cannot continue to inspire original productions, except perhaps through parody or understatement. The years he is given to create truly new and noteworthy compositions will be productive if he accepts the rigors such work entails and responds to the supercharged creative drive his contract with Satan releases.

In Goethe's poem, Faust himself proposes the condition that will determine his fate. The scholar who will leave his musty library to perform world-conquering, extra-terrestrial exploits is so eager to experience the utmost life can afford by engaging ceaselessly in exploration and effort in whatever arena, he asks Mephistopheles to take him immediately to hell if he ever pauses for even an instant to rest on his laurels:

Faust

When on an idler's bed I stretch myself in quiet,
There let, at once, my record end!
Canst thou with lying flattery rule me,
Until, self-pleased, myself I see,
Canst thou with rich enjoyment fool me,
Let that day be the last for me!
The bet I offer.

Mephistopheles

Done

Faust

When thus I hail the moment flying:
"Ah still delay—thou art so fair!"
Then bind me in thy bonds undying,
My final rule then declare!
Then let the death bell chime the token,
Then art thou from thy service free!
The clock may stop, the hand be broken,

The time be finished unto me!
(Act One, Scene IV)

Faust must continue to strive, to seek further and dive deeper, to build, explore, create, and achieve inexhaustibly. Once he loses himself in the moment and allows himself, however briefly, to feel a sense of fulfillment, he has no more worlds to conquer through infernal power and must be taken from the earth.

Adrian is not so bold as to make proposals of this sort during his fateful meeting with Satan, the only one recorded in the novel. The master lays out all the binding protocols in no uncertain terms. The major restriction is Adrian's renunciation of love in all its forms for the rest of his days. This recalls Alberich's forced celibacy in Wagner's *Das Rheingold* in return for possession of the gold which the Rhine maidens guard. The dwarf is told that once he shapes the gold into a magic ring, he will exercise supreme power world-wide. Dazzled by this prospect, Alberich, whose ugliness repels most women in any case, accepts the prohibition. Adrian is not ugly or repulsive, but he is cold, aloof, and self-absorbed. He has no choice but to agree to a loveless future if he is to be awarded "genius years" of creativity. The consequences of this sacrifice will be felt over time as not only sexual pleasure and paternity will be denied but also close friendships, intimacies, and attachments of every sort will be forbidden. On occasions when Adrian, in his innocence, yields to love in the hope that somehow his daemonic handler will permit an exception to his mandate, the results will be tragic. The icy cold that chills Adrian when Satan is in his rooms will radiate from the composer as well as the years pass and his loneliness mounts, endangering any to whom his affection extends.

This episode occurs in either the summer of 1911 or 1912, Zeitblom not being sure because the manuscript recording the scene is not dated. In these years just before the outbreak of World War I, Germans are becoming increasingly detached from the religiously inspired idealism that had undergirded moral and cultural aspiration since the Reformation. Under Prussian rule and its authoritarian certainty, Germans of all classes and faiths are increasingly nationalist, militarist, and prideful. The conviction of German superiority and uniqueness begins to be associated more and more with the armed forces and less and less with the scholars and philosophers who had made insight into moral truth the criterion for any claim to exceptionality. As we have seen, the theological students Adrian and Serenus befriend speak hardly at all of faith, hope, and charity during their excursions in the countryside; instead, the power and might of Germany are highlighted, to the exclusion of universal love and fraternity. In the theology classes Adrian attends, Satan and his works seem to receive more attention than Jesus and his teachings. The Middle Ages are invoked not as a period of profound faith and devotion but as a time when witches dabble in the occult and are burned, when women use sexual appeal in league with the devil to lure men to perdition, and when those on the margins of society are ostracized and feared. Outside the academy, Nietzsche's revaluation of morals extols the power of the primitive and the barbaric, exalts self-assertion over humility, cold impassivity over mercy toward those in need, and self-exaltation over self-denial, all of this resonating within influential social and political circles. In other words, the dark forces that are at play in Adrian's life are infecting the nation as a whole. Both the composer and the people are allowing themselves to savor the intoxication inspired by the possibility of world-transforming influence and power, just as Alberich is by the magic ring. Adrian is not connected formally to any military or nationalist bodies, his migraines keeping him exempt from service; nevertheless, he succumbs to the devil's blandishments and assurances of personal glory just as fully as the countrymen around him do to fantasies of national greatness that place "Germany over all." Conceptions like these will make many welcome war since conflict among nations will confirm German superiority as it toughens those engaged; for Adrian, tireless labor and lovelessness will have the same impact. The nation and the composer are united in following a trajectory laid out by fiends.

In 1914, war does come, to the delight of almost all. The Germans have elaborate plans, which their officers and troops strive to fulfill faithfully. In so doing, they overcome obstacles and adversity by any means possible. Thus, they violate treaty obligations, rules of engagement, and canons of civilization by invading neutral Belgium, committing atrocities against innocent civilians and clergy, and burning the university library at Louvain, including priceless medieval manuscripts; later on, Germans will use poison gas against their enemies, allow submarine attacks on neutral vessels, and work to destabilize entire nations, such as Imperial Russia (Communism) and the United States (Mexican irredentism), all this in a desperate attempt to win a war they have entered feeling invincible. All such measures prove unavailing, however, as a coalition of allied powers, including Russia until 1917, Great Britain, France, and the United States after 1917, finally defeat Germany and its partner, Austria-Hungary, decisively. The victors impose harsh peace terms, essentially blaming Germany for starting the conflict and punishing its people for the excesses of its government and its military.

Worse will follow. The excesses of the 1914–18 conflict began mostly as responses to unexpected developments or pressures that commanders had to combat on the spot with whatever means was available, and, as the war dragged on with victory nowhere in sight, such responses became more extreme and inhuman out of desperation. In the years between the ratification of the Versailles Treaty in 1919 and the outbreak of the Second World War in 1939, the satanic grip on the battered German people grows stronger, pulling them farther away from religion, tradition, and humane values. War crimes that were occasional and spontaneous in the First World War are integral to the German high command's planning during the Second World War, particularly in connection with the invasions of Poland and the Soviet Union. This descent into barbarism comes as a result of the accession of the National Socialist Party and its leader, Adolf Hitler, to political supremacy in Germany in 1933. Nazi ideology is permeated with presumptions and prejudices wholly in line with the witches' brew of primitive tribalism and cruelty emphasized by Satan in person to Adrian in connection with new music and in steady Nazi propaganda to the German people as a whole. Hitler's most fanatical followers, the members of the SS led by Heinrich Himmler, wear death's head emblems and tout the superiority of the Aryan race, from which they believe the German people are descended. Those not fortunate enough to have forbears like these elite white and blond supermen and women are, ipso facto, hopelessly inferior and worthy only of subjection. In the case of the Jews, however, subjection is not enough. In Nazi thinking, the Jews have spawned everything from Christianity to Communism that has worked or is working to mongrelize the pure-blooded German people through foreign infestation and wipe away all traces of ancient Aryan customs and rites. As even Luther asserted, the Jews are a tribe of conspirators looking always for ways to undermine the individualistic values of German social, familial, and political life, replacing them with supra-national collectivist structures designed to crush personal striving and exceptionality. Ultimately, Jews from all over the European territories conquered by Germany between 1939 and 1941 will be at first imprisoned in "concentration camps" where, in theory, they can "concentrate" on the errors in their thinking and correct them, but, ultimately, are being sent to these places only to be executed *en masse* since they have been born irredeemable. Homosexuals, Communists, gypsies, and naysayers in general, suffer similar fates. Like Adrian, the Nazis are denied love, frozen by their attachment to a leader whose hatreds are of truly Mephistophelean dimensions.

PART FIVE

As his narrative resumes, Serenus Zeitblom briefly leaves Adrian and 1912 to describe what he sees and hears around him in April 1944, the year marking the beginning of the end of World War II and Nazi Germany. In the Bavarian countryside where he resides, Zeitblom, a German patriot but never a Nazi sympathizer, hears the thunder and feels the ground shaking from "the terrors of almost daily air raids upon our beleaguered Fortress Europa" (252), a designation he amends later to "our prison, our madhouse?" (253). He notes with concern how the Russian counteroffensive in the east is steadily driving the Germans out of cities and territories they had captured and held since 1941 and how on the other side of the world, America is producing "an absolutely crushing abundance of war material" (252) that must prove decisive over time. The arrogant assumption that "war is a German prerogative" (253) is being challenged daily. Serenus finds some consolation in the fact that Adrian is "safe from the days we dwell in" (253), having died in 1940. His lifelong friend and biographer now bears with fortitude "the burden his shoulders were spared" (253), imagining he can still respond to "the always cherished desire to serve, to help, to protect him" (253). He could not save Adrian from succumbing to the "glamor of evil" in his lifetime, and the story he resumes cannot be altered, but Zeitblom is at peace with himself and with his memories.

When Adrian returns to Germany in 1912, he immediately makes arrangements to live in the quarters the Schweigestill family of Pfeiffering had shown him during an outing in the countryside years before. This is the residence and surrounding area that Zeitblom earlier had compared to Adrian's "childhood home" (25), where the two friends spent happy days. Before leaving Munich permanently, Adrian also secures the services of a copyist to prepare the manuscript of the opera, *Love's Labour's Lost*, upon which he had been putting finishing touches. Adrian appreciates the solitude and privacy his new rooms provide, affording him the right conditions for composition and reflection. Nevertheless, visitors abound, mostly men and women the composer had met in Munich and who find "his cool, reserved person, shy despite his haughtiness . . . far from unattractive" (259). Though he is not worldly, Adrian welcomes the bits of news, witty commentary, and entertainment these guests bring. In a remarkable coincidence, Serenus Zeitblom is offered a teaching position at the nearby "Freising Academy" (261), enabling him to see Adrian as often as both could wish.

The manuscript of *Love's Labour's Lost* arrives soon after Adrian has settled into his new surroundings. The copyist attaches a letter containing nothing but praise for the work and offering astute observations on particular parts. Adrian, however, already has put this composition behind him, asking only that Zeitblom send the score to Wendell Kretschmar, far to the north in Lubeck. Kretschmar will use his connections to arrange a performance but not until the following year when, as it happens, war is raging. This politico-military reality is too much to overcome. The fact that Adrian has based an opera on a play by Shakespeare ruins its reception in Germany. Most of the audience in Lubeck ostentatiously leave the theater before the work's conclusion, and local critics are dismissive. Only one commentator, "an old music-professor" (263), reacts differently, pronouncing the opera "a work of the future, full of profound music" (263) that should surely be appreciated in the coming years. In Adrian's lifetime, though, only three performances will be staged.

The composer does not let this setback discourage him. He moves ahead, first setting poems by Blake and Keats to music, as if daring his countrymen to reject his offerings again, but then concentrates on a German poem "of the highest rank" (265), Klopstock's *Spring Festival*, which is more like a "religious hymn" (265) than a lyric lament. Adrian's score turns it into "a thrilling piece of work" (265) that still only "a minority" (265) praise but, "through the efforts of some courageous conductors friendly to the new music" (265), receives numerous performances. Serenus admires aspects of the work but at the time cannot penetrate the composition's "inward necessity, its purpose, informed by fear, of seeking grace in praise" (265). Only after reading years later Adrian's account of his encounter with Satan "in the stone-floored sala" (265) in the Italian hills could he place in context this "plea to God, an atonement for sin, a work of *attritio cordis*" (266).

This plea does not lead Adrian back to God or to faith. He becomes instead more like his father at this juncture, inclined to speculating on extreme locations and events in nature and, for a time, putting composition aside. Zeitblom remembers Adrian's relating in great detail, for instance, a tale about exploring the depths of the sea in the company of an oceanographer. Since Adrian lives nowhere near the sea, his adventure is a leap of the imagination, a tour de force facilitated by his infernal master that will give Adrian a mind-altering glimpse into the grandeur of creation. Based as it is on science and data, Adrian's experience is analogous to the breakthroughs German physicists were making in atomic theory and the like at about the same time. Adrian's account seems eerily accurate. As he and his guide descend in their vessel to great depths, Adrian describes "solid blackness all round, the blackness of interstellar space whither for eternities no weakest sun-ray had penetrated" (268) and how he and his companion's conveyance are shedding a light never before grasped by "the creatures of the depths" (268) crowding all about. Despite Zeitblom's "lack of interest" (269) in such phenomena, Adrian goes on about "his experiences of the monstrously extra-human" (269), moving from the ocean's bottom to the vastness of space, wherein "our utter insignificance to any larger view; the almost undiscoverable situation not only of the earth but of our whole planetary system . . . within the vortex of the Milky Way" (270) is apparent. The same "Professor Abercocke," who had guided Adrian through the sea's darkness, is also steering him "among the stars" as "his mentor" (272).

The composer continues with a reference to the expansion of the universe after what astrophysicists will later call the Big Bang originated all that now exists. Adrian seems to have at his fingertips encyclopedic knowledge about this phenomenon, concluding with certainty that "the cosmos, at least for a long time, more precisely for nineteen hundred million years, has been in a state of furious expansion—that is, of explosion" (272). By this point, the humanist Zeitblom has heard enough. He protests that his friend's conception does not "stir one to a feeling of the majesty of God or give rise to any moral elevation" (272). He argues that the civilizing virtues, "piety, reverence, intellectual decency, religious feeling, are only possible about men and through men and by limitation to the earthly and human" (273). Man is "no mere biological being" (273) who is brought into existence by some cosmic force akin to a billiard stick knocking balls haphazardly. Quite to the contrary, man is special and chosen because "to him the Absolute is given, the ideas of truth, of freedom, of justice; that upon him the duty is laid to approach the consummate" (273). This strong defense of classical humanism is in direct conflict with a scientism that degrades the human race to a soulless condition more like inert matter. Such thinking is, in Serenus's view, stimulated by the "devil's juggling" (272).

The former theology student is unmoved by his faithful friend's dissent, dismissing Serenus's assertions as grounded in anachronistic constructs. He calls the philologist's position "pure Middle Ages," and based on "a cosmology proper to Kaisersaschern" (273)—that is, backward and juvenile, amounting only to a stubborn refusal to accept the truths revealed by science. Serenus is disturbed by Adrian's "persisting in the whimsical pretence of a personal, direct, and special knowledge about the affairs of heaven and earth" (274). Years later, Zeitblom will be able to place the composer's cold and crushing conceits in perspective. He will realize that Adrian at this time was preparing a one movement "orchestral world-portrait" (275) that would move in an entirely different direction from "the spirit of humble glorification" (274) of his *Spring*

Celebration. This “cosmic music” (274) arises from the same dehumanizing conclusions about man’s importance Serenus found so disturbing then. The work’s essence is “mockery” (275). Its “luciferian sardonic mood, a sneering travesty of praise” (275), reflects in music Adrian’s “preoccupation with the immeasurable extra-human” (275). His art is ceasing to be seminal and experimental in a positive sense but is evolving toward “a virtuosity antipathetic to the artist mind, a blasphemy, a nihilistic sacrilege” (275).

Three conclusions may be drawn from this dramatic episode. First, Zeitblom is correct in regarding Adrian’s immersion in the depths of the sea and in the explosive origins of the universe as somehow the devil’s work. The mentor and guide for Adrian’s voyages is indeed Satan, the same being that permits Goethe’s Faust, to transcend all limits in fantastic ascents toward the heavens and descents into mythological underworlds where he meets the likes of Helen of Troy. But Goethe’s subject grows more human in the sense Zeitblom understands, as he uses the superhuman powers Satan has endowed him with in part two for the betterment of others, to a point where by the end of the epic, Faust can merit salvation. Adrian’s explorations of the cosmos, however, reinforce the cold, loveless egotism Satan has mandated ever since their encounter in Italy. Adrian’s response to his mentor’s tutelage is a “mocking” work inspiring no broadening of sympathies nor any reaching out to “brothers” as in Beethoven’s *“Ode to Joy.”*

A second conclusion follows from Serenus Zeitblom’s eloquent affirmation of humanism’s ideals. His arguments may be viewed as a ringing endorsement of German higher thought, dating from Luther’s insistence on the primacy of faith and the necessity of a believer’s personal commitment in living out this faith as a pre-condition for salvation, extending through Kant and his confidence that moral absolutes exist and that philosophers can access them by rising above earthly phenomena and through Fichte, who assures German youth that with proper education they, too, can intuit these same absolutes. Zeitblom is the exponent of constant striving toward higher realms, while Adrian is aligning himself more and more with Nietzsche's rejection of all such effort.

The composer is not alone. A final conclusion concerns the character and direction of German culture in Adrian's creative years. A surprising number of acquaintances in his social circle arrive by their own routes at the same disparaging propositions Adrian formulates after his experience of cosmic marvels. One such is Dr. Chaim Breisacher, a "polyhistor who knew how to talk about anything and everything" (279). True to his principles, Zeitblom is repelled by this man's glib dismissal of the idea of cultural progress and considers him an "intellectual intrigant" (279). Breisacher, for instance, sees "the development of painting from the primitive flat to the presentation of perspective" (279) as wrong-headed, and "the change-over of music from monody to part-music, to harmony . . . [as] an acquisition of barbarism" (280). He is likewise unimpressed with the evolution of Judaism over the centuries, considering "King David, King Solomon, and the prophets . . . already debased representatives of an exploded late theology" (281), which had lost all vital connection to the "genuine folkishness" (281) that had animated the earliest tribes. This primitive consciousness nourished "the cult of the effectively present national god, the general concept of the metaphysical power of the folk" (282) that by the time of Solomon had been completely lost with Elohim "exiled into the sky" (282) and no longer "ahead of the people in a pillar of fire" (282). In true Nietzschean fashion, Breisacher denies the reality of sin, arguing that "the genuine religion of a genuine folk" (283) does not recognize sin or punishment. "All morality," he avers, derives from "a misunderstanding of the ritual" (283) governing behavior among the folk.

Zeitblom finds this "frightfully clever playing of atavistic cards" (284) ominous. Breisacher's theorizing leads to "something revolutionary; something more disrupting than any liberalism" (284) and is totally alien to everything Serenus espouses. What the Jewish scholar is proposing is one more variation on what Adrian is trying to communicate in music and what, in the years after 1918, the Nazis will keep stressing in their propaganda, to wit, the primitive is preferable to the sophisticated, whether in religion, art, or politics, since conventional morality is stifling, conventional harmony in music is outdated, and conventional political life is tone-deaf to the needs of the masses. A return to the folkish style of thinking and living is the only way to break the chains of modernity that are so devitalizing. In a chilling admission years later, Serenus realizes that "through this very Breisacher" (284), he "first came in touch with the new world of anti-humanity" (284) that would soon be in the ascendant and lead to, among many horrors, the demonization and systematic murder of Breisacher's compatriots. The poison Satan offers Adrian Leverkuhn is being passed around liberally.

The Rodde family Adrian stayed with in Munich for a time is also infected, as will be revealed in stages over time. Introduced earlier, its members are the Frau Senator, wife of the late political leader, and her two daughters, Clarissa and Inez. After the Senator's death, it became harder and harder for the three to maintain the well-ordered lifestyle of a respectable bourgeois family. Even though the Frau Senator still "retains remnants of upper middle-class elegance" (286) in her Munich apartments, she mixes these amenities incongruously with "the bohemian air of her salon" (286), at whose gatherings a wide variety of academics, artists, and intellectuals mingle. This "hybrid milieu" (286) cannot interest the daughters, who are polar opposites. Even if she lacks "what one calls theatre blood" (285), Clarissa likes the company of actors and artists and appears sometimes in the provinces in supporting roles requiring little actual stage time. Inez, by contrast, seeks "the psychological security of an assured bourgeois position" (286) and views marriage as a means to acquiring such. For both sisters, whose fates will be tragic, the traditional values modeled by Serenus Zeitblom, emphasizing rigor, faith, morality, and regard for others, will be, in Clarissa's life, largely irrelevant, and for Inez will be subsumed within an all-encompassing "security" that makes no demands. The stout-hearted burgher determination and strength of will are not recognizable in these women, whose total life experience will illustrate how the best in German culture has been lost to laxity and indifference.

A professor at the Technical Institute in Munich, Dr. Helmut Institoris, "from a solid Wurtzburg family" (287), considers Inez Rodde a good marriage prospect. But though his pedigree seems right, Institoris too has been lured into the same dangerous style of thinking Breisacher finds invigorating. He lectures on "aesthetic theory and the history of Renaissance architecture" (287) from an idiosyncratic point of departure. Institoris dwells on the "brute force" (287) the era supposedly prized and whose exercise gave Italy's powerful families the resources to sponsor great artists and commission beautiful works. This emphasis on the primitive and instinctual is at odds with the professor's "delicate and nervous" (287) make-up but is perfectly consistent with the glorification of barbarism already embraced by Adrian and Breisacher. Institoris' aesthetics, highlighting "beautiful ruthlessness and Italian poisoners" (289), at least on the surface, does not seem compatible with the "pessimistic moralism," inclining Inez toward "a strictly orthodox, modish, economically well-upholstered marriage" (289). This fact causes Zeitblom, who will remain Inez's friend and confidant for years to come, to consider a union between the two scarcely "plausible" (288). He detects instead signs of attraction between Inez and the violinist Rudi Schwerdtfeger, whose charm and sex appeal radiate "sweet unthinking life itself" (297). Notwithstanding, Inez will let her need for comfort and security overcome any romantic inclinations and will marry Professor Institoris, a choice that, as the judgmental like to say, will have consequences.

The exaltation of the primitive and the barbaric that scholars like Breisacher and Institoris promote is by no means a point of view that only eccentrics share. "The first glowing August days of 1914" (299), in fact, reveal the German nation as a whole accepting enthusiastically the prospect of a two-front war against the British and French in the west and the Russians in the east. Unlike many in France, for instance, where the scale of death and destruction in the months to come will be monumental and "*malheur*" (299) is the favorite term for what is happening, the

Germans are mostly jubilant. They feel "joy at being released from dull every day and from a world-stagnation that could go on no longer" (299); they look forward to "yielding to unbridled instinct" (299), the surrender to Satan that will release any inhibition or hesitation among those ready to perpetrate mass slaughter. Zeitblom has been called to the colors as a "reserved vice-sergeant major" (299), and while ready to do his duty as a patriot, is not "at ease in" (299) the atmosphere of frantic mobilization and eager expectation all around him. He worries about the ardent young recruit who "if he thinks of himself as a sacrifice by which the old Adam is put away and from which in unity a new and higher life will be wrestled, then our everyday morals will be outbid by the abnormal and must be silent" (300). But the intoxication of some "new breakthrough" (301) is too much for "everyday morals" to prevail among multitudes engaging in "war against everybody, to convince everybody and to win" (301). The same world-altering destiny that Adrian believes will bring about his artistic "breakthrough" motivates the German armed forces to fulfill a duty imposed by "sacred necessity" (301), nothing less than facilitating through German leadership and power the process by which "the world was to renew itself" (301). Zeitblom admits that even "a superior individual" (301) would find it easy in such a time "to lose himself altogether in the general" (301) excitement.

Just such "a superior individual" is Adrian, usually so detached from happenings like this war hysteria. "To say good-bye" (303) to Adrian before his deployment, Zeitblom visits him at Pfeiffering. During their conversation, Serenus confesses his misgivings about how Germany's "breakthrough to world power" (306) requires "an outbreak of war" (306) that in turn leads to a violation of international law as German troops invade neutral Belgium. He knows this action has not occurred through error or impetuosity since it has been part of the general staff's war plan for years. He stresses that his nation must be "ready to make good" (307) in some way the "wrong" (307) so strongly condemned by the rest of Europe. He can say no more, however, because Adrian cuts him off abruptly. Then, to Zeitblom's dismay, the reclusive artist, his oldest and best friend, takes the opposite position by asking "who denies that a real break-through is worth what the tame world calls a crime?" (307). Serenus counters that "craving to break through from bondage" (308), as Germany envisions itself doing, is rooted in "a psychology threatened with envelopment, the poison of isolation, provincial boorishness, neurosis, implicit Satanism" (308). This point hits home because, again, the condition Serenus ascribes to a whole people is almost identical in each detail to the factors disturbing Adrian's own mental processes. The composer responds to Serenus as he always does to any who disturb him deeply:

> *The look he cast on me was the look, the familiar one that made me almost equally unhappy, no matter whether myself or another was its object: wordless, veiled, coldly remote to the point of offensiveness, followed by the smile with closed lips and sneeringly dilating nostrils—and then the turning away.* (308)

Throughout his time at the front, Serenus remains haunted by this parting.

Dr. Zeitblom's service is in Western Europe, where five German armies are advancing into France, with overcoming French and British resistance and capturing Paris as the ultimate goal. Once the capital is taken, the enemy will be forced to sue for peace and the fighting will cease. Notwithstanding the example of Napoleon in 1812 waiting outside Moscow's gates for a peace delegation that never appeared, the Germans expect victory and capitulation before the leaves turn. There is reason for such optimism as the invading armies make steady progress and achieve objectives laid out according to timetable. Zeitblom is not given to flights of fantasy, but even he describes these days almost rapturously: "We advanced as though on wings. It was just as we had dreamed: by the favour of the god of war, at destiny's nod, we were borne as on pinions" (310). But this forward momentum, apparently irresistible, comes to a screeching halt when, as autumn approaches, French and British counterattacks throw the Germans off course in certain key sectors. The ripple effect shakes the High Command's confidence; their "order to retreat" (310) strikes Zeitblom and most of his comrades, who know only the local successes they have been enjoying, as incredible. The "chance of a lightning triumph" (311) has vanished, never again to be offered. The "rotting, decaying, misery-creating war" (311) that rages on will become impossible for either side to win decisively, because the defensive positions of the combatants are too strong and too deep to be overpowered, no matter the numbers or resources of their attackers. Zeitblom is spared the full four years of pain and suffering that follow. He is "mustered out" (311) after contracting an infection that forces him to leave the filthy trenches, where his condition could rapidly deteriorate. The gentle scholar considers his military duty "fulfilled" (312) and welcomes the opportunity to "serve . . . the cause of education" (312) instead.

He and Adrian are reunited soon enough. Their relationship, however, is still strained, and Zeitblom admits his inability to connect with Adrian, whose "painful lack of response" (312) and "increasingly productive isolation" (312) form the background that will color the two friends' interactions from this point on. Adrian is aloof and distant with others as well. Two female friends, whom Zeitblom refers to as "the Nackedey" and "the Rosenstiel" (313), as if they are pets of different breeds, are devoted to Adrian. They are drawn by a quasi-maternal need to address "his aloneness, the nonconformity of his life" (313), so different from normal living. Though these women are skillful and resourceful, making every effort to keep Adrian "taken care of so far as the essentials were concerned" (314), their selfless service evokes no more emotional reaction than Serenus's care and concern. The composer "simply accepted the tributes and devotion of these followers of his with the utter heedlessness of his nature" (314).

With regard to his work, however, Adrian is focused and moving steadily forward to achieve a creative breakthrough, "a dizzying upward surge" (315) that will yield his powerful *Apocalypsis cum Figuris* (315) a few years later. Now he is working on "brilliant marionette fantasies" (315) based on the *Gesta Romanorum*, "the old book that passes for the source of most of the romantic myths of the Middle Ages" (315). One of these tales involves an Oedipal union of a mother and her son, a future pope, who later absolves her from her sins and frees her from the devil's grasp. In a style reminiscent of Orff's *Carmina Burana*, the composer lets marionettes make "the bizarre, and particularly the farcically erotic" ((319) overcome "the moralizing and priestly" (319) seriousness of medieval lore. Just as in his previous works, Adrian strives to have "all the arts of counterpoint and instrumentation . . . disappear and melt together . . . [in] an intellectually winged simplicity" (321). He works toward "a break-through from intellectual coldness into a touch-and-go world of new feeling" (321) that will allow music "to find her way to the folk" (322) and thus be revitalized. Not surprisingly, Zeitblom is uneasy about this aspiration, since he has little trust in "the folk" that Breisacher and Institoris exalt in such reckless ways. He fears that if the new music's duty is to address "the needs of the crowd, of the little man, of small minds" (322), the revived art Adrian envisions will lead to "the murder of mind and spirit" (322). Serenus tries to take some comfort in what he feels is Adrian's insincerity, not believing that this aloof artist could ever want to appeal to the masses. Even so, with or without the composer's contribution, the same devil that has taken over Adrian's soul will in time seduce the German people, scores of whom will sing patriotic songs, march in lockstep, and repeat Nazi propaganda slogans with mindless ease.

If Adrian Leverkuhn is giving himself to Satan in order to gain the energy, strength, and support that will make an artistic breakthrough possible, and if other Germans are flirting with evil to restore a mythical past where Aryan might ruled and moral restraint was unknown, Inez Rodde, now by marriage Inez Institoris, so apparently proper and correct, is surrendering to sexual needs of almost Proustian depth and urgency. As

Zeitblom observed earlier, Inez has married Dr. Institoris, "that rather limited teacher of aesthetics, wrapped in his dreams of beauty and brutality" (327), for reasons other than love. She has made what her mother considers "a good bourgeois settlement" (324) that will provide comfort, security, and the right environment for child-rearing. This reasoning is not in itself a result of daemonic influence; we have already mentioned the decidedly practical considerations that led Martin Luther to propose to a former nun, and even Serenus Zeitblom, the moral conscience of the novel, speaks about his marriage in businesslike terms. As noted in the introductory section, sexual longing plays far less of a role in German culture than, by comparison, in Italian or French literature, art, and music. Faust's pursuit of Gretchen, for instance, is more creepy than romantic, and its tragic outcome leads to shame and repentance. Manon Lescaut, by contrast, never lets conscience upset her as she leaves De Grieux, who desires her passionately, in misery. What Inez Institoris does is subvert the bourgeois German ideal of conjugal contentment built on household harmony, joint prayer, well-brought-up children, and constant attention to duty and detail in favor of a Latin emphasis on sex, usually outside of marriage, as the most necessary and vitalizing experience known to man or woman, a fount of inexhaustible pleasure, as well as mind-numbing misery if one party fails or ceases to respond to the other's entreaties. This immersion in passion will bring for Inez, as for Julien Sorel and Emma Bovary, both ecstasy and sorrow beyond limit.

With typical German intellectual acuity, Zeitblom realizes early on in Inez's marriage "that despite her nostalgia for it, the bourgeois life had no real viability for her" (327). The "immaculate eight-roomed apartment" (328) Inez shares with her husband is picture perfect, "a pattern establishment of German bourgeois culture " (328), with the right books, the right artwork, the right furniture, the right carpeting, and so forth on display. There is, however, no individuality, no personality, no original touch in any of these rooms. When children arrive, the "light, bright room" (329) is likewise furnished and decorated in the same conventional style, becoming "the very pattern of a children's paradise, correct in every detail" (329). This Potemkin-like home is nothing but a backdrop, a stage setting that is well-cared for but lacking in warmth or any hint of being lived in and enjoyed.

Serenus believes Inez Institoris began her love affair with Rudi Schwerdtfeger "not long after her marriage" (331) and "as disillusioned wife she fell in love with him, in full consciousness and with utter abandonment to feeling and desire" (330). Over time, her effort to conceal the affair and to maintain the fiction of a happy bourgeois union has strained Inez to such a degree that it "deepened the two furrows between her blond brows until she looked almost maniacal" (331). But Inez cannot help herself, determined as she is "to possess the elusive, and, at last, at last, not only once but for confirmation and reassurance never enough, to see it in the state that suits its worth, the state of devotion, of deep suspiring passion!" (333). Her hopelessness in controlling such emotion is like an addict's compulsion, or like the archetypal woman of medieval superstition, whom the teachers in Adrian's theology classes highlighted as the devil's favorite instrument, the one being who could lead a man to endless sin. Inez also embraces the Latin conviction "that inward worthiness could only fulfill itself, realize itself in fleshly desire . . . that it was at once the highest and the most indispensable happiness to keep them together" (333).

Such intensity of feeling, however, cannot be summoned up again and again without slowly becoming diminished. Exhaustion and repetition lead to something like "burnout," a condition that cannot easily be cured. Inez confides in Zeitblom, "the intimate friend, the good man" (332), one night while her husband is away from the house. She ends her lengthy confession of repeated adultery, given in words "soaked in a sensual bliss" (333), with a chilling prediction. She is sure Rudi will break off the affair eventually: "But then woe to him! And woe to me!" (335). The passion that draws Inez irresistibly to her lover now, will, when Rudi leaves her, cause the same irresistible need to become twisted and transformed into incurable and fatal malice.

This painful but pivotal conversation, and the aftermath that Zeitblom will have to record later, makes the author pause in his narrative, if only to change the subject. He does so by leaving Munich, circa 1917, and returning to Germany in the summer of 1944, just after the Allied invasion of Normandy, to assess how his country, guided collectively by the same dark forces that have taken control of lives dear to Serenus, is faring in its epic struggle against overwhelming military odds. The disintegration Inez and Adrian will endure over a span of years is, in Germany's case, accelerating daily. Zeitblom senses that "a judgment . . . such as once fell on Sodom and Gomorrah" (336) is threatening national annihilation. From his solitary Bavarian retreat, so reminiscent of Adrian's at Pfeiffering and in an entirely different universe than the battle zones, the humanist scholar can only speculate on the terrible pressures German troops are under on three separate fronts. The British and Americans are advancing in northwestern France and Belgium having established a secure supply station in Cherbourg; other British, American, and Allied armies are moving up the Italian peninsula; and the Russians are nearing Minsk, whose fall is imminent. The gentle man of peace, Dr. Serenus Zeitblom, cannot bear the thought that if "the dam should break . . . and there were no more hold against the boundless hatred that we have fanned to flame among the peoples round us" (337), Germany will be laid waste, and the "dictatorship of the proletariat" (339) will ensue. But, waxing indignant over the misery brought by Nazism, the scholar avers he would rather be ruled by the proletariat than by "the scum of the earth" (340), who have for so long been "destroying the things of the spirit" (340) and leading Serenus's people to perdition "according to their beastly will" (340).

Zeitblom resumes the narrative he had broken off in 1917, as an earlier world conflict is nearing its end. He remembers his friend Adrian around this time falling seriously ill, almost in concert with "the national misfortune" (342) even though the composer's "remoteness from outward things" (342) makes a linkage like this hard to support. Stomach cramps, headaches, nausea, and other afflictions combine to keep the composer immobilized. He cannot bear the light, so he stays "entire half-days in a densely dark room" (343). Adrian's pain and suffering make the touchy artist more bitter and scornful than usual. He ridicules the concept of "an immortal soul" (344), for instance, as "a perfectly absurd wish" (344), since "it is much more soothing to know that after death one will be the foam on the sea, as Nature wills" (344). He also will not agree with his doctor's recommendation that he arrange "for a consultation with a higher medical authority" (345), regarding this as useless because, true to form, Adrian is sure "that he, more or less alone, out of his own nature and powers, would have to get rid of the evil" (345). Meanwhile, Frau Schweigestill provides "humanly wise and motherly care" (345) to keep her difficult tenant as comfortable as possible.

Violinist Rudolf Schwerdtfeger is also attentive to Adrian, whose "favour and good will" (347) he treasures. He even considers concern for his friend's "more or less helpless state" (347) as a pretext to "conquer a coolness, dryness, and ironic withdrawal" (347) in Adrian that had always bothered Rudi. At this juncture, the two are moving in opposite directions, Adrian in a downward spiral and Rudolf, the lover of Inez and the newly appointed "leader in the Zapfenstosser orchestra" (348), flying high, at least to all appearances. Regarding Inez, Rudi admits the affair but insists Inez provoked it, attaching herself to him "like a drowning person" (349) and demanding his love. He has obliged by "doing his knightly duty" (349), in other words, his obligation rather than his pleasure. He needs to escape through music the entrapment he suffers with Inez. Adrian can help him undergo a "purification" (350) by composing a violin concerto "for him, if possible, with all rights of performance reserved." (350). Rudi outlines the structure of the proposed piece generally, stressing that the final form and order of themes and movements can be as Adrian wishes so long as the concerto "will make people cry" (350) and compel Rudi to "brood over it and love every note like a mother" (350), as if the work were a child born of the two artists' "platonic" (350) union. In "the defencelessness of solitude" (351), Adrian cannot resist such an ardent appeal and will indeed present his friend with the desired composition. Unlike most of Adrian's mature works, the concerto will be melodic, virtuosic, and popular.

Rudi, however, will have to be patient. In the spring of 1919, Adrian suddenly recovers when "the illness lifted like a miracle from off him" (352), leading to "an unintermitted flow of almost breathless productivity" (352). Zeitblom links the two phases of the composer's experience as necessary elements in the creative process. The suffering brought by illness has led Adrian to plumb the depths of the human condition, reaching nearly to hellish despair. This grueling period is succeeded by "a healthy and creative epoch" (352) that is "by no means a time of enjoyment, but rather in its own way one of affliction, of painful urgency, and compulsion" (352). What Adrian will attempt now is worlds removed from the romantic violin concerto Rudi Schwerdtfeger has requested. Adrian is, instead, taking on a project that has grown out of the morbid visions and agonies brought on by mental affliction. He will try to sum up in music the apocalyptic tradition of prophecy and eschatology extending from the Old Testament's *Book of Ezekiel* through the New Testament's *Book of Revelation* and including various medieval contributions, most notably Dante's *Divine Comedy*. The work will be an oratorio tying these components together, with special reference to the conceptions realized in "Durer's series of woodcuts of the Apocalypse." (354). The work will be entitled *Apocalypsis cum Figuris* and will be, in effect, an apotheosis "of the whole literature" (357).

Zeitblom is awed by the sheer scope of this ambitious undertaking. He is at the same time undergoing a personal crisis of confidence that makes him receptive to an artistic portrayal of cataclysmic upheaval. The end of World War I has confirmed for this sensitive observer a shattering realization: the world he regards as his "extended spiritual home" (352) is ending. He sees too many signs that "the epoch of bourgeois humanism" (352) will soon be no more and "the world would enter into a new, still nameless constellation" (352), the germ of which he had felt as "an awful sense of destiny" (353) as early as the beginning of the war. The Nazi movement is in fact beginning to spread its propagandistic simplifications about Aryan superiority, national self-assertion, and liberation from ancient bonds, all to be brought together in the *Ubermensch*, who lives and acts in an amoral void. What Adrian has "robbed from the depths" (355) to give his composition necessary weight, Serenus has intuited in his interactions with those caught up in the new world order taking shape all around him.

Adrian labors over his monumental work with a creative energy stimulated by daemonic infusion. He devotes sometimes ten hours a day to composition, as the "haunting and hunting inspirations" (359) proliferate and take musical form. In just "four and a half months" (359), most of the oratorio is complete. But the strain of such difficult and demanding days takes a toll. Adrian suffers a relapse of his illness as he approaches the work's end, "that frightful finis . . . which, so far from being a romantic music of redemption, relentlessly confirms the theologically negative and pitiless character of the whole" (360), which makes Adrian's great achievement an apt, if unwitting, artistic contribution to the advent of a new era.

"Theologically negative and pitiless" describes well the world views espoused by many fellow citizens who have had little knowledge of or contact with Adrian Leverkuhn. Zeitblom has already introduced us to scholars, philosophers, writers, and ordinary men and women who have largely rejected the moral values and teachings that have guided the course of German history and thought since the Reformation, preferring, on the contrary, to embrace instinctual drives of primitive times that leave no regard for considerations like charity or sympathy in the pursuit of power or pleasure. As a participant in discussion groups meeting in the home of Sixtus Kridwiss, a collector and art lecturer, the staunch defender of bourgeois decency and restraint meets other "members of the intellectual life of Munich" (362) who are cut from the same cloth as Breisacher and Institoris in loudly rejecting all the principles Zeitblom treasures. He feels an instinctive revulsion as he listens, for instance, to Daniel Zur Hohe, a precursor of Heinrich Himmler, who leads paramilitary "troops prepared to die for the subjection of the globe" (364) through "riotous terrorism" (364). There is also Professor Georg Vogler, a literary historian who evaluates writers "from the point of view of racial origins" (363), as if no one can say or do anything except what "his real, concrete, specific corner of the Reich" (363) dictates. These and fellow "advanced" thinkers share a murderous contempt for individuals too stubborn or too humane to respond to their satanic siren song proclaiming "a general indifference to the sufferings and destruction of human beings" (365) with contrary views.

To Serenus, these "men of education, culture, science" (365) are guilty of a form of treason against "the values of culture, enlightenment, humanity" (365) he and his humanist forbears have always espoused. They are also quick to condemn the postwar Weimar Republic, built upon liberal concepts like tolerance and respect for diversity, viewing it as "a bad joke to be dismissed with a shrug" (365) and expecting its overthrow any day by the thugs their divisive rhetoric has emboldened. These people collectively have surrendered to Satan as fully as Adrian has individually, but they have received nothing for their capitulation comparable to the composer's artistic stimulus. Instead, these *poseurs* are motivated by "fables, insane visions, chimeras" (366) that justify their advocacy of tyranny as fully as their successors in brown shirts will. When Zeitblom in one discussion argues that "a thinking man" should make "truth and not the community his goal," he is met with stony silence since his listeners all think "the far higher court of violence, authority, the dictatorship of belief" (368) should define truth. They would allow Zeitblom's "thinking man" to search for truth zealously only so long as at the end of the quest, he validates what "the authority of the community" (369) has already prescribed. The gentlemen speak approvingly of a "deliberate rebarbarization" (370) they see as inevitable and purgative. The coming "renunciation of all the humane softness of the bourgeois epoch" (370) will lead to "the purification of society and the race" (370) say these cultists, a cleansing that will leave Aryans masters of the world once again.

Zeitblom is convinced that even though the Kridwiss attendees are "talking nonsense," they have "laid their fingers on the pulse of the time" (371) and are in accord with the arc of history. They will be "on the crest of the moment" (371) the *Zeitgeist* appears, a moment the decent humanist dreads and fears. Serenus admits to a degree of complicity in the injuries to the spirit his visits to the Kridwiss colloquies are causing. But while he goes deliberately and faithfully to these sessions, he does not do so primarily to hear foolish and menacing pseudo-intellectuals pontificate. Zeitblom attends because what this group's members keep preaching serves as "a cold-blooded intellectual commentary upon a fervid experience of art and friendship" (371)—that is, Adrian's *Apocalypse*. Zeitblom realizes this powerful work reflects the tenor of the times and "in spirit" (372) echoes in its subject and structure the same conclusions the speakers highlight in their analyses. Underlying both are the devil's urgings.

Zeitblom cites numerous examples to illustrate the parallels between the composer's musical style and structure and the themes stressed in the Kridwiss home. The post-bourgeois aesthetic preferences among the scholars and teachers, for instance, are much the same as Adrian's. Serenus recalls how many in the Kridwiss circle hailed "the passing of the dramatic form into the epic, the music drama . . . changing to oratorio, the operatic drama to operatic cantata" (372). These advocates of the primitive and the instinctual welcome new musical forms that actually are ancient but can be revived to resonate with the new age's emphasis on "the absolute, the binding and compulsory," (372). Such a revival will lay upon the composer and the listener "the pious fetters of pre-classically strict form" (372) which "Bach's and Handel's harmonic art" (372) later outgrew. Zeitblom worries about Adrian's absorption in this aesthetic and "his claim in time to the sphere into which he had plunged" (373), the netherworld he is destined for in eternity. The humanist scholar says simply: "The revival of ritual music from a profane epoch has its dangers" (373). It does not mean a revival of faith but rather a reversion to "a stage of civilization not only priestly but primitive" (373), exactly the "pre-cultural" (373) jungle world of the Aryans.

Adrian's eerie conception evokes this same world in end times of sound and fury. The composer employs "the gliding voice, the glissando" (374), which Serenus describes as "a barbaric rudiment from pre-musical days" (374), to create the effects of "howling" (374) in instrumentation and "shrieking" (374) in some vocal passages. The tenor who narrates in music the "horrid happenings" (377) of each section is actually a counter-tenor with "an almost castrato-like high register whose chilly crow, objective, reporter-like, stands in terrifying contrast to the content of the catastrophic announcements" (377). Leverkuhn also employs parody, as when music with "inaccessibly unearthly and alien beauty of sound, filling the heart with longing without hope" (378), is sung by a children's chorus welcoming souls to hell. These "tones of spheres and angels" (379) become transformed into "hellish laughter" (379). For Zeitblom, the effects of individual passages like these, combine to make the *Apocalypse* as a whole "oppressive, dangerous, and malignant" (375), an artistic structure filled with brilliant, moving, and highly original components but ultimately terrifying because all these devices are in the service of fiendish ends.

What is playing out in German higher thought and in Adrian Leverkuhn's compositions is corrupting citizens of modest attainment as well. Members of the Rodde family, as we have seen, have conflicting attitudes toward and understanding of the classic bourgeois values upheld in the late Senator's household. The Frau Senator has embraced in her Munich apartments a quasi-Bohemian lifestyle, giving precedence to eccentricity and the avant-garde. As we have noted, her two daughters largely disdain this approach, with Clarissa staying aloof and looking down on her mother's predilections and Inez remaining firmly bourgeois, at least outwardly. Clarissa is pursuing a career in the theater, but because "her natural talent was not equal to her ambition" (380), she has made little progress, with "the larger theaters of the Reich" (380) ignoring her completely. As the months pass with only minor parts in out-of-the way venues providing her with minimal sustenance, Clarissa finds it difficult to resist "the demands of her own femininity" (381). She fends off some advances, earning the scorn of rejected suitors. Eventually, "a little the worse for wine" (381), she succumbs to the advances of "a pseudo-Mephistopheles, a . . . back-stage hanger-on . . . by profession a criminal lawyer" (381). Pseudo or not, this devilishly inspired person will manage to have an impact on Clarissa quite as enormous and quite as tragic as Esmeralda's on Adrian.

Despite the "scathing self-contempt" (381) her affair generates, Clarissa tries to move on. She continues to appear in small roles in Pforzheim, just over the border from Alsace, now a province of France as a result of the Treaty of Versailles. One evening she meets "a young Alsatian business man" (382) named Henri, who has seen and admired her in performance. Clarissa and he fall in love immediately and are soon planning an engagement and wedding. This gentleman is "the light of his family's eyes" (382), whose members express concern about a hasty decision that will bring "an itinerant actress and a *boche*" (382) at that, into their midst. Clarissa pays little heed, feeling "confident of success" (382) in calming Henri's family's anxieties. She begins looking forward to "a bourgeois happiness" (383) like her sister's, secure and proper within "a new frame into which she would be transplanted" (383). In a few short years, she expects her children to be "prattling in French" (383).

Like Inez, Clarissa is defining "bourgeois" by possessions, comforts, satisfactions, and advantages. This is a corruption of genuine bourgeois values and ways of living. The emphasis in German tradition since the Reformation has always been on the practice of moral virtue to exhibit faith in action. Piety, charity, order, respect, fidelity, and modesty are the outward signs of an inner acceptance of and confidence in the grace that opens up the soul to a faith-filled life. Clarissa is not manifesting anything like such an understanding. She is focused only on rewards and benefits per se, skipping the hard work and day-to-day commitment to virtuous living required in German burgher culture. Serenus Zeitblom, friend of the Rodde family and exemplar of middle-class moderation and restraint, shows in his steadfast regard for and loyalty to Adrian, a far more difficult and demanding artist than Clarissa, how necessary selflessness is in keeping important relationships happy and healthy. For Clarissa, as well as her mother and her sister, the soul of bourgeois living has been tarnished by absorption in what pleases oneself rather than in what improves oneself and helps others.

The high hopes and expectations Clarissa has entertained from the start of her relationship with Henri will not be borne out by events. The aptly characterized "pseudo-Mephistopheles" who has stolen her virginity learns of Clarissa's engagement. He promptly blackmails her in true stage villain fashion. In return for his keeping silent about her past, Clarissa must yield to "his will" (383) wherever and whenever he wishes. Clarissa feels she has no choice except to do as ordered and become a sex slave to gain "a present peace" (383). But no peace is gained. Clarissa's putative fiancé soon receives an anonymous letter explaining all that has occurred between her blackmailer and Clarissa. It has the desired effect. Henri's registered letter response contains no suggestion of "unshakeable faith and love" (384). Clarissa is with her mother in Pfeiffering when the lethal missile arrives. Upon reading the letter, she says nothing but "with a blank, dazed look and fugitive smile" (384), she runs quickly to her room. There, Clarissa swallows "a dose of cyanide large enough to kill a regiment and dies instantly" (384). She had carried this poison with her wherever she stayed, indicating that depression leading to despair could afflict her at any time. The cyanide was kept in a "book with the death's head on the lid" (383), another satanic touch.

At her sister's funeral, Inez Institoris, now no longer the lover of Rudi Schwertdtfeger, is comforted by a number of women who have befriended her in recent times. These are a varied group of mostly unattached writers and performers, who resemble Clarissa and who rely on morphine to get them through hard times. Inez believes "that pain is an indignity, that it is shameful to suffer" (386), more evidence that carrying one's cross and trusting in the Lord no longer guides the thinking of worldly citizens. Notwithstanding his long acquaintance with and affection for Inez Institoris, Serenus finds her "deeply offensive" (387) when he realizes what she and the other women are resorting to more or less regularly. The withering away of sturdy German virtue and will and their replacement by lethal or addictive drugs is another indication of how successfully Satan's destructive inroads into the moral lives of ordinary Germans have borne forbidden fruit.

On the wider stage, something similar is occurring. The Imperial Germany that entered the First World War has ceased to exist at its conclusion, having been replaced by the German Republic, which conducts its business in the city of Weimar, well-known for its association with Goethe. This new political arrangement, dismissed with contempt by the atavistic intellectuals of the Kridwiss Circle, Serenus considers "an attempt, a not utterly and entirely hopeless attempt . . . to normalize Germany in the sense of Europeanizing or 'democratizing' it, of making it part of the social life of peoples" (388). The Weimar Republic may be the embodiment of bourgeois values such as popular sovereignty, respect for minorities, and equality before the law, but even so, many Germans, still attached to authoritarian political and social structures and practices, see the Weimar government as a protective shield for revolutionary elements manipulating levers of power behind the scenes. In the arts, too, unconventional styles and innovative theory are gaining traction but little popular support. Leverkuhn's *Apocalypse*, for instance, is "denounced as a specimen of cultural Bolshevism" (389) by conservative critics when it receives its first complete performance in Frankfurt in 1927. In places like Munich, where the Nazi movement is starting to coalesce, "the nationalistic-Wagnerian-romantic forces of reaction" (389) set themselves against artistic developments they see as foreign-inspired and corrosive. The same transvaluation of values affecting the personal lives of families like the Roddes, is being introduced into the cultural life of the nation.

Nevertheless, at least on the surface, the political and artistic advances of the post-war years make the decade of the 1920s an ideal time for Adrian Leverkuhn to come out of the shadows. Zeitblom records numerous achievements and advances during this period. A prominent music publisher, Edelman, for instance, seeks out Adrian in Pfeiffering to secure rights to the still unfinished *Apocalypsis cum Figuris* for the publisher's house in Vienna. Dr. Edelman also brings Adrian into contact with Frau von Tolna, a wealthy Hungarian noblewoman who admires Adrian's work. She takes charge of efforts to make "the hermit of Pfeiffering" (391) better known within the larger artistic and social worlds, particularly those inhabited by patrons able to commission works and finance productions. Though Mme. de Tolna is present at many performances of Adrian's works, and though she is seen in Kaisersaschern, Oberweiler, and Pfeiffering, the two never meet. They correspond, however, and Frau Von Tolna takes on the role of "protecting deity, an Egeria, a soul-mate" (392) for the lonely and needy artist. Early on, she sends him a ring, "a jewel of great beauty and . . . incalculable value" (393), dating from the Renaissance. It contains "in the tiniest Greek characters" (393) lines of poetry describing "with unearthly terror the sign of an epiphany of the god [Apollo] at his shrine" (393). A figure of "a winged snake-like monster whose tongue was clearly arrow-shaped" (393) lies beneath. Adrian is so taken by this ring he always wears it while working. In fact, "during the writing of the whole of the *Apocalypse* he wore the jewel on his left hand" (393).

Zeitblom wonders if this ring could be "the symbol of a bond, a fetter, yes, of possession" (393), but to Adrian, the jewel is "a merely cloudy symbol of a personality, about whose features or individual traits" (393) the composer cares not to know since the two do not meet. His patroness, however, in her own way, does communicate interesting items, references, suggestions, and the like to Adrian throughout their acquaintance and offers her rooms in Vienna for his personal use whenever she is absent. Although Zeitblom does not explore this relationship any further, it can be hypothesized that the ring with the snake-like monster allows its wearer to access the underworld, as Adrian does for his *Apocalypse,* and that the woman who almost haunts Adrian in these days is a representative of those dark realms sent to watch and keep "on task" this devil's servant.

An altogether different personality is Herr Saul Fitelberg, an "international business man and concert agent" (397) who shows up at the composer's door in Pfeiffering "one lovely day in late summer" (397) in 1923. Serenus happens to be there as well and records the long monologue Herr Fitelberg, "naively persistent, profuse of promises, rebuffed by no reserve, certainly superficial" (397), forces his two listeners to endure. "Endure" may not be quite the right verb, since Serenus at least finds their visitor "an engaging type" (397), but certainly the American-style salesmanship this cosmopolitan talent scout subjects Adrian to is intense and high-pressured. Though Adrian's works have not yet been performed often or widely, Fitelberg has heard or heard of them and been impressed. He is enthralled by the possibility that "Monsieur Saul" could "discover a genius and as his manager introduce him to a social world always and above all avid for new things" (397). In the impresario's mind, lifting Adrian out of "the retreat where genius created and suffered" (397) will be good for both parties.

Herr Fitelberg thereupon pulls out all the stops to achieve such an outcome. Although Serenus is present throughout the "sales pitch," Fitelberg pays little attention to him, focusing exclusively on "his proper prey" (398) right from the start. Dressed "in elegant summer clothes" (399) and speaking and gesturing with an "easy manner and lightness of touch" (399), this maestro of contracts and commerce is irrepressibly charming, fluent in several languages, sophisticated, and insightful. Zeitblom remembers that "whatever Adrian or I interpolated or replied played scarcely any role" (399) in the meeting, so his hosts leave the stage entirely to their guest. Fitelberg begins by flattering Adrian and appealing to whatever hidden ambition the artist may be harboring, i.e., to leave his comfortable little Pfeiffering nest and see the great world he knows of only through Mme. De Tolna's notes and ministrations. Herr Fitelberg promises to do

Since none of these consequences can be realized, the original pact's terms remain in effect. Fitelberg's failure resembles Mme. De Tolna's decision not to grow close to the composer, both characters' interactions confirming that Adrian is still subject to the devil alone. Nevertheless, dynamics like these will come into play again in different forms and with different actors in the years ahead. As we will see, the results will not always be in accord with Adrian's infernal "baptismal promises."

PART FIVE

A different promise is fulfilled shortly after Adrian's eventful meeting with the agent.

Adrian completes the *Violin Concerto* Rudi Schwerdtfeger had asked him to compose exclusively for the violinist's use. To Zeitblom's surprise, the composer of so much "ruthlessly radical and uncompromising work as a whole" (409) provides his friend with a richly melodic showpiece in the romantic tradition Adrian has always regarded as outdated. The concerto is "dedicated to Rudi personally" (409), and Adrian actually appears in person at the work's premier in Vienna. Although the concerto is unusual in having "three *tonalities* built into it" (409) with "no key signature" (409), its "heavenly" (410) passages make the arrangement appealing to audiences. Zeitblom is not quite sure what to conclude about this composition's immediate acceptance; he finds it "half-respectful, half-caricature" (410) since some of its lyricism comes close to "mockery" (409). It is also, like Adrian's choral parts in *Apocalypse*, extremely demanding technically. "Beads of sweat" (410) form when Rudi has to work his way through certain sections of the concerto.

Zeitblom knows that this uncharacteristic virtuoso piece has taken its unique form only because of Rudi's "tireless, self-confident perseverance, put off by nothing" (415), a success Serenus describes as "a conquest" (415). Since "the polarity of the partners, the intellectual antithesis between them" (415), makes their cooperation in such a joint project hard to understand, Zeitblom looks for a deeper explanation. He speculates that Rudi's "wooing of Adrian" (415) must be based on the violinist's need for Adrian's friendship, a gift that could and should "develop, elevate, improve" (415) the younger artist's life and character. Zeitblom even goes so far as to suggest that Rudi's "native gift of coquetry" (415) may have produced in Adrian "signs of ironic eroticism" (415) that neither man could acknowledge. Whatever the case may be, what Zeitblom calls "the apotheosis of salon music" (410) Adrian creates for Rudi marks a personal and artistic turning point for the composer. In a conversation with friends later, Adrian speaks up for emotional reactions he has hardly ever praised: "Idealism leaves out of count that the mind and spirit are by no means addressed by the spiritual alone; they can be most deeply moved by the animal sadness of sensual beauty" (414).

Adrian Leverkuhn has been, as Zeitblom reiterates, "bewitched" (416) by Rudi's persistent and reckless advances. The aloof composer is unable fully to grasp what has happened but much against his will and his compact with Satan, he has allowed love for someone, no matter its nature, to enter his life finally. The highly accessible *Violin Concerto* is a catalyst for Adrian's entrance into the "world" and its many dimensions he had previously walled himself away from to concentrate only on crafting decidedly unworldly compositions. He leaves his monastic-like quarters in Pfeiffering, for instance, to accompany Rudi to two concerts in Switzerland featuring the concerto. Both performances are well-received, with the audiences insisting "on the appearance of the composer, who gratified his interpreter by appearing repeatedly hand in hand with him to acknowledge the applause" (417). Zeitblom is not present on either of these occasions and can only record with astonishment "this twice repeated unique event, the exposure of the recluse in person to the gaze of the crowd" (417).

The recluse does more than wave to theater audiences. In their post-performance euphoria, Adrian and Rudi attend a party hosted by "Herr and Frau Reiff, an elderly, wealthy, childless pair" (418), known for their interest in and support of "coming musical events" (418) and the artists involved in their production. The composer and the soloist are placed at table next to a woman neither knows. She is "a young, or still young professional woman, Mlle. Godeau, a French Swiss" (418) "designer . . . who sketched and worked out for the smaller Paris opera and vaudeville stages . . . the figurines, costumes, and settings which then served as models for costumiers and decorators" (419–20). Though Zeitblom does not observe this first encounter between Adrian and Marie Godeau, his "eyes dwelt long upon her in anxious scrutiny" (419) later on, so he can "summon up in painstaking love the figure of this woman" (419) who will play such an important role in Adrian's life going forward. Marie is, in a word, an incarnation of innocence comparable to Goethe's Gretchen but without her peasant constrictions. Serenus cannot say enough about Marie's features, dwelling on "the loveliest black eyes in the world . . . black as jet they were, not large, indeed, but with a clear and open shine from their dark depths" (419). He remembers "nothing artificial, no make-up about her, no accentuation by borrowed colour" (419). She has a "native genuine sweetness" (419) and a "not precisely frequent smile [and] still less frequent laugh" (419) that confirm her feminine maturity. Serenus uses the word "sympathetic" (419) as an all-encompassing adjective: "from head to foot, in every feature, with every word, every smile, every expression of her being, she corresponded to the tranquil, temperate, aesthetic, and moral climate purveyed by this word" (419).

Adrian is clearly smitten with Marie, whom he engages at the Reiffs in conversation about composers and productions she is familiar with through her work and that Adrian knows only through scores and recordings. He approaches their relationship almost theoretically at first, telling Zeitblom he is nearly forty years of age, "warning enough not to put off" (422) marriage for very long and not to expect a woman like Marie to come into his orbit again. Serenus is thrilled to imagine Marie "as Adrian Leverkuhn's life partner" (423), not least because her presence will quickly edge Rudi out of the composer's everyday life. Marie will also allow "the world" (423) to "come near to him in her, the world from which he shrank" (423) until lately. This world can arrive "in the most serious, friendly guise, awakening confidence, promising fulfillment, encouraging him to abandon his recluse state" (423).

But romantic excitement of this sort and the fantasies it stimulates must engage the world as it is and people as they are.

Adrian's detachment from life's rough and tumble affects his judgments. Zeitblom is surprised, for example, by his friend's insouciance. Adrian seems to think Marie will accept a proposal from him, whom she has just met, without question or delay. Adrian also takes little note of the fact that at the Reiff dinner, Rudi spoke often with Marie and her aunt and that both women found him charming. Adrian's lifestyle does not make room for decoration, remodeling, convenience, comfort, and so on, all aspects of normal middle class living. There is, too, no mention of money, upon which any serious life choices must depend.

Adrian's emotional embrace of the world he has long avoided and a potential spouse who will bring so much good to him from that world causes one supremely important fact to be ignored completely. When Adrian made his arrangement with Satan, he agreed explicitly not "to love." The composer already has come very close to breaking his compact by letting Rudi Schwerdtfeger into a friendship involving personal affection as much as artistic partnership. Now Adrian is going far beyond *sorge* and jumping into the domain of *eros*, whose power he has experienced only once, a long time ago. The stage is being set for one or more catastrophes, such as are inevitable in Greek tragedy.

Like Oedipus, Adrian will act in ways that lead to his own downfall. His natural shyness makes him shrink from direct contact with Marie, so when he wishes to invite Mlle. Godeau and her aunt to join him and a few friends "to do the honors of Munich" (425), Adrian asks Serenus Zeitblom to make the request. He explains that the idea was originally Rudi Schwerdtfeger's, but Adrian wants the ladies to think it really is his, which they will if Serenus, his best and oldest friend, calls on them. Though this explanation is hardly convincing, Zeitblom does as he is asked, and aunt and niece react "with enthusiasm" (426) to the proposal for an excursion. Serenus knows Adrian's shyness is inhibiting, but still he wonders why his friend cannot make an effort to overcome this socially disabling tendency and just "address himself to her [Marie] direct, ring her up, even go to Munich" (426) or the like. He does not realize until later that Adrian follows in courtship "a pattern . . . of sending to the beloved . . . and leaving it to someone else to speak to her" (426). This preference for indirection and the use of others as spokespersons seems for now only an awkward but harmless idiosyncrasy, but as Adrian's relationship with Marie grows more serious, the composer's manipulations will become self-destructive, resulting in multi-dimensional fatality.

All of this, however, will be worked out in the future. The excursion into the Bavarian countryside turns out to be as pleasant as Adrian could have wished. The party enjoy a train ride through the mountains outside Munich, during which Adrian periodically gazes at Marie in admiration and compliments Rudi fulsomely on his performances of the composer's concerto, "calling his playing masterly, consummate, simply incomparable" (428). Adrian's aloofness breaks down throughout the trip as he allows love to evoke the most generous sentiments. Rudi adds to the travelers' joy when, during a stop at an inn, he joins a small group of musicians entertaining the guests, takes the violinist's instrument, and plays "magnificently" (429), even including "some snatches from the cadenza of 'his' concerto" (429), all this to the "open-mouthed" (429) astonishment of the other players. The day ends with a visit to "Linderhof, the small rococo castle of Ludwig II" (430), the patron of Wagner and the victim of mental illness that left him in his last years under the control of specialists who reduced him to the status of an assisted living patient. Adrian cannot yet make any connection between the "Mad King's" helplessness and the long decline from greatness he will himself endure in the years ahead, but there will be similarities. For now, the excursion comes to a mutually agreeable end, with Adrian summoning up the courage to join "aunt and niece in a taxi to their pension" (433), returning home on "the usual eleven o'clock train" (433) as happy as he ever was or could be.

As Serenus Zeitblom prepares to narrate the story of Adrian's marriage proposal to Mlle. Godeau, he pauses briefly to bring the reader back to the present and to Germany's awful plight. His nation is on the verge of being squeezed to death by powerful armies advancing from east and west. The end is now inevitable, with the battered Wehrmacht able to mount only feeble delaying actions that do little to retard its enemies' two-front advance: "Rats grown fat on corpses house in the rubble of our cities; the thunder of the Russian cannon rolls on toward Berlin; the crossing of the Rhine was child's play to the Anglo-Saxons; our own will seems to have united with the enemy's to make it that" (434). As military defeat looms, Serenus looks back to Adrian Leverkuhn's apparently happy situation "after that so memorable excursion" (434) through the same lens he has been watching Germany collapse. Though he was not at Adrian's side during those days, he insists that "the frightful intimacy" (434) he and Adrian shared over a lifetime enables him to act as "an eye-and ear-witness" (434) to what actually occurred then.

Two days after the Bavarian trip, Adrian asks Rudi to visit him "as soon as possible, for the matter was pressing" (434). Though the violinist is scheduled to perform with the Zapfenstosser Orchestra that evening, the "always compliant" (434) Rudi arrives at Pfeiffering at 4:00 p.m. Adrian quickly confesses his strong attraction to Marie Godeau, stressing that he cannot consider their recent time together "as a mere episode" (435); on the contrary, he must be with her and "have her about" (436) all the time. Adrian has, in other words, tasted of the forbidden fruit and fallen in love, in direct opposition to the vow to forswear all love Satan forced him to take years before. Adrian's reasons for violating the promise are altogether normal and understandable. At age forty, he would certainly "like a real home, a companion congenial in the fullest sense of the word; in short, a warmer and more human atmosphere round him" (436). Such a state of affairs will surely bring the composer "good and fine things for his working energy and enthusiasm, for the human content of his future work" (436). In response, Rudi makes a telling point when he reminds his friend that the word "human" is "incredibly unsuitable" (436) for an artist whose music has always "owed its greatness to its inhumanity" (436), a characterization exactly appropriate to its origins in a gift from hell. Adrian now, however, is being powerfully drawn away from such inhuman heights and depths, preferring instead the ambience of the warm, melodic, and "humanly inspired work" (436) Rudi has performed "already three times . . . before the public" (436). A life with Marie Godeau will keep both husband and wife firmly grounded in that same sphere. Adrian thinks Rudi's ardent friendship "released the human" (437) in Adrian for the first time, allowing the lonely hermit to experience the "human warmth" (436) he had so long suppressed.

Rudi understands how Adrian's desire to marry Marie could be a natural development of what his friendship inspired. He is not at all prepared, however, for what Adrian asks next. Admitting that his "awkwardness" (437) in making a face-to-face marriage proposal to Marie and his fear that a letter might seem so inappropriate for such a personal matter it could provoke a negative response that would "hurt" (437) terribly, Adrian asks Rudi for help. If he will act as Adrian's "advocate for happiness" (437) and propose to Marie on the composer's behalf, Adrian is sure the handsome and charming ladies' man can find the right words, make the best case, and persuade Marie to marry Adrian. All this may be true, but Rudi is clearly uncomfortable playing such a role. He suggests Zeitblom instead, but Adrian insists that "such a sober-sides as my Serenus" (438) could not perform such a sensitive task as effectively as Rudi. Only Rudi can speak to "her, gently, appealingly . . . try if she, well, yes, could love" (438) Adrian. The composer shows genuine need and cannot bear a refusal.

Rudi then makes his own confession. He makes Adrian aware that his good friend "is not indifferent to her [Marie] either" (439), proclaiming Marie "the nicest, loveliest feminine creature . . . that has come [his] way" (439). He admits to having had tea with Marie and her aunt prior to the excursion, which, as Adrian knows, Rudi first suggested. Under Adrian's questioning, the man about town avers that he has not "thought of" (439) making a marriage proposal of his own yet nor will he ever "simply seduce her" (439). Such talk would cause a prudent man to think twice about placing all his hopes for conjugal bliss in Rudi's hands, but Adrian is too far down the slippery slope to hesitate. He accepts Rudi's assurances and then reiterates his plea in a more demanding fashion, almost like a senior commander entrusting his adjutant with a mission that might have fatal effects for either man. Adrian bluntly tells his envoy-to-be to "sacrifice" (440) any budding interest in Marie for the sake of their friendship and "as a final contribution to the merit" (440) Rudi has gained by awakening the composer's "humanity" (440). In other words, Rudi's gift has to keep on giving regardless of pain or sorrow. With dutiful obedience to the great artist he respects and admires, Rudi agrees to do as Adrian wishes and offer the service and sacrifice the older man requires. The two then take leave of each other at the train station, never to meet again.

The denouement is, in one sense, predictable. This *opera bouffe* substitution of one for another fails in its purpose as it must, but there is no resolution that will bring joy to all concerned as musical comedy dictates. A letter from Rudi arrives days after the friend whose love and loyalty Adrian does not question has agreed to sacrifice his own interest in Marie to advance the artist's proposal. Its contents are as shattering as the news Clarissa Rodde could not absorb when a similar note was delivered. What actually occurs during Rudi's encounter with Marie, who says what and who replies how, cannot be known for certain; Serenus, however, is sure he can with reasonable accuracy reconstruct the dialogue between Rudi and Marie, just as he has done with the pivotal conversation between Rudi and Adrian.

Rudi's letter reveals that Marie rejected Adrian's proposal outright and accepted his instead. Serenus realizes the great master of composition fumbled this affair badly, losing "friend and beloved at one blow" (441). He also senses that "a reality harsher, colder, crueler" (442) than anything a comic opera creator could devise has been intertwining the fates of Adrian, Rudi, and Marie regarding this proposal gone awry. All three have been or will be "sacrificed" in some way. A fourth participant, Inez Institoris, Rudi's former lover, will make a shocking and deadly intervention right after what would be the violinist's last performance in Munich to bring the tragedy to its awful end. Presiding over and orchestrating the step-by-step destruction of all that Adrian and company had expected is the infernal being who commanded the composer to serve him alone and now is bringing collateral damage to everyone connected to Adrian's betrayal and punishment.

In Zeitblom's version of what transpires between Rudi and Marie, the meeting taking place between the two leads to no definite conclusion. He believes that Marie's aunt greets Rudi first as he arrives at "the little vestibule of the pension" (443) she and her niece occupy. Rudi reveals he is carrying an important message for Marie from "a third party" (443). Zeitblom imagines Tante Isabeau reacting to this information with "a mischievous smile" (443), as if only Rudi himself has something to say to her niece.

Once alone with Marie, according to Serenus, Rudi does as he was directed. He describes Adrian's strong feelings for her, notes the unusual pleasure he took in their experience together during the excursion, and informs Marie that this composer of genius, of whom "the public would only slowly become aware" (443) begs her consent to a marriage that could only bring the best to both.

In Serenus's mind, this wholly unexpected proposal must have disturbed his hostess. She asks if she has heard correctly and when assured she has, the proud and proper Mlle. Godeau offers "a distinctly cool, distinctly mocking comment" (443) to the effect that "it was certainly very kind of him [Rudi]" (443) to share this with her on behalf of "Dr. Leverkuhn" (443) whose "scrupulous delicacy" (443) prevented his doing so himself. Rudi is embarrassed and quickly realizes his message is not being well-received: "Her manner expressed sheer surprise and umbrage—and that both startled and secretly pleased him" (444). Now things move in an opposite direction as Rudi allows his own pent-up emotions to come to the surface. When Marie denies that the "reverence" (444) she feels for Adrian can give rise to "any feelings that could form any basis of a union" (444) in matrimony, Rudi is relieved. He blurts out "Marie" (444) with emotion, indicating "that he was not himself indifferent to her" (444). Marie shows "amazement at his use of her first name" (444), a familiarity he was not entitled to presume and bids Rudi farewell.

Rudi leaves not without hope. He composes a letter to Marie explaining that with Adrian now having "no prospects of success" (445), he, Rudi, can release "the loyally controlled feelings" (445) of deep affection he has for her and declare for himself how much he loves her. Tante Isabeau accepts the letter for Marie, who at first wants to send it back, but then listens as her aunt reads it to her. She does not reply. Days later Rudi visits when Marie is out. He appeals to her aunt, who refers to her niece's "proud nature but full of deep feeling" (445). Tante Isabeau then promises to "spare no pains to represent to her niece the uprightness of his [Rudi's] conduct" (445). Her gentle proddings have an impact. Even though Marie is not in agreement about "the uprightness of his conduct" (445), she is drawn to the challenge of spending a life with such a charismatic and electrifying man. She vows to "love the breaker of hearts …" (445) and "to domesticate the wild-fowl she had caught" (446). In less than twenty-four hours the news travels all through Munich's cultural and social circles that "Konzertmeister Schwerdtfeger and Marie Godeau were an engaged pair" (446). They will marry in Paris, where Rudi henceforth will "devote his services to a new musical group being organized, called the Orchestre Symphonique" (446).

Rudi's "presence at the next concert" (446) of the Zapfenstosser Orchestra takes on the character of a "farewell performance" (446), bringing "all Munich" (446) to the theater. Among the audience are friends of both the violinist and Adrian, including Schildknapp, Jeanette Scheurl, and Dr. Serenus Zeitblom. Inez Institoris is also present, sitting "rather far back, in a frock so simple as to look almost poverty-stricken" (446), incongruous attire for one so sensitive to social protocols. As the concert proceeds, Rudi concentrates on his instrument and the score, avoiding the "many curious eyes" (446) focused on him. Once the last selection, Wagner's *Overture to Die Meistersinger*, concludes, the audience erupts with "crashing applause" (446) that grows louder as the conductor asks "the orchestra to stand up" (446), taking care to "put out his hand gratefully to his Konzertmeister" (446). This gesture and the affirmation of the assembly are undoubtedly the high points of Rudi's tenure as the leader of the Munich ensemble.

This concert will become a "farewell" in more senses than anyone present could ever imagine. After the performance, Serenus walks to the Theresienstrasse "to pick up a tram for Schwabing" (447). As he takes his seat, he notices that none other than the star of the evening's show, Rudi Schwerdtfeger, is sitting nearby, as is Inez Institoris, who is in "the middle of the tram, diagonally opposite" (448) the man with whom she had carried on a passionate love affair for many years. How these three individuals have managed to take the same train back to their homes and have somehow seated themselves so near to each other is hardly a coincidental circumstance. The fiend who has been guiding the earthly life of Adrian Leverkuhn has made this arrangement for his own purposes. The love that Adrian has felt, first for Rudi, who brought amity into the cold household in Pfeiffering, and then for Marie, who promised erotic arousal and conjugal attachment, must be punished. Marie's rejection of Rudi's appeals on Adrian's behalf and her embrace of the violinist in Adrian's stead, have effectively suppressed the composer's tender feelings for her or anyone else. But Satan is not content with inflicting misery on Adrian alone. The accomplice has to pay a terrible price as well. Inez Institoris has been brought to the tram to play the role of "woman scorned." To the horror of all who witness the crime, Inez aims a loaded pistol squarely at her former lover and empties its chambers into her helpless victim. With wounds all over his body, the charmer extraordinaire dies on the way to the hospital, thereby ending any possibility of reconciling with Adrian. The "convulsively sobbing" (450) Inez is apprehended and taken away immediately, an instrument no longer of any use to Satan. What had once seemed like comic opera ends in tragedy, with blood gushing and tears flowing.

As he does when recounting events or experiences in Adrian's life or within his narrow circle that elicit overpowering emotional response, Dr. Serenus Zeitblom once again suspends his narrative for a time to report on what is happening in Germany contemporaneously, if only to catch his breath. In so doing now, though, he gains no relief. Germany in late 1944, like Adrian twenty years before, is part of a "tale . . . hastening to its end" (452). In impotent fury, the humanist professor in his "Freising hermitage" (452) laments all that he and his countrymen and women have had to suffer since the Nazi accession to power so fatally twisted the arc of that proud nation's development:

> *Our "thousand year" history, refuted, reduced ad absurdum, weighed in the balance and found unblest, turns out to be a road leading nowhere, or rather into despair, an unexampled bankruptcy, a descensus Averno lighted by the dance of roaring flames.* (452)

The "dance of roaring flames" consuming the Reich will devour Adrian Leverkuhn as well, as Zeitblom's memoir moves steadily forward. In spite of the revulsion aroused by the "sinful issue" (452) of Germany's "infamy" (452) and by the evil consequences radiating in every direction as a result of Adrian's pact, Serenus will not cease to love his country or his friend. Toward Adrian, especially, "a great German man and artist" (452), Zeitblom reaffirms his "love, full of fear and dread, yet eternally faithful to this German whose inscrutable guiltiness and awful end" (452) prefigure his nation's descent. Both Germany and Adrian require, like Goethe's Faust, a cleansing from "the everlasting mercy" (452), the amplitude of which no mortal can fathom. As we shall see, only Goethe's version of the Faust myth includes such a redemptive outpouring.

Returning to the days following the murder on the tram, Zeitblom recalls Adrian's pained and listless response to all that has been occurring, starting with the shattering letter from Rudi. The composer once again separates himself from the public and, with the exception of Serenus and a few other acquaintances, keeps the world at bay. When his *Apocalypsis cum Figuris* is performed in Frankfurt "about a year after the frightful events" (453) in Munich, Adrian cannot "bring himself to break through his usual retirement" (453) and attend the concert in person. Without Rudi Schwerdtfeger's bracing stimulus, Adrian is becoming a recluse once again. In the case of the *Apocalypsis* performance, his absence will have a lasting impact because Adrian will not enjoy any other opportunity to "hear the work, one of the two chief monuments of his proud and austere life" (453). This life is now turning "idle and void" (454). The composer suffers from "a dearth of ideas" (454) and "a mental stagnation" (454) that will not lift. Adrian describes his current condition as "a dog's life, a *vie végétale*, without past or future, root or fruit, an idyll too idle for words" (454). Physical illness succeeds psychological distress. Adrian is even compelled on doctor's orders to miss his father's funeral.

With the onset of 1927, however, just as after the cataclysm of World War I, Adrian's health suddenly and inexplicably improves. He seems finally "to have overcome the ship-wreck of his life plans" (455) and actually struggles "to keep his poise in the storm of ideas rushing upon him" (455). He composes at first mostly chamber music, all of it characteristically intricate, complex, imaginative, and original. One of these works, a string trio, is "scarcely playable" (457), presenting so many difficulties, it is "mastered technically only by three virtuosos" (457). In the midst of this creative ferment, whose "sufferings" (458) tempt the composer to wish for a return of "the peaceful incapacity of his former state" (458), Adrian begins to sketch out a new oratorio called *The Lamentation of Dr. Faustus*, which will eventually join the *Apocalypsis* as one of the two larger masterpieces of Adrian Leverkuhn's career. There is, however, on the horizon, another "priceless and heart-piercing" (459) experience of love that will arise within Adrian and then be lost, causing sorrow that will make the torments of the creative life he is currently combating almost nothing by comparison.

Adrian's master must reign in the composer's heart just as absolutely as he does in hell's dark depths. So far, Satan's pride of place has been threatened twice, once through Adrian's fondness for Rudi and then through his intense attraction to Marie Godeau. The love shown in friendship and the love aroused by erotic desire have touched Adrian deeply and drawn his attention away from the musical achievements his demonic pact demands he dwell on exclusively in his lifetime. Consequently, these affections have been abruptly and irrecoverably taken from him. Satan has also augmented almost beyond endurance the creative energies released after Adrian's recovery from breakdown to stimulate his productivity. The composer, nevertheless, cannot suppress completely the powerful emotions evoked by love, no matter how distracting and no matter the consequences for himself and others. Thus, when Ursula Schneidewein, Adrian's sister, falls seriously ill in 1928 and asks her brother to care for her youngest child, five-year old Nepomuk, while she undergoes treatment "in a sanitarium in the Harz Mountains" (460), Adrian readily agrees.

Not only Adrian but everyone in Pfeiffering who meets Nepomuk, or "Echo" (461), as the little boy calls himself, finds the child enchanting. Zeitblom pulls out all the stops in his portrait of Nepomuk and his impact on the whole Schweigestill household. Nepo has, he writes in retrospect, the features of "a fairy princeling" (461), and he seems like "a guest from some finer, tinier sphere" (461). Serenus confesses that "after fully seventeen years" (462), he cannot think of his "adorable little subject" (462) without tearing up. The boy is not only charming and polite; he is mature beyond his years, instinctively showing stern discipline when it comes to eating, sleeping, playing, and so on. He lights up the larger community of Pfeiffering as if heaven-sent, radiating "a state of bliss, a constant heart-warming gaiety and tenderness not only to the farm but to the village as well, and even as far as Waldshut" (464). The apothecary, the shoemaker, the clerks in the general store offer Nepo "the same rapturous reception" (465). The pastor presents the child "a colored picture of the Lamb of God" (465) after hearing him pray like an angel, and the schoolmaster feels uplifted "after talking with him" (465). Zeitblom goes from calling Nepo "this little ambassador from childhood and fairyland" (466), to "this pure and precious being" (466) dwelling somehow outside of time, to, finally, "an envoy and message-bearer" (467) from God Himself.

Adrian does not go quite so far in his regard for his nephew. He leaves the "ecstasies to simpler folk" (467), preferring to treat "the little one with a delicacy and warmth, smiling or serious as occasion called it out; without flattery or fawning, even without tenderness" (467). Zeitblom remembers how his friend would not "caress the child, scarcely even smooth his hair" (467). Nevertheless, even though chastened by his previous failures in trying to connect intimately with others, the cool and reserved artist undoubtedly feels paternal love for Nepo, a love less expressive or emotional than his prior affections but grounded in Adrian's need to help guide, form, and lead his charge down paths that will encourage the boy's development in all the right ways. The aloof artist here has to work not with combinations of notes or instruments but with flesh and blood humanity brought into his life fortuitously and presenting him with possibilities of inspiring and nurturing healthy growth.

Adrian senses soon that Echo has limitless potential that his uncle can try to actualize. His nephew is a prodigy, a young boy who can think, feel, and speak like a young man, a child, in other words, who resembles Adrian himself as a child. This is confirmed when Adrian allows Echo to scan "the drafts of the scores of Ariel's songs" (470) from Shakespeare's *The Tempest*, his latest project. Uncle Adrian patiently explains the myths and legends of the spirit-world that underlie these songs. Echo recognizes and likes especially "the place in the notes where the dog says 'bow-wow' and Chanticleer cries 'cock-a-diddle dow'" (470). Nepo also wonders about the slave imprisoned for twelve years by "the wicked witch Sycorax" (470). The ageless one wants to know how old the little spirit will be when he is freed. Adrian assures Echo that spirits do not age; this one is "the same child of air" (470) as before. This reassures Echo, who will too remain innocence incarnate during his entire stay with Adrian.

Adrian likes to observe Echo in the evening as he lies in bed saying his prayers. These prayers are not the standard texts children memorize and recite by rote each day. Their origin is a source of mystery to everyone in the household. That they are another indication of precocity, perhaps divinely directed, is clear, however, because their content encapsulates Christian charity so consistently and concisely, as in this example:

Mark, whoso for other pray
Himself he saves that waye.
Echo prayes for all gainst harms
May God hold him too in His armes.
Amen (472)

The style is reminiscent of the ancient dialect Adrian used in his recounting of Satan's visit to him in Italy. It is as if Echo is in contact with and communicating for today primitive Christianity's pure and pristine spiritual essence. Adrian and Serenus marvel that one so young should "pray for us all" (472), not just himself. Adrian, after all, concluded a pact with Satan that basically excludes any possibility of his subject's praying at all, let alone for others. The pact requires self-absorption, not self-giving. For Adrian's master, it is ominous that this little gift of God is saying and doing things at a very young age that are beginning to inspire in Adrian a new love, grounded in charity (*caritas*) and, for this reason, even more abhorrent to one who cannot allow such an aspiration to take hold in a creature he owns. The fiend will strike once more.

The child who can teach Adrian and company truths as compelling as those the young Jesus shared with the learned elders in the temple in Jerusalem is victimized by what at first seems like a violent recurrence of the measles he had contracted months before. The "seraphic little being" (473) who has "been the joy of the house" (473) since his arrival, finds it difficult to eat, tolerate light or noise, or listen to music. Soon he avoids "the high-summer sunshine of yard and garden" (473) altogether, and, like his uncle in the middle of a migraine attack, spends his days in a dark room. Adrian is sickened by what is happening, appalled that his nephew, who has been brought to "the country to strengthen his health" (474) is deteriorating rapidly. When the local doctor examines the boy, he cannot "conceal his fear that a more serious illness" (474) could be taking hold. Nepo gets worse, with vomiting, fever, and head pains so severe the child shrieks in agony. These terrible cries are "a martyrdom to all who" (474) have to endure them. Dr. Kurbis now detects symptoms of "cerebral-spinal meningitis, inflammation of the meninges" (474), a disease medical science in his day cannot cure. He then pulls fluid from the spinal canal to test the diagnosis, a procedure that brings Nepo temporary relief. Dr. Kurbis recommends that Adrian arrange "a consultation with a physician from the capital" (475), because Nepo's is "a case for a higher authority" (475). Reflecting on these words later, Serenus senses "a gloomy irony" (475), since there is no higher authority on earth that can surpass that of the Almighty, by whose special favor this angelic child has been brought into Adrian's household. The boy Jesus was not snatched and taken away to be crucified the moment he had finished his dialogues in the temple. Why then is Nepo being given over to the infernal torturers?

A specialist arrives from Munich and quickly sees that Dr. Kurbis has been correct in his analysis. Since he is helpless to arrest the disease's progress, he tries to prepare the household for the inevitable by laying out the stages through which Nepo's spinal meningitis will have to pass over the coming days. Relief from his agonies will come, he says, with "a clouding of the consciousness" (476), which will "grow progressively worse" (476), leading to a coma from which Echo/Nemo will not emerge.

In the midst of all this, Adrian stays mostly alone in his quarters, becoming as the days wear on more and more distraught. With Serenus Zeitblom finally arriving at Pfeiffering "four days after the onslaught of the disease" (476), Frau Schweigestill asks him to go immediately to Adrian first because the composer has been "talking crazy-like" (476). As he does so, Zeitblom is confronted by a man clearly in distress: "Shockingly pale," and with "the same red eyes as the rest of the household" (476), Adrian is in a state resembling Hamlet's after the prince discovers that his uncle murdered his father and married his mother shortly thereafter. His world is collapsing all around him in similar ruin. As Serenus approaches, the composer insists that he make the sign of the cross, as if his friend were entering Dracula's chambers. But though the abbot's room is not a vampire's lair, it is far worse: the dwelling place of Satan, the sadist supreme, who is "taking" (477) Echo to himself. This horror leads Adrian to mince no words in an agony combining defiance and guilt and distilling all the pain of a life devoid of any lasting love. His sorrow overflows in outbursts like this:

> *Take his body, you have power over that. But you'll have to put up with leaving me his soul, his sweet and precious soul, that is where you lose out and make yourself a laughing-stock—and for that I will laugh you to scorn aeons on end. Let there be eternities rolled between my place and his, yet I shall know that he is there whence you were thrown out, orts and draff that you are! The thought will be moisture on my tongue and a hosanna to mock you in my foulest cursings!* (477)

Recriminations aside, however, Adrian knows he is ultimately responsible for Echo's fate, so he engages in self-laceration as well: "What a sin, what a crime" (477) "that we let him [Echo] come, that I let him be near me, that I feasted my eyes on him!" (478). Zeitblom tries to reassure Adrian he is not to blame, that "a blind dispensation" (478) would have taken away "the dear child, perhaps too dear for this earth, wherever he chanced to be!" (478). His uncle's "loving-kindness to him" (478) cannot have been anything but life-enhancing for Echo in the short time they were together, but these words do not comfort. Adrian's despair is rooted in the fact that "loving-kindness" from him is fatal. It destroys anyone who accepts such poison. Adrian now ordains that "the good and noble" in humanity must "be taken back" (478), sounding like Hamlet damning marriage. Serenus does not quite understand what has to be "taken back" (478). The composer answers cryptically: *"The Ninth Symphony"* (478). In other words, the *"Ode to Joy"* and all its wondrous praise for the best in human experience, such as its invocation of universal brotherhood and faith in a gracious God, must be "taken back" so as not to burden humankind with hopeless aspirations and ideals. And on this inexpressibly inconsolable note, the drama ends. "Nepomuk Schneidewein, Echo, the child, Adrian's last love" (479) dies the next morning.

The personal sorrows and sufferings Adrian Leverkuhn is forced to undergo are matched by those of his nation in the last months of World War II, a dark reality Zeitblom must face as he pauses his biography once again. The spring of 1945 is bringing unremitting loss and despair. The Russians are approaching the center of the capital as "the horrible man" (480) who has asked his people over and over to strive and sacrifice beyond human capacity, adds to the impossible by ordering "his soldiery to drown in a sea of blood the attack on Berlin and to shoot every officer who speaks of surrender" (481), as if there is still the possibility of bringing about some kind of stalemate. Hitler's delusions are not shared by anyone else, least of all his closest associates, who "now rage and kill themselves" (480). The horrors of the Holocaust are also being exposed, leading Zeitblom to conclude that "all that is German now stands forth as an abomination and a warning" (481). This "Christian and humane man" (482) cannot help hurling "curses on the corrupters of an originally decent species of human being, law-abiding, only too docile, only all too willingly living on theory, who thus went to school to Evil!" (482). In so stating, Serenus connects the demonically inspired disintegration of the German people's character and virtues with the equally daemonic assault on Adrian's spirit.

With nothing but horror and misery everywhere around him, the author returns to 1929–30, "the last years of . . . [Adrian's] rational existence" (482). These are years of "monstrous creative activity" (483), with Satan supplying "an almost excessive energy and an unexceptionable state of health" (483) in compensation for inflicting shattering losses. Creative inspiration, after all, is what the composer chose in return for his surrender to the Prince of Darkness. With the hour glass marking the composer's "genius-years" of time starting to ebb, "productive absorption" (483) is imperative. To be sure most of these precious hours are devoted to composition, Adrian declines all visitors, enjoys no diversions, and lets the outfits "worn to evening parties and on public occasions" (484) remain hanging in a closet. He takes a break from his labors only for "regular, indispensable long walks . . . to get the air into his lungs" (484) and "for an afternoon rest in a darkened room" (485) to relieve migraine attacks.

The product of all this concentration and effort is *The Lamentation of Dr. Faustus*, Adrian Leverkuhn's "utmost work" (483). Zeitblom calls it "a beloved work" (485) and "a buried, forbidden treasure" (485) deserving in 1945 "to be sung from our very souls" (485) since the *Lamentation* is "the most frightful lament ever set up on this earth" (485). It should be for Germany at war's end what Beethoven's *Ninth Symphony,* which Adrian wanted "to take back" as his nephew lay dying, was for post-Napoleonic Europe. This work constitutes the composer's long-desired "break-through" (485), the necessary reversal of hundreds of years of musical development that has declined in the twentieth century to nothing beyond "calculated coldness" (485). The *Lamentation* "is expression itself" (485); despite its subject matter, this forbidding work opens up "the soul" (485), radiating "a warmth and sincerity of creature confidence" (485) that paradoxically can lead a beaten and mourning people to "the birth of freedom from bondage" (486) in the same way as "earlier music, to which it links itself across the centuries, sought to be a liberation of expression" (486) in art.

The *Lamentatio*n is the obverse of the *Ninth Symphony,* particularly in relation to the *"Ode to Joy."* Leverkuhn's "mammoth variation-piece of lamentation" (487) is in complete opposition to Beethoven's "variations of exultation" (487). The culmination of this cantata is Faust's farewell to earthly life, which, "as his hour-glass is running out" (487), like the composer's, he shares "with friends and familiars" (487). All join in feasting and drinking for most of a day. As night approaches, Faust announces his fate "in an address both dignified and penitential" (487). The magician descends into hell not accompanied by a seraphic choir, as in the *Apocalypsis*, but by "an orchestral piece in the form of grand ballet—music and galop of fantastic rhythmic variety" (489), a *"Dance of Death"* for Faust, for Adrian, and for Germany all together. A "symphonic adagio" (489) ends the work, an *"Ode to Sorrow"* (490) that denies all possibility of "goodness, joy, hope" (490) for Faust, for the composer, and for the German people, who have made the same infernal promises.

At the very end, a neighbor engages in "a pious effort to convert" (490) Faust, an intervention similar to Gretchen's plea to the Virgin Mary in Goethe's poem. Speaking through the magician, Adrian emphatically rejects this possibility because after all he has done, witnessed, and lost, "with his whole soul he despises the positivism of the world for which one would save him, the lie of its godliness" (490). This Nietzschean contempt for "false and flabby middle-class piety" (490) leaves the composer who strove for a "break-through" from conventional musical forms and the fervid countrymen and women who reveled in their liberation from the morality of the herd, with no destiny other than utter extinction. Serenus Zeitblom recognizes all of this, admitting "to the very end no consolation, appeasement, transfiguration" (491) in this terrifying finale. At the same time, however, he detects behind the cantata's fading notes "a hope beyond hopelessness, the transcendence of despair" (491) that lingers in the wake of all the horror Adrian has brought up from the depths. The gentle scholar cannot accept the finality of Faust's fate nor that of his friend or his nation. He insists on revealing "the miracle that passes belief" (491) in this haunting evocation:

> *For listen to the end, listen with me: one group of instruments after another retires, and what remains as the work fades on the air, is the high G of a cello, the*

> *last word, the last fainting sound, slowly dying in a pianissimo-fermata. Then nothing more: silence, and night. But that tone, which vibrates in the silence, which is no longer there, to which only the spirit hearkens, and which was the voice of mourning, is so no more. It changes its meaning; it abides as a light in the night.* (491)

Notwithstanding, the comfort Serenus feels as *The Lamentation*'s finale concludes will soon be replaced by more and greater pain. The gathering of Faust and his friends that precedes the doctor's descent into hell will now be reproduced by Adrian, who, on the pretext of performing on the piano "characteristic parts" (492) of his new work, invites some thirty friends, acquaintances, admirers, scholars, and musicians to Pfeiffering in May of 1930. Among these is Serenus Zeitblom, his oldest, most loyal, and most caring friend, who is uneasy about this event and, at first, thinks he should "remain away" (493). Among other concerns, he fears that the man who has spent most of his adult life "alone in his refugium" (493) cannot be comfortable being stared at by "all the eyes of a mixed gathering" (493) and will hesitate and falter in consequence. Nevertheless, Serenus's "anxious sense of duty" (493) wins out, and as he has done so often in their times together, he will "be present and watch over everything" (493).

As the guests mingle "in the Nike Salon" (493) of the Schweigestill compound on a Saturday afternoon in spring, Zeitblom notices that most seem not to be aware that their host is among them, seated "at the heavy oak table in the center of the room" (494) with "his back to the light, and . . . dressed in his everyday clothes" (494). Adrian has grown a beard, but this alone cannot account for so many attendees' failure to recognize or acknowledge the composer. It slowly dawns on Serenus that Adrian Leverkuhn "must have changed" (495) profoundly under the weight of his pain, losses, illnesses, and creative toil. This realization causes him to turn pale and to break into a cold sweat as his anxiety for his friend mounts. He who has come to "watch over everything" worries that what he is about to see and hear may be impossible to manage or control.

Adrian does not begin well. Serenus remembers how he "often mis-spoke . . . and in correcting one mistake made another . . ." (495). Leverkuhn also utilizes "a sort of elder German" (495) dialect "with its defects and open sentence-structure" (495), an anachronistic version of the language the composer had used repeatedly in his account of the meeting with Satan in the Italian hills. For Serenus, this connection is unsettling. After thanking members of his audience for coming to be with him and apologizing for the constant "yauling and bauling" (496) of the dog Suso as so many strangers passed by him into the hall, Adrian asks everyone to "not take and receive in evil part" (497) the "full confession" (497) he is about to make. He repeats Faust's words in the cantata about "the houre glass" (497) expiring, at which time Adrian "shall both body and soul everlastingly be his and fall in his hands and his power" (497) forever. Though "his" is not yet identified, Adrian's listeners are becoming uncomfortable, with some showing "a look of dark foreboding" (497). Serenus's worst fears are being acted out in full view and in words he is helpless to silence.

What comes next is hardly imaginable. Adrian's candor spares his guests no ugly detail. He can "no longer hide" (497) from "the good and godly folk" (497) in front of him that since age twenty-one he has been "wedded to Satan" (497) simply to "win glory in this world" (497). His compositions have, therefore, "with his help come to pass" (497) and are, in essence, "divel's work, infused by the angel of death" (497) and "justly regarded with mistrust" (497) by so many who hear them. No one can fathom such an outburst, which seems to connect Dr. Leverkuhn with the realm of the occult and sorcery. Is this man of genius hallucinating? While Adrian sits "in dead earnest" (497), many look toward Serenus "inquiringly" (497), hoping he can explain what is taking place before their eyes. But the man who is there to help his friend get through this unfamiliar function has been immobilized since Adrian began speaking, unable to say or do anything and wishing only that the composer "would soon begin to play and give us notes instead of words" (497).

But the words keep coming in a torrent of self-reproach and admission of guilt. Adrian tells everyone how "Hetaera Esmeralda" (498) was the catalyst that set the twenty-one-year-old student on a downward spiral, "a butterfly" (498), who "as she charmed . . . so she bewitched" (498) the naïve youth inflamed by desire. Sexual union with Esmeralda brought syphilis, which Satan cured in return for ownership of Adrian's soul. Esmeralda was the fiend's instrument, just like an enchantress in a medieval folk tale, but she did not by herself cause Adrian suddenly to fall from grace. He reveals that "long before [he] dallied with the poison butterfly" (499), [his] soul in high mind and arrogance was on the way to Satan" (499). Since he "was born for hell" (499), the time Adrian gave to the "study of divinity was secretly already the beginning of the bond and the disguised move not Biblewards, but to him, the great religiosus" (499). His motive was to "pass beyond all this and get to the break-through" (499), which, he was sure, only "the divel as guest" (499) could bring about.

Adrian continues to reminisce, like a proud actor recalling his greatest moments on stage. He describes next "the parley with [Satan]" (500) in Italy, which brought him "four and twenty years" (500) of enhanced creativity, allowing Adrian to "be capable of the work" (500) that would, as a whole, constitute the artistic "break-through" he longed to achieve. He also reminds his hearers that from the time he became the devil's disciple, he "might love no human being" (501). This prohibition he defied when Nepomuk came to live with him and the composer grew to love the child. Adrian confesses to murdering the boy at Satan's "merciless" (501) command, using his "own proper eyes" (501), because "when a soul is drawn violently to evil, its gaze is venomous and like to a basilisk, and chiefly for children" (501). As if this monstrous act were not enough, Adrian compounds the horror by confessing to a second murder, that of Rudi, "the trusting one" (501), whose friend and intermediary he had been. His death at the hands of Inez Institoris Adrian considers also willed by him since he had desired through Rudi's good offices to enter "the wedded state" (501), clearly an "apostasy from him [Satan] and a trick for atonement" (501).

Throughout these "confessions," guests have been walking out, unable to endure or process Adrian's mountain of woe. One of these is "little Helmut Institoris" (501), who exits "in silent protest, white, his underlip drawn across his teeth" (501), undoubtedly sickened that his wife should have been used by the devil and his minion for the murder of Rudi but probably not suffering any self-reproach for his own advocacy of a proto-fascist extremism that would, on a national scale, lead to countless acts of violence far more brutal and far more systematic than the isolated deed of one woman scorned.

Adrian winds down finally by stressing, almost as compensation, that even if he has been, admittedly, "a murtherer, enemy to man" (501) and so on, he has also always been "a worker and did never arrest . . . but toiled and moiled and produced hard things" (501). He speaks of the possibility that such steady labor and industry might somehow be to his "credit" (502), for he "applied [himself] and obstinately finished all" (502) as the German guild masters of old did. But Adrian ends by acknowledging the bitter truth that his fateful embrace of evil for no other purpose than self-exaltation has made any "possibility of Grace and pardon" (502) for one who did so dare, "an impudent calculation that makes compassion unpossible" (502).

The great strain building on what he has put himself through and what he has had to recall in scorching detail, has visibly affected the composer. As he finally moves to the piano and opens the score of *The Lamentation of Dr. Faustus*, his audience, now much reduced, expects a measure of relief, an expectation that will not be fulfilled. Adrian opens his score to a part of the composition he first "heard from the lovely instrument of Satan and which in part the knowing children sang" (503), probably "the closing movement of the piece, where the choir loses itself and which sounds like the lament of God over the lost state of His world" (491) that so moved Serenus. Nothing, however, is heard except “a wail” (503) from Adrian that precedes his collapsing on the floor. He has suffered a “paralytic stroke at the piano” (505) that will leave him with only “the burnt-out husk of his personality” (505) for the remainder of his life. This dramatic fall will conclude the “genius years” for which this benighted explorer of the darkest realms sacrificed everything.

EPILOGUE

Adrian regains consciousness twelve hours after being stricken. Dr. von Hosslin, the specialist treating him at "his private hospital for nervous diseases" (505) near Munich, informs Serenus and Schildknapp, who have taken charge of Adrian, that the composer is suffering the effects of "a disease of the brain which could only run its course" (506). Its progress would mitigate to a degree "the crass manipulations" (506) now apparent, and lead to "quieter, though unfortunately not more hopeful phases" (506). The end of this great artist's life will, in other words, replicate the experience of his nephew, whose screams ceased only as death drew near. "After three months' treatment in the Von Hosslin establishment" (507), Adrian reaches "a degree of composure" (507) sufficient to permit his return "to private care in quiet Pfeiffering" (507). When Serenus visits shortly afterwards, however, his friend is not welcoming, offering instead a look of "gloomy repugnance" (507) that becomes "menacing" (507) the longer Zeitblom stays. Notwithstanding, Serenus performs a duty he cannot evade no matter the atmosphere in the room: he sends a letter to Elsbeth Leverkuhn, at Buchel, informing her of what has occurred and requesting her presence at her son's bedside. She responds immediately, setting up a pieta-like encounter soon to follow, whose emotional impact, especially upon Adrian, Zeitblom can hardly bear: "Anything more fearfully touching or lamentable cannot be imagined than to see a free spirit, once bold and defiant, once soaring in a giddy arc above an astonished world, now creeping broken back to his mother's arms" (506).

Adrian is informed of his mother's impending arrival but does not react as if he understands what he has been told. Yet it seems that he does know Frau Elsbeth is on the way because "when he was supposed to be asleep" (507), he leaves his lodgings without telling anyone. Adrian is discovered shortly after "standing up to his neck" (507) in a pond at the edge of the property, a pond strikingly similar to the one near Buchel that he and Serenus had waded in as children. To Zeitblom, an attempted suicide like this shows that "a remnant of his pride" (506) still stirs in Adrian's wounded spirit, forcing him to try even desperate measures to escape the mutual pain maternal solicitude will inflict. Serenus also considers the possibility that Adrian's attempted self-sacrifice is rooted in an "older theology" (508) asserting that "those who had invoked the Devil could save their souls by "yielding their bodies" (508). He quickly rejects this supposition, however, since Adrian has long given up any hope of redemption and would not, in any case, resort to an expedient crushing to any mother, who "would prefer an irresponsible son to a dead one" (508).

Frau Elsbeth appears after this crisis has played out, "bent on taking her lost and erring son back into childhood" (508), which is to say back into innocence. Their reunion is deeply moving, as Adrian shakes with emotion while "resting his head on the breast of the woman he called *Mutter* and *Du*" (508). On the train taking Adrian, his mother, and an attendant back to Thuringia, however, the intimacy between mother and son is suddenly shattered when Adrian suffers "an unexpected seizure" (508), leading to "an outburst of rage against his mother" (508). This compels "Frau Leverkuhn to retire to another apartment" (508) for the rest of the journey. Although Zeitblom considers this only "an isolated occurrence" (508), it may well have been a calculated attempt to keep Adrian's master at bay. Too strong a response to his mother's love could provoke the fiend once more to intervene and use Adrian's filial devotion to justify matricide, a final and most horrible "murther." But no lightning strike of this nature follows, allowing Adrian to spend his last days in Buchel "as the most docile of children" (508), buoyed by familiar sights, happy memories, and a mother's tender, loving care.

Dr. Serenus Zeitblom recounts what will turn out to be a concluding visit to Adrian Leverkuhn in 1939 "after the conquest of Poland, a year before his death, which his mother, at eighty, still survived" (509). He comes upon his friend lying on a sofa with his hands "crossed on his breast, like a saint's on a medieval tomb" (509). His gray beard and "hollow face" (509) heighten Adrian's resemblance to one of the ecclesiastical grandees El Greco portrayed so compellingly. Serenus muses on the irony of this prisoner of Satan "presenting a picture of the utmost spirituality just there, whence the spirit had fled!" (509). He might also have added "whence the spirit had been corrupted." For an instant, Adrian gazes upon his oldest and most faithful friend "with an unspeakably earnest look, so searching as to be almost threatening" (509), a last look that in its satanically inspired intensity bears comparison with so much of the riveting and intimidating eye contact the soaring artist and the down-to-earth scholar have exchanged over the long years of their acquaintance.

Adrian dies in August 1940, at age fifty-five. With what Zeitblom calls "that remnant of a life" passing on, the professor too has to make radical adjustments, since his own life's "essential content" (509) for so many years was formed through his relationship with Leverkuhn. Another being's existence is altered by Adrian's loss. At the composer's burial service, Serenus is joined by Adrian's relatives, a few friends of long years standing, and "a stranger, a veiled unknown, who disappeared as the first clods fell on the coffin" (510). The shape shifter of innumerable disguises and masquerades whose "craft and guile" had captured Adrian for all eternity had to be sure his subject was really dead.

In 1940, Nazi Germany was at "the height of her dissolute triumphs" (510), just as Adrian had been years earlier. She was "about to gain the whole world by virtue of the one pact she was minded to keep, which she had signed with her blood" (510) in the same way Adrian had. From the perspective of Zeitblom's present, 1945, and his knowledge of all the "horrors" (510) his nation has inflicted and endured since the war's early successes, he asks how or when his beloved people "will reach the bottom of the abyss" (510) and exorcise the demons that have brought them to ruin. Serenus is haunted by the fact that Adrian Leverkuhn died without benefit of such an exorcism. Throughout his tale the good doctor has linked Adrian's personal story with his country's experience. The final sentence of *Doctor Faustus* expresses Serenus's anguished hope against hope that somehow the two principals of the novel, with whom he places himself as a fellow sinner, can be forgiven and be returned to the bosom of their creator cleansed of their guilt through love: "God be merciful to thy poor soul, my friend, my Fatherland" (510).

Review Requested:

We'd like to know if you enjoyed the book. Please consider leaving a review on the platform from which you purchased the book.